# The Country Music Encyclopedia

# The Country Music Encyclopedia

## BY MELVIN SHESTACK

THOMAS Y. CROWELL COMPANY

NEW YORK

ESTABLISHED 1834

The publisher thanks the following for permission to use excerpts from printed material: *Esquire* magazine, for Melvin Shestack's interview with Charley Pride, copyright © 1971 by Esquire, Inc.; Folkways Records, for Mike Seeger's essay on bluegrass and Harry K. McClintock's letter to "Nicholas"; *Music City News,* for Geoff Lane's interview with Willie Nelson, copyright © 1973 by *Music City News;* Simon & Schuster, for *The Nashville Sound* by Paul Hemphill, copyright © 1970 by Paul Hemphill; Triangle Communications, for Ed Miller's interview with Glen Campbell, reprinted from *Seventeen,* copyright © 1969 by Triangle Communications, Inc., all rights reserved; *TV Guide* magazine, for Neil Hickey's article on Roy Clark, copyright © 1973 by Triangle Publications, Inc., Radnor, Pa.

**Library of Congress Cataloging in Publication Data**

Shestack, Melvin.
   The country music encyclopedia.

   1. Country music—Dictionaries. 2. Musicians, American. 3. Folk music—United States. I. Title.
ML102.C7S5        784'.092'2 [B]        74-9644
ISBN 0-690-00442-7

Designed by Judith Woracek Barry and Marshall Henrichs

Manufactured in the United States of America

ISBN 0-690-00442-7
   2   3   4   5   6   7   8   9   10

# Introduction

DRIVING SOUTH FROM Cheyenne to Denver not too long ago, I picked up a hitchhiker. He was about sixty years old and was wearing new sneakers, green ones, decorated with red stripes. "Pretty nifty," he said proudly. "Only two dollars at J. C. Penney's." His face showed the history of the West. His shirt was a castoff Union Oil Company special, with "Grover" embroidered over the left pocket. He carried a broken suitcase and a pair of almost-new western boots, with "Grover" embossed on the side of each boot. "That's my name," he confided. "Grover Woodbury. I'm part Cherokee and I come from Miami. Miami, Oklahoma, that is. I like to travel. I just left a gas station job in California and I'm going to New Mexico, since I never been there. Some guy I worked with told me that New Mexico was like Italy. I worked in an Eye-talian hospital during the war. Married me a New Jersey woman night before I left for the war and she disappeared. We didn't even have one night together. I was drunk and so was she. Where you headin', Mister? Why you got them whiskers? You a de-partment store Santy Claus?"

The disc jockey on the car radio announced that he was going to play several songs by Tom T. Hall. Grover said, "You ever heard of Tom T. Hall?" I nodded and he looked incredulous. "He sure knows how to tell stories." We kept quiet, listening to Tom T. Hall sing "Margie's at the Lincoln Park Inn." Margie is the mistress of the narrator of the song, who waits for him nightly at the motel bar, while the faithful wife in the kitchen is ignorant of her husband's extracurricular activities. "What a mess that guy's in," I said, starting conversation again. "Oh, no," Grover replied. "He's really a lucky man. He has his wife *and* Margie lovin' him. Hell, I'm fifty-six years old next day before Christmas and in all my life I never had one woman, even the New Jersey woman, who loved me for me. I never had no love what I didn't pay for."

There was a moment of silence. Then Grover said, "Hey, you like country music?"

"Yes," I said.

"And you live in New York City?" he asked.

"Yes, but where have you been living the last five years?"

"Los Angeles, Albuquerque, Chicago, and for a while in Council Bluffs, Iowa."

"They're all cities."

"Well," Grover said, "you can't hardly make a dollar in the country no more."

"Think about all those country songs about cities," I said.

"Well," he agreed, "you're darn right. Country people are livin' in cities now."

Country music is *all* over. As this is written, country music is some of the most popular in America. Many rock stars are returning to country. Conway Twitty returned to country in the mid-sixties. Freddy Weller, once a stellar attraction with Paul Revere and the Raiders, now sings country exclusively. "Country music is no longer strictly rural, as the name implies," claims an announcement from the Country Music Association, "but has become the folk music of the working classes. In many respects, country music can rightfully claim the distinction of being America's only native art form." Country music has blanketed America. "The music has grown up," says singer George Hamilton IV, "and public taste has become less interested in sophisticated uptown songs. There's been a meeting place. Country had a bad connotation when I was a kid. It's a good word now." Country fans run the gamut from truck drivers and college kids to farmers and suburban housewives. Abroad, nobody does better than country artists. The country jamboree in Wembley, England, outdrew any rock festival held in the same place. Willie Nelson is a big star in Norway, and the all-time hit pop tune in Japan is "The Tennessee Waltz," and Jimmie Rodgers ranks with native Japanese stars in volume of record sales. New York's station WHN plays country music exclusively and is one of the most popular stations in the Northeast. Numerous country concerts have been planned at Madison Square Garden, based on the success of Tammy Wynette's concert at Philharmonic Hall. Max's Kansas City, where the Andy Warhol crowd hangs out and where the kinkiest pop stars can be seen every night, hosted the introduction of Waylon Jennings and Willie Nelson to sophisticated New York audiences. "If they like country music in New York," one Nashville songwriter told me, "then country music really is what we've been saying it was for the last fifty years—the gen-u-ine American music."

Most of the people who produce country music have rural roots, still. Songwriter John D. Loudermilk says, "Take me. I was raised in the country and can remember taking a bath in the kitchen with the radio on top of the icebox playing country music. Most of us have, somewhere in our background, the sound of a banjo being plucked or a fiddle being played. But we're not satisfied with three chords and bass and a steel. That's our heritage, but we want to offer a whole lot more."

That heritage is several hundred years old. The early Scotch-Irish settlers brought their music with them to Canada, to the Appalachians, and to the ever-onward American West. The frontier people were conservative and they clung to their old music tenaciously, but change comes with new environments, and though the roots of the music remained, the instruments were new. "New homemade instruments (zither, guitar, banjo) created new sounds such as bluegrass," writes Paul Hemphill in *The Nashville Sound*. Hemphill continues:

> *Negro slaves in the South, the Civil War, hard religion, industrialization, and the necessity to leave home to find work had their effect on a music that had always been simple and topical. Then came the westward migration into Louisiana and Texas and on toward California, and the music carried west by these settlers was influenced by the new life they faced and the people they met: the Cajun, the cowboy, the Mexican, and even the touring Hawaiian musician. And the changes kept coming. Woodie Guthrie sang about the migrant farm*

*laborers, Jimmie Rodgers about the railroads and "goin'
to California," the Carter Family about the virtues of
toughin' it out until you get to heaven, Gene Autry about
the lonesome prairie. Then, finally, came the modern
period: borrowing from Negro blues and spirituals and
jazz, the world wars, migration into the big northern
industrial towns, Roy Acuff's paving the way for solo
singing stars, Eddy Arnold's toning down of country
music, Elvis Presley and rock-and-roll, drums and electric guitars onstage at the Grand Ole Opry, the steel
guitar, the use of tapes in recording studios, and, most
recently, the slick country-pop sounds of such stars as
Glen Campbell and Chet Atkins and Roger Miller. You
can sit in the audience at the Opry on almost any
Saturday night and see a cross section of nearly every
American musical form pass across the worn old stage:
bluegrass from Appalachia (Bill Monroe and the Bluegrass Boys), honky-tonk from east Texas (George Jones),
gunfighter ballads from the Mexican border (Marty Robbins), Cajun music from Louisiana (Hank Williams, Jr.),
Negro rock-and-roll (Bob Luman), spirited mountain
spirituals (Wilma Lee and Stoney Cooper), cowboy songs
(Tex Ritter), and pop music (Leroy Van Dyke). Let the
Country Music Association and the scholars talk all they
want to about country music being the only pure form of
American music; what they should say is, country music
is the purest hybrid music we have in America. If it was
simple and moving and earthy, country music borrowed
from it. Country music is today, just as it was some 500
years ago, the folks' music.*

For years I have been trying to formulate a definition of
country music. I sometimes say country music "articulates
the feelings of the nonarticulate," which is rather pomp-
ous. Mrs. Jo Walker, the grand and gentle woman who is
the executive director of the Country Music Association,
says, "We used to spend a lot of time trying to define what
a country song was. A committee was even appointed to
work up a definition. We finally gave up." Kris Kristofferson says, "If it sounds like country, man, it's country."
Tom T. Hall disagrees: "Look at rock star James Taylor,"
he says. "And his song 'Country Road.' He's singing
through his nose like the rest of us, and he sings about a
country road, but it never goes anywhere and he never gets
off it. If he makes that much noise, you'd believe something
would happen. In country it does."

Christopher Wren, author of a biography of Johnny Cash and Moscow correspondent for *The New York Times*, says:

*Country music is really a story, told plain, of people trying to get along the best they can. It is music from the ground up, where the lyrics override the melody, and the tune itself is built to a guitar rather than a piano. Country music is traditionally rural southern in its origin, conservative in its politics (but with a stubborn streak of gut liberalism), blue collar in its economics, blatantly patriotic, fundamentalist about God, and nostalgic about Jesus. It distrusts urban wealth and intellect, but tolerates homegrown vices like boozing and philandering when accompanied by a footnote that they don't come free. If the songs sometimes wallow in self-consciousness, they hold no patent on mediocrity. When the songs are good— and they so often are—something incisive about ourselves as a people shines through. This, like the black soul wail, becomes the real folk music, not what the scholars dissect. The Nashville Sound is a misnomer. Country music is really the American sound.*

I have been interested in country music all my life—at least from late boyhood, when I listened (like most country artists) to Grand Ole Opry on Saturday nights and was fascinated by the music. It was a lonely occupation for me, in upstate New York. My contemporaries preferred Vaughan Monroe and Harry James and Frankie Laine (who often sang country-rooted songs). Through the friendship of Vern Young (see my entry on Hank Williams), who was a local country singer and owner of a record shop in Rochester, I learned a great deal about country music, and as I grew older, and my collection of records grew enormous, I began to attend concerts wherever I happened to be in the country. During my years at Fort Bliss, Texas, I listened to country music exclusively, and travel has always been a part of the jobs I held, and if a country star was appearing anywhere I happened to be, I attended the performance. Often, my journalistic assignments were focused on country performers, since for a long time I seemed to be the only one in New York City interested in country music.

Times have changed, happily, and the country fan has come out of the closet. The very people who used to scoff at my record collection are now eager to borrow records no longer commercially available, to tape for their own listening pleasure. Some years ago, when I was working for a general magazine with a huge circulation, I asked my boss to assign me to cover Johnny Cash, who was going to sing at Folsom Prison. "Johnny *who*?" I was asked. "Who'd be interested in that story?" A few weeks ago, this same editor, now with another national magazine, sent a reporter to interview me about country music. He was planning a cover story on the subject. The reporter asked me, "I don't know much about country music, what should I concentrate on?"

I answered, almost without thinking, "The people who make country music. Once, when I was in college and I was writing a paper on poetry, I asked my professor the same question. He answered, 'Study the poets themselves as well as their work and then you'll begin to get an understanding of what poetry is all about.' " In writing *The Country Music Encyclopedia* I have tried to do that very thing and I hope I have been successful. I have concentrated on the people who *perform* (and quite often write) country songs, the men and women whose lives are devoted to entertaining the ever-growing country-music-hungry public. In rereading the 100,000-plus words in this book, I realize that I have omitted much. Thousands of people make up the country-music industry who aren't performers or who have never made the country hit parades. There are executives and producers and publicists and impresarios and musicians and guitar makers and bus drivers and executives of the Country Music Association who in their own right are impressive, interesting, creative, and imaginative people, deserving of credit for their efforts on behalf of an art form they believe in and have worked for. The Fred Roses and Wesley Roses and Harlan Howards and Francis Prestons and Billy Sherrills and Jack Clements and scores of other Nashville luminaries certainly are interesting enough to have entire books written about what they do—but in *The Country Music Encyclopedia* I have mentioned producers, arrangers, record company executives, and songwriters who don't record themselves only in their direct relationship with artists who record and perform. I have been held down by space requirements and the knowledge that the reader is primarily interested in the *star*; since country music is a *commercial* art form, it is the stars who sell records, and the stars who draw the crowds. Hence, I have concentrated on the stars, using as a criterion the record-popularity charts in *Billboard* and *Cash*

*Box* magazines. There are numerous artists who make a good living and have their followings and personal fan clubs but whose songs never seem to appear on the charts. I have sadly overlooked, in most cases, this genre of performer.

"Bein' a country singer ain't easy," one young hopeful told me at the King of the Road motor inn. "There's only one way to make it in this business, and that's to have a hit record. You can be the greatest singer in the world, but if you don't have a hit song, you might as well join a church choir." It is a cruel, hard fact of country-music life. And country music deals with the cruel, hard facts of life. That's why it is so popular with the average man and woman in America, and why country music is so important. "We're in such a mess right now that our music must reflect the turmoil that we're going through," John D. Loudermilk says. "We need dialogue. Decent dialogue. Country music can be the real vehicle from which the broadsides come. I want to tell the world how the guy in the filling station feels. It's vital that people know how he feels." The country singer or country songwriter knows, because chances are he's worked in a filling station himself. Or has been (like Tammy Wynette) a hairdresser. Or driven a truck (like Freddie Hart). In reducing the entries in this book into statistics, I would say that the average male country singer was born in the Southeast in poor or modest circumstances. He worked from the time he was old enough to walk and learned his music on his own. The average female country singer is also generally self-taught. They are all self-made men and women who work long hours, seven days a week, years on end, to entertain their fans. They sacrifice their own comforts (most country singers spend 250 nights a year in a *bus*) to bring their songs to the world. They get paid well and live well but rarely forget their early roots. Most successful country artists, men and women, are wedded to the land, and the first thing they do when they make some money is to buy land near their birthplace. They represent what is often called the backbone of America, and for the most part they live up to their images. They are dedicated, these country singers. I have talked to scores of them in the course of writing the book, and have been impressed by their intelligence and understanding of life's problems. I have read every book I could find on country music, and thousands of magazine articles, scholarly theses, and newspaper stories. I have visited Nashville as often as possible. I hope the reader will find more than just a few facts about the life of his favorite country performer. I have attempted to portray a part of America often neglected by scholars—the artists most appreciated by the people, because they come from the people themselves, and always relate to them. They are of America—of the people, for the people, and by the people. I feel fortunate to have walked among them.

—MELVIN SHESTACK
*New York City, 1974*

# Contents

The Country Music Encyclopedia      1

Discography      325

Country Radio Stations:      377
   United States, Puerto Rico,
   and Canada

A Sampling of Country Songs      395

Photo Credits      409

# The Country Music Encyclopedia

# A

## ACUFF, ROY

BORN: September 15, 1903, Maynardsville,
    Tennessee
MARRIED: w. Mildred Louise
CHILDREN: s. Roy Neal

The King is what they call him, and though there are a couple of pretenders to the throne, he hasn't yet been deposed or abdicated. When I first saw him in Carlsbad, New Mexico, back in 1953, he announced that his favorite numbers were "Loop the Loop," "Rock the Baby," and "Walk the Dog," all of which he still performs at the Grand Ole Opry. His scepter is a fiddle bow which he balances sometimes in unkingly fashion on the end of his nose. This is one of the tricks he's been performing along with his songs at the Opry for almost forty years, and insiders in the business claim that Roy Acuff is the closest thing country music has to a father figure. He is a thin, wispy man with an ingratiat-ing smile and lively eyes. If something worth-while happens in the country music industry, musicians in Nashville often say, "Roy would like that" or "That would please Roy." Acuff is a millionaire several times over and has been a performer, songwriter, band leader, publisher, world traveler, businessman, and even a guber-natorial candidate. He started off traveling with a medicine show, fiddling and singing, and dispensing an exotic tonic that he recommends even today. The songs he made famous during the 1930s and World War II became as strongly symbolic of country music as had the blue yodels of Jimmie Rodgers before him.

His father, Neill Acuff, was a lawyer and Baptist minister. Neither occupation brought much money to the Acuffs, and Roy spent his first years on a tenant farm in the foothills of the Smoky Mountains. When he was sixteen, his family moved to Knoxville, Tennessee. At Cen-tral High in Knoxville, Acuff became a star

athlete, winning no less than thirteen letters. He was good enough to be claimed by the New York Yankees, who sent him to their summer training camp in Florida. Unfortunately for baseball, he suffered a serious sunstroke, which ironically came during a fishing trip and not at training camp. The stroke ended his sports career and Roy turned his interest toward music. He had always sung during church services, and along with the influence of his fiddle-playing father, this early religious musical training proved to be the predominant influence in his musical career. He first entered the world of show business in the early 1930s as an entertainer for Doc Hower's Medicine Show. The star, Clarence Ashley, taught Acuff valuable show-business techniques. He worked with a small group called The Crazy Tennesseans, playing on WNOX in Knoxville. "Most of those days we played backwoods schoolhouse one-nighters with twenty-five-dollar total gate receipts," Acuff recalled.

In his early career, Acuff had not yet developed a set style, and a few of his records, like "Yes, Sir, That's My Baby," were of a pop nature. But by the mid-thirties he discarded these attempts at middle-of-the-road-music and settled on the mournful, wailing style that was traditional and natural to his mountain-music heritage. And this made him famous. By 1936, through the efforts of the perceptive talent scout Arthur Satherly, Acuff signed with Columbia Records. He changed the name Crazy Tennesseans to Smoky Mountain Boys because he thought the title was "derogatory to my native state. One of the songs with which he is still most strongly identified, "The Great Speckled Bird," was on his first recording. This somewhat metaphysical hymn by someone called "Rev. Gant" was set to the melody of A. P. Carter's long-popular "I'm Thinking Tonight of My Blue Eyes." (Some years later this melody was the basis for not one but two country superhits: Hank Thompson's "Wild Side of Life" and Kitty Wells's "Answer to Honky-Tonk Angels.") Also from Acuff's first recording session came a song which probably helped him make his first million, "The Wabash Cannonball."

Roy Acuff: The once and future king.

In 1938, after trying for five years, Acuff was accepted as a performer at the Opry. He became the first *singing* star of the Opry, beginning the trend away from emphasis on the old string bands. During the war years Roy Acuff and Grand Ole Opry became synonymous. Acuff's Opry repertory, heavily weighted with sacred and traditional mountain-style melodies, hasn't changed much since the forties. In a period when country singers sported spangles and wildly decorated western wear, Acuff and his musicians wore plain sports clothing. There is not a single "cowboy" number in his repertory. He still prefers numbers like "The Great Judgment Morning" and "All the World Is Lonely Now." Many of his most popular songs, including "Beneath the Lonely Mound of Clay" and "The Precious Jewel," were composed by Acuff himself. "When Roy Acuff raised his voice in his mournful, mountain style," writes historian Bill C. Malone, "he seemed to suggest all the verities for which Americans were fighting: home, mother and God."

But Acuff's popularity was not confined to native American audiences. His records have been sold by the millions all over the world. During World War II Ernie Pyle corroborated Acuff's international fame in a report filed during the battle of Okinawa. On attacking a position held by marines, Pyle claimed, a Japanese banzai battalion employed a battle cry which it believed the zenith of insults: "To hell with Roosevelt, to hell with Babe Ruth, to hell with Roy Acuff."

Largely through the business acumen of his wife, Mildred, Acuff built his immense personal fortune by investing in a number of enterprises, including the Roy Acuff Dunbar Cave Resort near Clarksville, Tennessee. Recently he has been involved with the opening of Opryland (he has two museums in the park), a giant entertainment complex and amusement park near Nashville, which will become the permanent home of Grand Ole Opry, instead of the Ryman Auditorium.

When an interviewer once asked Acuff if he felt badly about the Opry moving, he replied: "I want you to know how *strongly* I feel about it. You see, so many people have been saying, 'Oh, this is where the Opry started. We don't want to destroy everything' ... they don't know! They're just talkin'. Why, some people think it was under a tent once. It wasn't. It was never under a tent. It started in the studio at WSM and they moved it out to a little theater out on Eighth Avenue. Then they moved it back to Fatherland Street, where you walked down a sawdust trail and sat down on a board. That's when I joined 'em. 1938. You didn't pay no money to see it. Didn't cost a dime. You all knew where you could get a ticket . . . at the National Life and Accident agent. Pretty soon we outgrew that and they moved us into the War Memorial. We were only there a couple of years and we outgrew that. And only then did we move to the Ryman Auditorium. But a lot of people think that the Ryman Auditorium was where it started, that this is the home of country music. Well, they just don't know. They don't see what I see.''

Probably the most important of Acuff's enterprises is the Acuff-Rose Publishing Company, founded in 1942 and the first publishing house devoted exclusively to country music. The late Fred Rose was originally a pop writer for belt-'em-out singers like Sophie Tucker (Rose wrote her trademark hit, "Red Hot Mamma"), but he was one of the few who made the complete transformation from city to country music. He often recalled how he once stood backstage at the Opry one night, watching Acuff, with tears streaming down his eyes singing a tragic song about a dying child, "Don't Make Me Go to Bed and I'll Be Good." The company proved to be the nucleus for Nashville's later rise to eminence as the major music-publishing center in the world. Hank Williams was one of the first stars discovered by Acuff-Rose (now run by Rose's son, Wesley).

Once, in the 1940s, when the then Governor of Tennessee declared that "hillbilly music was disgraceful," Acuff decided to run for governor himself. He never made the governor's mansion, but he did acquire the title of King of Country Music. And, like most kings, he tends to be conservative and traditional. His dislike of hippies and their life-style is widely reported, but he insists he is open to change. "There's no reason any group with the hippie dress—long hair, beards, dirty clothes—couldn't sing on the Opry. But it wouldn't be accepted as if you or I should walk on as we are in our good American way of life." He proved his tolerance by agreeing to record a three-record album with the Nitty

Gritty Dirt Band. (The United Artists album, "Will the Circle Be Unbroken," which also includes among its participants Earl Scruggs, Merle Travis, Mother Maybelle, and Doc Watson, has been highly successful.)

When an interviewer asked Acuff about the recording session with the Nitty Gritties, he replied: "Well now, let me make myself clear to you. I have no respect for hippies. I'm clear about that. I have no respect for them because I don't think they have respect for anything. So that's the reason I dislike the hippie attitude. Wes Rose called me and asked me if I would consider going into the studio with the Nitty Gritty boys. And I said, 'Wes, I have no objections to doing anything, at any time with anybody, if they want to do it and in the right way.' Now, I have never met a finer group of boys than the Nitty Gritty boys. They're just as fine as they could be. I haven't seen them . . . their faces was covered! I didn't know if I was in the studio with boys eighteen or thirty-eight or fifty-eight! I couldn't tell! I'm serious about it! I didn't know if they were boys, men, or maybe girls! You cover your face and you hide all your character. I dunno. When I went in the studio, they took me at my word. I said, 'Fellers, they call me one-time Acuff, now let's get it over with.' And we did it . . . one take and that was it. But really, they really were a good group of boys. I would have liked to see them."

Nonetheless, Acuff maintains that country music "is down to earth, for the home—not to get all hepped up and smoke a lot of marijuana and go wild about. The music is full of Christianity and sympathy and understanding. It helps make people better."

In November 1962 Roy Acuff was elected as the first living member of the Country Music Hall of Fame.


## ALAN, BUDDY

BORN: May 23, 1948

Being the son of a fabulously successful man has its built-in problems. Buddy Alan's daddy is Buck Owens, country superstar, TV host, and king of the Bakersfield, California, division of the country-music world. His mother, Bonnie Owens (now Mrs. Merle Haggard), is a star in her own right. Buddy is almost a mirror image of

Buddy Alan: It's only a matter of time before Buck Owens' talented son will be able to use his full name.

his celebrated father and sings in the same earnest, yet strident, western honky-tonk style. His future success depends on how derivative he wants to be; how much he is willing to grow artistically and develop an image that will reflect his musical heritage without smothering his individuality.

## ALLEN, REX

BORN: December 31, 1924, Willcox, Arizona
MARRIED: w. Bonnie Lindner
CHILDREN: s. Rex, Jr.; Curtis, Mark; d. Bonita

A jaded critic once wrote that if you tossed a "pinch of Gene Autry, two tablespoons of Roy Rogers, a half-cup of Jimmy Wakely, and two shakes of Tex Ritter into a bowl, stirred until well-mixed and then baked for an hour, the result would be Rex Allen." There's a grain of truth in the writer's cynicism, for Rex Allen came to prominence at the tail end of the singing-cowboy era when the movie-industry moguls were searching for imitations. But as a cowboy, Rex Allen was no imitation. His acting ability certainly surpassed that of Monte Montana and Sunset Carson, and his voice was full and rich. Having been born and raised in Arizona's cattle country, Allen learned to ride and rope as part of the standard operating procedure of growing up. He was a rodeo bronc rider and bulldogger in his teens, and though he always played the guitar and sang, it was his fellow cowboys who suggested that singing might bring in better prize money than calf roping. Live radio was still booming in the 1940s, and Allen managed to get a job entertaining on WTTM in Trenton, New Jersey (a northern state where country music has always had status). He became a local star, garnering sufficient attention to win him an offer from the *WLS National Barn Dance* in Chicago. Rex Allen spent five successful years in Chicago, leaving to host his own TV show in 1950. Within a few months the *Rex Allen Show* rated seventh in national ratings and Rex Allen's rendition of "Crying in the Chapel" for Decca made the top ten in the record charts. Republic Pictures signed him to a movie contract, and he made a film every six weeks for several years. During this time he also appeared in feature roles for Twentieth Century-Fox and began a long association with Walt Disney Productions. In the 1960s his popularity as a singer waned somewhat, though he had a hit with "Don't Go Near the Indians" in 1962. Nowadays, his clear voice, which has been described as "western intelligent" as opposed to "sidekick hillbilly," can be heard narrating TV documentaries, often for Walt Disney. Rex Allen often makes appearances at rodeos when he is not managing his hotel in Acapulco or his 360-acre ranch in California. He has been cited as Rodeo Man of the Year (1965) and Arizona Man of the Year (1966), and he was elected to the Cowboy Hall of Fame in 1968. A songwriter as well as singer, Allen has published more than 300 songs.

## ALLEN, ROSALIE

BORN: June 27, 1924, Old Forge, Pennsylvania

The "queen of the yodelers" during the 1940s and '50s, Rosalie Allen was among the first successful women country singers. An older brother (over her parents' vehement objections) taught her to play the guitar and yodel. In her teens she sang at a variety of amateur contests, where Denver Darling heard her, and he invited her to join his *Swing Billies* show in New York. During World War II Rosalie conducted her own hillbilly show in New York, then joined Zeke Manners' show, which starred Elton Britt. Her great fame came as a partner of Elton Britt. Among their hits: "Soft Lips," "Game of Broken Hearts," and "Tennessee Yodel Polka." Her solo efforts on RCA Victor included "I Want To Be a Cowboy's Sweetheart" and the superhit "He Taught Me to Yodel." Though she generally remained in the northeast, Rosalie Allen was a frequent visitor to Grand Ole Opry. In the 1960s she had her own New York TV show, was a disc jockey on WOV, and opened a record shop, Rosalie Allen's Hillbilly Music Center. She hasn't been too active in recent years and now lives quietly in suburban New Jersey. She is married and has one child.

## ANDERSON, BILL

BORN: November 1, 1937, Columbia, South Carolina

MARRIED: w. Bette (divorced) (d. Terri Lee, Jennifer Lane); w. Becky

Late in 1957, a twenty-year-old University of Georgia junior climbed to the roof of the hotel in Commerce, Georgia, where he was a summer disc jockey and sports-page stringer for the *Atlanta Constitution*. Thinking about the temptations and frustrations that come to heartbroken souls who venture into the big city in quest of some kind of solace, he wrote:

A bright array of city lights as far as I can see
The great white way shines through the night
For lonely souls like me.
The cabarets and honky-tonks flashing signs invite
A broken heart to lose itself in the glow of city lights.

"It took inspiration to write that song," Anderson recalls, "if you have any idea of how many city lights there are in Commerce, Georgia." Anderson, who had been singing since high school, made 500 records of the song and one somehow reached the attention of Ray Price in Nashville. Price liked it, and his rendition of "City Lights" became one of the giant country hits of 1958. Anderson, whose business acumen has long impressed Nashville (if not always favorably), proved his shrewdness even then, convincing Decca to give him a contract, using his obvious talent for writing hit songs as a weapon to make them use him as a singer.

When Anderson received his A.B. in journalism a year later, he moved to Nashville for good. He impressed Hubert Long—a promoter and the president of the Moss-Rose Publishing Company—and within twenty months Anderson was considered "a boy to watch" and a regular member of Grand Ole Opry. In 1963 he wrote and recorded a sweet ballad/recitation called "Still," and Anderson began receiving the first of the seemingly endless presentations of awards, trophies, plaques, and citations which fill his kingly house in Tennessee. Thus far he has written more than 400 songs, which he

Eddy Arnold: "The Tennessee Plowboy" in black tie and tux.

singer, and he identifies himself with the Nashville scene. Yet, as Bill C. Malone, a professor at Wisconsin State University, writes, Arnold "is representative of the many country singers who after an initial period of success become dissatisfied with their original rural style and strive to achieve a more polished and smoother approach. In so doing they may become more accomplished, self-conscious vocalists, but with an attending loss of rustic simplicity and sincerity. By the mid-fifties Eddy Arnold could no longer be pictured as strictly a hillbilly singer." He had greatly modified his vocal delivery and was appearing in sophisticated supper and night clubs throughout the country, but his appeal to country fans began to wane. From 1948, when *Billboard* magazine first began its top-ten listings, until 1963, he led all country performers with a total of fifty-three top-ten tunes, thirteen of which—including "Cattle Call," "Bouquet of Roses," "Don't Rob Another Man's Castle," and "Make the World Go By"—reached the number-one position.

Arnold was one of RCA Victor's big names and sold records in the millions. Yet, in 1973, he left Victor to join MGM. A company spokesman claimed that "his records just weren't selling. He may have been king, but there isn't much room for royalty these days." MGM, on the other hand, feels Eddy Arnold is going to soar to new heights in the mid-seventies. Though hardcore "purists" in the country business feel that Arnold is being somewhat traitorous by crossing over to pop (When Arnold stepped onto the stage at the 1969 Grammy Awards Banquet he was greeted with a chorus of *bwok-bok-bok* chicken calls, a reference to his going into the fried-chicken business. A friend said, "It wasn't entirely done in good humor"), other critics feel that Arnold has been the catalyst easing country music's penetration into the urban marketplace.

Arnold was born a farmboy and earned an extra fifty or seventy-five cents a night playing the guitar at square dances. His earliest memories are of hard times. When he was only eleven, his father died and he eventually had to quit school to work the farm. At eighteen he landed a job singing on a radio station in Jackson, Tennessee. He worked with Pee Wee King and the Golden West Cowboys for almost three years ("I sold song books and swept out the auditoriums"); then he got married. At the same time he sang in a style reminiscent of Gene Autry. He was influenced (as was Marty Robbins sometime later) by the smooth renditions of blind performer Pete Cassell, of station WSB in Atlanta, who was a relatively popular artist in the late 1930s. Arnold joined station WTJS in Jackson, Tennessee, in 1942, where he was a tremendous hit. It wasn't long before he was discovered by Grand Ole Opry, and by the time he was thirty years old, he could celebrate his birthday by having had nine top-ten records that year.

Arnold now lives the life of a gentleman farmer, performing occasionally and investing in businesses which include an auto agency, a music publishing company, a realty company, and apartment houses. Arnold claims that all he wants to do is sing. He is also adamant about his stylistic changes in country music: "Once we cut out the by-cracky nonsense and give respect to our music, then people will respect us."

Nashville paid its respects to Arnold by electing him to the Country Music Hall of Fame in 1966.

## ASHLEY, CLARENCE "TOM"

BORN: September 29, 1895, Mountain City, Tennessee

DIED: June 2, 1967, Mountain City, Tennessee

MARRIED: w. Hettie Osborne

Only a few papers out of the immediate area of Mountain City carried the obituary of Clarence "Tom" Ashley, but a surprising number of Nashville and Hollywood stars made the trek there for his funeral, as did a number of New Yorkers, southern political personalities, and other notables. He was one of the most outstanding and historically important musicians from the golden age of early country music. He recorded more than seventy sides of old-time music during the 1920s and 1930s for Columbia, Victor, Okeh, Vocalion, Cennett, and others. He made records with the Carolina Tar Heels, Byrd Moore and his Hotshots, and the Blue Ridge Mountain Entertainers. Many contemporary "hard" country artists consider Ashley their musical "godfather."

There weren't many professional country musicians before Grand Ole Opry. In the early 1920s few southern people had phonographs, and the main sources of entertainment in rural areas were circuses and medicine shows. In the

tradition of Fiddlin' John Carson and Uncle Dave Macon, Tom Ashley joined the medicine shows when he was only sixteen, picking the banjo, singing ballads and comic songs, and telling funny stories. "After his first few summers on the circuit," writes biographer Ralph Rinzler, "Tom hitched up with a fellow named Doc Hower with whom he worked regularly until the beginning of World War II, and Tom's extraordinarily animated recountings of the Doc's pitches complete with lurid tales of little girls consumed by worms who could have been saved by one small bottle of Mokiton Tonic (Tom describes the taste as approximating that of strong unsweetened wild cherry or aromatic bitters) are as entertaining as the best of his tunes."

Not long after Ashley had been brought into the troupe, another young boy was hired on, and Hower instructed Ashley to teach him the ropes. Ashley did, including the skits, jokes, and songs. The boy was Roy Acuff, and he remained a close friend of Ashley's until his death.

Ashley remained with the medicine show until the first years of World War II, when he joined Charlie Monroe's (the brother of Bill) Kentucky Pardners as banjo picker and troupe comic. Lester Flatt was also with the group during this period. Ashley moonlighted on occasion with the Stanley Brothers, who lived nearby.

Clarence Ashley once explained how his life "was like a flower that bloomed twice"—in the early years in the mountains and again in his late years with the new city audience. During the 1960s Ashley was a major attraction at many folk festivals: Newport, Chicago, New York, Los Angeles, and in England. He introduced his friend Doc Watson to the city audiences. Clarence Ashley's most popular banjo number was "The Coo-Coo Bird." Ashley's music always reflected the old-time country sentiments and was aimed at giving an understanding of rural experience.

## ASHWORTH, ERNIE

BORN: December 15, 1928, Huntsville, Alabama

MARRIED: w. Elizabeth Rose

CHILDREN: s. Mike, Mark Paul; d. Rebecca Gail

Ernie Ashworth's songs were recorded by Little

ATKINS, CHET

Jimmy Dickens and Carl Smith in the 1950s, and he was considered somebody to watch. His own recordings, like "Billy Worth" for MGM, didn't catch on and Ashworth returned to Alabama to work for the space program. Wesley Rose (of Acuff-Rose Publishing Company) had faith in Ashworth and managed to bring him back to Tennessee with a contract from Decca. Singing under his own name, he had two quick hits: "Each Moment" and "You Can't Pick a Rose in December." During the late sixties Ashworth toured successfully in this country and in Europe, and made guest appearances on a number of TV shows. Although he was nominated as Most Promising Young Artist by several music trade papers in 1963 and 1964, at this writing he doesn't seem to be a candidate for the Country Music Hall of Fame.

## ATCHER, BOB

BORN: May 11, 1914, Hardin County, Kentucky
MARRIED: w. Margerite Whitehill
CHILDREN: s. Robert Whitehill; d. Mary Christopher, Cecily Ann

Kentucky-born Bob Atcher defected from medical school to become one of country music's numerous stars. For many years he was undisputed western "king" of Chicago and the Midwest. He was the mainstay of the *WLS National Barn Dance* and star of his own TV show. During the late forties he had a number of moneymaking records, some of them his own compositions: "Money, Marbles, and Chalk," "Don't Rob Another Man's Castle," and "Why Don't You Haul Off and Love Me." Atcher's billing included a "singing partner" called Bonnie Blue Eyes (Atcher's theme was "I'm Thinking Tonight of My Blue Eyes"). He gave up the throne to become mayor of Schaumberg, Illinois, eventually becoming a director of the Schaumberg State Bank and director of a successful advertising agency. To many old-time country fans in Chicago, Bob Atcher still ranks with Roy Acuff and Tex Ritter.

## ATKINS, CHET

BORN: June 20, 1924, Lutrell, Tennessee
MARRIED: w. Leona Johnson
CHILDREN: d. Merle

During the early days of country music, most Nashville musicians could neither read nor write music. They were improvisers—men of instrumental flexibility who could easily adapt themselves to any style. These musicians were a small, tight group playing with each other so often (at radio concerts and on the road as well as at recording sessions) that they became intimate with each other's styles as well as with the vocalist's nuances. Musicians from New York, watching informal Nashville musicians at work, were always amazed how they could anticipate each other's moves. The most eminent and important member of this informal group was Chet Atkins, one of the world's most honored guitarists and chief of RCA's country-music division. During the early 1960s Atkins appeared at a Nashville club called The Carousel with a group including pianist Floyd Cramer, drummer Buddy Harman, bassist Bob Moore, and guitarists Grady Martin and Hank Garland. This group produced a distinctive instrumental pattern very different from early country instrumentation, characterized by relaxed, tensionless feeling and a loose, easygoing beat. It became widely known as The Nashville Sound. The ubiquitous fiddle of mountain music was tossed out, the guitars provided a beat not unlike that of rock-and-roll, and the piano added a cool, "uptown" quality. Atkins is generally credited with injecting this sound into commercial country music. Moreover, he is universally considered Nashville's master musician and all-around authority. "If Chet likes it," it is often said, "it'll sell."

Nobody denies that he is the most influential man in Nashville. When Chet Atkins was asked by *The New York Times* to comment on his appointment as RCA Records' Division Vice President in Charge of Popular Artists and Repertoire in Nashville in March 1968, he said: "The difference is that I'll be able to play the guitar more. I'm really a guitar player; I just stumbled into the office job years ago. But, I've got to practice and I haven't had time for it. I looked around for material for everyone so I sort of neglected myself."

For a dozen years Atkins has been doubling as both performer and manager of RCA's Nashville office, and has been juggling his schedule to include almost weekly concerts annually all over the country—appearances that range from accompanying symphony orchestras to "picking"

13

Chet Atkins: He's discovered more stars than most astronomers.

at hard country festivals. He has appeared as a soloist at the Newport Jazz Festival, before President John F. Kennedy at the White House, and on numerous TV variety shows from Ed Sullivan to *The Kraft Music Hall.*

Among the scores of artists discovered by Chet Atkins are Don Gibson, Floyd Cramer, Connie Smith, Dottie West, Charley Pride, Roger Miller, Boots Randolph, and Roy Orbison. He has produced more than thirty of his own albums, many of them featuring his own compositions.

Atkins was born in the Clinch Mountain country of Tennessee near Knoxville. His father taught piano and voice. Jimmie Rodgers' records were played on the family's windup phonograph. Somewhere in his childhood, Atkins traded an old pistol for an old guitar. By the time he finished high school he had acquired proficiency on the instrument and was broadcasting from WNOX in Knoxville with Bill Carlisle and a group billed as The Dixieland Swingers. He later did radio stints in Cincinnati, Raleigh, Richmond, and Denver. Finally, he returned to Nashville to work with the Carter Family. RCA's Chicago-based Steve Sholes, hearing a transcription of Atkins' "Canned Heat," offered him a contract by mail, and Atkins began his long association with RCA Victor.

Atkins is one of the most versatile musicians in America. His guitar techniques are varied. He is a virtuoso classical, traditional, modern-jazz, flamenco, pop, and of course, country guitarist. "The basic style I play," Atkins says, "was started by a colored guy in Kentucky" (Jim Mason, a black guitarist who played a "choke" style of guitar). Mason taught it to a white coal miner, Mose Reger, who in turn taught it to Ike Everly, father of the Everly Brothers. Reger also taught Merle Travis, who had a great influence on Atkins' playing. (Atkins' daughter, Merle, is named after Travis.) Atkins likes the heavy use of vibrato on the Spanish guitar. He claims to have been influenced by Les Paul and Django Reinhardt, among others. He is interested in the "physics of sound" and has invented an instrument to aid guitarists called the magic bass.

To his closest friends he is known as Chester, and Paul Hemphill, author of *The Nashville Sound,* describes him as "an icy-veined, wry-humored, conservatively dressed refugee from the mountains with pale blue eyes and high Cherokee cheekbones and the demeanor of a small-town undertaker." Like several other "Mr. Nashvilles," Atkins has invested in sound properties and is one of the Music City millionaires. His wife still cuts his hair. He reads poetry and philosophy.

Not long ago, he and songwriter John D. Loudermilk took their wives on a Caribbean vacation cruise. "We got to singing and playing one night," Atkins recalls, "and the next day one of the people who'd been sitting around listening came up to me and said, 'Say, you sure can play that guitar.' I thanked him, and then he said, 'I'll tell you one thing, though, you ain't no Chet Atkins.'"

Chet Atkins was elected to the Country Music Hall of Fame in 1973.

## AUTRY, GENE

BORN: September 29, 1907, Tioga Springs, Texas
MARRIED: w. Ina May Spivey

With the release of Al Jolson's *The Jazz Singer* in 1927, it was only natural that sound would be added to the second-feature western then gaining popularity. Nat Levine, a producer at Republic studios, struck the moneymaking chord. He decided to combine the western's fast-paced, no-time-for-sex plots with the pleasant but innocent interludes provided by a cowboy who sings. After considering a Broadway actor who could sing but not ride a horse, and a Hollywood actor who could ride a horse but not sing, Levine picked Gene Autry, who could sing and ride but had no acting experience. In his first film, a Ken Maynard western, he was cast as a "tuneful cowpuncher." It was a tiny part, but he sang, and the heavy fan mail indicated that the public wanted more of the tuneful cowpuncher, and the singing film cowboy leaped into music and film history. Autry is one of the most successful figures in the history of American show business. He began as a singer in the style of Jimmie Rodgers; his songs did not have a true western flavor. He became one of the most highly paid stars in Hollywood. He is a millionaire many times over through brilliant investment of his money. He owns countless acres of real estate, particularly in Oklahoma;

Johnny Bond, left, and Pat Buttram helped their boss, Gene Autry, reach millions over the airwaves.

buildings in several states; chains of gas stations, hotels, radio stations, and TV production companies; and at one time or another, owned major sports teams including the Los Angeles Angels baseball team. He became a championship golfer. At one time, *Variety* reported, Autry owned more than 300 pairs of fancy cowboy boots and as many "western" outfits. A joke in Hollywood, during the Autry heyday, told of Autry in a film, facing disaster and talking to himself: "Them bandits have beaten my mother, ravished my girl, burned down my house, killed my cattle, and blinded my best friend. I'm a-gonna get 'em if it's the last thing I do—but first, folks, I'm going to sing you a little song."

Autry was born in Tioga Springs, Texas. His grandfather was known locally as the "singing Baptist minister," and he taught little Gene (who was then known by his given name, Orvon) to sing hymns because he needed a youngish voice for his church choir. Gene liked to sing—but not only hymns. By the time he was seventeen he sang in local nightclubs, passing a plate around for collections. ("I never made more than fifty cents a night," Autry recalls.) Like many southern singers, he joined a medicine show and worked from time to time with the Fields Brothers. His first instrument was the

saxophone, but Autry liked to sing too much to just play an instrument. He traded the saxophone for a guitar. Autry's father had purchased a ranch near Achille, Oklahoma, from which Gene would drive cattle to the railroad station. He became interested in trains and the telegraph, and learned how to send and receive in the Morse Code. Eventually, he was good enough to work the midnight-to-eight shift as telegrapher for the Frisco Line in Chelsea, Oklahoma. That's where the "story" of Gene Autry really began. One night, a man entered to send a wire. Autry says: "Seeing my guitar, he requested that I sing 'They Plowed the Old Trail Under.' Then the stranger sang a version of 'Casey Jones' for me. After he left, I saw the wire was signed 'Will Rogers.' Will came in several times after that and gave me great encouragement. 'I think you have something,' he told me. 'Work hard at it and you may get somewhere.' "

Using a free railway pass, Autry rode a chair car from Tulsa to New York, and carrying his guitar, he auditioned for recording companies. He made a few songs for American Record Company and then Victor hired him to record for them as Oklahoma's Singing Cowboy. He returned to Tulsa, where he hosted his own show, and then, with his records catching on, was engaged by the WLS Barn Dance in Chicago, where he was a smash hit. A number of Gene Autry songbooks appeared; his records were advertised in a full-page ad in the Sears Roebuck Catalog. The Gene Autry "Roundup" guitar ad reminded the possible buyer that Autry became famous "simply because he learned to play a guitar while on the ranch." His first superhit was a song he wrote with Jimmy Long, "That Silver-Haired Daddy of Mine," which sold half a million discs in 1931—a record for the period. Other popular Autry hits of the thirties included "A Gangster's Warning," "My Old Pal of Yesterday," and even a labor song, "The Death of Mother Jones," which chronicled the story of a famous radical labor leader.

It was because of this recording and radio success that Nat Levine chose Autry to be the singing cowboy for Republic studios. An ingredient of the Autry films was the natural way in which songs were worked into the plot. Going beyond simply stopping the action and providing music around the bunkhouse (although there was plenty of that, too), Autry's songs moved the action right along. In *Mexicali,* he exposed a group of crooked businessmen with the words of the song he sang over the radio. In *Tumbling Tumbleweeds* he used a song to decoy the bad guys into shooting at a dummy rigged and operated to look like him singing. Musically, Autry moved from Jimmie Rodgers-type songs to "western" motifs: "Riding Down the Canyon," "South of the Border," and "Empty Cot in the Bunkhouse." Autry's popularity stimulated other movie makers to present a variety of versions of the singing cowboy, but Autry, and really Autry alone, established the stereotype of the heroic horseman who was equally adept with gun and guitar. He was world-famous. His visit to Dublin, for example, in 1939, just prior to World War II, brought a million people into the streets. In November 1941 the town of Berwyn, Oklahoma, changed its name to Gene Autry, Oklahoma. During World War II Autry enlisted in the Army Air Corps. He served with distinction in the Far East, clocking as much time flying cargo and supply planes over enemy territory as he had done riding his horse, Champion, in films.

After the war Autry turned to TV and signed with Columbia Records, where his all-time best sellers were produced: "Rudolph the Red-Nosed Reindeer," "Frosty the Snowman," and "Peter Cottontail." "Rudolph" still brings in a barrel of money every Christmas.

Autry was elected to the Country Music Hall of Fame in 1969.

It would be easy to say that Autry didn't have much of a voice, that most of his songs were silly, that he wore absurd clothes in his films, and that he had little impact on serious culture. Women didn't scream at his performances, teen-agers have never torn his clothes (these days he wears civilian clothes, mostly), and his old records don't fetch $200 each at memorabilia shows. But to a generation or more of Americans, Gene Autry is *the* cowboy. And in a way, the cowboy is symbolic of America. No man can have a more intensive compliment.

# B

## BAILEY, DeFORD

Charley Pride was not the first black performer in country music. DeFord Bailey, "the little crippled boy," was a hunchbacked Nashville bootblack who could play the harmonica "like it was the most important thing in the world." Realizing how good he was, Bailey auditioned for the *WSM Barn Dance* and was quickly signed up by George D. Hay, "The Solemn Ole Judge" and founder of Grand Ole Opry, and became a very popular performer. This was at a time when blackface-minstrel humor was integrated into the Opry's fare, and two of the major blackface stars were known as "Lasses" and "Honey" and were white. Bailey was probably the first artist ever to record in Nashville. He cut eight sides for RCA Victor on October 2, 1928. But despite his popularity, Bailey disappeared from the Grand Ole Opry roster. In 1945 Judge Hay wrote: "That brings us to DeFord Bailey, a little crippled colored boy who was a bright feature of our show for about fifteen years. Like some members of his race and other races, DeFord was lazy. He knew about a dozen numbers, which he put on the air and recorded for a major company, but he refused to learn any more, even though his reward was great. He was our mascot and is still loved by the entire company. We gave him a whole year's notice to learn some more tunes, but he would not. When we were forced to give him his final notice, DeFord said, without malice, 'I knowed it wuz comin', Judge. I knowed it wuz comin'.' DeFord comes to the show now and then to visit us. We are always glad to see him—a great artist."

Bailey doesn't agree. He says he was a "mascot" all right, but he didn't think his rewards were so great or that he refused to expand his repertoire. Bailey doesn't think that the Opry people are glad to see him or that he gave up his career "without malice." When asked about the Opry he says, "Go ask them about it." Writer Paul Hemphill visited Bailey's shoeshine stand a few years ago, when the harmonica player was approaching seventy. Hemphill asked him to play: "Bailey reached beneath his apron and fished a gleaming chrome harmonica from his coat pocket. He blew it clear of dust and held it in his left hand, crossing his ankles and leaning on one of the platforms with his right hand, and as he stood like that looking out over the excavated corner lot across the street in this neighborhood where he had spent his whole life, he began to play 'John Henry.' Yes, he still can play. When he'd had enough of 'John Henry,' he played 'Fox Chase,' one he was famous for, a tune that simulates all of the sounds of a pack of hounds after a fox. He can play the hell out of a harmonica, DeFord Bailey can . . ."

When asked if he'd like to play professionally and cut records again, Bailey said wistfully, "There ain't no future in it. I ain't got no future, anyway. Ain't no future for nobody seventy years old."

# BALLAD

A ballad is a simple narrative composition of verse in marked rhythm, suitable for singing. Generally ballads are story songs, often dealing with love themes. (See COUNTRY MUSIC.)

# BARE, BOBBY

BORN: April 7, 1935, Ironton, Ohio
MARRIED: w. Jeannie
CHILDREN: s. Robert; d. Carla

Bobby Bare's biggest hit was in 1963. His version of Mel Tillis' "Detroit City" sold more than one million records, and it still graces a number of his "best of" albums. "Detroit City" tells of the boy from Appalachia who comes north to Detroit, ostensibly to make his fortune. He does find a job, but his heart remains in the southland and he feels that life is pretty crummy: "By day I make the cars, by night I make the bars." A depressing song—but very affecting and sensitive, and a soulful rendition by Bare.

It isn't surprising that Bobby Bare could feel the depression of the song. He was a child of the Depression and life for the Bares was bare as Mother Hubbard's cupboard. The farm was on the least productive land on the Ohio side of the Kentucky-Ohio border. There was no work, and food was so scarce that Bobby's sister was put up for adoption. He never knew what it was to have free time during his childhood. He worked on farms, as a bundle boy in a clothing factory and as an ice-cream peddler. In the early 1950s, with less than $30 to his name, he headed for California, hopefully to make a name for himself in music. He had always sung, mostly for free at bars and on local radio stations. But as soon as he got to California he was drafted. The day before he entered the service, he taped some of his own compositions and sent them off to record companies. One of them, "All-American Boy," became a big hit. (He sold the rights for only $50, which seemed like a lot for a private E-2 in the army.) But the success of the number opened some doors when he was discharged, and in 1963, after "Detroit City," his success was assured. Bare's friends in the music business call him The Bare, which is kind of a misnomer—it connotes something fearful, and Bobby Bare has the reputation of being a nice guy in a business where nice guys don't always come out on top.

He comes out as a "nice guy" in his songs, too—with a tone of quiet, intimate emotionalism. During the years he has been labeled "pop" or "folk-country" or "folk-pop." His records have made the middle-of-the-road and pop charts, but Bobby Bare considers himself a "country singer." He has one of Nashville's drier senses of humor. He and his wife, Jeannie, once came to a birthday party for Tom T. Hall and his wife, Dixie. Bare's gift for Tom was an empty picture frame captioned "The Phantom." When the package was opened, Bobby exclaimed, "Darn, he got away again." For Dixie, who operates one of Tennessee's more successful dog kennels, there was a kitty-cat—a live one.

Among Bobby Bare's hits: "Streets of Baltimore," "Miller's Cave," and "Come Kiss Me, Love." He appeared in a small role in the movie *A Distant Trumpet.*

Bobby Bare: From "Detroit City" to superstardom.

# BEAVERS, CLYDE
BORN: June 8, 1932, Tennega, Georgia
MARRIED: w. Louise

Like many country singers, Clyde Beavers knew what it was to go hungry as a child, to work before he was nine to help keep his poverty-stricken family's Georgia farm from failing. His parents finally gave up, and the children were taken in by neighbors and friends. Beavers managed to finish his schooling, somehow, and as soon as he was old enough, enlisted in the air force. He'd always sung and put songs down on paper, and he impressed enough people in the air force with his ability to realize he might have something. When he was dis-

charged, he became an Atlanta disc jockey, writing and performing on the side. His big hit, "Man in the Glass," was recorded in 1957 for Mercury. He also recorded and wrote for Decca and Hickory. And, in 1961, Grand Ole Opry beckoned Clyde Beavers to Nashville and a position as a performer on the Friday night spectacular. This often means fame and fortune for an artist. In Beaver's case it meant a steady job. Clyde Beavers is certainly on the country-music scene. He has a nice voice, but he hasn't had a chart hit for some time, and in Nashville, that's "going hungry."

## BEE, MOLLY [Molly Beachboard]
BORN: August 18, 1939, Oklahoma City, Oklahoma

Can you imagine this: If Molly Bee had been born a few years later, and had come to popularity during the rock and surfing eras in California, she would never have had to change her name. Molly Bee was born Molly Beachboard, of the Oklahoma Beachboards who became the Arizona Beachboards when Molly was a wee tot. The Beachboards encouraged little Molly to entertain, and before long she was a singing and dancing tot, belting Hank Williams songs on Rex Allen's Tucson radio show. The Arizona Beachboards became the Hollywood Beachboards, and little Molly (nobody would ever ask her to join a basketball team as center) auditioned for Cliffie Stone's *Hometown Jamboree* TV show. She was only eleven, but Cliffie Stone signed her up, and the Los Angelanos took to her like sports cars to freeways. *Hometown Jamboree*, like many early, live, local TV shows, had its problems. Its cardboard sets often ripped during the performance, props wouldn't work, and the sound went dead. But it was a fine show, nonetheless, introducing to the California southland a number of talented country performers: Billy Strange, Billy Liebert, Jeannie Black, Leon McAuliff, Red Sovine, and the superb guitar of Merle Travis. The late Spade Cooley was a regular, and any Nashville wanderer in the Los Angeles area managed to get on the show. But among all this talent, the dancing and singing tot prevailed, and many listeners referred to the show as the "Molly Bee hour."

She was short and cute and American as chile and beans, and her popularity was only rivaled by *My Little Margie's* Gale Storm. Molly Bee, it was reported, smiled the moment she popped out of bed and continued smiling during her entire cheerful day, singing cheerful songs. (Even her big hit, "Miserable Me," was sung with a smile.) Leaving *Hometown Jamboree* in her mid-teens (people hardly noticed that she wasn't eleven any more), she added a bit of vigor to the *Pinky Lee Show* and then as one of Tennessee Ernie Ford's brightest pea-pickers, singing all the time, mostly for the MGM label. Her personal appearances broke all records during the 1950s. She appeared in summer stock with Alan Young and Buddy Ebsen. And she appeared in a number of films, including *The Chartreuse Caboose*, one of the worst pictures, if not *the* worst, ever to be produced in Hollywood. As country music and its fans grew more sophisticated, Molly Bee's popularity diminished somewhat, but she can be seen from time to time on TV variety shows whenever a need arises for a thirty-five-year-old dancing and singing tot.

## BELEW, CARL
BORN: March 21, 1931, Salina, Oklahoma
MARRIED: w. Kate May
CHILDREN: s. Robert Gene

Elvis Presley's single of "Lonely Street" is often included in the "biggest-selling records of all time" lists. It also was a hit for a number of other performers—country, rock, and easy-listening variety. Just about the only performer who didn't cash in on the song was Carl Belew, who wrote it. His authorship, however, opened some doors and started his career as a singer/writer. Belew, who supported himself by plumbing and construction work and grueling one-night stands in rinky-dink honky-tonks, finally gained a regular spot on the *Louisiana Hayride* show in Shreveport. In 1955 he co-authored the cross-the-board hit "Stop the World," which was followed by an equally profitable "Hello, Out There." His contract with Decca seemed secure, and crowds were drawn by the name of Carl Belew. But audiences are fickle, and Belew's 1966 album, "Am I

That Easy to Forget?" seemed to be prophetic. The current Schwann LP catalog of stereo recordings doesn't even mention his name.

# BLUEGRASS

Bluegrass is often lumped generically with "country music," because of the similarity of sounds. But there is a difference, which Mike Seeger points out in this essay written for Folkways Records:

"Bluegrass, the term, came into use in the early 1950s, originally referring to the music of Bill Monroe, from Kentucky, the Bluegrass State, and his Bluegrass Boys, a group that for twenty years has appeared on the Grand Ole Opry in Nashville and made records for Bluebird, Columbia, and Decca. Bluegrass describes a specific vocal and instrumental treatment of a certain type of traditional or folk-composed song.

"Vocally the style is characterized by high-pitched, emotional singing. In duets, Monroe's high tenor voice is dominant in volume and interest in harmony above the lead part, using unorthodox, often modal- and minor-sounding intervals, probably influenced by his childhood church singing as well as by early country musicians such as the Carter Family. Often a third, or baritone, part is added, usually below the lead voice, and in gospel songs there is often a bass singer. Harmony in parallel thirds, popular in more formal music, is rarely used, and Monroe's tenor (harmony) often seems to be a separate and superior melody. The singers are also the instrumentalists.

"Instrumentally, Bluegrass music is a direct outgrowth of traditional hill music styles, its two most distinctive features being that it has no electrified instruments and that it uses a five-string banjo for lead or background in all songs. The guitar players, most commonly also the lead singer, supply the band with an open—not 'slap' (or rhythm) style—chord background, much like the Carter Family style, with a few melodic runs such as Lester Flatt's famous G run, but rarely take an instrumental lead. The five-string banjo is played in a style like that of Earl Scruggs, who introduced his new style on Monroe's early Columbia records. See Folkways record 'Banjo

Songs and Tunes Scruggs Style' FA2314 for more on this. The fiddle player uses odd double stops and slides that vary from breakdown to country blues, a smooth style initiated largely by the Florida fiddler Chubby Wise, also on the early Monroe Columbia records. Monroe's mandolin playing is driving and syncopated, and like the fiddling, is influenced by both blues and breakdown styles. The string bass supports the guitar by picking on the downbeat with an occasional lead, and the bass player usually is dressed in a ridiculous costume and provides the comedy skits and songs.

"The songs themselves are mostly built on traditional patterns, four-line verse, three or four chords, and in simple 2/4 or 3/4 time; instrumentals are usually in a breakneck 4/4 time, and like the songs, are performed with great skill. Often new songs are made from the old with a change of words, harmony, treatment, or pace. The subject matter is most usually unsuccessful love but also covers home, Mother, catastrophes, religion, and almost anything else under the sun. Monroe has written a large number of his own songs, as do many other artists.

"Bluegrass is directly related to the old corn-shucking-party banjo and fiddle music as well as the ballad songs and religious music of the southern mountains. With the influx of the guitar, mandolin, and string bass from the cities of the deep South in the early 1900s, mountain people such as the Carter Family, Blue Sky Boys, and especially in this case, Bill and Charlie, the Monroe Brothers, began adapting old songs previously sung unaccompanied or with banjo and fiddle to the new instruments (with likewise new singing styles) and made these songs acceptable as a performance. There were several other bands in this era that could also be called pre-Bluegrass: the Mainers with their four-piece band and (sometimes) smooth singing, and Byron Parker, who even had a banjo picker, Snuffy Jenkins, who played a style much like Earl Scruggs and came from the same area in North Carolina.

"But not until Bill Monroe, Earl Scruggs, Lester Flatt, and Chubby Wise came together after World War II did the bluegrass band take its classic and most competent form. When the records of this group were released, old-time music and especially five-string-banjo picking were in decline, and the early Monroe Columbias plus his show on the Opry brought new attention to the old-time music. Several groups such as the Stanley Brothers who had been playing old-time music with thumb-style banjo started working more towards bluegrass.

"Lester Flatt, a singer and guitar player, and Earl Scruggs, the five-string-banjo picker, formed a five-piece band, the Foggy Mountain Boys, with a style much like Monroe's but more polished, and featuring Earl's banjo picking and Lester's singing. Mac Wiseman sang revised old sentimental songs with his clear tenor voice; Jesse McReynolds picks the mandolin somewhat like Scruggs with a flat pick; Jimmy Martin features novelty songs; the Osborne Brothers specialize in smooth, close trio singing and their own banjo and mandolin styles; Don Reno plays an expert, jazzy, harmonic plectrum banjo style (as opposed to Earl's melodic style), which is also more suited to his slow dance songs and has gained many converts; the Stanley Brothers feature good old-time bluegrass music.

"By about 1953 bluegrass music reached its height of popularity, with no less than ten different bands on commercial records. And many smaller amateur bands sprang up through the South, perhaps one in every town of 1,000 population. With such competition and with advanced recording techniques, bluegrass changed more quickly. 'Bluegrass' became more a means of distinguishing any type of traditional music from the run-of-the-mill performance by the steel guitars of the Nashville Philharmonic and, later, hillbilly rock-and-roll. Bands are now called bluegrass that contain one element of the original style, for example, the Louvin Brothers' singing and playing (but not their electric and Hawaiian style guitars) or Charlie Monroe's singing (despite his electrified band members) or any number of combinations of less than the five main instruments such as a banjo-fiddle duet, two guitars, a bass and banjo duet, etc. etc.

"Bluegrass, like other types of music, is constantly changing and searching for combinations that will give its practitioners something new and put them a step ahead of the competing groups. Flatt and Scruggs now include in their band a dobro guitar, fretted Hawaiian-style with a steel bar, unelectrified and often played like a banjo. Other bands have experimented with duets on instrumental and instrumental breaks and with adding mouth harps, pianos, organs, tipple, or accordion, but so far only the dobro and instrumental duets have been accepted into the style. The trend in singing is away from the country twang toward smoother, more widely acceptable harmony. One of the greatest changes brought about in bluegrass is the new method of 'hi fi' recording and pressing of records and the use of the echo chamber, which gives the full orchestra sound, destroying the home-made effect.

"Also changing is the bluegrass audience. Old-time hill music has always appealed to the individualistic mountain people since it is deeply rooted in their tradition and they feel that it is an expression of their preserving that tradition. But many of these have come to prefer the more sophisticated music of the commercial country music bands, or even rock-and-roll. Many city-bred people, however, have been hearing and buying records by the bluegrass artists, this being part of the urban revival of folk music. It is mainly a musician's music and is appreciated even by many commercial musicians (including Elvis Presley, whose first release was Bill Monroe's composition 'Blue Moon of Kentucky'), who consider it a desirable part of all country music."

# BLUES

Blues generally are songs about miseries and the sad part of life, sung in twelve-bar stanzas of three lines each. In this form, the repetition of the first line gives the singer an opportunity to extemporize the third line in any manner he chooses. I once asked Duke Ellington to tell me about "blues" music. "My friend," Ellington said tolerantly, "blues is something you feel and sing, not describe." As Peter Guralnik writes, in *Feel Like Going Home*: "blues take in a lot of territory. If you confess to liking it, you open yourself to any number of responses. Oh, Louis Armstrong, someone will say. Bessie Smith. B. B. King. Ten Years After. Any one of them will be correct because within a fairly narrow framework there exists a real multiplicity of styles. But if it's country blues that you're talking about, despite all the exposure and attention which has been lavished on the blues in recent years, it's unlikely you're going to make yourself clear. . . . Country blues, which was at first considered too disreputable to record, remains to this day too funky in a pejorative sense to merit serious attention.''

"In its most well-defined and distinct phase, the blues form developed in the period between 1885 and World War I," explains historian Bill C. Malone, "and in fact paralleled and derived from the hardening of racial segregation in the South. Developing out of the old worksongs and spirituals, the blues came to be the expression of the Negro's outlook on life. Arising out of poverty, oppression, and the numerous miseries and injustices which the Negro experienced, the blues had taken on a fairly established form by 1920." Before any record company decided to exploit blues, black singers were performing their varied arts all over the South. This secular music provided the base for rock-and-roll as well as rhythm-and-blues, and many of the earliest white country musicians listened to and were influenced by this kind of music—especially Jimmie Rodgers and Hank Williams. Jerry Silverman has described the white country blues as a hybrid type of song, "the product of the mingling of the Negro blues, the southern mountain ballad, and the cowboy song."

## BOGGS, DOCK [Moran L. Boggs]
BORN: February 7, 1898, Dooley, Virginia

During the folk boom of the 1960s, Mike Seeger introduced a number of "natural" Appalachian musicians to folk-festival audiences. Among the best of these was a mild-mannered banjo virtuoso named Moran L. "Dock" Boggs. Boggs, who started playing as a child, learned his two-finger, one-thumb style from "a colored man that used to be around Norton, Virginia. He played with his forefinger and next finger." Boggs developed that style into what has been described as "fine art." He married, at age twenty, a woman whose religious peculiarities included a fear of banjo playing as venal sin. Brunswick records attempted, in 1927, to get Dock Boggs to record for them, but his wife was adamant, and Dock sold his banjo and went to work in the coal mines, which his wife believed was "a more honorable way to earn a living." He didn't even

touch a banjo for many years, his picking fingers swollen and scarred from operating a coal-cutting machine. But he listened to music, and at a country/folk festival in 1954, after forty-one long years in the mines, he was persuaded to play one song by Mike Seeger. No longer able to resist any more, Dock Boggs has been recording for Folkways, influencing banjo pickers and pleasing himself and audiences ever since.

## BOND, JOHNNY [Cyrus Whitfield Bond]
BORN: June 1, 1915, Enville, Oklahoma

One of the great singing "sidekicks" of second-feature westerns, his real name is Cyrus Whitfield Bond, but everybody calls him Johnny. He appeared in hundreds of films, mostly with Gene Autry, Roy Rogers, Tex Ritter, and Hopalong Cassidy, but also in major feature productions like Wilson with Alexander Knox and Gallant Bess and Duel in the Sun. One of his 300 published songs is the all-time western classic "Cimarron." He also wrote "Tomorrow Never Comes," "I'll Step Aside," and "I Wonder Where You Are Tonight." His first instrument was a ninety-eight-cent ukulele, bought from the Montgomery Ward catalog. He was a member of the Jimmy Wakely Trio, the Pop Moore Oklahomans, and the Gene Autry Ranch Gang. He was a featured performer on Gene Autry's radio show for fourteen years. Though teenagers don't run after him for autographs and his name on a poster won't guarantee a full house, Johnny Bond still writes and records, nowadays for Starday.

## BOOTH, TONY
BORN: February 7, 1943, Tampa, Florida

Tony Booth has had a couple of chart hits, "Irma Jackson" and "Cinderella" among them. He is part of Buck Owens' Bakersfield gang, and a regular performer at southern California's Palomino Club. A lot of country fans in and around the San Fernando Valley turn out to listen to him sing watered-down country songs in a pleasant, professional manner. Thus far, however, there are no strong vibrations that he will grow into either a new Elvis or a latter day Ray Price. He does have his following and his records sell, but it will be a while before we know if Tony will be booked into Country Music Immortality.

Tony Booth: A "Buckeroo" with his own following.

## BOWMAN, DON

BORN: August 26, 1937, Lubbock, Texas

Don Bowman calls himself the "worst guitarist in country music," and though he presumably plays well (like Jack Benny with the violin), he is one of country music's few singing comics. "Chit Atkins, Make Me a Star" was his major hit, and the fans call for it again and again. (Actually "Chit"—or Chet—Atkins, the great guitarist and country-music talent scout, made Bowman a star by signing him with RCA in the mid-sixties.) Bowman travels with a number of country shows, both singing and telling jokes, and has made the charts with "Giddyup, Do-Nut," "Folsom Prison Blues No. 2," and "Poor Old Ugly Gladys Jones."

## BRITT, ELTON [James Britt Baker]

BORN: July 7, 1917, Marshall, Arkansas
DIED: June 23, 1972

Late in 1942, in the darkest days of World War II, President Franklin D. Roosevelt invited a young "hillbilly" singer to the White House to personally entertain him and a few close friends. It was the first time a "country" singer, according to anyone's memory, had been invited to the White House, and the song Elton Britt sang was "There's a Star-Spangled Banner Waving Somewhere," which recounted the story of a crippled mountain boy who yearned to do his part in the war effort. The song, written by Bob Miller, was released as the "B" side of one of Britt's Bluebird records. It became the one song that surpassed all other World War II patriotic numbers in popularity, and the one that revealed to music company executives the latent interest, on the part of non-southerners, in "hillbilly" music. Britt's recorded version sold one million records (a phenomenal figure in those days) and remained popular almost until 1944. Elton Britt, billed as the "highest yodeler in the world," became the first rural singer since Vernon Dalhart to record a song of national hit proportions which transcended the bounds of most musical categories. (Interestingly enough, the song was eventually rewritten as "The Ballad of Francis Powers"—about the unfortunate experiences of the pilot of the first U-2 shot down by the Russians.) Britt was not a one-hit star: In more than twenty years he turned out 627 singles and 60 albums, mostly for RCA Victor.

Born James Britt Baker in the Osage country of Arkansas, he was a member of a musical family. His mother sang and his father fiddled. Elton played a five-dollar Sears Roebuck guitar. His ambition was to become a construction engineer, but Arkansas was badly hit by the Depression, and while in high school Elton picked cotton, dug potatoes, and hoed corn—all for seventy-five cents for a twelve-hour day. On weekends he sang at clubs for not much more money. Meanwhile, R. S. McMillan, the California industrialist and hillbilly music fan, had founded station KMPC in Los Angeles and was eager to sign "authentic" talent. Scouring the back country of Texas and Oklahoma in search of talent, McMillan eventually found the Britt

cluded high school, college, and some years in art school—a rare background for a "down-home" country comedian. "When I graduated from college in 1936, there wasn't any demand for commercial artists," Campbell says. "I'd have starved to death if I'd followed it." Always ready with a quip, Campbell auditioned for and won a spot on the *Mid-Day Merry-Go-Round* radio show in Knoxville, Tennessee. Other members of the cast included Roy Acuff, Chet Atkins, Pee Wee King, Eddie Hill, Homer and Jethro, and the Carlisles. When World War II broke out, Campbell joined the navy, returning to Knoxville with his own TV show. Archie Campbell introduced a number of future stars on the show, including Carl Smith, Carl and Pearl Butler, and Flatt and Scruggs. "Many

people think I'm only a comedian," Campbell says wistfully, "but there's more than one Campbell who can sing. Glen doesn't have a monopoly. I've made a lot of money from record sales. Some new *Hee Haw* fans aren't aware that I sing. I've had several big hits on the country charts" ("Dark Side of the Street" with Lorene Mann and "The Men in My Little Girl's Life"). He is chief writer and "top banana" of *Hee Haw,* the most successful syndicated TV show in the United States and Canada. He still paints, is active in civic affairs and Republican politics (for eight years he was a member of Knoxville's school board), and plays golf for charity. "I try not to let the fact that I'm a college graduate show," Archie Campbell says. Archie Campbell records for RCA Victor.

Archie Campbell greets visitors to *Hee Haw.*

Glen Campbell: From Arkansas to Hollywood, a housewives' delight.

## CAMPBELL, GLEN

BORN: March 22, 1936, Delight, Arkansas (sometimes gives birthplace as Billstown, Arkansas)

MARRIED: w. Billie Jean

CHILDREN: s. William Travis; d. Kelli Glyn

In 1968 Glen Campbell was generally acclaimed —because of the number of awards he received and the volume of his record sales—the top country singles and album artist. He hosted a popular CBS-TV series and began an acting career. "Not since Elvis Presley's ascendancy more than a decade ago,'' wrote Vernon Scott for UPI, ''has a young soloist come along to capture the mass audience with such effectiveness as Glen Campbell.'' Nashville's reaction to Campbell's success was shaky. There were many who were appalled by his friendship with the Smothers Brothers and other ''hippies'' and by his desire to be on the pop charts. Others believed he opened up country music for a new audience. ''They don't know how to classify me,'' Campbell says. ''Some of my records are listed as country, some as pop. I don't fit into the usual country music, sweet music, and rock categories.

''When I first started out, people used to ask how come a country musician was playing George Shearing. Musicians like Shearing have meant a lot to me. Django Reinhardt, he really tore into the guitar, and Tal Farlow. And people like Marty Robbins and George Jones in country music. I've always admired Sinatra's way with a song—'Come Fly With Me' and all those. I've enjoyed jazz. I think Nat 'King' Cole and Gary Burton are great. Some people make the kind of music a man in the street understands, and they can win great popularity; but some are too deep —the average person can't understand what they're saying.''

Whatever else he is, Glen Campbell was born country—in the ''ragged corner of southwestern Arkansas.'' Campbell says, ''We lived in the sticks so things were very quiet. We didn't even have a tractor and the kids had to do all the chores. There were twelve of us. I was the seventh kid.''

Campbell left school in the tenth grade to play in a band in Wyoming, but it didn't work out. ''I finally had to hitch home and I had to give up my guitar to pick up enough money.'' In a long interview with *Seventeen*'s Edwin Miller, Campbell recalls that he later went off with an uncle, Dick Bills, ''and played with his band for four or five years—all kinds of sweet and country music —in Albuquerque, New Mexico. I finally quit the band in 1958. We had some words about a piece we did. He said he had been playing it for eighteen years or whatever it was, and he knew what he was doing, and I said that after so long he ought to, and resigned. It wasn't anything I could have gone on with anyhow, being a member of the family. The others could foul up and then he'd turn around and give me heck on

what I was doing with the guitar. I formed my own band then, Glen Campbell and the Western Wranglers, and we played together for a year and a half or so. That's when I met my wife, Billie, who's from Carlsbad, New Mexico. I fell for her as soon as I saw her. I've always been like that. I don't like to do any window-shopping. I know what I want as soon as I see it, whether it's a wife or a shirt in a store. It took me six months to persuade her, and that's been it ever since.

''Someone had promised me a job in Los Angeles, but I worked for two weeks and didn't get paid. We had a rough time in the beginning. I was playing with a band and traveling, making maybe eighty dollars a week, which just about covered my expenses on the road. Billie had to get a job to help pay the rent. Finally I began to get studio recording sessions. If you're good, you can get lots of work. One year I played in 586 sessions, and of all those records there were only three hits. I sat down and analyzed what the trouble was with the others. There was a lot of good music there, but out of all those singles I worked on that year only three of them had lyrics that meant something! The main thing that makes for a hit song is that it tells a story; you get caught up in the lyrics.

''In 1961 I had a hit record called 'Turn Around, Look At Me' on a little label. The next year I signed with Capitol and had one record, 'Too Late to Worry—Too Blue to Cry,' that hit the charts. They didn't follow it up with an album for about five or six months, by which time it was all forgotten. And that was it for five years. Finally I got tired of doing things their way. They always wanted me to have patience, but I was through with that. I went up to Voyle Gilmore, a nice guy who was in charge of Artists and Repertoire at Capitol at that time, and blew my stack and told him what I thought of the company and how things had worked out. Then I went to the heads of all the departments at Capitol and told them what I thought of their operation too. It worked.

''By the next spring they let me make records the way I wanted to do them, and a month or two later I had my hit, 'Burning Bridges.' Then came 'Gentle on My Mind' and 'By the Time I Get to Phoenix' and 'Hey, Little One.' Now they put out my albums so fast they crowd each other.''

Actually, although Campbell was making $75,000 a year as a busy studio musician, and did make a few hit singles, it wasn't until 1967 that he emerged as a star with his rendition of "Gentle on My Mind." The song, written by John Hartford, a friend, and co-performer with him on the Smothers Brothers summer TV show, has become a classic, and Campbell uses it as a theme song on his show. Today the gentle Campbell has a lot of other things on his mind. He owns land in San Diego and apartment buildings in Los Angeles. He plays golf with Bob Hope and other luminaries. He no longer drives a "solid gold Cadillac," but his country smile cost more than $3,000 worth of jacket crowns. If he is not a country singer, he certainly is a singer with country roots. "If I can make a forty-year-old housewife put down her dish towel and say 'Oh,' why then, man, I've got it made."

In 1973 Campbell's album "I Knew Jesus Before He Was a Superstar" was on the country, easy listening, and pop hit charts. He obviously has it made. Why is it then, in my personal collection of more than 2,000 country albums, not one is by Glen Campbell? I guess it's because I'm not a forty-year-old housewife.

## CARGILL, HENSON
BORN: February 5, 1941, Oklahoma City, Oklahoma

Atlantic Records seems to have big plans for Henson Cargill, whose name, at this writing, is not yet a household word with country fans. He is over thirty, a late age for a "big buildup" (especially after having been signed by two other labels. Cargill didn't like Monument, it is said, and asked for his release from them, and Mega, which produces good records from time to time, isn't the most promotion-minded company making records), and he doesn't want to live in Nashville. He lives in Oklahoma and operates a ranch near Stillwater, where he writes songs and tends his 150 head of cattle. He has had a number of hits: "Skip-a-Rope" brought Cargill's name to the fore and got him a job on Cincinnati's TV *Country Hayride*, which he left after thirty-nine weeks, because it was taking too much of his time. His first song for Mega, "Pencil Marks on the Wall," was an immediate success, as well.

Henson Cargill: He's more at home on the range.

The grandson of O. A. Cargill, Sr., the mayor of Oklahoma City, and the son of celebrated Oklahoma trial lawyer O. A. Cargill, Jr., Henson Cargill could have been a trial lawyer or politician. Instead he went to Colorado State University to study animal husbandry, and though married (in his senior year of high school), worked his way through school, refusing financial aid from his family. Cargill was always interested in music, having played the guitar and sung from childhood, but didn't consider music seriously until he returned to the ranch after college. He hauled cattle for his brother and worked as a deputy sheriff in Oklahoma County. He was a deputy when he met Harold Gay, leader of The Kimberleys, who encouraged him to develop his own singing style and to do some studio work. The Kimberleys worked the Northwest and convinced Cargill to give up crime fighting to sing with them. "There were five-shows-a-night jobs," Cargill recalls, "and constant travel. But it was experience and an income." After a gig at the Golden Nugget in Las Vegas, "pretty good for a fellow with no record," Cargill went to Nashville, looking for a producer who would record him. Don Law, an independent who had formerly worked for Columbia, liked Cargill, and through Law, publishers began to pitch songs to Cargill. One of these songs was "Skip-a-Rope," and the record became number one on the country charts. At this juncture, many people in Nashville are observing the "singing deputy's" career with interest.

## THE CARLISLES

### Bill Carlisle

BORN: December 19, 1908, Wakefield, Kentucky

MARRIED: w. Leona

CHILDREN: s. Billy; d. Sheila

### Clifford R. Carlisle

BORN: March 6, 1904, Wakefield, Kentucky

MARRIED: w. Henrietta

CHILDREN: s. Thomas R.; d. Violet L.

If Jimmie Rodgers "founded" American commercial country music, then the Carlisle brothers helped give it shape. Performing through the late twenties and thirties, they excelled in every type of country song, both honky-tonk and gospel. They were noted for their humorous tunes, and in person they also sang a number of risque songs, unusual for country (Cliff Carlisle, the oldest brother, had left home early and joined the Keith Vaudeville Circuit, where he picked up this kind of material, which he later turned into country songs like "Is Zat You, Myrtle"). Cliff Carlisle was one of the first to play the dobro guitar and was considered one of the best three or four steel guitar players in the 1930s. He accompanied Jimmie Rodgers on a number of records.

"Me and my brother Bill," Cliff Carlisle said in an interview in the early 1960s, "come from the old school. We didn't have any silver spoons in our mouths." Their farm was a tobacco sharecrop operation complete with badly constructed log cabin. "Many a winter the snow would come through the cracks." The only entertainment was the Sunday songfest by all the Carlisle family—brothers, sisters, mother, and father. Cliff decided to become a professional musician, and as soon as he was old enough, he appeared in all the amateur shows he could enter and finally joined the Keith Circuit as a singer. He worked with guitarists Wilbur Ball and Fred Kirby. And Cliff and Kirby (who sang too) had the first yodeling duo in country music (brother Bill later accompanied them). Cliff Carlisle's playing influenced a number of steel guitarists, and Buck Graves, who played with Flatt and Scruggs during their heyday, will tell anyone who asks that his guitar "contains parts of Carlisle's old dobro."

When Bill Carlisle was old enough, he joined Cliff, and from 1930 until Cliff's retirement in 1947 the Carlisles recorded for every major label in the country. Their repertory contained a number of fine hobo songs: "Ramblin' Jack," "Just a Lonely Hobo," and "The Girl in the Blue Velvet Band." The brothers joined Grand Ole Opry in 1954, and when Cliff retired, Bill remained as a single, with a major hit, "What Kinda Deal Is This?", as late as 1966.

## CARSON, FIDDLIN' JOHN
BORN: (?) Fannin County, Georgia
DIED: 1935

Lots of contemporary bluegrass performers talk about their debt to Fiddlin' John Carson, and old-timers fondly tell stories about his life as an itinerant mill hand, house painter, cotton picker, and full-time fiddler at medicine shows in the South. There is a "Carson style" of fiddling, too —but there's disagreement as to the origin of the term, and Carson is a very common Appalachian name. In his youth, being small of stature, John Carson was a professional jockey, but his name doesn't add much to the annals of thoroughbred racing. However, John Carson was a country music pioneer. He was the first country musician to be recorded commercially. Ralph Peer, then of Okeh Records, came to Atlanta to record musicians in June 1923. He chose several bands, including Warner's Seven Aces, the Collegians, and black pianist Eddy Heywood's group. But the recording session with John Carson was the event that made country-music history.

Bill C. Malone, in his scholarly history of country music, recalls the day: "With the recording of Fiddlin' John Carson on June 14, 1923, Ralph Peer made his initial venture into the unexploited field of country music. When Peer listened to the two songs which Carson chose to record—'The Little Old Log Cabin in the Lane' and 'The Old Hen Cackled and the Rooster's Going to Crow'—he responded as one might expect of a northern urbanite upon first being initiated into the exotic world of southern folk music. He thought the singing was awful and insisted that only Carson's fiddle tunes be recorded. Polk C. Brockman, an executive with Okeh Records, however, understood the Georgia entertainment market and realized that the small farmers and mill workers enjoyed Fiddlin' John's vocalizing as much as his instrumental virtuosity. Brockman offered to buy five hundred copies of Carson's first recorded and unpressed numbers immediately. Unable to conceive of a regional or national market for such items, Peer issued the record uncatalogued, unadvertised, unlabeled, and for circulation solely in the Atlanta area. By late July 1923, when the first shipment of five hundred records had been sold and after Brockman had

ordered another shipment, Peer acknowledged his early mistake and gave the recording the label number 4890, a move which placed the songs in Okeh's popular catalogue and gave them national publicity. In November, as sales continued to mount, Carson was asked to come to New York, where he recorded twelve more songs and signed an exclusive Okeh contract.

"Fiddlin' John Carson, therefore, became the first hillbilly performer to have his selections recorded and marketed on a commercial basis. This was the real beginning of the hillbilly music industry. Peer now remembered the recorded but unreleased tunes of Henry Whitter, who had earlier persuaded New York Okeh executives to test-record some of his numbers. Two songs, "Lonesome Road Blues" and "The Wreck on the Southern Old 97," were released in late November with the number 40015. The popularity of these songs, plus that attained by Fiddlin' John Carson and Eck Robertson, encouraged other record companies to cash in on the popularity of native white performers as a means of bolstering lagging sales capacity."

And that's why Fiddlin' John Carson is remembered.

## CARSON, MARTHA LOU
BORN: March 19, 1921, Neon, Kentucky
MARRIED: h. Xavier Cosse
CHILDREN: s. Rene Paul

Country music used to be associated with barns and haylofts. Today, among other things, it's much more honky-tonk and neon. And it was in Neon, Kentucky, that Martha Lou Carson was born. Martha Lou Carson was one of the early queens of country music: a big draw at the *Renfro Valley Barn Dance* in Kentucky and state fairs all over the United States. In the forties she sang on all the country radio shows, and in the fifties on the country TV shows. She was also a member of Grand Ole Opry. Martha Lou Carson recorded for RCA, Capitol, and Cadence, and for a short time de-countrified and tried the supper club circuit, where she experienced a modicum of success. Late in her career she de-citified and gospelized a couple of big original hits: "I Can't Stand Up Alone" and "I'm Gonna Walk and Talk with My Lord." Her big standard was "Satisfied." Lots of young people on Nashville's music scene have never heard of Martha Lou Carson, but she had her day.

## THE CARTER FAMILY

### A. P. Carter
BORN: Maces Springs, Virginia
DIED: November 7, 1960, Maces Springs, Virginia

### Maybelle Carter
BORN: May 10, 1909, Nickelsville, Virginia

### Sara Carter
BORN: July 21, 1899, Wise County, Virginia

### June Carter (see JOHNNY CASH)
BORN: June 23, 1929, Maces Springs, Virginia

Since colonial times, singing families have been part of the American musical heritage. Few of these families have had the impact on musical style that the Carter family had. They established a close-harmony technique that has become the pattern for all subsequent groups. The first time I saw Mother Maybelle was at New York's Village Gate; she had been brought to Greenwich Village by *Cavalier* magazine for its first folk-music awards. She stole the show from a number of then more popular city-folk performers. I have seen her several times since, mostly singing on the Johnny Cash tour. She never disappoints. There are many things I have to say about the Carter family, but they are much better said in the following magazine article by Billy Edd Wheeler, the great songwriter and performer, who is a friend of the Carter Family (and whom I first met way back in 1960 when he was living in Brooklyn, New York, of all places).

"She is short, but she casts a long shadow—long and a half-century wide. Her voice is shy and unassuming, but it has boomed over the loudest air waves of her time and made her a household sound. She is so modest that digging facts out of her is like digging clams on a rocky, clammed-out Maine shore at high tide, because many of these facts would sound like compliments to herself and she is not, and never has been, on an ego trip. She is like the bass in a good band: you never know she is there 'til she

The Carter Family: They set a style for picking and singing.

stops pickin'. Yet thousands imitate her guitar licks and a handful of Nashville's elite acknowledge her as a master, a creator, an originator, and an influence on their own style. She is Maybelle Addington Carter, Queen of Country Music.

"She gave Chet Atkins one of his first steady jobs back when people said 'Chet Who?' This was when Mother Maybelle and the Carter Sisters were playing the *Tennessee Barn Dance* in Knoxville, after the Original Carter Family had split up, and the girls and Mama had gone on to Richmond to begin anew, to see how hard show biz can be (they had two radio shows a day and did personal appearances just about every night).

"It was 1949 and Mother Maybelle and her daughters got an offer to come to Springfield, Missouri. 'We asked Chet if he wanted to come along and work with us.' ''I sure would,'' Chet said quickly. ''I'm starving to death.''

" 'Chester had his trailer hooked to his car. He unhooked that trailer and we took off. He was with us for three and a half years. He went with us to the *Ozark Mountain Jubilee* in Springfield, played with us 'til after he went with RCA here in Nashville. We brought him here with us and we had a time getting him in here. The guitar

35

players tried to keep him out. They was afraid he'd take their work away from 'em, and he did eventually, but he couldn't play with nobody else but us for about six months.'

"Floyd Cramer is another Nashville picker who admits (or brags, for Floyd is big enough to) that some of his unique piano style came from Mother Maybelle and the way she slurred the bass notes playing her guitar.

" 'There's a little lick I get on the autoharp when I jump the key, you know, that Floyd says influenced his piano playing too,' she added shyly, with a little embarrassed laughter.

"Sitting in her son-in-law's home, Johnny-come-lately-Cash, and listening to him play tapes made from transcriptions of the Original Carter Family broadcasts over XERA, XEG, and XENT in Texas from 1938–42, the influences keep popping up.

" 'Hear that?' Johnny Cash says, rewinding the portable Wolensak. 'Those patterns, repeats, coming in on certain phrases of that hymn —the Carter Family was doing that in the thirties. Gospel groups were making it popular in the forties and even the fifties.'

"A. P. Carter, Maybelle's cousin and the man of the group, had a way of coming in when he felt like it, when the spirit moved him or when the song needed a lift, singing bass harmony (though many of the notes were too low and his voice just naturally trailed off to nothing), repeating a key word, while Maybelle echoed him with her higher harmony.

" 'I'm thinking of doing an album using some of these old Carter Family transcriptions,' Johnny Cash continued. 'I'll do the narrating and pick out the best things from their different periods. Listen, here's June singing when she was ten.'

" 'Honey!' June protests, blushing. 'You don't have to play that!' But he does, knowing she'd have clobbered him if he hadn't, for the tapes are fascinating documents of American musical history. The announcer, Brother Bill, barks out businesslike: 'And now here's one of the Carter girls, pretty little ten-year-old June Carter, to sing for you. What are you going to sing, honey?'

" 'I thought I'd sing "Engine 143." ' Johnny Cash almost breaks up when June starts in, 'Along came the FFE, the swiftest on the line,' and for the rest of the evening he was like a child

on Christmas morning, each new song a delightful revelation. There were 190 of them and we sampled a good many.

"It was a treat for me too, for frankly I didn't know that much about Mother Maybelle—though I knew she was a member of the Country Music Hall of Fame, and I knew there was a style of playing named after her, the famous 'Carter Lick,' and I knew that they had erected a monument at Bristol, Virginia-Tennessee, to the Original Carter Family and Jimmie Rodgers, and I knew that she had a famous son-in-law and was mother of three of country music's most talented and beautiful girls, Helen, June, and Anita.

"But that is not knowing someone. That's the way the public knows many of its legends, only superficially. What I was learning now was about the warmth of the woman, the fabric of her personality, and the love that everyone has for her, not just her family, but everyone who has been associated with her. The one thing everyone agreed on, the key to her greatness is her deep humility. She is completely oblivious to how great she is.

"There is one other thing that came out about Mother Maybelle and that is her physical strength. When they say, 'She is a trouper,' they mean that today, in her sixties, she will sit up all night and pick and sing, if there is anyone who'll sit with her.

"But with all her touring and trouping, she has always been a mother first and an entertainer second.

" 'When mother invited you for supper, she cooked it, not a servant or a cook,' Helen says proudly. 'The wheat thrashers loved to eat at our house. And when a play was given at school, a Carter girl got the lead, 'cause Mama was the best seamstress around.

"She still raises a garden and she still cooks. She's a legend but she is still paying her dues. Billy Wilheit of the Hubert Long Talent Agency says they booked her twenty-eight times between January and June of this year, but to hear her tell it, she ain't doing much.

" 'Mother would be happy if she could just die on stage,' Helen said.

"Maybelle Addington was born in Copper Creek in southwestern Virginia on May 10, 1909, in a land of small creeks, limestone rocks, rolling hills, rail fences, and cellars full of cabbages and potatoes. She was one of ten children born to Margaret and Hugh Jack Addington.

"On the other side of Clinch Mountain were the Carters. Bob and Mollie Carter had eight children, eldest being Alvin Pleasant, or A. P., who became known as a collector of English and Irish songs, grew up to be jug-eared and tall and handsome, and, in 1915, raided the Copper Creek side of the mountain of a buxom, dark-eyed, beautiful girl named Sara Dougherty who sang in a low, almost male voice. She was Maybelle's first cousin.

"In 1926 A. P.'s brother, Ezra J., crossed the mountain too, on a hunting trip—not for deer or bear or turkey, which were plentiful, but for blue-eyed gentle Maybelle, who could play the banjo and the autoharp and the guitar and, because there weren't many other pickers around, developed a style of finger playing wherein she worked rhythm and lead at the same time. They were married and came back to settle in Maces Springs, neighbors to A. P. and Sara.

"So they were ready when in 1927 A. P. came home and said he had run into Ralph S. Peer in Bristol and that word was going out to all mountain communities for musicians and singers to come in and audition to make records for the Victor label.

"Out of those who came and were lucky enough to be paid $50 per song recorded, two names were standout hits—the Carter Family and a young boy named Jimmie Rodgers. The Carter Family records must have sold well, for in 1928 Peer called them to Camden, New Jersey, for additional recording, paying them now $75 per song. In May they recorded 'Wildwood Flower,' a song A. P. 'worked up' for them, 'John Hardy,' 'Forsaken Love,' and others. In February they returned to New Jersey again for the recording of 'Little Moses,' 'Lulu Walls,' 'Diamonds in the Rough,' and 'Foggy Mountain Top.'

"In 1938 they made the long trip to Del Rio, Texas, where they did the transcriptions described earlier, over the Mexican border radio stations, with 500,000 watts, the most powerful in the world. They had crept quietly from the hills and now were blazing across international skies. Hillbilly music was evolving.

" 'The second year I went out to Texas,'

Mother Maybelle told me, 'I took Anita. This was '39 and she was four. She'd sing duets with me and sometimes solo. We worked for Consolidated Drugs (Peruna and Kolorbak) out of Chicago—they paid for the broadcast time—and when I came home Christmas, 1940, I was asked if I had any other kids that could sing. I said I've got one, Helen, but I won't promise you about the other one, June.

" 'I went home and I started to work on them kids. I put June on autoharp and Helen on guitar and in two weeks they'd memorized fifteen songs. He put them on the show and give 'em $15 apiece a week, and that was big money back then. They was still in school, too.'

"A. P. and Sara separated in 1933, and Sara married Coy Bayes in 1938 in Brackettsville, Texas, moving with him to California, though she continued to sing and record some with them. In 1942 the Carters moved to Charlotte to work for WBT, and the following year they broke up. They had recorded some 300 songs for different labels, but no albums, though they were to see many albums put together in various packages later on.

" 'We recorded with Jimmie Rodgers in Louisville in 1932, not more than a year before he died,' Maybelle says. 'In fact, he wasn't able to play his guitar very much, he was that sick, so I played for him and he sang. I had to play like him, you know, so everybody would think it was him. But it was me.' Again that embarrassed laughter.

"The Carter Family moved to Richmond, then on to Knoxville, where they picked up Chet Atkins, and on to Springfield where they did their network show and another radio show every day and the hard work continued, and finally to Nashville and tours of Germany (where Helen said Mother Maybelle once went to sleep while standing picking on stage!) and tours with Johnny Cash, the man she had blind faith in even before he made it big.

" 'Me and my husband, we just figured there was a lot of good in Johnny. He used to come out to the house when we was living at Two Mile Pike—he'd come in and out—June was beginning to work some with him then. After we moved over on Summerfield I just fixed him a room and let him come and go when he got ready. He stayed off and on two or three years.

" 'I knew he was having a little problem with

some things, you know, and me and my husband talked about it. We figured we had to stick by him, and that's what we done. There were some things he did that we wouldn't o' put up with with a lot of people, I guess. I said sometimes I'd go off and come back and I wouldn't know if the house would be burned down or my doors broke down, or what. (That laugh again.)

" 'But if he ever tore up anything, he always fixed it. Once he broke the foot off my bed. I come in one day and he had him a bunch of books and rope and . . . I don't know what all, some glue, and he fixed that bed. I thought, now that thing won't hold. But it never has come loose.

" 'I know he was taking a pretty good bunch of pills. I'd try to keep him from going out. I'd just sit and talk with him. He'd just get up or go back to bed, or just ramble around. But I knew if he ever got hisself straightened out, he'd be one of the biggest artists going.'

"She loves Johnny Cash and is proud of him, and it is obvious he loves her and is deeply proud of her. He has hung around her doorstep, like many others, for a long time, drinking at the free-flowing tap of one of the deepest springs in American folk and mountain music. She loves her girls, too, and her husband, Ezra, and that love is returned in full measure. It is not a gushy kind of affection, not the backslapping variety, but strong and silent and reticent and sure. It's like money in the bank, you know it is there, but you don't overdraw on it. They give each other a lot of slack.

"Mother Maybelle played an important part in 'working up' the songs A. P. discovered or brought in, especially in arranging them, though only the man's name was put on the label in those days. Their harmonies were church-influenced, and because they used autoharp and guitar, most of the old ballads had to be taken out of their modal keys to lend themselves to instrumental band accompaniment.

"Mother Maybelle has survived several eras, from the beginnings of country and western music, through ragtime, jazz, big bands, rock-and-roll, all the way through to today's middle-of-the-road or country-metropolitan sounds.

"Mother Maybelle is still paying her dues. She is booking on her own again, with the girls, Helen and Anita, and with Helen's son David, sometimes, and beautiful fourteen-year-old Lorrie, Anita and Don's girl [Don is Sara Carter's son].

"If, in the past, they'd had one of today's super managers, the Carters would probably be rich several times over. But A. P. used to book them and he never bothered to read the fine print of a contract. Also Ezra, or "Pop Carter" as he has become known affectionately by those around him, helped out with some of the booking. But they were never interested in money. They loved what they were doing. The songs were important. It was a natural way of life. Nor have they reaped the mass adulation of superstars or been publicized for the legends they are.

"Not that Mother Maybelle has gone unnoticed or is not loved by the country-music community. She is. Deeply. It's just that the praise has been as quiet as she has. People like Joan Baez have stirred interest by recording some Carter material, like 'Little Moses,' and the Nitty Gritty Dirt Band used Mother Maybelle on a recent double album called 'Will the Circle Be Unbroken?' She was written up recently in *Newsweek* and is beginning to be booked in more and more colleges.

"And she is not trying to make a comeback. She is a trouper. She is just acting natural, the way she always has. She is there, she always has been and she always will be. And age is taking its toll, though she doesn't show it. She has to tell you about it. 'I can't play the way I used to because of arthritis in my fingers. So I don't use the guitar as much. I play the autoharp.' And she is not complaining. She is just being natural, as always.

" 'Can you imagine the stages she has played on?' Nat Winston [a writer on musical subjects] asked me. Yes I can. I can see them, everywhere from London's Palladium to Carnegie Hall, from Newport's Folk Festival to those little school stages lighted on each side by kerosene lamps. And I can see Ezra, her husband, though I never met him during my interviews. And I know he has stuck by her and sacrificed just as she has all these years, with never a cross word between them.

"I can see Ezra crossing Clinch Mountain and bringing back a talented, beautiful woman with music in her fingers that everyone who meets says is 'truly a lady.' And I can see him sharing quietly in her glory and being proud, content to stay out of the limelight with his books and his

decided to resurrect a song he had written for Kay Starr that Kay had turned down. Patsy Cline didn't like it, but encouraged by Decca executives and Hecht, she agreed to do a tape of "Walkin' After Midnight."

"Patsy talked about her Blue Ridge Mountains, hunting, fishing, and about her mother," Hecht recalls. "Always of her mother, and how she hurt not being able to do for her mother all the things she wanted to. She really got to me then. Here was a girl, attractive but plain, simple but complicated, with a heart as big as the mountains that made her eyes shine each time she spoke of them.

"Paul Cohen, then president of Decca Records, scheduled our recording session at the Owen Bradley Studios in Nashville in the fall of 1956. It was then I realized that Patsy was never completely happy with anything she recorded. 'Please, let's try it one more time,' was her classic statement after listening to her playbacks. No matter how close she came to perfection, she was always eager to do it better.

"Before 'Walkin' After Midnight' was ready for release, Patsy happily informed us that she had, finally, been successful in auditioning and being accepted as a contestant for Arthur Godfrey's *Talent Scouts*, slated for January 28, 1957.

" 'But, God,' she said, 'New York! That town scares me to death.'

" 'It's just another town with a few more people in it,' I said. 'You'll do just fine.' But it wasn't the giant city that frightened Patsy Cline —it was New York's people.

"I tried to assure her that people are alike the world over. 'Maybe,' she said, 'but New York people aren't like country people. They dare you to make them like you. Country people are different. They try hard to like everybody.' When I reminded her that I wasn't a country person and that I liked her she laughed and said, 'Maybe you're right, but those New Yorkers still scare me.'

"In New York City, something happened that was to change, not only Patsy's and my outlook about the country music field respectively, but something that was to provide, also, a major turning point in both our lives. And I must name here one who is perhaps least credited with but most responsible for Patsy Cline's acceptance in that ivory-towered city.

"Janette Davis, herself a singer and regular with Arthur Godfrey, carefully reviewed Patsy's entire repertoire in an effort to help Patsy choose material which, in her opinion, would best demonstrate her talents on the show.

" 'We went over thirty songs,' Patsy confided, 'and still, Janette asked if I had any other material.' She went on to say that she finally uncovered copies of the best two sides she had just recorded for Decca, and which were yet unreleased. (Patsy showed these last because it is forbidden for any singer to publicly perform recorded material before planned release dates.)

" 'So Janette and I went over them,' she said —'first, the side I picked, "Poor Man's Roses," then "Walkin' After Midnight." '

"Janette Davis advised Patsy to do the latter song on the show, saying that its bluesy sound fit her voice and style. 'Okay,' Patsy said via long-distance telephone, 'I give up—I surrender. It's four against one now.'

" 'Four against one?'

" 'Sure,' she laughed. 'The record company, you, Janette Davis, and Arthur Godfrey. Four against one.'

" 'Well, God bless Janette Davis,' I said, 'and Arthur Godfrey too.'

" 'First thing I'm gonna do,' she added, 'when I get back to Nashville, is record that song again.'

"Astonished, I asked her why and she said, 'Because I like it! I really like it now. And we're gonna win with it.'

"And she did win with it. On that evening of January 28, 1957, she strode before the cameras that were ten million eyes, and this complicated and simple and brave girl from the country sang her heart out for an eternity of two minutes ten seconds, froze the applause meters, brought the audience to their feet, to her feet, and for the first time I saw Patsy Cline cry.

"That she conquered New York was diminished only by the degree to which that giant place was to focus a second look on country music. An embarrassed Decca Records rushed the release to a clamoring market. It became an immediate smash million seller, followed by 'She's Got You,' 'Heartaches,' 'Cry Not for Me,' 'Fingerprints,' 'Sweet Dreams of You,' 'Leavin' on Your Mind,' 'Crazy,' and a host of others, including 'I Fall to Pieces,' which was, ironically, her last recording.

"The rest, they say, is history. But it is there between those pages of her brief career that the little-known disappointment and pain and disillusionment served to develop to maturity one of the meaningful voices of our time. For Patsy Cline knew how to cry on both sides of the microphone. And the why of it all, explained by many, understood by few, is slowly becoming a legend unparalleled by any country entertainer since Hank Williams." In 1973, Patsy Cline was elected to the Country Music Hall of Fame.

## COCHRAN, HANK

BORN: August 2, 1935, Greenville, Mississippi

MARRIED: w. Jeannie Seely

Hank Cochran was a big star in the 1960s. Almost every country hit chart had his compositions on it. Patsy Cline made "I Fall to Pieces" a smash, and his own record of "Sally Was a Good Old Girl" was played on all Top Forty stations. Willie Nelson made some money by singing Cochran's "Willingly," and Burl Ives had a country hit with "A Little Bitty Tear." Ray Price recorded Cochran's "Make the World Go Away," and Jeannie Seely—Jack Greene's singing partner and Cochran's wife—did well with his "Don't Touch Me." Cochran's still writing away, but he never made it as a singer, and though he probably has fortune, super fame has escaped him.

## COOLEY, SPADE [Donald C. Cooley]

BORN: 1910

DIED: November 23, 1969

Donnell C. Cooley, called "Spade" by everybody and by himself "the king of western swing," led the most popular country dance band in southern California in the 1940s and had a popular radio show emanating out of the Venice Ballroom in Santa Monica, California. He was the author of "Shame on You" and other country hits and was one of the leaders of the country-music community on the West Coast, appearing on shows with Tex Williams, Cliffie Stone, Brenda Lee, Red Sovine, and many others. He was considered (almost) on a par with Bob Wills (the real "king of western

swing") and Hank Thompson and his Brazos Valley Boys—those were the days when trumpets and fiddles were added to western music and good old boys and their ladies shuffled to tunes like "Take It Nice and Easy" and "Joshua Tree Stomp." By the late fifties, people stopped dancing to western music, and as friends of Cooley's say (kindly), "Spade went kinda sour." Sour enough to murder his wife, Ella Mae, just like he was a character in a country song. The lawmen came and took Spade to prison, where he continued fiddling for his cellmates. On the day they paroled Spade, he appeared publicly, fiddled a tune, and dropped dead of a heart attack. I'm amazed that Tom T. Hall hasn't written a song about it.

## COOPER, WILMA LEE and STONEY

### Wilma Lee:

BORN: Valley Head, West Virginia

MARRIED: h. Stoney Cooper

### Stoney:

BORN: October 16, 1918, Harmon, West Virginia

MARRIED: w. Wilma Lee Leary

THEIR CHILDREN: d. Carol Lee Cooper (Snow)

The music library of Harvard University contains most of the recordings of Wilma Lee and Stoney Cooper. They are often called the most authentic mountain singers in America. Stoney was born in the part of West Virginia where the famous singing Learys lived. He played the fiddle before he was twelve and the guitar shortly after that. Before he finished high school, he joined the Leary Family Singers, performing at church functions. He and Wilma Leary hit it off musically and romantically, and they became an official duo. Leaving the family, they struck out on their own—but during the Depression years Stoney had to supplement his income as a singer by working for a beer company in Wheeling, West Virginia. By 1947 they were regular cast members of the radio station WWVA (Wheeling, West Virginia) *Jamboree*, and in 1954 they joined Grand Ole Opry. They have recorded for Hickory, Decca, and

Columbia. There are those country and blue-grass enthusiasts, and I am one of their number, who feel that Wilma Lee and Stoney Cooper are unparalleled in their field.

## COPAS, COWBOY [Lloyd Copas]
BORN: July 15, 1913, Muskogee, Oklahoma
DIED: March 5, 1963, Camden, Tennessee
MARRIED: w. Cathy

In 1954, when I was stationed at Fort Bliss, Texas, and was editor of *The Fort Bliss News*, I learned that Cowboy Copas was going to appear at a honky-tonk bar in Ruidoso, New Mexico (when that town wasn't the lively horse-racing and skiing resort it is now). Among the first country records I had bought as a kid was Cowboy Copas' rendition of "Filipino Baby," an odd song about a South Carolina sailor who falls in love with a "dark-skinned Filipino" and returns after the war to join her "in her little rustic cottage in the far-off Philippines." The song had been a major hit for Copas, and along with Ernest Tubb and Hank Williams he had been one of the hillbilly superstars of the late forties, generally singing honky-tonk-style songs. I had always loved them and I wouldn't miss a chance to see him perform. It never dawned on me until I saw him in Ruidoso that Copas was on the decline, that he hadn't had a hit in some years and was reduced to playing honky-tonks. The audience was made up of bored Mescaleros from the nearby reservation, a number of servicemen from the various bases which skirted the area, and some local cowboys who kept chattering throughout the perform-ance. When Copas came to what could only generously be called a stage, alone with his guitar (there was no band, and no microphone—it was that kind of high-class establishment) I thought, How *old* he is. He was forty-one at the time (the age I am now). He wore an Ernest Tubb–style white Stetson and a checked cow-boy shirt. He sang "Filipino Baby" and "Ten-nessee Waltz" and kept telling us how happy he was to be in Ruidoso, New Mexico. But nothing he could say could make him anything but a tragic figure. The big star, on his way down,

playing to a hundred people in the middle of nowhere.

Tragedy is a consistent theme in country music, and tragedy seems to stalk country singers. Cowboy Copas was 1948's top country star. By the early fifties he couldn't sell a record, and when, at the turn of the sixties, his record "Alabam" catapulted him to new fame and a younger, more appreciative audience, he was killed in a plane crash.

Cowboy Copas was born and raised on a small ranch in Oklahoma. Before he was ten, he played the guitar. At sixteen, he hitchhiked to Cincinnati to try out as a singer and picker. He met an Indian fiddler named Natchee, and the two began to win prizes at fiddling contests (which were very popular in the Ohio River Valley in the late 1920s). To promote their duo, Cowboy Copas appeared as a free singer on radio stations. He had a number of offers to remain as a local star and accepted one in Knoxville, Tennessee, in 1940, returning to Cincinnati a few years later as a featured performer on *Midwest Hayride,* where King Records signed him up. His big hits of the 1940s were "Filipino Baby," "Honky-Tonkin'," "Tragic Romance," and "Texas Red." Pee Wee King convinced Copas to join his band as a sideman on Grand Ole Opry. Copas recorded "Tennessee Waltz" and "Kentucky Waltz," both making the top ten of 1948, followed by "Tennessee Moon." Although "Strange Little Girl" sold some records in 1950, Copas was unable to get a song on the charts after that, and audiences, fickle as they are, forgot about him.

For an entire decade he played volunteer firemen's carnivals, small-town bars, and bene-fits. Then, in 1959, Don Pierce of Starday Records offered Copas a chance to record a song called "Alabam." It was 1960's number one hit for more than forty weeks. Copas rerecorded his big smash "Signed, Sealed and Delivered" and it sold better than ever. "Flat Top" also made the charts. Copas rejoined Grand Ole Opry and crowds came to his con-certs. It all ended on March 5, 1963, in the air crash eight-five miles west of Nashville. Cow-boy Copas, his son-in-law Randy Hughes, Hawkshaw Hawkins, and Patsy Cline were on their way to a benefit performance in Kansas for the family of country disc jockey Jack Call, who had been killed in a traffic accident.

## THE COUNTRY GENTLEMEN
### Leader: Charles Waller

Charles Waller has led The Country Gentlemen for more than fifteen years, singing and guitar-picking in front of a group that has undergone personnel changes without losing steam. Waller was born in Louisiana but has lived in the Washington, D.C., area since he was a teen-ager. The nucleus of the group is composed of Waller and his two partners, Doyle Lawson and Bill Yates. Lawson plays mandolin, sings tenor, and handles arrangements of the group's materi-al, which leans toward pop-flavored bluegrass. Lawson hails from Kingsport, Tennessee, but also makes his home now in the D.C. area. Yates sings and plays bass. A Virginia boy, he also lives in the D.C. area, which is becoming a stamping ground for bluegrass bands. The group is usually augmented by Rick Skaggs on fiddle and Mike Lilly on five-string banjo. Kentucki-ans by birth, they also live in the D.C. area. In 1972 the group signed a contract with Vanguard Records.

on public display at the Country Music Founda-tion's Hall of Fame in Nashville, Tennessee:

| | |
|---|---|
| Fred Rose (songwriter and publisher) | 1961 |
| Jimmie Rodgers | 1961 |
| Hank Williams | 1961 |
| Roy Acuff | 1962 |
| Tex Ritter | 1964 |
| Ernest Tubb | 1965 |
| James Denny (executive) | 1966 |
| Eddy Arnold | 1966 |
| George D. Hay (executive) | 1966 |
| Uncle Dave Macon | 1966 |
| Jim Reeves | 1967 |
| J. L. (Joe) Frank (executive) | 1967 |
| Red Foley | 1967 |
| Steven C. Sholes (executive) | 1967 |
| Bob Wills | 1968 |
| Gene Autry | 1969 |
| Original Carter Family (May-belle, A. P., and Sara) | 1970 |
| Bill Monroe | 1970 |
| Art Satherley (executive) | 1971 |
| Jimmy Davis | 1972 |
| Patsy Cline | 1973 |
| Chet Atkins | 1973 |

## COUNTRY MUSIC

Country music is the catch-all term for a com-mercial American popular music with strong southern (and sometimes western) roots. It developed out of the reservoir of ballads and folksongs brought to North America by the earliest English immigrants and through the years absorbed influences from other musical sources, until it emerged as a force strong enough to survive in an urban society. (See the introductory essay on country music.)

## COUNTRY MUSIC HALL OF FAME

Every year a nominating committee selects from ten to twenty candidates for the Country Music Hall of Fame. An electorate of 250 industry leaders (artists, executives, journalists, produ-cers, etc.) then chooses one of the nominees as the new Hall of Fame member. The members are memorialized on bronze plaques, which are

## CRADDOCK, BILLY "CRASH"
BORN: June 16, 1939, Greensboro, North Carolina
MARRIED: w. Mae
CHILDREN: s. Billy, Jr., Steve; d. April

Billy "Crash" Craddock has been around for a while, starting to record back in 1958, for the Date label ("Ah, Poor Little Baby"), which got him a contract with Columbia and appearances on Arthur Godfrey's *Talent Scouts* and Dick Clark's *American Bandstand*. He was offered parts in movies and roles on Broadway (*Bye-Bye, Birdie*), but he claims to have turned them all down in favor of country music and stock-car racing (hence the nickname Crash). For Cartwheel Records he hit the charts three times in a year with "Knock Three Times" (number three for seventeen weeks), "Dream Lover" (number five for fourteen weeks), and "You Better Move On" (number ten for fourteen weeks). ABC Records has picked up his con-tract and promises big things for Billy "Crash." Time and the public taste will tell.

The Country Gentlemen: Bluegrass for the masses.

Billy "Crash" Craddock has begun to discover his niche in country music: country rock.

## CRAMER, FLOYD

BORN: October 27, 1933, Shreveport, Louisiana

Floyd Cramer's distinctive piano style has dominated country music for well over a decade. He has recorded more than two dozen albums for RCA Records since Chet Atkins brought him to Nashville in 1955. Cramer says he became interested in music when he was five years old. His parents responded by buying a piano. As a teen-ager, he played throughout Louisiana, supporting local groups, until the early 1950s, when he joined the popular *Louisiana Hayride* show. By the time he reached Nashville he was backing Elvis Presley, The Browns, and Jim Reeves, as well as other country stars who passed through RCA's Nashville studios. His first single, "Last Date," sold a million copies in 1960, causing a stir on both country and pop charts.

49

Cramer compares his piano style to Mother Maybelle Carter's distinctive guitar lick, which involves the judicious "slurring" of certain notes. Cramer calls his technique a "whole-tone slur."

Floyd Cramer: He rode the *Louisiana Hayride* to Nashville.

## CURLESS, DICK

BORN: March 17, 1932, Waterville, Maine

"Nobody writes songs about cowboys anymore," Tex Ritter lamented recently, "but hundreds of songs were written this year about the truck driver." Dick Curless has probably recorded most of them. The truck driver, battling sleep, curved roads, fog, and faulty brakes, is probably the newest American working-class hero. And along with Dave Dudley, Red Sovine, and a few others, Dick Curless is one of the best

interpreters of this genre song. Unlike most country singers, Curless was born and raised in New England, singing in his late teens as The Tumbleweed Kid in an unlikely place: Ware, Massachusetts. The name Dick Curless became known during the Korean War. As The Rice-Paddy Ranger, he was the most popular performer on the Armed Forces Korea Network. In 1957 his version of "Nine-Pound Hammer" won first prize on the Arthur Godfrey *Talent Scouts* show, but nothing much happened, and he returned to Rockland, Maine, where he sang locally. In the mid-sixties Curless met Dan Fulkerson, who had written a song called "A Tombstone Every Mile." They paid for cutting the record and released it under the name Allagash Records, and it began to move. Capitol eventually bought the master record and the song became one of the major hits of 1965. Curless followed this, for Capitol, with "Six Times a Day," and in the ensuing years he has had numerous hits. He has been a member of the Buck Owens show and performs in other shows all over the country. He is one of the few country stars who lives permanently in New England.

# D

## DALHART, VERNON [Marion G. Slaughter]

BORN: April 6, 1883, Jefferson, Texas
DIED: September 15, 1948

One of the first country artists to attract national attention, Vernon Dalhart began recording for the Victor Company in 1917, turning out mostly pop songs and light opera selections, which he recorded under a wide variety of pseudonyms. When his popularity began to decline in the early 1920s, Dalhart switched to singing songs more in line with his country origins (having been raised on a ranch). He asked Victor executives if he could record a "hillbilly" song. They consented, and the fortunes of all involved soon changed for the better. From 1925 to 1931 Dalhart scored with a string of country melodies, most notably "The Wreck of the Old 97" and "The Prisoner's Song."

He is credited with introducing the wailing steel guitar sound as an essential element in country arrangements through his affiliation with guitarist Frank Ferara, who claimed to have introduced the Hawaiian guitar sound to American music in 1900. Dalhart worked for many years with Carson Robison, the composer of standards like "My Blue Ridge Mountain Home" and "Life Gets Tee-Jus, Don't It?", and he recorded many of Robison's songs.

Red Sovine and one-eyed Dick Curless: "Big mother truckers . . ."

## DAVIS, DANNY

BORN: April 29, 1925, Dorchester, Massachusetts

Danny Davis is a trumpeter from a proper Massachusetts family whose mother was an opera coach. He attended the staid New England Conservatory of Music on a four-year scholarship. He knows Beethoven from Bach. He is acquainted with the finer nuances of Renaissance court music. He is also a prominent country musician as well as an independent producer. Danny Davis created the Nashville Brass and turned it into the top big band in country music. Only in existence since 1968, it has won every award given by the Country Music Association and some Grammys as well. Danny Davis plays the lead instrument—either trumpet or flügelhorn. The rest of the band includes drums, bass, two trombones, two trumpets, and occasionally voices. There is frequently a rhythm banjo.

Danny Davis joined RCA Victor in 1965 as a pop artist and repertoire producer. At fourteen he was a trumpet soloist with the Massachusetts

All State Symphony Orchestra. He was hardly out of his teens when he joined the Bobby Byrne orchestra on CBS and then played with Gene Krupa, Bob Crosby, Hal McIntyre, Art Mooney, and Freddy Martin. At first he just played the trumpet. Later he doubled as a singer with Vincent Lopez, Blue Barron, and Sammy Kaye. Danny Davis occasionally surprises audiences when he suddenly begins to sing. Some years ago, when he was with Freddie Martin, he recorded a solo, "The Object of My Affection." After a stint at MGM, where he guided the careers of Herman's Hermits and Johnny Tillotson, he came to RCA to work with Lana Cantrell and Nina Simone before joining guitarist/producer Chet Atkins at RCA's Nashville offices. At first he had a desk job as an executive producer, but the success of the Nashville Brass forced him to forego his administrative position. Danny Davis is reputed to be a super swell guy and obviously has demonstrated an honest affection for country; nonetheless there are a number of critics who feel brass has no place in country music.

Danny Davis: A dash of brass in country music.

Jimmie Davis: Gospel-singing former governor of Louisiana.

## DAVIS, JIMMIE (James Houston Davis)

BORN: September 11, 1902, Quitmann Louisiana

MARRIED: w. Alvorn (deceased)

CHILDREN: s. Jim

Jimmie Davis is proudest of his several awards over the years from various gospel organizations naming him the best white male sacred singer. And these days his songs are mostly sacred songs, on Decca. Unlike most country singers, Jimmie Davis has both a Bachelor of Arts and a Master's degree. And his education helped, obviously, because he served two terms as governor of Louisiana (1944–48 and 1960–64). However, people often forget the names of past governors, and Jimmie Davis' immortality will be based on a song he wrote and recorded—probably the one country song of which the words are known by just about every American: man, woman, or child. It's called "You Are My Sunshine," and it's brought a lot of gold sunshine into the ex-governor's wallet.

Jimmie Davis was elected to the Country Music Hall of Fame in 1972.

## DAVIS, MAC

BORN: January 21, 1942, Lubbock, Texas

MARRIED: w. Sarah

CHILDREN: s. Scotty

Mac Davis' songs have already been cut by more than 150 artists including Elvis Presley, Nancy Sinatra, Bobby Goldsboro, Kenny Rogers, Glen Campbell, and O. C. Smith. He sings his songs, too, with more regularity these days. Until recently he's been classified as a folk-rock artist, but Davis claims he's country, rooted in country, born in country, and "feels" country. He's a Texan, and legend has it that Texans, though noted for a proclivity toward exaggeration, don't really lie. So, the fan must accept that the homespun Lubbock, Texas, lad is the real McCoy. (Not Charlie, of course.) His version of his own composition "Baby, Don't Get Hooked on Me" has done quite nicely and is still played as an "extra" on many country stations. Davis started playing the guitar when he was about fifteen, "though I was probably making up melodies when I was only five or six years old."

"I knew I had that gift," he told Jay Ehler in a magazine interview. "I didn't realize by any means that's what I wanted to do. But I can remember riding in the back seat of the family car, and entertaining myself by whistling and making up songs. My daddy started me off singing in the church choir as soon as I was able to hold the hook up, I think I kind of learned to write from that."

Before he could play the guitar at all, Mac had already mastered the blues harp and bongo drum.

At fifteen he left home in Lubbock and went to Atlanta. He left because, by his own admission, he'd realized he was becoming a real hood. He'd been hanging around with a bad bunch of kids, and was in trouble continually.

"I really felt that if I had stayed there I was gonna end up in trouble, that I'd wind up in prison or be a ditch digger all my life, or something. At this point my grades had degenerated and I was just a hoodlum. I didn't have any ambition and I had a big picture of having to go across the street to college—we lived directly across the street from Texas Tech. I wanted a college education. Nobody in my family, except for an uncle, had ever been to college.

"I'd been to Georgia once and I saw trees. I decided I wanted to live in a place that had trees in it, unlike Lubbock. So when I left home, I struck out for the big city of Atlanta.

"I still thought singing was sissy stuff. I took the college boards in Atlanta and started attending Emory University. That was a big mistake, 'cause I ran out of money and ambition at about the same time. I majored at Emory in Beer, with a minor in Rock-and-Roll.

"When I was growing up in West Texas, we didn't have rock-and-roll stations. We didn't have rock-and-roll music until I was about thirteen. I'd always listened to country music. In fact, that's my roots. I never heard anything but country music—Hank Williams, Eddy Arnold, and Ernest Tubb—until I was thirteen or so.

"When rock-and-roll came along, we had a sound we called 'Tex Mex'—Buddy Holly. I used to go down to a place in Lubbock called the Bamboo Ranch and dance to Buddy Holly music all night for twenty-five cents. This was back in '55 before he ever had a hit—about the time Elvis came onto the scene. Actually, I think Buddy was tryin' to sound a little like Elvis."

Mac wanted Elvis to sing the first song he wrote. Elvis was his strongest musical influence back then. Later he began listening to the Coasters, and found that he, too, could write novelty songs. He wasn't giving much thought to being a songwriter, though. At the time he was employed as a statistician.

"A lot of people, writers, feel they've got to starve to be funky," he says. "Well, I just don't believe that. I think if a fella gets a job and works and keeps himself happy, then he's in a position where he can be objective when he writes. He can sit back and look at himself objectively, rather than on the downside.

"I think the down-and-out attitude is fine . . . I just don't believe that a fella has to starve to be able to write good songs."

Mac formed a rock-and-roll band, and started playing at fraternity parties and high school hops in Atlanta. His band, named the Zots (from the comic strip "B.C.") learned to play a few of his novelty songs. It sang dirty, drunken backroom ballads. "Sort of white Doug Clark and

Mac Davis: A Lubbock lad who loves music.

the Hot Nuts," says Davis. He never could get his songs to the Coasters.

Finally, Mac managed to get one of his novelty tunes recorded. He bumped into Sam the Sham's manager, and even though he had written the tune for the Coasters, he knew that Sam, hot at the time, could sing this type of novelty song.

"I sold my first song to Sam the Sham's manager in a public restroom in Nashville, Tennessee. The guy was standin' there. I figured I had him collared. So I buttonholed him right there and sang the song for him. I don't know whether he felt sorry for me, or if he was impressed by it. But they cut the record and it was released. It was called 'The Phantom Strikes Again,' and it was a really bad song. But everybody has to start someplace, whether it be at a public urinal or wherever . . .

"I went through a big rock-and-roll scene until I finally started writing songs that I thought made sense, songs that were really introspective. When I did this, the songs came out country. I said, 'I am a country boy, and there ain't no gettin' around it.' I wrote primarily about myself, things that had happened to me. I wrote some awfully sad songs, like 'Don't Cry, Daddy.' It was later done by Elvis.

"It was a song about me and my son. I exaggerated on it. But the idea originally came to me when I was sitting with my boy, Scotty, and he and I were watching television. They showed some scenes of some Vietnamese children who were burned and hurt. I started to cry. I'm a supersensitive person anyway. Scotty came over and started pattin' my hand and said, 'Don't cry, Daddy.' I changed the situation around and wrote around that one line. When Elvis did it, it sold 1.5 million."

Perhaps it's a bit surprising that Davis never used to consider himself a country artist. "I guess I give off a country image, just playing my guitar and singing, even if I sing 'Something's Burning' (which Kenny Rogers had a hit with), which is definitely not a country song. When I sing it, it comes off country.

"Country radio has been good to me. Better than I think I deserve. For example, 'Baby, Don't Get Hooked on Me.' I wanted to put out a record that could go both ways, pop or country. I didn't think 'Baby, Don't Get Hooked on Me' would get any country play at all, but it has."

Davis has recorded a number of little-label singles in Atlanta and one Capitol single release. Columbia has released his last three albums. He doesn't read or write music. "I'll always give Elvis credit as long as I live for having opened all the doors for me by singing my songs and givin' me a chance. When he cut 'Memories' it went top thirty and everyone started coming to me saying that was a gas of a song. I sent him a tape of 'In the Ghetto' and 'Don't Cry, Daddy.' He cut them and they both went number one. After that I never had any trouble gettin' in the doors no more."

## DAVIS, SKEETER [Mary Frances Penick]

BORN: December 30, 1931, Dry Ridge, Kentucky

MARRIED: h. Ralph Emery (divorced)

When Skeeter Davis left Dry Ridge, Kentucky, she was still officially Mary Frances Penick. Music was a vital ingredient in the Penick clan's (four girls, three boys) life, so it wasn't odd that Skeeter decided, very early in life, to be a professional singer. Unlike many show-business personalities, Skeeter had another ambition—to sing and live as a devoted Christian. And, she's accomplished both goals.

Anybody who knows her will tell you: Skeeter is a Christian. And she probably is one of the most widely popular of the female country singers in her appeal to groups outside the country audience. Although for some time she moved toward pop, her early recordings were genuinely country and recently she has again identified herself strongly with Nashville. Her career actually began in 1953, when with her schoolmate Betty Jack Davis she formed the Davis Sisters. Their version of "I Forgot More Than You'll Ever Know" made the top ten in early 1953, and the Davis Sisters were in great demand for personal appearances. In August 1953, while they were driving home from one of these, a speeding car plowed into theirs, and Betty Jack was killed. Skeeter tried to keep the act going with Betty Jack's sister, Georgia, but the tragedy was too intense, and she retired from show business for some time, emerging in the late fifties as a single, under the careful eye of RCA's Chet Atkins. Her 1959 hit was "Set Him Free," followed in 1960 with "I'm Falling, Too."

For a few years Skeeter Davis, forsaking gingham for gold lamé, was a regular guest on Dick Clark's show, Duke Ellington's show, and even sang on a Rolling Stones' special. She kept one foot in country with her regular appearances on Grand Ole Opry.

She married Ralph Emery, the popular Nashville disc jockey, but the marriage didn't work out. She has never remarried. And she has remained true to her faith: Skeeter Davis won't perform where liquor is served. She has given up her tobacco crop (she has a 200-acre farm). "I don't work clubs that sell alcohol 'cause it's not my bag. As a Christian, I think it's harmful to my body, and I love my body and I think my body is the Temple of God. And that's the same reason I quit growin' tobacco on my farm."

Skeeter Davis lives in a black colonial mansion in Brentwood, Tennessee. "It's a house that is distinguished by the living room," reports magazine writer Genevieve Waddell. "The walls of this room can best be compared to a junior high school bathroom—except that all the scribbled messages are clean."

"I didn't mean to turn my living room into this," Skeeter says. "It just happened. While I was waiting for the painters to come in, friends started writing messages on the walls. After a while, I couldn't erase the paint. The words are part of me, now."

Graffiti on Skeeter Davis' wall include: "Give to Mental Health, or I'll kill you" and "Don't get into Jesus but let Jesus get into you."

She owns an ocelot named Fred, twelve dogs, two Siamese cats, and a white dove in a gilded cage. Guests have to keep their ears open, because she talks at top speed. "I had this tree in the yard and my gardener said the tree was dead, but I tol' him to just water it and talk to it nice. But then, he looked at me like I 'uz crazy and said, 'Shoo, I ain't gonna talk to no tree.' "

Skeeter is constantly concerned about her fans. She passed out ham and biscuits, made by herself, from the porch of her hillbilly cabin at the 1973 Fan Fair (an annual Nashville event. Thousands of fans from all over the country pour into Nashville to attend an "open house" to meet their favorite artists).

"Last Christmas," she says, "my fan club gave me a cross with eighteen tiny diamonds in

Skeeter Davis: "I know I'm country. I can look at my bare feet and tell that."

it and I wear it all the time now. The members didn't know it, but that 'eighteen' is significant to me. That's how old I was when I became a Christian." Skeeter Davis sings in prisons and old folks' homes, and recently has undertaken a personal campaign to save the Grand Ole Opry house. She likes to encourage young songwriters. Her live-in secretary, Linda Palmer, has written a number of songs which Skeeter plans to record, and she listens to all tapes that are sent to her. "We've got to help young writers if the future is going to mean anything in country music."

Skeeter Davis has always had a difficult time convincing the world that she's "pure country." She earned her gold record with a rock tune, "The End of the World." In 1973 RCA re-released the song and it is played on country, rock, and easy-listening stations. "And I don't care who plays it," Skeeter Davis insists, "because I know I'm country. I can look at my bare feet and tell that."

57

## DEAN, JIMMY [Seth Ward]

BORN: August 10, 1928, Plainview, Texas
MARRIED: w. Sue Wittauer
CHILDREN: s. Gary, Connie, Robert

Jimmy Dean's big hit was "Big Bad John." He wrote it on an airplane in 1961, going to a Columbia recording session in Nashville. It sold more than 2 million copies and everybody said Jimmy Dean was "Mr. Country." He had a weekly TV show during prime time on ABC—actually it could be that he was the real forerunner of *Hee Haw* (same cornball humor, except he had a Jim Henson Muffet puppet dog named Rowf, who generally stole the show from Dean), *The Glen Campbell Goodtime Hour*, and Johnny Cash. Most of Dean's guests were more at home on Dean Martin's show than on Jimmy's, but for a while he was a big name on the scene, guesting on the late-night talk shows and occasionally taking over the MC chores for Merv Griffin, who was a New Jersey neighbor. Dean told *TV Guide* that when he was growing up, kids were always laughing at his funny poor clothes. "And I'd go home and tell Mom how miserable I felt being laughed at. I dreamt of havin' a beautiful home, a nice car, and nice clothes. I wanted to be somebody."

Jimmy Dean had his chance. After he left the service in 1948, he stayed in the Washington, D.C., area and formed a group called The Texas Wildcats. They were popular in Washington, and this led to a WTOP-TV morning show. The ratings were high, but sophisticated sponsors wouldn't back the show, and it folded. Dean hit the personal-appearance circuit. His voice was croony enough to gain acceptance with city audiences, and he appeared everywhere from the Holiday House in Pittsburgh to the Shoreham in Washington. He even traveled with the Ice Capades. He was signed by ABC-TV, but when his TV show finally died, so did his popularity. I took my family and some friends to dinner at the Tower Suite in New York shortly after his show died. Jimmy Dean, in a blue suit and lizard-skin cowboy boots, was seated near us. "That's Jimmy Dean," I told one of the teen-age children with us. "He's a country singer who had a show on TV." The teen-ager, from North Carolina, shook her head. "He's not country," she said, with conviction.

Jimmy Dean: Rode to fame on "Big Bad John."

# THE DELMORE BROTHERS

## Alton Delmore

BORN: December 25, 1908, Elkmont, Alabama

DIED: June 8, 1964, Huntsville, Alabama

## Rabon Delmore

BORN: December 3, 1916, Elkmont, Alabama

DIED: December 4, 1952, Athens, Alabama

The Delmore Brothers began on Grand Ole Opry in 1932 and lasted until cancer claimed Rabon. Alton composed more than 1,000 tunes, and Rabon more than 200. The major hit "Blues Stay Away from Me" was a collaboration of the brothers, and "Beautiful Brown Eyes" was the result of Alton's collaboration with Arthur Smith.

Historian Bill C. Malone considers them among the most important of country performers: "Their recording career lasted from 1931, when they signed with Columbia, until 1952, when Rabon's death broke up the duo. Their recording ventures included stints with Bluebird from 1934 to 1939, and with Decca and King after that period. The Delmore Brothers, important because of their use of traditional material, which was extensive, were more important because of their adaptation of Negro songs and rhythms. The Delmores were greatly influenced by deep-South Negro styles, which they incorporated in many of their songs. In contrast to most of the string bands of the period, the Delmore Brothers featured guitars (the six-string and tenor) as lead instruments. In many of their novelty and rhythm tunes they used a ragtime guitar technique similar to that of the Negro blues performer Blind Boy Fuller—an eight-to-the-bar progression heard in such songs as 'Step It Up and Go' and 'Don't Let the Deal Go Down.' The Delmore Brothers recorded a multi-assorted variety of country songs—most of them written by Alton Delmore—which included the sentimental favorites 'When It's Time for the Whippoorwill to Sing' and 'Southern Moon.' Their greatest popularity and influence, gained largely through performances on WSM, came from their performance of novelty numbers such as 'Brown's Ferry Blues,' and the greatest tribute to their work is the large number of Delmore Brothers songs still found in the repertoires of modern country singers."

# DENVER, JOHN

The first time I saw John Denver was several years ago in Carnegie Hall when a spokesman announced that Chad Mitchell was no longer with the Mitchell trio and his place was going to be taken by a "wonderful young singer" named John Denver. There were a number of howls and boos, but by the end of the performance there was applause, and John Denver has, ever since, faced generally appreciative audiences. When the trio called it quits, John Denver carved a name for himself as a writer and singer of country-style songs (for RCA Victor), which he performs in a high-pitched, folkish manner. His compositions, "Country Roads" and "Rocky Mountain High," among others, have been recorded by a number of hard country performers. His own versions are often played by country and western DJ's, and many country record collections probably contain a Denver album or two. Although he's a great booster of Colorado living, and apparently would "rather be a cowboy" than anything else, and is undoubtedly a splendid young fellow, in my not-so-humble opinion, John Denver ain't country, baby.

# DEXTER, AL

BORN: April 4, 1905, Jacksonville, Texas

MARRIED: w. Frankie

CHILDREN: s. Jimmie, Wayne; d. Helen Louise

Nobody remembers old Al Dexter these days, and word is that he's running a motel in Lufkin, Texas—and still collecting royalties for one of the all-time best-selling country songs ever written, "Pistol Packin' Mama." The lyrics—and there were endless verses—were simple:

Drinkin' beer in a cabaret
And was I havin' fun
'Til one night, I didn't drink right
And now I'm on the run . . .

Lay that pistol down, babe
Lay that pistol down
Pistol Packin' Mama,
Lay that pistol down.

Dexter says the song was inspired by the turbulence of the early days in the east Texas oil

John Denver: Country roads and Rocky Mountain highs.

fields. He wrote and recorded the song for Columbia and it was released in March 1943. Within weeks it had become the national song. Everybody was singing it, and the song ranked as one of the top three hits of World War II. Endless parodies of "Pistol Packin' Mama" were made up in camp shows and USO shows. Yet the song was not placed on CBS' *Lucky Strike Hit Parade* for more than six months. Angered, the publishers sued the program. *Life* magazine claimed the song wasn't used because the show's star, Frank Sinatra, couldn't sing it. Nonetheless, "Pistol Packin' Mama" sold 3 million singles in twenty-two months, and Dexter opened his own club, The Bridgeport, in

Dallas, where he sang his honky-tonk country blues to admiring audiences for many years. Dexter wrote and recorded a number of other songs, including the classic "Jelly Roll Blues" and "Honky-Tonk Blues."

## DICKENS, LITTLE JIMMY

BORN: December 19, 1925, Bolt, West Virginia

MARRIED: w. Ernestine (deceased)

CHILDREN: d. Pamela Jean

Jimmy Dickens, only four feet eleven inches high, walked tall for a number of years in the

60

country music world, singing loud and lively novelty numbers. Jimmy Dickens' material dealt with being the runt of the litter on the farm: "Take an Old Tater and Wait" and "Sleepin' at the Foot of the Bed." He sold a lot of records during the 1940s and '50s for Columbia, and prophesied (with Vaughn Horton's lyrics) that "hillbilly fever was spreadin' all around." He also wrote songs: "Sea of Broken Dreams" and "I Sure Would Like to Sit a Spell with You." Dickens had a brief spurt of supersuccess in the mid-sixties with his number-one chart hit, "May the Bird of Happiness Fly Up Your Nose." Everybody who is interested in country music has heard of Little Jimmy Dickens, and his name undoubtedly draws old-timey fans in rural areas who still play his happy novelty numbers. He is, as they say, a credit to country music. As they also say, there's no business like show business. Not one Jimmy Dickens record is listed in the 1973 Schwann catalog.

# THE DILLARDS

## Doug Dillard

BORN: March 6, 1937, Salem, Missouri

## Rodney Dillard

BORN: May 18, 1942, Salem, Missouri

## Mitch Jayne

BORN: July 5, 1930, Hammond, Indiana

## Dean Webb

BORN: March 28, 1937, Indianola, Missouri

Although Bill Monroe must be cited as having achieved the summit in making "bluegrass" a profitable subdivision of country, the valleys are filling with other talented ensembles. Most of the bluegrass groups come from eastern Appalachia, but one which achieved much critical success in the 1960s was the Dillards, an Ozark-born group with a wide following among folk and rock as well as country fans. Even though the group has for the moment disbanded, their records dating from the late sixties are listed in the 1973 Schwann catalog, which means they're still selling steadily.

# THE DIXON BROTHERS

## Dorsey Dixon

BORN: October 14, 1897, Darlington, South Carolina

## Howard Dixon

BORN: June 19, 1903, Darlington, South Carolina

DIED: March 24, 1961

Dorsey Dixon was a smash at the Newport (Rhode Island) Folk Festival in the summer of 1963, and he appeared at several subsequent festivals. In his mid-sixties at the time, Dorsey could, for the first time in fifty years, devote full time to music. Most of his life had been spent as a mill hand. Officials from the Folk Archives of the Library of Congress came to his house and he sang thirty-eight songs for them. He told the sound engineers that he wished his brother were alive to see that day. Piedmont, Vanguard and Testament produced Dorsey Dixon albums. But it was all too late.

Dorsey Dixon and his brother were among the great pioneer country performers and songwriters. Bill C. Malone, who has written extensively about the origins of American country music, considers them to be among the two or three seminal country brother acts and one of the first to feature the dobro guitar.

Writes Malone: "Howard and Dorsey Dixon came from Darlington, South Carolina, from the same type of textile-mill environment that produced such important country performers as Henry Whitter, Kelly Harrell, and Jimmie Tarlton. Although music was always an integral part of their lives, the Dixon Brothers were never permanently away from the mills. Howard died on the job, and Dorsey finally retired in 1951.

"Both brothers played instruments—Howard, the guitar, and Dorsey, the fiddle and guitar —from the time they were in their late teens, but, although they played semiprofessionally throughout the late twenties, they made no serious attempt at a professional career until the thirties. In 1931 Jimmie Tarlton, in one of his frequent forays through the country, stopped in East Rockingham, North Carolina, where he gained temporary employment at a mill where the Dixon Brothers were working. Because of this chance encounter Dorsey was inspired to develop a finger-picking style on the guitar and

Howard started playing the steel guitar, both in emulation of Tarlton. In 1934 the Dixon Brothers inaugurated their professional career with a performance on J. W. Fincher's Crazy Water Crystals Saturday Night Jamboree, carried over WBT in Charlotte, North Carolina. They recorded for only two years—a stint with Victor which began on February 12, 1936, in Charlotte. Although their recorded repertory of over sixty songs never earned them enough money to free them from textile employment, they introduced several songs (most of them written by Dorsey, a prolific songwriter) which have endured in country music: 'Intoxicated Rat,' the widely circulated 'Weave Room Blues,' and Roy Acuff's great hit, 'Wreck on the Highway,' which the Dixon Brothers entitled 'I Didn't Hear Nobody Pray.' ''

## DOLLAR, JOHNNY

BORN: March 8, 1933, Kilgore, Texas
CHILDREN: s. John Washington Dollar III

A check of the hit charts of the last three years will show that the same fifty artists' names are featured every week. These almost never change. Every once in a while, a new name hits the charts. Most often it's a one-song fluke, and the performer is never heard from again. Many performers who have this brief fame go back to their local area, and if they perform at all, it's done locally. Others never stop fighting. Johnny Dollar is that kind of performer. He has played every small town in America. He deserves the applause he gets. For a while he worked for Shelby Singleton, recording Shelby's songs: "West Texas," "Crawling Back to You," and others. They were good songs, but the Dee label couldn't afford to promote them, and Dollar was only making nickels and dimes. True to his name, he went into the money business—investments—in Oklahoma, but after five years the urge to perform was too great. He recorded "Lumberjack" for Winston, gaining enough attention for Columbia to pick him up for a while. In 1966, 1967, and 1968 Dollar made the charts with "Tear Talk," "Stop the Start," and "The Wheels Fell off the Wagon." These days the only chart he's on is Chart Records (with a truck-driving album, "Big Rig Rollin' Man"), but he keeps plugging and plugging, which is all to his credit.

## DRIFTWOOD, JIMMY [James Morris]

BORN: June 20, 1917, Mountainview, Arkansas

Jimmy Driftwood doesn't classify himself as a country singer, though he certainly has the sound and golden credentials. Brought up in the Ozarks, fiddling and picking before he was ten, he recalls that his first homemade guitar was built of "fence-rail, ox-yoke and bedstead." Jimmy's interest centered on historical songs and traditional ballads instead of commercial country, and he was a familiar figure at folk festivals. He deserves mention in country-music history because sometime in the early 1950s, Jimmy Driftwood took an old square-dance tune, "The Eighth of January," and fashioned a song out of it he called "The Battle of New Orleans." Johnny Horton recorded it for Columbia, and spurred a revival of historical country ballads. Many of Johnny Cash's songs were in this vein: "Don't Take Your Guns to Town," for example, and Marty Robbins' "Hanging Tree." Jimmy Driftwood still packs them in at the folk festivals and has recorded a number of splendid albums himself for Columbia.

## DRUSKY, ROY

BORN: June 22, 1930, Atlanta, Georgia
MARRIED: w. Bobbyee Jean Swafford
CHILDREN: s. Roy Frank III, Tracy

Roy Drusky has had a number of big successes: "Such a Fool," "Another," and "Any More." He is the archetype of the talented country singer who has not set the fans on fire, yet turns out capable and interesting work. Unlike other country stars, he didn't get the "music bug" until after high school, in the navy. He bought a guitar and taught himself to play. Though now interested in music, on his discharge he entered Emory College to get a degree in veterinary medicine. To make extra money he formed a band, The Southern Ranch Boys. They were so successful that WEAS in Decatur, Georgia, offered Drusky a daily fifteen-minute show, as well as a job as a country disc jockey, on the station. Starday Records signed Drusky in 1953, and it was goodbye veterinary medicine, hello Nashville. Columbia picked up his contract, and not much happened during that period. Drusky broke up the band and headed for Minnesota

Roy Drusky: An Atlanta, Georgia, boy.

Dave Dudley: Lets everyone know about his six days on the road.

and a DJ job in Minneapolis. At night he sang at the Flame Club, where Webb Pierce occasionally did a guest shot. Pierce liked Drusky and convinced Decca to let Faron Young sing Drusky's composition "Alone with You." It became a top-ten hit in 1958. Within a year, Drusky was back in Nashville, writing and recording. He has also been active in Nashville's social and professional life, serving on the board of the Country Music Association.

## DUDLEY, DAVE

BORN: March 3, 1928, Spencer, Wisconsin
MARRIED: w. Jean

Oh yes, big Dave Dudley, one of the great singers of trucking songs and deep-voiced hero of countless thousands of country fans. He was born and raised not in North Carolina or Texas but in the northern climes of Wisconsin, far from the country-music heartland. When he showed an interest in music as a child, his father bought him a guitar (with money saved from a World War I bonus) and Dave learned to play by watching other musicians at Saturday matinees. "The best I ever did in high school," Dudley admits, "was to be a backup guitarist in the school band." He was mainly interested in baseball (like Bill Anderson, Charley Pride, and Roy Acuff), and a semipro team snapped Dudley up as soon as he finished school. In 1949, as a pitcher, he won fifteen games for the Wausau, Wisconsin, team, and lost only three. He was purchased from Wausau by the Gainesville,

64

Texas, Owls (not the most famous team in baseball, but higher up in the hierarchy than Wausau), and it looked for a while as if he would make the majors, but he hurt his pitching arm and was invalided home to Wisconsin. With nothing to do but recuperate, Dudley started picking guitar again, visiting his friend Vern Shepard, DJ on station WTWT. Shepard asked him to sing "live," and Dudley the baseball player retired and Dudley the singer was born.

Within a few months he had his own program on WTWT, and forming a trio, played the Midwest. Just when his career was flourishing, Dudley, leaving an engagement at the Flame Club in Minneapolis, was struck by a car. He spent six months in bed and figured his career was over. Nonetheless, endowed with "true grit," Dudley bought time at a local studio to make a demonstration record of a song he liked called "Six Days on the Road." A friend, who supplied juke boxes with records, put it out on the Soma label. The song was picked up by midwestern disc jockeys, and then all around the country, and Dudley became a show business hero and a founding father of a type of song: the Truck-Driver Song. Country-music historian Bill C. Malone says that "Dudley affects a hard-driving, virile style of singing replete with mumbles and slurred expressions which make him sound like an adult Elvis Presley." Well, he might not have the following that Elvis has, but just say you're a friend of Dave Dudley at any truck stop—and see the treatment you get.

Among Dudley's other hits (mostly for Mercury): "Cowboy Boots," "Truck Drivin' Son of a Gun," and "What We're Fightin' For."

## THE DUKE OF PADUCAH, see
WHITEY FORD

## DUNCAN, JOHNNY

BORN: October 5, 1938, Dublin, Texas
MARRIED: w. Betty Fisher
CHILDREN: d. Anje, Leslie, Lori

Johnny Duncan has been on Columbia since 1967, when Don Law signed him to a contract. His work has made the charts on a regular basis, but not one of his records has clicked as well as "Sweet Country Woman" in 1973. He now travels with the immensely successful Charley Pride show and is developing a following of his own. Other Duncan hits include "You're Gonna Need a Man" and "There's Something About a Lady."

# E

## EDWARDS, JONATHAN

Jonathan Edwards is an example of a rock-oriented singer whose one fling into country, "Honky-Tonk Stardust Cowboy," popped him into the country charts and points out that one-timers sometimes get there. Although Edwards is a decent songwriter—indeed, he writes about 98 percent of the stuff he records—the song that brought his name to the fore was the composition of Darrell Statler.

## EDWARDS, STONEY

Stoney Edwards, a black country singer who lives on a California ranch (one of three blacks in the "star" category of country music, the others being O. B. McClinton and the great Charley Pride), has had moderate success with a number of original songs based on his love for country music as a child ("I was raised on Hank Williams"). Though he hasn't the following of Pride, nor the publicity backing being given to McClinton), Stoney Edwards is picking up a following among critics who enjoy his good voice and pure country phrasing.

## EVANS, DALE

BORN: October 31, 1912, Uvalde, Texas
MARRIED: h. Tom F. Fox (divorced); Roy Rogers
CHILDREN: s. Roy, Jr., John [deceased]; d. Robin [deceased], Cheryl, Linda Lou, Marion, Scottish Ward, Mary, Little Doe, Deborah Lee [deceased]

Stoney Edwards (right) studies an arrangement with Capitol Records' producer Biff Collie.

If Roy Rogers had to fight it out to be king of the cowboys, there is no doubt in anybody's mind that Dale Evans was, and probably still is, queen of the cowgirls. Despite her Texas birth, however, Dale started out as a torch singer. She married (don't let this shock you, everybody has a skeleton or two in some kind of closet) someone named Tom F. Fox when she was only sixteen, but left the marriage at eighteen and concentrated on her singing career. During the early thirties she sang on radio shows in Memphis and Dallas and finally became the vocalist with Anson Weeks's top Chicago band. As "the toast of the silk hat set" she headlined at the swank Chez Paree and appeared weekly on a CBS radio variety show, graduating to regular singing stardom on the immensely popular *Charlie McCarthy and Edgar Bergen Show.* All during this period she never climbed a horse or fastened a spur. When the movies beckoned, they made her a cowgirl: *Swing Your Partner* was the picture's name and it starred a young man named Leonard Slye, a member of the Sons of the Pioneers, a cowboy from Ohio who was being groomed as a new Gene Autry. They called him Roy Rogers, and he rode and sang his way to stardom. In 1947, sometime after Roy's first wife died, Dale married the singing cowboy and spent many years and many films being Mrs. Singing Cowboy. Nowadays she writes inspirational books, is sincerely involved in infinite good works, looks after any of her seven foster children who are home, and appears with Roy at rodeos, fairs, and special events for charities like the National Association for Muscular Dystrophy, the Red Cross, and the National Association for Retarded Children—and just about everybody in the world recognizes her. She never was much of a C & W singer, though.

## THE EVERLY BROTHERS

### Don Everly

BORN: February 1, 1937, Brownine, Kentucky

### Phil Everly

BORN: January 19, 1939, Brownine, Kentucky

On Friday, July 13, 1973, Don Everly, looking older than his thirty-six years, and having been a performer for twenty-eight of those years, and making no bones about his dissatisfaction with being "booked as a relic of the past," announced that his next appearance (at the John Wayne Theater of Knotts Berry Farm, Buena Park, California) would be his last public performance with his brother, Phil.

"It's over," Don Everly stated to reporters. "I've quit. I'm tired of being an Everly brother." A number of contracts were voided and a much-publicized European tour canceled.

At the performance, Bill Hollingshead, who runs entertainment for Knotts Berry Farm, decided to stop the show. Don wasn't anywhere up to snuff, he felt, and things could get worse. There have been conflicting reports on the evening's events. One national radio bulletin claimed Phil Everly smashed his guitar on his brother's head. Another claimed a free-for-all, with Hollingshead getting the worst of it. Actually, when Hollingshead stopped the show, an angry Phil Everly smashed his guitar, all right, but on the floor, and rushed off the stage. Don insisted he could finish the show alone, and Hollingshead agreed. In the middle of his first solo, a member of the audience shouted, "Hey, where's Phil?" First Don said, "I haven't seen him, pal. Do you know where he is?" Then, clearly and slowly so everyone in the audience could understand what he was saying, Don announced: "The Everly Brothers died ten years ago."

This is not the first time the Everly Brothers have split. Their relationship has been stormy for some time. In 1970 Don made a solo album for Ode Records. It didn't sell well. More recently Phil Everly released a solo album on RCA, "Star Spangled Springer." Friends claim that the "brothers just need a rest from one another. After all, they've been singing together since 1945."

It is true. When Don was six and Phil eight, they joined their parents, Ike and Margaret Everly, well-known country performers in the South and Midwest, on their radio show on KMA in Shenandoah, Iowa. They were part of the Everly Family Act, but when Ike and Margaret retired, in the 1950's, Don and Phil decided to strike out on their own. Nashville recalls that era with some horror. Rock-and-roll was taking hold, country was at a low ebb. One of the few bright spots was Ike and Margaret's kids, who were Acuff-Rose products, and whose records were played by both rock and country

The Everly Brothers and their families present a "super picker" T-shirt to Chet Atkins.

DJ's. Their first hit was "Bye-Bye Love" on Cadence, and it was a monster success. It's follow-up, "Wake Up Little Susie," did even better. (Felice and Boudleax Bryant and Acuff-Rose composed both those songs, and their relationship with the Everly Brothers during the late 1950's was mutually profitable. Among the other hits written by the Bryants for the Everlys: "Bird Dog," "All I Have to Do Is Dream.") Along with Buddy Holly, Elvis Presley, and Carl Perkins, the Everlys were fusing country singing with the strong black blues beat. If you listened behind the rock beat you could still catch the bluegrass-style harmony in the Everlys (they still have it to some extent). And their success made great inroads into country. Producers, to win the young audience back, listened hard to people like the Everlys, and there are some who claim that's how the new Nashville sound was really born.

F

## FAIRCHILD, BARBARA
BORN: November 12, 1950, Knoble, Arkansas

"I don't know if you've guessed it, but all this has messed up my head a little. I always said to myself," Barbara Fairchild told reporter John Pugh, "when I get a hit record, I want to be ready. When I got it I found out I still wasn't ready."

Barbara Fairchild's head may be in the clouds, but the rest of her is down to earth.

Down in the rolling plains of Nashville, to be exact, where she is kicking up a lot of dust with her record, "Teddy Bear Song." And finding the grass even greener than she had imagined.

"All the changes in my life since 'Teddy Bear' —it's almost unreal," Barbara began. "All of a sudden people are concerned about what I think, important people are calling me, Columbia Records even sent me flowers when I was in the hospital. It's hard to get used to making good money when before I was always worried about paying my bills. When I was a kid in the country the days just crawled by, especially Sundays. Now they just fly by. I'm on the go so much I don't have time to relax. I've got the money to do some of the things I've always wanted to, but now I don't have the time. They can think of

something for me to do twenty-four hours a day. Like in May, I was home three days. I've waited all my life for a record, so I could work, and I love it, but dragging suitcases, waiting for planes, and leaving my bag back at the motel can drive me crazy. But I love being twenty-two. I don't know why, I'm just glad I am what I am. Everything good has happened to me this year: a baby, a hit record. As long as I can remember, this is what I've wanted. It's almost freaky the way everything is falling into place for me so young. It's almost like somebody's watching over me."

Perhaps so. Songwriter Jerry Crutchfield, who gave Barbara her start in Nashville, says, "I've seen many artists that somehow never quite got it together. There would be a lot of

Barbara Fairchild: Teddy bears ain't kid stuff . . .

behind-the-scenes excitement over them, but they just never seemed to happen with the public. On the other hand, I've been aware of people in the business that seemed destined to accomplish certain things. I get the same feeling about Barbara. In fact, the second time I met her I told her I would positively guarantee her a record."

Barbara's second meeting with Crutchfield was even more productive than her first. At that time Barbara, with a friend, had come to Nashville from St. Louis to secure a recording contract. She was all of seventeen. They had been in Music City several days when Barbara's companion spied Crutchfield in a parking lot. "I know him!" she exclaimed. They cornered Crutchfield and chatted with him until he invited them up to his office for a quick listen-to.

"She had one song I liked," Crutchfield related, "so I told her to go home, write some more and come back. But the most impressive thing was Barbara's singing. She was only seventeen, but she sang with the conviction and experience of someone who'd been around a lot longer. She's the most refreshing new talent I've ever run into. She can handle many types of material. Most girl singers do one thing. Barbara can do several, all just as effective. Her country songs have been compared with Dolly Parton. She's also been compared to Teresa Brewer. She reminds me of a torchy French singer. I think this is the reason for all the comparisons."

"Any time a new artist comes along, he or she is bound to be compared to established singers," Barbara said. "Nobody's ever compared me to Dolly; I get compared mostly to Brenda Lee. In school I admired Brenda, knew all her songs, tried to sing like her until I finally realized the world didn't need two of us. Then I tried to follow Loretta Lynn, Connie Smith, and others. Out of all this came what I do."

Out of all this came "Teddy Bear Song," a unique song, which has defied categorization, swept the country, and mystified many insiders —including Barbara. "I really don't know why it was such a big hit," Barbara said. "I wasn't prepared for its being the record it's been. But it's a singable song, a simple song, and there may also be some degree of novelty factor involved. It's like 'Snowbird' in that it's a sad song, but a light feeling."

The same feeling one gets around Barbara. It is easy to imagine her incorporating Loretta Lynn into her singing, because of their remarkably similar personalities and mannerisms. "The first time I met Loretta she said, 'You're my favorite singer,'" said Barbara. "She started making such a fuss over me, and this was long before I had had 'Teddy Bear.' She asked me to come to the disc jockey convention and she let me stay with her the entire week.

"I don't see Loretta much these days; one of us is always gone. But I admire someone like that and I hope I can be that way. What scares you is when you see performers who start out loving the public, but change. I hope that never happens to me."

## FARGO, DONNA
BORN: November 10, 1949
MARRIED: h. Stan Silver

There's no doubt that Donna Fargo was country music's big success story for 1973: "The Happiest Girl in the Whole U.S.A." Grammy winner first time out. Only in the business less than a year, imagine. Her first album was on the charts for forty-five weeks and her second album climbed almost as high, and the record stores put in big advance orders for the third. She's had single hits every couple of months. The executives at Dot (not generally known as a country label, though it produces Roy Clark and others) are licking their chops in expectations of the BIG MONEY that comes when one of their artists becomes a superstar. "It's amazing the way Donna Fargo made it overnight," a Nashville agent wrote in a trade paper. "It proves that it still can be done."

Yes it can, but nobody knows about all those years Donna Fargo worked *before* anybody heard of her. She even had an album, which was released on the West Coast. Every high school graduating class has at least one kid who has a dream of making it in show business. Most of them take a route similar to Donna's—that is, invest money to record themselves and then impress a big label with the results. Last year more than 700 independent record sessions were produced in Nashville. The people wanting to cut a record pay anywhere from $800 to $3,000 for the session. In 1973 Donna's recording of her own song, "The Happiest Girl in the Whole

Donna Fargo: Still the happiest girl in the whole U.S.A.

U.S.A.,'' worked. It received, among other citations, the Country Music Association single-of-the-year award. The idea to invest money in a private session came from Stan Silver, Donna's manager, who knew the quality of his star and her ability to write and sing. He is her husband as well as manager. She was able to quit her job teaching English to perform full-time. I met Donna Fargo in London, Ontario, in the spring of 1973. Her career was in full swing, and she was heading a bill that night with Hank Williams, Jr., and Jan Howard. "We've been on the road so much, I'm used to it. We live in Nashville, but we're almost never there.''

"We have a house there, though,'' Stan interrupted. "We found it almost two-thirds built and we're finishing it. But we're on the road all the time. It's hard. We've been going since last June.''

Donna continued: "I stopped teaching last June. They let me quit three days early, so I could tour with Roy Clark. It was really exciting.''

I asked Donna about her teaching. "I'd always been interested in singing,'' she told me, "but I was trained as a teacher and I got a job teaching. A friend of mine introduced me to Stan, who has been in the music business for a long time. I sang for him and he said, 'You're a country singer.' Did you know Stan taught me to play the guitar? I told him I wanted to write songs and he said, 'Then write songs,' and I started writing.''

Stan interrupted: "Donna was head of the English department in her school and she helped accredit the school for the state. She was a fine teacher. They weren't happy when she left. They wanted her to teach teachers, too. That's how good she was." Donna squeezed Stan's hand and blushed. "I'm really shy," she confessed.

"Donna never told anybody about wanting to be a singer,'' Stan said. "But she's really a worker.''

"I guess you'd say I'm a very determined person. I learn by doing. When I wrote my first song about five years ago, I put down what I heard in my head. It didn't work exactly, but I wrote it over and over and it finally came out nearly like I wanted it.'' Stan explained how Donna's first record, for a company called Ramco, got a lot of Southern California airplay, but it was a small company and didn't have wide distribution.

"We're a real team. We work really well together,'' Donna said, proudly. She stopped for a moment. "You know, we're together all the time—and I mean all the time. In most families, the husband and wife work at different jobs. But lately our life has been so busy that we haven't had time to think about anything. Even about finishing our house, or building one next door for the band to rehearse in. We're always on the go.''

Donna claims there are religious overtones in her songs. "I went to a Methodist college—High Point in North Carolina. Did you know that I was scared to death to be baptized? Thought I would drown. I'm still a little guilty about having fun. And my life is fun. Especially since I met Stan.''

"Then you really are the happiest girl in the U.S.A.?'' I asked, almost joshingly, but she answered in a serious vein: "In the world, I think. That's how I happened to write the song. I wanted to make a statement about happiness. The idea sat up there, kind of ready to explode for about two months. Then, one Saturday night, in front of the fireplace, I didn't have any specific intention of any particular words but they just came out of me—'Good mornin', mornin'—good mornin', sunshine.' And the second verse just happened. Maybe it's because I'm a Scorpio. Things just happen to me.''

Donna doesn't wear "country style" clothing on stage. Her outfit generally is a simple pair of pants and a shirt, and although she plays the guitar, she moves around the stage too much for her to carry one during the act. She dances, prances, jumps, almost does cartwheels, and she has the ability to carry the audience with her every step of the way. Her style is very much her own, there is an originality in her voice. It rings like a bell at times and then drops without warning to a sexy, throaty quality—the effect is dazzling. It will be interesting to see if Donna Fargo remains a country star, or if the wicked temptations of the pop charts are still an unfightable magnet to super country performers. Others have succumbed. Donna says, "I just sing the way I sing. I don't know what kind of label you put on it.''

# FELTS, NARVEL

MARRIED: w. Loretta
CHILDREN: s. S. Narvel, Jr.; d. Stacia

"Drift Away" was one of the big hits of 1973. It was sung by Narvel Felts, who nobody had ever heard of, although he'd been singing and recording since 1956. Born in Arkansas and raised in Missouri, Felts was raised on a diet of Ernest Tubb and Roy Acuff, bought a Sears guitar, and at sixteen won a high school talent contest singing "Baby, Let's Play House," the Elvis Presley hit. By 1956 Mercury had signed Felts as a Presley imitator, and his rockabilly songs did moderately well. Then he recorded "Honey Love," which started a climb to the top until many station owners listened to the lyrics. "Compared to the words of today's songs," Felts now says, " 'Honey Love' would be too tame for *Sesame Street*." But the record was banned from practically every station in the country. Felts didn't give up. For a dozen years he traveled from label to label, keeping his rock-country style. "I just sing like Narvel Felts," he says. Johnny Morris, a former Missouri disc jockey, became head of Cinnamon Records, remembered Felts, and signed him, and the rest just might be country history. "Drift Away" did well, and a couple of Felts hits are on the charts now. At this writing he isn't a household word, but he has such a groovy name, how can he lose?

# FLATT, LESTER

BORN: June 28, 1914, Overton County, Tennessee
MARRIED: w. Gladys Lee Stacy
CHILDREN: d. Brenda Carolyn

Back in the mid-sixties I was one of three thousand fortunate New Yorkers who packed into Carnegie Hall to hear Flatt and Scruggs at their first big-city concert. The audience scared the daylights out of the staid Carnegie Hall ushers by shooping, hollering, and jumping up and down on the plush seats. Joan Baez, one of many celebrities in attendance, sat in front of me, and she shooped and hollered with the best of them. Backstage, I managed to talk to Lester Flatt, who was surrounded by autograph seekers. "I guess our music is for everybody," Flatt said. "If anybody told me I'd be playin' Carnegie Hall back a few years, I'd a called him a liar." When the musical marriage of Lester Flatt and Earl Scruggs broke up in the late sixties, it was hard to mention either name without provoking a speculative discussion. The rumors about the cause of the breakup were plentiful—differences over politics, philosophies, and publicity ... Earl's increasing involvement with his sons' experimentations in non-country music. But the relationship ended. "Music can't stand still," Scruggs said. Flatt didn't say much at all. He kept the group going, without Buck Graves, who joined Scruggs. And lately Flatt has been recording with Mac Wiseman, and has produced some fine if not great records. Lester Flatt isn't the genius Scruggs is with his fingers, but he's still among the top two or three bluegrass singers in America. And if he wants his music "to stand still," there are still untold thousands of fans who will come out to applaud him. Personally, I get the shivers everytime Flatt sings "Jimmy Brown, the Newsboy."

Flatt was a product of rural Tennessee, and learned to play the guitar "old-timey style." Like many other musicians of his day, he worked in textile mills, playing only on weekends. He turned professional, at the advice of just about everybody, in 1939, with a stint on WDBJ in Roanoke, Virginia. He joined Grand Ole Opry in the early forties, as a member of Bill Monroe's Bluegrass Boys (from Monroe's style came the name bluegrass to describe a certain type of country music. See BLUEGRASS). In 1945 a young banjoist joined Monroe, and Flatt and Scruggs was born. Within a few years they split from Monroe and started their own band.

Bill C. Malone, who has done as much studying about bluegrass and the urban folk revival as any man, wrote: "During the mid-fifties, while country music as a whole became more commercialized and akin to pop music, bluegrass music proliferated and moved strongly toward the performance of authentic and old-time country music. Although many bluegrass bands vied for recognition by the American audience, none equaled the success of Flatt and Scruggs. Flatt and Scruggs, with the Foggy Mountain Boys, took their brand of music into areas long alien to

Lester Flatt (far right) at the Newport Folk Festival when he was still a partner of Earl Scruggs (left).

country music and, more than any one group, implanted bluegrass music in the national music consciousness. Recording first for Mercury and later for Columbia, Earl Scruggs, the one-time farm boy from Flint Hill, North Carolina, and Lester Flatt, a former textile worker from Overton County, Tennessee, popularized bluegrass music in small southern hamlets and in metropolitan New York and from the stages of village schoolhouses and Carnegie Hall alike. They joined the Grand Ole Opry in 1955 and, using that institution as their Saturday-night base of operations, they toured all over the southeastern United States and appeared in towns and villages—some of them too small for a post office—sponsored by the Martha White Mills of Nashville. And as their popularity increased in the late fifties, their schedule of concert tours expanded to take in the entire United States from Boston's Jordan Hall to Los Angeles' Ash Grove. The success gained by the Flatt and Scruggs organization was paralleled by the rise in prosperity experienced by the Martha White Flour Mills. Cohen T. Williams, president of the firm that advertised Hot Rize (a self-rising ingredient found in the flour and meal), stated unequivocally that 'Flatt and Scruggs and the Grand Ole Opry built the Martha White Mills.'

"Although it is doubtful whether Flatt and Scruggs, who feel that their repertory has broadened into the sphere of musical eclecticism, now consider themselves to be part of the bluegrass movement, bluegrass devotees definitely believe that the songs recorded by the Foggy Mountain

Boys during the late forties and early fifties were among the most exciting in the entire bluegrass genre. These early Flatt and Scruggs recordings were characterized by verve and originality, with much of the instrumentation performed at breakneck speed and the vocals rendered in an old-fashioned, high, hard harmony by such singers as Everett Lilly and Curly Sechler. The group first gave notice of its distinctiveness with the recordings of such instrumental numbers as 'Foggy Mountain Breakdown' (currently known as 'The Theme from *Bonnie and Clyde*') and 'Pike County Breakdown' and a few Earl Scruggs originals like 'Earl's Breakdown,' 'Flint Hill Special,' and 'Randy Lynn Rag' (named after one of his sons). Songs of this type were often used as themes or fill-in numbers on country disc-jockey shows; in fact, they were quite often the only bluegrass songs included on the country radio shows.

"By the middle of the sixties the Flatt and Scruggs group had won success and affluence and their band had evolved into a well-coordinated, precision-like unit which, though almost flawless in its musical execution, lacked the fire and enthusiasm exhibited on the early Mercury recordings. Lester Flatt now characteristically pitches his vocals much lower than on such early recordings, as 'Jimmie Brown, the Newsboy' and 'Roll in My Sweet Baby's Arms,' and, possibly as a reaction against the Bill Monroe sound, the mandolin has been dropped from the Foggy Mountain Boys' instrumentation. In place of the mandolin a dobro steel guitar, played by Buck Graves, was added in 1955. Graves, known in his comedian's role as Uncle Josh, plays the dobro with a rapid picking technique similar to that of Scruggs on the banjo and did much to widen the basis of Flatt and Scruggs' popular appeal. Buck Graves, fiddler Paul Warren (who had earlier played with Johnny and Jack), bassist Jake Tullock ('Cousin Jake'), and Flatt and Scruggs exhibit an effortless stage presence and collective musical interaction that is a delight to watch."

Perhaps the outstanding feature of Flatt and Scruggs's popularity (and of the popularity of bluegrass music as a whole) was the interest and enthusiasm shown by people outside the usual country-music audience. People who had never evinced the slightest interest in commercial

country music before, and who in fact would have dismissed it as a crass and pseudo form of rural music, were now attracted to the bluegrass style and described it in superlatives. Greenwich Village and Washington Square habitués, college students at institutions like Fordham, New York University, Vanderbilt, and the University of Illinois, and people who considered themselves "folkmusic" partisans delighted in the bluegrass sound and tried eagerly to copy the Scruggs banjo technique. As the Flatt and Scruggs band roamed far and wide, Earl Scruggs's preeminence as a five-string banjoist was readily admitted everywhere. In 1959, Scruggs participated in the Newport (Rhode Island) Folk Festival—the only country musician to be included.

## FOLEY, RED [Clyde Julian Foley]

BORN: June 17, 1910, Blue Lick, Kentucky
DIED: September 19, 1968, Fort Wayne, Indiana
MARRIED: w. Axie Cox (deceased), Eva Sally Overstake (deceased)
CHILDREN: d. Betty, Shirley Lee, Jennie Lou, Julia Ann

Red Foley was elected to the Country Music Hall of Fame the year before he died. He is considered one of the "founding fathers" of modern country music. He was the first star to actually record in Nashville: March 1945, at Studio B, station WSM. He was a major star of the Grand Ole Opry and an important Nashville citizen. His daughter Shirley Lee is the wife of Pat Boone. Another daughter, Betty Foley (Cummins), had a brief, successful career in country. Her 1959 hit, "Old Man," on Bandera Records remained in the top ten for a long time. Red Foley always helped young talent. He was the first big star to hear Charley Pride (he was on tour in Montana) and convinced Charley to try his luck in Nashville. Other performers credit him with a boost, as well. Red Foley had a constant succession of superhits over the years: "Chattanooga Shoe Shine Boy," "Peace in the Valley," "Beyond the Sunset," "It Is No Secret," and infinite others.

Born and raised in Kentucky, he was a star

athlete and always had a good voice, winning an Atwater Kent amateur talent contest at seventeen. His mother was convinced Red would be a fine musician and hired a voice coach for him. During Red's first semester of college (Georgetown College in Kentucky) a talent scout for WLS in Chicago spotted him and offered him a chance to sing on the *WLS National Barn Dance* if he could get to Chicago. Borrowing $75 from his father, he made the trip, and never returned to school. Chicago in the early thirties was a stopping-off point for blacks on their way north. They played flat-top guitars with the neck of a broken bottle—and Foley learned his style of picking from them. In 1937 he left the *National Barn Dance* to start the *Renfro Valley Barn Dance,* and a few years later he costarred on the first national country show, *Avalon Time,* with Red Skelton. Decca signed him to a lifetime contract. It's estimated that he sold about 25 million records. Foley produced and starred in the *Ozark Mountain Jubilee,* on ABC-TV, for six years. He was Fess Parker's costar on the ABC-TV series *Mr. Smith Goes to Washington.*

He died of a heart attack in 1968, after a personal appearance on a Grand Ole Opry tour in Indiana, and Red Foley is always named in any list of the ten great country performers of all times.

## FORD, TENNESSEE ERNIE

BORN: February 13, 1919, Bristol, Tennessee
MARRIED: w. Betty Jean Heminger
CHILDREN: s. Jeffrey, Brian

Old Ernie Ford, a dead ringer for Grace Kelly's old man Prince Rainier ("they look the same, but their accents are different") and for many years *Mister* country music on TV and radio, and even in a couple of movies, has had an amazingly successful career. His trademark opening, "Howdy, pea-pickers," is familiar to several generations of Americans, and his rich voice and ability to put over songs (even some clinkers) has afforded him countless acres to cultivate solid gold peas. But it was rock-and-roll, strangely enough, which brought the voice of Ernie Ford to the collective ear of America. There was this song, "Sixteen Tons," written and recorded by the great Merle Travis in 1947,

for Capitol. (It was one of the first records I ever owned; I still have it, play it often—even though it's a 78-rpm—but apparently no one else bought it.) Then, in 1955, Tennessee Ernie Ford decided to record the song over a rock-and-roll background, or as he says, "a semi-rock-and-roll background." "Sixteen Tons" became one of the fastest-selling records in history, reaching the number-one position on the charts only four months from its first issuance, and only twenty days after its first appearance on the *Billboard* poll. From that time on, Tennessee Ernie was no longer a "country" star but a plain old universal star, appearing as a guest on shows where he didn't even sing country-style songs.

As a boy in Tennessee, Ford spent all his spare hours listening to country and western musicians. In 1937 he got a job as a staff announcer at a station in Bristol, Tennessee, at $10 a week. Everybody told him he had a marvelous voice, and in 1938 he entered the Cincinnati Conservatory of Music. Before World War II he worked for stations in Atlanta and Knoxville. He enlisted in the air force, became a bombardier, and while he was stationed in California, married Betty Jean Heminger. On his discharge, he became a disc jockey in San Bernardino, moving shortly afterward to KXLA in Pasadena, a country station featuring the live show of Cliffie Stone. Stone and Ford became close pals, and Cliffie Stone not only encouraged Ford's singing, but arranged for Capitol records to audition him. The audition was a success, and the result was "Mule Train" and "Smokie Mountain Boogie."

By 1955 Ernie Ford had his own CBS program and dozens of successful chart hits. His TV show, sponsored by the Ford Motor Company ("no relation") consistently made the top Nielsen ratings. At the very top of his career, Ford backed away from show business to spend more time with his wife and family. His records (especially the religious ones) still sell. He emcees country-oriented specials, and visits Nashville frequently. And people recognize him. I was in California once when Tennessee Ernie came out of a restaurant. It was many years after his TV show, but several people stopped what they were doing and stared, while others ran over for autographs. Tennessee Ernie is a Good Old Boy with no rural edges left—but he's still good.

Tennessee Ernie Ford: He can afford gold-plated peas . . .

## FORD, WHITEY [Benjamin Francis Ford]

BORN: May 12, 1901, DeSoto, Missouri

Whitey Ford—known to country-music fans as the Duke of Paducah—is another funny man who, like others in country music, started out as a musician. Upon his release from the navy in 1922, he founded a dixieland jazz band and toured the vaudeville circuit, at one point teaming with Bobby Van in a banjo duo. He later toured as a member of Otto Gray's Oklahoma Cowboys band, and took part in an early Gene Autry radio show on WLS, Chicago. Through the 1930s until 1942 he was star of NBC radio's *Plantation Party*, which he wrote, directed, and hosted. After a tour with the USO during World War II, he returned to the States and became a regular on the Grand Ole Opry, making numerous personal appearances on stage and television. He guested on national TV shows during the 1960s, too.

The Duke of Paducah usually closes appearances with the now-classic line: "I'm goin' back to the wagon, boys, these shoes are killin' me!"

## FRAZIER, DALLAS

BORN: October 27, 1939, Spiro, Oklahoma

Although born in Oklahoma, Dallas Frazier grew up around Bakersfield, California, where his family moved when he was still a child. He demonstrated a proficiency for music at an early age and was able to play guitar and trumpet before he entered his teens. When he was twelve years old he won a talent contest sponsored by Ferlin Husky, who was so impressed with the young man that he signed him to join his show on a national tour. One thing led to another, and soon young Frazier was appearing on Cliffie Stone's *Hometown Jamboree* TV show. A contract with Capitol Records followed shortly thereafter.

In the late 1950s Dallas Frazier moved to Nashville, where he continued writing and performing. In 1957 one of his songs, "Alley Oop," became a country hit and crossed to the national pop charts. A prolific composer, his songs have been recorded by many major country artists.

Younger artists, particularly George (Commander Cody) Frayne, credit Frazier with introducing them, through his pop releases, to the simpler melodies of the country idiom.

## FRIEDMAN, KINKY [Richard Friedman]

BORN: October 31, 1944, Rio Duckworth, Texas

"Cowboys and Jews," says Kinky Friedman, have a common bond. "They are the only two groups of people in the world to wear their hats indoors and attach a certain amount of importance to it." Kinky Friedman is probably, next to Charley Pride, the most unlikely country singer in America—and both, in their ways, are pioneers. They also prove the universality of country music among all groups of people. Kinky is both Jew and Texan, and is strongly rooted in the qualities of each. The backstage workers at Grand Ole Opry in the spring of 1973 were a little worried when Kinky was invited to perform. Kinky doesn't look—well, for want of another word, wholesome. But the fans went wild, and that's success in the country business. Kinky Friedman is an original, in an unoriginal world.

Kaye Northcott, in the *Texas Monthly,* was one of the first people to write about Kinky Friedman: "What can I say to prepare you for Kinky Friedman? Kinky is a funny, Jewish country-western poet. He's the only recording star in Nashville who buys his clothes at the Hadassah Thrift Shop.

"Kinky's songs transgress so many cultural borders that he can offend Jesus Freaks and Jews and goat ropers and women's libbers in the same song. Then, in the next breath, he will finagle everyone's forgiveness with a verse so poignant that you know there's a heart of gold thumping under his blasphemous exterior. Kinky is just a nice Jewish overachiever who had the curious fortune to spend some of his formative years in Texas' cowboy country, some in various academic communities and some in the monsoon area of Borneo. He was bound to be a little schizy.

An unlikely candidate for the country circuit, perhaps, but Kinky Friedman and his group—The Texas Jewboys —have impressed Opry crowds and college audiences alike.

"Kinky, born Richard, and his younger brother, Roger, who performs some business functions for his brother, are the sons of a speech therapist and an educational psychology professor. Tom Friedman teaches at the Austin campus of the University of Texas, and, during the summers, the whole family runs a camp for children ages seven to thirteen, in the Texas hill country. It's not a typical regimented, competition-prone Texas camp. Roger calls it 'a Franny and Zooey farm.'

"Country-western music, especially Slim Whitman, first caught Kinky's ear at camp. C & W was all he could pick up on the radio. He wrote his first song, 'Make My Coffee Blue,' at the age of thirteen. Tom and Mim Friedman had the foresight to encourage their elder son's penchant for weird rhyming and soon Kinky was performing for the camp children. 'I'd sing them to sleep in the bunkhouse. It was just like bedding down cattle for the night,' Kinky remembers.

"He broke . . . well . . . stumbled into records in 1966 with a locally pressed single—King Arthur and the Carrots singing 'Schwinn 24' and 'Beach Party Boo Boo.' The tunes were haircuts off the then-popular surfing songs by Jan and Dean. 'It was a good little record, but it never quite took off,' Kinky said.

"After college, Kinky trained for a Peace Corps project in Tanzania, but he was deselected, partially, he maintains, because of the notoriety he had gained from King Arthur and the Carrots. He tried again and was sent to Borneo to distribute seeds, but monsoons made it impossible to go upriver and play Johnny Appleseed, so Kinky stayed in the city and played Frisbee. He insists he introduced the Frisbee to Borneo, 'but the natives only used it to make their lips big.'

"Back in the U.S. of A., Friedman set up headquarters at the family ranch, Rio Duckworth, which is down the road from the summer camp, equidistant between Kerrville and Bandera. The decor at Duckworth reveals the Friedmans' eclectic (real bizarre) tastes. Among the most treasured items are the stuffed head of a Longhorn reputed to have originally hung in the foyer of the old Schreiner Bank in Kerrville; a drum with an interior light that shows off a garish sunset scene on the drumhead; photographs of Charles Whitman and Slim Whitman,

hung side by side in the kitchen; a magnificent silver and bronze chess set from Lebanon; a portrait of Jesus with a 3-D effect; and a wood sculpture holding a yarmulke.

"When the Beaufords, as the Friedman brothers are wont to call themselves, are at the ranch, they sleep most of the day away and stay up all night playing chess and working. Kinky labors over his songs and Roger makes telephone calls, promoting his brother wherever he needs to be promoted. Rumor has it that they amassed the largest unpaid telephone bill in the history of the Hill Country Co-op before the phone was yanked out in February.

"Rio Duckworth is not Hollywood's or even Houston's idea of a proper Texas ranch, but it has the grey-green magic of the Texas hill country, the breezes smelling of cedar and the whippoorwills singing in the twilight. If the cow-country mystique has not moved Kinky to butt a saddle or mend a fence, it has affected his musical tastes and his metaphors. If he were pinned down, he probably would have to claim as his theme song 'Ride 'em Jewboy,' a country-western variation on the myth of the Wandering Jew:

Wild Ponies, all your dreams were broken
Rounded-up and made to move along
The loneliness which can't be spoken
(Just) swings a rope and rides inside a
    song

How long will you be driven relentless
    round the world
The blood in the rhythm of your soul

Ride, Ride 'em Jewboy
Ride 'em all around the ol' corral
I'm, I'm with you boy
If I got to ride six million miles

"Kinky spent most of 1971 trying to get his songs recorded in Los Angeles, but California just wasn't ready for him. The Jewish president of Warner Brothers Records said he'd like to give him a contract, 'But I don't know what I'd tell my mother.'

"With the exception of playing the pied piper at camp, Kinky has never been overly anxious to perform for audiences. He's not exactly a virtuoso on the guitar and he takes solace in the fact that Hank Williams could play only three chords. Besides, 'I don't want to be a star. I want to be a millionaire,'' Friedman says. During his eight months in L.A. he sang in public only twice, the most memorable occasion being at a celebration of Israel's twenty-third birthday. Kinky remembers, 'I went on right after a gypsy fiddler.'

"The best thing that came out of Kinky's Los Angeles experiences was a chance meeting with Chuck Glaser of the Glaser Brothers' recording studio in Nashville. After hearing some of Friedman's songs, Glaser urged him to move to Music City. Kinky left the West Coast lickety-split. 'In Hollywood I totalled my karma,' he wrote in 'Flying Down the Freeway,' a song about the exhilaration that came with leaving California.

Flying down the freeway (deedle de de)
Jettin' outa L.A. really set me free
Goin' back to nature in my Christler car
Flyin' down the freeway—gonna' be a
    star

"Things have gone all topsy turvy in Nashville. Kris Kristofferson is wearing full-length leather coats and singing about getting stoned. There's a black C & W star, Charley Pride, as well as Johnny Rodriquez, a Chicano star. Ever since Dylan's 'Nashville Skyline' album, rock & rollers and country singers have been mixing it up. One sees Commander Cody and the Lost Planet Airmen creeping up on the kicker charts while country-western stalwarts like Willie Nelson and Waylon Jennings are finding new and wildly appreciative audiences at places like Armadillo World Headquarters in Austin.

"This cultural cross-fertilization augured well for the group. What L.A. record executives were afraid to chance in 1971, three Catholic brothers from Nebraska recorded in 1972. Tompall, Chuck and Jim Glaser are known in their own right as a country trio, but they also own one of the more tasteful recording studios in Nashville. Their biggest hit was John Hartford's 'Gentle on My Mind,' which has provided them the royalty money to encourage other talented but atypical musicians. The Glaser Brothers are not Nashville hippies. To the contrary, they enthusiastically played at benefits for Richard Nixon last year. But, politics aside, they know good music when they hear it, even when it's attached to titles like "The Top 10 Command-

ments' and 'Get Your Biscuits in the Oven and Your Buns in the Bed.'

"Meanwhile, good things were happening for Kinky in New York. Commander Cody turned David Wilkes of Vanguard onto Friedman. Vanguard, which was just getting into the country music field, signed him. Kinky's first album, 'Sold American,' was recorded at the Glaser studio during the fall. The Glasers pulled together an impressive group of studio musicians and produced a genuine, sometimes innovative country-western sound. The album includes some stellar fiddle-playing by John Hartford, a somber church organ in 'The Top 10 Commandments,' a fine rumbling and whistling effect for 'Silver Eagle Express,' and a manic conversation sequence in 'Highway Cafe,' featuring Roger Friedman and Tompall Glaser as highway patrolmen describing an accident in which a semi-driver was squashed 'slicker'n owlshit.'

"Being gentleman of the night in Nashville gave Friedman the background for some of his more traditional country western songs, like 'Sold American.'

Faded, jaded fallin' cowboy star
Pawnshop's itching for your ol' guitar
Where you goin' ain't nobody knows
The sequins have fallen from your clothes

And everything's been Sold American
No place to go and Brother, no place to
    stay
Everything's been Sold American
Just let that golden Greyhound roll your
    soul away

"It was around Hanukkah when Roger took the final mixing of the tape to New York for the Vanguard people to hear. Vanguard had been a little uneasy about the record. The meat and potatoes of the label always has been classical music along with some solid, left-wing folkies like Joan Baez, Odetta, and Buffy St. Marie. Country-western was uncharted country for Vanguard. And there was the question of taste. There are lots of Jews in the record business, but Vanguard is the most Jewish label of them all. Everyone was nervous about the Jewboy bit. How would the Jewish rackers who stock the discount houses feel? How about the Anti-Defamation League?

81

"The troops crowded into one of the listening rooms for the preview. There were smiles of relief as the songs rolled out, one good one after another. And there was recognition of the plaintive, lonely quality of the Glaser Brothers' arrangements. By the end of 'Ride 'em Jewboy,' there wasn't a dry eye in the room. You could say that, at least in Vanguard's New York office, the album was a smash, a hit, a very big success. About fifteen New York Jews left the room feeling a tremendous rapport with faded, jaded cowboy stars.

"The album was scheduled for release in late March and Kinky premiered in Texas about the same time. 'I expect to sell two albums per Jew,' Kinky said optimistically. 'I'm going to give one third of the royalties to the JDL—the Jewish Defense League; one third to the ADL—Anti-Defamation League; and one third to the ABL—the American Bowling League.''

## FRIZZELL, LEFTY [William Orville Frizzell]

BORN: March 31, 1928, Corsicana, Texas

MARRIED: w. Alice

CHILDREN: s. Marlon Jaray, Rick; d. Lois Aleta

Lefty Frizzell's nomadic childhood led him from the turbulent oil fields of Texas and Oklahoma, where his itinerant father was a driller, to the flashy honky-tonks and tough dance halls of Waco and Dallas when he was hardly sixteen, to rough-and-tumble backroom rings of illegal Texas boxing clubs (where his record of southpaw knockouts earned him the nickname Lefty), to stardom in Nashville in the late 1940s, when he wasn't even twenty-one, to top-ten hits, a Columbia recording contract, Grand Ole Opry, and all the accouterments of success in show business.

Frizzell tells a story about his early recording days, when he and Hank Williams were the two hottest artists touring the country. "Hank kept telling me that I needed Opry. I knew that my manager, Jack Starnes, didn't want me to join the Opry at that time, so I told Hank, 'Man, I've got the number-one song in the nation, the number-two song in the nation, the number-six song in the nation, the number-eight song in the nation. Now, what do I need with the Opry?'

Lefty Frizzell: One of the greats.

"Hank said, 'Son, you've got one hell of an argument.' "

(A *Billboard* magazine dated October 27, 1951, charted four Lefty Frizzell songs in its first ten top-selling country records: 1. "Always Late"; 2. "Mom and Dad's Waltz" (which was the flip side of "Always Late"); 6. "I Love You A Thousand Ways"; 8. "Traveling Blues." Neither Presley nor the Beatles have topped Frizzell's record.) Frizzell did join the Grand Ole Opry eventually, but only stayed a few months, moving to California, where he became a regular on *Town Hall Party.* In the early sixties, now making the top ten less regularly, Frizzell's best sellers included "Long Black Veil" and his own "Saginaw, Michigan" (number-one hit in 1964).

Way back in the early fifties, while driving home from college, through Arkansas, I went 100 miles out of my way, over an icy road, to listen to Lefty Frizzell. I would drive 100 miles out of my way, today, to hear Lefty—only he's not appearing as often. Show business is a precarious profession, at best, and Lefty's career, during the early 1970s, seems to have trickled down somewhat. But there's a saying around the Texas oil country which, roughly translated from the Spanish, goes something like this: "Don't underestimate the big gushers, especially when they appear to give out. There's usually a lot of oil left in reserve." There's a gusher or two remaining in Frizzell, all right, and ABC Records has recently signed him to a contract (he was with Columbia for twenty-three years). "I'm writing again," Frizzell reports. "In fact, my first album for ABC will have several of my tunes on it. I have my own publishing company. I work enough dates to suit me and I am quite happy." Even if he never recorded another hit, Lefty Frizzell has already won his spurs as one of the all-time great honky-tonk singers in America. A lot worse things can be said about a man.

# G

## GENTRY, BOBBIE

BORN: July 27, 1944, Chickasaw County, Mississippi
MARRIED: h. William Harrah (divorced)

"Anybody can write one hit song," Will Rogers once said. "The trick is to keep turnin' them out." Well, Will, Bobbie Gentry isn't an *anybody.* She was only twenty-three, a philosophy graduate from UCLA (which we didn't hold against her) and a student at the Los Angeles Conservatory of Music (where she majored in theory, composition, and counterpoint) and a graduate of Palm Springs High School (though we were glad she was really a Mississippi girl). Oh, Bobbie. What memories you've given us: "Ode to Billy Joe" and the tragic specter of the Tallahatchee Bridge. You were an overnight success, the American dream. We bought your Capitol recordings. We watched you on TV, and many of us fell in love. You were black-haired and beautiful. Only you married that gamblin' man from Nevada. What was he? Forty years older than you. We forgave you that, too. We predicted it wouldn't last. We weren't crazy about your later songs, "Chickasaw County Child" and "Lazy Willy," and we waited for another smash. But the years are passing and you'll soon be thirty, and Bobbie, don't be one of those one-hit-song kids.

## GIBSON, DON

BORN: March 3, 1928, Shelby, North Carolina
MARRIED: w. Barbara
CHILDREN: Autumn Scarlet

Once, during the Beatle days, I was in Nashville, walking down the street with a friend, who pointed out the Biltmore Courts Motel. "Do you know what happened there?" he asked. "No," I said, fully expecting him to describe a horrible axe murder, or something like that. "Well, that's where Don Gibson wrote "Oh Lonesome Me."

At the time, when C & W was in a low period, a number of Nashville performers were hitting both the pop and country charts: Jim Reeves, Patsy Cline, Marty Robbins, and Don Gibson. Gibson, who came from western North Carolina, was originally a hard-country honky-tonker, but seeing the handwriting on the wall, evolved his style into a sophisticated, country-rooted rock-and-roll. "Oh Lonesome Me" was recorded by a number of performers, but Gibson's version made all the money. At the time he also wrote "I Can't Stop Loving You." (Just those two "valuable copyrights" are sufficient to establish Gibson as a country classicist.) During the rock heyday, Gibson appeared as a guest on a broad variety of TV shows and toured the country. As rock is fading into the sun, Gibson is again going country, and let's hope he can make it. He still can get into a song, and he can still sound as if he is going to burst into tears with every word.

## THE GLASER BROTHERS

### Chuck Glaser

BORN: September 3, 1933, Spaulding, Nebraska

### Jim Glaser

BORN: December 16, 1937, Spaulding, Nebraska

### Tompall Glaser

BORN: September 3, 1933, Spaulding, Nebraska

For several years, Tompall and the Glaser Brothers were a successful Nashville singing group, recording on their own and backing up a number of other entertainers (Marty Robbins, Claude King, Patsy Cline, Johnny Cash). Discovered in Omaha, where they had come 183 miles from their home in Holdredge for an Arthur Godfrey audition, they eventually emerged as regular Arthur Godfrey entertainers. They moved to Nashville, where they were invited to join the Grand Ole Opry family. They wrote songs and produced records, singly and together. Tompall provided Jimmy Dean with "Stand Beside Me," and Bobby Bare with "The Streets of Baltimore." Jim Glaser wrote "Sitting in an All-Night Cafe," and Chuck produced records for Decca and guided the careers of John Hartford and Jimmy Payne. They opened a studio in Nashville in which artists like Waylon Jennings record their hits. They continued to record together for Decca and MGM until 1973, when they dissolved their relationship as a singing group. That year Tompall's hit "Charlie" zoomed to the top of the charts, and after fifteen years in the business it seems he is destined for special stardom. "Charlie" is pretty unusual for a country song Dave Hickey wrote, since it deals straightforwardly with the viciousness of suburban social climbing. "Pinball and Jack Daniels," Tompall confided to Hickey, "are my vices and I can afford them. That's what you get when you're a millionaire and it turns out that's not what you want to be after all. All that work and that's not really what you want at all."

Tompall Glaser: "Pinball's my vice . . ."

Hickey writes: "The implication is that a lot of people who pretend to be a lot better do a lot worse. And whenever Glaser talks about business, at which he is very skilled, you can see the tensions which have developed over the years of being both the leader and the black sheep of a group of talented brothers who grew up in a large Catholic family in Nebraska. The reasons for the gradual dissolution of the Glaser Brothers become more and more obvious. It was a choice between breaking up a family or a musical group, and the family, as always, comes first."

## GRAMMER, BILLY

BORN: August 28, 1925, Benton, Illinois
MARRIED: w. Ruth
CHILDREN: s. Billy; d. Donna, Diane

Billy Grammer's been around a long time; he's a first-rate instrumentalist and sideman and during the 1950s traveled with such stalwarts as Clyde

The Glaser Brothers: Chuck, Jim and Tompall.

Moody, T. Texas Tyler, and Hawkshaw Hawkins. His gold record (1948) was "Gotta Travel On" for Monument, earning him a spot on the Opry team. In the early sixties Billy Grammer made it again with "Kissing Tree" and "Bonaparte's Retreat." Most recently, his name has appeared as one of the performers who barnstormed the south for the election of Governor George C. Wallace of Alabama.

## GRAND OLE OPRY

Grand Ole Opry is Nashville, Tennessee's, biggest attraction. Since 1925, when George D. Hay convinced station WSM (owned by National Life and Accident Company) that the world was ready for a "hillbilly" music program on radio, Grand Ole Opry has become *the* showcase for what has developed into country-western music. Broadcast every weekend from Ryman Auditorium in downtown Nashville, the Grand Ole Opry show has made the world aware of such luminaries as Minnie Pearl, Red Foley, Hank Williams, Roy Acuff, and hundreds of other country performers. It usually plays to a packed audience of 3,500 people, with another couple of thousand people waiting outside for vacant seats. It is estimated by WSM that every weekend people from at least thirty-eight states come to Ryman Auditorium, and it regularly draws more people from Alabama, Illinois, and Arkansas than it does from Tennessee. Although the show is no longer on a network, the syndicated version is listened to by approximately 30 million people every Saturday night.

Country artists perform at the Opry for almost no money, but to be invited to perform is worth its weight in gold. As one Opry regular says, "It means that you have arrived. It means that you have made star rank. It means that you are an 'official' country performer." There have been other "cradles of the stars" radio shows featuring country music—among them, *Louisiana Hayride* and *Town Hall Party*—but none have had the clout of Grand Ole Opry. In 1974 Grand Ole Opry moved from Ryman Auditorium to a modern auditorium in Opryland, the new multimillion-dollar pleasure park on Nashville's outskirts, fomenting a controversy as to what will happen to the old, un-air-conditioned, and much loved Ryman Auditorium. (See the introductory essay on country music.)

Grand Ole Opry: The Ryman Auditorium in Nashville.

Grand Ole Opry: The new Opry House at Opryland.

## GRAY, CLAUDE

BORN: January 26, 1932, Henderson, Texas

The "Tall Texan" is over six feet, five inches, and he's announced as "a man you have to look up to." Over the years he's had a number of hits for Decca, Mercury, and Columbia: "Family Bible," "I Never Had the One I Wanted," "Mean Old Woman," and Roger Miller's "My Ears Should Burn" are his biggies. Gray toured the country, successfully, with his excellent group The Graymen. In 1969 Claude Gray had a number of albums listed in Schwann's catalog. The 1973 edition lists none. As they say, there's no business like show business.

## GRAY, OTTO

BORN: c. 1890, Ponca, Oklahoma
MARRIED: w. "Mommie" (nickname, real name not available)
CHILDREN: s. Owen

Otto Gray is often called "the first singing cowboy," though hardly anybody will remember him today. According to *Billboard* magazine, Gray's band, The Oklahoma Cowboys, started performing in 1923. Like other "hillbilly" organizations, Gray advertised in *Billboard* and other music trade publications. The Oklahoma Cowboys were picked up by the RKO vaudeville circuit, and because of their "authenticity" were extremely popular in the northeastern states. A press agent traveled with the group. The Oklahoma Cowboys wore simple cowboy clothing, and toured in Otto Gray's $20,000 custom-built limousine, with (unusual for the period) a radio receiver and transmitter. The group included Otto, Wade Allen, Zeke Clements, and Whitey Ford, who became Grand Ole Opry's "Duke of Paducah." There are no extant records of the Otto Gray band, unfortunately. Its big hit on the stage was "She'll Be Comin' Round the Mountain."

Claude Gray: A man you have to look up to.

## THE GREENBRIAR BOYS

**Dian Edmonson**
**John Herald**
**Ralph Rinzler**
**Frank Wakefield**
**Eric Weissberg**
**Bob Yellen**

The popularity of Flatt and Scruggs, the Monroe Brothers, and others made considerable impact on the cities and colleges, and there are those critics who claim country's new popularity in urban areas is a result of the bridge built during the late 1950s and early 1960s by bluegrass bands. There were a number of "college" bluegrass bands born during that period, but the Greenbriar Boys was probably the most distinguished. Its lead singer, John Herald, had the power and driving tenor and tension of the best country singers. Banjoist Bob Yellen developed a personal style somewhat influenced by the Jimmy Martin band—a loping, erratically metered set of figures that inevitably set one's feet tapping. The group's records, produced by Vanguard, still stand up and are deserving of reissue. The original banjoist with the Greenbriars was Eric Weissberg, who left to join the Tarriers. (His most recent claim: "Dueling Banjos.") The Greenbriars' innovation in country-bluegrass was the addition of a female voice to the ensemble, Dian Edmonson, who appeared with the band during its numerous TV appearances.

## GREENE, JACK

BORN: January 7, 1930, Maryville, Texas
MARRIED: w. Barbara Ann Stidham
CHILDREN: s. Jackie Wayne, Forest Anthony, Mark Allen; d. Barbara Lynn, Jan Thomas

Jack Henry Greene worked in a glass shop, was a construction worker and a salesman. He was already thirty-seven years old when his first hit made the country charts: "The Last Letter." Before that, he was in the army, played drums and guitar, and occasionally did a vocal for Ernest Tubb's Troubadors. Tubb fans especially loved Greene, whom they nicknamed the Jolly Greene Giant (he's well over six feet tall). Occasionally, at the Opry, Greene duetted with Dottie West. "Love Is No Excuse" always

stirred the fans. Ernest Tubb often suggested that Greene leave the Troubadors to try out his luck as a single act, and when "The Last Letter" (which was on a Tubb album) gained a lot of air play, Greene took the chance. By the end of the sixties, Greene was a recognized star, with his first five releases all hitting the charts. Among them: "You Are My Treasure" and "Ever Since My Baby Went Away." These days the "Green Giant," jollier than ever, has teamed up with Jeannie Seely, and they're being introduced as "one of the great country teams."

Jack Greene: "The Jolly Greene Giant."

## GUTHRIE, WOODY [Woodrow Wilson Guthrie]

BORN: July 14, 1912, Okemah, Oklahoma
DIED: October 4, 1967

Some folks might think Woody Guthrie doesn't belong in an encyclopedia of *country* music because he's been so closely identified with the *folk* music scene. But that wasn't his fault. Guthrie's roots were firmly planted in country music, and if that isn't enough, he deserves a mention simply because he wrote so eloquently about *the* country, its wonders and woes. Woody Guthrie's father came to Oklahoma from Texas, where he had played guitar and banjo with several cowboy bands. Woody's cousin, Jack Guthrie, was a popular cowboy singer throughout the Southwest until his death in 1948. Woody made no bones about where he got the inspiration for many of his most popular songs. He got them from the Carter Family.

His reputation as a man who didn't mince words, and who didn't hesitate to write songs about unpleasant occurrences if he was moved to do so, is in keeping with the attitude of today's more outspoken country artists. When it came to describing crop failures, an outlaw's state of mind, or the simple joys of a country morning, Woody Guthrie was as country as anyone you can name. As the years go by, more country artists are using songs from Woody's extensive legacy. Woodrow Wilson Guthrie wasn't born in Muskogee, but he came pretty close.

# H

## THE HAGERS

### Jim Hager
BORN: Chicago, Illinois

### John Hager
BORN: Chicago, Illinois

The Hagers are identical twins, best known for their appearance on the *Hee Haw* show. Versatile, if not too forceful, as artists, they can sing country, folk-rock, blues, pop, and musical comedy, and they joke a little, dance, and have very straight long hair. The Hagers appeared first in Chicago's East Street, joined the Buck Owens show, and now commute from their homes in Los Angeles to do *Hee Haw* segments in Nashville. They record for Capitol.

## HAGGARD, MERLE
BORN: March 6, 1937, Bakersfield, California
MARRIED: w. Bonnie Owens

The country-music world has an odd resemblance to life in medieval Europe. Every nook and cranny is filled with "kings" and "queens" and "pretenders to the throne." There are about half a dozen claimants to the title "queen of country music" and as many for "king." Merle Haggard claims he's "king of nothing," but he has developed an army of loyal subjects none-

The Hagers: Identical twins and *Hee Haw* stalwarts.

theless. He is a regal performer. Few names in any field of show business can guarantee a full house. Haggard always plays to full houses. He is in the same league with Hank Williams and Jimmie Rodgers. He is a serious artist, and music critics have called him "the most important American singer in two decades." Musicology students and celebrated institutions are writing their theses on Merle Haggard, his songs and style. Paul Hemphill, the brilliant southern journalist, wrote about Merle Haggard in a magazine interview:

"Outwardly, Merle Haggard has changed considerably over the past two or three years since 'Okie from Muskogee' won most of the big Country Music Association awards for him and made him a true superstar of American music. Now he demands upward of $10,000 per show, lives in a $250,000 home on a lake outside Bakersfield, California, fishes from a fully stocked yacht, and travels with two $100,000 buses (one for his band, The Strangers; the other for him, his wife, and his manager). He is playing all of the big places now like Harrah's at Lake Tahoe, rather than the dinky nightclub circuit, and they want him for television and the movies. He can buy anything he wants, do whatever he wants to do, go wherever he wants to go. He has found the brass ring he was looking for during all those years of working the 'fighting' and 'dancing' clubs and playing country fairs and begging disc jockeys to play his records.

"And, from what I see, an amazing thing has happened. Rather than success spoiling the man, it has strengthened him. Five years ago he would come blowing into Nashville 'to do some howling' and be seen stumbling around Music Row like a lost soul, but today he has all but quit drinking. In the past he was a moody man who seemed terribly complex and haunted by all sorts of devils, but now he is as self-composed as any man I have ever known in show business. The money and fame have worked for him, not against him, giving him a self-confidence and a freedom he had never known. Not having to worry about paying the bills or becoming a success or otherwise proving himself, he now has the peace of mind to go on and become what my friend Streetcar and a lot of other people think he can be: an artist whose work should be every bit as lasting as that of a very few, such as

Hank Williams and Jimmie Rodgers. 'I tell you what,' says Kris Kristofferson, 'that man has already written some of the best folk songs that's ever been done. I think that now, when we speak of Merle Haggard, we aren't speaking about how he's going to come out on the CMA awards this year: we're talking about posterity.'

"It is really quite simple to me why Haggard did not have his head turned—did not sell his soul and his art—when success finally came. It is because he has remained true to his roots. He plans to die in Bakersfield, right there where his Okie parents migrated during the thirties. He would much rather be out fishing with some longtime crony than kowtowing around a network television executive on a golf course. His mother, who suffered during his boyhood days of wandering, still lives with Merle's family and is titular head of his fan club. His personal manager is an old boy named Fuzzy Owen. There is no telling how much money Haggard might be earning if he had a high-powered agent —but it was Fuzzy who virtually picked Merle up off the streets when he got out of prison and Merle respects that obligation. It is not in his system to forget where he has been and it is when he writes around those experiences—as in 'Mama Tried' and 'Branded Man'—that he is at his best.

"Those experiences are something else. Merle was born in 1937, when all the family was living among the sagebrush in a boxcar that had been converted by Mr. Haggard. The Haggards had bailed out of East Oklahoma along with many other burned-out farmers and rumbled up and over the Rockies to the promised land in California. Mr. Haggard was a hardworking, honest man, who had given up the fiddle when his wife, a stern member of the Church of Christ, objected to such carrying-on. At the age of nine, Merle had just begun to pay some attention to music when his father suddenly died. Mrs. Haggard felt perhaps too strongly her responsibility to raise her youngest son properly, and by the time Merle was fourteen he began skipping school and investigating the world on his own.

" 'It was the wrong thing to do,' Mrs. Haggard says now of her decision to put Merle into a juvenile home for a few days to frighten him into straightening up. He promptly escaped, getting himself a record, and for the next ten years he was into everything: bogus checks, escape, burglary, petty theft, pitching hay, stolen checks, riding the rails. 'Wild hair is all it was,' he says. 'You'd be surprised what a kid's thinking at that age. I mean, like the first time I got locked up I felt like I'd finally become a man. That's what it was all about. I was just trying to grow up.'

"If so, he did it the hard way. Late in 1957, Bakersfield authorities, tired of dealing with him, charged him with attempted burglary and escape and sent him off to San Quentin for six months to fifteen years. He spent three years there (and was in the audience the day Johnny Cash came by to perform), straightened up when he spent a week in solitary confinement next to the doomed Caryl Chessman, and drifted back home to Bakersfield.

"Off and on, between stretches in jail, Merle had gotten into music by writing an occasional song and picking guitar in roadhouses. When he returned from prison, Bakersfield was beginning to sprout a modest music industry—Buck Owens and others had built studios, and plenty of clubs featured live country music. Soon Merle was quitting his job as a laborer and going into the clubs full-time. And he met Fuzzy Owen, who eventually recorded Merle in a garage "studio" he had built. The first release sold 200 copies, but not much later, in 1965, Merle did 'All My Friends Are Gonna Be Strangers' and it made the country Top Ten. He signed with Capitol Records, rounded up a band, bought a station wagon, and hit the road. Within six years he had become a star—mainly on the strength of such autobiographical songs as 'I'm a Lonesome Fugitive' and 'Swinging Doors,' which strongly identified him with working people and the downtrodden. Then, of course, came 'Okie from Muskogee.'

"The story surrounding 'Okie' oozes with irony. In the beginning the song was written on a lark. 'We were riding through East Oklahoma and saw this sign that said "Muskogee" and somebody said, "I bet they don't smoke marijuana in Muskogee," and somebody else threw in another line,' Haggard recalls. 'We must have pretty much written the song in twenty minutes.' During the session when it was recorded, everybody kept breaking up over the lyrics ('I didn't think we would ever get it down,' says one studio musician).

"Before the record came out, Haggard sprang the song on a beery crowd of Green Berets at Fort Bragg, North Carolina. He was astounded when they tore the place up. Then came the release of the record and Haggard found himself in the middle of a controversy. In some quarters he was being hailed as a 'proletarian poet' (President Nixon wrote to congratulate him on the song), but elsewhere he was being castigated for capitalizing on Middle America's distaste for the hippie life-style. Just as liberals had begun to worship and respect Haggard as a folk singer in the vein of Woody Guthrie, he had taken what they felt to be a cheap commercial shot.

"It is my feeling that Haggard seems mildly embarrassed about having written 'Okie' and 'Fightin' Side of Me.' A man who has no taste for politics (he seldom reads, doesn't vote, and turns down invitations to appear on behalf of candidates), he simply wrote a couple of songs that in one way backfired on him. No doubt about it, they made him a superstar, 'Okie' becoming his first gold album. They thrust him into a prominence transcending the world of country music, and brought him untold riches, but they also taught him a lesson. The charges that he had gone commercial got in his craw. Cash was just beginning to be accused of getting away from *his* roots, allowing non-country acts on his television show, and Haggard didn't want that to happen to him. Many performers would have gone on to made a career of being a professional 'patriot,' but instead Merle next tried to do a song about an interracial love affair (which Capitol refused to record on the grounds it would be 'bad for my image').

"The uproar over those two songs was really only another progression in the slow but steady growth of Merle Haggard over the past decade. Only a man who retains his roots and keeps an inner calm can mature as he has.

"'I remember when he first came back to Bakersfield and began singing,' says Bettie Azevedo, Merle's secretary. 'Fuzzy had to show him how to stop twisting his mouth up so funny.' Back then, everything he sang came out sounding like Lefty Frizzell, who is still a hero to him. He went through a long period then when he was terribly shaky in front of crowds, perhaps the most difficult problem he has had to overcome. Then he was leaning too heavily toward songs about boozing and unrequited love, which he began to break away from when he started going to his own background for material with such numbers as 'Hungry Eyes' and 'Mama Tried.' His marriage to singer Bonnie Owens was a stabilizer ('He's an Aries, very restless, and I have to remember that'), and his acceptance by longhairs in spite of their dislike for 'Fightin' Side' and 'Okie' gave him the confidence he needed to branch out. His re-creations of the sounds of Bob Wills and of Jimmie Rodgers represent some of the purest country music I have ever heard (to be authentic, he taught himself to play the fiddle in six months for the Wills album).

"What we have now is a man on the verge of becoming a complete musician, able to do it all —and in almost any medium. The catalogue of songs he has built up and continues to build runs the gamut—re-creations of greats like Rodgers, gospel songs, hard beer-drinking classics, sweet love songs, even impersonations—and he may have already reached the point of being the most flexible country singer on the scene. 'Let's face it, most of us aren't singers,' Bill Anderson once told me, 'we're stylists.' Dave Dudley does truck-driving songs, Marty Robbins does gunfighter ballads, Cash does prisons and hard times. But Merle Haggard has run through them all and was last seen working on a Dixieland album. His one weakness, as I see it, is an inability to make his personality come across on television; he simply doesn't have the flair for showbiz and hopping around that the screen calls for. There is a feeling around Nashville that Haggard will never achieve the spectacular success—financially, in particular—that Cash enjoys. A major reason for that, they say, is because he isn't good enough for TV and doesn't have the distinctive physical presence of Cash. Almost unspoken, though, is a deeper reasoning: that Haggard, unlike Cash, lacks the drive to go all the way. 'I really think,' admits Bettie Azevedo, 'that Merle dreams of the day he can stay home to fish and write songs.' It is frustrating to anyone, up to and including executives who want to make a lot of money for Merle, to locate him when he is back home in Bakersfield. Capitol is forever having to reschedule recording sessions in Los Angeles when Merle doesn't show up. Merle even walked out on an Ed Sullivan show, back when he really needed it, because they wouldn't let him

sing what he wanted to sing, the way he wanted to sing it. He doesn't like to hang around with important people in show business, preferring to be alone, or with members of his band or with his family. He is, in short, his own man. Those very qualities which make him a beautiful man could be the same qualities keeping him from being a super-superstar.

"The last time I saw Merle was during the past summer, when he was making a short swing through the South. He had played at George Jones and Tammy Wynette's outdoor place in Lakeland, Florida, rushed to Nashville for some recording, and had a date in Columbus, Georgia, before driving all night to Huntington, West Virginia, for another. At four o'clock in the afternoon Merle and Mel Tillis, who was also working the show, sat in Merle's bus outside the Columbus Coliseum talking about songs and other writers and whatever.

" 'I thought you was gonna quit the road, Merle,' Tillis was saying.

" 'I *was* getting pretty tired there,' said Haggard.

" 'She's a booger, all right.'

" 'Kinda got my second wind now, though. Got stale for a while, but then my tax bill came in.'

" 'How's that?'

" 'Had to pay half a million to Sam for last year.'

"A girl reporter from the local paper came by to interview Haggard ('I understand you write some of your own songs, Mr. Haggard'), followed by a couple of disc jockeys and then a pair of good old boys who wanted to audition a song for Merle right on the spot ('Tell you what, send me a tape so I can give it a fair shake'). He talked about the movie he may star in ('Sort of a *Grapes of Wrath* character'), played his latest record on the stereo, then reached for his fiddle and played a few strains from Bob Wills's 'Faded Love.' It occurred to me to ask him what he is shooting for, what he would like to be remembered as.

" 'I never thought about that,' he said, squinting and looking absent-mindedly out the window of the bus. The Coliseum was filling up very early, and it looked like a sellout. 'A writer, I guess. Somebody who did some living and wrote songs about what he knew. Just like Jimmie and Hank did. That's all.' "

Merle Haggard: None of his friends are really strangers.

# HALL, CONNIE

BORN: June 24, 1929, Walden, Kentucky
MARRIED: h. John

During the fifties Connie Hall was one of the contenders for "queen of country music," but she never became more than a lady-in-waiting. Among her hits for Mercury were "Bottle Me In" and "Where Do We Go from Here?" She went to Decca, recorded "Fools Like Me" and "Yellow Roses," and then went to a new label called Musicor, and for the last few years, relative obscurity.

# HALL, TOM T.

BORN: May 25, 1936, Olive Hill, Kentucky
MARRIED: w. Dixie Dean

I'd just told Old Paint good-bye, and leaving Cheyenne, I was speeding southward toward Denver in a rented Dodge Dart, the radio blaring. I stopped for an aging gray-haired hitchhiker. He was wearing sneakers. New ones, green, with three red stripes on them. "Pretty nifty," he said proudly. "Only two dollars at J. C. Penney's." His face showed the history of the West. His mouth was largely unburdened of teeth, and those that were left showed the stains of a lifetime of tobacco. As he entered the car, the disc jockey on the radio announced that he was going to play a number of songs by Tom T. Hall.

"Tom T.," the hitchhiker said. "I love his songs, man. I wish he could sing better. But it don't matter how he sounds. He knows about people. Take that country jail song. I been two weeks in a country jail and that's the way it really is. I'm going to New Mexico. Some guy I know told me that New Mexico was like Italy. I was a medic in an Eye-talian hospital during the war. Married me a New Jersey woman night before I left for the war and she disappeared. We didn't even have one night together. I was drunk and so was she."

The next song played was "Margie's at the Lincoln Park Inn." (Margie is the mistress of the narrator of the song; she waits for him nightly at the motel bar, while the faithful wife is ignorant of the affair.) "What a mess that guy's in," I said, resuming the conversation.

"Oh, no, man," the old hitchhiker replied. "I know that song and it makes my goddam heart

break. That feller's a lucky man. He has his wife and Margie lovin' him. Hell, I'm fifty-six years old next day before Christmas and in all my life I never had one woman, even the New Jersey woman, who loved me for me. I never had no love what I didn't pay for. Tom T. Hall writes them songs for the likes of me. He knows what it's all about. He's a good old boy, I'll bet."

The old hitchhiker was probably right, but Tom T. Hall is no longer a "good old boy," even if he likes "old dogs, children, and watermelon wine." (Johnny Cash said if people keep writing songs like that, country music's "here to stay.") Hall is too sophisticated, too subtle a writer. He avoids sudsy anguish songs and concentrates on hard subjects like a telephone book, being hungry, a switchblade knife, Watergate. The Arizona critic Tom Miller says that Hall's forte is "taking personalized, lightweight experiences and transforming them into heavier implications."

I watched a reluctant Carnegie Hall audience, including a coterie of rock music critics, generally hostile to country performers, being won over by Hall. The songs, though about country performers, religion, a man who taught him to play the guitar, made sense to the audience, who gave him a noisy standing ovation and undoubtedly bought a Tom T. Hall album the next day. Hall, I think, after a number of conversations with him, won't ever "cross over"—he has taken contemporary experience and brilliantly kept it within the country medium. I think he is an important man to watch on the Nashville scene. He certainly has one of the more inventive minds in the business. And there's no doubt he has the artist's involvement in his work.

In a magazine interview, Hall told Jay Ehler: "Songs are my children and none of them, to me, are ugly. They are bits and pieces of what's going on. So many people have done what my songs are about. People enjoy them because the people in them don't get out of character. They're true to life. Normally my favorite song is the one I just wrote."

Ehler's interview continues: "Tom T. Hall's musical career began in his hometown, Olive Hill, Kentucky, with a group he had formed when he was about sixteen, Tom Hall and the Kentucky Travelers. At first the Kentucky Travelers just played schoolhouses in the area, but when a local radio station opened up, Tom

Tom T. Hall sings on Grand Ole Opry while Jeanne Pruett and Archie Campbell listen.

went over and asked the owner if he and his group could sing. They got the job. It didn't pay anything at first, but Tom was still living at home and he had saved up a little money to get by on, so he did the radio show regularly.

"Tom had written a song for a local firm, the Polar Bear Flour Company, or at least the company made use of it after it became popular in the area. The company also signed up the group, at a small salary, to play the radio show regularly. Then the Travelers' manager, an old-timer, died and the group disbanded. Tom was

retained as a disc jockey because he had sold so much flour.

"When he was twenty-one, he recalls, 'It was summertime, and in Morehead, Kentucky (where the station was located), you walked out on the street and it looked like the opening scene in *Hud*. The wind and the dust and nothing's happening. I guess I was the hottest thing there, the number-one disc jockey, but that was a nothing thing so I joined the army. I came in and told the station manager I was quitting. He said I couldn't leave 'cause we were getting ready to sell all this flour. I told him I would be back. He asked me, When? I told him in about three years. There wasn't too much he could do, really. He told everyone he'd fired me.'

"While he was in the army Tom decided to be a writer. 'I had it in my mind to be a journalist or a novelist because I liked to read a lot. I managed to finish high school while I was in the army. I had dropped out when I was sixteen to work in a factory because my father had been accidentally shot. He was on a fishing trip with an uncle of mine. My uncle went to shoot a fish in the water, but the limb he was resting on broke and he slipped and shot my father.

" 'After the army I went to Roanoke College and studied journalism. Somewhere along the line I discovered I was a better songwriter. I sent some songs to Nashville and they were recorded. Before I knew it, I had a songwriting contract, and a year later, the publishing company, New Keys, asked me to come to Nashville. I was with them for about eight years before I formed my own company, Hallnote. I wanted to call it Hallmark so I could say, "Record a Hallmark song when you care enough to hear the very best." But I didn't. I was afraid I'd get sued.

" 'After my first three or four successful songs, people wanted me to start to record. The problem with recording is not finding people who can sing and entertain but finding the songs you can relate to. And at that time Nashville was just beginning to catch on to the idea of signing the writers who also sing. So they'd ask me and I'd say, "No, I don't want to be an entertainer." I had a weird thing in my head about it. I just wanted to write. I didn't want to start recording until I heard people in Nashville say, "There's Tom T. Hall, he's a writer." So for three or four years I just hung around and wrote songs. I had enough money to live on from my royalties. It gave me a license for freedom. I could come and go as I pleased, travel, go camping or fishing. I didn't have any set hours or meetings. I wasn't married at the time. All I had to do was think about things, sing and write.'

" 'Harper Valley' was the most successful song Tom Hall wrote. He's told the following story many times. 'A woman had asked me to write a "tell it like it is" song. A lady in my home town was a swinger. She would have little beer parties—people singing and dancing till three o'clock in the morning. The community disapproved of it. They spanked her child in school because they figured the woman wasn't a fit enough mother to discipline her kids. So one day the woman happened to walk in on a P.T.A. meeting and told them all off for preachin' one way while being hypocrites themselves. I was impressed; this woman just walked in there and wrote everyone off, putting them in their place.' [And he wrote a song about it.]

" 'Then Jeannie C. Riley got hold of the song, recorded it on a Friday night, and by Tuesday it was the talk of the town. It surprised me. It was like walking down the street and suddenly you bend over and pick up $100,000. It makes you nervous. I did a lot of interviews explaining that song, which I don't really like to do. When I explain a song, I end up making a chapter out of what was originally a paragraph.'

"Hall's first number-one song was back in 1964—it was called 'Hello, Vietnam.' He was trying to relate how the young men felt going off to this 'new' and then unknown war. It was a patriotic song written years before so many people were down on the war, or even before many knew how to pronounce the word 'Vietnam.'

"Tom Hall still lives in Nashville with his wife, Dixie. He records there and spends roughly three days a week there, but the photograph on his latest album cover—showing all the participating artists and musicians—suggests that he's not entirely happy with the rapidly developing superstar syndrome and the inevitable commercialization of the country-music capital.

" 'One thing that bothers me about Nashville,' he says, 'is that like New York and L.A., we've priced ourselves a lot higher. I'm not against the pickers making a lot of money, but it costs so much to do a session nowadays that we've driven away all the little creative people. It's hard to experiment any more. And after all, that's what music is, trial and error—one record out of a hundred makes it. We've sacrificed a lot for the sake of profit."

"The complaint is an all too familiar one in Nashville today. Newcomers find it increasingly difficult to get work, though as Tom Hall points out, 'A new writer can still come to Nashville and make it because A & R people know a good song. It's not hard to get your song heard even in a town full of writers.' But for the would-be performer, the kid from the Midwest who plays guitar, knows all Chet Atkins' records by heart, and has saved his money for a one-way bus ticket to Nashville, it can be pretty cold and lonely. Recording costs being as high as they are, not many people are willing to risk money on an inexperienced musician. When they can hire somebody they know can cut it, why take a chance with a newcomer?

"Tom Hall preferred Nashville about eight years ago. 'It was a big workshop, where a lot of people were digging music and people. Everything was free and easy. But now we're being computerized like everywhere else. It used to be that you'd yell at a guy on the street and pitch him a song. Now it's like you make appointments. I don't like the formality. I can't communicate my ideas in somebody's office at some appointed time. But if I sat on the hood of a car somewhere and picked my new song for him, while he smoked a cigarette and drank a beer, I'd be able to relate more naturally.

" 'But some of the changes taking place in Nashville seem to travel in a circle. They'll add an instrument for example, then they'll get tired of it and put in another one. Dobros had been dead for twenty years in country music, but now they're a heavy thing and everyone is using them. But we'll get tired of that. What you have to realize is that there are only so many ways you can make music, only so many instruments. You can stretch them, push them, pull them, electrify them, but we got to the point for a while when there was too much electricity and not enough person. I think that's why tastes cycled back again to Kris Kristofferson, James Taylor, and so on, singing about people, me and you. People have to go back to the origins, back to the days of guys with lutes traveling around the countryside singing about what is going on.

" 'I personally don't like the idea of changing to please people. If I can't do what I want to do to be successful, then I don't want to be in the music business. I wouldn't change my style to make a buck. I'm a songwriter because that's what I do. It has a lot to do with luck. Maybe I am where I am today because of all the BAD breaks I had. It's all relative. People tell me I'm a successful songwriter, maybe if I had better luck I'd be Elvis. I just do what I want. It's up to other people to judge me.' "

## HAMBLEN, STUART

BORN: October 20, 1908, Kellyville, Texas
MARRIED: w. Suzy
CHILDREN: d. Veeva Obee

Do you remember Stuart Hamblen in those third-feature Republic, Monogram, and PRC westerns? He was the really bad guy, always playing cards, who left the game, no matter how much he was winning, when the chief villain, in a suit, would say, "All right, boys, saddle up." And Stuart Hamblen wrote nifty songs like 'I Won't Go Huntin' with Ya, Jake, but I'll Go Chasin' Women." Then, out of the blue, in 1952, Stuart Hamblen decided to run for president—against Dwight D. Eisenhower and Adlai Stevenson—on the Prohibition party ticket. Hamblen lost by about 26 million votes, but he'd found a new life, and a turn in his career. For a while he joined the Billy Graham organization, singing in praise of his newfound faith, and he wrote a number of religiously oriented country songs, most of which did quite well as sung by Hamblen and scores of others: "Open Up Your Heart and Let the Sun Shine In," "It Is No Secret What God Can Do," "This Old House," and "Remember Me, I'm the One Who Loves You" (Ernest Tubb scored with that one for Decca; Hamblen did well with it for Columbia).

## HAMILTON, GEORGE, IV

BORN: July 19, 1937, Winston-Salem, North Carolina
MARRIED: w. Adelaide Watson
CHILDREN: s. Edwin Peyton, George V; d. Mary D.

In 1966 George Hamilton IV, only nineteen years old, managed to get a contract with ABC-Paramount records, recorded a tune, "A Rose and a Baby Ruth," and became a pop star overnight. He was in college at the time (University of North Carolina) but succumbed to show-business lure by accepting a job with WMAL-TV in Washington, D.C. (Unlike other stars, he didn't give up college, but enrolled at American University in Washington). During this period there wasn't a teen show on which Hamilton didn't guest-shot: *The Steve Allen Show, The Patti Page Show*, Jimmy Dean, and many others. "Country was always my love," Hamilton admits, "and somewhere along the line, I made the transition to country music and I've been there ever since." Obviously, country claimed Hamilton, too, and by 1959 he was appearing regularly on Grand Ole Opry. Since 1961 he has been recording for RCA, and he sings his country hits ("West Texas Highway," "Break My Mind," and "Abilene"—a number-one hit) in a folksy, pop manner. Hamilton is often called country music's worldwide ambassador because he travels extensively and has sung in German, Japanese, and other languages. He is especially popular in Canada and Europe. Hamilton wears his hair short and neat and wears vested, Ivy League suits, button-down collars and striped repp-silk ties, looking more like a professor than a country singer.

## THE HARDEN TRIO

**Arleen Harden**
**Bobby Harden**
**Robbie Harden**

For a while, Jim Ed, Maxine, and Bonnie Brown seemed to have no competition as a country family trio, but when they split up, an Ozark-based family group from England, Arkansas, who had been featured on the *Ozark Mountain Jubilee* show and on *Louisiana Hayride* arrived on the Nashville scene. The Hardens joined Grand Ole Opry and recorded a number of successful sides for Columbia: "Poor Boy" (written by Bobby Harden), "Don't Remind Me," "Husbands and Wives," "Seven Days of Crying," and "Let It Be Me." In 1968 they released a record called "Everybody Wants to Be Somebody Else." Apparently, each of the Hardens identified with the words of the song, because they disbanded the group and went on to be "somebody else." With the exception of Arleen, who has had a number of relatively successful records, the sum of the Hardens seems to have been more successful than the individual parts.

George Hamilton IV: Dresses like a professor and sings sweet songs.

## HART, FREDDIE

BORN: December 22, 1930, Kochapoka, Alabama

For a man with only a second-grade education and a fourth-degree black belt in karate, Freddie Hart has come a long way. When he was fourteen he lied to a Marines' recruiting officer and joined up in time to take part in the World War II invasion of Guam, Iwo Jima, and Okina-wa. When he got out of the marines he taught Karate at the Los Angeles police-academy. "I practice karate for health's sake," Hart says. "I believe in singing, not fighting, but I jog a couple of miles every day and I can jump in a pool and swim all day long. You know how it goes, if the heart ain't pumping right it is like a bad carbure-tor."

Hart doesn't reveal much about his back-

Freddie Hart: He's got a black belt—in love.

ground. He was one of fifteen children born to a poor Alabama family. When he was little he kept running away. "The first time at seven," he recalls. "I would go to houses and ask for a job. Sometimes people wanted to know where I lived. I would tell them just around the corner or just a couple of blocks down the street. I was a thousand miles away from home. I scattered around the country. Did just about every odd job you can name. Cotton picking, sawmilling, pipeline work in Texas. For two and a half years I was a dishwasher in a Hempstead, New York, restaurant. That was after I had been in the service. Worked my way up to second cook. Somehow I always wrote songs and I managed to get one wrote for George Morgan—'Every Little Thing Rolled into One.' Freddie Hart appeared on *Town Hall Party* in Compton, California—sort of a West Coast version of *Louisiana Hayride*, and a terrific proving ground for future stars (Buck Owens is another alumni, as is Lefty Frizzell). He records his hits for Capitol and he has been on the charts constantly since 1959, when "The Wall" reached twenty-fourth position for a month or so. In 1971 "Easy Loving" hit the number-one spot, selling over a million singles, and put Freddie Hart on the country map. Hart owns and operates a truck line, and runs a ranch filled with hundreds of registered breeding bulls and forty acres of plum trees. Not many people realize he runs a school for orphans and handicapped children. "This man's bag is love in its truest form," he claims, and people who know him say it's so. He sings nicely, too.

Hawkshaw Hawkins: Died in a plane crash.

# HAWKINS, HAWKSHAW [Harold F. Hawkins]

BORN: December 22, 1921, Huntington, West Virginia
DIED: March 5, 1963, Camden, Tennessee
MARRIED: w. Jean Shepard
CHILDREN: s. Harold Franklin II, Don Robin

"It is a wonder more of us aren't killed," an Opry musician at Hawkshaw Hawkins' funeral said. "We rack up so much mileage in the air and on the road. It was inevitable that the law of averages would catch up with some of us. It is unfortunate." Hawkins, along with Patsy Cline, Cowboy Copas, and Randy Hughes, was killed in a plane crash near Camden, Tennessee. Hawkins' act included his deftness with an Australian bull whip, but that wasn't why the fans adored him. The deep-voiced singer was respected by his fellow artists as well as the paying customers. His recording "Sunny Side of the Mountain" is often considered one of the score of "really great ones." His theme song, "Slowpoke," was his big hit, for King Records, in 1952. Hawshaw Hawkins was Appalachian born and bred, but he looked to the West for his style, which was slightly derivative of Ernest Tubb, and he affected decorated cowboy outfits, which somehow looked less gaudy on him. At his death, "Hawk" had been around a spell, and he was just beginning to give promise of greater range. He had just recorded "Lonesome 7-7203" (by Ernest's son, Justin) and it was doing well in the cities.

Hawkins, in true country fashion, had traded five trapped rabbits for his first guitar. By the time he was fifteen, he was performing at a local radio station, and his career was about to blossom when World War II erupted. He spent the war in the Pacific theater, singing from time to time, on Manila's WTUM. Postwar days found him in Wheeling, on WWVA with his first recording contract. He cut "Slowpoke" for King, and his career catapulted. His records still stand up and remain popular. Hawkshaw Hawkins maintained a stable of Tennessee walking horses and was in the process of grooming them for horse shows when the plane crashed. He left his pregnant wife, Jean Shepard, also an Opry star, and a son, Harold Franklin II.

## HEE HAW

When CBS canceled *Hee Haw* in 1972, some skeptics (read "young moderns") thought Middle America's beloved show—a mixture of country music and cornball humor—was doomed. But its owners, Youngstreet Productions, decided to produce the show themselves. A calculated risk, yes—but one that has certainly paid off. *Hee Haw* is now shown in prime time in over a hundred markets, and reaches a total of about three hundred markets.

Like *Laugh In, Hee Haw* is made up of short segments and put together by computer. Twice a year the cast assembles at WLAC studios in Nashville for about six weeks. There they film enough segments to make up thirteen complete shows.

Besides its best-known stars, Buck Owens and Roy Clark, the names of *Hee Haw*'s other characters are almost household words by now: Grandpa Jones, the Hagers, Archie Campbell, Junior Samples, Gordie Tapp, the late Stringbean (David Akeman), and a host of beauties including Gunilla Hutton and Barbie Benton—and, of course, Beauregard, the bloodhound.

*Hee Haw:* It brought country music into America's living rooms.

## HELMS, BOBBY

BORN: August 15, 1933, Bloomington, Indiana

MARRIED: w. Esther Marie Hendrickson

CHILDREN: s. Bobby Bun, Randy Scott; d. Debbie Kay

Country stars start young, and by the time he was thirteen Bobby Helms was a local celebrity, pickin' and singin' the way he did on Bloomington's WWTV. Grand Ole Opry flew him to Nashville every month or so, to appear on Saturday night, and he was a mainstay of midwestern country concerts. *Cash Box* magazine called Bobby Helms "the number one country singer of 1957." He had a superhit, "Fraulein," and no matter what TV show you tuned in, whether Ed Sullivan or Dick Clark (he appeared seven times that year), you could bet on catching Bobby Helms belting out "Fraulein." The next year was fairly good, too. "My Special Angel" was in the top ten. And then that "something" happened, and Bobby Helms hasn't been heard from much, at least as a vocalist. He keeps writing, and like the rest of us, sits by his radio waiting for Christmas, when country DJ's pull out for a few holiday replays his standard, that great country Christmas classic "Jingle Bell Rock."

## HILL, GOLDIE

BORN: January 11, 1933, Karnes County, Texas

MARRIED: h. Carl Smith

CHILDREN: s. Carl, Jr., Larry Dean; d. Lori Lynn

Two big hits of 1953 were "I Let the Stars Get in My Eyes" and "Say Big Boy," both by a twenty-year-old Texas girl from *Louisiana Hayride* named Goldie Hill. Decca planned big things for Goldie. For a couple of years she toured, recorded and sang: "Yesterday's Girl," "Looking Back to See," and "Make Love to Me." The great country artist Carl Smith, who was on several of her tours, obviously took the last song to heart, and married her in 1957. Goldie retired, just like that, and raised a family, which includes two sons and a daughter. Goldie and Carl have a ranch, quarter horses, and a herd of black angus. The stars no longer get in

her eyes. "I'm just pläin Mrs. Smith," Goldie says, "a farmer's wife from Franklin, Tennessee."

## HOLLY, DOYLE

BORN: June 30, 1936, Oklahoma City, Oklahoma

Originally a member of Buck Owens' Buckaroos, Doyle Holly decided to go out on his own as a single. In 1973 he had a hit song, "Queen of the Silver Dollar" (written by Shel Silverstein for Dr. Hook), which was extremely popular with disc jockeys. Whether or not he can live up to his maiden performance is something only time can tell. But he has a nice, soft, interesting style, and ol' Doyle is a master picker.

Doyle Holly: Once a "Buckaroo."

# HOMER AND JETHRO

## Homer [Henry D. Haynes]
BORN: July 27, 1918, Knoxville, Tennessee

## Jethro [Kenneth C. Burns]
BORN: July 27, 1923, Knoxville, Tennessee

Many people have thought Homer and Jethro were brothers. They're not, but they may as well have been. Born on the same day, but not the same year, and in the same town, they teamed up as children and have remained together through the years. Their act hasn't changed very much, either. They were knocking folks out on WNOX, Knoxville, when they were still wet behind the ears, with their brand of deadpan country humor, and they've kept 'em laughing right through the 1960s with frequent appearances on national television, including a series of commercial spots for—what else?—corn flakes.

While they've earned a solid reputation as country humorists, Homer and Jethro are also first-rate musicians. Their stock in trade has been to produce hilarious cover versions of songs made popular by other country artists, and their success is based, in part, on the excellent musical backing they've supplied. They brought a bit of country to the national pop charts on more than one occasion, scoring with "Baby, It's Cold Outside" (with June Carter), "How Much Is That Hound Dog in the Window?" and "I'm in the Jailhouse Now." This exposure certainly helped Homer and Jethro gain a wider audience than they would have otherwise, and it did nothing to diminish their popularity as country artists. It just provided them with more things to laugh about. And who else but two lovable clowns could have gotten away with having a best-selling album (in 1958) called "The Worst of Homer and Jethro"?

Jethro, left, is about to feed Homer some raw country music.

## HONKY-TONK

Throughout the entries I have used the descriptive term "honky-tonk" to describe a certain kind of country song. Honky-tonks are what southerners and southwesterners call a kind of funky blue-collar bar where decor is secondary to drinking and where country music is played, either live or on juke boxes. Dave Hickey, who writes country songs, claims that someone once told him that "honky-tonks were where a white man could get killed by his own kind while listening to country music." Honky-tonk songs, generally accompanied by a band featuring loud, strident steel guitar, deal with life's seedier problems—drinking, death, crime, and adultery and other varieties of illicit love. (See COUNTRY MUSIC.)

## HORTON, JOHNNY

BORN: April 30, 1929, Tyler, Texas
DIED: November 5, 1960, Milano, Texas
MARRIED: w. Billie Jean Jones

Poor Johnny Horton. He gave strong indications of becoming a really big country star. As "the singing fisherman" (he reputedly had magic powers with a rod and reel) of *Louisiana Hayride,* he exhibited the versatility to sing any kind of song. His specialty, however, was honky-tonk, and "I'm a Honky-Tonk Man" was a successful hit of the mid-fifties. Horton grew up in East Texas, sang in clubs and local radio stations, and caught the eye of Tillman Franks (a first-rate bass player as well as manager who has taken a number of unknowns and guided them to stardom: David Houston and Claude King, among others), who convinced Horton to specialize in saga songs. Franks was right, and "The Battle of New Orleans," "Sink the *Bismarck,*" and "Springtime In Alaska" all hit the charts in a big way. Then tragedy struck. Horton was killed in an automobile collision near Milano, Texas, ending his career, Oddly enough, his widow, Billy Jean, was the widow (and second wife) of Hank Williams.

## HOUSTON, DAVID

BORN: December 9, 1938, Shreveport, Louisiana

David Houston (and everybody in Nashville I checked with said it's true) is a descendent of both Sam Houston and Robert E. Lee, which means he probably could run for governor of a number of southern states if he wanted to give up singing country songs. There is no reason for him to do this: He is in the top-ten list of stars with the most consecutive number-one records on the country charts. From March 1967 through June 1968, David Houston remained on the top of the charts with "With One Exception," "You Mean the World to Me," "Have a Little Faith," and "Already It's Heaven." During the previous years he topped the charts with "Mountain of Love" and "Almost Persuaded," [recorded, like all his songs, on Epic Records.] He grew up in Bossier City, Louisiana, where his parents were great friends of the 1920s singing star Gene Austin ("My Blue Heaven"). Austin encouraged a singing career for young David, and by the time he was twelve, Horace

David Houston: An artist of Epic proportions.

Logan, producer of *Louisiana Hayride,* put David Houston on the show and not long afterward he became a regular. During this period Houston was still not sure about a musical career, and he enrolled at Centenary College in Shreveport, singing on weekends. Epic Records convinced him to make a single, "Mountain of Love," which turned into a mountain of riches for both the company and David Houston, and he's been singing ever since. From time to time, he sings duets with Barbara Mandrell which are occasionally as sweet as any music ever produced.

## HOWARD, JAN

BORN: March 13, 1932, West Plains, Missouri
MARRIED: h. Harlan Howard (divorced)

In 1968 Jan Howard's album for Decca was titled "Count Your Blessings, Woman." Jan Howard's blessings have been pitifully few since that time. She split from her husband, songwriter Harlan Howard. Two of her three sons are dead. One was killed in Vietnam, and another committed suicide. Nonetheless, her spirit hasn't been broken, and her performance improves all the time. For a long time she was a featured artist on both the traveling and the TV versions of *The Bill Anderson Show.* Most people, given the circumstances of Jan Howard's life, would have opted for the security of the successful Anderson bandwagon. Instead, in 1973 Jan Howard struck out on her own. I happened to catch one of her first solo appearances, in Canada, and she sang clearly and beautifully, her style more country than pop (during the late fifties, she had a definite "California" sound), including her big hit, "Evil O' My Mind," and "A World I Can't Live In." The audience was with her every minute and demanded encores. She absolutely crushed a front-row heckler with wit and grace.

Always interested in a musical career, Jan Howard defected from her native Missouri, headed for California and show business, met and married Harlan Howard, raised a family, and sang on her husband's demonstration re-

Jan Howard: Delights country audiences.

cords. An executive of Challenge Records liked not only Harlan Howard's songs but Jan's voice, and before long she supplemented housewifing with singing and recording, and she has continued to do so with enthusiasm and talent, to the delight of country audiences around the world.

## HUSKY, FERLIN

BORN: December 3, 1927, Flat River, Missouri

No use listing Ferlin Husky's wives. He's been married six times already, at this writing, and makes no secret about it. "That may be too many wives for one man," a friend of his says, "but then Ferlin's three people." Which is true: Ferlin Husky has recorded, successfully, as Terry Preston and as Simon Crum—and at times, Preston and Crum records have outsold the Husky product. His big hit "Gone" was a flop as recorded by Preston but a hit when sung by Husky. Go figure it out! Ferlin adds to the confusion by occasionally spelling his name "Huskey" on some recordings. I saw Ferlin Husky in person a few years ago, coming out on the stage in an outrageous lavender-and-lace Lord Byron shirt, making a little fun of the audience and telling some awful stories about himself. But as soon as he started singing "Sweet Misery," the audience stopped mumbling and everybody was transfixed.

Husky is a highly regarded showman in Nashville and there are as many Ferlin Husky anecdotes as there are beer glasses in Music City. Officially, he was born in Flat River, Missouri. Sometimes, though, Ferlin will tell interviewers he was born in Hickory Grove or Cantrell. Whatever the town, he grew up in rural Missouri, attending school and helping with the chores. When he noticed a guitar on a neighbor's porch, he asked his parents to get it for him. There was little money, but his father was willing to trade a hen for the instrument. When the chicken refused to lay eggs, however, Ferlin had to return the guitar and didn't have another until he could afford to pay for it. His actual entry into the music business was as a disc jockey. His rich voice was perfect for radio, and when he landed in Bakersfield, California, in 1949, he thought

Ferlin Husky: Alias Simon Crum, alias Terry Preston.

the name Ferlin Husky sounded "made up and unreal," so he called himself Terry Preston. Bakersfield was coming of age as a country-music recording center, and "Terry Preston" was introduced to singer Jean Shepard, and the result was a record called "Dear John Letter"—

the number one hit in 1953. Ferlin wrote a song at that time, dedicated to the late Hank Williams: "Hank's Song." For some reason, he decided to record it under the Husky name and it was a hit. "I was doing some country humor then, as Simon Crum," Husky recalls, "and I decided that two identities were enough. So I dropped Preston but kept Crum." Only Ferlin Husky remains unconfused about his background. What is not confusing is his talent. Since 1955 Ferlin Husky songs have been on the country charts almost without a miss. Several, including "Gone," "I Feel Better All Over," and "Wings of a Dove," have been number-one hits. He records for Capitol records and his albums should be in every country collection. In 1958 he starred with Faron Young in what was probably among the six worst movies ever produced in Hollywood: *Country Music Holiday.* You won't believe this, but his leading lady was Zsa Zsa Gabor. (The Dolly Parton of Budapest, maybe?)

# I

## IAN AND SYLVIA

### Sylvia Fricker
BORN: September 19, 1940, Chatham, Ontario, Canada
MARRIED: h. Ian Tyson

### Ian Tyson
BORN: September 25, 1933, British Columbia, Canada
MARRIED: w. Sylvia Fricker

Ian and Sylvia, survivors of the folk-music days of the late 1950s, produced a series of first-rate albums, often folk-oriented but with strong country roots. Ian, a lumberjack and rodeo cowboy before trying to win his spurs as a singer, has always been "country."

Sylvia Fricker, who hails from a section of eastern Canada where country is the most popular music, has a clear, resonant voice, with miles of range. Her version of "Trucker's

Cafe" makes any other pale into insignificance. When the folk bubble popped, Ian and Sylvia's fortunes continued to rise. For a spell, they formed a country rock group, Great Speckled Bird, and Ian hosted a country TV show, headquartered in Nashville and featuring a number of Canadian country artists like Murray McLaughlin and Gordon Lightfoot. Ian's big chart hit: "Four Strong Winds." Sylvia's: "You Were on My Mind." In late 1973, Max's Kansas City, a New York honky-tonk bar, advertised the personal appearance of Sylvia Fricker, mysteriously billed as "formerly of Ian and Sylvia."

## IVES, BURL
BORN: June 14, 1909, Huntington, Illinois
MARRIED: w. Dorothy

One of the most talented men of the century, Burl Ives has extended his achievements far beyond the borders of country music, though he is anything but a stranger in Nashville. For the record, Burl Icle Ivanhoe Ives began performing at four, had mastered the banjo in high school, and was a football player in college. In true "on the road" American fashion, Burl decided to see America with his guitar, hitchhiked and worked and sang for his supper. He was even thrown in jail, in Utah, for singing "Foggy, Foggy Dew" in public. In New York he met producer George Abbot, who put him in *The Boys from Syracuse.* Ives also convinced CBS to give him his own radio program, *The Wayfaring Stranger,* and this is how America became aware of "The Big Rock Candy Mountain" and "The Blue Tail Fly." Ives joined the army, sang his way through World War II, went to Hollywood, earned Academy Awards, made hugely successful records, wrote books, and gave speeches on conservation for the Department of the Interior. In the early sixties he turned out a couple of successful country songs, "A Little Bitty Tear" and "Call Me Mr. In-Between." He has recently "returned to the country."

Rich Wiseman reported on the "new" Burl Ives in a magazine article: "Burl Ives, pipe in hand, sat back comfortably in his favorite chair in the sitting room of his Hollywood Hills home. For the benefit of the visitors, his secretary started the tape recorder. In a few seconds, the

Burl Ives: Payin' his dues again.

110

strains of Ives's latest record filled the room. Midway through the song, visibly moved by the words, he started singing along.

'Payin' my dues again
Singin' the blues again
Seems like the sun don't shine
I'm so far down
And it's so hard to start all over
Knowin' where I've been
Payin' my dues again'

" 'The song is important to me,' Ives, sixty-four, said later, his clear blue eyes twinkling. 'In a way I am starting my life all over again.'

"While Burl Ives, the internationally loved 'wayfaring stranger,' has made major changes in his life in recent years, it appears the sun *is* shining on him. For example, he has found Dorothy, a woman he adores (they were married in 1971), and his new philosophic bent, based on Chinese thought, has done wonders for him. 'I don't get all hot and bothered about the world going to hell anymore,' he said.

"And, after concentrating on acting the last few years, he has returned to his first love—singing. And he's singing country songs. In fact, it was country music that lured Ives back to the recording studio and concert stages. 'Payin' My Dues Again' is the title song of his recently released country album.

" 'Dorothy and I started listening to the Ray Scott show on KLAC (the 50,000-watt Los Angeles country-music outlet) every night before we went to bed,' Ives explained. 'And I was impressed.

" 'I think people are looking for a basic truth. And while country music might not be sophisticated musically or lyrically, its conceptions are very basic and human. In other words, there's no hair on it.'

"Ives wet his feet in country's waters last summer when he played the first country-fair dates of his career. The response was great. 'For the first time in my life, I truly enjoy personal appearances,' he said.

" 'You know, Americans are the doingest people in the world,' Ives said. 'When I got back here after traveling around the world years ago, the energy here nearly floored me. Other people go to bed when it turns 8 P.M. Here you come to the first truck stop and the joint is swinging.'

"Ives is very pleased with his album. 'I had never given recording the attention it deserves,' he said. 'But I did with this album. On the whole, it's pretty good. But I'm not as good as Waylon Jennings—not yet.' "

## JACKSON, STONEWALL

BORN: November 6, 1932, Tabor City, North Carolina
MARRIED: w. Juanita Carmene Wair
CHILDREN: s. Stonewall, Jr.

"I was born third of three children, the sixth day of November 1932," writes Stonewall Jackson, "to Mr. and Mrs. Waymond David Jackson, in a railroad shack, in a railroad and logging settlement near Tabor City, North Carolina.

"My daddy was an engineer that had worked his way up to this position from a job he took at a very young age on a maintenance crew. Cancer took his life at twenty-eight when I was two years old. Before his death he christened me Stonewall Jackson named for Thomas Jonathan Jackson, as the family tree traces back to the general.

"Of course, this left my mother a widow with three children to feed. Being already poor didn't help much, except being poor sometimes makes you just a little better braced for life. We lived in the house between two and three years with my daddy's mother and step-grandfather while my mother worked day work in tobacco or hoeing in the fields. The kind of work my mother and oldest brother could do in this part of the country, in North Carolina, could have been more plentiful, so she decided we would go to Georgia where my daddy's only living brother had a farm. In Georgia there is also cotton work as well as the tobacco. So we hitchhiked our way to South Georgia. For those who don't know what hitchhiking is, that is getting there any way you can—including walking. A toy red wagon carried most of our belongings. Me being a little over four, I caught a nap now and then on top of the wagon. Up to this point, due to my age and memory, most of this story was gathered from the family and elderly friends. Although I do remember parts of this long tiresome dirty, hungry trip to Georgia. Like the long ride on an old rickety wagon and a time when for a small boy I was my hungriest. A farm family gave us some food and we spread an old quilt down along side the road like a picnic. The years that followed were hard and easy to remember.

"Finally we reached my uncle's farm near Moultrie, Georgia, when I say my uncle's farm it may sound like I mean the world's richest landowner—not so—he was a man only making a decent living by very hard work for his own family. He wanted to help what he could—so we moved into an old shack on his place and my mother and oldest brother went to work in the fields while Waymond, the middle-aged of the three kept me and with God's help we survived. I recall I was plowing at the age of eight and pulling a crosscut saw in the woods by nine. We got by the best we could like this, saving all we could in the summer, so us boys could go to school in the winter, all getting a minimum education.

"When I was sixteen I wireworked my way into the Army by having my birth record changed. At this time I had been playing guitar about two years and had several songs that I had written myself. My Army career didn't last very long—Uncle Sam got wise to me and out I went. At this time my mother had a new husband and family so I felt pretty much on my own at least I already had been since I was fourteen. I went on up to North Carolina and lived with my grandmother until I was seventeen and then I joined the Navy.

"This is where most of my country music career started. I started writing more and I found my fellow sailors had quite an interest in my style of singing and picking. 'Don't Be Angry' and songs like that put my sailor pals to sleep many nights. I had the use of a real good guitar. The Captain of my ship the U.S.S. *Kittywake* loved country music so he let me borrow and keep his guitar extensively. This was a great help since the crew and myself enjoyed the playing and singing. The Captain rigged up a sound system and when we had movies aboard he allowed me to put on a short show just before the movies.

"By the time I came out of the Navy in 1954, I wanted to make country music my career. Realizing it takes a lot of money and time, in most cases, to get started, I was scared to tackle the job broke. I took my mustering out pay which is not enough for such an undertaking and went back to South Georgia—with intentions to work day and night and save me up some money, so I could go into Country Music, and work I did. I got myself a half-crop farm and worked as fast and hard as I could work. Beside my regular crop I'd work Saturday afternoon and at night and Sunday after church. I was only trying to fulfill my goal the only way I knew—hard work.

"I farmed this way all summer and in the winter I cared for the big end of a two man chain saw in the swamp, lending a helping hand to the paper industries cutting pulpwood. In two years I'd saved enough I thought to try to make it in Country Music. I had a little money and a 1955 pickup truck. With a truck I had a home—so giving my folks my other belongings, I headed for Nashville, Tennessee.

"The first thing I intended to do was to get some songs cut by the leading artists. So, on my way in to Nashville, I checked in at the York Motel across the street from Acuff-Rose Publishing Company. The next morning I went over to see Mr. Rose, the son of the late Fred Rose, that gave Hank Williams his start. We cut some dubs on 'Don't Be Angry,' 'Gettin Older,' and several others. Mr. Rose seemed to like the songs so he took two or three for publication and to play to the other artists. I went back to my room and in about an hour I received a telephone call from Mr. Wess Rose. He told me he had called WSM Radio, the station that owns and operates the Grand Ole Opry, and told them about me and asked if they would set up an audition for me the next day and asked me if I'd like to try out for the Opry. I was more than stunned and told him I sure appreciated his interest and I'd try to do my best.

"The next day found me and my pickup truck at WSM Radio Station. Being a lad straight from the country made it a bit difficult finding my way around in even this large a city. When I found WSM Studios, I asked the receptionist about the audition and where I could find Mr. George D. Hayes (Judge Hayes) as he is known 'The Solom Ole Judge.' The receptionist went down the hall and came back with Judge Hayes. Mr. Hayes

Stonewall Jackson: Sang country on the high seas.

greatly appreciate Ernest Tubb, Wess Rose, Judge Hayes, Dee Kilpatrick and Country Music loving people all over the world for their interest, help and support.

"Then came the happiest years. I had my first number one record in 1958 with a George Jones song named 'Life to Go.' I also married a Nashville girl, the former Juanita Carmene Wair, who has been a great help to me in my career. Nineteen hundred and fifty-nine brought me my first million seller, 'Waterloo.' Then came my son, Stonewall Jackson, Jr., born June 23, 1960.

"Due to the lack of funds, which a lot of us understand, I didn't get a start in country music at a real young age. I auditioned for the Grand Ole Opry at the age of twenty-three, at an age when many singers are well on their way. I am glad I have had the chance to contribute what I can to country music, this being the music I have loved all my life. I don't spend much time worrying over the hard times, as I am too busy being thankful for the better ones."

## JACKSON, WANDA

BORN: October 20, 1937, Maud, Oklahoma
MARRIED: h. Wendell Goodman
CHILDREN: s. Gregory Jackson; d. Gina Gail

In Japan Wanda Jackson is really big stuff, and her "Fujiyama Mama" is a standard country hit (they love country music in Japan). Wanda is popular in Germany as well. Her "Santo Domingo" wowed them in 1965, and still finds its way to country juke boxes in Munich and Dusseldorf. She has remained true to the old country sound, with echoes of Molly O'Day and Kitty Wells. Oklahoma is very much a part of Wanda Jackson's voice, even though she more or less grew up in California.

Her parents, Oklahomans, down and out, migrated to California along with thousands of their neighbors, settling in Bakersfield. Although Tom Jackson earned his living as a barber, he was a musician, and after work he toiled many patient hours teaching Wanda the guitar. By the time she was nine years old, she played the guitar and the piano and could read music. The family, having prospered somewhat in California, returned to Oklahoma, where Wanda went to a high school only a block away

took me into one of the sound rooms and said 'now try not to get too excited son, just take your guitar and show me what you can do.' I told the Judge 'I'm not used to playing for anything this important and I sure was nervous. I said I'll just stand over in the corner and sing like I was home just singing for the family or some friends.' When I was through with two songs, he left and went down the hall and came back with the station manager and had me sing a song for him. Mr. Dee Kilpatrick was the station manager at that time. After that they signed me to a contract with the Grand Ole Opry and set up the auditions that got my contract with Columbia Records. I appreciate the fact that I was the first and only artist ever signed to the Grand Ole Opry without being in great demand and with several hits to his credit.

"Ernest Tubb took a great interest in me and helped me quite extensively by taking me on the road shows with him before I had a record out. I from a radio station which ran a talent contest. Wanda entered, won first place, and as a high school sophomore starred on her own program, prompting the great Hank Thompson, an Oklahoma boy himself, to offer her a spot recording with him. The song, "You Can't Have My Love," was a major hit in 1954, and when Wanda graduated from high school, she toured with Thompson and Elvis Presley. Wanda Jackson became one of the first country performers to "make it" in Las Vegas, drawing capacity audiences for weeks at a time to the Golden Nugget, the Silver Nugget, and the Show Boat. Hank Thompson recorded her own composition "Knocking Our Hearts Around," and her own hits included "In the Middle of a Heartache" and "The Box He Came In." Wanda, who specialized in female honky-tonk—songs with words like "If you want some barroom swinger, I'm not the one . . . 'cause I don't think a girl's gotta drink to have fun"—has recently recorded a gospel album for Word and plans to devote more of her time to religion. Her albums for Capitol have done very well. Wanda Jackson has never succumbed to the lure of Nashville and lives with her husband, Wendell Goodman, in Oklahoma City.

## JAMES, SONNY [James Loden]

BORN: March 1, 1929, Hackleburg, Arkansas
MARRIED: w. Doris

If you're old enough to remember "Young Love," you've listened to Sonny James, the "southern gentleman." "It's Just a Matter of Time," "Empty Arms," "Running Bear," "A World of Our Own," and "I'll Never Find Another You" are familiar names among the endless list of Sonny James's successes. My aunt, who listens to middle-of-the-road stations eighteen hours a day, claims there are only a very few country singers she can abide. "I like the ones like Eddy Arnold and Sonny James," she claims, tolerantly. "I mean the ones who don't *sound* like country singers." She's right. Sonny James often sings "country songs," but he modifies them for acceptance (which he certainly has earned) from a wide public, whose collective ear deafens and shrivels from what we purists call "high country art." There's no

crime in what Sonny James does. Many of his very successful contemporaries, faced with a dwindling country audience in the post–Korean war days, aimed toward the rock-pop sound. My protestations notwithstanding, Sonny obviously still considers himself a country singer and Nashville still claims Sonny James.

Reporter Robert Adels wrote a magazine article about Sonny James, a story which omits the anecdote of four-year-old Sonny getting a brand-new silver dollar from Kate Smith for winning a singing contest.

" 'The Southern Gentleman' is an example of the name living up to the man. The tall, distinguished-looking country balladeer does more than simply fill the bill visually; Sonny James *lives* his title in all its appropriately quiet, respectable and gracious splendor.

"A true Southern gentleman is generally glib but becomes reticent when matters turn to the personal. This Southern gentleman would, at first, rather be interviewed in a Nashville hotel room than in his own suburban homestead, but he'll change his mind, given good reason. You don't hear much of his comings and goings from gossip, professional or amateur.

"So if Sonny James seems to be hiding from all but his closest friends, it's only to maintain that degree of privacy he deems essential to his lifestyle.

" 'Some people like to keep everything secret,' Sonny observes, sitting back on the couch from the Berkline den furniture bearing his nickname, which rings the hearth on the second floor of his stately home. 'Others want everything they do known to the public. I guess you might say I'm splittin' the difference.'

"His duplex's difference lies in the total independence of the two spacious floors: both have separate entrances and kitchen facilities as well as numerous bathrooms (which come close to outnumbering the closets) and bedrooms for an unusual piggyback effect, which proves most functional. When Sonny's family and friends come to stay, they're given a floor and the freedom to come and go as they please for the sake of everyone's privacy. It's how you might imagine the house of a Southern gentleman to look.

" 'Can you imagine a house like this without a fireplace?' Sonny asks rhetorically as he con-

Sonny James singing his hit "Running Bear" on a TV special.

structs a fine blaze. A Southern gentleman is after all a doer and not a complainer. Sonny had that fireplace put in because he thought it should be there. Because he also had visions of living by a lake, he sometimes jokes about evicting his more low-lying neighbors in order to flood a large portion of the surrounding area. But a Southern gentleman is also practical and considerate. For water fun, Sonny and his petite, attractive wife, Doris, set out for Center Hill Reservoir's Clear Lake.

"Sonny and Doris spend much of their free time there, in the Tennessee recreational area. Their comfortably carpeted all-purpose boat is not far from the moorings of fellow country entertainers Jerry Reed and Porter Wagoner. The craft is fully equipped for skiing, cruising and fishing. When they want to spend the night, the Jameses rent a lodge or join one of their houseboated friends.

" 'Fishing's my favorite hobby,' Sonny continued, lured on by the mere mention of Clear Lake as the den fire crackled. 'You can fish all-year-round there; I go for the small-mouthed bass. But I go with the seasons as far as sports are concerned—baseball, basketball, football.' Revealing a special fondness for the autumnal game, James speaks of 'reliving the times back in high school when I was torn apart, head to foot, by halfbacks.' Two kinds of tackle—both the independent and relaxing realm of the angler as well as the rough-and-tumble team spirit of playing defensive and offensive end—are part of the sports-mindedness of Sonny James.

"Memories of his high school days recall earlier aspects of his Alabama boyhood.

" 'We never felt we were livin' out of a trunk at any time,' Sonny said, moving from the couch to the easy-chair. 'My sister Thelma and myself never missed a thing growin' up.' His parents were 'Mom and Pop' to everyone in their 'real hometown' of Hackleburg. Sometimes they uprooted their Loden clan for months at a time when an appearance on a radio-sponsored talent show won the musical family their own program somewhere in the South. James Loden was the youngest member of this Carter Family–type group; he didn't become 'Sonny James' until years later when Capitol Records' Ken Nelson began to take an active role in his solo career and tagged him 'The Southern Gentleman.' Sonny met Ken when his friend Chet Atkins informally invited Nelson over to witness a 'woodsheddin' ' session between the two musician pals back in 1952.

" 'He didn't just set me down and teach me right there,' Sonny explains with a gentle smile, 'but over the years, I learned to respect Ken and the way he handles artists. It was he who thought I should drop my family name, "Loden," because it sounded like too many other names—like London and Louden. Said people might get confused and wouldn't remember it. So he took "Sonny," my nickname from when I was small, and put it in front of my first name.

" 'At first I complained: "All my friends won't know who it is!" ' Sonny went on. 'But Ken said, "Sonny, the friends that know you now will be able to add two and two together." Little kids that can hardly speak can still say "Son-james!" so I guess it was a good choice.'

"By coming up with the Southern Gentleman title, Nelson proved he was more than just a good judge of character. He was also a man who was thinking ahead. 'Ken had that title put under the "Sonny James" on all my records,' The Southern Gentleman recalled. 'Now the two have become synonymous and I'm happy, because "Sonny" sounds like a child without something to make it mature. People who never met me know that with "The Southern Gentleman" I wasn't tryin' to be a teenager. After I passed twenty, "Sonny" by itself wouldn't have pleased me.'

"The Southern Gentleman began to talk of how he's pleased to be known as a singer despite his other musical abilities.

" 'I think that if I were a comedian,' he said, 'I'd want the comedy to overshadow anything else I might do. Whatever else I do as a singer is a mold around my singin'. You don't let any other area—be it banjo, mandolin or guitar—take away from what your career was built on.' A number of instruments have a special meaning to this singer who's played guitar on all his records. One is the first mandolin Sonny's Dad

fashioned for him when he was three. (It's now in the Country Music Hall of Fame.) Another is a guitar Pop Loden sent him in Seattle just before Sonny's National Guard unit was put on active duty in Korea in 1950.

" 'I wrote him for a used one,' Sonny recalls, leaping up to tend the fire once more, 'because I was pretty sure where we were going. Well, it very quickly became the company guitar—anyone who knew a G-chord played it. It's funny how an instrument can bring so much joy to a bunch of guys for fifteen months, but it can.' Members of the unit, mostly Sonny's high school chums, proudly emblazoned '252 Truck Co.' on its back and were rewarded with a bit of luck in return. Despite the dangers of guerrilla warfare as they hauled ammo to the lines and prisoners back, only one of their number was lost during that tour of duty. The Southern Gentleman was beginning to tell how his lone moments were often occupied with some of the first songwriting he had ever tried when, bounding up the spiral staircase from the lower house level, came Patches to change the subject.

" 'How would you like to meet a dog that sings "Happy Birthday" over the telephone?' Sonny queried, vigorously stroking, scratching and fooling with the two-toned white and black poodle who's only as aristocratic as he wants to be. 'I don't really teach him,' he explained, looking up. 'It started one night when he began to "sing" while I was watching Nixon on TV. I started to hum with him and he continued to do this trick. Now when I hum, he'll sing on command.' And Sonny proved his tale with a demonstration.

" 'Patches,' whom Sonny describes as a real 'inside dog,' was a gift from a minister friend. (The Southern Gentleman has quite a few minister friends, many serving as advisers on charitable matters.)

"Almost as close to him as his wife, family and dog are the Black Angus cattle he raises on the three ranches he owns in the Hacklesburg area. Sonny views them more as a hobby than as an investment. 'And it's only a two-hour drive down the Interstate for me to see 'em,' he adds, glowing.

"A phone call from Sonny's mother; the Southern Gentleman excused himself from the conversation. Later, he picked up a new train of thought in the living room, which serves as a

An interesting note: While Jesse was serving in Korea, he met Charlie Louvin, also a soldier, and they teamed up to entertain the troops. Unfortunately no recording of the duo now exists.

# JONES, GEORGE

BORN: September 12, 1931, Saratoga, Texas
MARRIED: w. Tammy Wynette
CHILDREN: d. Tamela

George Jones has never been called the "king of country music," though on occasion he's referred to as a "crown prince." For a long time he looked more like an insurance executive, with a crew cut, tie, and tweed jacket. These days, his hair is shoulder-length and his attire is more casual and he no longer feels like a member of the marine corps (which he was, by the way, during the Korean War). He is married to country superstar Tammy Wynette, some years his junior, who "fulfilled my lifelong dream" by marrying Jones. They have a successful act, which they climax by reenacting their marriage ceremony to music—a tableau which has brought both admonition and praise from country audiences. In 1973 an announcement that George and Tammy were splitting up had Nashville gossips busy day and night. All sorts of dark rumors permeated the Music City community: George was hitting the bottle. Tammy was hitting the bottle. They were hitting each other with bottles. None turned out to be true, and they are still together, happy as well as superstars. And George Jones, though he's had his ups and downs, is an gen-u-ine country superstar. He is number six of the top ten artists with the most charted record sides (sixty). He is in the top twenty artists with the most number-one records. He is number eight in the top ten country stars with the most consecutive years on the charts.

In the best sense of the word, George Jones is a *country* singer. "Of all the singers in the honky-tonk resurgence," writes country-music historian Bill C. Malone, "two individuals with styles deeply rooted in country tradition give greatest promise of achieving the kind of fame earlier won by such country music giants as Jimmie Rodgers, Hank Williams, and Roy Acuff. They are George Jones and Buck Owens."

George Jones of Saratoga, Texas, near Beaumont, has been influenced by a variety of earlier country styles and singers, and his devotion to country tradition is so strong that he has resisted most of the modern commercializing pressures. He is so firmly imbedded in the country tradition that even the addition of popular choral backgrounds cannot diminish the distinctive country sound of his voice." George Jones is a prime example of the thesis that traditional styles die very slowly. He grew up in Texas, but far from the cattle country. Saratoga is in the heart of the industrial-urban center of eastern, Gulf-coast Texas. His childhood coincided with the decline of rural ways in the area. His family was working class: His mother played the piano in the church and his father was also musically inclined, but was a pipefitter by trade, and a log-truck driver. Their religious attitudes were fundamentalist. "The Jones family," Bill Malone writes, "was typical of the rural Texas family that moved into the urban centers during the immediate prewar and war years and remained rural in everything but residence and occupation. The old rural values and attitudes, built up through the decades, would be a long time a-dying."

The years during World War II, 1941–45, were exciting ones in the area. Thousands of rural Texas families swarmed into cities like Port Arthur and Orange in search of work in the war plants. Entire city blocks were lined with taverns and dance halls, which "poured out a steady stream of hillbilly music" and young George Jones, like other young Texans of his period, listened to Floyd Tillman and Ernest Tubb. "I was both thrilled and influenced by them," Jones recalled to an interviewer. "My personal favorites, I think, were Roy Acuff and Bill Monroe. I heard them on Grand Ole Opry." There is still an Acuff influence in George Jones's singing. Listen to his phrasing on the high notes. George got his first guitar while he was in high school, and he began singing, at first for free and then for money at local clubs, in the classic tradition of country entertainers. His influence at the time was Hank Williams, and in his earliest jobs at a Beaumont tavern, "he affected a style very close to that of Williams."

Jones enlisted in the marines during the Korean War, and when he was discharged three years later, he planned to continue picking and singing intense, and because of his choice of songs, many of which he wrote himself. His recordings of 'Don't Stop the Music' and 'Just One More' are excellent examples of both the honky-tonk style and of Jones's own personal, emotional style.'' Among Jones's hundreds of hits: "White Lightning" and "Walk Through This World with Me." George Jones has sung country duets with several women singers: Brenda Carter and Margie Singleton among them. He now sings with his wife, Tammy, and the albums do phenomenally. But country critics feel that his best duet work was with Melba Montgomery. "We Must Have Been Out of Our Minds" and "Let's Invite Them Over" are among the great hits they sang together and are excellent examples of country songs "denoting the temptations and heartbreaks of illicit love." George Jones has recorded 400 songs, and there probably will be 400 more.

## JONES, GRANDPA [Marshall Louis Jones]

BORN: October 20, 1913, Niagra, Kentucky
MARRIED: w. Ramona Riggins
CHILDREN: s. Mark Alan; d. Eloise, Elise June

Everybody knows who he is now, since *Hee Haw*, but Grandpa Jones was one of the South's favorite entertainer-comedians for many years before he hit the networks. Not only is he a faithful advocate of old-timey country songs, but he is also a wonderful comedian, actor, and general all-around entertainer. Even when he was quite young he dressed in the garb of an old man and sported false white whiskers. He is an expert banjo player and has a never-ending storehouse of Appalachian mountain anecdotes, most of which have country audiences rolling in the aisles. "In a sense, Grandpa Jones might be considered the successor to Uncle Dave Macon," country-music historian Bill C. Malone writes, "through his maintenance of mountain banjo songs and styles."

Grandpa Jones grew up in the pre-depression era in Kentucky ("There was always a depression in Kentucky for poor folks") and his folks had a sawmill. One of the workers had a guitar, and eleven-year-old Louis Jones "would slip into the room where it was kept and try to play it

George Jones: A genuine superstar.

but didn't think he'd be able to make a career of it. Instead, he landed a job as a house painter. Starday records was then headquartered in Beaumont, and H. W. "Pappy" Dailey and Jack Starnes, who owned the company, were among the few record producers who weren't moving toward rock-and-roll, which was cutting into the country market at the time. Jones made a number of records for Starday, and "Why, Baby, Why" did well on the charts, but the incursion of rockabilly was devastating to the country market for so many years that Jones didn't really reach his audience potential until the very early sixties. In both 1962 and 1963 the nation's DJs named Jones Best Country Singer, and it was one of the few times that the recipient of this honor was not a member of Grand Ole Opry. "His success came," Bill Malone says, "because of his unique style, personal and when no one was around." Eventually he got his own guitar, and by 1929, now living in Akron, Ohio, he entered a talent contest, walking off with the $50 first prize. "I spent the money for a new guitar," Jones told an interviewer, "and in a couple of years I joined up with Bradley Kincaid's group." Kincaid was appearing on WLD, on the *National Barn Dance* radio show, and listeners wrote in asking about the new performer, whose voice on the air sounded "very old." This gave Jones the idea for the Grandpa character, even though he was only in his twenties. In 1937, with his new character overwhelmingly accepted by the public, Jones began his own band, The Grandchildren, and became the feature act on Cincinnati's *Boone County Jamboree* show, giving up the spot to join the army at the outbreak of World War II. When he was released from service he was asked to join Grand Ole Opry and has been there ever since. Although Grandpa Jones's songs don't get too high on the country charts, his records sell well, and he has recorded for King, Monument, and Decca.

## THE JORDANAIRES

### Leader: Gordon Stoker

> mmmmmmmmmmmmmmmmmmm!!!
> ah-ah-ah-ah-ah-ah !!!
> m-m-m-m m-m-m-m !!!

That's what the Jordanaires sing, quite often, and they make a pile of money doing it. Most new country recordings are characterized by background choruses. Just pick up *any* country album at random, and nine chances out of ten you'll find a note saying that the background choruses were by the Jordanaires. The Jordanaires (under the direction of Gordon Stoker, with some revolving personnel) started as a gospel group in 1949 but began making themselves known by backing Elvis Presley on his first recordings. Since that time they have been averaging three recording sessions a day, five days a week, fifty-two weeks a year. Each member of the Jordanaires makes at least $65,000 a year. The group also has, collectively, considerable outside business interests, including clothing stores, publishing companies, food concerns, and a recording studio.

## KAZEE, BUELL

BORN: August 29, 1900, Burton Fork, Kentucky

Buell Kazee was well educated, which set him apart from Clarence Ashley, Dock Boggs, and most of the mountain musicians of the 1920s and '30s. He had a college degree and musical training, was a Bible scholar and a minister. His records for Brunswick in the early 1920s— "Little Mohee," "If You Love Your Mother, Meet Her in the Skies," "John Hardy," and others—were extremely popular. Many Baptist ministers of the period felt singing was sinful, but Kazee entertained none of those convictions, and though he spent more than twenty years as minister of the First Baptist Church of Morehead, Kentucky, he never stopped picking and singing publicly. Many of the songs made popular by Pete Seeger and Joan Baez during the folk revival of the late 1950s, like "Darling Cory" and "East Virginia," are derived from Buell Kazee versions of the songs on Vocalion and Brunswick records. Kazee was a lifelong student of Elizabethan literature and ballads and adapted many to the idiom of the hills. The musicologist Charles Seeger (father of Pete, Mike, and Peggy) referred to Kazee's "Lady Gay" as "about the finest variant of the 'Wife of Usher's Well.'" Kazee's biggest hit was "The Waggoner Sod," which he performed over a galloping banjo background.

## KERSHAW, DOUG

BORN: January 24, 1936, Tiel Ridge, Louisiana

MARRIED: w. Elsie Carol

CHILDREN: s. Douglas James, Jr., Victor Conrad

The late Johnny Cash TV show (May It Rest in Peace) is credited with a number of things, including the introduction of Bob Dylan to country audiences and of country music to city audiences—but to me, the *Johnny Cash Show*

Doug Kershaw: The Cajun kid is proud of his roots.

signified my introduction to Doug Kershaw Looking like a bayou version of Tiny Tim and sawing away at his Acadian fiddle, Kershaw sings of life on the Mississippi Delta, of growing up as a poor Cajun boy, and of the wonders of the world to a boy from a place even most rural people call "the sticks." Few people know that Doug Kershaw went to college (McNeese State, Louisiana) and appeared on *Louisiana Hayride*, *The Ed Sullivan Show*, *The Dick Clark Show*, and a number of other national TV programs, all before 1960—and led a group called Pee Wee

Kershaw's Continental Playboys (with brother Rusty), or that he voluntarily gave up show business and entered the service for three years.

Rich Wiseman talked with Kershaw for a magazine interview:

"Not every Cajun singer/fiddler is invited to a President's inauguration, but Doug Kershaw, who performed before Pat Nixon at an earlier Washington function, was. And he had himself a good time. 'The Nixons are nice people,' he said. '*And they serve some good liquor!*'

"But just ask Doug if meeting the President is

one of the highlights in his career. He'll stick out his chin, his bayou brown eyes will pop wide open, and he'll answer in his best Louisiana swamp baritone: 'Hey, man, no no no.' And then he'll excitedly tell you about the show he did in Lake Charles, Louisiana, a few days later.

"It was to be Doug's first performance in the swamplands he had left seventeen years earlier for the Nashville bigtime. He had felt jittery. 'Why do you think we all go out and hustle?' he said. 'We want to prove ourselves to the people we've left. There is no greater feeling, bar none, than your parents and friends saying: 'Hey, man, you did it.'

"The homefolk had surfaced from the swamps in all directions to hear him. 'There were so many Cajuns you couldn't see the people!' Doug exclaimed. One Cajun present was his sixty-one-year-old mamma, Rita, who still lives humbly in Jennings, the town of 12,000 in which Doug was raised. The homefolk cheered and Mamma beamed.

" 'Things like that don't happen every day— when you can perform in your home where people accept you and where you can get your parents onstage and share something and let the whole world know you're proud,' he said.

" 'Proud' is a word that Doug Kershaw uses unabashedly to describe himself. Being accepted by his Louisiana neighbors validated the pride he feels, but it wasn't so long ago that Doug was ashamed of who he was.

"Cajuns are descendents of the Acadians, French Canadian settlers who were driven south to Louisiana in the 1700s by the British. Those who live and work in the swamps are poor people, and Doug's parents were no different.

"He was born in his parents' houseboat thirty-seven years ago at Tiel Ridge, a tiny island two miles off the coast. That's where the fish were congregating at the time, and Doug's daddy, a fisherman and trapper by trade, had to follow his livelihood. It was a hard life.

"To supplement his mother's fifty-cents-a-day income from washing and ironing clothes, Doug shined shoes.

" 'Did you ever see ten shoe-shine boys on one block?' he asked. 'You got to fight, man. I was too small to be much of a fist fighter. Besides it took too much time and I couldn't shine many shoes.'

"It was at the age of seven that Doug started playing his fiddle in earnest. He had learned to play the instrument on the sly while his dad and brothers trapped muskrats and minks during the day. 'I played it good enough not to get a whuppin' when I was caught,' he joked.

"Through determination, Doug and brother Rusty sang and played their way from Louisiana to Nashville and into a Grand Ole Opry contract by the time he was twenty-one. However, a volunteer stint in the Army took him away from Nashville for three years. When he returned, few remembered the name it had taken him years to build up.

"One day as he sat in his Nashville apartment, flat broke, he started thinking back to early childhood. Before he knew it he was writing a song that told of those years. The words to 'Louisiana Man' came easily. And, somehow, the raw, gutty sounds of that fiddle brought his hard bayou existence to life. The song was an immediate hit. It sold thousands of copies, and Doug estimates that 1,000 performers around the world have recorded it, the most recent being Japanese.

"The song solved Doug's financial problems and gave him the confidence to take a good look at himself and the stigma he had felt at being a poor Cajun.

" 'In the sixties I got to see a lot more of Doug Kershaw,' he said. 'Whether anybody heard it or not I got my feelings off my chest. I got to feelin' brave. And then one day I found out who I was. My name is Doug Kershaw and I'm a Cajun, and nobody can take that away from me. I got to where I could go to sleep and wake up with myself. Not many people can do that.'

"At Southern California's famous Palomino nightclub, 700 people, hippies and hillbillies alike, have jammed in to see Kershaw. Backstage, Doug is dressed in a red velvet Edwardian suit and fancy gold silk shirt. He looks as far displaced from Cajun country as one could be, but when one young female fan presents him with an old picture of his mamma lacquered on wood, tears well in his eyes and for a moment one can picture him as a child in tattered bluejeans.

"In a few minutes he is on stage, giving the crowd the knee-slapping, foot-stomping show his fans have come to love him for. He fiddles so fast and rough that one can't help but look for the smoke as he jumps about the stage like a

127

man possessed, his face flashing one outlandish expression after another. He performs a wild 'Orange Blossom Special.' And, of course, he finishes with 'Louisiana Man.'

"Doug feels he has a lot of surprises left in him. Getting out of the swamps is just a start. He wants to make movies, but he also wants to continue to record and perform in clubs, auditoriums and universities around the country. He said he hasn't performed to an empty seat in the last year and a half.

" 'I set my goals when I was quite young,' he said. 'I'll never quite reach my goals, but I'll come within finger distance.'

"And just what are Doug Kershaw's goals?

" 'That's something I won't reveal to anyone but me and God.' "

## KILGORE, MERLE

BORN: August 9, 1934, Chickasha, Oklahoma
MARRIED: w. Dorothy Lee
CHILDREN: s. Stephen, Kimberly; d. Pamela Ann

Once, when I was talking to Hank Williams, Jr., Merle Kilgore, who travels with Hank, Jr., and writes songs with him, and announces the show, came into the dressing room. He was behind me, and began talking like Johnny Cash, and I thought it was Cash—the imitation was that perfect. Kilgore, who wrote "Ring of Fire" with June Carter, often does Cash imitations as part of his act. They bring the house down. He's a big man—as big as Johnny Cash, anyway, with a friendly, if horsey, smile. He has black curly hair and wears crushed velvet tuxedos in blue and maroon. Kilgore has had parts in a number of western movies including *Five-Card Stud* and *Nevada Smith.* (He also wrote and recorded the title song for *Nevada Smith.*) Born in Oklahoma, he moved early in life to Louisiana. While still a teen-ager, he became a disc jockey and a member of *Louisiana Hayride.* By 1952 he was appearing on Grand Ole Opry. He was only eighteen at the time and wrote a song, "More and More," which eventually won gold records for both Guy Lombardo (Guy Lombardo???) and Webb Pierce. He also wrote "Johnny Reb" (a big hit for Johnny Horton), "Dear Mama" (high chart hit for Kilgore), "We're Talking It Over," and countless other songs. Kilgore

wrote "Wolverton Mountain" for Claude King. It's a song dealing with Clifton Clowers, a mountain man who tried to shoot any suitor who would come up Wolverton Mountain after his daughter. Clifton Clowers was actually Kilgore's uncle, but Kilgore assures one and all that most suitors got away, and his daughter finally did get married. Kilgore is one of those personable and attractive performers, with a lot of stage savvy, a lot of brains and personality and sophistication, who should do better than a lot of the little milksops who seem to appeal to the public.

## KINCAID, BRADLEY

BORN: July 13, 1894, Point Leavall, Kentucky

Bradley Kincaid, college graduate, Kentuckian, songwriter, was the first artist to introduce mountain songs on radio. Billed as The Original Authentic Folksinger, he sang "Barbara Allen" on his Saturday night show from Chicago for four straight years. There were always thousands of mailed requests. He was a mainstay of the *WLS National Barn Dance* in Chicago, singing his "mountain" songs (he hated the word "hillbilly") in a high, nasal tenor. He recorded for a number of companies; Brunswick, Gennet, and others. In those days no singer had exclusive contracts with record companies, and Kincaid and others sang under many labels and often under pseudonyms on a number of labels. When Kincaid retired, he bought a music store in Springfield, Ohio, coming back to performing briefly during the folk-music boom, producing a few albums for Bluebonnet Records, and appearing at folk festivals.

## KING, CLAUDE

BORN: February 5, 1933, Shreveport, Louisiana
MARRIED: w. Barbara Jean Coco
CHILDREN: s. Duane, Bradley, Jerone

Shreveport has produced a number of country stars: Carl Belew, Faron Young, and the personable and deep-voiced Claude King, for whom the Nashville prognosticators predicted a mammoth career. His first records were heavy hits for Columbia: "The Burning of Atlanta," "Big

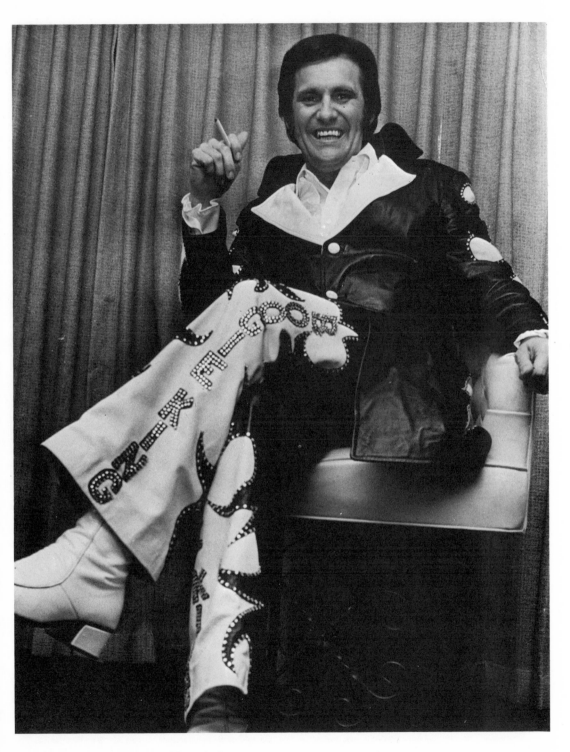

Merle Kilgore: Wrote "Wolverton Mountain."

Bradley Kincaid: ''Barbara Allen'' is his favorite.

says. "Up until now that hasn't been true because country was always held to a straight commercial basis. Now people are *listening* more, paying attention to lyrics, and this has enabled writers to open up more without the risk of losing their audiences. I think country music is going to get back to the earth and get back to the people. I've been lucky in that I've always believed in truism, simplicity, and have been able to transfer my feelings. I'm not a writer who can say, 'I've written thousands of songs'; I've only written two number-one songs. I started in country music as a guitar player and I didn't begin writing until one day I asked myself, 'What if something should ever happen to my hands and I couldn't play guitar any more?' I know it sounds weird, but when Hank Williams died on New Year's Day of 1953, I got the feeling that he passed something on to me. It was eleven years before I did anything with it, but since then I've always tried to remember that."

All Red Lane will admit about his background (I tried to get it from him when he came to pose for the picture on the cover of this book) is that he's from Texas. (He was actually born in Louisiana.) Critic Geoff Lane says: "Red is one of the few underground cats who actually looks like a good ole country hoss: clean-shaven, medium-length hair, fairly straight dress; all in all, the kind of guy any truck driver would be glad to have riding in his cab." Red Lane is a man to keep your eyes on.

## LEE, BRENDA [Brenda Mae Tarpley]
BORN: December 11, 1944, Atlanta, Georgia
MARRIED: h. Ronnie Shacklett
CHILDREN: d. Julie, Jolie

Brenda Lee's most recent hit is a song called "Nobody Wins," an odd sentiment for the *wunderkind* of rock-sometimes-country music. Although not yet thirty, the former Brenda Mae Tarpley has been singing professionally for twenty-two years and has had more than thirty consecutive "winners" on the charts, including "I'm Sorry," "Baby Face," "One Step at a Time," "Pennies from Heaven," and "Johnny One-Time."

Robert Adels, on assignment for a magazine interview, spent some time backstage at Madison Square Garden with Brenda Lee:

Brenda Lee: The little girl with the big voice is now the twenty-nine-year-old mother of two and is still a top entertainer.

"Thirteen has turned out to be a lucky number after all for Brenda Lee, despite its evil portents. Her recent set at Madison Square Garden's thirteenth rock-and-roll revival concert proved that the petite southern lady is still as loved in the Big City as she continues to be in country's heartland.

135

"Brenda Lee prefers the nightclub circuit to the packaged show itineraries of country and rock, so she approached this particular date with double doubts. Her own five-piece band had only one hour in which they could rehearse with promoter Richard Nader's own band, which played for the other performers on the bill, none of whom had one country ballad to their credit.

"As it turned out, the final result was personally rewarding for her. She summed it up this way in her hotel room the next afternoon: 'If you can quiet down 18,000 people, many of whom were on their feet the whole time Chubby Checker was doing his dances on stage, with a ballad—well, then you've really done something!'

"And after her biggest country song (Kris Kristofferson's 'Nobody Wins') and her biggest album ('Brenda'), Brenda's career shows hardly any signs of waning. It was thirteen years ago (that number again!) that she scored her first number-one record with 'I'm Sorry,' and thirteen years ago when she began to be recognized as a major country ballad singer. Although she opened her set in New York with her original version of 'Comin' On Strong' (now the Chevrolet commercial as sung by Tex Ritter) and closed with 'Kansas City,' these rousers only served as a frame for her mainstay—heartsongs.

"Now a twenty-nine-year-old mother of two, Brenda was first brought to Nashville from Atlanta at the age of twelve by her widowed mother; her three brothers and sisters naturally came along too.

"'I don't ever remember Mom acting the stage mother or anyone in the family being jealous of me. Really, I don't,' she recalls.

"Ten years ago, she married Ronnie Shacklett, now a building contractor in Nashville. Their two daughters, Julie, nine, and Jolie, four —'sometimes I wish I would have named the younger one something else'—inspired Brenda to begin a soon-to-be-published volume of poetry called *First Born*. 'When I'm lonely, I find comfort in writing about every walk of life,' she said. 'No, they aren't meant to be song lyrics. They're to be read as poems because that's how I wrote them.'

"Brenda doesn't write for a musical purpose, and since the success of 'Nobody Wins,' many top writers have been sending their songs to her and producer Owen Bradley. Some have even been known to phone up to ask if they could stop by to play her a few, but she's not particularly annoyed by their persistence. 'It just gives me a wider range of things to pick from,' she says. 'I never rely on any specific songwriters—I go for the song. At the concert, some of the people backstage like Bo Diddley even said they had things they were going to get to me.'

"It might seem so, but Bo Diddley—the black singer/guitarist who popularized a soulful, rhythmic sound which bears his name—is not really an off-the-wall source of material for Brenda, for she sees more of an analogy between her career and that of Ray Charles than of, say, Loretta Lynn.

"'I've attracted a country audience because of the material I usually choose to sing,' she explained, once again referring to the fact that she doesn't play the traditional country musicians' dates like fairs and multi-artist tours. As her husband Ronnie put it, 'Well, we just feel kind of "establishment," ya know?'

"In 1967, Brenda stopped recording altogether and did not start again for four years. 'I felt the business changing—moving away from what I wanted to do,' she said. And although she doesn't claim it has turned into a country balladeer's paradise by any means, she feels that the reception of 'Nobody Wins' means that things can go back in that direction.

"'Country music is increasingly being accepted by a wider range of people just for what it really is,' Brenda Lee, short but sharp, observed. And she's very much a part of that fact.''

## LEE, DICKEY

BORN: Memphis, Tennessee

Dickey Lee is often referred to as a "friend of Elvis" and "former teen-age rock star." He's no longer a teen, and country is his love these days, as reporter Gail Buchalter discovered:

"Dickey Lee has managed not to wear the weariness of the road on his face. He didn't wince, cringe, or give off any other signs of displeasure when asked why he is sometimes referred to as the 'world's oldest teen-ager' even

Dicky Lee: A sound crusader of country music.

though he is now in his early thirties. He explained that it was a label he acquired fifteen years ago when he was regarded as a teen-age idol, although he was attending college.

" 'I was going to Memphis State, majoring in commercial art. I wanted to be an entertainer, but you know how that is—I figured I probably never would make it. I had put out several records which didn't do anything until I recorded "Patches." ' "

"Dickey launched his singing career with a high school country band in the assembly halls and auditoriums of Memphis. But the country aspect of the group was short-lived. Elvis Presley had exploded, and any kid who played guitar was enthralled by rhythm. Born and raised in Memphis, there was no way for Dickey to escape this influence, and his band turned to rock-and-roll.

" 'I met Elvis when I was still in high school and had put out my first single on a fly-by-night label. The strange thing was that it outsold Elvis' first single on Sun Records. I was visiting at his house when someone there suggested he give me a helping hand. He replied, "Dickey's off to a better start than I was when I began. I think he'll do all right on his own." '

" 'I went to his house several times after that and always brought a girl with me that I was trying to snow.' This time Dickey's smile went past his eyes and his mouth turned up mysteriously in a way faintly reminiscent of the Mona Lisa's, as he added, 'And you know, it usually worked.' "

"Unlike many entertainers, Dickey Lee is endowed with an unusual shyness. Today, having reached a point in his career where he is recognized in supermarkets and on the streets, he tries to keep away from the limelight once offstage.

" 'I don't like to be the center of attraction except when I'm on stage. I've got my hang-ups; I guess you could say a semi-inferiority complex. Sometimes I get a little scared because I think I'm not what a lot of people think I am. I never was hung up on the star trip and I get embarrassed when people try to put me on a pedestal—I don't belong there.' Dickey admits he had little confidence in himself when he started in the music business and was consequently led around by the nose by the pop disc jockeys. When they wanted any type of free promotion, Dickey was one of the first to be called. It was the typical story of when you're hot, you're hot, and when you're not, nobody gives a damn.

"One person who had little time for teen-age idols in Dickey's early recording days in Memphis was Jack Clement, now one of Nashville's most successful producers.

" 'Jack was an engineer there and at the time I thought he was a real bastard. We would go into the studio feeling like heroes and Jack wouldn't pay much attention to us. While we were recording, he would be sitting there reading a comic book or something, and it really deflated us. But I think that has been one of the things that has really helped me in this business, because every time I let myself get out of hand, Jack comes along and accurately tells me where I am, which has aided me in maturing.'

"When Jack Clement opened his own studio in Beaumont, Texas, he became Dickey's producer and was responsible for his number-one pop hits 'Patches' and 'I Saw the Light.' Dickey became involved with production work in Memphis, and Jack eventually persuaded him to work for him in his studios and publishing companies. Dickey had no desire to record again but ended up doing a session with Jack 'just for kicks.' The feel for country music which had been lying dormant began to flow, and although his first two singles received little attention, the next four songs established him as a legitimate country artist.

" 'I don't follow any set pattern in choosing the songs I cut—I just look for good material. "Ashes of Love" is an old country tune, while "A Never-ending Song of Love" was written by a pop artist a few years ago and was a big rock hit. I respect a lot of the old country tunes, but that doesn't mean I can't appreciate the new ones coming down the line.'

"Last month Dickey began working with Charley Pride and will be doing more dates with him this year. He considers it a great opportunity due to the additional exposure he will gain, but what he really would like to do most is get on the college circuit.

" 'I think country music could gain a wider acceptance in the college market if it was presented better. I've heard more great artists put on bad shows simply because they were forced to use faulty sound systems. I guess I'm on a crusade to upgrade the sound quality of country music. Not that I consider myself to be a savior—other guys are doing the same thing, like Freddy Weller and Joe Stampley. People like Johnny Cash and Glen Campbell have gone a long way to bring respectability to country music by the way they present it, and by the other people they have gotten involved in it.'

"There is now an ever-growing stable of artists who have made smooth transitions from rock-and-roll to country. Dickey Lee must surely rank among them. Early success in rock-and-roll has not lessened his stature as a performer in the eyes of country-music fans. Dickey Lee is above all a professional whose years of experience in the music business have enabled him to score swift successes in country music. Like many of his contemporaries, he may be just on the verge of his greatest musical achievements.''

# LEWIS, JERRY LEE

BORN: September 29, 1935, Ferriday, Louisiana

He has a number of vocal detractors and his behavior has been a modicum less than angelic, especially for a graduate of the Waxahachie, Texas, Bible Institute, but Jerry Lee Lewis cannot be faulted as a musician. He is a virtuoso in pop, rock, rockabilly, and gospel, and he stands high in the hierarchy of country, bringing his dynamite piano and violent emotion. For example, Jerry Lee Lewis can take the Jim Reeves hit "He'll Have to Go" and, using the

Jerry Lee Lewis: "I'm the greatest."

same words and music, change it into an entirely different kind of song. To see Jerry Lee Lewis in person is one of the better musical-consciousness-raising experiences of the late twentieth century.

Few writers have caught the essence of Lewis as well as reporter John Pugh did in the following article:

"He is called The Killer primarily because that is what he calls everyone else. Even so it would be an appropriate nickname—quite possibly the only appropriate nickname. Because Jerry Lee Lewis can leave you for dead at just about any game you want to play.

"Back in the mid-fifties Jerry Lee's music was something the world had never heard before. Then he was billed as 'Jerry Lee Lewis and His Pounding Piano,' and at that time that was like saying Marilyn Monroe has a nice shape. When he sat down at a piano it was like watching a karate demonstration by a man afflicted with *delirium tremens.* Dementedly pounding away, exhorting the Cool Generation to 'Shake It One Time For Me,' he was a father to, and became an overnight legend in, a music whose repercussions continue to reverberate into its third generation. Today he has toned it down—as far as he can ever be said to have toned it down—crossed over into another genre, and now lays down some of the most 'hillbilly' licks ever to grace the country-music scene.

"The pace of Jerry Lee's music may have slowed; his own pace hasn't. Following a recent show in Knoxville, Tennessee, in which he 'sent 'em on a rampage,' Jerry Lee boarded his private plane around midnight and flew to his beloved Memphis (about 400 miles). There, jumping off his plane almost before it had stopped, he hopped into a waiting limousine and sped to an after-hours club. Unscheduled to appear, he was forced up on the stage (this is like forcing a drink on Dean Martin), where he 'couldn't have knocked them any more dead if I'd used my fists.' Returning home with a dozen or so friends, he threw a party at which he was still going strong long after the sun had come up the next morning. In some fifteen to sixteen hours he was never once without a drink, and never once stopped talking or singing. The fifth of whiskey he consumed had no effect on him whatsoever. He never even burped. The furious, non-stop pace only reinforced him.

"And Jerry Lee certainly hasn't toned down his opinions. '*Elvis?* ' he explodes incredulously. 'Follow *me?* I guarantee you that if Elvis had his choice of being up in heaven right now, or coming on before me, he'd have to come on before me. There's no way Elvis can follow me. There's no way *anybody* can follow me. I've been the Greatest Live Show on Earth for the past fifteen years, and I'll keep on being the Greatest Show on Earth until they put me six feet under. And even then I might still find a way to keep hanging it in.'

"Jerry Lee came out of Ferriday, Louisiana, much the same way Elvis Presley came out of Tupelo, Mississippi, Johnny Cash came out of Dyess, Arkansas, and Carl Perkins came out of Jackson, Tennessee. His area was the richest mixture of music in America—the country, folk, and particularly indigenous Cajun of the white man, the blues and jazz of the black man. While growing up, he spent many long nights in places like Haney's Big House and Junior's Club, raptly absorbing it all. When he made his move at age twenty-one, he was ready to take on the world. The world just wasn't ready to take on him.

"In the mid-1950s music was undergoing—and, consequently, causing—an upheaval comparable to Vesuvius in all its glory. Country music and rhythm and blues had secretly married. Their offspring—which nearly devoured both parents—sprang forth not only fully grown, but demanding to head the family. By arousing, exciting, or outraging everyone who viewed or heard it, rock-and-roll got its way. And no one aroused, excited, or outraged more than the 'Memphis Mauler' himself—Jerry Lee Lewis. He was denounced as a work of the devil by his elders, and regarded as a godsend by youngsters.

" 'I don't remember much about my early days, but I know I came out jumping and I've been running ever since,' Jerry Lee recalls. 'First time I ever sat down at a piano I played a tune on it, so my father mortgaged the house to buy me a used piano. In two weeks I taught myself how to play it. I started giving shows when I was just a kid. My father would load that old piano onto his truck, we'd drive somewhere, he'd unload it, I'd give a show, we'd pass the hat, he'd load it back on again, and we'd go home and see what he had got.

" 'Then in 1956 my father and I sold thirty-three dozen eggs, got in our old car, and headed for Memphis to get an audition with Sun Records. We got there just in time to miss Sam Phillips (founder of Sun), who had gone to Nashville, and they wouldn't let me in. I told them I was going to get an audition if I had to sit on the doorstep for three weeks. Finally, Jack Clement took me in and we cut a tape. Then he told me to come back a month later to see what Sam Phillips thought.

" 'A month later I came walking in the door and Jack Clement looked up and said, "Jerry Lee Lewis! I was just fixing to call you. Sam heard the tape and wants to cut a session on you." So I cut "Crazy Arms" and "Whole Lotta Shakin' Going On." Then when the record came out, they banned it because it was "vulgar." Every radio station in the country banned it.

" 'Then one night I was doing a show in Alabama. Judd (Sam Phillips' brother) came backstage, introduced himself, and told me he was going to take me to New York, get me on national television. "Whole Lotta Shakin' " would sell a million, and break me into one of the biggest ever.

" 'So we got up there and Judd took me around to *The Steve Allen Show*. We walked in and the man there said, "Well, Judd, what can you let me have? Have you got any pictures or records?"

" 'Judd said, "No."

" 'The man said, "What have you got?"

" 'Judd said, "I got my boy here."

" 'How many records has he had?"

" 'He's had one."

" 'How long had it been out?"

" 'About seven months."

" 'How many has it sold?"

" 'About 30,000."

" 'The guy turned around to somebody else there and said, "How do you like that? Here's a salesman without a damn thing to sell." Then he said, "You got your boy, huh? What does he do?"

" 'He plays piano and sings."

" 'The man looked at Judd like he was crazy. He said, "You mean you came all the way from Memphis to show me a kid who plays piano and sings?"

" 'I just sat there blowing bubble gum, reading a funny book. I was still an innocent babe. I'd only been married twice. This guy looked at me and I looked at him. Finally he said, "Okay, kid, let's see you play piano and sing."

" 'I said, "Judd, what do you want me to do?"

" 'Judd said, "Just cut loose on 'Whole Lotta Shakin'.' "

" 'I walked over the piano, and this guy sat down and put his feet up on his desk like he was going to get a big laugh. The minute I started in on "Whole Lotta Shakin'," this guy came up out of his chair, and came creeping up on me, and got down behind me, and just crouched down there looking over my shoulder the whole time I was playing. When I finished, he said to Judd, "I'll give you $500 if you don't show him to anybody else! And bring him back first thing Monday morning. I want Steve to hear him!"

" 'We went back Monday morning, Allen heard me and said, "I want him on the show this week!" We went on that week, signed for two more appearances, and the only time Steve Allen ever beat Ed Sullivan in the ratings was when he had me on the second time.

" 'We got back to Memphis and Judd had the girl at Sun send the record to every DJ in the country, telling them that I had played it on *The Steve Allen Show*, and for them to start playing it on the radio. It started selling 50,000 to 60,000 copies a *day* on that little independent label. Then I cut "Great Balls of Fire" and it sold a million the first ten days it was out. "Breathless" and "High School Confidential" sold well over a million. Everything I put out was selling a million. I was King of the Rockers. Then I married Myra.'

"Myra Gale Lewis was Jerry Lee's third wife. She was also his thirteen-year-old second cousin. Sooner or later that was bound to mean trouble. It came in England in 1958.

"Jerry Lee: 'I stepped off the plane in London and they (the press) pounced on me. They looked at Myra and said, "Who's this, Mr. Lewis?"

" 'I said, "That's my wife."

" 'They said, "Your wife?"

" 'I said, "Yeah, and what's more, she's my cousin. And what's more, I've had two other wives and never got a divorce from any of them." That's when they started coming on strong. One paper said I had married my nine-year-old cousin, another one said it was my twelve-year-old sister . . . they had *me* confused who I'd married for a while. It got so ridiculous there were 100,000 people outside my hotel waiting to look at me. I was eating in my room and went to open a window—this was about two or three stories up—and there was a man hanging on a rope with a camera. I raised the window, drug him in, and said, "Here man, get your picture." He took his picture and I slung him out. The publicity and the crowds got so much that my promoter said, "There's no sense doing a tour after all this. Let's go home." We came back to Idlewild (Kennedy) Airport and I had a bigger reception waiting for me than Clark Gable when he was king.'

"But despite his bravado, an unforeseen disaster awaited Jerry Lee upon his return. As he tells it, Sun Records had panicked over the matter and done the biggest cut and run since Rhett Butler told Scarlett O'Hara he didn't give a damn. Jerry Lee: 'I got back home and asked Sam how "High School Confidential" was doing. He said, "It's not doing too well." I came to find out he hadn't even sampled a DJ! The record still sold a million anyway. But they were trampling each other to death at Sun looking for a place to hide. Judd had it squashed here and nobody wrote it up, but they still wouldn't stand behind me. If I had had some backing from the label, the whole thing would have blown over in three months.'

"And so, as quickly as it had begun, it was over. Jerry Lee still had a contract with Sun and he says he made them live up to their recording obligations, but he got no air-play and little retail distribution. At twenty-three years of age, and after only two years on center stage, Jerry Lee Lewis became rock-and-roll's first has-been. In a rare reflective moment, Jerry Lee said, 'It might have all been for the best. If I'd have kept going like I was back then, I'd be dead by now.'

"For all intents and purposes, however, he was dead. A change in labels—to Smash, a subsidiary of Mercury—in 1963 and Herculean efforts at a comeback produced little. His only real source of income was live shows—mostly in clubs that featured talent either on the way up or on the way down. Jerry Lee had been up.

"Trouble is, it is impossible to convince *him* of all this. He insists that despite the radio blackout his records still sold well. And, to use his favorite reiteration, 'The whole time I never quit working, never quit packing them in.' There is some truth in both these claims, but both are still exaggerations. What really kept him going all those years was his love for performing and his unshakable conviction that the Second Coming of Jerry Lee Lewis was imminent.

"A sideman who was with him in the lean days said, 'He always told me, "Stick with me, Hawk. I'm going to get back up there. If I don't get another rock hit, I'll get one in country." '

"In 1967 he made good his boast. Country music, a former fortress of constancy, was at last undergoing changes—changes not so sudden and dynamic as those that produced rock-and-roll, but just as definite, nonetheless. Country fans were getting little hard country music, and hungrily snatched at any available morsel. Jerry Lee served them a banquet fit for a king in the form of 'Another Place, Another Time,' a classic lament about an ole boy who goes down to a honky-tonk looking for a woman, finds one, thinks he is going to score, then sees her slip away for reasons never made quite clear, and is left facing ' . . . a sleepless night waiting for another place, another time.' The country DJs picked up on the record. It shot up to number one, and in one fell swoop Jerry Lee had gone from rock-and-roll purgatory to Hillbilly Heaven.

"It is ironic that Jerry Lee would stage his comeback in the music he played such a large part in almost destroying. It would seem even more ironic that he sees nothing ironic about it. But this characteristic style of reasoning greatly defines him, for he is a maze of complexities and contradictions.

"A few at random. He is literally possessed by a gigantic ego concerning his ability and talents, yet he lavishly praises nearly all other entertainers. He says he lives only to please his audiences, yet he has had some of his most angry moments with audiences he felt did not show him the proper respect. He talks with great authority about women, citing his four marriages as ample justification, yet in private moments he wonders if he really knows anything about them. His compassion knows no limits, yet to anyone who upstages him—however temporarily—he can be unbelievably base. He operates on an even, if greatly accelerated, keel, yet he can become suddenly, inexplicably, totally, and often violently irrational. He is a deeply religious person who periodically expresses misgivings concerning his boozing, wenching, hell-for-leather way of life, yet he will not, or cannot, bring himself to modify a single aspect of his character.

" 'Jerry Lee lives his life on a much larger scale than the average person—even the average show business person,' says a former sideman. 'Consequently, everything he does—the good, the bad, the indifferent—is done on a much larger scale.'

"Jerry Lee makes it plain that he has never run for cover on seeing the storm clouds brewing. 'I am what I am,' he said. 'I've always said what I wanted to say, done what I wanted to do, and been what I wanted to be. I've never tried to hide anything. Everything I've done has been out in the open. If people don't like that, then that's their problem.' But, basically, he sees himself as merely an earnest person striving to make his peace with the world, who has been beset by evil forces at every turn—and has still managed to prevail. 'I've been picked on, abused, sued, jailed, ridiculed, persecuted and prosecuted,' he said. 'But I never let it bother me. You know why? Because I beat every one of them. Besides, these people are not the real buying public. My public has always stood by me.'

"When Jerry Lee says he lives just to please his audiences he is at his sincerest. Put him in front of an appreciative audience and he is supremely happy. 'Just point me to the piano and give me my money,' he will tell promoters, 'and in fifteen minutes I'll have 'em shaking, shouting, shivering, and shacking.' It is that rare time when these are not forthcoming that all hell breaks loose. In Detroit, for example, he stopped his show, and to a couple of fans who expressed displeasure, shouted, 'Listen, Killer, if you don't like it, that door back there swings both ways.'

" 'It's been blown out of proportion,' said a former sideman. 'Out of a hundred shows, it would only happen maybe once or twice. Of course, when it did, we all wanted to fall right through the stage.'

"Jerry Lee: 'If I'm up there doing my best to entertain people, they should show some consideration and shut up, and let me entertain them. Nobody made them come to the show,

and nobody's making them stay. If they don't like it, there are exit signs all over the place. I demand respect from my audiences, and if I don't get it, I give 'em a good cussing. I'm not the only entertainer who does it, either. But I'll also sign autographs and talk to the fans, whereas a lot of performers won't. Heck, I love my audiences.'

"In what could probably qualify as a prime example of doublethink, he steadfastly maintains both positions—particularly the latter.·He is amazingly accessible to his public, enduring—even welcoming—impositions that would have any other entertainer calling for the police. Wherever he performs, his dressing room is always filled with friends and neighbors whom he knows from somewhere or other, and there is much backslapping and handshaking, much talk of mutual friends, much inquiring about the health of respective relatives and much reminiscing about former good times. Barring the need for a fast getaway, he will stay until he has answered the last question, signed the last autograph, and posed for the last picture, displaying a patience, endurance, and amiability that are utterly astounding.

"Most—if not all—of his difficulties stem from his having two different audiences: country and rock. He does, indeed, love his country audiences. With his rock audiences he is not so sure. 'His native Southern people are the ones who stayed with him when he was down,' says a friend, 'and they're the ones who rode him back up again. He's automatically accepted by them. The rock audiences always seem to have a "show me" attitude, and I don't think he likes this much.'

"All observers agree that Jerry Lee's ego is uniquely exceptional. Though everyone has some comment on it, perhaps Jack Clement's statement best sums it up.

" 'Jerry Lee—and this is true of most outstanding performers—doesn't have an ego because he's a performer; he's a performer because he has an ego, and the applause and acclaim are his way of having it constantly gratified.'

"There are, of course, other reasons. Because of his overnight fall from grace, Jerry Lee has never felt his achievements in rock-and-roll were properly honored. Even worse, he saw a former Sun artist and fellow Memphis resident

—Elvis Presley—be accorded the esteem he always perceived as being, for the most part, rightfully his. To this day it remains in his mind as a gross injustice.

"Jerry Lee: 'I told Conway Twitty one time that there have only been four stylists. The first was Al Jolson, the second was Jimmie Rodgers, the third was Hank Williams, and the fourth was Jerry Lee Lewis. By stylist I mean somebody who created his own style and his own type of music that hundreds of entertainers have tried to copy and failed, simply because they weren't that person.'

"There is also another aspect of his certitude that has never been fully understood. His ego offers him veritable life sustenance, and, more than anything else, is responsible for his being Jerry Lee Lewis. It takes a hell of an ego for a kid from Ferriday, Louisiana, to come to Memphis and *tell* them he is going to get an audition come hell or high water; it takes a hell of an ego to endure seven or eight years of oblivion and never give up; it takes a hell of an ego just to *do* some of the things he does on stage. Without this, despite everything else he has going for him, he *would* be just a guy who plays piano and sings.

"Besides, some of it—particularly that which is often displayed on stage, is an outrageous put-on. Jerry Lee decided long ago that if he were going to be so miscast when all he was trying to do was set the record straight, then he might as well play the role, and—what the heck—have a little fun doing it. This decision shows in his regal countenance, in the way he whips out his silver-plated comb and ceremoniously flicks his sideburns, and in the way he often follows a boastful statement with a knowing look or a quick, sly smile.

"What he does take seriously—to the almost total exclusion of everything else—is music. Jerry Lee is a very single-minded person, and his mind never strays far from music. If he isn't playing music, he's listening to it; if he isn't listening to it, he's talking about it. Approach him about something other than music, and he just isn't very interested.

"His knowledge of music is all-encompassing. 'He's got the most remarkable memory concerning music I ever saw,' says a former sideman. 'If he were put to the test, I think he could recall nearly every singer and every song

that has ever been recorded.' Literally obsessed by the musical past, he has acquired an inexhaustible record treasure trove, and will sit for hours totally transfixed by anything from Gene Austin to Jimmie Rodgers to Cole Porter. An original 78 by someone such as Jimmy Wakely or Margaret Whiting can render him speechless —something no other power on earth has yet been able to do. Blissfully mindless of the almost unbearable static and distortion, he regards his old records in much the same way an antique-lover regards that which most other people refer to as junk. 'Considering what they had to work with, they made better records back then, just like they made more durable, longer-lasting cars in 1942 than they do in 1972,' he says. 'Besides, this is where I get a lot of my stuff.'

"This same preoccupation with music also carries over into his personal life, dominating his every decision and action. He always carries some of his 78s on the road with him. An unostentatious person offstage, he affects little of the trappings and glamour of a celebrity, partly because of his relatively simple tastes, but more so because he feels that it would somehow adversely affect his historical significance in the musical hierarchy. 'When they look back on me,' he says, 'I want them to remember me not for all my wives, although I've had a few, and certainly not for any mansions, or high living or the money I made and spent. I want them to remember me simply for my music.'

"'People come to him all the time with business deals and propositions,' says a friend, 'and he very attentively hears them out, and then very politely turns them down, and very graciously thanks them for their time and interest. Then, as soon as they leave, he pulls out another box of 78s.' Seeking some kind of a nest egg, however, he does dabble in real estate ('It's the only thing that doesn't depreciate. Other than me'), and a pro football game—particularly one involving the Dallas Cowboys—can lure him away from his record lode. But that's about it. Anything else outside of music he has little comprehension of, less interest in, and no time for.

"Excepting his family and friends. When his mother died a year ago, he plunged into a tailspin which he took many long, hard months to pull out of. No one is certain just how many various relations he helps over rough stretches, but it is a considerable number. He was raised in a time and place where a family was an all-embracing, cohesive, loving, guiding, helping, understanding *unit*. To this day it remains the single most important influence on him, accounting for his boundless compassion, fierce loyalty, and overwhelming generosity.

"His friends come in a close second. Actually he views and treats everyone as a friend, mostly due to his innate conviviality, but also because he perceives it as his Christian duty.

" 'I was raised in the Assembly of God Church and taught to believe in the church and, even more so, the Bible,' he says, as if reciting the multiplication tables. 'The Bible teaches us two things: that everyone is equal in the eyes of God, and that we're supposed to help our fellow man in every way possible. If you're going to be a Christian, this is where you should start. You can't turn anybody down or hurt anybody, and still call yourself a Christian. You're supposed to believe in the worth and dignity of every human being, and look for every person's good points. Now, I'm not perfect; I've made my mistakes. But at least I'm trying to do that much.'

" 'I'd come back to the motel dead to the world,' says a former sideman, 'and pretty soon the phone would ring, and it'd be him, and it'd be the same thing every time. "Hey, Killer, this is Jerry. What are you doing?''

" 'I was sleeping.''

" ' "Well, hell, get out of bed and come on up and have a drink.'' Pretty soon I learned that "come on up and have a drink'' meant "you better get your ass up here, the party's starting.'' '

"And once one enters Jerry Lee's lair for a night of fun and games, there is absolutely no escaping until he is ready to call it quits, which is usually six to eight hours and a mind-boggling quantity of whiskey later. By then even his indefatigable energy has abated, and he is ready for a few hours sleep before getting up and starting the cycle over again. His private moments are rare, his introspective ones almost nil. He lives simply to live.

"The one time he tried to change his *modus operandi*, it ended in a complete flop. In the latter part of 1970, Myra Gale filed and won a

divorce suit. As is par for the course with anything involving Jerry Lee, there were all sorts of stories, rumors, charges, and counter-charges. The upshot of it all was the statement that Jerry Lee had seen the error of his ways and had turned to the church in an attempt to 'get my life in order.' He forsook cigars, whiskey, nightclubs, and young ladies not bearing his last name. This announcement came as a complete surprise, sent shock waves throughout the music world, and was the cause of endless speculation.

"It lasted about two months.

"Shortly thereafter he explained. 'Yeah, Killer, I'm back to smoking, drinking, playing in clubs, and running around with women. I sure ain't going to run around with no men. I meant it when I said it, and I was going good there for a while, but I just couldn't keep it up. I tried and failed. At least I'm man enough to admit it.'

"A new love and passage of time, however, rapidly helped soothe his tribulations to the point where several months later he was able to announce: 'In the last three or four months I've never been happier. It's the first time in twenty years that I've been really free and I'm really enjoying it.'

"Less than two months later he traded his short-lived freedom for his fourth wife. 'Best thing that ever happened to me,' he said. 'In one week I went from rags to riches.'

"Right before his recent marriage he was asked why he had such a compulsion to be married when it appeared that he was not especially suited for the ties of matrimony. 'Well, Killer, that's something I've wondered about myself, and it's one question I can't answer. I don't know if I'm a one-woman man or not.'

"Perhaps the following exchange best summarizes Jerry Lee. Recently, he was asked by an observer if there had ever been anyone like him before.

" 'Nope! Absolutely not! Never been another Jerry Lee Lewis!' came the staccato replies.

" 'Do you think there ever will be?'

" 'I certainly hope so,' came the totally unexpected response.

" 'Why?'

" 'Well, Killer,' he said, pausing to take a long puff on his cigar and ruefully contemplate his momentarily-empty glass, 'just think what a dull world this would be without a Jerry Lee Lewis in it.' "

## LINDSEY, LA WANDA

BORN: January 12, 1953, Tampa, Florida

La Wanda Lindsey, another of the country-music *wunderkinds*, made her first record when she was only fourteen years old. Born in Tampa, Florida, where her father was stationed at the air base, she moved to Savannah shortly after her first birthday and grew up in the area. "We were living in Savannah, Georgia, and my daddy and mamma had a band, and I started off singing with the band. I never knew anything else. Daddy was with the radio station there and it was country. So, I just never knew anything but country."

La Wanda Lindsey has recorded a number of hits for Chart Records: "We'll Sing in the Sunshine," "Picking Wild Mountain Berries" (a duet with Kenny Vernon), and "Partly Bill."

## LOCKLIN, HANK

BORN: February 15, 1918, McLellan, Florida
MARRIED: w. Willa Jean Murphy
CHILDREN: s. Maurice; d. Margaret, Beth

Hank Locklin, with his distinctive tenor voice, is one of Ireland's favorite singers. He returns to Ireland again and again and plays to huge crowds, and he is credited with the popularization of American country-western music on the Emerald Isle. Hank Locklin was also elected mayor of McLellan, Florida, his hometown, some years ago. When he was picking cotton as a seven-year-old boy, and working on highways for the Works Progress Administration during the Depression, he never thought he'd be a star in a foreign country, a public official, and a regular on Grand Ole Opry. All during the hard years of the Depression, he never gave up hope of becoming a professional musician. His big professional break came in 1942, when he made his concert debut at the Community House in Whistler, Alabama, followed by appearances at a number of southern radio stations. As a soldier during World War II he continued singing at camp shows, and after the war he joined the cast of *Louisiana Hayride*. Hank Locklin made the

Hank Locklin: Ireland's favorite country artist.

charts in 1949 for the first time, with "The Same Sweet Girl," followed a few years later with "Let Me Be the One." He joined Grand Ole Opry and RCA shortly thereafter, and has had top-selling hits ever since, including "Please Help Me, I'm Falling," "Geisha Girl," "Happy Journey," and numerous others. Locklin has

146

resisted the lure of Nashville. He lives in his native Florida, where he collects old victrolas, cylinder records, horse-collar mirrors, and wood stoves. Locklin occasionally buys and sells race horses, and his eighty-seven-year-old mother, who lives down the road from him, will tell any visitor how she "taught little Henry to pick the guitar."

## LONZO AND OSCAR

### Rollin Sullivan
BORN: January 19, 1919, Edmonton, Kentucky

### John Sullivan
BORN: July 7, 1917, Edmonton, Kentucky
DIED: June 5, 1967, Nashville, Kentucky

### Ken Marvin
BORN: June 27, 1924

### David Hooten
BORN: (Birth date not available)

Lonzo and Oscar have been one of country music's most successful and longest-running comedy teams. Rollin Sullivan remains the original Oscar. His brother, John, played Lonzo for many years, but he was *not* the original Lonzo. However, the Sullivan brothers are remembered by most country music fans as Lonzo and Oscar since it was this duo that charmed and entertained Grand Ole Opry audiences for many years.

John and Rollin Sullivan had toured the South as a successful brother act during the late 1930s. During a stint on a radio show on WTJS, Jackson, Tennessee, they met Ken Marvin, another musician with a knack for comedy. Marvin and Rollin got together to form the original Lonzo and Oscar team. Marvin's voice, in fact, is heard on the duo's hit recording of "I'm My Own Grandpa," although the tune was written by the Sullivan brothers. Marvin and Rollin stayed together as Lonzo and Oscar until approximately 1945, with various interruptions for war time service. Then Marvin retired, and the duo was reformed by the Sullivan brothers.

This is the team which played the Opry for years, rolling cornball gags across America

Lonzo and Oscar: Changing partners.

before *Hee Haw* was invented. Throughout this period the Sullivan brothers toured the land with various country shows and made numerous appearances on network television. In 1967 John Sullivan's death in Nashville ended the brother act.

Within months Rollin Sullivan made up his mind to continue the Lonzo and Oscar routine. He chose David Hooten as a replacement for his brother, and Lonzo and Oscar became a reality once more. Hooten, incidentally, bears a distinct resemblance to Ken Marvin. This new team continues to perform on the Opry and tour the country, as well as appearing on the *Ed*

147

*Sullivan Show,* the *Kate Smith Show,* the *Porter Wagoner Show,* and the *Bill Anderson Show,* singing old favorites like "You Blacked My Blue Eyes Once Too Often" and "I'm My Own Grandpa."

However, the new Lonzo and Oscar have become less of a comedy attraction since they signed with the General Recording Corporation, an Atlanta, Georgia, firm. Their latest appearances and record releases have featured tender ballads, Lonzo's superb mandolin playing, and Hooten's pleasant guitar strumming. But Lonzo and Oscar are still liable to set the audience howling with laughter at any moment.

## LORD, BOBBY

BORN: January 6, 1934, Sanford, Florida
MARRIED: w. Violet Mozelle
CHILDREN: s. Robert, Jr., Cabot Wesley; d. Sarah

Bobby Lord began his career as a "teen-age jazz singer" on Paul Whiteman's TV show in the early 1950s but turned to country while he was a student at the University of Tampa. A regular on the Red Foley TV show for some years and a popular star for Columbia and Hickory records, he inaugurated his own widely syndicated show in the mid-sixties. An Opry stalwart, Bobby Lord is also a practicing Christian and has written a book on country music and Christianity. His most popular hit: "Hawkeye."

## LOUDERMILK, JOHN D.

BORN: March 31, 1934, Durham, North Carolina
MARRIED: w. Gwen Cooke
CHILDREN: s. John, Ricky, Michael Phillip

Once upon a time, while trying to produce a country show, I suggested the name John D. Loudermilk to the promoter.

"Who?" he asked.

"He's out of sight," I answered, in the jargon of the mid-sixties.

"His name wouldn't draw flies," the promoter said.

"He'll be a big star," I predicted, with bravado.

I was wrong. John D. Loudermilk has not yet become a big country star, but then, he's hardly forty years old. During the past years Loudermilk has been a department-store clerk, telegraph messenger, paper boy, carpenter's helper, steam-shovel oiler, tobacco farmer, factory worker, hosiery-mill worker, janitor, shoeshine boy, lifeguard, cotton-gin worker, door-to-door Bible salesman, window dresser, sign painter, commercial artist, TV cameraman, photographer, part-time vendor at football games, and hit songwriter. He also remains a fine singer, but he dislikes touring, though he has made some personal appearances recently.

Loudermilk came from a religious family in Durham, North Carolina, and his first musical experience was beating a Salvation Army drum. By the time he was thirteen he had a local radio show under the name of Johnny Dee, playing for square dances. Eventually, after a spell at the University of North Carolina, he became a staff musician at WTVD in Durham, where he had the opportunity to sing one of his own compositions on the air. "A Rose and a Baby Ruth." Listening in was another student at UNC, George Hamilton IV, and the subsequent recording was a smash. Loudermilk moved to Nashville. "I was prepared to give the town one year. If it didn't work," Loudermilk recalls, "I was ready to go back to Durham to work in my wife's daddy's hardware store." Guitarist Chet Atkins, who also runs the RCA country-music division in Nashville, agreed to meet him; Loudermilk uttered a prayer; and the meeting was a success. He became an assistant to Atkins, eventually writing a number of hits like "Abilene," "No Playing in the Snow Today," and Stonewall Jackson's biggie, "Waterloo." Virtually everybody in Nashville has recorded Loudermilk's "Break My Mind," and there's hardly a Johnny Cash performance in which "Bad News" isn't sung. "Tobacco Road" has been recorded by at least forty artists. When Loudermilk does perform, he does it alone, with a guitar, no backup, no choruses—just John Loudermilk, on a chair, singing.

He recorded a number of albums for RCA Victor, but "Elloree," recorded for Warner Brothers, is unlike any other country album produced and well worth buying. When he is not writing or singing, or collecting old railroad dining car lamps, Loudermilk, a devoted hurricane freak, travels to sites of impending hurricanes so he can be present as they boil up on the Atlantic coast.

## THE LOUVIN BROTHERS

### Charlie Louvin
BORN: July 7, 1927, Rainseville, Alabama

### Ira Louvin
BORN: April 21, 1924, Rainseville, Alabama
DIED: June 20, 1965, Jefferson City, Missouri

Gospel music has a number of styles. The greatest exponents of what might be called electrified "bluegrass talking gospel" were Ira and Charlie Louvin during the late 1950s. They considered themselves country-western singers, but their two-tenor harmony derived more from classic Appalachia singing than from the Nashville Sound. "Love Thy Neighbor as Thyself," for example, is an original Louvin composition and is often sung now by college bluegrass ensembles. While talking of sin and Satan and fallen souls, the Louvins' songs always show hope for salvation and the feeling that there is some good in everybody. Many country scholars feel the Louvins were the finest "purist" singing team in country music history. "When we sang gospel songs," Ira Louvin said, "we meant every word." On Father's Day, 1965, Ira Louvin was killed in an automobile accident in Missouri. Four days later, tears in his eyes, Charlie played the little town where his brother died. He sang many of the songs that the brothers had sung together (a number of these have been put together on a Capitol album, "The Great Gospel Singing of the Louvin Brothers").

The Louvins were celebrated for their story songs. "Satan Is Real" was probably their most requested. It tells the story of a man in church who stops the preacher's sermon to testify that the world should fear Satan, for "Satan is real." He tells of his past life when he was a happily married man and a community leader, but Satan led him from the paths of righteousness and ruined his home and family.

There is a straightforward "artless" quality to the Louvin brothers' art. Their arrangements are almost nonexistent. They just sing in perfect harmony. Their voices, on a cut like "Make Him a Soldier," are so alike that when the

The Louvin Brothers: Only Charlie (on the right) survives.

talking parts occur, it is difficult to tell whether Ira or Charlie is speaking. After Ira died, Charlie took on a singing partner but eventually became a single, and he has recorded numerous hits for Capitol and has sung a number of duets with Melba Montgomery.

## LULUBELLE AND SCOTTY

### Lulubelle [Myrtle Eleanor Cooper]

BORN: December 24, 1913, Boone, North Carolina
MARRIED: h. Scott Wiseman

### Scotty [Scott Wiseman]

BORN: November 8, 1909, Spruce Pine, North Carolina
MARRIED: w. Myrtle Eleanor Cooper

For a quarter of a century, Lulubelle and Scotty were familiar names to thousands of country fans in the Midwest, singing every week on the *WLS National Barn Dance* from Chicago. They often sang Scott's compositions: "Mountain Dew" (which he co-wrote with Bascom Lamar Lunsford), "Between You and Me," "Remember Me," and a host of others. During the 1950s Lulubelle and Scotty appeared on Grand Ole Opry's TV show and a number of other TV variety programs. During this period Scotty kept going to school, and when he received his M.A. from Northwestern University in 1958, the Wisemans retired to North Carolina, where Professor Wiseman now teaches speech. During the late thirties, Lulubelle and Scotty starred in a number of lighthearted Hollywood musicals, including *Country Fair* and *Swing Your Partner*.

## LUMAN, BOB

BORN: April 15, 1937, Nacogdoches, Texas
MARRIED: w. Barbara
CHILDREN: d. Melissa

Bob Luman has both friends and enemies in Nashville. He definitely has a rock beat and makes no bones about the kind of country music he cares about. Nevertheless, he is on Grand Ole Opry, though to some traditionalists it is almost sacrilegious. (Wesley Rose, of Acuff-Rose Publishing Company, says, "That kind of music has no place on the Opry.")

Paul Hemphill, in his lively book, *The Nashville Sound*, writes: "Almost everybody in Nashville likes Luman. He is a little heavy around the middle, with merry blue eyes and a good word for anybody (you get the idea his 'feud' with Acuff, et al., is merely good business, like the feuds of pro wrestling). His marriage appears to be in better shape than most of those in Nashville, and he is obviously more careful about his money than the majority of country stars: although he doesn't write, and his biggest single ('Let's Think About Living,' 1960) earned only $30,000 for him, he has a sprawling home across the street from Johnny Cash's $250,000 palace on Old Hickory Lake in Hendersonville. Since he doesn't write and hasn't had the really big record sales, he has to knock himself out on the road from Boston to Sacramento to keep up with the bills.

"The biggest event in Bob Luman's life came while he was in high school in Kilgore, Texas. He had a cowboy band and was interested in entertaining, but his major interest was baseball (the following spring, after graduation from high school, he was scheduled to report to the Pittsburgh Pirates' minor league camp in Florida). All of that ended, though, when a girl in his school came to class one day and breathlessly described an entertainer she had seen the night before. 'She was really knocked out,' Luman was saying. 'She said, "You ain't gonna believe this guy." I got so interested I told my girl we were going to go, and we did. Man, I *didn't* believe it. This cat came out in red pants and a green coat and a pink shirt and socks, and he had this sneer on his face and he stood behind the mike for five minutes, I'll bet, before he made a move. Then he hit his guitar lick, and he broke two strings. Hell, I'd been playing ten years and I hadn't broken a *total* of two strings. So there he was, these two strings dangling, and he hadn't done anything except break the strings yet, and these high school girls were screaming and fainting and running up to the stage, and then he started to move his hips real slow like he had a thing for his guitar. That was Elvis Presley when he was about nineteen, playing Kilgore, Texas. He made chills run up my back. Man, like when your hair starts grabbing at your collar. For the next nine days he played one-nighters around Kilgore, and after school every day me and my girl would get in the car and go

Bob Luman: He rocked the Grand Ole Opry.

wherever he was playing that night. That's the last time I tried to sing like Webb Pierce or Lefty Frizzell.' Luman gave up his baseball dreams just as quickly as he ditched the hard country-and-western music he had been raised on, and turned his life around overnight. Shortly after that he won a talent contest and was taken on as a regular by *Louisiana Hayride* in Shreveport to replace Cash, who had just heard the call from the Opry. After recording 'Let's Think About Living' and 'Great Snowman' and a string of other records that had decent sales, plus logging some time at the clubs in Las Vegas where his rockabilly style was a smash, Luman became a regular on the Opry and moved to Nashville in 1965.

" 'I don't have anything against Acuff and those guys,' Luman said as he ordered another beer. 'They're just doing their own thing. But I think there's a place for all of these different styles in country music, and I get a little hacked off at some of those who don't like what I'm doing.' "

A lot of audiences apparently like what Luman is doing, and he's been booked at a number of clubs usually barred to country musicians. His records have consistently made the charts, but only a few, like "Let's Think About Living," have made the top ten. Luman records for Epic.

Judy Lynn: Queen of the Rodeo.

## LYNN, JUDY

BORN: April 12, 1936, Boise, Idaho
MARRIED: h. Jack Kelly

Judy Lynn is truly "queen of the rodeos," where she leads the parade (she's a real, live, honest-to-goodness western girl, so why not?) and sings and yodels quite marvelously. Often she sings her hits "Footsteps of a Fool," "My Tears Are on the Roses," and "Honey Stuff." Judy Lynn (no relation to Loretta) has had a number of awards showered on her over the years: Among them:

Queen of the Snake River Jamboree (1952)
Miss Idaho (1955)
Runner-up in the Miss America contest (1955)
Best-dressed Female Vocalist (*Pioneer* magazine, 1955)
*Billboard*'s Most Promising Female Country Vocalist (1955)

And, she's toured with Gene Autry, Eddy Arnold, Eddie Fischer (Eddie Fischer?), Rex Allen, and Elvis, and was co-host with Ernest Tubb on the first coast-to-coast Grand Ole Opry show. She now records for Amaret.

## LYNN, LORETTA

BORN: March 14, Butcher's Hollow, Kentucky
MARRIED: h. Oliver V. (Mooney) Lynn
CHILDREN: s. Jack Benny, Ernest Ray; d. Betty Sue, Clara Marie, Patsy Eileen, Peggy Jean

"Loretta Lynn can't read well enough to pass the written test for a driver's license," Pete Axthelm wrote in a cover story for *Newsweek* (June 18, 1973), "and her syntax and pronunciation are subjects of frequent jokes among her friends. ('Every time folks start tryin' to fix up my talkin',' she moans, 'it messes up my singin'.') But Loretta learned something up in that bleak hollow that few entertainers ever acquire: an indomitable strength and warmth that she transmits in every word—tender or funny, plaintive or defiant—that she sings. Others may be more polished or complex, but to her fans Loretta Lynn is the quintessential country girl."

Loretta Lynn, one of the handful of "undis-

Loretta Lynn: Mooney Lynn admires Loretta's beans.

puted queens of country music," was a mother at fourteen, a grandmother at twenty-eight. She started out washing other people's clothes and picking fruit as a migrant worker. Today she owns an entire town, and has an annual income that surpasses that of the President of the United States and probably beats that of any corporation chairman in America. She is closest to her husband, Mooney Lynn, who bought one of her pies at a church supper, and despite her young age, decided to marry her, against her parents' wishes.

Loretta Lynn described her early years to reporter Steven Fuller in a magazine interview.

" 'Well, I told my mother *who* had walked me home when I got in the house. She got all upset, and said, "Oooh, he's too old for you, and not only that, he's the meanest thing around. He's got a real bad reputation." But I never thought too much about it.

" 'Well, the next night here he comes with that jeep. What with our house settin' up on a hill, Daddy always had to pull the horse and sled up the hill in the wintertime, ya know, but he came right up that hill with that jeep and scared me to death. About two or three days later,

153

though, he got me to ride in it. Every night after that he came to see me, and we went together one month and got married the tenth day of January.

" 'That was the funniest thing you ever heard in your life. I told my mother. I says, "We're gonna git married," and she says, "No you're not." I says, "Well, why not?" She says, "You're too young." Well, Mooney, my husband—I call him "Doo"—worked in a coal mine. It was a Friday night and he'd just got a real good check. He says, "We better get married right away and not wait," 'cause he had this big check. I told him he'd have to talk to Mommy and Daddy about it and that they wasn't actin' too good about it. So he went out on the porch, and my Daddy went out on the porch, and Doo asks him and he says he'll have to ask Clara, my mother. Mommy sent him back out to ask Daddy and this went on for about an hour. He was runnin' from the porch to the bedroom, and they wasn't gonna go for it. I told him that he's gonna have to catch 'em together. So Doo was settin' in the front room when Daddy walked in off the porch and went in the bedroom. Doo went in there and said he'd like to marry me. Daddy said that I was awful young to even be thinkin' about gettin' married. Doo said he knew that, but he'd take real good care of me. Daddy made him promise not to take me very far away from home. Mommy says, "I don't want you bein' mean to her. I don't want you to whip her, ya know." Doo says, "Awww, I'll never do that." So we got married. Seven months later we moved three thousand miles away from home.'

"Loretta and Doo went to Custer, Washington, where they lived for the next eleven years. Loretta had her first child there shortly before she turned fifteen. The next one was born in Kentucky when they returned home for a short visit. Then numbers three and four were born in Washington, all before Loretta turned eighteen. Eight years after that, Loretta gave birth to twins, and thus far that's the entire family.

"In those eleven years, Mooney Lynn worked at a variety of jobs, doing construction work and busting broncs, which he had done before he'd gone into the army. Loretta raised the kids and sang them to sleep every night. Mooney thought Loretta had a pretty good voice, so he urged her to write some songs and

to try and learn the guitar. Which she did. She taught herself how to play and she wrote a song called 'I'm a Honky-Tonk Girl.' Mooney arranged for her to sing the song locally. At one of her performances, in a grange hall, a man from Vancouver heard Loretta and arranged for her to cut a single of the song. Loretta and Mooney *and* the man from Zero, the tiny Canadian label, were so poor that they did the distribution themselves.

" 'I sent the song off myself to I don't know how many disc jockeys along with a little note explaining about myself. But it went over real big 'cause the record stores were callin' up the radio stations and tellin' them to get the record off the air 'cause people were buggin' them to death about the record. They wanted to buy it and nobody had it.'

"Loretta was a local success, but the Lynns were still poor. Mooney decided that they should go out on the road and try to promote Loretta themselves. 'We went on tour drivin' from radio station to radio station in an old Mercury. We didn't have enough money to stay anywhere, so we slept in the back of the car and ate baloney and cheese sandwiches. I remember I had one good dress. When we were drivin' I'd just wear jeans or something, but when we were comin' to a radio station, I'd hop in the back seat and put on my dress. Then we'd go inside and do a radio interview. Afterwards I'd change back into blue jeans and we'd drive on to the next station.'

"The touring continued, even though Loretta wrote one local hit after another. Eventually she appeared on *The Buck Owens Show*, and finally cut a single which made the top ten in Nashville. This got her a promotional trip to Nashville, where she signed a contract with Decca Records. That was ten years and thirty albums ago.

"Today, Loretta seems to be creating her own modern-day dynasty. She and Mooney have built their own little corporate conglomerate. Besides the seven-man, one-woman organization that travels with her, she owns three publishing companies for her songs, which number in the hundreds, since she writes much of her own material. In addition, Mooney runs the Loretta Lynn Rodeo, which travels all over the world and is one of the largest rodeos in existence.

" 'There's about two hundred cowboys and

cowgirls,' Loretta explained. 'The top cowboys travel with the show just about all the time and there's all kinds of acts. The first time I ever went to a rodeo I didn't like it because there was so much time between every act. You'd sit like five minutes before anything else happened. But in our rodeo it all goes real fast; that's the only way I'd have it. It's got every act you could imagine, there's clowns and trick riders, then sometimes I do a show. Just about everything you'd want to see we got in the Loretta Lynn Rodeo.'

"Then there's a chain of Loretta Lynn Western Stores, which sell all the usual western apparel but carry an entire line of mod clothing too. Loretta loves the clothes the kids wear today and confesses she takes a 'heap of 'em' home with her every time she visits one.

"The latest addition to the Lynn realm is United Talent, Inc., a Nashville-based talent agency which specializes, naturally, in country artists. Loretta started the agency a year ago but only recently teamed up with Conway Twitty, her sometime singing partner, to make it a joint venture.

" 'I started my talent agency myself,' Loretta says, 'but in about two or three months Conway talked to Mooney, and Conway wanted to go into it with us. I wasn't very enthused about it at first, but Conway's such a nice guy, and if there's anybody I'd like to be in business with, it would be Conway. I've had it a year. Conway's been with us about five months now.'

"Recently four new recording artists were signed up by United Talent. Songwriter and singer Ray Griff, who wrote 'Patches,' is one. Also Anthony Armstrong Jones, Stu Phillips, a regular member of the Opry, and L. E. White, who has written number-one hits for both Loretta and Conway.

"Loretta's success in country music has enabled her to help two of her younger sisters and a brother get into the business.

" 'Six or seven years ago I hired my brother, Jay Lee Webb, to go on the road with me. He played lead guitar for me and drove the car we had at the time. Since then I got him on Decca Records and he's doin' quite well for himself right now. My two sisters, Peggy Sue and Crystal Bell, used to sing with me too. We all were just called the Loretta Lynn Sisters and they never had a name of their own. Then I sent

them out on their own. They didn't like it too good at the time, but I did it for their sake, not mine. Crystal sings more pop than she does country. The first record she had, I wrote for her. It was called "I Cried the Blue Right Out of My Eyes." She sold 45,000 copies of that one. Peggy does real country. She sings a lot like me. Peggy sings with her husband and she has two albums out now. Since I let her go, she hasn't done as good, but she's not worried. She works good when she goes out on stage, but she don't work with disc jockeys and write letters to them the way she should. Crystal likes to sing, but she doesn't like the travelin' and signin' autographs and meetin' people. But that's what helps. If I'm feelin' good, I'd rather sign autographs than do about anything. I think that's what keeps me goin'. Sometimes I'm feelin' bad and somebody comes up to me and says, "You've just made my night," and I get to feelin' better and better.' "

## McAULIFF, LEON

BORN: January 3, 1917, Houston, Texas

One of the great western swing steel guitar players, Leon McAuliff was part of W. Lee "Pappy" O'Daniel's Light Crust Doughboys until fellow doughboy Bob Wills lured him away to play with his new Texas Playboys. He made more than 200 recordings with Wills and 40 under his own name. In the 1950s and '60s McAuliff starred on his own TV show in Tulsa. His composition "Steel Guitar Rag" is a classic instrumental number. McAuliff has often voiced his opinion on Nashville's reluctance to accept western music, preferring the "country" designation, "and yet the influence of western music can be found in country themes, the dress of the performers, in the instrumentation and rhythm." Among the Leon McAuliff chart hits: "Panhandle Rag," "Cozy Inn," and "Shape Up or Ship Out," and the last time on the charts was in 1964 with "I Don't Love Nobody" for Capitol. McAuliff is the coauthor of "San Antonio Rose.'' He appeared in a number of western movies in the early 1940s.

# McCLINTOCK, HARRY K. [Haywire Mac]

BORN: October 8, 1882, Knoxville, Tennessee
DIED: April 24, 1957, San Pedro, California

Harry Kirby McClintock, under the name Haywire Mac, was the first recorded singing cowboy. He had a radio show on KFRC in San Francisco as early as 1925 and recorded for Victor from 1927 to 1931. McClintock was a tough old bird, full of great self-contradictory stories. I first learned about him from a magazine called *Adventure,* which featured a section called ''Songs of Trail, Mountain, and Fo'c'sle,'' edited by McClintock. I was in college in Los Angeles, and learning that McClintock lived in San Pedro, I drove down to visit him and spent a memorable afternoon listening to him sing his bawdy verses of ''Hallelujah, I'm a Bum,'' which he claims to have written, as well as ''Big Rock Candy Mountain.'' Mac wasn't too happy with treatment given to ''Big Rock Candy Mountain.'' ''They made it into a goddam kid's song,'' he complained. '''Big Rock Candy Mountain' was a song about hoboes looking for young boys, or jockers as we called 'em, to travel with them on the rails. It was a wooing song about a never-never land.'' When Mac sang about brutal railroad cops, rattling freight trains, and lonely hours, the authentic voice of experience shone through. There was nothing phony about Haywire Mac (whose work is available now on Folkways Records). I only met him that once, but he was a fantastic letter writer and I saved his letters for years, only to have them stolen from my room at the Pickwick Arms Hotel in New York in 1963, where I was living with precious few possessions when my first marriage dissolved. Mac wrote other letters. One of them was to a man named Nicholas, who presented it to Folkways Records:

''I made first waxing of such songs as RED RIVER VALLEY, JESSE JAMES, SAM BASS, CHISHOLM TRAIL, WHEN THE WORK'S ALL DONE THIS FALL, COWBOY'S LAMENT, BURY ME NOT ON THE LONE PRAIRIE, TRAIL TO MEXICO and many others. I had plunked a guitar and warbled my ditties for many years in cowtowns and mining camps from Bisbee to Nome and I added to my repertoire whenever possible.

''In April, 1925, I got my big break. I was handed a whole hour on radio K-F-R-C, San Francisco, Monday through Saturday. The program was aimed at the children and its immediate success surprised hell out of me—and everybody else.

''There never was a kid that didn't like cowboys and Indians and the daddies of my youthful audience had nearly all knocked around this western country in their own youthful days.

''Some Indian friends dropped in occasionally and sang their own songs to the thump of a knuckle-drum. There was Tall Pine, a Sioux from the movie lots, Joe Longfeather, a tall handsome Blackfoot who was selling automobiles, Silver Cloud, a Laguna and a copper smith in the Santa Fe railroad shops and Evening Thunder, a Pima who was a pretty good middleweight pugilist.

''I had written a few hobo songs in my rambling days and the radio listeners liked them too. I was signed by Victor in 1927 and was under contract for four years.

''Well—maybe you remember what things were like in 1931. All the phono companies quit recording and drew on their 'backlogs' for a couple of years.

''Now for the autobiog you asked for. Born in Knoxville, Tenn., October 8, 1882. Was a 'boy soprano' in choir of St. John's Episcopal church until voice changed.

''Ran away from home to join Gentry Bros. Dog and Pony Show—at age 14. When season ended I hoboed to New Orleans. Was lucky enough to meet Captain and owner of a small stern-wheel steamer that was laid up for the winter. The old boy was glad to have a trustworthy person to leave aboard when he stepped ashore to catch up with his drinking. I got comfortable quarters and most of my meals.

''One night I edged into a waterfront saloon where the crew of a British steamer were filling themselves with beer and the evening with song —a good old custom that still survives among the limeys. Someone called on me for a song and I obliged. I scored a hit. I sang, it seemed, for hours. I'll never know how I got back to the boat but in the morning I shook something like three bucks in nickels, dimes and quarters out of my pockets. I had made a discovery that shaped my life. No one who can sing need ever go hungry.

"When I hit the road again in the spring I faced the world with confidence, movies, juke boxes, radio and TV were far in the future and even a ragged kid, singing without accompaniment, could pick up the price of bed and breakfast in almost any saloon, anywhere.

"Came the war with Spain. I latched on to a troop train bound for Chicamauga Park, near Chattanooga, Tenn. Hired by a hustling circulation manager I built up a newspaper route, and as I ate at army chow lines and slept in the hay at the supply base, I had no expenses and I prospered.

"Army teamsters and packers were civilian employees in the Army of that day. I was fascinated by the packers, a bunch of tough, competent westerners, and I hung around with them until I was a pretty good hand myself. It was claimed that Army chow killed hundreds of soldiers that summer but I thrived on it. And in the autumn of 1898 I was hired as a full-fledged buck packer for the Quartermaster Corps and shipped to the Philippines.

"For two years I helped freight ammunition and rations to the troops beyond reach of the wagon trains. The going was rugged at times; we were frequently under fire and we carried Colt 45's for defense. But we figured that we were far better off than the soldiers; *we always ate* and we drew fifty bucks per month instead of the $15.60 of the buck private.

"I was shipped to China and hiked from Tientaing [Tientsin] to Peking with the Allied Relief Expedition, composed of American, British, Russian, French Colonial, German and Japanese units. Something like 22,000 men were in the outfit and 10,000 were Japs. . . ."

# McCLINTON, O. B.

BORN: April 25, 1940, Senatobia, Mississippi
MARRIED: w. Jo Ann
CHILDREN: s. Drexel

O. B. McClinton followed Charley Pride and Stoney Edwards as a black entry in the country-music sweepstakes. His first interview went to Carol Offen of *Country Music*:

O. B. McClinton was inevitably compared at first with Charley Pride, but McClinton is creating his own strong following.

" 'I was brought up believing that only white folks sang country and western music,' he explained. Although he came from a middle-class family, not very typical of blacks in Mississippi, his parents' fears were very typical. 'My mother was a little black lady from Mississippi. She couldn't see the white folks accepting me singing white folks' music.'

"So Obie did most of his singing 'behind closed doors,' when no one was around. He lost a lot of odd jobs after he left home in his teens, 'because they always found me singing instead of working.' When he decided to try a career in music after graduating from Rust College in Holly Springs, Mississippi, it was in rhythm and blues, not country. But it didn't go very well.

" 'Hard as I tried, it just wasn't me. You know, when black people used to ask me, "Don't you like soul?" I'd say, "Yeh, I like it, but it won't sound like soul when I sing it." ' "

"Obie had tried to cut a rhythm and blues record on and off for ten years. 'They almost convinced me I couldn't even sing,' he recalls with a laugh. He discovered that even though he couldn't sing it, he was good at writing it, so he turned his attention toward songwriting and also worked as a disc jockey on WDIA in Memphis. It was only when he decided to stick to the kind of singing he knew best that the doors began to open for him on Music Row.

"While he was in the Air Force in Okinawa in '67, a friend brought him a record album and told him he was 'in for a shock.' 'He knew how much I loved country music,' Obie explained, ' 'cause he always heard me singing songs by Merle Haggard and Charley Pride—even though I didn't know it was Charley then. He played me this record without letting me see the cover; it had songs on it like "Snakes Crawl at Night." When he showed me the cover, I really couldn't believe my eyes. I was like the lady who saw Charley at a concert for the first time and he could hear her squeal, "He is!" '

"Obie decided right then and there that if Charley Pride could make it, so could he.

"He came back from overseas, made some demo tapes, and made the rounds of country producers. Since he wanted to get 'a real true opinion' of his abilities, he told producers that the artist on the tapes was a buddy he was stationed with in South Carolina. 'He's got a real unique sound,' a producer told him. 'You think you could get him over here to talk to me?' Obie decided to have a little fun with him. 'Sure I probably could,' he told him. 'One thing that might surprise you he's black.'

" 'Really, no kidding?'

" 'Yeh, in fact, he's about as black as I am,' Obie told him.

"But that's as far as it went at the time. O. B. McClinton apparently wasn't ready yet. He was busy turning out R&B hits for artists like James Carr and Otis Redding. Later, he ran into Al Bell, executive vice-president of Stax Records, when he was in Muscle Shoals, Alabama, and played some tapes for him. Bell liked what he heard and made Obie an offer. This one, he said, he couldn't refuse. He would be Stax's first country artist, on their new Enterprise label. That was in January '71.

"Obie's first album, 'O. B. McClinton Country,' was one he'd rather forget. 'As far as I'm concerned, I've only had one album,' he says quite seriously, referring to the second. Obie produced the second album himself, along with Tommy Strong. The difference is apparent.

" 'A lot of people have asked if that was really me on that first album. If I had continued like that, the first album would've been my last, for sure. It just wasn't the real O. B. McClinton.'

"The *real* O. B. McClinton has a deep rich voice and an upbeat style. He likes variety in his music and the new album includes both love ballads and fast tempo numbers, plus two novelty tunes. Onstage he likes to move—correction, *dance*—to the music.

"It was getting close to showtime and Obie had to leave.

"When I saw him later, the spotlight was onstage as the MC gave a brief introduction to an 'up and coming star' on Stax Records. Just offstage, a figure in a white suit was shadow boxing in the darkness and a few stifled giggles could be heard from nearby.

" 'And now, would you please welcome . . .'

"The figure leaped onto the stage.

" 'Ladies and gentlemen,' said O. B. McClinton, 'the rest of this evening's show is brought to you live—and in living color.' He went right into his number, 'Don't Let the Green Grass Fool You' and the audience loved every minute.

"No doubt about it, that was the *real* O. B. McClinton."

## McCOY, CHARLIE

BORN: March 28, 1941, Oak Hill, West Virginia
MARRIED: w. Susan
CHILDREN: s. Charlie, Jr.; d. Ginger

The sideman of sidemen, Charlie McCoy has brought fame and glory to the previously unacclaimed heroes of the Nashville sound by stacking up hit after hit with his solo instrumental albums and award after award from various associations. He is probably the only country instrumentalist who has ever had four consecutive LPs at the top of the charts. And for two years in a row, he's walked off with the Country Music Association's award for Instrumentalist of the Year.

Charlie McCoy: A musician's musician.

When Charlie McCoy started out in the music business, he was hoping to go solo—but as a singer, not an instrumentalist. What changed his mind? "Well, I had nine records flop in a row. That'll do it."

He arrived in Nashville in '59 to audition for producers, but at the time he was singing and playing rock-and-roll, and as he recalled later, was "completely bombed out." So he went back to college in Florida, still thinking about the Nashville sessions he'd seen. A year later he heard that Johnny Ferguson was looking for a guitar player, so he packed up and headed for Nashville only to find that he'd arrived too late. But Ferguson did need a drummer, so "I ran out

and bought a set of drums and hired on." He learned to play them while working with the group—"probably the most frightening and worst musical experience of my life."

McCoy went to work for Stonewall Jackson as a drummer and soon began doing sessions as a harmonica player. "This was when I really began getting into country music and out of drumming. It was a challenge," Charlie says, "since no one had figured out how to make a harp fit into hoe-down- and fiddle-type tunes." Besides harp, Charlie plays vibes, organ, guitar, and bass on sessions he's booked on.

He signed with Monument Records (his present label) in '63 but continued to work in rock

159

groups on and off. In the late sixties he began making his own solo albums as an instrumentalist. His career has been uphill all the way since then.

## MACON, UNCLE DAVE [David Harrison Macon]

BORN: October 7, 1870, Smart Station, Tennessee

DIED: March 22, 1952, Readyville, Tennessee

It was more than twenty years ago, but I remember it well—my first visit to Grand Ole Opry. Pee Wee King and Red Foley were there as well as the Duke of Paducah and Eddy Arnold. There was also a very old man, wearing a beat-up hat and carrying three banjos. He was Uncle Dave Macon, and even at eighty years of age, he was able to hold his audience, handling his banjo the way a monkey handles a peanut. His voice was weaker than when I had heard him on radio as a child, but he still sang, told stories, preached, and picked with virtuosity. And Dave Macon was the chief singer of Grand Ole Opry before the coming of Roy Acuff.

David Harrison Macon grew up in post–Civil War Nashville. His parents owned a boardinghouse which catered to theatrical people, and young Dave learned songs, stories, and instrumental techniques from the vaudeville performers who stayed there. But he didn't plan to become a professional entertainer himself. Instead he went into the hauling business: The Macon Midway Mule and Wagon Transportation Company. He ran the business, profitably, until World War I. (The company is immortalized in his recording of "From Earth to Heaven.") Macon had always performed—but for free. A farmer who wasn't a favorite of Macon's asked him to perform at a party, and Macon,

Uncle Dave Macon: Uncle Dave said it all.

"just to be ornery," asked a $15 fee. The farmer surprised Macon by paying on the spot, and a talent scout for the Loew theater circuit, who happened to be a guest at the party, convinced Macon to do a one-nighter in Birmingham for $35. He never returned to the hauling business. In 1926 he joined Grand Ole Opry. He was fifty-six years old, and brought with him to commercial country music the skills he'd picked up in vaudeville and minstrel shows. "He also brought a wide variety of complex frailing and picking styles which modern banjoists might well envy," country music historian Bill C. Malone writes. Ralph Rinzler, another critic, says: "With the exception of the Carter Family, Uncle Dave preserved more valuable American folklore through his recordings than any other folk or country performer." He recorded songs he learned from white and black river workers and haulers he'd known personally. "Way Down the Old Plank Road" is one of the best chain-gang songs, and his "Buddy, Won't You Roll Down the Line" treats the bitter labor upheavals in Tennessee in the 1880s, in which the workers condemned the use of convict labor in the coal mines. Uncle Dave often appeared with a popular group called The Fruit Jar Drinkers. Roy Acuff is credited with saying, "When Uncle Dave died at the age of eighty-two, a bit of America died with him, and certainly part of the Opry." He was elected to the Country Music Hall of Fame in 1966.

## MADDOX, ROSE [Roseea Arbana Brogdon]
BORN: December 15, 1926, Boaz, Alabama

During the 1940s and early '50s, Rose Maddox and her brothers Cal, Henry, Fred, and Don were billed as "the most colorful hillbilly band in the land." The Maddox Brothers and Rose affected gaudy, spangled costumes and performed in a strident, highly emotional, traditionally "hillbilly" style, suggestive of the emotional pitch of gospel singing at a fundamentalist camp meeting. The brothers turned out a number of hit records for King, Columbia, and Capitol. Among their successes: "Tramp on the Street," "Philadelphia Lawyer," and "Gathering Flowers for the Master's Bouquet." In the early sixties, Rose Maddox teamed with Buck

Owens to produce a number of successful duets —"Loose Talk" and "Mental Cruelty" among them.

## MAINER, J. E.
BORN: July 20, 1898, Asheville, North Carolina
MARRIED: w. Sadie Gertrude McDaniel
CHILDREN: s. J. E., Jr., Glen, Earl, Charles; d. Carolyn, Mary

The folk-music revival of the early 1960s brought a number of old-timey country performers out of hiding, among them J. E. Mainer and his Crazy Mountaineers, who with the Carter Family and Gid Tanner and his Skillet Lickers are considered almost "holy" by bluegrass fans.

Country-music historian Bill C. Malone writes: "J. E. Mainer was yet another country entertainer who came out of a textile mill environment and, until he became a professional entertainer in 1932, music for him was never more than an amateur diversion, although he earned a modest reputation in western North Carolina as a consistent winner at fiddlers' conventions. In 1932 J. E., Wade, an old friend and guitarist named Daddy John Love, and Claud (Zeke) Morris began performing over WBT in Charlotte, North Carolina, as J. E. Mainer's Crazy Mountaineers, a name inspired by their first sponsor: the Crazy Water Crystals Company, whose Charlotte representative, J. W. Fincher, was a consistent employer of hillbilly talent. Although the personnel of the Mainer organization changed from time to time (eventually including Homer Sherrill, Steve Ledford, and two of Zeke Morris' brothers, Wiley and George) the four original members remained the nucleus of the group.

"The Mainer repertory, first recorded on Bluebird in 1934, included an amazing number of traditional songs, including many zestful fiddle breakdowns such as 'Run Mountain' and 'What'll I Do With the Baby-O?' The Mainer group, performing with great gusto and abandon characterized by whoops and hollers, evoked a tangy backwoods atmosphere while they ranged from raucous novelty tunes to southern gospel songs. Although they featured many vocal offerings—such as 'John Henry' (a well-done version of Uncle Dave Macon's earlier rendi-

161

tion) and the influential 'Maple on the Hill' (performed by Wade Mainer and Zeke Morris) —Mainer's Mountaineers remained primarily an instrumental organization. For the student of folk music the Mainer organization's extensive traditional repertory and perpetuation of old-time country fiddling marks them as one of the most important groups in the country-music history.''

## MANDRELL, BARBARA

BORN: December 25, 1948, Houston, Texas
MARRIED: h. Kenneth Dudney
CHILDREN: s. Matt

Barbara Mandrell, five feet tall, weighing ninety pounds, and cute as a button, cuddled next to the Teddy Bear Girl, Barbara Fairchild, on a hill outside of Nashville, where they were gathered to pose for the cover of *Country Music* magazine. Barbara Mandrell laughed, pulled up the leg of her bell bottoms. "Can I show you a little leg?" she said, smiling. "That's all I have you know, a little leg."

"I was born in Houston, Texas, on Christmas Day, 1948," she told writer John Fergus Ryan in an interview for a magazine article. "My family moved a lot and I've lived in a lot of places, but I grew up in Oceanside, California. My father was the owner of a music store and my mother was a music teacher. I learned to read music before I could read English.

"I could play the saxophone, the steel guitar, and the banjo by the time I was in the fifth grade. When I was in the sixth grade they used to get me out of school to play with the high school band for contests and things like that.

"I was just eleven when I made my first public appearance. It was at the Palmer House in Chicago. I played the steel guitar at a musical instruments sales convention. I don't call that my first professional job because I didn't get paid for it. My first professional job came right after that when I went on *The Joe Maphis Show* at the Showboat in Las Vegas.

"I was really too young to even be allowed in the place. I had a certain path I was supposed to follow to get to my dressing room and to the stage. I wasn't supposed to go anywhere else in the club. I didn't get into any trouble, though. I did what I was supposed to. Besides, I had my Dad with me and he took care of me.

"After that, I was on the *Town Hall Party* TV show in Los Angeles. That was *some* experience! That show was four hours long and filmed live!

"By then, my family was living in Oceanside, California, and that's where you could say I spent most of my childhood. I was Miss Oceanside when I was sixteen. I toured with *The Johnny Cash Show* and was on *The Red Foley Show.*

"My family had a band then, Mom, Dad, my two sisters, Louise and Irlean, and me. We were called the Mandrells and we made two trips to the Far East, to Korea and Vietnam.

"I've had two teachers, besides my mother. One was Mr. A. R. Lambson, who was the high school choir director in Oceanside, and all I had from him were group singing lessons, and then there was Norman Hamlet, who was a family friend in California. He used to come to visit when I was just a little girl and he taught me to play the steel guitar. He plays steel with Merle Haggard now.''

When she was eighteen, Barbara married Kenneth Dudney, who had been drummer with the Mandrells. He was then an ensign in the navy, in flight training, and she was just getting ready to graduate from high school.

They got married two weeks before her graduation so that they could be together before she went back to the Far East on another tour.

"After my husband went overseas with the navy (he is now a pilot for Governor Winfield Dunn of Tennessee)—I was about eighteen at the time—I more or less retired from show business after having been a professional entertainer for seven years. I moved to Nashville because my parents were living here. I was through with show business, but the temptation was too much. I got a two-week job appearing at a place called The Black Poodle in Printers' Alley—it's called something else now—and after two nights I had six offers of recording contracts, three from major companies. I signed with Billy Sherrill of Columbia Records because I knew he was a winner.''

Barbara's sister Louise is married and lives in Texas. Her sister Irlean, age seventeen, still lives at home, is finishing high school by correspondence and special tutor, and travels with

Barbara Mandrell: Loves to sign autographs.

*The Barbara Mandrell Show* as drummer in the band.

"*The Barbara Mandrell Show* consists of me, my Dad, Irlean, and sometimes Momma and the three members of my band: Buddy Leach on guitar—Buddy just got married and we had to leave on a tour the morning after his wedding—Rick Boyer on the bass, and Julian Earl Tharpe on the steel. Julian is president of the Nashville Steel Guitar Players Club.

"We travel three weeks out of every month. If I'm making a long trip away from home, I take my son, Matt, with me.

"In our act, my dad and I do a little comedy. He kids me and things like that. For instance, I sometimes wear a purple jump suit and when he sees me he does a double take and says, 'She looks like a ninety-pound grape!'

"I spend so much of my time on the bus. I catch up on my sleep, I answer my fan mail, and I do my own hair. I have to do it every day.

"But it's all worth it! I love to entertain live audiences! I'm not just a singer! I'm an entertainer! That's why I make records, to make it possible for me to meet people in person and have live audiences.

"I love to sign autographs and meet my fans. Sometimes I'm the only one in the show who will come out afterward and sign autographs. I feel funny, sometimes, coming out by myself, but those fans don't let you feel funny long. I just love it when some little boy asks, 'Can I hug your neck?'

"Coming down after a show is what's hard. I get excited, keyed up, doing my act. Afterwards, I've got to come down. I can come down easy enough if I can just go somewhere and sit down and drink a Coke and rest for a few minutes.

"When we travel, my family and my band, we're tame. Nothing wild ever goes on in this bus! I won't even let my band members wear blue jeans while we travel because you can't tell a nice pair from a ratty pair. When we get out at truck stops to eat, I want us to look like true professionals. I don't allow drinking of any sort when we're on tour. I won't even let my band have as much as one beer before a concert. If a fan smells one glass of beer on your breath, as far as he's concerned, you're drunk. Musicians have enough bad image to overcome as it is.

"I won't let them smoke on stage, either. Not even in the wings. Nothing looks worse to me than to see someone on stage or waiting in the wings smoking.

"My rules make it hard sometimes to get good musicians. We never practice or rehearse. When we have a new song to learn we just run through it while we're riding until we get it down. That's the way we learned 'The Midnight Oil.' We just got together in the back of the bus and went over it until we had it.

"When I go in for a recording session, I have no idea what I'm going to record. All the songs I record are selected by Billy Sherrill, my producer at Columbia Records. And I don't rehearse, either. I go in cold, after maybe five minutes looking at the music. That's the way Billy wants it. No rehearsal. Just record them the first time I sing them."

It apparently works, since she's had numerous songs on the charts since her debut, the most current being "Midnight Oil." Barbara Mandrell often sings in duet with David Houston.

## MAPHIS, JOE AND ROSE LEE

### Joe Maphis
BORN: May 12, 1921, Suffolk, Virginia

### Rose Lee Maphis
BORN: December 29, 1922, Baltimore, Maryland

THEIR CHILDREN: s. Jody and Dale; d. Lorrie

Joe and Rose Lee Maphis were among the most popular performers of country music during the post–World War II years. Like many country stars, Rose began early. By the time she was fifteen she had her own program in Maryland, *Rose of the Mountains.* Joe was a mainstay on a number of midwestern "hayride" shows. When he married Rose, they moved to California, where they were featured on Cliffie Stone's *Hometown Jamboree,* and then were regulars on *Town Hall Party.* They recorded for a number of companies, composed background music for several TV series, and backed a number of superstars like Rick Nelson and Tex Ritter. For a time they traveled the country circuits and earned a modicum of fame, but their old-timey approach hasn't caught on with the more sophisticated country fans. Few of their records reached the charts, and lately they haven't been heard from much. It's reported that they are living in California.

## MILLER, JODY

BORN: November 29, 1941, Phoenix, Arizona

Jody Miller, pretty as a western sunset, all buttons and bows, and improving with every record, won a Grammy for her "Queen of the House" in 1965 and has been consistently professional ever since. "Jody Miller is most certainly a top-ranked major leaguer," critic Robert Adels writes. "Because her records never throw you any curves, they never fail to knock you out. She's at least Queen of Consistency—

Jody Miller: Many observers believe she is only beginning to receive the full acclaim that her talents have long merited.

and that's no title to sneer at." Jody Miller grew up with music. She has four singing sisters and her father was a fiddler. When the Miller family moved to Oklahoma, Jody and two friends formed a group called The Melodies and worked steadily at local clubs. Aiming at a musical career in California, Jody Miller left Oklahoma for Los Angeles, but an auto accident only twenty days after she arrived sent her to the hospital with a broken neck. "I didn't think I'd survive," Jody recalls, "but I did, and I went home." Folk singer Tom Paxton had a popular show in Oklahoma City and he asked Jody to make a guest appearance. She did, and was a success. When she was fully recuperated, she began singing, and playing the ukulele, at clubs all over Oklahoma. One night when she was guesting at The Jester, in Norman, the Limelighters dropped in after their own appearance nearby, liked Jody, and convinced her to try Hollywood once more. Actor Dale Robertson liked her singing, brought her to Capitol, and they let her record a single, "He Walks Like a Man," which was a country-flavored pop hit in 1964. This was followed by "Queen of the House" and a fine career in country music. Jody Miller lives in Oklahoma part of the time and summers in Ruidoso, New Mexico, where she seriously raises quarter horses. Epic is her label.

## MILLER, ROGER

BORN: January 2, 1936, Fort Worth, Texas
MARRIED: w. Leah Kendrick
CHILDREN: s. Roger, Jr.

"Roger is uncomfortable most of the time," his friend William Price Fox, Jr. (author of the novel on country music *Ruby Red*), reports. "It's as if his skin is too tight for him. He can spot insincerity from twenty yards. He is used to it. He is sad about it. 'That girl smiles too much ... no one's that happy. Maybe her brain's been turned.' Fox says that Miller's coterie is a "strange mixture of beards, frauds, and disc jockeys, and silent staring Texans just passing through." Miller claims that "everybody's my best friend. There's so many stickers on my windshield I can't even see out. Man, I ain't got time to breathe."

In 1965 Roger Miller's "King of the Road" took the world by storm. There was no doubt

Roger Miller: He's calmed down with age.

Bill C. Malone, "eventually made him the leading exponent of that instrument in country music. His style, which has changed greatly through the years and is largely the result of his own improvisation and experimentation, was initially based on fiddle styles. In his mandolin playing, Monroe tried to emulate the continuous flowing notes of the fiddle, but he was always an experimentalist and improvisor and his style became jazzier as his commercial career progressed."

In 1927 Bill's brothers Birch and Charlie organized a band and asked him to join them. For three years they appeared throughout the South and Midwest, and then they joined station WWAE in Hammond, Indiana (Monroe has always liked Indiana and runs a country-music park at Bean Blossom). Birch quit the group before Charlie and Bill began recording as the Monroe Brothers. From 1936 to 1938 they recorded sixty songs for Bluebird, both gospel and country, "that in style of performance stand as important precursors of modern bluegrass style," says Malone. Their hard-driving style served as an inspiration to scores of future bluegrass musicians. Featuring only Bill's mandolin and Charlie's guitar, the Monroe Brothers were smaller than most contemporary country bands. "Many of the elements of bluegrass music—the high harmony singing (performed by Bill), the bass guitar runs, the hard mandolin style—could already be heard." During these years Bill Monroe always sang harmony; he didn't sing solo until he had his own band on Grand Ole Opry in 1939.

In 1938 Charlie and Bill parted ways, each forming his own band. Bill Monroe called his group The Bluegrass Boys, never realizing that he'd coined a generic phrase. The original Bluegrass Boys included Cleo Davis, Art Wooten, and Amos Garin. The alumni of the Bluegrass Boys have included Lester Flatt, Earl Scruggs, Don Reno, Gordon Terry, Carter Stanley, Mac Wiseman, Jimmie Martin, and Sonny Osborne.

Until 1945 the banjo was conspicuously absent from the Bill Monroe unit. In 1942 David "Stringbean" Akeman joined the group, but his banjo was used for rhythmic purposes and played no prominent role. But when Earl Scruggs joined Monroe, he brought with him the sensational technique that brought the five-string banjo back into the fore, and it has been a major lead instrument in bluegrass ever since.

Bill Monroe was elected to the Country Music Hall of Fame in 1970.

## MONTANA, PATSY [Rubye Blevins]
BORN: October 30, 1914, Hot Springs, Arkansas
MARRIED: h. Paul Rose

Patsy Montana was the first female country singer to record a song selling more than a million records ("I Want to Be a Cowboy's Sweetheart"—1936). She was a mainstay of the *WLS National Barn Dance* from Chicago, remaining on the show for more than twenty-five years. Patsy Montana is considered one of the best yodelers in country-music history. She retired from show business in 1959, though country-western buffs still collect her records.

Patsy Montana: "I Want to Be a Cowboy's Sweetheart."

## MONTANA SLIM  see CARTER, WILF.

## MONTGOMERY, MELBA

BORN: October 14, 1938, Iron City, Tennessee

MARRIED: h. Jack Solomon

What a wonderful southern name it is: Melba Montgomery. Cornelia Wallace told me she has been a fan of Melba's ever since they once sang together in some kind of country show in Europe. I remember the great country duets of George Jones and Melba Montgomery ("We Must Have Been Out of Our Minds") and the big Montgomery hits of the early sixties: "Hall of Shame" and "The Greatest One of All," with Melba's genuine country phrasing and odd use of the dobro guitar. Now, after some years of quiet and motherhood, and living in Florence, Alabama, Melba's back with a new label, Elektra, and a big hit, "Wrap Your Love Around Me." A few days after the record was released, more than 6,000 singles were sold in Atlanta in one day. It was Melba's first recording in eighteen months. Melba and her guitar-playing husband, Jack Solomon, wrote "Wrap Your Love Around Me." Peter Drake produced it, and the Elektra officials feel Melba will catapult back to country queendom on the song. (She was named Most Promising Female Vocalist by the Country Music Association in 1963.) Melba Montgomery looks like a queen—with regal Tudor cheekbones and long, glistening Plantagenet hair. She could easily play Mrs. Macbeth or the strongest daughter of King Lear. There is a real strength—and warmth—in Melba Montgomery. She was raised on farms in Tennessee and Alabama, always wanted to sing, and in 1958 entered the Pet Milk amateur contest in Nashville. She won the contest and a job as part of the Roy Acuff's Smoky Mountain Boys. After four years, she signed with H. W. "Pappy" Dailey, the veteran record executive then working for United Artists, and a music-hungry public has been grateful ever since.

Melba Montgomery: Looks like royalty.

## MORGAN, GEORGE

BORN: June 28, 1925, Waverly, Tennessee
MARRIED: w. Anastasia Paridon
CHILDREN: s. Matthew; d. Candy Kay, Bethany Bell, Liana Lee, Loretta Lynn

George Morgan started right at the top, at the age of twenty-three, with a superhit called "Candy Kisses" (the biggest hit of 1949), and he joined Grand Ole Opry right away. Not only was George Morgan's version of the song in the top ten, but Eddie Kirk, Elton Britt, and Cowboy Copas all had successes with his composition and the royalties poured in—Morgan was the country man of the year. Within the next two years he kept on the top of the charts with "Crybaby Heart," "Please Don't Let Me Love You," "Rainbow in My Heart," and "Room Full of Roses." Although George Morgan has continued recording, his career seems to have leveled out. After a long association with Columbia he left in the mid-sixties, and has since recorded for Starday, Stopp, and Decca. I listen to old George Morgan records from time to time. They're good, and it's not too late for him to make a big hit again.

## MULLICAN, MOON

BORN: March 27, 1909, Corrigan, Texas
DIED: January 1, 1967, Beaumont, Texas
MARRIED: w. Eunice

Moon Mullican was one of the great country pianists, utilizing a two-finger, right-hand style of playing that earned for him, during his successful career, the title "king of the hillbilly piano players." He sang and played for King, Decca, Starday, and a number of minor labels. He toured with a number of great country artists including Hank Williams, Jimmie Davis, Ernie Ford, and Red Foley. His compositions include the superhits "Jole Blon," "Jambalaya," "I'll Sail My Ship Along," and "Sweeter Than the Flowers." He died of heart failure in Beaumont, Texas, in 1967.

## MURRAY, ANNE

Anne Murray is yet another Nova Scotian (Hank Snow and Wilf Carter are two of the others) who is carving a niche in country music. Often billed as "the Singing Sweetheart of Canada," or ". . . here she is, Miss Snowbird herself," Anne Murray is vocally displeased with her peaches-and-cream image. "Mine has been the wholesome-girl-next-door, apple-cheek-Annie thing," she told a Canadian audience (which included Prime Minister and Mrs. Pierre Trudeau), "and I want you people to know that under these clothes and behind this facade, this body is a mass of hickeys."

Anne's public personality comes from several factors. She grew up with five brothers and a minimum of emotional discomfort in Nova Scotia, and graduated from college as a physical education teacher. "I feel totally liberated," she told *Rolling Stone*'s Judith Sims. "I have no reason to burn my bra; I've just never had any problems." Moreover, she *looks* healthy, with her blonde hair, blue eyes, and robust figure. "People think I'm a goody-good because I look that way. I'd like to shock them now and then, just to make them realize that I'm normal." She also has refused to "do the show-biz number." Anne Murray lives in Toronto. She won't move to southern California or Nashville, despite the obvious business advantages. And she chooses "unknown" Canadian songwriters for her albums. Moreover, she is nonchalant about her career: "If another record happens, it does. If not, we'll get on to something else. Some groups get to the point where they have to make it. They start treading on toes and screaming at people. But I figure, what do I need with another gold record. I already have one. I've done that already. It sure is easy to live with yourself that way."

Her singing career started when she needed money for a car and auditioned for *Sing-Along Jamboree*, a Canadian TV show. She got the job for the summer, but Brian Ahern (now her producer), who was musical director of the show, insisted that she quit schoolteaching and sing full-time. "I thought he was crazy," Anne told Judith Sims. "Singing was something you did in the bathtub and around bonfires." Nonetheless, she cut a record for Arc, a Canadian company. Capitol heard it, and "Snowbird"

Anne Murray: Wants to retire at thirty and make babies.

resulted the next year, followed by the gold record she is so blasé about, and then *The Glen Campbell Show.* In Canada, Anne Murray isn't usually called a country singer, though the Nashville publicity is making them more aware of her in that category. "The guys in my band can play country music, pop, jazz, anything," she says. She has just hired the legendary Lenny Breau as guitarist. She sings in an earthy, sometimes breathlessly husky style, which is popular with audiences. "I don't care much about clothes," she says. On stage she's barefoot and usually wears shirts and pants. "I'm there to sing, not to do a fashion show. I guess I want people to accept me for what I am. I'm not a square and I'm not a freak. I'm an ordinary girl who has drives, ambitions, and desires like everybody else. I mean, nobody could be quite as good and straight as I'm sometimes made out to be."

Anne Murray is a beer drinker and says she'll quit the business at thirty to get married and have children because a career and marriage don't mix. Those are famous last words, especially for a potential superstar.

# N

## NELSON, RICK

BORN: May 8, 1940, Teaneck, New Jersey
MARRIED: w. Kristin Harmon
CHILDREN: s. Matthew, Gunnar; d. Tracy

Rick Nelson, who grew up before our eyes, playing himself on his parents' television program for fourteen years, has become one of the steadiest-selling artists on the country-music charts. No wonder. If country music is as American as apple pie, *The Adventures of Ozzie and Harriet* reflected the ideal American family, at least in the minds of people who shared the Nelsons' middle-class style of life. "Ricky" Nelson, as he was then called, was the image of everyone's little brother. A cute kid who could sulk without being obnoxious, Ricky didn't cause much of a stir until his sixteenth birthday.

roots'' on wax. The phenomenal success of the "Circle" album not only boosted the reputations of the Dirt Band and the other participants, it also helped stem the tide of mediocrity, lush orchestration, and commercialism that was threatening to turn *country* music into a memory.

# O

## ORBISON, ROY
BORN: April 23, 1936, Wink, Texas

Roy Orbison became an international star in the 1950s, appearing on many TV shows, singing "The Great Pretender" and "Pretty Woman" and "Dream Baby." He also wrote hits for the Everlys, Buddy Holly, and Jerry Lee Lewis. His trademark was dark glasses and black suits. He is another graduate of Sun Records. Though the teeny-boppers chased him in the fifties, his name isn't drawing in the country crowds these days, which is too bad. Roy Orbison still sings a mean song, and his older albums are sought by collectors. An interesting bit of trivia about Orbison: He went to college with Pat Boone.

## THE OSBORNE BROTHERS

### Bob Osborne
BORN: December 7, 1931, Hyden, Kentucky
MARRIED: w. Patsy
CHILDREN: s. Robby, Wynn; d. Tina Renea

### Sonny Osborne
BORN: October 29, 1937, Hyden, Kentucky
MARRIED: w. Judy Rose
CHILDREN: s. Steve Russell; d. Karen Deanna

I will start this entry with an admission of my prejudice: I am an unabashed Osborne Brothers fan—have seen them perform a number of times and listen to their records often. So it is difficult for me to dislike their electrified instruments and

take a stand on their music, which is often considered "controversial." Bluegrass purists feel the Osbornes are "too commercial," and some country stations won't play their records because "we don't play bluegrass." The controversy doesn't stop the Osbornes from playing, and they've made a success of whatever you call their music. They perform regularly on Grand Ole Opry and work at least one bluegrass festival a week during the summer months, spending the rest of the year touring on their own, or occasionally as part of country entertainment package shows. In 1973 the Osborne Brothers appeared with Merle Haggard at Harrah's Club at Lake Tahoe, one of the major entertainment spots in the world. They were the first bluegrass/country group ever to play there, and they broke an eleven-year attendance record (previously held by Sammy Davis, Jr.). They also entertained at the White House (even though Sonny Osborne tried to cancel the engagement—not for any political reasons, though; he has always refused to fly, and to make the engagement, a plane ride was necessary. He finally submitted, made his first flight, and does admit "a slight preoccupation with the amount of play in the plane's wings").

Not too many years ago, the only vehicles the Osbornes traveled in were the taxicabs they drove to supplement their income. Brought up on country music (and bluegrass), the brothers learned to play the banjo and mandolin by the time they were in high school. Sonny was only sixteen when they appeared on station WROL in Knoxville, Tennessee, and began to make appearances throughout the Midwest. In 1959 they added the five-string-banjo talents of Benny Birchfield and made their campus debut at Antioch College—a milestone in bluegrass history: neither the Osbornes nor any other bluegrass group had ever even been on a college campus. Folk music was the rage, and hardly anyone knew what bluegrass was, and the Osbornes were used to playing in honky-tonk bars, not on a liberal college campus. The concert, played to an almost-full, curious house, started out slowly (half the audience left), and then, toward the end, the audience went wild. Word of the success of the concert spread through the bluegrass world, and within a year bluegrass was a major thing with the college kids.

Back to the controversy: Much of the criti-

The Osborne Brothers: They took the Midnight Flyer to Nashville.

cism leveled at the Osborne Brothers stems from the electrification of their sound, heresy for bluegrass (in the same way, Bob Dylan's fans were upset when he was backed with an electrified rock band—which became The Band). In 1971, while the Osbornes were performing at the Flame Club in Minneapolis, the crowd was unattentive, paying more attention to their talking and drinking than to the entertainers. Angered, Sonny went out to his car and retrieved an electrified five-string dobro which he had been carrying around. Plugging into the amplifier used by the steel player whose band played alternate sets with the Osbornes, Sonny turned up the volume and "peeled the paint off the wall." To his surprise, the crowd loved it, and listened carefully. The Osbornes say that going electric was not a matter of preference for electric over acoustic sound: "It was basically a device to project the sound of the instruments with sufficient force that they would not seem weak" contrasted to loud country bands with whom they shared the stage.

The Osbornes record for MCA. Among their hits: "Rocky Top," "Midnight Flyer," "Georgia Pinewoods," and many others.

## OVERSTREET, TOMMY

BORN: September 10, 1934, Oklahoma City, Oklahoma
MARRIED: w. Nancy
CHILDREN: s. Thomas Cary; d. Elizabeth Nan

Tommy Overstreet has had a number of hits since 1969, including "Heaven Is My Woman's Love." He's been in the business about six years and audiences seem to like his quiet, country style. He sings with a minimum of histrionics, and Dot Records calls him a "top-notch performer." In a sense, having musical ability, Overstreet was "born" to country. His father was a district manager in Texas for the National Life and Accident Insurance Company, the owner of Grand Ole Opry. Moreover, a family cousin was Gene Austin, the popular star of the 1930s ("My Blue Heaven" was his theme song), and Tommy Overstreet patterned his life after "Uncle Gene," as he was called. When he was thirteen, his parents bought him a $13.50 Harmony guitar. At fourteen, he landed a role in

a Houston summer stock production of *Hit the Road* in which he gained critical success and the job of replacing rock idol Tommy Sands on a Saturday morning TV show in Houston. While in high school, he appeared on the Slim Willet TV show, forming his own band to play the local air bases and clubs. He studied radio and TV production at the University of Texas, spending summers on the road with "Uncle Gene." Then Uncle Sam came around and invited Overstreet to sing for the army for two years, after which he moved to Los Angeles, worked for Pat Boone as a writer, and signed with ABC Records as a pop singer, cutting the first master record produced at Bradley's Barn in Nashville:

Tommy Overstreet: Rides the Nashville Express.

"There's a Little Bit of Devil in My Angel." Dunhill didn't release the record, feeling it was "too country." Tommy Overstreet left Dunhill, California, and pop music and returned to Texas; then he went to Nashville to work as professional manager for Dot's Nashville office. He handled the work of several artists, and it wasn't until 1970, when he recorded "If You're Looking for a Fool" (a fourteen-week chart hit), that his career began to take off. "Gwen (Congratulations)" was among the big hits of the year. His next four songs made the charts and his success seems assured. Overstreet's band, The Nashville Express, is noted for its twin steel guitars.

## OWENS, BONNIE

BORN: October 1, 1932, Blanchard, Oklahoma

MARRIED: h. Buck Owens (divorced) (s. Buddy, Mike); h. Merle Haggard

The former wife of Buck Owens, now the wife of Merle Haggard, and former singing partner of both, Bonnie Owens first came to fame as one of Arizona's most popular teen-age yodelers. She has had a number of chart hits, among them "Why Daddy Don't Live Here Anymore" and "Consider the Children."

Bonnie Owens: A star in her own right.

## OWENS, BUCK [Alvis Edgar Owens, Jr.]

BORN: August 12, 1929, Sherman, Texas

MARRIED: w. Bonnie (divorced)

CHILDREN: s. Buddy, Mike

During the 1973 Disc Jockey Convention in Nashville, I overheard three California DJs at Ireland's Restaurant. "If Haggard is here to be on the Country Music Association awards show, then Buck won't come," said one.

"He'll be here, all right," the second DJ answered. "But not until Haggard leaves."

"What do their managers do?" the third DJ interjected. "Plan their itineraries according to their feud?"

Whatever the reasons behind the feud (and there are numbers of rumored ones, including the fact that Buck Owens' ex-wife is now Mrs. Merle Haggard), both Buck Owens and Merle Haggard claim Bakersfield, California, as their own territory. In Nashville some people call it Buck-ersfield. Sometimes it is called Nashville West, but in any case, ever since the Okies and other broke and busted and homeless *Grapes of Wrath* citizens from the dust bowls of Oklahoma, Texas, and Arkansas arrived in California to seek their fortunes, Bakersfield's own brand of country music has been growing.

And as Jeff Young wrote in a magazine article, it is out of this tradition that Buck Owens emerged:

"Like so many others, Alvis Edgar Owens, Jr. ('Buck' from quite early) was an immigrant from America's heartland. Sherman, Texas, in the early thirties was a hot dusty town up near the Oklahoma border, and Buck's father was a hardworking sharecropper when Buck was born in 1929. The family's small frame house had only dirt floors and no electricity. Theirs was not an easy life, but not an untypical one for workers in the area.

"Buck was an early worker, and through the eighth grade, he tramped into the fields of cotton and maize, both before the school bell rang in the morning and after it rang in the late afternoon, to help out with the grocery bills at home. He grew up big and strong early, and the summer following the eighth grade, he worked full-time 'doing a man's work for a man's pay,' as he is fond of saying.

"It was also that year that the Owens family picked up what was left of its windblown stake and drove an old car to Tempe, Arizona, looking for a better life in more fruitful fields. Buck started Mesa Union High that fall, but quit after six weeks and went back to work as a truck driver, a ditch digger, a hay baler, a fruit swamper, anything that had to be done and that he could do. The war was on, and for a strapping, towheaded young man too young for the army and World War II, jobs were plentiful. He lived with his folks until he was seventeen, the year he married Bonnie.

" 'I don't know why I got married,' Buck recalled. 'I just wanted to, I guess. Why does anybody get married?' He was married just long enough to have two sons, Buddy and Mike.

"Music had entered his life quite early. His mother played piano in church for as long as he can remember, and he was hauled off to sing each Sunday. Soon after the family moved to Tempe, his father went out one afternoon and purchased a rickety old piano that he set up in the family parlor. That's when Buck learned to play. They also got an old radio, and Buck, for the first time, heard country music on the airwaves early in the morning and late at night after the work was done—music pulled in from the powerful Mexican stations and the one in Coolidge. Buck's early favorite was Bob Wills, along with Red Foley and Roy Acuff. The radio in the house also filled another function. Buck had purchased a battered old electric guitar when he was fifteen, and his father soldered a jack into the back so that Buck could practice with amplification. It wasn't much but it was enough, and Buck practiced. By the age of sixteen, he was performing in the honky-tonks.

"His first booking was in Eloy, Arizona, the toughest town he had ever seen. He stood on a stubby wooden platform barely six inches off the beer- and blood-stained floor and witnessed his first really hairy barroom brawl, a roaring fight that saw beer bottles by the dozen bounc-

Buck Owens: He put Bakersfield on the map.

ing off heads and walls. Buck's eyes opened to the size of bright silver dollars and he continued to play for more than a minute. But things kept getting worse, and as the bottles flew closer to his own head, he put down his guitar and tried to sneak off. The owner spotted him and ran after him hollering, 'Keep playing! Keep playing! You can't quit!'

"Even the joints, however, were few and far between in Arizona, so in 1951, at age twenty-one, Buck packed up his family in another old car and headed out on Route 66 for Bakersfield. He had kin there, and he had heard there were places to play his music. In Bakersfield he found a home and neighbors that were his kind.

" 'I first hired Buck as a guitar player,' said country-western promoter and musician Bill Woods. 'That was around '53. That's what he was selling himself as. A guitar player. He played a few casual nights with my band when I was at the Blackboard in Chester. It was a rough-and-tumble place back then. Drinkin' & Fightin' clubs had taken the action away from the ballrooms by then. Hell, there were no admission prices at the clubs, and you could get drunk and dance and whoop it up until you were crazy. It got pretty mean sometimes. A fight-and-lick-your-wounds-type club. But the music was damn good.

" 'By then the trend was toward small bands. That's pretty much how it was when Buck was with me. I had a small band and a singer by the name of Billy Mize. Now, Billy left me one night on short notice, went to Los Angeles to make it *big* on his own, and I told Buck that he was going to have to sing, and he threw a fit. He hated to sing because people *stared* at him, and all he wanted to do was play guitar. But I made him sing. And he did, but *only until Billy gets back* he always said. But Billy never came back, and Buck would walk off madder than a wet hen each night. But the crowd loved him. *More Buck.* Always *more Buck.* That's when I knew he was going to be a big star. He had the talent, the drive, everything.'

"While Buck was working Bakersfield by night, he was also traveling to Hollywood by day to play sessions at the famed Capitol Towers for a multitude of Capitol recording stars, including Tennessee Ernie Ford, Tommy Sands, Stan Freberg, Kay Starr, Sonny James, Gene Vincent, and Tommy Collins. He got his session break when he toured with Tommy as a lead guitarist. It was an easy step into session work after that. By this time, he knew he wanted to get into the country-music business as more than a session man, and it looked as if the best way was as a songwriter. He had knocked on doors to try to make records himself, but people always asked, 'Got any songs?' They said they had plenty of singers, but they needed material. Buck began writing, and people began to take an interest in him.

"After a minor contract with Pep Records ('The guy sold over a thousand of my records out of the back of his car') Buck finally hooked up with the people that knew him best in the business. Ken Nelson, the famed country producer at Capitol Records, signed Buck in 1956.

"His career didn't exactly break immediately. In fact, it was three years before Buck scored his first hit, 'Under Your Spell Again,' but from there, Buck Owens reached the top of the country-music field with his recording of 'Act Naturally,' a record that turned country music's musical head.

" 'I'd always been criticized,' Buck says, 'because I used too many drums on my records, but when this one broke, it changed a lot of people's minds. I think I always felt more beat than the country-music people who grew up in the East. I mean, I was influenced by all the greats, but I never played the schools and the churches and those type of affairs where people sit down. From Arizona to Bakersfield, I played dances in VFW halls and ballrooms and clubs, and those people wanted rhythm. They wanted to dance. I was also influenced by a lot of early rock-and-rollers: Chuck Berry, Carl Perkins, Fats Domino, Elvis, Eddie Cochran. Eddie Cochran, in fact, used to come into the Blackboard when he came through town, and I even played a couple of dates with Gene Vincent. I used to do a lot of rock at the Blackboard, anyway, so the rhythm came natural to me. I felt it.'

"Just as 'Act Naturally' was beginning to climb the national charts, Buck received a phone call in Bakersfield one day that was to change not only his life but the life of the caller.

"Jack McFadden in 1963 was a longtime-aspiring West Coast promoter who lived on the periphery of the big time. Today he is a distinguished down-home and graying man who commands attention. He smiles easily, can talk business a mile a minute, and is always ready. His career in the entertainment industry began as an eager ticket taker at a small theater in Sikeston, Missouri, when he was only twelve. The owner had several theaters throughout Missouri, Tennessee, and Arkansas, and he would periodically visit the theater where Jack worked. The owner took a liking to the boy and on one occasion took him to a corner grill near the theater, bought him a hot dog and Coke, and asked him what he wanted to be. It took Jack fewer than five seconds to answer. He wanted to be in show business. Not as an actor or performer, but still in show business.

"By the time Jack McFadden was twenty, he was managing movie theaters and radio stations in San Francisco. Later, in Stockton, California, he managed an appliance store, an auto dealership, and more radio stations. It was in 1954 that Jack first met Buck Owens.

" 'I'd been around Buck, and had seen what he had done in the years since I had first met him at the Blackboard. He was an aggressive and hardworking man. I called him that afternoon in '63 just to say "hello," but as we talked that afternoon, the subject of me handling Buck exclusively came up. We agreed to meet that afternoon to talk about it in more detail. That's how it all began. I knew a manager can only do what an artist will let him do, and after talking with Buck, I knew he was like I was. He was hungry. Not only for money, but to get things done. This is what I had looked for all my life. He had both feet on the ground. Realistic and positive.

" 'In 1964 I predicted Buck would have eleven number-one records in a row, but I was wrong. We had *twenty seven*.' Jack leaned back behind his massive walnut desk and lit up a cigarette. 'You know, Buck and I were driving to Las Vegas one day, and Buck asked me, "What's your main ambition in life?" "To make you a millionaire!" I answered.' Jack looked coolly around the spacious mahogany elegance of his thick-carpeted office and then leaned forward with a handsome smile. 'It don't take much to figure out why either.'

"Jack McFadden is not only Buck's manager, he is also one of Buck's biggest fans, even after all these years. He believes that Buck's next big move is into the movies.

" 'Almost everything that we planned,' he confides, 'we wrote down on paper a long time ago. A list of things that we wanted to do. And do you know, it has all happened, and in almost the exact order that we planned it. During the original negotiations, we decided that all my time would go to Buck. But there was so much activity going on around him after he broke that we knew it all had to grow. We had to help other people.'

"Thus it was that Buck Owens Enterprises was formed, a foundation upon which Buck's growing empire could grow even more. In 1965 Buck and Jack took their first big step in diversification. Both saw a need for a central West Coast country booking agency to handle country acts exclusively. They formed OMAC, a booking agency to develop a stable of known stars and an agency that would give the artists the best results. OMAC immediately signed Joe and Rose Maphis, Wynn Stewart, Merle Haggard and Bonnie Owens, Freddie Hart, Rose Maddox, and other West Coast–based country acts.

"Jack's son, Joe McFadden, has taken over the controls of OMAC. Although Jack still handles Buck exclusively, and the Buck Owens All-American Show, OMAC handles the individual bookings of each of the Owens entourage, including Sheb Wooley and Red Simpson. Joe McFadden's office is right next to his dad's, but it is smaller, with less-tuft-per-inch carpeting, a smaller desk—less a place to live than to work.

" 'When an artist comes to Buck Owens Enterprises,' Joe explained, 'and wants to be represented, he usually comes for the whole ball of wax. OMAC handles his or her individual bookings, but when he or she goes out with Buck on the road, that's my dad's territory. Freddie Hart, on the other hand, has no business dealings with Jack. He's separate from the Buck Owens shows altogether. I handle all his bookings. For the most part, however, like I said, it's usually the whole ball of wax, like Susan Raye or Buddy Alan or the Buckaroos, or Kenni Huskey or the Brass. Most of them even live in Bakersfield, like a family unit. It just makes things easier, and it gives us a base. People aren't spread out all over and out of touch.'

"With his developing stable of artists under

one business umbrella, Buck then set out to get all his publishing rights under the same roof. He formed Blue Book Publishing in 1967. Prior to Blue Book, Buck was signed with Central Songs, but when so many artists, ranging from Dean Martin to Peter and Gordon to Ray Charles to the Beatles, started doing Buck's songs, it only made good business sense for Buck to channel all that money being made into his own business.

"Buck Owens Productions was the next arm of the empire to be established. It handles the *Buck Owens Ranch Show* and the two radio stations that Buck owns, one in Bakersfield, KUZZ-KZIN, housed in the Owens building, and KTUF-KNIX in Phoenix. Mike Owens, Buck's youngest son, manages Buck Owens Productions, but at one time, like his brother, Buddy, he was the janitor and then a DJ for the radio station in Bakersfield.

"The *Ranch Show* these days is seen in seventy-plus markets across the country, and is shot at WKY-TV in Oklahoma City. Several times a year the Owens entourage flies to Oklahoma City and in one madcap week puts together months' and months' worth of shows by working virtually around the clock. The shows are edited in Oklahoma, but the musical tracks are prerecorded in the Buck Owens Studios in Bakersfield. It's all handled like clockwork. As Buck says, between *Hee Haw* and the *Ranch Show* and the way TV overlaps, he can be seen on TV sometimes six times a week.

"Virtually all of Buck Owens' needs are now taken care of by Bakersfield. (Except for the audiences and the few sojourns to Oklahoma.) Sitting in his thoroughly masculine, interior-decorated office with dark walnut furniture, thick gold carpet, black leather chairs, a couch, a fully outfitted bar, and a grand piano, it's hard to think of Buck as a country boy. The crew cut he sported for so long is gone, but the eagerness is still there in his eyes as he leans back in his chair and smokes his pipe. This is 'the man who put Bakersfield on the map.' He is looking through a one-way glass window looking out on North Chester Avenue.

" 'No, I can't really see Bakersfield becoming a music capital,' he says thoughtfully, and narrowing his eyes. 'For that we're gonna need to see more growth and the growth will have to

be more people producing things, pressing records here, that sort of stuff. The big labels will have to come in. Otherwise, it's just my organization and me. We're gonna have to have more competition, more quality product. A lot of people believe that Bakersfield will develop into that, but I haven't seen it as yet. It's like spread a rumor and watch it grow. But then I kinda like it as it is. It's a quiet little town with few hassles. You can concentrate here on what you're doing. I can never concentrate in Nashville.'

"When Buck says he'll stay *here*, he may mean it in a more literal sense than just living in Bakersfield. Buck knows that with all his record successes, and more recently with the success of *Hee Haw* and his own *Ranch Show*, that so much exposure sometimes hurts an artist. He seems more than prepared to take himself away from the center spotlight that he has held for so many years. His records aren't automatically number ones anymore, and last year he ranked number sixteen of *Billboard*'s Top Country Artists. In the last few years, Buck Owens the stage figure has by choice taken a less prominent place in the life of Buck Owens the person.

" 'There's a certain mystery that must remain about an artist, if you're going to continue,' Buck said. 'When you become a household word and everybody can see you as much as people have seen me over the past few years, it takes away the mystery. I know that Glen Campbell's record sales are down. His TV show has hurt him in that respect. Same with Roger Miller and Jimmy Dean. TV almost killed them as far as record sales, and even personal appearances.' He leaned forward, cocking his head with a Buck Owens smile. 'The biggest record buyers are women, right? If they're listening to somebody sing on the radio, who knows what's going on in their head. But if they see that person a lot, well, it changes them. It removes that essential mystery.' He pauses a moment, his eyes twinkling as he looks you square in the eye. 'Image is a very strange and touchy thing. Especially in country. The audience out there wants to know if you're fish or fowl. But if you as an artist don't know, then you're in trouble. If you have a record that breaks over into the pop category, that's okay, but if country people think you've gone over into the pop area totally, then they'll think you deserted them, and then you do have a problem.

" 'When I released "Bridge Over Troubled Waters," *whew*, did I get letters about that. One minister from Missouri got all over me for singing a *dope song*, of all things. He was really uptight about that. But at the same time, I get requests to do that song every show. People love it. I will admit that I went after a much broader audience with "Bridge," but my belief is that you always have to be yourself. I would like to enlarge my audience. I would like to just sing and not really be labeled as pop, country, or whatever. But it's not easy. I can do gut-bucket country and some people will say I'm regressing, while others will say, "Now you're cooking." But I don't lose any sleep over it. I do things with sincerity and honesty. If they like it, great. If they don't, I'm sorry, but I'm not going to go jump in a lake or anything.'

"Producing now takes up most of Buck's time. He's always out looking for new talent, checking on an act that someone told him about, checking new presentations that he may be able to incorporate into the Owens Enterprises, making plans that will enable him to stick closer to Bakersfield.

" 'I've planned for a changeover from being known as Buck Owens, the guy who plays the clubs, who makes the records, who goes out and beats the road, to Buck Owens who is known as a producer, a coordinator. That's what I'm working on now. The most satisfying part of everything I'm into now is producing and watching the acts that are signed to me grow. Susan Raye. Freddie Hart. Buddy. The Brass. I watch their record sales, and if they move, I get five times as much satisfaction out of watching their records than I do mine.'

"Buck says that country music needs a czar, like baseball or football.

" 'You've got to have organization and planning. I don't think any Joe Blow should be able to call up and book anybody but maybe the top five country acts. Promoters should be licensed and should belong to an organization. Country music is a business, and it should be recognized as such.'

" '*Centered in Bakersfield*?'

"Buck laughed and shifted in his chair. 'You know, when I identified with Bakersfield, I was trying to tell all those people who believed you had to go to Nashville to cut a hit country record that I didn't believe that. I don't believe that any more than I believe you have to go to Memphis to cut a blues record. I believe if you've got the right material, the right people to perform, that you can have a hit record.' He winked. 'And I thought it might be popular to be an underdog to Nashville. America loves underdogs, and God knows if you're in country and don't do *it* in Nashville, you're an underdog. You sure are.'

"Buck is quick to add that there is no animosity between him and Nashville. In the early sixties, in fact, he was going to move there at the request of the late Nashville promoter and booking agent Hubert Long, 'the only man who could have gotten me there.' But Ken Nelson talked him out of it, and Jack McFadden swears that keeping Buck in his home environment was an 'instinctively shrewd move.' Bakersfield, at first, wasn't that sure, especially the people who court Buck for his attention today.

" 'At first the city looked upon me with some disdain. I was, in their eyes, a hillbilly with manure on my boots who had gained some sort of national recognition. They came around very slowly at first. Today, of course, it's a different story. Today the people, the politicians, seek to have your home phone number, but I suppose it's a normal thing. The city is full of typical American people. They take a wait-and-see attitude about anything that's new, or that they don't understand.

" 'The golf tournament is a good example. It's recent. Last year it was tough. We didn't get city cooperation from certain areas which might have made it easier. But I think we showed them something. This year we received much more help. In fact, the city fathers can't do enough. Now they're happy to have the movie stars. It's something they've never seen before. I only hope it doesn't rain for the damn thing.'

"It did rain that Saturday morning, and the wet drove everybody into the clubhouse for a mad celeb-filled party before the golfers could tee off again at noon. Back on the course, Mickey Mantle hit the pill a mile, Charley Pride cracked jokes every third step he took, and Buck played with a bad sore on his back that just about killed him every time he swung. But you never would have known it. It all went off like clockwork. And Joe McFadden won the tournament in some of the ugliest golf shoes ever worn at the Bakersfield Country Club.''

Gram Parsons: "Grievous Angel."

190

# P

## PARSONS, GRAM

BORN: November 5, 1946, Winter Haven,
Florida
DIED: September 19, 1973, Joshua Tree, California

"When Gram Parsons died on September 19 of last year, country music lost a force that much of the industry never knew existed," Dave Hickey wrote in April 1974, in a review of Parsons' second, and last, solo album. For many country music fans, it *was* probably the first time they had ever heard the name of the young man whose single-minded determination was largely responsible for introducing country rhythms to the youth culture of the 1960s.

Parsons' career could be described in the same terms Hickey used to describe his music—"sweet and sad." It was also very short. Parsons died at age twenty-seven in a motel room in Joshua Tree, California, shortly before the release of his last album, aptly titled "Grievous Angel." It features the sparrow-like singing of Emmylou Harris, a young Alabama beauty with a silken voice, and it is full of "sweet and sad" country music. The funny thing about Gram Parsons is that although he was raised in Waycross, Georgia (where his father sang under the name Coon Dog Conner with local bands), Parsons' love affair with country music didn't blossom until he enrolled in Harvard University in 1966. He felt out of place, and only lasted four months, but in that time he met several students who were fascinated with his rural origins.

"They actually reintroduced me to country music after I'd forgotten about it for ten years," Parsons later admitted. Those friendships resulted in the formation of The International Submarine Band, a country-oriented group that didn't last long, but it brought Parsons' name to the attention of a band called The Byrds, who at the time were the nation's premier rock-and-roll attraction. The Byrds had *leaned* toward country in some of their arrangements, but when Parsons accepted an invitation to join them on their next album, he brought them full circle.

The Byrds' album, "Sweetheart of the Rodeo," included only two songs written by Parsons, but it was full of wailing, mournful steel pedal guitars, fierce picking, and an ambience far removed from the acid rock that dominated the "youth market" in 1968. One cut, "Drugstore Truck-Driving Man," managed to incorporate every country lick imaginable. It was delivered with the same finesse the best Nashville sessionmen could have offered, and the lyrics were aimed directly at the same hypocritical attitudes Tom T. Hall later took to task in "Harper Valley P.T.A." The album is now regarded as one of The Byrds' finest efforts.

Parsons left The Byrds, however, after refusing to accompany them to South Africa on a tour. He floated around the West Coast, jamming at country bars with Chris Hillman, Chris Ethridge, and steel pedal whiz "Sneeky Pete" Kleinow. They soon formed The Flying Burrito Brothers, outfitted themselves at Nudies Rodeo Tailors, and recorded a classic album, "The Gilded Palace of Sin." The group didn't evolve as Parsons hoped it would. It was still a hybrid mixture of rock and country that he found unsatisfactory, so he left to pursue a solo career. The Burrito Brothers cut three more albums without him.

Parsons played talent nights at The Palomino in L.A. for two years after that, trying to work out a style that suited him. He found it eventually, and with the aid of Emmylou Harris, three members of Elvis Presley's band, and fiddler Byron Berline, he turned out two solo albums, "GP" and "Grievous Angel," both for the Warner Brothers label.

"Both of them reflect Parsons as a coherent and gifted country solo artist," Hickey wrote in his review. "Both albums are evenly divided between Parsons' songs and country songs by other writers, and the selection is as personal as the original material. The first album contains lovely cuts of "Streets of Baltimore" and "We'll Sweep Out the Ashes in the Morning," and the second contains fine versions of "Hearts on Fire," Tom T. Hall's "I Can't Dance," and the Louvin Brothers' "Cash on the Barrelhead," plus a really beautiful version of Boudleaux Bryant's "Love Hurts."

"Gram Parsons was a sweet singer and he never found a place when he was alive," Hickey concluded. "But I hope his music finds a place in the canons of country music; I know, at least to my own certainty, that if Gram hadn't stuck it out at The Palomino, if he hadn't bridged the two worlds by himself, it would be a lot harder today for many country artists to find an erstwhile pop audience.''

Bud Scoppa, in a review of "GP" for the rock journal *Rolling Stone,* had this to say about Parsons' music: "His central theme has always been that of the innocent southern boy tossed between the staunch traditions and strict moral code he was born to, and the complex, ambiguous modern world. He realizes that both are corrupt, but he survives by keeping a hold on each while believing neither.''

Parsons' death was attributed to a heart attack. Like most musicians, he lived hard. Like some great country artists, he died young.

# PARTON, DOLLY

BORN: January 19, 1946, Sevierville, Tennessee

MARRIED: h. Carl Dean

Someone, writing about the Porter Wagoner TV show some years ago, mentioned "the girl singer Dolly Parton," who sang in a "quivering Appalachian soprano." The "girl singer Dolly Parton" has become a country superstar—and no wonder. I am not given to compliments (some of the entries in this volume will attest to that), but like Black Sambo's tigers, I melt into butter when I hear her sing. It would be unfair for me to go on. Instead, I am reprinting a piece by Jerry Bailey which says it all:

"Rooms have a way of growing smaller when Dolly Parton walks in. It has nothing to do with physical dimensions but with psychological comparison. She could wear pajamas to a banquet, and many formally attired persons there would feel improperly dressed. In her presence, women tend to fidget with their hair and adjust their clothes; men stiffen uneasily and stare noticeably at the object of their admiration. She has a way of destroying one's composure, though it seems entirely unintentional.

"When she walked into the dressing room of a Nashville TV station one recent evening, I thought my chances for survival would have been better had she instantly been transformed into a man-eating grapevine. It is somehow impossible for this reporter to get mentally prepared for her. With her four-inch heels and mounds of blonde hair, her height came to threatening dimensions, though she would stand only five feet with plowed earth beneath her toes. She was wearing tight-fitting blue pants, revealing curves reminiscent of Marilyn Monroe, and moved with the carefree innocence of a country schoolgirl. Her perfect face, highlighted with skillfully applied makeup, reminded me of a seasoned, passionate woman and, at the same time, a tender childhood sweetheart. On this particular evening, she wore seven rings on her fingers.

"She extended her hand in the friendly, frank manner of Tennessee hill folks.

" 'Hi, I'm proud to meet you,' she said, like a magician breaking a hypnotic trance. She pulled up a folding chair uncomfortably close, and smiled eagerly. After a meaningless greeting, I found myself fighting with paranoia, in spite of hours of preparation for the interview. After some fumbling with my tape recorder, I ventured a half-question.

" 'Uh, I suppose you get tired of telling your life story.'

" 'Sometimes, but not tonight,' she replied, still smiling eagerly. I had almost hoped she would say she was too busy to talk to me. Just in the nick of time, Porter Wagoner walked in and began putting the final touches to his sparkling clothes before the wall of mirrors. It was a welcome distraction.

"Dolly watched him for a moment and then asked, 'What are you going to give me for Christmas?'

" 'Another chance,' Porter replied.

" 'Another chance! That's what you gave me last year.'

" 'Last year I gave you a Cadillac, a diamond necklace, and another chance,' Porter said. He had earlier estimated that he had given Dolly five rings, two Cadillacs, and two necklaces during the years she had been with his show. He turned to me and grinned mischievously: 'Dolly was born in Frog Alley until she put Sevierville on the map.'

"Porter's joke held a lot of truth. Dolly Parton, who at her present age of twenty-seven is the pride and joy of the *Porter Wagoner Show,* was the fourth of a dozen children born to a farmer-turned-construction-worker in Sevier

Dolly Parton lectures to a songwriting class at Vanderbilt University.

County, Tennessee. Her mother and father married while still in their mid-teens, but, as Dolly once said, 'they done pretty well.' Her earliest memories are of a place back in the Smokies called Webb Mountain. The family had moved there when she was three, and stayed, scratching out a living by raising just enough food for their own survival, for five years.

Later, they moved around the country for a while and then settled in the Caton's Chapel community 'on a little farm, well, not too little, about forty or fifty acres,' where they lived until she graduated from high school.

'' 'I started writing songs before I could even write songs—before I ever went to school, when I couldn't write or read or spell. I used to make up songs and my momma would write them down for me. She said I was making up songs before I was five, but at that age I used to beg her to write them down so she could read them back to me. When I was about seven years old I

started playing the guitar. It's all I've ever known.'

"Dolly made her first guitar from an old mandolin and two bass-guitar strings. She had the strings keyed up in some way so she could play a melody and form chords, and she wrote a lot of songs with that guitar.

'' 'I got a real one when I was eight years old. My uncle gave me a little Martin. It's really the one I learned to play on. Of course, it had full strings where I could learn full chords. When I was twelve years old, I was away from home in Knoxville one weekend and didn't have my guitar. While I was gone, my guitar got loaned out and it broke. That hurt me real bad. It had the side busted out and the neck broke off. I guess some kids had jumped up and down on it —I never did know what happened. I put it away and said when I got enough money, the first thing I'd do was have my guitar fixed so I could play it again.'

193

"It is perhaps entirely understandable that many of Dolly Parton's most ardent fans have tended to exercise their eyes at the expense of their ears. It is as if the fact that she is a genuine country singer with a unique style and repertoire is only a secondary feature. But to play down the importance of music to Dolly Parton would be to not understand Dolly Parton. She may not have worked especially hard to quash the myth that beautiful blondes and brains do not run together, but a few minutes' conversation with her would be enough to convince any skeptic that she has a good head on her shoulders, a vivid imagination, and a great dedication to succeed as a musician.

"And apart from her music, there is another very important influence in her life which dates back to her childhood.

"To the people in the communities where Dolly grew up, religion was both recreation and duty. In words that one of his granddaughters would use in a song someday, the Rev. Mr. Owens 'preached hell so hot that you could feel the heat.' Two years ago a song about this subject became one of the top ten country songs in the nation, and in it Dolly Parton tried to convey the spirit of the way it was in her grandfather's church in the hills.

"Before she ever left for Nashville, she was singing in church with her granddaddy, and it did not take Dolly long to start singing something besides hymns. She sang well enough that one of her uncles, Bill Owens, managed to get her on the radio in Knoxville before her eleventh birthday.

" 'Dolly was singing around home all the time,' Owens said. 'She'd sing while she washed dishes; she'd sing when she put her younger brothers and sisters to bed. And even then she sang good! All of a sudden the thought came to me that I should take her to the Cass Walker (a renowned Knoxville disc jockey) broadcasts.

" 'This particular show was originating downstairs. When Dolly started to sing, announcers and other people from all over the building came in, announcers from upstairs and everywhere, just to hear this new talent. She was an instant hit, and Cass hired Dolly on the spot.'

"It was shortly after this that she cut her first record. It was on the Gold Band label, a small company in Lake Charles, Louisiana. The song was called 'Puppy Love,' written by Dolly and her uncle. The record went nowhere.

"She began high school in Sevier County in 1959, and one of her school activities was playing the snare drum in the band. But her main interest was still country music, and it touched all aspects of her life. By the time graduation rolled around in 1964, definite steps had been taken to launch her in the music business. Bill Owens, his wife, and young son moved to Nashville about two weeks before school was out and found an apartment. Dolly was to live with them until she could establish herself. She graduated on Friday night and, the next day, boarded a bus for Nashville.

" 'When I moved to Nashville I lived with them (the Owenses) for about five months. He was working some on the road with Carl and Pearl Butler. After a while, I got a contract with Monument Records and Combine Music. They gave me an advance and paid me so much a week, so I moved out and got my own apartment. I lived by myself until I got married. There were some hungry days back then, I tell you. I had hot-dog relish and mustard in my refrigerator, but that's all I had to eat for about three weeks at one time. The only time I ever got a really good meal was when I was on a date, and I didn't date anybody in the music business that much, because I didn't want to get a reputation. Not that I would have done anything to get one, but you don't have to, really.'

" 'I say it in a joking way, but that's really the only time I ate—if somebody would take me to his momma's for Sunday dinner, or if we would go to a show. I mean, I was taught well and was a big girl, but I didn't want somebody to say "Yeah, so and so went out with her," when I went somewhere to get something done. I just felt like that was the thing to do, so that's why I ate mustard and hot-dog relish.

" 'I met my husband the same day I got to Nashville. When I left Sevierville, I had taken a bunch of dirty clothes with me, because I was in a hurry to go and didn't have all my things ready. That particular day I was at the laundromat and I got me a cola and I was walking down the sidewalk, just looking around, you know, because I'd never been to the city. I was fascinated. I'd been to Knoxville, but I'd never lived in a city.

" 'Being from the country, I was real friendly, because everybody in the country knows everybody else. Everybody's your neighbor. Well, I just went out walking and I saw this boy go down the street in a white Chevrolet, a '65 Chevrolet. No, it was a '63; we had a '65 later. I spoke to him and he spoke back. I wasn't doing it to flirt, although I might have been in a way. He was real friendly too, and he turned around and stopped, and we got to talking and he asked me out.'

"Uncle Sam was soon to declare an intermission in the courtship, but almost exactly two years later, Dolly Parton married the driver of that white Chevrolet. His name is Carl Dean. He is now thirty years old and a partner in his father's asphalt-paving business.

"Those two years while Carl was in the military were probably the roughest and most decisive of Dolly's career. Not only did she go hungry often, but her music was equally unfulfilling. The first records she made after coming to Nashville were based on rock music, which is about as foreign to the Smokies as a lobster dinner.

" 'Monument Records was doing what it thought was best at the time. My voice was so strange, and still is. They didn't think I could possibly sell any country because they thought I sound like a little girl. They didn't think I could sell any hard message song or sad story, because nobody would believe it. But I always wanted to do it, so I told them after a while that I was either going to do what I felt that I could do in my heart or I was going to have to leave. I got to do country. I would love to have a song that would go pop, but I would want it to be country-oriented. I wouldn't want to aim it right at the pop field. I think I've got some songs that could go pop. You never can tell nowadays.'

"Dolly proved her point about the acceptability of her singing country songs. Monument gave her the go-ahead to record more country records. She came up with a hit song called 'Dumb Blonde,' selected for her by Fred Foster. She followed it with one of her own songs, 'Something Fishy.'

"Then one afternoon, at home in her apartment, Dolly received an unexpected phone call from Porter Wagoner.

" 'I had never seen Porter Wagoner in person. We were big fans of his back home and watched his show on television. I never had met any real big stars; I had met a lot of people, but no stars. He called me one day and told me who he was, and I just couldn't believe it.'

"She thought Porter wanted to see her about one of her songs and took her guitar along for the appointment. She had a lot of songs out around town at the time and was trying to get someone to record them. Porter and Norma Jean, the girl he had on his show, had several. She had heard that Norma Jean liked one of the songs especially well. But Porter wanted to tell Dolly that Norma Jean was getting married and moving to Oklahoma. He was considering replacing her with Dolly Parton.

"Porter has told the story of that first meeting many times.

" 'Dolly came to my office, but she didn't really know what we were going to talk about. She brought her guitar. And she sang a song for me, a song about everything being beautiful. She had written it. And this song told me so much about her. I knew if a person could sit down and write a song like that, they'd have to have a real soul inside 'em.'

" 'If I seem to ignore you, it's because Porter doesn't like to see me talking while he's singing,' Dolly said as we watched Porter during the taping, and I began to understand just how seriously Porter and Dolly regard each other's music. It's important to Porter to know that Dolly takes his artistry seriously, and while one is singing, the other reacts as if a sacrament is being performed.

"In the summer of 1967 Dolly began appearing on the Porter Wagoner television and road shows. Those first few months were torture for her, because at each appearance, she felt people wanted to see someone else, namely Norma Jean. Porter sensed her anxiety and began singing with her on the bus before their shows, trying to help her relax. He liked her interpretation of songs and decided to cut a record with her. From those efforts came a success bigger than either anticipated, and from that success came a work load for Dolly that only a person with a lifetime of determination could handle."

# PAYCHECK, JOHNNY [Donald Lytle]
BORN: May 31, 1941, Greenfield, Ohio

Johnny Paycheck, the bantam cock of country music, the "Ohio Kid," tough and determined, burst onto the Nashville scene in the mid-sixties with hits written for Webb Pierce, Skeets McDonald, and Sheb Wooley. Then he disappeared as fast as he had catapulted to prominence. In an

Johnny Paycheck: "The Ohio Kid" made it, lost it, and made it again.

exclusive magazine interview in 1973, John Morthland told the story:

"Little more than five years ago, after serving apprenticeships with Faron Young, Ray Price, and George Jones, he was considered one of the most promising new stars in all of country music. He had been nominated, on the basis of one single, in every category of the 1966 NAR-AS (National Association of Recording Artists) Awards, and, while he hadn't won in any of the finals, his records were selling. He was very much in demand for personal appearances, and he was being talked about like a potential successor to George Jones for the 'king of country music' crown. How much more promising can a man still in his twenties be? Well . . .

"About three years ago, after all that promise, he was living destitute in Los Angeles, unable to record, living hand-to-mouth, doing just a little picking between bottles at a few local dives. He went about virtually unnoticed, seemingly without a friend in the world. His career, if it could still be called that, was at a dismal, all-time low. But . . .

"Was it only a year ago that he made his comeback with '(Don't Take Her) She's All I Got' at the Disc Jockey Convention in Nashville, where an audience of several thousand rose as one to give him a long standing ovation for his performance? Yep—one year—that's all it's been, and the story doesn't end there . . .

"For in the last year or so, country-music audiences have welcomed him back just as enthusiastically. Since 'She's All I Got' Johnny has had four straight hit singles and three successful albums. He's working twenty-five nights a month, and it looks for sure as if there's no stopping him now.

"The Johnny Paycheck comeback is one of the most heartwarming stories in recent years, but in order to get its full effect, we have to see what he came back from. And that story begins fifteen years ago, when a nineteen-year-old Johnny Paycheck, then known as Donald Lytle, showed up in Nashville from the farm country of Greenfield, Ohio, with the music of Hank Williams and Lefty Frizzell ringing in his ears.

"It wasn't his first trip there—when he was fourteen, he'd given in to the wanderlust he felt all his life and hit the road. He hitchhiked, rode freights, and bummed around, but that lasted only a month before he returned home. He'd come to Nashville again when he was sixteen, again failing to make any headway.

"But this time he was determined to make it or bust in Nashville. Buddy Killen of Tree Publishing heard him sing, and the next thing he knew he was recording a couple of singles for Decca under the name Donnie Young, one of several pseudonyms he'd been using. Both records bombed, as did two more for Mercury, and so Donnie Young took a job with Faron Young. He played bass and sang tenor, warming up Faron's audiences for the star; he also recorded such tunes as 'Face to the Wall' and 'Country Girl' with Faron.

"That lasted about a year, because Donnie Young was still a restless soul. He moved over to Ray Price's band, holding down the same job for the next three years off and on, recording 'Heart Over Mind' and 'Twenty-fourth Hour' with Ray. Then, from 1962 to 1966, Donnie Young fronted the Jones Boys for George Jones. It was the longest time he'd ever held a job.

"'It's hard to say why I stayed with him so

much longer,' Johnny says today. 'I guess I really liked him. I mean, I liked them all, don't get me wrong, but there was just something about him. I guess we were so much alike. I liked his music and I liked him as a person and the whole bit. You know, I had a terrible drinking problem most of my life—I now have it whipped—but during those years I drank all the time and roared and had a big time. George was that way then, and him and I was like two peas in a pod. He'd fire me one night and hire me back the next day, that kind of stuff. His phrasing and mine are quite a bit alike, too, although I was singing that way from the time I was a kid. But he came out first and was *the* George Jones, and after I went to work for him, I probably was influenced quite a bit; I'd be wrong if I said I wasn't.'

"That vocal influence became apparent in late 1965, when Donnie Young changed his name to Johnny Paycheck and formed a partnership with Aubrey Mayhew. Johnny would sing and Aubrey would take care of business matters. The first big single was a Hank Cochran tune, 'A-ll.' They leased it to Hilltop Records, and it went high up the charts, earning Johnny all those NARAS nominations. It was time to go it on his own, with Mayhew as business partner. They started a new label, Little Darlin', which at various times included steel guitarist Lloyd Green, the Homesteaders, Bobby Helms, and even the first sides by Jeannie C. Riley.

"But there was no doubt about who was the label's star. Johnny broke into the top ten in 1966 with 'Lovin' Machine' and again the next year with 'Juke Box Charlie.' A selection of material from that period is available on 'Johnny Paycheck's Greatest Hits' (Little Darlin' SLD-8012), an album of some of the very finest country music of the mid-sixties, but one you'll probably have to search the drugstore bargain bins to find. Johnny's songs then were a monument to the honky-tonks, their neon and juke boxes, fast women and whiskey.

" 'I liked those songs then, because I *lived* those songs. "Juke Box Charlie" and so forth, that's the way I was living, and I identified with those songs. I still kinda like them, but I don't identify with them anymore. I still do some of them, but mostly because I get a lotta requests for 'em.

" 'Those were my big years, but I didn't know how to handle it,' he continues. 'I was drinking like crazy, and wasn't taking care of business at all. I was very bad. Mayhew and me finally separated; we just dissolved the partnership. He went his way, and I went mine, so to speak.'

"Exactly what happened with Little Darlin' is so tied into a morass of legal complexities that it's hard for anyone except a lawyer to understand. Johnny displays a lack of bitterness when he talks about it, but the gist of it is that Little Darlin' went out of business and Johnny Paycheck was left holding a stack of bills that it would take him two and a half years to pay off. Worse yet, he still had certain attachments to the Little Darlin' organization that made it impossible for him to make records for anybody else. In late 1968, he left Nashville for self-imposed exile in Los Angeles.

" 'I'd lost everything, and was really depressed and not giving a damn about anything. And I spent two and a half years in the gutter. I still had those ties with Little Darlin' and as long as those ties were there, nobody would touch me. At the same time, there really was no such thing as Little Darlin' anymore,' he remarks, shaking his head at the memory of it. 'I had to resolve that, and it was almost impossible. I had planned to keep going in country music, but I didn't know how. There was nothing I could do, and I just had to let it work itself out. I was strictly on my own through that period. I had nobody. Matter of fact, nobody wanted nothin' to do with me because of the other stuff.'

"The 'other stuff' was his drinking, which had reached enormous proportions. He had started as a youngster, when he ran with a much older crowd, and just kept drinking more and more as he grew older. Pretty soon he was taking pills in large quantities as well. When he says he spent most of that time in Los Angeles in the gutter, he means he was at the absolute rock bottom—he was too wasted to do more than occasional picking in various seedy bars. One foggy day blurred into the next, and virtually overnight, he'd gone from being The Next Big Thing to being Nobody.

"Reprieve finally came in late 1970, when Nick Hunter, a CBS distributor in Denver, tracked Johnny down to tell him Columbia was interested. Billy Sherrill, Columbia's man in Nashville, had once made the statement that if he could ever get his hands on Johnny Paycheck, he'd make him the biggest thing in the country. Hunter felt that this might be the time, and urged Johnny to come to Denver.

" But first I had to get myself squared away, and I did. I thought many times I wasn't going to make it at all, but every time I thought of it, it made me mad. I just wouldn't give up,' Johnny stresses. 'I finally got to the place where the booze was killing me, and I just had to get away from it. I woke up one morning, and I don't know how a man knows these things, but I just *knew* that I was gonna die if I didn't quit. And so I just quit—from that day forward, I never touched nothin' again. I knew I had a good shot on the CBS thing, and that helped me. Once I got a hold, I just wouldn't let go.'

"When he got to Denver, Johnny worked a club while Hunter and Billy Hall, a music publisher, were trying to help Sherrill get Johnny signed with a new label. After some complex wheeling and dealing between companies, everything was finally sorted out and Sherrill signed Johnny to Columbia's subsidiary, Epic.

"Then it was Sherrill's turn to put up or shut up. He now had to make good on his earlier statement. It took him nearly five months to find Johnny just the right song, because he wasn't going to take any chances. '(Don't Take Her) She's All I Got' was released just before the Disc Jockey Convention, and took off. Johnny was on his way back, but it took the convention to put him over the top.

" 'I don't know if I can tell you how it felt at that convention. I was very surprised at the reception I got. I thought that because the record was hot at the time I'd get a nice welcome, but I wasn't prepared for what they did. There was 10,000 people there at the CBS banquet dinner, and I did the song and they gave me a standing ovation, which to me is the ultimate a man can get, especially from his fellow workers. I was the only one on the whole show they did that for, and it was very gratifying. They did the same thing again this year, and it's really terrific. That's about the only way I can describe it.'

"From there the word spread, and Paycheck has had a number of big hits, including the smash 'Mr. Lovemaker.' ' "

## PAYNE, LEON

BORN: June 15, 1917, Alba, Texas
MARRIED: w. Myrtie Velma Cormier
CHILDREN: s. Leon Roger; d. Rene A., Patricia Lee, and Myrtie Lee

Leon Payne is one of the great country-western songwriters, and during the 1940s, particularly, his records sold well. Like other blind musicians, Payne mastered a number of instruments in his childhood—guitar, organ, trombone, drums. He began performing as a one-man band, joined Bob Wills and the Texas Playboys, remaining with them several years. Despite his blindness, he hitchhiked to performances, and occasionally was introduced as "Texas' blind hitchhiker." One of his great songs, "Lost Highway" (a Hank Williams hit), came out of this period. His most popular song, "I Love You Because," was sung by a number of performers, including Elvis Presley. Since his heart attack in 1965, Payne has been living in San Antonio.

## PEARL, MINNIE [Sarah Ophelia Colley Cannon]

BORN: October 25, 1912, Centerville, Tennessee
MARRIED: h. Henry R. Cannon

Though country music has moved "uptown" (as they say around the bar at Tootsie's Orchid Lounge in Nashville), country humor is pretty much still in Minnie Pearl's make-believe town of Grinder's Switch. Not only country-music fans but many other Americans love Minnie Pearl and laugh at her broad humor on how to "ketch fellers" and the comings and goings of her "Uncle Nabob." Originally a dancer and a teacher of drama, she won local recognition for her flair for comedy, and by the time she was twenty-eight, she was a regular on Grand Ole Opry. She has been synonymous with the Opry ever since. Her costume, a wide-brimmed hat with the tag still on it and an old-style "mountain wife" dress, is as familiar a fixture in American folk humor as Charlie Chaplin's tramp suit. Minnie Pearl has written a cookbook and run a chain of franchised restaurants, and as one of the most respected women in the Nash-

Minnie Pearl sent this photo as a Christmas card in 1973.

ville community, both in and out of country music, she is constantly active in good works. In 1966 she hit the charts with a top-ten hit, "The Answer to Giddyap Go."

## PERKINS, CARL

BORN: April 9, 1932, Jackson, Tennessee
MARRIED: w. Valda de Vese
CHILDREN: s. Steve, Stan, Greg; d. Debra

Johnny Cash was the MC at the 1973 Country Music Awards TV show, but the first musician on the stage was a lean man in black, carrying an electric guitar. There was a smattering of applause from those who recognized him. On this night he was backing Johnny Cash. His name would never be mentioned on the air, and the millions of people watching at home wouldn't know that the guitar player was one of Nashville's original living legends, the great Carl Perkins, one of the founders of rock-and-roll. "That man wrote 'Blue Suede Shoes,'" a woman sitting next to me told her daughter. "He used to be a number-one star."

"Sometimes it's nice to be number two," Perkins once admitted to Patrick Carr, who wrote the following magazine article in 1973:

"In the spring of 1970, Carl Perkins and Johnny Cash stood on a little two-foot-high stage in the Green Room of the White House playing 'A Boy Named Sue' for the President of the United States sitting about three feet away from the end of Cash's nose. Now, as Perkins puts it, Richard Nixon is 'just marked with one of them faces. He can be happy and he don't show it,' and with him sitting there, his hands folded in that Presidential fold and his chin stuck up towards the two old friends on stage, it wasn't exactly the kind of date a man might choose to do just for the fun of it. But there was dignity and politics and a man's art at stake in that room . . .

"'Then I thought, "Well I'm gonna look at him,"' Perkins recalls. '"I'm just gonna look him right in the damn eye"—thinkin' he'd be lookin' right at John . . .'

"But when he took his eyes off the neck of his electric guitar and forced himself to do it, Carl Perkins saw to his horror that the President was looking right at *him*.

"'He's supposed to be lookin' at John,' was Perkins' first thought. 'He ain't supposed to be lookin' at *me*.'

"For the past seven years, Carl Perkins has been playing guitar for the *Johnny Cash Show*, going on before Cash and warming up his audiences. Carl Perkins works for Johnny Cash —but there's more than that to it: The two have a lot in common, like being born with next to nothing in the hard days of the Depression, about thirty miles from each other (Perkins in Lake County, west Tennessee, Cash across the Mississippi River in Arkansas).

"In the oak-paneled conference room of the Cedarwood Publishing Company in Nashville, Perkins is remembering those days as a sharecropper's son on one of the big cotton plantations. Now he's sitting in a leather chair, a tall, strikingly handsome man, high-cheekboned and tanned and big-chested—a tough character, strong—in a sharp, close-cut midnight blue stage suit, remembering the black folks he'd share a hoe with back in those days when he was only a kid of eight or nine. 'I listened to them sing in the field; it was a *natural* thing,' he recalls.

"'Uncle John would start it off: "oooooooooooooooooooooh . . ." Then sister Juanita three or four rows across would pick it up—"Yeeeeeeeeeeaaaah . . ." And then someone else would begin: "*Gonna lay down my burden*—"

"'They made the music with their *mouths*,' he says. 'I'd join in and take a verse, and then every evenin' after supper I'd ask my daddy's permission to go on to Uncle John Westbrook's shack across the plantation.' There he'd watch as the old black man sang the blues and picked on a beat-up acoustic guitar that as often as not didn't have a full six strings to its credit. Sometimes the strings there were had knots in them, so Uncle John couldn't slide down a fret: he'd have to push the string up and hit an octave between notes. 'That got to me,' says Perkins. 'I said, "*that's* the way *I* want to play."' So he did, and when he moved away from Lake County to Jackson, Tennessee, he took that guitar with him—for payment of $3 to old John Westbrook.

"At the age of fourteen, he had saved enough to buy a single-speaker Fender amplifier and an electric pick-up for his roundhole Gibson. He bought a stand-up homemade bass fiddle for $25

Carl Perkins: A "founding father" of rockabilly.

from some boys who lived over the hill and taught his younger brother Clayton to play it. With Jay Perkins on rhythm guitar, that made the Perkins Brothers Band a reality. They were pretty good, and were soon winning amateur contests around the area. Then one day in 1955, Carl heard an Elvis Presley record on the radio.

" 'Hey, wait a minute, boys, have you heard this record by *Evelin Presley* (or somethin' like that)? He's playin' just like *we* do!'

"Memphis, Tennessee—the home of Sam Phillips' Sun Records—was seventy-five miles away. Carl's 1940 Plymouth had hardly enough rubber between itself and the road to make it over the next hill, let alone a trip like *that*, but as luck would have it, there was in the locality a man by the name of W. S. Holland—and he, in addition to being a drummer, was an only child and the owner of a big, black 1948 Cadillac. The band gained a drummer and transportation, and two weeks later they were down in Memphis with Sam Phillips, who was impressed by the fact that these boys might just fit right into the new kind of music he was making with Elvis

Presley, Jerry Lee Lewis, Charlie Rich, Roy Orbison—and John Cash.

"But the big break came one night when the Perkins Brothers were playing a Jackson club date and Carl happened to overhear a conversation going on down in front of the stage.

" 'Don't step on my shoes!' said this young man (with the hair, the clothes, and all the characteristics common to the new, affluent, rebellious and *fashionable* rock-and-roll generation) to his date.

" 'That just bugged me,' says Carl. 'I couldn't sleep. So I went downstairs and I started to write a song about this guy and his shoes. Then I thought of the old nursery rhyme—"One for the money, two for the show, three to get ready and four to go"—where you used to put your head against a tree and the others would go hide . . .'

"He wrote the words on a brown paper potato bag there in the living room of the two-up-two-down Government project house where he and his wife and their first two children lived. The next morning he went across the street and borrowed a telephone.

201

" 'Mr. Phillips? I got a new song. It's called "Blue Suede Shoes." ' "

" 'Is that like "Oh, Them Golden Slippers"?' "

" 'No, this cat don't want nobody *steppin'* on his blue suede shoes.' "

" 'I can't picture it.' "

"Carl went ahead and sang 'Blue Suede Shoes' to Sam Phillips over the phone. 'When can you come on down?' said Phillips.

" 'Blue Suede Shoes' was a mighty song. Not only did it have that *beat* for which kids all over America were waiting in line at record stores, but it was also the first song by a white man that caught the essence of the new youth in all its spunky yet narcissistic glory—and it had that 'Go, cat, go!' tag on it, put there completely by Perkins' mistake on the first take in Memphis (he meant to sing 'Go, *man,* go!'). Sam Phillips predicted that those three words would soon be on the lips of every rock-and-roll kid in America, and they were.

"Then, on March 22, 1956, when 'Blue Suede Shoes' was number one on the charts and Elvis Presley's 'Heartbreak Hotel' was number two, Carl's car hit a man in Dover, Delaware. Jay Perkins was killed; Carl's neck was broken, his skull fractured—and Carl's moment had come and gone. He never made it to New York to become the first rock-and-roller on syndicated TV—in fact, he watched Elvis perform his record-album version of 'Blue Suede Shoes' on the *Jackie Gleason Show* from his hospital bed, and he never again made such a successful 'youth' record.

" 'Six years ago this past November, I threw a pint whisky bottle into the Pacific Ocean and John Cash threw in a bottle of pills,' says Carl, pulling hard on a filter-tipped cigarette and leaning back in his good leather chair. (Looking at him now, in peak form, you realize how fearsome this big, hard man must have been when he was drinking.) 'We shook hands and to this day we haven't touched a thing.'

"It was the end of a long and harrowing time, the point at which Carl decided to do something about the nagging realization that he had to get away from a *bad* booze habit. Like many a poor boy from the cotton fields, he had come close to burning himself out on one drug or another in the fast, hard world of show business.

" 'I've been with John for seven years now,' he says, 'and on many occasions I've *leaned* on John. I've asked him, "Are you goin' to take a pill?" and he's said, "Are you goin' to drink a beer?" "Nope, not if you don't," I've said. So we've waded out of a deep dungeon between us.

" 'Since Cash and I quit, it's brought us much closer to God because we *couldn't* go out there alone: we were too scared. There's something about the stage—when that spotlight shines on you, you *know* who you are. It's frightening, it never ceases. When I used to drink I'd get keyed up and I'd say, "Here I *come*, man. Let me *out* there." But it wasn't until I quit that I found it hard to go out.' "

## PHILLIPS, BILL

BORN: August 28, 1936, Canton, North Carolina

MARRIED: w. Nita June Rich

CHILDREN: s. William George

Bill Phillips is a nice fellow from North Carolina, born and bred in "hard country" country. Between 1964 and 1971 he had fourteen hits with Decca on the country charts, including "The Company You Keep" and "Little Boy Sad." He travels with the *Johnny Wright–Kitty Wells Family Show* and their fans love him, too. And no wonder. He's friendly and courteous, and this comes across in his singing.

## PIERCE, WEBB

BORN: August 8, 1926, West Monroe, Louisiana

MARRIED: w. Audrey

CHILDREN: s. Webb, Jr.; d. Debbie

It was a broiling-hot west Texas day and we were marching from Fort Bliss to a firing range, full pack and rifle, double-time. Our merciless first sergeant denied our request for a ten-minute break until we passed a roadhouse, from which a jukebox was blaring "There Stands the Glass." The sergeant said, "Okay, boys, take ten." When I asked him why he got "soft" all of a sudden, he said, "Soft, hell. It's just that I never miss the chance to hear Webb Pierce." Apparently millions of other country-western fans of the 1950s and 1960s agreed with the sergeant, for Webb Pierce was a country king for a long time: Only Eddy Arnold has had more chart hits than Pierce, and Pierce is in the top

Webb Pierce: He can spot a hit.

ten of artists with the most consecutive number-one records as well as with the greatest total of number-one records. He is number three as the artist with the most consecutive years on the hit parade, with songs like "Wondering," "Slowly," "In the Jailhouse Now," "Back-Street Affair," and scores of others. All in all, he's had sixty-eight songs in the "hit" category.

Brought up in rural Louisiana, he made his mark there before heading for Nashville. While working as a salesman for Sears Roebuck he sang locally, getting favorable attention and finally landing on Shreveport's *Louisiana Hayride*, during the days when Faron Young, Goldie Hill, Jimmy Day, and Floyd Cramer were regulars. "Then I got a Decca recording contract, and I had this song, 'Wondering,' which hit big. And so, after that song hit—and I had another hit, too, called 'Don't Do It, Darling'—then I got an offer to come to Nashville and be on Grand Ole Opry, and that's how it started."

Pierce is very proud of his ability to spot a hit song. "Yes, sir. I predicted 'Sunday Morning Coming Down' was gonna be a hit when Ray Stevens first did it. It should have been a hit then, but Johnny Cash got the song across because he was so hot on television. You can take that television network, and you can sell almost anything with all that power behind you. That's a great song. I always liked it long before Cash recorded it. I predicted that other song of Kris Kristofferson that Ray Price had out, 'For the Good Times,' too. That's a great song."

*How do you spot a hit?*

"That's a good question. It's just something . . . you have to listen to a song. If you like it, you feel it, you record it, and you wait for the public to make a hit out of it for you. It's up to the public. If they like it, it's a hit. If they don't like it, it's not a hit. You never know when you put one out what's gonna happen."

*But certainly your sixty-eight hits have something in common. What would you say are the ingredients of a hit song?*

"Well, it's different things that make a song a hit. One of the things is you sing about the things people think about the most, but don't talk about. That becomes an emotional outlet for the people, and they feel they have a friend in the song. They like it, they buy it, they play it, they sing it, because it's something that seems to fit their purpose."

*How important do you think the melody is?*

"The melody is important, but the lyric is the most important thing—the words to a song. You can develop a liking for the music. Once you like the words, you like hearing the words, the music will just grow on you."

*Are there any subjects in particular that people buy in a song lyric?*

"Not any special subjects . . . that is, there are special subjects, but there are many of them. I think people like songs about back-street affairs. It's a proven fact that they bought that 'Back-Street Affair' of mine. I think the reason that song hit is that there were a lot of people having back-street affairs, and it was something they were keeping hidden. Then, when the record came out, it became an emotional outlet for them. They hear somebody singing about back-street affairs, they kind of smile and say, 'That's us, honey. Let's play that one. Let's buy that one.' You know. There were enough people saying 'That's us, honey' that it sold a lot of records and got a lot of plays. 'There Stands the Glass' is another instance. There's a drinking song that I just figured would hit, because 75 per cent of the people in the world drink. You know, they take a drink at some time or other. They drink sociably, and some drink to extremes, but 'There stands the glass, Fill it up to the brim' . . . they like that song. It's still one of the most-requested songs I've ever recorded.

*But, Webb, there are so many barroom songs that have also become hits.*

"'There Stands the Glass,' though, is like the national anthem of barroom songs. It's the top of all. There's a lot of barroom songs, that's true, but 'There Stands the Glass' conquers all of them. It's a proven fact that anywhere an artist goes, if he plays a barroom, they're gonna ask him to play 'There Stands the Glass.' That song took care of all the drinking songs when it happened. Every artist—of which I know every artist in the business—and every one of them tell me the same thing: 'Webb, that song of yours, "There Stands the Glass," if I play a barroom or a nightclub, I have to sing that song. If I don't, they'll kill me. They've gotta hear that song.' And they ask me, 'How is it with you?' I say that's the first thing they ask for. I say people can walk up to me an' say, 'I'd like for you to sing that song.' And I say, 'I know, "There Stands the Glass,"'" and they say,

'How'd you know?' I say, 'That's what everybody else wants, I figured that's what you'd want, too.' ''

Success has not stopped Pierce from performing. "I'm on the road again," he says, "but just on weekends. Weekends, two or three days is enough. And I'm doing that because the public still seems to want me out there. I'm tired of the road. The only part you enjoy is when you're doing the show. This traveling is a man-killing job. Staying in hotel rooms, being away from your family, taking a chance on getting killed, flying from here to yonder." Pierce's major activity these days is helping his young daughter, Debbie, in her career as a country singer.

## PILLOW, RAY

BORN: January 30, 1937, Lynchburg, Virginia
MARRIED: w. Jo Ann
CHILDREN: s. Dale, Daryl Ray; d. Selena

Ray Pillow tried out for the National Pet Milk Talent Contest in Nashville some years back, and lost. He went home to Virginia, graduated from college, and sang in clubs, gaining enough local fame to get him a contract with Capitol. He recorded "Thank You, Ma'am," which was a fair hit (number seventeen on the charts for ten weeks), and joined Grand Ole Opry. He was named Most Promising Male Country Artist of 1966 by *Billboard* magazine and starred in a movie called *Country Boy*. He has a pleasant voice and a coterie of fans, but these days he doesn't seem to be the Pillow that country fans want to dream on.

## POSEY, SANDY

BORN: Jasper, Alabama

Sandy Posey recorded "Born a Woman," which sold more than a million records for MGM and is not exactly a country song. But she claims kinship to Elvis Presley, Jerry Lee Lewis, and Mac Davis, who all "possess that quality of being at home in any music." "Bring Him Home Safely to Me" did well on the country charts in 1971, and in 1973 "Happy, Happy Birthday, Baby" began a slow climb. Sandy Posey also received good marks from European critics on her recent tour, where she was on a bill with

Tom Jones and Engelbert Humperdinck. She records for Columbia.

## PRESLEY, ELVIS

BORN: January 8, 1935, East Tupelo, Mississippi
MARRIED: w. Priscilla Beaulieau (divorced)
CHILDREN: d. Lisa Marie

Probably the most famous alumnus of L. C. Hume High School in Memphis, Tennessee (class of 1952), Elvis is one of the few people in the world who doesn't need a last name. There is only one Elvis, and he is claimed by every branch of popular music—including country. Actually, he's only had five number-one hits on the country charts, and these were probably simultaneously number one on the pop charts as well. There are those who claim Elvis is not a country singer, but as a nameless Nashville cynic once said, "I don't know one Grand Ole Opry star who wouldn't share billing with Elvis in Madison Square Garden, the Hollywood Bowl, or any of the big, hard-to-fill houses in America. Elvis *always* has a sold-out sign hanging on his concerts." Nonetheless, country purists believe his influence corrupted country music.

Paul Hemphill explains it in his book *The Nashville Sound*: "Nashville, by the early fifties, had established itself as country music's spiritual headquarters and business was booming. There was little experimentation with the music, although some singers—notably Eddy Arnold, a country boy who had once clowned around in a checkered suit with the Pee Wee King band—had managed to take some of the corn out of the music and had begun reaping royalties from pop charts. Country music was sailing right along, doing its own thing, having a ball, until—*Elvis*.

"Rock-and-roll changed everything, of course. Or, at any rate, the forces that rock-and-roll represented changed everything. Rock sneaked up on everybody and hit before anybody realized what was going on. What was going on was, the kids were taking over. Until the fifties, a teen-ager had stayed in his place. No money, no rights, no nothing. Go to school, mow lawns, in by ten, graduate, don't smoke, marry a *nice* girl, get a *nice* job, talk *nice*, join

the Rotary, shut up, have babies, have grand-children, collect social security, die. Big deal. You had Korea now, the first of the lousy little wars. You had the atom bomb now. You had the fallout from World War II, which meant unprecedented affluence and more liberal morals and the gnawing thought that maybe the world *won't* go on forever. It marked the beginning of an era that only now is coming into full blossom: an era in which the majority of Americans are below twenty-five years of age, an era that finds nudity in clubs and on movie screens, an era where marijuana is likely to be legalized, an era where any high school girl who hasn't been laid by her junior year gets funny looks, an era where baseball and Old Glory and the Lions Club and crewcuts and apple pie have gone out of style, an era where sixteen-year-olds set clothing fashions for the whole world, an era where the old man is a fink. In the fifties, in other words, the kids took over. And their leader was a snarling ex-hillbilly musician by the name of Elvis Presley.

"The term 'rock-and-roll' had been first used in 1951, but it was around '54 when the music reverberated across the country and nearly wiped out everything else. It was, technically, a blend of country blues and boogie and jazz and gospel and what was called, in the South, 'nigger music.' Realistically, it was teen soul. Elvis Presley had been raised on a farm near Tupelo, Mississippi, and had known them all. He was country, Negro, jazz, blues, gospel, all of them rolled into one. He thumped a bass fiddle onstage at the Opry at one point, and wailed Assembly of God songs back home at another point. When he went to Memphis in 1954 and got a recording contract with Sun Records, after hacking out a living as a truck driver, he recorded a sort of country-jazz-gospel-nigger-good ol' boy-race-blues number and the world was ready for him. Elvis was saying to hell with Korea and the old folks. He was saying groove it because tomorrow you may die. He was right there on the *Ed Sullivan Show*, wearing black leather, making love with his guitar, sneering at the folks, bawawawawawaw-anging all of those watts through an amplifier, being preached about on Sunday, having his clothes torn from him in Chicago, *taking over.* And these kids, the ones who had all of the money for things like records and transistor radios and black leather

jackets and electric guitars, bought him. And a guy named Harold Jenkins, who had led a hillbilly band called The Cimarrons while he was in the army in Japan, came home and heard this Presley, who had come from only forty miles away from *his* hometown of Friars Point, Mississippi, and changed his name to Conway Twitty and went rock-and-roll and hit the road in search of *his* fortune. And the others, many of them former country musicians, quickly fell in line: Bill Haley, Jerry Lee Lewis, Roy Orbison, Johnny Cash, Buddy Holly, the Everly Brothers. (All but Haley and the late Buddy Holly have more or less returned to country.)"

The Presley story has been told countless thousands of times in periodicals, books, and TV documentaries, and by word of teen-age mouth in countries from Scotland to Zambia. If anyone in the world doesn't know who Presley is, he probably is a deaf lama in Ulan Bator.

One of twin boys (the other died at birth, and there are those close to Elvis who say he harbors a great guilt about his departed sibling and that is the reason he can't really enjoy his phenomenal success), Elvis grew up in Mississippi and Tennessee singing at camp meetings, home, and for friends. In mid-1953, while working as a $35-a-week truck driver, he decided to record one of his songs to help him get club work in the area. He went to the offices of Sun Records, in Memphis, and Sam Phillips recorded him and liked what he heard.

In a magazine article about Sam Phillips, John Pugh describes Phillips' version of the Elvis beginnings: "In the meantime Elvis had come into the studio. I recorded him and got a moderate response. Elvis did not break overnight. I traveled widely and got encouragement from only two DJs. The white disc jockeys wouldn't play him because he sounded too black, and the black disc jockeys wouldn't play him because he sounded too white.

"In those days a radio station was either top ten, 'hillbilly,' or what was euphemistically called a 'race' station, and there was no programming deviation whatsoever. As Elvis was neither fish nor fowl, no one would take a chance on him. And for good reason; the first DJ, for example, who played Elvis on WSM—home station of the Grand Ole Opry—was fired for his temerity.

"Sam did two key things. He gave records to

the juke-box operators who were going through the transition from 78s to 45s. Their number of slots had suddenly quadrupled on the new machines and they were hungering for any new product. Sam also *gave away*—albeit reluctantly —free records to the radio stations. The latter practice was unheard of at that time, but both efforts brought results. People punched Elvis' number on the juke box out of curiosity, liked what they heard, and began demanding the record. A grateful disc jockey, awed by Sam's largesse, would take a gamble, give Elvis a spin, and get an overwhelmingly favorable reaction that the programming director couldn't ignore. And so, bit by bit, this new cat on this new label with this new music began being heard and accepted.

"There were even a couple of factors operating in Sam's favor. Back then it took three weeks for a record to arrive in the South and Midwest from Los Angeles, two weeks from New York. This time lag could kill a record before it ever got started. Sam, sitting in centrally located Memphis with his own pressing plant, could have his product all over the country in less than half the time. He literally ran circles around the majors in distribution.

" 'Elvis' records began to sell and I knew I had a powerhouse,' Sam continued. 'I called Jim Denny and Jack Stapp about getting Elvis on the Opry. They suggested we go to *Louisiana Hayride*. That was the first time I had ever seen Elvis in professional circumstances. After the first song, he had them on their feet. I had never seen anything like it before. Then we had him at a park concert in Memphis with Slim Whitman. Slim was one of the biggest artists in the country. I noticed the size of the crowd was larger than usual, but I had no idea until the show started they had come to see Elvis instead of Slim.

" 'It was then I began to get calls about Elvis' going to another label. I couldn't understand it,' said Sam, 'because I had never said anything about Elvis' leaving, and he had never said anything to me about it. I called a promoter, Tom Parker, and said, "Somebody's putting out this story, because I've heard it too many times."

" 'He said that it wasn't he and that he didn't know who it could be. We talked on and he said, "By the way, is he for sale?"

" 'I said, "Anybody I got is for sale, but I can't go into it over the phone."

" 'He said, "I'll fly down and let's talk about it."

" 'He came down, we talked it over, and I got the impression he was the one who had talked out of school. Anyway, I laid the deal on the line.

" 'He said, "That's awfully high, but let me see if I can raise the money."

" 'In the meantime I had to call my distributors and set them straight. I told them I had a great bulwark of talent potential, and that I had to have the money to sustain them. I certainly wasn't going to take it and run.

" 'Parker put up the money and we consummated the deal in the fall of 1955. I took the $40,000 and plowed it back into the company so I could get into the record business like I wanted to. I had no idea Elvis was going to be so astronomical, but I've never regretted selling him [he went to RCA]. The sale was agreeable with everybody.' "

The rest of the story, as they say in show biz, is history. Elvis is now about forty years old, he has had smash hit after smash hit, and all his ho-hum movies make money. He has been a soldier in Germany and he has married and divorced. He has a baby daughter. He is good to his old friends and to his family. He divides his time between Memphis and Los Angeles. Colonel Parker keeps Elvis a mystery, a shadowy figure whose only personality is that of the man in the wild suits, shaking and rocking on the stage with fans screaming.

When Presley appeared in Madison Square Garden in 1972, Parker allowed a press conference (less than half an hour) in which reporter Patrick Carr recalls: "Elvis was the epitome of the vagabond Vegas Prince he has become since he quit being the world's chief threat to maidenly virtue and the moronic hero of a score of formula Hollywood movies. He was dazzling, bronzed, and magnificent, but he was also warm, humble, easygoing, and completely unaffected, playing Elvis Presley, the living legend funnin' the boys.

" 'First of all, I plead not guilty to all charges,' was his opening remark, just to let the press know that bygones were bygones, and now he and they were playing the same game.

After all, had he not proved beyond a shadow of doubt that he could master any set of rules they cared to play by, and come out bigger and brighter than ever? Had he not crossed the Showbiz Sweepstakes finishing line, laps ahead of the competition—heavy-metal kids, hairy Liverpudlians, prime-time crooners and all—on a steed of solid gold and pure American savvy?

" 'Why have you never performed in New York before?' asked Geraldo Rivera, ABC News whiz kid.

" 'Ur . . . I think it was a matter of not getting the proper building,' the king replied with a wide grin and a glance toward Colonel Tom. Pure nonsense, of course, but just the right reply.

"Dozens of telephone calls made by this reporter, asking just that question in various forms, revealed no more likely reason. On any subject of even a faintly controversial nature, nobody close to the Elvis organization had anything to say but good news couched in the vaguest terms—as usual, for the Colonel is no respecter of the press's desire for candid revelations. You can speculate, of course: mutual hostility between the Colonel and the moguls of Madison Avenue, fear that Elvis might not succeed beyond every wildest dream, difficulty in finding the right deal . . .

" 'Mr. Presley, why do you think you have outlasted any other pop performer?'

" 'I take vitamin E.'

" 'I hear from everybody in the business that you really are a shy, humble, wonderful human being. Are you?'

" 'I don't know what makes them think *that*—y'know, this gold belt . . .' Elvis stood up, pulled back his dazzling, powder-blue Regency jacket, and exposed the belt. Flashbulbs and laughter exploded through the room. It was pure corn, but they loved it.

" 'I'm reminded of the *Ed Sullivan Show*,' shouted the chic lady reporter who had asked the previous question.

" 'So am I,' replied the star, 'that's why I'm sitting down now.'

"Did he still use hair grease? No, he gave up that greasy kid's stuff years ago. Did he feel modest these days, after all that stuff he used to do? Well, he was 'tame' compared to what they do now, he just 'stood there and jiggled.' Did he have anything to say about other popular acts? Naw, he couldn't possibly criticize another performer. Did he have anything to say about the Vietnam war or Women's Lib? 'Naw, I'm just an entertainer, honey.'

" 'Elvis, after forty-seven gold records and fifteen years at the top, what are you going to do now?'

"Elvis leaned forward, flashed a coy expression, and said, 'Punt.'

"Why did he go back to the live stage? Well, he missed the closeness of a live audience—something the Garden's enormous barn supplies with difficulty—and just as soon as he could get out of his MGM movie contracts, he had headed for the stage again. His next aim after his American tour was to visit Britain. Except for his years in the army, Elvis has never been outside the United States, even for a vacation.

"Why had he not agreed to an authorized biography? (The only comprehensive work, by Jerry Hopkins, was decidedly unauthorized. Hopkins didn't end up paying $25,000, the price the Colonel used to make a habit of asking for an Elvis interview.) 'I don't feel that it's time yet,' answered Elvis.

"After twenty minutes the press conference was beginning to drag; Elvis was answering questions evasively. Enter Colonel Tom, the absolute master of all Presley affairs, aside from musical direction.

" 'I'd like to live up to my reputation of being a nice guy,' said the Colonel, tongue firmly planted in cheek, 'but *this* is *it*, folks.' Elvis stood up, waved once, and strode offstage—instantly.

"As the audience filed out of the Mercury Ballroom, and Elvis headed back to the two penthouse floors which the Colonel had selected for maximum security, a team of the Colonel's sidekicks gathered up the discarded souvenir books, ballpoints, and calendars. It was a reflex action from all those years of practice at concert halls across the nation.

"And that's what we know about Presley.

"Is he country?

"Let's take the word of a record company executive: 'Elvis Presley may not be hard country in the tradition of the Maddox Brothers and Rose, but we know that people who buy country records buy Presley and they don't buy the Allman Brothers or Neil Diamond.' "

## PRICE, KENNY

BORN: May 27, 1931, Covington, Kentucky

Known affectionately, according to his record company, as The Round Mound of Sound, Kenny Price sings smooth ballads and offbeat, humorous country songs in a deep baritone reminiscent of his idol, Red Foley. Kenny's a big man in country music. He tips the scales around 300 pounds and stands over six feet tall.

Born and raised on a farm near Covington, Kentucky, Price learned to play guitar at an early age. By the time he was fourteen years old, he was ready to make his debut on WZIP radio in nearby Cincinnati, Ohio. Following high school and a two-year tour with the army in

Kenny Price: "The Round Mound of Sound."

Korea, Price attended the Cincinnati Conservatory of Music, something he had never considered before entering the service. But while performing with a USO show in Korea, the audience response convinced him to pursue a musical career.

In 1957 he became a regular performer on Buddy Ross's *Hometowners* TV show on WLW, Cincinnati. This led to a spot on the popular *Midwest Hayride.* In no time at all, Price was established as *Hayride*'s lead singer, and his popularity grew throughout the Midwest. He recorded for Boone Records, a regional label, and scored a big hit with his version of "Walking on New Grass." This was followed by other releases that produced considerable commercial success, including "Happy Tracks" and "Pretty Girl, Pretty Clothes, Pretty Sad."

With each release, Price gained more fans, eventually attracting the attention of RCA Records' executives, who thought he warranted exposure to a national audience. He joined RCA in 1969, and many of his early songs for Boone Records were re-released on his new label. Among the albums he's recorded for RCA are "The Red Foley Songbook" and "Northeast Arkansas Mississippi County Bootlegger," both of which offer a fine introduction to Price's talents as a country artist.

## PRICE, RAY

BORN: January 12, 1926, Perryville, Texas
MARRIED: w. Betty B. Greb
CHILDREN: s. Clifton Ray

Danny Thomas, on the Merv Griffin TV talk show, turned to Merv and described his wife's favorite song, and then he sang a few bars of the number himself, in Danny Thomas style—a combination of the Broadway musical comedy and the middle-of-the-road TV variety show schools of singing. "We have someone from Nashville who has a big hit with that song," Merv said, and Danny Thomas, good actor that he is, feigned surprise, even though at the start of the show Griffin had announced that his "great, good friend Ray Price is going to be with us." Price, dressed in a natty pearl-gray, western-styled business suit, sang, without his guitar, and to the cocktail-lounge accompaniment of Griffin's house band. "Oh, that hillbilly music," Danny Thomas said, warmly shaking Ray Price's hand. "No wonder it's so popular, with people like Ray singing big hits."

Well now, Danny: It's *country* music, and Ray Price has been around since he sang *hillbilly* music. In 1950, when I was in Dallas for the first time, I accidentally listened to a program on station KRLD called *The Big D Jamboree* and heard Ray Price. "He's as good as Hank Williams," I thought at the time, and I called the station to find out how to get his records. It was difficult to find recordings in Los Angeles on the Bullet label, but I managed, and I listened to them until they almost wore out. "If you want to hear pure, honky-tonk country," I told my friends, "listen to Ray Price." And when he joined Grand Ole Opry and began recording for Columbia, I placed a standing order at my record dealer's to always put aside Ray Price albums. But it was a very different Ray Price from the man who appeared on the Merv Griffin show. *That* Ray Price has violins (not fiddles—violins!) in his group now and appears with symphony orchestras.

The former hillbilly Ray Noble Price was born in Perryville, Texas. Like everybody else (Jim Reeves was growing up some miles away) in Cherokee County, he listened to Jimmie Rodgers, the Carlisles, and others of that variety. When he graduated from Adamson High School (his family had moved to Dallas) he thought about a musical career, but World War II intervened and he spent four years in the service, and in 1946 he entered North Texas Agricultural College in Arlington. He studied hard, not yet sure of a career, but appeared as a singer locally and on the KRBC *Hillbilly Circus* in Abilene. At that time his style was strongly influenced by Hank Williams (whom he had met, and from whom he had received personal encouragement). He recorded some songs for Bullet and appeared on the *Big D Jamboree,* but still entertained thoughts about ranching until segments of the *Big D Jamboree* were broadcast on the CBS radio network and letters poured in wanting to know who "Ray Price" was, and Columbia signed him. His first two offerings were biggies: "Talk to Your Heart" and "Don't Let the Stars Get in Your Eyes," followed by the equally big "I'll Be There" and "Release Me." During this period he billed himself as The Cherokee Cowboy, and with the death of Hank Williams managed to get remnants of Williams' band, The Drifting Cowboys, to back him up in a group called The Cherokee Cowboys. "Hank Williams may be dead," critic George Gordon wrote, "but in a sense he lives through the work of Ray Price. He is obviously the successor to Hank. But Price has steadfastly refused to be typecast, and he has developed into one of the most individualistic of country singers, with a style heavily influenced by blues music." In fact, Price has been so individualistic that by the late sixties, when country music had shifted back radically toward the honky-tonk style, he began regularly performing songs in the pop style which he had so vehemently rejected in the late fifties.

Nowadays, nobody can accuse Price of using a whining-steel-guitar sound to back him up. He sings middle-of-the-road. It seems to work, though, because Price records hit after hit. "Crazy Arms," which he recorded in 1956, holds the third-place title for records of longevity on the country charts. It remained for forty-five weeks. Only Bobby Helms's "Fraulein" and Hank Williams' "Cold Cold Heart" have beaten it out. Price also has a number of other hits which hold titles for longevity—and is number seven in the top ten artists with the most record sides on the country charts (fifty-seven until 1971). He is in the top twenty artists with the most number-one country records, and number six in the list of artists with the most consecutive country hit-parade tunes. His Country Music Association and Grammy and other country-music-oriented awards are too numerous to mention. Ray Price has recorded (excluding the early Bullet days) exclusively for Columbia. They consider Ray Price one of their more important artists, and there's a reason. But he's no longer a hillbilly.

# PRIDE, CHARLEY

BORN: 1938, Sledge, Mississippi
MARRIED: w. Rozene

Charley Pride, immaculately tailored in a Victorian pearl-gray suit and never relaxing his now-famous gap-toothed smile, pushed through the crowd of well-wishers at the 1973 Country Music Awards show, his departure postponed briefly by three people at the stage door. "Can

211

Charley Pride: Still hitting home runs.

we talk to you for a minute, Charley?'' said the father, a rangy man in farmer clothes. "We got all your records,'' said the mother, a thin-lipped, grim woman in a worn print dress and men's oxfords. She ran her hand through hair which had never been touched by a beautician. "We listen to you all the time,'' the son said, handing a stub of paper to be autographed. The son, his front two teeth missing, spoke haltingly. "You're our favorite. We drove 125 miles hopin' to talk to you.'' Charley Pride hurriedly signed his name. "Aren't you folks nice,'' Charley Pride said, smiling and disappearing into a cluster of black Cadillacs. "You really drove that far?'' I asked the father. "Oh, you bet,'' the son replied. "You like black country singers?'' I asked, provocatively. "Black?'' the son asked. "Oh, you mean colored. Well, you know, we never much think about that when we listen to Charley. He's the greatest singer since Hank Williams, we think.''

It is a long time since RCA cautiously produced Charley Pride's first album, not showing his face. Now Pride is probably among RCA's top three properties, country or pop. Within two years of his first album he had eight number-one records (including "I'd Rather Love You,'' "Is Anybody Goin' to San Antone,'' "Afraid of Losing You Again,'' and "Kiss an Angel Good Mornin' ''), putting him in the top ten of country artists with the most number-one hits.

"Everywhere I go, people want to know two things,'' Pride always tells audiences, making light of his shading. "They want to know, 'Charley, how did *you* get into country music?' and 'Charley, how come you don't talk like you *supposed* to?'' He says he owes it all to Hank Williams, but there are many critics who feel he sings Hank Williams songs better than Hank did.

A few years ago, I heard Charley Pride and convinced *Esquire* to let me interview him. He was appearing as a "special guest" on the *Johnny Wright–Kitty Wells Family Show* in Newark, New Jersey (another then-underrated performer, Willie Nelson, was also a special guest, and during the course of the evening I was treated to a couple of Pride/Nelson duets). Charley Pride was the last to appear as a solo, and I asked the stage manager why a special guest would not have been highlighted on the show sooner. He looked at me and laughed.

"You haven't seen Charley Pride, have you? Well, nobody, but nobody, can follow Charley Pride."

At the time, Charley Pride told me about his background: "I was born in Sledge, Mississippi, and as a kid I always dug country music. Nobody in my family was musical. I memorized all those country songs and sung them. My family thought I was crazy. My sister would ask me, 'Why you singin' this music? It ain't gonna get you nowhere.' I said I didn't care if it got me anythin', I loved it. I bought my first guitar when I was fourteen years old, I think, and I played for my own fun. I never had any intention of being a cotton picker, no sir, but I didn't think music was the way out. So at seventeen I left Sledge to play baseball for the Negro American League, with Detroit and the Memphis Red Sox. Then I went into the army and I played afterwards for a time with the Los Angeles Angels. I ended up in Helena, Montana, playing semipro ball and working as a smelter for Anaconda's zinc complex. Every once in a while I'd sing between innings and the crowds seemed to like it. Some folks who had a nightclub heard me and soon I was playing baseball, smelting, and singing at nights. I thought it was a pretty good life. Then one night [country singer] Red Sovine came into the club, told me I should look him up in Nashville, but I wasn't ready. I wanted to play for the majors, anyway, and decided to try out for the Mets. I ordered six bats (W-166 Brooks Robinson models) with my name on them and took time off from the smelter to go to the Mets training camp. To make a long story short, [Casey] Stengel didn't seem to know I was coming and I overheard him saying that he wasn't running a goddamn tryout camp. They let me try out anyway, but I wasn't good enough, so on my way back to Montana I stopped in Nashville at one in the morning, and woke up Red Sovine and told him I was here. Red told me to go to Cedarwood, where Webb Pierce booked out of. I made a tape which was listened to by a Nashville record producer, Jack Clement, who was looking for a Negro entertainer. They liked the tape, but they wanted to dress me up funny and bill me as George Washington III, but I told them I wouldn't be no clown for nobody, that I was going to sing under my own name. Anyway, the tape got to Chet Atkins."

"Chet Atkins," I reported in *Esquire*, "one of the most successful guitarists in the business, is also big man for RCA Victor in Nashville. When Jack Clement brought him the Charley Pride tape, Atkins thought he was good enough to record and brought the tape to a meeting of A & R men. 'All the top creative brass at RCA,' he recalls. 'I played the record and everybody agreed he was worth signing up. Then I told them he was black. Pure silence. Finally, someone broke in, "He's great, though. Let's take a chance." And the rest is history. A lot of people believed we were making a mistake, that disc jockeys in the deep South wouldn't play him. That he wouldn't get any promotion. They were wrong.'

"Atkins believes Charley will become one of the all-time greats, 'and not only in country music.' He says that superstars like Hank Williams or Frank Sinatra have a certain intangible edge. 'Put Charley Pride on the worst p.a. system in the country and it doesn't matter. He'll penetrate. That's greatness. Few have it. Charley does.'"

A lot has happened for Charley Pride since. "Country music accepted him," writes Peter McCabe in a magazine article, "just as easily as Charley Pride had accepted country music. Not only did it accept him, it made him number one in its ranks in terms of record sales and voted him 'Entertainer of the Year.' The electricity is still quite apparent to anybody in an audience whenever and wherever Charley Pride is about to walk onstage. And seventeen albums later, Charley Pride's records are every bit as good and as rich in quality and material as his first album.

"Where does he go from here? As the latest in a line of country-music stars—Jimmy Dean, Glen Campbell, Johnny Cash—to bring country music beyond its traditional environs to an even wider audience, the next logical step seems to be a TV show. And maybe that's what Jack Johnson has in mind, though if he has, he ain't sayin'.

"Charley has a simple explanation for all his success.

" 'I feel music is just like buying and selling groceries, or insurance, or anything else,' he says. 'The better the product you've got, the better people like it and the better you can sell it. If it's got good lyrics and a good melody, I can do a much better job of selling it. But I have to

Charley Pride: Believes in love.

really like a song. I have to feel that I can put my heart into it because I sing from feelings, I mean from the heart.

" 'Why do I do mostly love songs? Well, I believe in love, for one thing. And some of the songs that I've recorded remind me not only of situations that other people have been in, but of situations that I've been in. And I just *love* ballads. I don't believe music should be used to promote politics, or religion or whatever, but that's only my own individual feelings on it. I want to make that clear. And I am a staunch individualist.

" 'I think that explains a lot about why I'm in country music. I said to myself, "Why can't I sing the kind of music I love?" I believe you should be your own individual self and not be molded into what somebody thinks you should be. I love to talk and visit with people, all people, but it was a long time before I would even venture to talk because I was afraid of saying "they does" instead of "they do," until I learned how to listen and observe, and even now I'm still learning. People say, "Where did you go to school?" I say, "Sledge Junior High." They say, "No, I mean college. Where did you learn to speak this well?" I say, "Self-taught. Observing. Listening." Because I make people my business.

" 'I'm a very curious person. I'm a Pisces. We're curious people. I believe in astrology. I've always started with the basis, "Well, we're both Americans." I've done that since I was old enough to learn a lyric.' "

Pride belittles his significance to most interviewers. He obviously loves his craft, and all his energies are devoted to it. He refuses to speak for any minority group and he doesn't see himself as a phenomenon. Peter McCabe says that Pride "thinks of himself as a plain, average guy who grew up in Mississippi, picked cotton, was blessed with a voice, wanted to be a baseball player but happened to make it as a singer after he didn't make it in baseball. He plays down the uniqueness of his situation in country music."

Musicologist Jules Siegel thinks differently. In a letter to me, which I printed in its entirety in *Esquire*, Siegel writes: "In order to understand the significance of Charley Pride, you need first to understand that music, like speech, is a form of communication that uses many languages, many dialects, many vernaculars, many accents. The musical language of white Middle America is Country & Western, which has been traced back to the English folk song of the seventeenth century and earlier. The other great popular musical language, rhythm-and-blues, comes from Africa; the most popular recording stars of our time have sung in a synthesis of these two great traditions. Elvis Presley was a white country boy who sang with a black accent. The Beatles were white English boys who sang in the idiom of Presley and other rock-and-roll performers. Bob Dylan was a white American poet who chose to combine the country voice with the black style. These performers have been translators standing between black and white; and explaining one side to the other. Until now, the black message has mainly flowed through white translators to the white audiences. Its effect has been overpoweringly great. Those of us who watched and felt what Presley, the Beatles, and Dylan did to American consciousness remember that that potent sound, still only five years old, was followed by the great wave of revolution we see sweeping the country today. If that was what happened when the voice of the black people was heard secondhand, we can only guess what may result when a black man like Charley Pride sings directly to Middle America in its authentic language, vernacular, dialect and accent.

"Charley Pride may not yet have chosen to deliver any special message, but he has proved that it is possible for a black man to sing in a white voice. When he or those who come after him begin to instruct as well as entertain, white Middle America will be changed forever.' "

## PRUETT, JEANNE
MARRIED: h. Jack Pruett
CHILDREN: s. Jack; d. Jael

In 1971, when she finally made the charts with a number-66 hit (for six weeks) called "Hold On to My Unchanging Love" (her own composition, by the way), nobody in Nashville thought that she would be named one of the "new" stars of the year at the 1973 Country Music Awards show. Her hit "Satin Sheets" catapulted to the top of the charts, and brought Mrs.

"contented, dedicated housewife," whose musical needs were satisfied by writing songs for Marty Robbins Enterprises. "I have a couple of teen-age kids," Jeanne says, "and I felt my first obligation was to the children God sent me and put in my charge to raise as best I could. But those children do have a way of growing up."

Jeanne Pruett was born in Alabama, the daughter of a full-time farmer. Among her earliest memories are Saturday trips to town to sell home-grown products and then hurrying back home to listen to the Grand Ole Opry. Because of her farm background, she claims, gardening is a major activity. Each year she raises tomatoes "for the Pruetts and all their neighbors." She has won twenty major prizes for her rosebushes. Marty Robbins has recorded a number of Jeanne Pruett songs: "Count Me Out," "Waiting in Reno," "Christmas Is for Kids," and "Lily of the Valley." Other Pruett compositions: "One-Woman Man" and "One Day Ahead of My Tears." Besides singing and writing, Jeanne Pruett is active in two PTAs and a Federated Woman's Club, and she has been a model for a Nashville department store. Her major charitable activity is the School for the Blind in Donelson, Tennessee. She claims she is the happiest woman in the music industry, and husband Jack says she is a great cook. Jeanne Pruett will not admit whether or not she sleeps on satin sheets.

Although Jeanne Pruett had been writing hit songs for other artists for several years, she just recorded her first single, "Satin Sheets," in 1973 and had a number-one hit.

Pruett fame and a chance for fortune. Some weeks prior to the CMA Awards show, she was a guest performer on Grand Ole Opry and was stunned to hear the announcement, at the same time the audience heard it, that "Jeanne Pruett would become an Opry regular." It's been a long wait.

The Pruetts, as a family, have a musical proclivity. Jeanne's brother Sammy is a musician, and her husband, Jack, is a picker for Marty Robbins. But until recently, Jeanne was a

# R

## RAINWATER, MARVIN
BORN: July 2, 1925, Wichita, Kansas

Back in the mid-fifties, the Arthur Godfrey *Talent Scouts* program was one of the ways to instant stardom. Among the country stars who won first prize on the show are the late Patsy Cline (who was just named to the Country Music Hall of Fame) and Marvin Rainwater. Rainwater—American Indian, World War II navy pharmacist's mate, and former veterinary student at Washington State University—tried out for Godfrey's TV show, was accepted, sang his own composition, "Gonna Find Me a Bluebird," and won a week as the star of Godfrey's morning radio show and a recording contract with MGM. "Gonna Find Me a Bluebird" was a major hit, reaching third place on the country charts in 1957 and lasting almost six months. In the two subsequent years, Rainwater recorded "Whole Lotta Women" and "Half Breed," both popular with the public.

He joined the cast of station WWVA's *Jamboree* in Wheeling, West Virginia, and regularly appeared on Red Foley's TV show. Then, in the mid-sixties, Rainwater's bluebird seemed to elude him, and though he travels regularly and has some following, he has never reached the heights expected of him. Interviewed recently in upstate New York, where he was playing at a small club, Rainwater said he probably should "update his style" but didn't think

it was possible at this late date. "But I keep singing. That's all I ever really wanted to do."

## RANDOLPH, BOOTS [Homer Louis Randolph III]

BORN: Paducah, Kentucky
MARRIED: w. Dee
CHILDREN: s. Randy; d. Linda

Boots Randolph began playing the ukulele when he was about ten years old. Although he was born and raised in Paducah, his family moved to Cadiz, Kentucky, before moving again to Evansville, Indiana, where they settled down. He learned to play trombone while in elementary school in Cadiz, but he switched to the saxophone while a member of the Central High School Band in Evansville. "It was easier to

Boots Randolph: "Mr. Sax" plays country horn.

play than the trombone while marching," he recalled.

He began appearing throughout Indiana with local combos in the early 1940s, playing his sax, although he was still a teen-ager. He enlisted in the service toward the end of World War II. Upon his discharge, he returned to playing clubs in the Midwest, until the late 1950s, when he collaborated with James (Spider) Rich on the song "Yakety-Sax," which combined the various styles of music Randolph had been exposed to—jazz, gospel, blues, and country. Chet Atkins, the famous guitarist and RCA Records talent executive, heard a tape and signed Randolph to a contract. Randolph left RCA in 1961 to join the Monument label, on which he still records. He lives outside of Nashville with his wife and family. He is one of the most popular artists in the country market—although his chosen instrument is more associated with jazz and pop. His music is a good example of the influence country has exerted on the pop style, and vice versa.

## RAYE, SUSAN

BORN: October 8, 1944, Eugene, Oregon
MARRIED: h. Jack Wiggins

Susan Raye was discovered by Buck Owens and his manager, Jack McFadden, in Portland, Oregon, when she was a teen-ager singing on a local TV show, *Hoedown*. She is now an installed resident of the Owens home territory of Bakersfield, California, a permanent member of the Owens All-American Show, and a star of growing stature in her own right.

"I went to the club I often sing at," Susan recalls with her radiant and now famous smile, "to see Buck play when he was in Portland. I was introduced to somebody called Jack McFadden. I didn't know who he was, but apparently someone had told him about me. We sat and talked for a while, and then, when Buck went on stage, Jack asked if I wanted to go up and do a couple of duets with Buck. *That's* when I found out who Jack was. Well, I was nervous to say the least, but I went up on that stage and sang some songs with Buck, and both Jack and Buck liked the way I sounded. That was the beginning."

It was almost two years later before Susan signed a contract with Buck and actually got into the Owens act. Buck and Jack bided their time until they felt she was ready for the big time.

"I was young and inexperienced when I first met them, and I honestly think that they both felt I wasn't ready to make a real serious go of it. Buck told me later he didn't want to ruin my life by getting me into the pressure of travel and all the things that go with the hard work of trying to make it before I was ready. So I worked around Portland, a few dates in Las Vegas, and grew up both professionally and personally. Jack kept in constant touch with me the whole time, but didn't put me under any pressure. Then one day, they asked me to come visit them in Bakersfield."

When Susan arrived, she sat and talked with Jack and Buck, and the two men decided that she was ready to join the Owens gang officially and begin touring and recording. They also suggested she move to Bakersfield.

"I talked it over with my mother for about ten minutes," Susan laughs, "and we both figured *why not?* If I was going to be singing, I might as well be with the best. So I went home to Portland, packed up my belongings, and drove back to Bakersfield."

Susan's first single, "Maybe if I Close My Eyes," was released in September 1969 under the management and guidance of Buck.

"I probably could have started out by doing a duet with Buck, but he decided he wanted me to make it alone. Still, he picks all my material, does all the producing, makes all the decisions. And I'm grateful, because he knows a whole lot more about the business than I do."

Her trust has been well founded, because she has had hit after hit, including "L.A. International Airport," "Pitty Pitty Patter," "Wheel of Fortune," and, of course, the duets that she now does with Buck that have made them one of the hottest new duos in country music today.

## REED, JERRY

BORN: March 20, 1937, Atlanta, Georgia
MARRIED: w. Priscilla Mitchell
CHILDREN: d. Sedina, Lottie

On a rainy, slate-gray spring day in Nashville, a crowd gathered outside of Tootsie's Orchid

Lounge, a honky-tonk bar frequented by truck drivers, tourists, good old boys, and country-music stars (it's right close to Ryman Auditorium). Tootsie's walls are papered with record-album covers and notes and pictures, and owner Tootsie Bess, a beehived woman of indeterminate age, has been known to be a character of sorts herself ("Some picker once got drunk," a Tootsie's regular confided to me, "and right in front of everybody decided to exhibit the reason he had this big reputation for being a hotsy-totsy lover, see. And Tootsie, she don't take none of that, and she tooked this club out and ruined his love life for some time to come"). A huge truck wired for heavy electronic performance was parked outside. Busy technicians with ear-phones and microphones and wrapped in wires buzzed in and out of the bar, while a huge crowd gathered, apparently unperturbed by the downpour. Fathers held children on their shoulders so they could see, and I asked one spectator what was happening. "Hey, man, *Jerry Reed's in there.*" Inside, Jerry Reed, filming a sequence for NBC's *Music Country* (which he more or less "hosted" during the summer of 1973), is sitting on the bar, laughing and singing his theme

Jerry Reed: "When you're hot—you're hot!"

song and big hit, "When You're Hot, You're Hot" (number-one country song in the nation for fifteen weeks in 1971). The people in the bar listen intently. They've heard "When You're Hot, You're Hot" dozens, perhaps a hundred times (DJs still play it as "country gold"), but it doesn't matter. "Where Reed is there's electricity," one of the NBC men said. "He's like a 300-watt bulb in a room full of 60-watt lamps. You can feel it. He buzzes."

Reed was wearing a faded Levi suit, with sneakers. His curly blond hair is unfashionably short and he never stopped smiling. "Hey, that was great, Guitar Man," Tootsie beamed. A lot of people in Nashville call Reed Guitar Man after the smash hit he wrote for Elvis Presley. For more than ten years, Jerry Reed has been the artist that many other musicians in Nashville have been touting. As of 1973, he enjoys star status as a top RCA recording artist, a producer, a writer, an actor, a TV star, and when his schedule permits, an "added attraction" on the elite *Festival of Music* package with Chet Atkins, Floyd Cramer, and Boots Randolph. "Jerry Reed has been able to synthesize the best of southern black blues talk songs and translate them into an art form totally acceptable to a wide, nonethnic audience," English music critic Bernard Henry wrote in 1970. "He is an artist on the level of Louis Armstrong, Duke Ellington, and Johnny Cash. And, he's just at the beginning of his career and is growing."

His career started in Atlanta, when, as a teenager, he worked long, grueling days as a laborer in cotton mills and as he told me, "performed nights in gin mills." Reed was friendly with a policeman who knew Atlanta promoter-publisher Bill Lowery, who listened and liked him and convinced Capitol Records to hire him as a writer in 1955 when he was only eighteen. Brenda Lee liked his songs, recorded them, and spread the word about Reed. His career was interrupted by two years in the service. He returned to Nashville in 1961 and has shown that when you're hot, you can keep being hot by working and writing. Among Reed's superhits: "Amos Moses," "Georgia Sunshine," "Alabama Wild Man," "Tupelo, Mississippi Flash," and scores of others. Reed claims to be a "singer, picker, and writer in that order" and says he likes the "home life." This includes professional-quality golfing, fishing, and "ex-

ploring other people's thoughts about life, religion, philosophy, and other heavy subjects."

## REEVES, DEL

BORN: July 14, 1933, Sparta, North Carolina
MARRIED: w. Ellen
CHILDREN: d. Ann Delano, Kari E., Bethany

Born and raised in North Carolina, Del Reeves went to California to find "country gold," appearing on numerous country TV shows in the Los Angeles area. By the late 1950s he had his own TV show and had made a number of appearances in Las Vegas. He composed several songs with his wife, Ellen, which were recorded by Carl Smith and Roy Drusky. The biggest hit of this period was "This Must Be the Bottom." Reeves prefers singing to writing and has had a number of big hits on the country charts, including "Girl on the Billboard" (number one for twenty weeks in 1965), "A Dozen Pair of Boots," "The Philadelphia Phillies," and "Workin' Like the Devil (for the Lord)." Reeves loves to entertain. In 1973 he fell off a horse and injured his leg, which forced him into a hospital and a cast, but despite the doctor's orders, Reeves told reporter John Duggleby, "I haven't missed a show since the accident."

In a magazine interview, Duggleby writes: "Not that he ever missed that many before. Del is one of a dwindling breed of performers who treat their audiences as old friends, and he could never let an old friend down.

"The people who turned out to see Del and the Good-Time Charlies that night were small-town Iowans who had spent the day watching a summer rainstorm turn their centennial celebration into a swampy catastrophe. They were hoping that the Reeves show would salvage the somber proceedings. For the band, it was just another road engagement, one of over 160 concerts they will play this year. 'Hell, we're takin' it easy,' Del laughed. 'Last year we did 235.'

"The concert hall was a leaky old circus tent erected on the flattest and driest ground available. The Good-Time Charlies started the show, struggling for balance on a makeshift stage that sloped so much that when guitarist George Owen leaned into the microphone, he nearly tumbled into the first row. But the show contin-

Del Reeves: His good-time image is accurate.

ued, with the help of Billy Cole, the all-night DJ on station WHO, Des Moines. Although Billy's rendition of 'Folsom Prison Blues' could have wrung a smile from the Man in Black himself, most of the crowd was resigned to shivering in their wet clothes and scraping their muddy shoes on the bleachers throughout the first set.

"After an intermission, the Good-Time Charlies returned, this time with Del leading the way. The tent came to life; the band shifted gears, the crowd switched from nose-blowing to toe-tapping, and even the rain stopped for this North Carolina trucker's son. After sailing non-stop through two numbers, Del paused to greet the audience. He glanced at his injured leg, then down the sloping stage. 'I guess you could say

we're playing under a handicap tonight.'

"'Yeah,' echoed George Owen, 'we're sober.'

"Back on the bus, Del finished an Old Milwaukee out of his refrigerator and quickly propped his swollen leg on a pillow. The band staggered in one by one, and he thanked them, declaring that they 'played their guts out tonight.' He probably tells them that every night. 'I guess the good-time image people get of me is pretty accurate,' he said. 'We joke around a lot on stage and play mostly happy music, because I think people should have fun at our concerts. *We* do.'

"The mention of music, the ice-cold beer, or maybe the combination of both seemed to

221

replace the energy the evening's concert had drained, and he recalled that he had always wanted to be a musician, idolizing the late Hank Williams. 'A lot of stuff we played tonight were old country standards,' he mused. 'You can call it folk or whatever you want, but it's just *old country music.*'

"By now, Royce Kendall had come over from his Winnebago, and the two road veterans began to talk about the state of country music today. Royce claimed that despite the hard-luck stories about making it big in Nashville these days, it is actually much easier to land a recording contract than it used to be. 'People gripe about having to pitch tapes, but back when I got started, the producers wouldn't listen to *anything*,' he said.

"Del agreed. 'There might be more people in Nashville now, but there are also a lot more opportunities. They're crying for young people down there, and trying to create a new star every day.' He attributed this in part to the growing number of frustrated rock disc jockeys who switch to country stations and try to combine elements of both into genetic misfits labeled 'pop country' or 'contemporary.' 'It's nice that country music is becoming more popular,' he added, 'but I wish some of these stations had more of a taste for what they're playing.'

"Billy Cole, one of the few DJs that Del *does* respect, popped his head into the door to bid the gang farewell before returning to Des Moines and his show. Del quickly reached under his seat and produced a copy of his latest album, 'Del Reeves Presents the Good-Time Charlies.' 'Let me circle my best ones, Billy,' he obliged, selecting a strong vocal here and a good fiddle tune there, until almost every song was engulfed by a red ring.

" 'You always were the modest type,' laughed Billy. 'Does anyone play on this album besides you?'

"Finally, the equipment was loaded and the bus was ready to roll—this time to Nashville, where Del and the gang were headlining the Grand Ole Opry the following evening. After explaining the directions to an all-night supermarket where they could replenish their beer supply, I asked Del what the future held for the band.

"He thought for a second, then smiled. 'I'm not sure,' he said, 'but most likely it's gonna be another 235 days of the same thing.' "

## REEVES, JIM

BORN: August 20, 1924, Panola County, Texas

DIED: July 31, 1964

MARRIED: w. Mary Elizabeth White

Perhaps if Jim Reeves had made it with the St. Louis Cardinals he would be alive today. Country music—and he told this to interviewers time and time again—was a "second choice." But during his days as a star pitcher for the University of Texas, he hurt his leg (Roy Acuff also suffered an injury, keeping him from a baseball career). "And I traded my glove for a guitar," Reeves said. "Of all the country-pop singers of the late fifties and early sixties," historian Bill C. Malone writes, "Jim Reeves, before his death in an airplane crash in Tennessee on July 31, 1964, had perhaps the greatest ability to appeal to popular audiences without at the same time losing his sense of country identity." In the years since his death, Jim Reeves albums have continued selling briskly. Reeves was a prolific entertainer, and the large backlog of unreleased recordings which were made available to RCA by his wife, Mary, made production more simple. And recently developed engineering techniques have been applied to these recordings, giving them an eerie contemporary sound. At least, I find them eerie, knowing that Reeves died before the Nashville Sound came into wide acceptance. But I buy Jim Reeves records, too. And I've seen Jim Reeves sing "He'll Have to Go" (one of the ten all-time-great country recordings, in my opinion) at a concert in Washington, D.C., in the early sixties, and though I can't seem to articulate it here, I know why Jim Reeves fan clubs still flourish, and why the constant re-recordings are popular. Maybe it was because he was a "popular" or "city" singer, with a lot of country left in him, and maybe that's what we Americans all are, and Reeves was a conduit to that rural past. Who knows? But there is no doubt of the authenticity of Jim Reeves's country credentials.

Panola County was the same east Texas area that produced country star Tex Ritter. Reeves's father died when he was only ten months old. His mother raised him and his eight brothers and sisters. "I learned early," Reeves told an interviewer, "that farm life is hard, almost too hard unless you find diversions." Reeves's diver-

Jim Reeves: Still selling millions of records.

sions were baseball and country music. He first began playing the guitar when he was six. A guitarist friend, Bill Galloway, recalls many musical sessions they had together, but Jim Reeves always felt that baseball held more promise. He was a star athlete at Carthage High School and the University of Texas, and while playing for the Henderson team in the East Texas League (a St. Louis farm team) he injured his leg. Though he considered himself a good singer and guitarist, Reeves decided that if baseball was out, he would use his "good voice" as an announcer on radio, and he managed to get a disc-jockey job on KGRI in Henderson, Texas. On weekends he played at local clubs, and for a short time he played lead guitar in Beaumont, Texas, in a group headed by the late hillbilly honky-tonk pianist Moon Mullican. Reeves grew more interested in music at this time, and recorded a couple of songs for local studios. One of these was "Mexican Joe" on the Abbott label. "Nobody was as surprised as I was," Reeves recalled, "when it made the country hit parade and stayed there." The success of the record gained him a bid from *Louisiana Hayride* and a contract from RCA Victor. From 1955 to 1968 (four years after his death, mind you) Jim Reeves had one or more top-ten records every year, and though he's been dead since 1964 he's still in the top ten of artists with the most charted records.

At the start of his career Reeves's style was fashioned after Hank Williams and he used honky-tonk instrumentation. But his voice really wasn't suited to this style. He had, as Bill Malone describes it, "a mellow, resonant quality which his supporters like to describe as a 'touch of velvet.'" With the popularity of country-pop, Reeves's voice was well suited for the new genre, and when he dropped traditional instrumentation for a softer quality, he attracted numbers of adherents from the pop-music audience. But Reeves claimed loyalty to country audiences, and his two most popular songs, "Four Walls" (depicting a man forsaken by a girl who loved the honky-tonk life) and "He'll Have to Go" (about a man phoning his girl friend who is sitting with a pick-up in a bar), are the quintessence of country song. Jim Reeves was elected to the Country Music Hall of Fame in 1967.

## RICE, BOBBY G.

BORN: July 11, 1944, Boscobel, Wisconsin
MARRIED: w. Alice Briskey
CHILDREN: d. Tamara, Connie

Bobby G. Rice hasn't been long on the country scene and is one of those young fellows who found his way to country over that rock-y road. He was brought to Nashville by producer Johnny Howard to record a country version of his composition "Sugar Shack"; Royal American released it, and several subsequent songs that Rice wrote and recorded: "Hey, Babe," "Lover, Please," and "Mountain of Love." In 1973 Rice was signed by Metromedia Country and produced his composition "You Lay So Easy on My Mind," a first-rate song that was picked up by a number of major stars and is an indication that even though Bobby G. doesn't make it heavy as a performer, he has a lot more fine songs in his clever brain.

## RICH, CHARLIE

BORN: December 12, 1932, Colt, Arkansas
MARRIED: w. Margaret Ann

Charlie Rich was the big winner at 1973's Country Music Awards ceremonies with his song "Behind Closed Doors," which was named Best Country Song of the Year. His LP with the same name won the Best Album plaque, and Rich himself was named Best Male Singer of the Year. The music press called it "an overnight success," but Charlie Rich has been around for twenty-five years, singing all the time. Yet, not one of the four or five books available on country music even mentions Charlie Rich—not even Bill C. Malone's, and he is tremendously thorough in his coverage. A few days before this was written, I sat next to Charlie Rich at NBC studios in New York. He was in town to tape a country concert. He spoke about "not fitting in" to country and said that his songs are "crossovers," which means they cross over from the country music best-selling charts into the pop music charts, which are generally more lucrative. "I know I'm popular in the South," Rich said, "but 'Behind Closed Doors' broke wide open. It shows how strong the new-type country music is." Rich claims

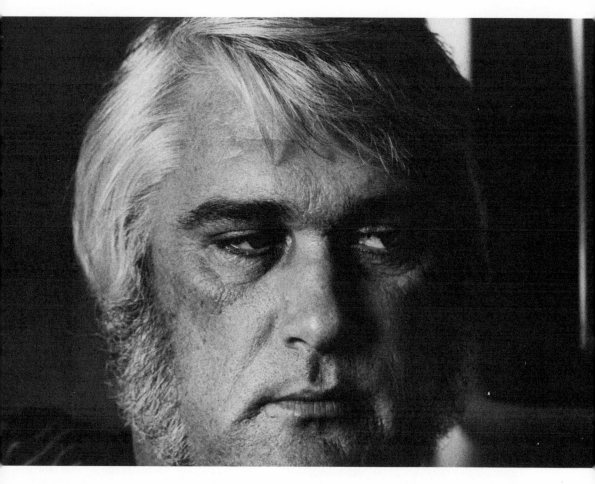

Charlie Rich: Possibly, the *ultimate* song stylist.

this "new" country has "a lot more freedom musically and lyrically from the older style, which is why it appeals outside the regional markets."

Rich rose to fame as one of the classy rockabilly artists to record for Sam Phillips' Sun label in Memphis. As writer Charlie Burton reported in a magazine interview: "Sam has become a legend for being with his microphones in the right place at the right time, and his important 'discoveries' have included, in the blues field, B. B. King, Howlin' Wolf, and Junior Parker, and in the country/rockabilly field, Elvis Presley, Roy Orbison, Jerry Lee Lewis, Carl Perkins, and Johnny Cash. But of all the exceptional artists that Sam Phillips has

recorded, it is an oft-quoted observation of his that it was Charlie Rich alone who had the kind of talent it would take to equal the success of his most fabulous discovery, Elvis Presley.

"One reason for the failure of this prediction —on a commercial level, anyway—was Phillips himself. By the time Charlie hit big with 'Lonely Weekends,' Sam had lost two of his biggest artists—Elvis to a deal with RCA and Jerry Lee Lewis to a public scandal. Johnny Cash was about to leave for Columbia, and when Charlie was sorely in need of promotion, Sam was devoting his time to projects he felt demanded more of his time. The other major reason for Charlie's lack of major commercial success is that Charlie just seems to lack the kind of determination and drive it takes to become a star in the music business.

"Charlie's wife, Margaret Ann Rich, his biggest fan for the past twenty years, says, 'I know that's been a problem with Charlie. I try to tell him, get yourself with a big booking agency. Go on the road for one year. JUST ONE YEAR. I know he'd hate it, but it would be good for him. But he just says no. He'd rather stay home and spend time with his family—he's real proud of the kids. And besides, that's the way he was brought up. That's the way he's always been. His family was a strict religious family—Missionary Baptist—and he's just never been able to resolve the difference between *that* life—the church life—and *this* life.'

"Margaret Ann waves her arm in the direction of the picture window overlooking one of the seamier sides of Nashville town. Charlie, who has been slouched in a chair drinking a Scotch and water while Margaret Ann has been talking, says nothing, but the volcanic expression on his face confirms what Margaret Ann has just said.

"Charlie Rich was born December 12 ('Or was it 14?'), 1932 ('Or was it 1934?'), in the little village of Colt, Arkansas, population 312. 'It's just a little big for my size,' says Charlie. He picked up his money picking cotton until he found he could do the same by picking up a horn—his was a musical family anyway—and he began playing tenor sax in the high school band. Charlie says that he got a lot of the 'bluesiness' in his music from playing the saxophone. He developed a strong liking for jazz—Stan Kenton and Oscar Peterson were his favorites—and also for Margaret Ann, another jazz fan, whose favorites included Stan Kenton's girl vocalist, June Christie, and Billie Holiday. Margaret Ann says that in high school, and later in college, Charlie was good in music and lousy in just about everything else. He entered the air force, where he was stationed in Enid, Oklahoma, and on the base Charlie started playing in a jazz group—piano and a little scat singing. After hours, when he was off-duty, Charlie would go into town to 'moonlight' with another little band that had a featured vocalist named Margaret Ann.

" 'Charlie often says that those three years he spent in the air force were the most valuable years of his life, musically speaking; there were so many good musicians there,' says Margaret Ann.

"When Charlie left the air force in 1955, he went back to picking cotton for a while, to support his wife and new little kid, and tried his hand at a little farming. But Margaret had an idea that Charlie would be happier making music, and she suggested that he make a tape for her to take around to different recording studios. Margaret took the tape they made—songs like 'River, Stay Away from My Door'—across the river to Sun records. Sam Phillips wasn't in, but his musical arranger Bill Justis was, and he listened to the tapes. Margaret Ann says it was probably best that Bill Justis heard Charlie first—he had a better background in jazz than Sam, and could probably dig what he heard more. Justis did like the sound, and Charlie was hired as a session man and part-time arranger, playing on tunes by Ray Smith and Johnny Cash, and even providing the piano part for his own composition 'I'll Make It All Up to You' for Jerry Lee Lewis when Lewis' own technique made it hard for him to learn the strange progressions in the key of E-flat. An early Rich recording, 'Whirlwind,' failed to click, despite a small promotional tour up North, but it was one of Charlie's own tunes that hit, and 'Lonely Weekends' is to date his biggest song, recorded by artists from Jerry Lee to Bill Anderson to the English rockers 'Them,' featuring Van Morrison on vocals.

"Charlie Rich followed 'Lonely Weekends' with a song called 'You're Gonna Be Waitin',' but it was too much like 'Lonely Weekends' and it flopped. He did score with one more tune while at Sun, the drinking song 'Sitting and Thinking,' but after Sun had set, around 1963, he was spending most of his time in various small lounges and down-and-out clubs. In fact, that's what Charlie has been doing for most of his twenty years in the music business.

"Much of Charlie's work for Sun has been reissued on two albums: 'Lonely Weekends' and 'A Time for Tears.' 'Lonely Weekends' contains Charlie's best-known, early work and all his early hits, including the magnificent rhythm-and-blues tune 'Who Will the Next Fool Be?' which has since been recorded by black rhythm-and-blues singers like 'Little' Esther

Phillips and Bobby 'Blue' Bland, and also by James Taylor's blues-singing brother, Alex Taylor. 'Break-up' is on that album, too—a big hit for Jerry Lee, though I'll take the desperate drive of Charlie's version any day, and also 'Stay.' 'A Time for Tears' has more obscure, but nonetheless interesting, sides cut for Sun, including the great Rich composition 'Midnight Blues' and an engaging little piece of rockabilly fluff, 'Good-bye, Mary Ann.'

"When Sun folded, Charlie signed with RCA's rhythm-and-blues affiliate, Groove, for a couple of years and then switched over to RCA itself for one year. He had two hits while he was with RCA: 'Mountain Dew' and a version of the old Jimmy Reed blues, 'Big Boss Man.' Charlie got along great with his producer at RCA, Chet Atkins, but despite Chet's expertise at production, and the talents of Bill Justis and Anita Kerr on the arrangements, he never reproduced a cohesive sound while with RCA. Oh, there were some fine moments—perhaps the most inspired performance ever of Lonnie Johnson's old rhythm-and-blues hit 'Tomorrow Night' was made by Charlie while at RCA. But in 1965, RCA and Charlie came to an amicable parting of ways.

"In 1965 Charlie produced some of the finest recordings he has made to date. Even Margaret Ann got to sing in the sessions on Charlie's new label, Smash. Jerry Kennedy, Charlie's Smash producer, showed up one day with a rhythm-and-blues novelty song written by a then fairly obscure songwriter named Dallas Frazier. The song, of course, was 'Mohair Sam,' and it became Charlie's second BIG hit. Those early sessions for Smash also produced an excellent album, 'The Many New Sides of Charlie Rich,' and included Charlie's 'Dance of Love,' which has since been recorded by Tom Jones—twice ('We're very grateful,' says Margaret Ann with a wan smile)—some more of those early, goofy Dallas Frazier songs like 'Moonshine Minnie' and 'She's a Yum Yum,' and one of the most brilliant songs of the Rich career, written by Margaret Ann, 'Down and Out.'

"There were more records for Smash—an album called 'The Best Years,' but, with tunes like 'Tears a-Go-Go,' it was nowhere near the quality of 'Many New Sides.' Record sales fell off at Smash, and once again Charlie found

himself switching labels—this time to Hi Records, a subsidiary of London, set up to record various Memphis acts like Bill Black and his combo, and saxophonist Ace Cannon. The association was a brief one, but it produced another album, 'Charlie Rich Sings Country and Western.' From Hi, Charlie moved to Epic Records, where he remains to this day. His first Epic single was a classic, a Curly Putman song with narration written by Joe Tex, 'Set Me Free.' The album of the same name was mighty dismal, but things have been looking steadily up since then. Charlie's hits are getting progressively bigger: 'July 12, 1939,' 'Life's Little Ups and Downs,' 'Nice 'n' Easy,' 'A Woman Left Lonely,' 'A Part of Your Life,' and 'I Take it on Home,' and his albums keep rising in consistency and quality, probably as Charlie's producer, Billy Sherrill, begins to understand more the varied and complex talents of Charlie Rich, and seems to apply his special commercial touch extra carefully and tastefully to each new Charlie Rich record. With the increasing success of his electrifying 'live' shows on the roof of the King of the Road motel and at various college and country concerts, his magnificent *Best of Charlie Rich* album and the release of 'Behind Closed Doors,' it looks like we are in the midst of the Third Golden Age of Charlie Rich, and one that will, hopefully, last this time. With the rise of the 'new' breed of country star, perhaps after twenty years Charlie Rich's time has finally come.

"Peter Guralnik, in his book on the blues, *Feel Like Going Home*, claims that at first Charlie Rich sounded very much like Elvis Presley. 'But if anyone fulfilled the artistic promise which Elvis originally showed it is probably Charlie Rich. The music that he does, his approach to the music, his ability to make each song a unique and personal vehicle for individual expression is something which in a way is lost to the star who is as much concerned with panoply as performance, who is forced by his image to be something he is not. Where Elvis is stiff and forced into a mold which is not entirely of his making, Charlie Rich is free to be whatever he likes. He feels none of the terrible restraints of stardom.' "

Jeannie C. Riley: Wishes it hadn't happened so quickly.

## RILEY, JEANNIE C.
BORN: Anson, Texas
MARRIED: h. Mickey Riley (divorced)
CHILDREN: d. Kim

Alice Joy was the first to record "Harper Valley PTA," on a demonstration record. It was a real gut-country song about middle America hanky-panky. But it was Jeannie C. Riley who made the Plantation record—and Jeannie C. is a big star because of it, with a big band, hit records (fourteen on the charts in two and a half years), and a big home in Brentwood, Tennessee, where the stars live. She also has a lovely little daughter and an ex-husband who runs a gas station with the ex-husband of another country queen. "Harper Valley" helped make its author, Tom T. Hall, rich and famous; it was a gold record in Canada and Australia, as well as the United States, selling 4,800,000 singles in all. Jeannie C. bought a purple Cadillac, studied how to walk and talk on stage at a Los Angeles charm school, and before she was twenty-one years old rode down the main street of her home town, Anson, Texas, on Jeannie C. Riley Day.

Writes Carol Offen in a magazine article: "The story is almost legendary by now. Although Jeannie had already been in Nashville for two years (she'd been doing demo work for Little Darlin' Records, and had even toured with

228

the *Johnny Paycheck Show*), she was still an unknown in August '68. She was working as a secretary at Jerry Chesnut's Passkey Music Company. Chesnut, a close friend, had given her the job 'mainly so I could get experience. I was the worst typist he ever had, he always told me.'

"Producer Shelby Singleton first heard Jeannie's voice on a demo tape she'd made for Paul Perry, then her manager, and a disc jockey at radio station WENO, who was working for Singleton part-time. Shelby told him he'd heard a certain song done by a girl whom he hadn't signed, yet he thought the song could be a hit. 'This girl's voice is perfect for it,' Singleton told him. 'You get whoever she is over here and we'll cut a number-one record.'

"Jeannie insists she shared Shelby's enthusiasm for 'Harper Valley PTA' from the start. As soon as she finished the recording session, near two in the morning, she telephoned her mother in Texas. 'Mama, I just cut a million-seller,' she told her calmly. 'Oh, yeah, I've heard that before,' her mother replied, assuming her excitable daughter was getting her hopes up falsely again. Jeannie had called Texas many times before to say she'd be having a record out soon. 'But this time I was certain,' Jeannie says. 'I called her back the next night and said, "Mama, forget what I said about the record sellin' a million . . . it's gonna sell three."'

"Six days after 'Harper Valley PTA' was released, Jeannie had to quit her job to go out on tour. A month later, she was singing it live on the *Ed Sullivan Show*. And then the floodgates opened: a Grammy Award for Best Female Country Vocal Performance, a Country Music Association Award for Single of the Year, four gold records, more television appearances, and even her own network TV special followed. The public wanted to see the singer of 'Harper Valley PTA.'

"What the public got was an attractive miniskirted performer in boots, socking it to 'em with more songs of that ilk. Plantation (Shelby Singleton's record label) was glad to oblige with 'The Girl Most Likely' and other 'sassy' songs, as Jeannie terms them. Her first album on Plantation, 'Harper Valley PTA,' included titles like 'Satan Place,' 'Mr. Harper,' and so on.

"'I was willing to go along with it 'cause it was all very exciting to me,' she said sadly. 'I

just took it all as part of the game, but all the while I was doin' it, it was nothin' but an act—a *front*.'

"Jeannie and Shelby may have known it was an act, but the public didn't. 'I was just tellin' a story in those songs, but I soon found out people thought that's what I was really like. It's not like me to be sarcastic or suggestive. But that's the kind of material they started expectin' of me,' she added.

"Translated into hard facts, what it all meant was that a love ballad like 'There Never Was a Time' didn't do nearly as well for Jeannie as did 'The Girl Most Likely,' which was a number-one hit after 'Harper Valley.' Nor did it do as well as its flip side, 'Back Side of Dallas,' a song about a prostitute. And, more recently, her version of 'When Love Has Gone Away,' perhaps her best vocal performance on any release, never got off the ground. 'The public will accept a gimmick from me, but I want to be accepted for *me*,' she said.

"'Frankly, I've been very fortunate to be able to keep up my house and car 'n' all these past few years, without any big hits,' she said. Although she no longer plays nightclubs, Jeannie's concert schedule hasn't slackened; she averages about fifteen days on the road a month —in the summer as much as twenty-one days. The reason? 'I know there are people more talented than I am, but I think mine is more a personality thing,' she said in a soft voice. 'I believe I can give a Christian testimony in song, not by doing gospel—'cause that limits your audience—but simply by doing wholesome, meaningful material. I think that's where my place is.

"'Of course I owe a lot to "Harper Valley,"' she said wearily. 'But I only wish it hadn't all happened so quickly. I realize now it would've been much better for my career if I'd had a few hits before that came out.'"

## RITTER, TEX [Woodward Maurice Ritter]

BORN: January 12, 1907, Murvaul, Texas
DIED: January 2, 1974, Nashville, Tennessee
MARRIED: w. Dorothy Fay Southworth
CHILDREN: s. Thomas Matthews, Jonathan Southworth

Tex Ritter in *Ridin' the Cherokee Trail* (1941).

Nobody in the Nashville community was better liked than Tex Ritter. The official Grand Ole Opry picture book says, "If the country-music industry ever has the opportunity to choose a new addition to the faces on Mount Rushmore, Tex Ritter would probably be the candidate." He became the first living person (1964) to be named to the Country Music Hall of Fame. Writer Paul Hemphill says that "if Tex Ritter couldn't add a little class to country music with his lordlike voice and Rock of Gibraltar car-riage, nobody could." And in a sense, Tex Ritter, singer of western ballads, writer of great songs ("When You Leave, Don't Slam the Door" and "High, Wide, and Handsome" among them), and Broadway star (*Green Grow the Lilacs*), was one of the first men responsible for bringing "country" to the "city." Tex Ritter had come to New York from rural east Texas, and his tradition was rural southern, but he was a Texan, and to eastern urban dwellers he had to be a cowboy and he tried to live up to the part.

"With his thick Texas accent and his storehouse of cowboy lore," reports country-music historian Bill C. Malone, "Ritter was a New York sensation." Of the three great singing cowboys —Roy Rogers, Gene Autry, and Tex Ritter— only Ritter, the college graduate and historian, had the image of a "real" working cowboy who sang "authentic" cowboy songs. And even those three- or four-odd Americans who might not have heard of Tex Ritter by 1952 learned about him at that time when he sang the title song for the Academy Award–winning film *High Noon.*

Ritter told his story on tape to magazine writer Kathy Sawyer in 1973:

"I was born in Panola County, Texas—deep east Texas—about forty miles from Shreveport, Louisiana. I was the youngest of six children, three boys and three girls. My father was a farmer, a cowboy—everything at one time or another.

"I went to school in a two-room schoolhouse. It was really only one room, but they had it partitioned to make two rooms because on Sunday the partition came down and it was a church. It was about 250 yards from our house, and usually the schoolteachers lived with us because it was closer to the school.

"Well, when I was very young, we had the old-time singing school that was prevalent in that part of Texas. For three weeks we had this singing school and there were itinerant singing teachers. P. O. Stamps was one of them who taught in east Texas. He later went to Dallas and formed the Stamps Quartet. And the citizens of the community would pay him to conduct the school. I suppose it was the forerunner of public-school music.

"My family sang a lot. Out of three boys, I was the youngest. My two older brothers were very good singers. There again, it was mostly church music. But usually they wouldn't let me sing with them, because I couldn't sing well enough. I remember once my mother said it would be nice if her boys would sing. So we got up in front of the fireplace and sang about a half a song, and the others stopped and said, 'Mama, would you make him sit down?' About the time we left east Texas, my voice started changing. I started really singing old cowboy songs as I grew older.

"I went to law school for one year, and then I went one year later to Northwestern in Chicago. I'd been in New York for a couple of years and then I went back to Chicago to Northwestern.

"Well, I went to Houston first, trying to sell life insurance, and I didn't do too well. I drifted around and went back to my brother-in-law in Ohio. He had always told me that a year or two in the East would be good for a Texas boy, because it moved a little faster and gave you a different outlook. That was what I had in mind, getting a job in New York. I didn't plan on singing, although I had my cowboy songs that I sang, but it never dawned on me during those years that you could really make a living singing, because all I knew was church singing and the quartet in the glee club. I had no idea of ever being in show business. It was during the Depression years and I came to New York in '29 when people were jumping out windows and selling apples and everything else. I had no money. I tried to get a job—one oil company wanted to send me to China, one oil company wanted to send me to Venezuela, but I wanted to stay in New York and study voice. It was pretty grim to see people jumping out of windows—well, I didn't actually see it; but I know I was pretty hungry, real hungry.

"Well, there was a western show with cowboy songs, so I went over there and they brought in a lady who they thought was an authority, which she was, and she said, 'This boy's authentic.' So I sang four songs and understudied the part of Franchot Tone.

"After that I went home, and when I came back, I got on the radio—WOR, *The Lone-Star Rangers.* During the next few years I was on WINS, then we had a program for children called *Cowboy Tom's Roundup.* It was an older man, an Indian boy from Oklahoma, and me. We did five characters and had a script every day.

"After the Cowboy Tom thing broke up, I had a thing on WHN called *Tex Ritter's Campfire.* It was on once or twice a week. And then I had another show once a week called the *WHN Barn Dance* in 1934. WHN has gone country now. It's a great thing because we've been trying for years to get to New York.

"I was in a couple of plays, aside from *Green Grow the Lilacs,* that later became *Oklahoma.* It was a folk play of Oklahoma at the turn of the century, while it was still a territory. It was beautifully written. *Oklahoma* still kept the dialogue, and the prose had a rhythm to it, kinda like poetry. They followed the book rather closely, except they extended the ending a little. It was done in sets that turned; first the living room, and then the smokehouse, and then the hayfields. Then when they changed the scenes we were out there singing cowboy songs. And then the girls did one segment, and the boys— we did two. But instead of the square dancing, they put in the ballet; and the cowboy songs were scored by Richard Rodgers. They followed the book pretty closely. That was a nice era.

"After *Green Grow the Lilacs* I was in a couple of more ill-fated things, the revival of *The Roundup,* which had been a play. Then I was in a thing called *Mother Lode,* a play about the discovery of the city of San Francisco. It wasn't too long after that when I went to Hollywood to make a Western.

Tex Ritter talks to a Spanish dancer played by Rita Cansino in Tex's fourth film, *Trouble in Texas.* The seventeen-year-old actress was making her dramatic debut. In future films she was known as Rita Hayworth.

"Some eight years ago I moved to Nashville. I had been coming in and out of here for a number of years. About all I had left in California—I hadn't made a picture in some fifteen years—was my family. I was being booked out of here on my personal tours, and I kept a car here and my musicians lived here. They would meet me in different places. I would fly back to the Coast and they would meet me in another town a week later or whatever and all of my activities were kind of centered here. Then they called me to join the Grand Ole Opry. So I came, and then my family came two years later.

"But politics—I've always been interested in politics, but I had never considered running for anything myself. Then people from east Tennessee came to my house on a couple of occasions and asked me to enter the race for United States Senate, so I did that. It was a great experience and I don't regret it at all. [Tex Ritter also ran unsuccessfully for the governorship of Tennessee.]

"I don't think anyone is ever satisfied with his accomplishments. Some of the greatest accomplishments in the world have been performed by old men, so you're never washed up. You can always accomplish something. But you'll never do it if you retire and just sit. Certainly not. When you do that, you die.

"When I was a kid, the kids would eat after the adults finished. They would talk and eat and talk and eat. Then the things would be cleaned away—this was not the family; this was a big gathering with all the relatives—and then we would eat. Then we'd go out on the front porch. The men would talk and pick their teeth and pitch horseshoes. Then they'd dwindle away, and some of the older men were left—maybe grandfather or a great uncle—just sittin' and lookin' into the distance.

"You couldn't wait until you got old, because you wondered what great thoughts they were thinking. And you'd say, Well, I hope someday that I can be a grown man and sit on the front porch and gaze into the horizon and think these great thoughts. Then when you get older you do that. You sit on the porch and look into the horizon and you think exactly what they thought, those great profound thoughts. You know what they were? Nothing. Ha!"

# ROBBINS, MARTY

BORN: September 26, 1925, Glendale, Arizona

MARRIED: w. Marizona

CHILDREN: s. Ronnie

"He doesn't look much like his publicity pictures," is the way writer Al Reinert describes Marty Robbins. "The boots he wears, with two-inch stacked heels, just boost him up to about five feet nine inches. He's short and wiry, hard-muscled, like a lightweight wrestler or a welterweight boxer, and his hair's getting longer now, mussed and matted and sun-bleached to a color that's almost strawberry roan; the mustache barely slips around the corners of his mouth in the hint of a handlebar, giving him the appearance, altogether, of a wizened old Robert Redford, a Sundance Kid who's spent twenty years robbing banks. His eyes, even hidden behind the bronze-tinted glasses, are open and honest, quick, flashing and dancing in all directions at once."

Reinert was present while Robbins was trying to earn a starting position in one of the key races of the National Association of Stock Car Racing Winston Cup Grand Nationals. "He'd brought his guitar to the garage this morning and, in the wet hours while they waited out the rain, played and strummed and whanged away at old favorites, joined on choruses by pit crews with nothing to do." Marty Robbins is more than a country-western singer. He's a race-car driver, a hard-hitting, tough-as-nails driver, who in 1972, at Daytona's 500, hit a difficult bump and slammed head-on into the concrete outer wall of the track at 150 mph, spinning and flipping, all the while trying desperately not to smash into A. J. Foyt. The car was wrecked, but Marty, unhurt, remarked "It was pretty embarrassing." Later that night he entertained by singing, among other songs, his big hit, "El Paso," a ballad he had written and recorded in 1959, about a man who was killed fighting for the love of his sweetheart, who hustled at a border joint. "El Paso" is a typical western ballad, made-up but with authentic roots. Robbins' recording of it was a hit, zooming to the number-one position on the country charts for sixteen weeks—and this was unusual because the song lasted well over four minutes; it was probably one of the longest songs ever to make a hit parade. It also made Robbins so much money that he virtually quit personal appearances for a year because of tax considerations. Now about forty-eight years old, Robbins owns four music-publishing companies, a 600-acre ranch, racing cars, real estate, cattle, and a house his band members privately call Marty's Ramada Inn.

It wasn't always easy. Robbins had scores of jobs before stumbling onto a music career. "I'm in this business," he told free-lance journalist Larry L. King, "because I despise honest labor." "He was ditchdigging in Arizona when a local country-western bandleader offered him $10 to play substitute guitar," King writes, "and he kept the job. One night in a roadhouse tavern, he sang, and the house roared. Robbins claims that he didn't know he could sing: 'I'd seen every Gene Autry movie as a kid and tried to imitate him, but not seriously.' He formed his own group and began to work rodeos, political gatherings, radio stations, and high school gyms. Grand Ole Opry signed him in 1953. His first big hit, for Columbia Records, 'Singing the Blues,' was at the top of every country chart." And, he's been on the charts since 1953. He is number ten of the artists with

the most consecutive years on the charts and is number eleven as the artist with the most charted record sides. Robbins considers himself a country-western singer but his songs often appear on the pop charts: "A White Sport Coat and a Pink Carnation" and "Teen-Age Dream" both were monster hits with the rock set in the 1950s.

For all this success, Robbins still is somewhat insecure: He told Larry L. King that he did "little" television because it scared him, and he worries when his songs aren't smashes. "When did I know I had it made? Hell, I haven't got it made yet. I dropped a bundle building a racetrack in Nashville; then some oil deals turned sour. And the damned federal government can ruin a man in thirty minutes."

In 1964 Robbins came out for Barry Goldwater for president, and in the 1968 presidential election he was solidly behind Alabama governor George Wallace (who is a personal friend). "A farm boy of simpler and older times," King called him, and said his friends feel that Robbins would like to be a frontier sheriff: "He'd enjoy a frontier shoot-out every day." His favorite songs are about hangings and dance-hall girls,

Marty Robbins: Hard ridin', fast drivin' country star.

and he has written a western novel which he hopes to turn into a film, starring Marty Robbins.

"Playing the road," Robbins says, "is just like robbing Wells Fargo. You ride in, take the money, and ride out." He is besieged with fans, and wherever he goes they follow him, asking for autographs, bringing their children with them to introduce them, wanting to shake his hand. Robbins takes it all in his stride, though this quote has often been attributed to him: "Bless the country fan. They'll do anything for you, except to leave you alone."

There has been much talk lately about the waning of rock-and-roll as one of the reasons for the country-music boom. Critic Dave Hickey believes a more powerful reason for the current enthusiasm is the vacuum left by the retirement and/or eclipse of the great ballad singers of the forties and fifties. "For those who grew up on Frank Sinatra, Nat King Cole, Tony Bennett, and Frankie Lane, country balladeers like Ray Price, Eddy Arnold, and Marty Robbins provide the only lively source for this kind of music available on the airwaves today." Hickey and other critics believe that Marty Robbins has one of the really beautiful voices in country music, and sings in the best 1950s style.

In reviewing Marty Robbins' first record for MCA (he left Columbia after a twenty-year stint there), Hickey summarizes Robbins' musical life: "The album is really a sampler of all the many kinds of singing Marty Robbins does best. There is the requisite saga ballad, looking back to his gunfighter days, 'A Man and a Train'; a beautiful, if old-fashioned, rendition of the Nat King Cole standard 'Pretend'; a more contemporary ballad, 'San Francisco Teardrops,' which has some really nice nightclub piano; an uptempo country tune called 'Up to My Shoulders in a Heartache,' which is so slickly produced it almost glitters; and finally, a group of songs done in the classic Marty Robbins mariachi style. It is not that Robbins sings these songs better than he does the others, it is just that nobody but Robbins can bring off this kind of number with nearly as much class. His rendition of Kris Kristofferson and Shel Silverstein's 'The Taker' is the best rendition of the song I have heard—likewise his version of Lobo's 'Las Vegas, Nevada' and his own 'Martha, Oh, Martha.'

"I would be less than honest if I said that what Marty Robbins sings is my kind of music, but I would be less than a critic if I didn't allow that there is no one who sings this kind of material better or more beautifully."

## ROBISON, CARSON J.

BORN: August 4, 1890, Oswego, Kansas
DIED: March 24, 1957, New York City

No one would have been more pleased with the universal acceptance of country music than Carson Robison, called the "granddaddy of the hillbillies." Born in Kansas and popular locally as a singer, he gained fame as one of the first western singers on radio and on RCA Victor records. He often sang on the same program as pioneer hillbilly musicians Frank Luther and Vernon Dalhart. During the thirties and forties he wrote his most popular songs: "Life Gets Tee-jus, Don't It?", "My Blue Ridge Mountain Home," "Wreck of the Number Nine," "I'm Going Back to Whurr I Come From," and "Settin' by the Fire." He also wrote "Barnacle Bill the Sailor"—which has become, with slightly changed words, one of the great bawdy songs of the twentieth century.

## RODGERS, JIMMIE [James Charles Rodgers]

BORN: September 8, 1897, Meridian, Mississippi
DIED: May 26, 1933, New York City
MARRIED: w. Carrie
CHILDREN: d. Anita

On August 4, 1927, a new singer, who would later be called The Singing Brakeman, recorded in a third-floor hotel room in Bristol, Tennessee. The equipment was primitive, but the voice was confident, even though it belonged to a sickly, down-and-out former railroad drifter. Jimmie Rodgers had practically stumbled into producer Ralph Peer's hotel room and demanded to be recorded. Peer was reluctant, but finally agreed to two songs only. That first recording was to mark the beginning of a career which was to

235

Jimmie Rodgers: He *is* country music.

change American music. Even today, forty years after his death, Jimmie Rodgers' records are selling briskly—and around the world. In Japan, a country where Rodgers is amazingly popular, his records are still played on the radio. Practically every big-time country-western star has recorded "the songs of Jimmie Rodgers." Every year in Meridian, Mississippi, there is a big Jimmie Rodgers celebration, drawing fantastic crowds. He was the first member of the Country Music Hall of Fame, elected in 1961.

John P. Morgan, a professor at the University of Rochester's medical school and a long-time student of the music of Jimmie Rodgers, traced the Singing Brakeman's career in a magazine article:

"Forty years after Jimmie Rodgers' death, his imitators—conscious and unconscious—constitute a music industry. And yet although 30,000 people attended a twenty-year memorial celebration in 1953 at Meridian, Mississippi, most Americans have little idea of his identity. Every one of his eight reissue RCA Victor albums sold over 30,000 copies within a year of release, but catalogs of country-western records still mix his record listings indiscriminately with those of another Jimmie Rodgers ('Honeycomb' and 'Bimbombey').

"Jimmie (James Charles) Rodgers was born September 8, 1897, in Meridian, Mississippi. His father, a section foreman on the Gulf, Mobile and Ohio railroad, raised him alone after his mother died when he was four years old. The rootless life of a section boss prevented much formal education for Rodgers; he had his last encounter with school at age fourteen, then began work on the railroad as a water boy in the Meridian yards. He began to learn songs and song fragments from black railroad workers, who may also have taught him to play banjo and guitar. Young Jimmie sang alone, picking up the steady tempo that helped keep the workmen together as they labored. During work breaks he sat and listened, while the crew gossiped, laughed, joked, and relaxed. Often the whole crew would break into a song that everybody knew, and Jimmie would sing along too. These early railroad songs and stories would serve Jimmie well in later life, for he never forgot them.

"Jimmie Rodgers had almost no formal education. Instead of learning stories he was living them, as an assistant section foreman, a full-time railroad employee. During the next fourteen years, until tuberculosis forced his retirement, Rodgers worked as a flagman and brakeman throughout the Southwest, mainly on the Meridian-to-New Orleans run.

"In 1925, having experienced one nearly fatal pulmonary hemorrhage, he sought other work, although he later made one or two other attempts to hold railroad jobs. In those days music was an occupation for men too infirm for hard labor: Rodgers qualified. He began touring a medicine show circuit playing guitar and banjo with a repertoire of popular music—the waltzes, dance tunes, and sentimental songs of the time.

"From Meridian he moved to Asheville, North Carolina, seeking a climate more suited to his health and hoping to find work as a musician —alone at first, but later with his wife, Carrie, and daughter Anita. (Another daughter had died six months after she was born in 1923. Rodgers was in New Orleans at the time, looking for work. When he heard the news several weeks later, he was so broke he had to pawn his banjo to get home.) In Asheville, he worked as a city detective until 1927, when he landed a job on WWNC. It was only when he was desperate that he turned to singing. He worked with a small string band (his 'hillbilly ork') for only a few weeks before the 'Jimmie Rodgers Entertainers' were canned from the airwaves. Despite this snub, he and his band continued playing in and around Asheville.

"In July and August of 1927 Rodgers made a trip to Bristol, Tennessee, on the Tennessee-Virginia border. There, within the space of a few days, Ralph Peer of the Victor Talking Machine Company made the first recordings of both Jimmie Rodgers and the country-singing Carter Family in a third-floor hotel room. Peer was a smart man. He had arranged for the folk-singing Stoneman Family to accompany him and had convinced the local newspaper editor that his and the Stonemans' presence was news. What probably attracted Rodgers and the Carters was a half column on the front page of the *Bristol News Bulletin* that began by stating:

MOUNTAIN SONGS RECORDED HERE
BY VICTOR COMPANY
NOTABLE PERFORMERS OF THIS
SECTION AT WORK AT STATION,
THIS CITY

237

"Ralph Peer, the Victor representative, later became Rodgers' manager and the first to suggest that Rodgers bring some of his own songs to record. More important in country-music history, however, is the fact that Peer was responsible for the first commercial recording of a 'hillbilly' performer. (In 1923 in Atlanta, Peer and Polk Brockman, both then working for Okeh Records, had recorded Fiddlin' John Carson doing 'Little Log Cabin in the Lane' and 'The Old Hen, She Cackled, and the Rooster's Gonna Crow.' There is some argument, but this is generally accepted as the beginning of recorded country music.)

"Rodgers contacted Peer and made the necessary arrangements for the audition. But the other band members were apparently jealous of Jimmie's personal success. They struck out on their own, changed their name to The Tenneva Ramblers, and convinced Peer to record them without Jimmie. When Jimmie found out, he was shaken. He had thought they were all loyal. But the next day Jimmie talked with Peer, who was reluctant to record him. Peer finally agreed to let him record only two songs. The date agreed upon was August 4, 1927.

"Jimmie Rodgers had only two chances. His choice of songs had to display every bit of musical talent he had. Of all the songs he had ever performed, he picked a lullaby, and a sentimental ballad he'd written about a friend who died in the First World War: 'Soldier's Sweetheart.'

"Essentially, Rodgers staked his future on an old-time lullaby, and an outdated war ballad, pathetic in its very simplicity—when he had a daring novelty like 'T for Texas,' with its blue yodels those city people at the mountain resort raved about. Carrie pleaded with Peer to let Jimmie record 'T for Texas,' but Peer stood firm: only one test record. The conversation was cut short when Jimmie suffered a mild coughing spasm.

"Before they left, the man from New York did two things that astonished both Jimmie and Carrie. First Peer thrust his hand into his pocket and gave Jimmie a twenty-dollar bill, then a contract. Jimmie Rodgers was now a recording artist for the Victor Company, under contract. The same day Peer recorded Jimmie Rodgers, he recorded a hillbilly group from Virginia, the Carter Family.

"Ralph Peer was, above all, a businessman. His generous gesture was to bring him rich rewards. Several months later, Rodgers received his first royalty check for $27, and his career was underway. His next recording session, also directed by Peer, was at Camden, New Jersey. Following Peer's suggestions, he brought songs authored by himself and his sister, Elsie McWilliams. At this session, he recorded the first of the twelve blue yodels, 'T for Texas.' Phrased in the now-familiar twelve-bar blues pattern, the song ended each three-line stanza with the high-pitched, quavering yodel which became his trademark.

"Strangely enough, the following six-year period before his death is hardly as well documented as this first recording session. He rapidly became the most widely known commercial country entertainer, recording a total of 111 songs, more than half of which are available on the RCA reissue albums. These included the twelve blue yodels and other identically formed blues; a variety of sentimental songs (many of which began as popular city tunes) about Mother, Daddy, and home; songs of cowboys and the lonesome prairie in which he personified the western image, adopting Texas as his home state (though unlike many who followed him, he seldom affected western dress on stage). He continued, and made more visible, the country tradition of train songs, often mixed with tales of the hobo, and in the blue yodels and other songs he lamented love gone bad. Finally he wrote and sang about the disease that killed him in 'The TB Blues' and 'Whippin' That Old TB.'

"During those brief six years, Jimmie worked a variety of tent show and vaudeville circuits mostly in the Southwest, with co-acts including repertory players, Will Rogers, Ben Turpin and even a fan dancer called Holly Desmond. Although the plans were often made, he never toured north of the Mason-Dixon line. He built a lavish home near Kerrville, Texas, which he eventually had to leave—fancy living and medical bills were too costly. He moved to San Antonio until near the end of his life and worked twice weekly on KMAC radio out of the Blue Bonnet Hotel.

"May of 1933 found him recording in New York City, where Dwight Butcher, who became one of his earlier imitators, recalls visiting him. He says that Rodgers was so weak, a cot was provided in the studio so he could rest between takes.

"Jimmie Rodgers died May 26 at the Taft Hotel in the company of a recently hired private nurse. On the death train that took him home to Mississippi, engineer Homer Jenkins pulled his whistle to a low moan as the train entered Meridian, a final tribute from fellow trainmen to the 'Singing Brakeman.'

"Simply in terms of record sales, Jimmie Rodgers' impact was astonishing. In a career coexistent with the Depression, he sold more than 5 million 78-rpm records (although probably not the popularly quoted 20 million) at one dollar each. These sales were almost entirely to impoverished rural southerners at a time when national phonograph record sales were declining precipitously. During those hard years, only the Carter Family approached his popularity.

"Singers like Ernest Tubb and Hank Snow consciously modeled their careers after him; Gene Autry, Bradley Kincaid, Lefty Frizzell, and even the Australian Hawking Brothers recorded Jimmie Rodgers tributes or memorial albums; Merle Haggard recently recorded an extremely well done tribute album, 'Same Train, Different Time.' But this impact goes even deeper than sincere imitation, for Rodgers introduced elements which now, forty years after his death, are regarded as conservative and unchanging aspects of country music.

"Rodgers' wide use of styles, his emphasis on nontraditional material, and his eminence as a recording star lead many academic students of folk music to totally ignore him. The city 'folk' revivalists of the sixties thrilled over performers like Frank Proffitt, Doc Watson, and Flatt and Scruggs, but completely ignored Jimmie Rodgers. Paul Siebel, a contemporary city performer who plays country music, tells how he completely emptied a Greenwich Village, New York, coffeehouse by singing and yodeling a Jimmie Rodgers song.

"Rodgers also solidified the use of country music for its 'reassurance' function, seeming almost to catalog the memories and wishes and experiences of small-town and rural America. His songs mourned for the mother and dad and home left behind, expressed sentimental feelings for love gained and lost, romanticized the plight of the hobo and railroad workers. He didn't single-handedly establish these as the predominant values in country music, but he certainly was one of the first to state them so explicitly.

"He also probably introduced Hawaiian bands and styles to country music. The dobro and pedal steel guitar styles used today were probably originated by musicians like Jimmy Tarleton and Cliff Carlisle, who heard Rodgers perform with such groups as Lani McIntyre and his Hawaiians.

"Rodgers was not the first to yodel on record, but his yodeling style became one of his principal characteristics and that of future country music. His yodeling may have derived from touring Swiss musicians, but he modified and used it almost as a structured white expression of emotionalism equivalent to the moaning and wailing styles of black singers.

"Rodgers was not merely a co-user of the blues, he also had much to do with fixing the form. Although generally neglected by historians of the blues, his adherence to the twelve-bar, three-phrase form helped promote and sustain this as the most common blues vehicle and made country music say, 'Blues, How Do You Do?'

"His election as the first member of the Country Music Hall of Fame was singularly appropriate because, even forty years later, he *is* country music.''

## RODRIGUEZ, JOHNNY [John Raul Davis Rodriguez]

BORN: December 10, 1951, Sabinal, Texas

"Oh, the girls,'' my Nashville informant confided to me, "how they turn out to see Johnny Rodriguez. And, there's a really big young star who just divorced her husband, and she makes no mistake who she's after now.'' But Johnny Rodriguez is something more than the newest musical heartthrob to nubile country fans. "If you thought Johnny Rodriguez was just another pretty voice and Nashville's official Chicano hillbilly, listen to his new album,'' writes songwriter and critic Dave Hickey. "Johnny's first album was undoubtedly one of the best things to come along in a while. He paid all his dues, hit all his notes and paid homage to all his sources in that album, and demonstrated that he was a full-blown, first-rate country ballad singer—the

Johnny Rodriguez (center) with his "discoverers," Happy Shahan (left) and Texas ranger Joaquin Jackson.

only ballad singer, with the exception of Stoney Edwards, who could sing in the Merle Haggard tradition and do honor to his master." Johnny Rodriguez has had two major hits in less than a year: "Pass Me By if You're Only Passing Through" and "Thumbing My Way to Mexico." He has a long contract with Mercury, and people in Nashville like him.

Three years ago, he only looked forward to a life of poverty. The late sixties weren't too happy for John Raul Davis Rodriguez. His family was poor, and after graduating from high school he had little to look forward to. His brother, Andy, had taught him to play guitar, but Johnny, wary of the frustrations of a strug-

gling singer, preferred the life of a drifter, and he picked and sang under shady trees or in small local cafes. His fine talents were discovered accidentally, and the story has become one of a score of special Nashville-style legends: When he was eighteen, he was hungry and broke in Garner State Park, Texas. Looking for a deer to shoot, Rodriguez found, instead, a frisky goat (goat meat is a staple among Texas' Mexican population), and he rustled it and skinned it, and while it was cooking over a fire, he was arrested by state trooper Joaquin Jackson. In jail for rustling, Johnny played his guitar, and Jackson was impressed enough with Rodriguez' voice to drive him to Brackettville, Texas, and introduce

240

him to James T. "Happy" Shahan, owner of a popular tourist attraction called Alamo Village. Shahan listened to Rodriguez sing and hired him for his summer shows, which involved wrangling horses, getting shot off of stagecoaches, and singing with the Alamo Village Band. On Labor Day, 1971, country singers Bobby Bare and Tom T. Hall visited Alamo Village and heard Johnny sing. Hall suggested that Rodriguez come to Nashville to see him, and Rodriguez, nervous and insecure, didn't feel ready to meet the challenge of Nashville. Then, when Johnny's father died of cancer and his brother was killed in a car wreck, his family was left with financial obligations that were almost impossible to handle. With eight dollars in his pocket and a plane ticket, Rodriguez headed for Tennessee. At the very moment he was en route to Nashville, Tom T. Hall's secretary was calling Texas to find him, to offer him a job as a guitar picker with Hall's band, The Storytellers. After a few months, Hall presented Rodriguez to Mercury Records' A & R man, Roy Dea. "It took Roy about half a song to make his decision," Hall recalls. "When Johnny started singing a chorus in Spanish, Roy broke in and offered him a contract, right on the spot." And Johnny Rodriguez became the first Mexican-American country-music star.

## ROGERS, DAVID

BORN: March 27, 1936, Atlanta, Georgia
MARRIED: w. Barbara Ann
CHILDREN: s. Anthony Kyle; d. Tonya Lynn

David Rogers' thirteen-year-old son already has his own band. But Rogers would prefer him to go through college and be a doctor—"that's what my own father advised me to do twenty years ago," Rogers recalls, "but I chose to ignore the advice." Instead he pursued a musical career, which has been rewarding to him and to his multitude of fans. "Nonetheless," Rogers says, "my son would be better off with something more secure." In January 1973 Rogers became the first country artist to sign with Atlantic Records. The success of "Just Thank Me" and "It'll Be Her" helped establish Atlantic as a country label—and it's done something for Rogers as well. Though his singles at Columbia Records made the charts, and some of them

in the top ten, "fame has been long in coming."

"It is simply a matter of getting lost in the crowd," he insists. But his sound hasn't changed. Rogers sings soft ballads, generally produced by Pete Drake. "I do need to do some uptempo material though. I can't just do twenty minutes of ballads on stage." Rogers and his band have now put 100,000 miles on his super-bus. Not long ago, he used a station wagon and trailer. "I don't know now if I can afford to keep the bus, but it's essential," and he considers it a status symbol. With his father's words still echoing in his ears, he likes to park the bus in front of his house once in a while. "Y' know it's got my name all over the thing."

David Rogers, soft-spoken and unassuming, prefers to sing soft love ballads.

David Rogers began playing clubs in Atlanta when he was sixteen. He played nights, and sold pots and pans door-to-door during the daytime. His favorite place to play was the Longhorn,

241

owned by Kathleen Jackson (who is now his manager) and her husband. Many country greats played there before it was torn down in the early sixties, and Roger Miller once lived in the club's back room. Before buying the Longhorn, the Jacksons had owned a grocery store. Their bread man, a fellow with musical aspirations named Pete Drake, urged them to buy a club and give him a job in it. The Jacksons bought the Longhorn and gave Drake a job (Drake subsequently became one of Nashville's great sidemen and producers). When Rogers, who had been singing regularly in the club, decided to go on the road, Kathleen Jackson decided to help. "Neither of us knew much about the business," Rogers recalls, "but we figured we'd learn along the way." Rogers cut a demo tape, and Mrs. Jackson sent it to Drake, who was in Nashville. Drake suggested Rogers do a "real session tape" in Nashville—an expensive proposition. Kathleen Jackson paid for it, Drake arranged it, and when Frank Jones, an A & R man at Columbia, heard it, Rogers was awarded a five-year contract. One of Rogers' hits was "I'm in Love with My Wife," and Nashville considers the Rogers family one of the happiest couples around Music City. They live in a modest home in nearby Donelson, Tennessee.

## ROGERS, ROY [Leonard Slye]

BORN: November 5, 1912, Cincinnati, Ohio

MARRIED: w. Arlene Wilkins (deceased); w. Dale Evans

CHILDREN: s. Roy, Jr., John (deceased); d. Robin (deceased), Cheryl, Linda Lou, Marion, Scottish Ward, Mary, Little Doe, Deborah Lee (deceased)

There will always be a battle, among fans of singing movie cowboys, as to who is the real "king." Most probably agree that Gene Autry holds the title. Others insist that Tex Ritter is the "uncrowned" monarch, and a huge segment ignores both Autry and Ritter and offers its fealty to a son of a shoemaker from Duck Run, Ohio, born Leonard Slye but known and loved by one and all as Roy Rogers.

I've seen Roy sing, act, and perform a number of times, but I remember the first time, back in 1950, when he opened a new shopping center in the San Fernando Valley. Shopping centers were then a new phenomenon and movie stars often cut the opening ribbon. I was there with a friend of mine who worked for NBC News. It was terribly hot and uncomfortable, and the first signs of what is now called smog were settling over southern California. "There comes Trigger," my friend said, pointing to a horse van. A blonde girl with eye shadow and wearing pedal-pushers led Trigger out of the stall. A bald man with a pencil-thin mustache was combing Trigger's lordly mane. After all, Trigger was the "king of horses" (if you discounted Autry's Champion). Then Trigger performed a very unregal act, an act of biologic necessity, forcing the girl to run into the van for a broom and pan to clean the area where the ribbon was going to be cut. Rogers, at this moment, came out of his dressing-room trailer, witnessed his horse's stomach distress, and remarked, in what seemed to me total seriousness, "Trigger, you should know better than that." Then he apologized to the people standing around. "Trigger usually doesn't do things like that," he said, wiping some beads of sweat from his face, smearing his makeup. Rogers wore a snow-white Stetson and a Nudie-made suit of many swirls and sequins, and carried two enormous pearl-handled six-shooters in a thick, brocaded leather holster belt. His boots were red, white, and blue, faced with stern leather imperial eagles. It all looked very uncomfortable, and I knew at the time that Will Rogers would have had something witty to say about it. Roy Rogers mounted Trigger, and with a huge pair of papier-mâché scissors cut the ribbon as a toothy announcer said, "Here he is, folks, Roy Rogers, the *king of the cowboys*." From that moment on, I was never sure about Rogers' wit, but I do know that he's an official good guy and a fine practicing Christian, and that with his wife, Dale Evans ("queen of the cowgirls"), he is involved in a multitude of works to make the world a better place in which to live.

Jack Parks, a writer and film historian who has long been a student of the Rogers-Autry phenomenon, writes the following: "Roy Rogers (then Leonard Slye) had come with his father to California as a migratory fruit picker. Playing at first with a number of western groups (Uncle Tom Murray's Hollywood Hillbillies, The Rocky Mountaineers, The International Cowboys, The O-Bar-O Cowboys, and The

Roy Rogers serenades Dale Evans in a 1943 film.

Texas Outlaws), he became the lead singer in a group called The Pioneer Trio and was calling himself Dick Weston. In 1934, when Autry was appearing in the science-fiction western serial *Phantom Empire*, the group changed its name to Sons of the Pioneers.

"Rogers stayed with the group for the next three years and did occasional bit parts in Columbia's Charles Starret westerns. Somebody at Republic noticed him, and he was signed with the same studio that was starring Gene Autry. So, for the next several years, Rogers played and sang a kind of second guitar to Autry's top billing.

"Rogers was really being groomed by the studio as another Autry, and so, after his first star billing in *Under Western Stars,* he did get his own pictures. But even though Rogers' films had their own distinctive style by remaining traditional historical and action westerns, they were never given as big a production or advertising budget as those of Autry. In addition, any new, popular hit song that was bought by the studio to be featured in a film always went to Autry. Friction did develop between them behind the cameras. Autry even quit the studio for a time but came back under a new deal. From then on he and Rogers shared the spotlight at Republic, although Autry probably was still more popular with country-western audiences, until the Second World War.

"Autry joined the army, and Republic put all their money into promoting and starring Roy Rogers, billing him as 'king of the cowboys.' But there being a war on and all of that, Republic did hedge their bet. They signed Monte Hale as a backup singing cowboy—just in case Roy got drafted. He didn't, though, and so remained secure—with his saddle throne and Stetson crown—as 'king of the cowboys.'

"Unfortunately, as with the rest of the world after the war, things just weren't the same in the tuneful West of the film. Autry returned to movies but went over to Columbia Pictures instead of to his old stompin' grounds on the Republic lot. And the old rivalry between him and Rogers was never really the same. Pictures with singing cowboys were still popular, and they were being made just as well—even though for some tastes they were being made with a little too much comedy and a little too many musical production numbers.

"But something else was creeping in, in the late forties and early fifties, and as a consequence, first Autry and then Rogers quietly rode not into the sunset but into the television set. Whether it was the returning GIs, or the younger generation of kids, or whoever, somebody wanted to see more obvious sex and more explicit violence in film. The tried-and-true formula of the musical western just couldn't take these two new—and completely foreign—ingredients. It was like alkaline water in a desert water hole.

"After Iwo Jima or Omaha Beach, who could believe again in a hero who captured the villains with his songs instead of with his bloodied fists? Or who, after they'd seen 'Paree' a second time, wanted to again believe in a hero that wanted to loosen the strings on his guitar instead of the buttons on his heroine's blouse?

"Even so, for two whole generations there would be memories. In 'Cowboy Buckaroo' Mason Williams expressed it best. And most appropriately with song and guitar:

'I was raised on matinees
on Saturday afternoon
Looking up at
Hoppy, Gene, and Roy
... Oh, boy,
And I grew up thinkin'
the best a man can do
Is be a rootin'-tootin'
straight-shootin'
cowboy buckaroo.' ''

# RUSSELL, JOHNNY

One of the more popular hits of 1973 in rural America was a song called "Red Necks, White Socks, and Blue Ribbon Beer," sung by Johnny Russell. He is a heavy man—almost 300 pounds, according to his press notices—but he makes light of his girth. "Since the album bearing the song's title came out with my picture on it," he joked, "the letters from girls who said they liked my music and wanted to marry me have dwindled." Critics who have seen Russell on the Wheeling, West Virginia, *Jamboree* show, Grand Ole Opry, or the touring Charley Pride show have generally raved about his performance. "If Guy Lombardo plays the sweetest music this side of heaven," reported writer Ellis Nassour, "then Johnny must sing it. I've never seen anybody stop a show like he did. He's Hank Williams, Sonny James, and Eddy Arnold —and Tennessee Ernie Ford too, all rolled into one."

Russell's career in country music was generated from a string of talent contests, country radio shows, and backwater tavern dates, from which he went on to better clubs and an occasional appearance at Grand Ole Opry. He got a job running the Wilburn Brothers' Sure-Fire Music Publishing Company and wrote songs on the side, one of which guitarist and RCA talent executive Chet Atkins liked. The late Jim Reeves recorded it, and then Buck Owens cut another of Russell's compositions called "Act Naturally," which was recorded by none other than the Beatles. It became a pop monster hit.

"'That sudden, newfound fame threw me into a dither,' Russell admitted, according to Ellis Nassour. 'I really wasn't happy, and I figured that was the time to do something about it. I loved—and love—writing songs, but my greatest joy comes from performing.

"'Now that I can look back, the amazing thing is the number of people who said No when I came to them to sing. I had written songs for Loretta Lynn, the Wilburns, Del Reeves, Burl Ives—even Patti Page. And, if I say so myself, I was a darn good song plugger. And since I was good at these two things—plugging and writing —I guess the powers that be figured, "Why, heck, let him keep doing what he's good at." But, you see, they forgot one thing. They forgot I carry a lot of weight in this town!'

"That he *literally* does," says Nassour. "Besides being a man of large proportions—stemming from an insatiable appetite for fried okra, butter beans, fried chicken, and cornbread— Russell is also a warm, outgoing, kind, and delightful person.

"'Hi, sweetheart,' he exclaims as he sticks his head into Connie Hurt's office at RCA. (She's secretary to Jerry Bradley, producer and head of RCA's operation in Nashville.)

"'Hi, how's your diet?'

"'I got off that thing.'

"'Why'd you do a thing like that?'

"'Well, you told me losing weight wasn't gonna do me any good anyway!'

"Almost as an afterthought he adds, 'You wanna take me to lunch?'

'Now, Johnny, be nice. You said you were off your diet and I only get paid every two weeks.'

"It has been a long, if not necessarily hard or frustrating, climb for Russell, who was born in Sunflower County, Mississippi, and raised in California. Besides the early influences of fried chicken and cornbread, there was also a great love of country music, especially as sung by such greats as Ernest Tubb and Lefty Frizzell.

"Russell's debut album, 'Catfish John/ Chained,' is one of those rare LPs on which every cut is excellent. Five of Russell's six country-chart singles are included (one of these, 'Mr. Fiddle Man,' was co-written by Johnny and his wife), along with a very winning version of 'The Jamestown Ferry' and two excellent new songs, 'My Mind Hangs On to You' (which is reminiscent of 'I Can't Stop Loving You') and 'It Sure Seemed Right,' penned by Johnny and his brother Michael.

"'I've made great strides in the last eight months,' Johnny said to me recently, 'but I don't feel a damn bit different. I guess the best thing to do, if you want to keep your head, is not to pay attention to any of it, but to just keep on going like you always do. I have seen how success affects the big-timers. Sometimes that stage seems to take hold and last forever. I don't want that to happen to me.

"'This business will warp your mind, *if* you let it. It was a lot better when they pitched songs without demos and tapes. They used to just pick a song out on a guitar and sing it for you. Now you go through a board of review.'

"That afternoon I sat in a small room at RCA as Johnny listened to new material. He was attempting to be all business, but he had a captive audience.

"'Johnny, let me play you a song that really fits you,' one songwriter declared.

"'Fit me! Heck, man, nothin' fits me.'"

∫

## SAGA SONG

One of the most popular forms of country songs, especially during the 1950s, was the "saga," or story, song. It resembled in style the old-time English folk ballads and historical ballads that described a real event. In 1958 the Kingston Trio, a college-aged folk-singing group, recorded the old mountain murder ballad "Tom Dooley." The song attained number-one position on the *Billboard, Cash Box,* and *Record World* hit charts and inspired the recording of similar ballads. Johnny Horton recorded "Springtime in Alaska," which (in the tradition of Robert Service's Klondike poetry) told the tale of a prospector killed in an arctic tavern brawl. Johnny Cash's "Don't Take Your Guns to Town" related the adventures of a young cowboy who disregarded his mother's admonitions and was killed when he came to town. Marty Robbins gained much of his fame, at the time, with "Hanging Tree." Jimmy Driftwood composed his own lyrics about Andrew Jackson's victory over the British at New Orleans during the War of 1812, and Johnny Horton's version of the song, "The Battle of New Orleans," was a major hit. He followed it with "Sink the *Bismarck*," "Johnny Reb," and "The Battle of Bull Run." Carl Smith told his saga, "Ten Thousand Drums"; Eddy Arnold sang "Tennessee Stud"; and Hawkshaw Hawkins' "Soldier's Joy" was a big hit, as well. The saga song, as a major country genre song, subsided somewhat in the 1960s. Lefty Frizzell recorded "The Long Black Veil" (which also was recorded by Joan Baez and the bluegrass ensemble The Country Gentlemen), and Marty Robbins' "El Paso" was very popular. During the Vietnam war, country singers for the most part defended the war (as opposed to the urban folk singers), but none of the saga songs about this war have become major hits.

## SCRUGGS, EARL

BORN: January 6, 1924, Flint Hill, North Carolina
MARRIED: w. Louise Certain
CHILDREN: s. Gary, Randy, Steve

"My daddy died when I was four," Earl Scruggs once explained to me in the New York office of Ren Grevatt, his publicist. "They told me my daddy was asleep, and that was what death was. So I used to lay on a rock with my eyes closed and pretend I was dead. And I'd walk around with my eyes shut. But I knew that wasn't death. What I decided, I think then and there, was that I wanted to live long enough so my kids would understand death. And I've been lucky."

Earl Scruggs is probably *the* virtuoso banjo picker in the world. Growing up in Cleveland County, North Carolina, a stronghold of banjo enthusiasm during the Depression-ravaged 1930s, Scruggs learned to play the year his banjo-playing father died. "I played the banjo because it was something I enjoyed doing." It also was something other people enjoyed listening to, and were willing to pay money for. When he was fifteen he played on a Gastonia, North Carolina, radio station with a group, and played duets with a fiddler named Dennis Butler. Before and during World War II, Scruggs worked at a factory. Earl recalls: "At that point I went to work at the Lily Thread mill for forty cents an hour, seventy-two hours a week. I thought I was getting rich. I did very well, was able to buy my first automobile after a while." Having an automobile allowed him to look for steady radio work, and in 1945 he found a job picking on morning radio on Nashville's WSM. "There was a boy from near my hometown working with Bill Monroe. His name was Jimmy Shumate," Scruggs says. "He was playing fiddle with Bill and he wanted me to go to work with Monroe's group. Well, I was never the type to jump from one thing to another just because someone asked me to. When John Miller, who was in Monroe's band, decided to get off on the road for a while, I took an audition with Bill and he gave me a job—on Grand Ole Opry.

Two years later Scruggs left Monroe with another band member, Lester Flatt, and they began an operation of their own called The Foggy Mountain Boys: "We were workin' from Florida to Canada," Scruggs recalls, "and had to be back for the Opry every Saturday night, which meant travelin' in a '41 Chevrolet automobile, on the road day and night. So I had kinda worn down from that and I had full intentions of quittin' completely. Then the same night that I bid 'em good-by, Lester turned in his notice and we got talking how we'd be dissatisfied gettin' out completely." Instead, they formed a band: Flatt, Scruggs, the late Cedric Rainwater on bass, and fiddler Jimmy Shumate. Guitarist Mac Wiseman signed on soon and the boys settled in Nashville. They joined Grand Ole Opry in 1955 and began spreading the gospel of bluegrass to America— from the campus at Harvard to Carnegie Hall, from Pumpkin, Iowa's, town hall to Panther Hall

Earl Scruggs with sons Gary (left), Randy (center), and Steve (right).

in Fort Worth, Texas. Untold thousands of kids bought banjos and began to imitate Earl Scruggs. "The Ballad of Jed Clampett," the tune that Flatt and Scruggs did for *The Beverly Hillbillies*, became the only bluegrass hit ever to be number one on the country charts. Their albums sold to people who had never considered buying a country album. And Scruggs-style banjo playing became the style most copied.

Scruggs passes off his style by saying that "I'm just a picker." But his style is unique. When he was a young child, he fell under the influence of two country musicians, Snuffy Jenkins and Smith Hammett. "Smith was a distant cousin of mine. I heard him play three-finger style when I was only five. I thought it was the prettiest playing I ever heard. So I tried

to reproduce the sound on my own banjo. Then one day I was fingering the old tune 'Reuben' when I shouted to my momma, 'I found the roll, Momma. I found it.'" According to country-music historian Bill C. Malone, this three-fingered roll has caused Earl Scruggs to be considered to "have the same relationship to a five-string banjo that Paganini has to the violin. By sharply accentuating the melody line, Scruggs makes it stand out clearly in a shower of notes."

In 1969 the country-music world was shocked to hear that Flatt and Scruggs were splitting as a team. Earl Scruggs maintains the separation was "friendly and amicable." He says, "I wanted to change the sound a bit. What Lester wanted was apparently the same style he's playin' now. My

247

sons Gary and Randy were gettin' pretty professional in their own rights and we were pickin' at home, and I had created a lot of interest in the sounds we were gettin'. Prior to that, Columbia Records and our producer had changed our style of music, which was sellin' real well, actually. But I really thought I'd stuck to the same type of music quite a while and I wanted to broaden the span of the banjo a little bit because I'd worked with some people on different occasions, some jam sessions, especially when I picked with King Curtis on a TV show called *Folksong USA*. That along with a few other musicians on brass and piano and some electrical instruments. I just wanted to join in on some of that stuff.'' Scruggs says that ''music can't stand still. I've always been for progress and keeping up with the times.'' His new group, The Earl Scruggs Review, is what Scruggs calls a ''no-cubbyhole, category-free, barrierless approach to music.'' The revue consists of Earl; Gary Scruggs, a philosophy graduate of Vanderbilt University who plays electric bass, harmonica, and guitar; Randy Scruggs, who plays guitar, slide guitar, and bass and who helps arrange the music; Steve Scruggs, the youngest member of the family and the rhythm guitarist; Jody Maphis, son of famous Nashville guitarist Joe Maphis; and Josh Graves, probably the world's finest dobro player.

Troy Seals once recorded with his wife, pop singer Jo Ann Campbell, but now he's embarked on a solo career—and the future looks brighter.

## SEALS, TROY

BORN: November 16, 1938, Big Hill, Kentucky
MARRIED: w. Jo Ann Campbell
CHILDREN: s. TJ

Troy Seals is one of the Nashville hopefuls, both as a singer and songwriter, and one of the many young people who are drifting into country from rock and pop. His first country album was released in 1973.

Born in Kentucky, only a few miles from country star Red Foley's hometown, Troy, like Foley, got his guitar at thirteen, formed a band, played on radio, and started writing country songs. He met and married pop singer Jo Ann Campbell, and they both joined the *Dick Clark Revue* and recorded as a pop duet for Atlantic. ''It was at that time that I decided to leave the music business,'' Seals says. ''We didn't like the pop-music business and life on the road can

be a drag.'' For over a year Seals worked for a construction firm in Indianapolis, but eventually he drifted to Nashville, where with Don Goodman and Will Jennings he wrote ''Girl in New Orleans'' (for Sammi Smith) and ''You Almost Slipped My Mind'' (for Kenny Price). When Atlantic opened a country line, Seals was one of the first artists signed. The Nashville smart-money set feels he's a comer.

## SEELY, JEANNIE

BORN: July 6, 1940, Titusville, Pennsylvania
MARRIED: h. Hank Cochran

Jeannie Seely is married to songwriter Hank Cochran (he wrote ''I Fall to Pieces'' for Patsy Cline) and sings duets with the Jolly Greene Giant, Jack Greene. Her first big hit, ''Don't

Touch Me'' (written for her by Hank Cochran, naturally), brought the Seely name to the attention of pop-music fans as well as country buffs. The record won Jeannie Seely the 1966 Grammy Award for Best Country Female Vocalist. "The only thing country about Jeannie Seely," a Nashville gossip columnist wrote at the time, "is her soul. She's slick, uptown, polished. But the little blonde girl in the miniskirt has crashed the Calico Curtain. Her performance and manner have literally demolished the outdated gingham image of Nashville women."

Jeannie Seely grew up in Titusville, Pennsylvania. Although she wanted to be a singer, she studied commercial law, economics, public relations, banking and finance at the American Institute of Banking in Oil City, Pennsylvania. At the age of eleven she started singing on a weekly radio program in Meadville, Pennsylvania, and throughout her tenure as a student at Townville High School she worked radio and TV and amusement parks throughout the area. Some of the shows she appeared on were fairly important, like *Midwest Hayride*, and eventually

Jeannie Seely: The other half of the Greene team.

she moved to Los Angeles, where she joined Four Star Music as a songwriter and as a performer for its subsidiary, Challenge Records. When she moved to Nashville in 1965, she found part-time work with Ernest Tubb ("Ernest didn't have a regular girl singer and sometimes the show demanded one, so I would go along"). Jeannie was rooming with Porter Wagoner's secretary and learned that Norma Jean, who was the regular female member of Wagoner's touring show, wanted to devote more time to domesticity. "It just happened to fall into place. Porter hired me to take Norma Jean's place on the road." Monument Records signed her, and she left Wagoner to book as a single.

In 1969 she joined the Jack Greene show as a full partner. Greene, whose duets with Jeannie Seely on Decca have won them numerous honors, including a number of Grammy nominations, credits her with originating the idea for their highly polished, widely acclaimed stage show, packaged more like a Las Vegas revue than the usual informal, almost catch-as-catch-can program some country performers prefer. Jeannie Seely has been a member of Grand Ole Opry since 1967, and has appeared, as a single, with Greene on most of the major country TV shows. As a writer, she penned "It Just Takes Practice" for Dottie West and "Enough to Lie" for Ray Price. Both Connie Smith and Willie Nelson recorded "Senses," and Faron Young, Jack Greene, and Norma Jean all scored with "Leavin' and Sayin' Good-bye." In 1973 Jeannie Seely wrote "Can I Sleep in Your Arms Tonight, Mister?" (with a tiny help from the traditional "Red River Valley"), which, at this writing, is climbing over its chart competition and has promise of becoming a country classic. During 1969 Jeannie, who once hosted an armed forces radio show, toured military bases in Southeast Asia, Europe, England, and Hawaii.

# SHAVER, BILLY JOE

Billy Joe Shaver is probably the singer-songwriter most mentioned by Nashville's younger entertainers. Many of them, like Tom T. Hall, have recorded his songs, and Waylon Jennings recorded a best-selling album called "Honky-Tonk Heroes" which features Billy Joe Shaver's songs—"Old Five-and-Dimers" and "Black Rose" and "Omaha, Nebraska." Shaver moves in the Kris Kristofferson–Willie Nelson–Leon Russel circle, and his future success should be assured. One of his songs, "Black Rose," has been mildly controversial: It deals with a white man loving a black girl ("The Devil made me do it the first time, the second time I did it on my own . . ."), and it is a song which is neither maudlin or condescending. Songwriter and critic Dave Hickey, an outspoken admirer of Billy Joe Shaver, recalls Shaver's singing at the Dripping Springs Festival in Texas. "I not only heard a man singing good songs, but a man singing them in my language. Evidently, I wasn't the only one who felt that way, because when Billy finished singing there was more noise than I would have expected, even from the crowd of cowboys sipping Lone Star out front. When the applause kept up, Billy smiled with a little more sincerity than he had walking out. I think, at that particular moment, Billy Joe was the only person backstage or onstage who was surprised by the applause. But then again he was also the only person who had made that long and lonesome run.

" 'Hell, I just thought I'd mention
That my Grandmaw's old-age pension
Is the reason why I'm standing here to-
  day.'

Hickey continues: "Twenty years earlier and 120 miles north, Billy Joe Shaver had stood up on a cracker-barrel in the general store at Emhouse, Texas, and sung for his supper—entertaining the locals in hopes that his songs would encourage the store-owner to extend credit to his grandmother. Now, a year and a half after that moment at Dripping Springs, Billy Joe has released his first solo album on Monument, produced by Kris Kristofferson with notes by Tom T. Hall; he has had songs cut by Kristofferson, Hall, Jerry Lee Lewis, Bobby Bare, Johnny Rodriguez, and Dottie West (to name a few) and has had Waylon Jennings cut an entire album of his songs called 'Honky-Tonk Heroes,' a rare honor for a young songwriter.

He has a few less debts now, and one new ulcer, and if you should run across him and he

Billy Joe Shaver: The devil made him do it.

doesn't seem appropriately happy with all of this success—well, you need to get to know Billy a little better, or rather, get to know that there are things inside him you will never know. As Tom T. Hall put it, 'His thoughts run deep and black,' and it's not so much that the success he has had isn't enough, it's just that success isn't his goal. He is much less concerned with making his songs sell than he is with making them true, making them poetry, and much less concerned with being a successful performer than he is with being a successful human being —with figuring a way a man can live according to his own lights in 1973.

"Sometimes it makes him seem a little crazy. As country star Red Lane said about him, 'He's spent so long with his gift messing his life up, it's gonna be hard for him to make his talent work for him rather than against him.' And given the fact that he is a sweet-tempered country boy by nature, watching Billy being blown this way and that by his talent and his feelings is a little like watching a cowboy riding a bronc he can just barely handle. Sometimes he's grinning and right on top of it. Sometimes he's just barely holding on. But he's still on top, and he's made some long runs between helping hands.

"The first big helping hand, and to Billy Joe the most important, was a young English teacher, Miss Legg, at Las Vegas Junior High School in Waco, Texas. She recognized Billy's talent in its early stages and encouraged him to write poetry. And even though he quit school in the tenth grade to join the navy, he kept on writing poetry, dedicating many of these early poems to the young teacher who encouraged him. After the navy, Billy came back to Texas and sort of gravitated toward the Quarter in Houston, which at that time was populated by many folk singers and poets. It was during this stay that Billy came under the influence of Willie Nelson, and Nelson's songs helped him make up his mind that he would become a songwriter.

> " 'Willy, you're wild as a Texas blue
> norther,
> Ready-rolled from the same makings as
> me,
> And I reckon we'll ramble till hell freezes
> over,
> Willy the Wandering Gypsy and me.'

"Having made up his own mind, however, it was a number of years before he convinced anyone else, and during this time he made it by cowboying around Waco and finally working steady in a sawmill there. And it wasn't until an accident took off the fingers on one hand and nearly took his life, that he took up playing the guitar. (Those people who like to think Billy tends to do things the hard way have pretty good evidence in this incident.)

"Finally, with Willie Nelson's encouragement, he took off for Nashville to hustle his songs in person; in fact, he took off several times, always coming back empty-handed until country singer Bobby Bare heard his songs, liked them, and took him on as a contract writer at $50 a week. Billy realized he had found one of the few jobs available that paid less than punching cattle, but he came to Nashville anyway. That was six years ago and now he's an overnight success, but he's still a poet.

"I once asked if he thought there was any particular reason that after so much work, he should all of a sudden begin to break—if the music industry had to change before his songs could be recorded. Billy shook his head. 'Naw, I don't think things have changed much. I just put so much into the songs, some of it was bound to get out.' "

## SHEPARD, JEAN
BORN: November 21, 1933, Pauls Valley, Oklahoma
MARRIED: h. Hawkshaw Hawkins (deceased) (s. Don Robin Hawkins, Harold F. Hawkins II); h. Bennie Birchfield (s. Corey Birchfield)

One of the really big songs of the Korean War period was "Dear John Letter" sung by Ferlin Husky and Jean Shepard—a soulful and sad talk-song by an unfaithful girl friend to her soldier lover: "Dear John, how I ha-a-ate to write . . ." (number-one song on the country charts for twenty-three weeks). It had servicemen crying in barracks from Pusan to West Berlin, in B-29s and on destroyers in the Mediterranean. Jean Shepard was heralded as the "small girl with the big voice," and promises of stardom echoed in the wings of Grand Ole Opry. She married the great country singer Hawkshaw

Jean Shepard: A "Dear John" letter launched her career.

country artists, Red Simpson was raised in a family that enjoyed getting together to make music just for and by themselves. He wrote his first song, called "The Chicken House Boogie," when he was fourteen. After a stint in the Navy during World War II, Red headed for Bakersfield, California, to try his hand at playing country music. One of his first jobs was as relief man for Buck Owens' show at the Blackboard Club in Bakersfield. When he wasn't on stage, Red augmented his income driving an ice-cream truck. He has written many songs with Buck Owens, including "Sam's Place," "Gonna Have Love," "Heart of Glass," "Kansas City Song," and "I Want No One but You." One of his biggest recent hits was called "I'm a Truck," which he didn't compose. He sure doesn't look like a Good Humor man, though.

Red Simpson: He drove a truck—an ice-cream truck.

Hawkins (who was killed in a 1963 air crash, leaving her with two small boys) and recorded a succession of songs, many of which made the country charts, but none of them was a blockbuster like "Dear John." After twenty-three albums and infinite singles, Jean Shepard (one of ten children, who started singing with her own band when she was only fourteen and cut her first record, with the help of country singer Hank Thompson, when she was only fifteen) had a career which seemed to be slipping away. Then Bill Anderson wrote "Slipping Away," Jean recorded it—and her career zoomed. She was nominated for a Grammy for Best Country Female Vocal Performance of the Year, revamped her act (with the help of Benny Birchfield, her new husband and father of her smallest child), and organized a full-time band, The Second Fiddles. She is determined not to let her professional life slip away.

## SIMPSON, RED [Joseph Simpson]
BORN: Higby, Arizona

Red Simpson was never actually a trucker, but his songs about truckers, trucks, and life on the road have won him a wide audience among today's kings of the road. Like many other

Cal Smith: "The Lord knows . . ."

## SMITH, CAL

BORN: April 7, 1932, Sallisaw, Oklahoma
MARRIED: w. Darlene

Cal Smith has been on the charts just about every year, but never as successfully as in 1973, when he recorded Bill Anderson's "The Lord Knows I'm Drinkin'," a fine song about a "backslidin' Christian in a neighborhood bar." And the Lord knows that Cal Smith's career is booming, too. Born in Oklahoma, Smith always wanted to sing, and he got his first nightclub job in San Jose, California, in the early 1950s. For several years he was a disc jockey in San Jose (station KEEN) and was a regular member of *California Hayride*, with time out for Uncle Sam and for an almost-fatal accident. "Much of whatever success I have," Smith claims, "comes from my years with Ernest Tubb." He was front man and featured vocalist for Tubb, and like many other Tubb alumni (Jack Greene is another), he has done well. Among Smith hits: "Drinking Champagne," "It Takes All Night Long," "You Can't Housebreak a Tomcat," and "Heaven Is Just a Touch Away."

## SMITH, CARL

BORN: March 15, 1927, Maynardsville, Tennessee
MARRIED: w. Goldie Hill
CHILDREN: s. Carl, Jr., Larry Dean; d. Rebecca Carlene, Lori Lynn

I had lunch recently with two pop-music critics. They asked me about the varied "kings" of country music. I mentioned Roy Acuff and George Jones and Johnny Cash, whom they all knew and whose work they admired. Then I said, "Carl Smith." "Come on now," one of them remarked, "how come I don't know him, if he's so successful?" Well, Carl Smith is in the top twenty artists with the most number-one country records, is number *three* (after Eddy Arnold and Webb Pierce) among artists with the most charted record sides, and only Hank Snow has been on the country charts more consecutively. He has sold more than 15 million records. He is about the number-one country star in *Canada*. His TV show, produced and distributed in that country, pulls top ratings. When he appears at the Calgary Stampede, fans from all over Canada flock to Alberta to see their favorite country singer. And among the countless thousands of American fans who buy his records and flock to his concerts, he is a hero. He is basically a ballad singer, like Eddy Arnold or Ray Price, but he maintains the basic honkytonk instrumentation as his backing. Carl Smith retains the unspoiled and pleasantly unsophisticated quality that the traditional country fan still looks for in a singer, but although he is not nasal or high-tenor, the urban fan either hasn't taken to him or is unaware of his work.

By the time Carl Smith was thirteen, he had entered his first amateur contest, and buoyed by the reaction of the crowd, he decided that country singing was his future. When he was hardly out of his teens, he managed to get a spot on WROL in Knoxville. A hitch in the navy intervened, and after eighteen months he returned to WROL, appearing on his days off on other stations in Augusta, Georgia, and Asheville, North Carolina. These, remember, were the pre-television days, when every southern city had at least three or four live country-music shows on radio. Country singers Molly O'Day and Archie Campbell, also working on WROL, encouraged Carl Smith, and in 1950 he was invited to join Grand Ole Opry. His first record for Columbia was "Let's Live a Little," probably the major hit of 1951. (He hit the charts with two other numbers in 1951, "If Teardrops Were Pennies" and "Mr. Moon.") For the next ten years, when Carl Smith was *Mr.* Country, hardly a week passed without his name gracing the charts. He appeared on every major country show, and starred in two films, *The Badge of Marshal Brennan* and *Buffalo Guns.* He traveled throughout the United States and to all of Canada's provinces. He has entertained in Europe and the Far East. And he has produced classic country hits like "Loose Talk," "Foggy River," "I'm Drifting into Deep Water," and "It's a Lovely, Lovely World." If someone came to me and said, "I can only buy twenty-five country albums and that's all I'll ever buy—suggest the best performers," I would, without a doubt, include an album called "The Best of Carl Smith."

Smith married Goldie Hill, who was a country star in her own right. She has willingly retired from the business and helps Carl raise his herd of prize quarterhorses, cattle, and children on their ranch outside of Nashville.

## SMITH, CONNIE

BORN: August 14, 1941, Elkhart, Indiana
MARRIED: h. Jerry Smith (divorced), Jack Watkins (divorced), Marshall Haynes

It's been almost ten years since Connie Smith soared to the top of the country charts with her very first record, "Once a Day." She was a pleasant, naive twenty-three-year-old who learned, all too quickly, that hit records don't necessarily bring happiness. During the past decade she's been divorced from two husbands, she's been the object of gossip and rumors, and there are stories of broken contracts and major lawsuits. "I got to where I never opened my mouth 'til I got on stage," she told writer Kathleen Gallagher, "and then I never opened it again 'til the next show. I lost all my joy. But now I am getting the joy back once again, and I am singing around the house a lot more than I used to."

Connie Smith was one of fourteen children. She was born in Indiana, but grew up in West Virginia and southern Ohio, where her always-on-the-move family (Poppa was an alcoholic) sent her to at least eight different grade schools. When her father was drunk, he beat her. Most of the time, she was neglected. Fourteen children clamoring for parents' attention is a difficult situation for a sensitive child. "I felt like I kinda grew by myself," she says. She was a country-music buff from the time she was very little, and as she grew older, she kept on singing—publicly, if possible—but didn't give much thought to a professional career. She married, settled down, and sang in the shower. Then, in 1963, she decided to enter an amateur singing contest at a Columbus, Ohio, amusement park. Bill Anderson happened to be there, liked what he heard, and asked her to join his group. What happened next is one of the legendary Nashville stories. He wrote a song, "Once a Day," which Connie recorded for RCA Victor; it reached the top of the charts during the Disc Jockey Convention in Nashville, and she was signed for TV appearances and a long-term recording contract.

She followed up her first hit with "Tiny Blue Transistor Radio," "I Can't Remember," and "I Never Once Stopped Loving You," writes Kathleen Gallagher, and in 1966 she was named Most Outstanding Female Country Vocalist by both *Cash Box* and *Record World*. She has fond memories of those early years: "To me, the biggest thrill was getting to hear myself on the radio for the first time. I was driving the car, and I nearly ran off the road. We were heading in towards Nashville, and the reception was poor, so I stopped the car, and my husband tried to get the radio to work better."

Her other big thrill was her first appearance on Grand Ole Opry. "I always thought it was just an old saying about someone's knees knocking, but when I got out on the stage, my knees really knocked," she said, laughing. "To the people, the record is the song, but to the performer the 'real' of it is when you are performing it live.

"I very seldom learn my songs before I record; it keeps 'em simple. To me, singing is like telling a story, and if you can't hear all the words, you've missed part of it."

Even in the first years of success there were troubled times, however. "I wanted to quit real quick when I first went out on the road and left Darren," she said. "When you leave your two-

Connie Smith with her new husband, Marshall Haynes, after marriage in Jimmie Snow's church.

year-old son crying at the window and playing your songs on the stereo, it's not so much fun.''

Things began to slide. "I had no foundation," she said. "It was an experience to travel over 100,000 miles a year on the road when you weren't used to leaving your own town. I couldn't face the reality of life, and I became bitter when the people I admired didn't act the way I expected them to off the stage. I signed several contracts and had to buy my way out of most of them. I came to mistrust everybody. Then I kept getting miserable myself and blamed it on the business. You just look for excuses anywhere, outside yourself.''

Her first marriage failed, then the second. She has admitted to close friends that she considered suicide. Fortunately, she saw a psychiatrist and started attending the church of Rev. Jimmy Snow (country singer Hank Snow's son), and she is now a committed Christian, happy, and with a new husband and a new baby. "I don't think I could have lived the last five and a half years if I hadn't found God," she said. "I've had a chance to live my life over." And it seems to be a good life: Connie Smith recently signed a new recording contract with Columbia which guarantees her the right to do one gospel album each year, plus two country albums with two gospel songs each. Among Connie Smith's past hits: "If I Talk to Him," "Ain't Had No Lovin'," "Just One Time," and "Cincinnati, Ohio.''

## SMITH, SAMMI

BORN: August 5, 1943, Orange, California

A couple of years ago Sammi Smith recorded (on Mega) "Help Me Make It Through the Night." It was a Grammy Award winner, with sales exceeding 2 million records. Thus far Sammi Smith hasn't repeated the commercial success of that release, but she has become an "underground" star in Nashville. When Waylon Jennings and Willie Nelson gave their special, much-touted two-man concert during the 1973 Disc Jockey Convention in Nashville, they asked Sammi to join them, and that's heavy company, man. Everybody who saw her in person agreed that no recording had yet caught Sammi's "magic." When she came to Nashville, to write and record for Columbia, times

were difficult. "I didn't know much about the business then," she says. She wrote "Sand-Covered Angels" and other songs, and recorded "well outside what the industry considered country," songs by John Hartford and John Sebastian, as well as Carl Perkins. Many of her efforts did well. "So Long, Charlie Brown, Don't Look for Me Around" managed to garner some chart action, and "He's Everywhere" was played by a number of leading disc jockeys. "Then You Walk In" and "For the Kids" both did fairly well. Sammi Smith is a female counterpart of Willie Nelson and Waylon Jennings and Billy Joe Shaver and that gang in that they have strong country roots but are interested in creating a new type of American music. She's worth watching.

Sammi Smith clowns around with drummer Paul English of Willie Nelson's band.

## SNOW, HANK [Clarence Eugene Snow]

BORN: March 9, 1914, Liverpool, Nova Scotia

MARRIED: w. Minnie Blanche

CHILDREN: s. Jimmie Rodgers Snow

Hank Snow! To many people, especially country-music fans over forty, that name epitomizes the best, the zenith, in American music, even though they know the little fellow is only a naturalized American. (For all intents and purposes, Snow *is* an American and embodies all the virtues of devoted patriotism and love of country. As one critic said, "Hank don't sing notes and bars, he sings stars and stripes.") He is one of the surviving giants of "Jimmie Rodgers country" along with Ernest Tubb and maybe one or two others. He sings about railroads and aggressive women (which can't keep a good man down) and the rockin', rollin' ocean. He is conversant with the "Queen of Draw-Poker Town" and has taken a honeymoon on a rocket ship. It is difficult for me to write critically about one of my two or three heroes, and though there are country musicians with more musical knowledge, more tonal variety, I am absolutely knocked out by his faultless articulation, his unmistakable mellow voice with its masculine resonance.

I'm not alone in my admiration. The people are on my side. He had at least one record on the country best-selling charts for twenty-two consecutive years (1949–1970); only four other artists in country-music history have topped his total of sixty-plus records on the charts; and one of his songs, "I'm Movin' On," remained on the charts for an almost-unheard-of forty-four weeks (only Bobby Helms's "Fraulein" and Hank Williams' "Cold, Cold Heart" lasted longer). Hank Snow refuses to betray country tradition and has resisted the hit-parade syndrome. When some of the newer, frankly "hipper" country musicians have run their course, DJs will still be playing Hank Snow.

I've never met him—and I consider this one of the flaws in my life—but Nashville's brilliant photographer Marshal Fallwell, Jr., has (and I envy him for it), and has sensitively recorded the meeting:

"Country comedian Minnie Pearl asked me if I thought Hank Snow was a funny man. I had called her to get some information and maybe a few stories on him. 'I think he's one of the funniest men alive,' she said. 'Oh, I don't mean in a slapstick kind of way. He's not a clown. He's got this dry humor, this quiet humor, that just cracks me up. I've known him for a long time, and that's what I remember him for: the good times we all had.'

"I had been told—by people who didn't really know him—that Hank Snow was cold and humorless. And to be truthful, it's easy to get that impression when you first meet him, especially in Nashville, where so many people are their own publicity agents, ready to gladhand you and call you 'buddy' the first time you meet. Hank Snow doesn't come on that way. When you see him on the stage at the Opry, bright as a Christmas tree in his embroidery and sequins, playing one of his beautiful guitars, you are looking at a real pro. Watch his eyes. They are not starstruck or full of a stagy emotion, but are looking right back at you, calmly and clearly. Merle Haggard does the same thing. Both command your absolute attention before you know what's happening, and they do it quietly, without jumping around and screaming.

"Once backstage, Hank goes straight to the dressing room. The first time I met him, the tiny room was packed with hot, sweaty people, myself included. There was, as always, a party atmosphere backstage. Hank was in a corner by himself, putting his instrument into a very expensive-looking case. A string that had broken onstage dangled uselessly against the frets. People milled about him busily, but he went calmly about what he was doing, not aloof or holier-than-thou, but businesslike. He shook hands with me and looked significantly at my tape recorder, as if to say that in the midst of this noise and confusion was not the time or the place for an interview. So, I gave him my name and phone. A few days later, at 8 A.M., he called and set up our first talk.

"Hank Snow's Rainbow Ranch is a few miles north of Nashville, not far from Maybelle Carter's home (Maybelle, of the famous singing Carter Family, is a close friend of Hank's wife, Min). A white, Western-style rail fence surrounds a lovely house set among trees and flower borders. The whole place gives a feeling of quiet and solitude. Around back is a stable and a field which was once a pasture for horses.

Hank Snow: a long way from the rockin' rollin' ocean.

Shawnee, Hank's trained horse and part of his act in earlier days, is buried there.

"Adjoining the house is Hank's office. Among the furnishings are several stuffed animals, something that puzzled me for a while since Hank claims never to have killed anything. It was here that our conversations took place.

"His story is extraordinary. He is fifty-nine years old and one of America's most respected folk singers; has been with the same record label, RCA, since 1936; has remained happily married to one woman for the same amount of time; has been a member of the Opry for twenty-three years; did all this without getting involved with alcohol to any great extent and not at all with drugs; has no complaints; and

would do it all over again. 'I'm not even really religious,' he says, 'although I believe in God and the Bible. Maybe I ought to be, since my son is a preacher.'

"As he warmed up, and as he talked about his life and struggles, he showed himself to be a deeply sincere and passionate man, a man who had been paying his dues even as a child. As a matter of fact, perhaps the most astounding thing about Clarence Eugene Snow is that he survived his youth at all. He was born in Nova Scotia in 1914. When he was eight, his family split up, sending one of his sisters to work in a shirt factory, two into orphanages, and himself to his grandparents' home. Hank wanted to live with his mother after she remarried, but his

259

stepfather made it painfully clear that he was not wanted. So, at the age of twelve, he went to sea as a cabin boy. The story almost ended there.

"In the North Atlantic, off the southern tip of Nova Scotia, there is an island called Cape Sable, known as The Ocean's Graveyard. One night, the gales blew 100 miles per hour and churned the seas mountain-high. 'You tell someone the seas get that big and they don't believe you,' Hank says. 'That night, they wouldn't let me on deck, so I went below and did the best I could. Everybody on deck had ropes around their waists so they wouldn't wash away. Once the captain was washed off the prow of the ship and back on the stern. Anyway, the next day, we learned that 122 men from neighboring ships had lost their lives. Nearly all were from one town called Blue Rocks.'

"At sea, though, the worst dangers were icebergs, ocean liners, and sharks. This was before the shipping lanes were moved southward after the *Mauretania* disaster. As for the sharks, Hank says the sailors would catch them in a kind of noose, kill them with axes and throw them back in the sea. He doesn't seem to mind so much the memory of the sharks being killed. 'They were a danger to us, you know.'

"Life at sea had its high points, too. The sailors would throw nickels to see little Hank sing and dance. For once, he was appreciated— they were his family. And the sea was beautiful. One time, he remembers, the small fishing vessel he was on was trapped in solid ice from horizon to horizon. All they could do was wait. 'The sun on that ice would almost blind you; and I can still see the seals on the ice, thousands of them, all over the place. I'll never forget it.'

"When life as a cabin boy became too much of a drudge, Hank returned to his mother—for the last time. His stepfather threw him out again, so he went to work at a fish plant until he wound up in the hospital with a ruptured appendix and doctor's orders not to work for a year. His stepfather saw that he was back at the fish plant in three months. When the work proved too hard for him, he took a job at a stable. It was here that he developed his love for animals of all kinds, especially horses.

"After having worked on a salt steamer for eleven days, Hank took some of the money and bought himself his first guitar, a T. Eaton Special. For hours he would sit in front of a Gramophone listening to Jimmie Rodgers' records, trying to copy the chords. Rodgers, of course, was the most important single influence on Hank's music. Much later, he was to record an entire album of Rodgers' compositions; he even named his only child Jimmie Rodgers Snow.

"In 1935 Hank wrote radio station CHNS in Halifax, Nova Scotia, for an audition, which he got. To his amazement, he was told to report that very evening with a 'theme song' ready for his first broadcast. Hank didn't know what a theme song was, but he came anyway. Bang. He was a star. The show was called *Clarence Snow and His Guitar* and paid him precisely nothing. As a matter of fact, in order to eat, he went on welfare. To his embarrassment, the welfare department set him to work sweeping the streets —in front of the radio station. For this work, Hank earned $2.50 per week and some milk.

"The following year he married Min. Min was a blue-eyed girl he met at a Halloween party and fell desperately in love with. When he left the church, he had fifty cents in his pocket. He had spent $150 to make sure the wedding was a good one. 'Why not?' he says. 'I knew it was going to be the only one I'd ever have.'

"That same year he began what has so far been a thirty-seven-year association with RCA. The first sides for Victor were 'Lonesome Blue Yodel' and 'Prisoned Cowboy.' Since that time RCA has released about eighty albums of Hank's music and such a large number of his singles that this reporter is afraid to try to count them. But there were more dues to pay, and deadlier sharks than he'd ever seen as a boy. From 1936 to 1942 Hank cut a few more records, but realized the need to build himself a reputation. He worked a little too hard at it, became weakened and nearly died from a bad case of pleurisy. These years, however, saw Hank's records—about nine in number now—being played more and more across Canada.

"From 1942 to 1944 he made a number of tours for a chain of theaters across the country. These gave him the priceless experience of being in front of mean, raunchy audiences that weren't going to swallow just anything they were given.

"Hank's first venture south into the United States (he is now a citizen) came at the urging of a fan named Jack Howard, a music publisher from Philadelphia. Hank's first visit netted him, besides some exposure arranged by Howard, a successful introduction to station WWVA in Wheeling, West Virginia. By 1946 Hank had enough money and sufficient hopes to buy himself a tent, a couple of trucks, a new Buick, and a beautiful horse he called Shawnee. Shawnee was to become a major part of Hank's act in the years to come.

"That was also the year the sharks came back. The Singing Ranger, a name he'd picked up somewhere, was flying high. He had money in his pocket and the stars were all out for him. He thought. His first trip to Hollywood was comparable to the first time a gambler holds the dice. If his luck holds, he'll make a fortune. In 1947 he returned to Canada after a short, tantalizing visit to Hollywood. His following was in Canada, so he went back to make enough money for a second assault on Hollywood. In 1948, he bought some new equipment and a $2,000 silver saddle for Shawnee and returned. After a few bleak summer months, his savings were gone and he was $3,000 in debt. He has been taken for just about everything he had. Desperate again, Hank drove to Dallas, where he had some friends. When he got there, he had Shawnee, a wife, a baby, and $11 to feed them with.

"However, in Texas, Hank had a couple of allies: a lady named Bea Terry and a DJ named Fred Edwards at station KRLD. Through their faithful efforts, Hank's records started to take off across Texas. Even so, what money he was to realize from club and concert dates for the next months went to repay the loan company in Hollywood. He hocked his diamond ring and his movie camera. At one point, he had to buy food with a Canadian five-dollar bill he found in his wallet.

"So, in 1949, Hank returned to Canada, where his fans were just as loyal as they'd always been. Canada seems to have pulled Hank Snow out of deep water several times. That fall, when he moved back to Dallas, he found that he'd become a star. He had saved $6,000 from dates in Canada and was clear of debt. When he played the Sportatorium in Dallas, all previous attendance records were broken when thousands of his fans showed up. That year, the song Fred Edwards and Bea Terry had plugged so hard, 'Brand on My Heart,' was voted the most popular song played over KRLD.

"Shortly thereafter, in Fort Worth, Hank met Ernest Tubb, also a disciple of Jimmie Rodgers. Tubb brought Snow to Nashville, and in January of 1950 Hank became a member of the Grand Ole Opry. He's been there ever since.

"The early fifties were Hank Snow's true heyday. During that period he cut his theme song, 'I'm Movin' On,' and 'Rhumba Boogie,' 'Golden Rocket,' 'Bluebird Island' (with Anita Carter), 'Tangled Mind' and 'I Don't Hurt Anymore,' among others. He has had other hits than these, of course—'Miller's Cave' and 'Big Wheels,' to name just two. Hank's most recent albums are 'The Best of Hank Snow,' 'Hank Snow Sings Grand Ole Opry Favorites,' and 'The Legend of Ol' Doc Brown.' My own particular favorites among the recent releases are the two instrumental albums he has done with guitarist Chet Atkins. On the second of these, 'C. B. Atkins and C. E. Snow—By Special Request,' Chet joins Hank in singing the old hit 'Poison Love.' His recordings for RCA and his road tours have kept him busy ever since, although lately he has been doing only about eighty-five days a year on the road.

"Recording companies aren't in the least sentimental. If you fail to be of use to them, they drop you, no matter how many hits you've had in the past. Snow is indeed a rare bird because he has been with one company for so long, churning out the albums and singles, obviously making money for himself and the company. And somehow he has managed to do this without changing his music to fit modern fads in production or studio techniques. His style is still as clean and uncomplicated as it was in the beginning. There is a purity to it that many good artists have lost trying to be fashionable.

"But the question remains. What kind of man is it that made such an improbable and hazardous life work out so well? The answer is not easy to give. But there are clues. First, he has no visible crutches. He seems to have ironed out any glaring emotional difficulties some time ago; or maybe he was just too busy staying alive to have time for problems. 'I used to drink,' he says, 'but I gave that up because it was controlling me, not the other way around. I drank for one reason—to get drunk. But I've *never* taken drugs. Nope, I don't have any problems that way.'

"On this same subject, he told some sad stories about the times he went on tour with Hank Williams to back Williams up in case he failed to show. 'One time, we hired a guard for Hank's door so he couldn't get any liquor. But he just leaned out the window and threw a ten-dollar bill to someone in the street and asked him to get him a pint. When the guy came back, he tied the end of a bedsheet to the bottle, and Hank just hauled it up.'

"There isn't a trace of humor in Hank's voice when he tells these stories. When it comes to human tragedy, he is truly without humor. I suggested that perhaps the life of a performer on the road could become too much to endure—endless hotels and restaurant food, and so forth. Hank said, 'Hell, what's wrong with that?' Then I remembered what kind of life he'd had before he became a performer, the gales off Cape Sable, the fear of a lonely death from peritonitis without anyone who cared for you, and having to shovel salt for days in order to buy a guitar. Anything would be better than that.

"The other clue to his character is the presence of the stuffed animals in his office, something that had puzzled me at first. Hank has always loved animals: Shawnee, a pet dog, the seals on the ice. I think he sees them as images of himself as he once was, a helpless, vulnerable creature in a world that is not very nice, a world full of sharks.

"After the interview we went outside to do some pictures. By the garage, he called to an old man, who was fiddling with one of the cars. 'Squirrely, I want you to do something for me.' After he'd sent him on his errand, we walked around to the front for some pictures by the gate. 'Squirrely's a faithful man. He's been with us for a long time, helping out.' Hank waved his hand, taking in the entirety of Rainbow Ranch, and said, 'Squirrely's got a home here for as long as he wants, for the rest of his life.'

# SONS OF THE PIONEERS

The most famous "western" group of singers called themselves Sons of the Pioneers. Per-

haps, more than any other ensemble, they hung on the "western" idea projected in the Roy Rogers/Gene Autry movies, and dozens of imitators popped up in their wake. The three original members of the group, which was formed in 1934, were: Roy Rogers (Leonard Slye) from Ohio, Bob Nolan from Canada, and Tim Spencer from Missouri. When Rogers left the group to become a movie cowboy, the personnel of Sons of the Pioneers expanded. Nolan wrote a number of fine songs, including the classic "Tumbling Tumbleweeds" and "Cool Water." Among the more famous alumni of Sons of the Pioneers are comic Pat Brady and Ken Curtis, the "Festus" character on TV's *Gunsmoke.*

# SOUTH, JOE
BORN: Atlanta, Georgia

Joe South is one of the new breed of southern-born singer/songwriters who has applied simple country rhythms to a variety of sophisticated themes that deal with the way people are—not as they were yesterday, or as he wants them to be, but as they are today, living amidst the complexities of modern life.

"Today songwriting is something powerful," he told an interviewer in 1971. "You can put something into people's minds they will never forget. It's like writing a three-minute book."

Joe South's songs bear witness to his statement. In 1970 the National Academy of Recording Arts and Sciences (NARAS) honored Joe with two of its Grammy awards for "Games People Play," voting it Song of the Year and Best Contemporary Song. Barely three minutes long, "Games" contained the best elements of southern "closet preaching," a simple, sensible exposition of life's peculiarities, set to an infectious, sing-along melody.

Joe drew on an old Indian aphorism for inspiration in writing "Walk a Mile in My Shoes," another example of country philosophizing at its best, set to music.

Joe learned much from his mother, who had a meager education but managed to fill composition books with her poems. The first songs Joe wrote were her poems set to music. Music, and communication, are Joe's chief interests in life. He is an accomplished technician in the record-

Sons of the Pioneers: Still tumbling along.

ing studio, who once built his own radio studio at home, broadcasting a mile and a half, filling neighbors' requests for songs. He's been a country DJ, a producer, and a sessionman, and has even worked on the assembly line at a record-pressing plant.

He lives on the outskirts of Atlanta, in a comfortable new home. He hopes to see Atlanta turn into another major recording center, like Nashville. With songs like "Games People Play," "You Never Promised Me a Rose Gar-

den," "These Are Not My People," "Children," "Fool Me," and "Don't It Make You Want to Go Home," it appears Joe South is capable of bringing that vision to reality through his own talent and energies.

Other songs he has written include "Down in the Boondocks," "Hush," "Untie Me," and "Birds of a Feather," a regional hit that launched his solo career in 1968, after years spent playing, writing, and producing for so many other artists.

## SOVINE, RED [Woodrow Wilson Sovine]

BORN: July 17, 1918, Charleston, West Virginia

MARRIED: w. Norma Searls

CHILDREN: s. Roger, Bill, Mike; d. Janet Carol

The late Spade Cooley introduced Red Sovine the first time I saw him, at the Riverside Rancho in Riverside, California, in the early fifties. Tex Williams and Cliffie Stone were also on the bill, and I remember the night clearly. I described it to Red Sovine, backstage at a New Jersey theater, a couple of years ago. "Those *were* the good old days," he sighed. "Country music was a big happy family then. You knew all the performers—all over the country—and even their families. Now you share billing with folks you've never met before, nice folks but they haven't grown up in the country."

Woodrow Wilson Sovine grew up "country." Before he was seventeen, he already was picking at local clubs in the Charleston, West Virginia, area. At seventeen, he joined Jim Pike and His Carolina Tarheels on their WCHS program in Charleston, moving after a few years to the WWVA *Jamboree* in Wheeling. When Hank Williams left *Louisiana Hayride* to join Grand Ole Opry, Red Sovine replaced him and took over his *Johnny Fiar Syrup Show* radio program. Webb Pierce was on the show at the time, and Sovine and Pierce often sang together, with hit recordings of "Little Rosa" and "Why, Baby, Why?" In 1965 Sovine climbed to the top of the country charts with "Giddyup, Go" (on Starday). It lasted for twenty-two weeks as top winner, has become Sovine's trademark, and is considered one of the seminal trucker songs.

## STAMPLEY, JOE

BORN: Springhill, Louisiana

Joe Stampley, the success story from Springhill, Louisiana, first made the country charts (way down, number seventy-five, but charted nonetheless) with "Take Time to Know Her." Then came "Soul Song" and a chance for success in country. Stampley, who started recording at fifteen, was the moving force of the rock group The Uniques, who worked for the Paula label. "Not Too Long Ago" sold about half a million

Joe Stampley: Likes Louisiana living.

records for the Uniques, and then the group sold 600,000 copies with "All These Things."

But Joe's roots were not in rock, and the break for him in country came in his hometown: "One day my little boy told me that the kids were teasing about him liking a girl from Springhill named Quanette McGraw, who sat next to him in the fourth grade. I thought the name so unusual I used it in a song along with the Arkansas town of Smackover." The end result was that "Quanette McGraw from Smackover, Arkansas" sold 35,000 copies and put Stampley into country. And his star seems to be climbing. But he hasn't moved to Nashville. He likes living in Springhill, Louisiana.

# THE STATLER BROTHERS

### Lew C. DeWitt
BORN: March 8, 1938, Roanoke County, Virginia

### Philip E. Balsley
BORN: August 8, 1939, Augusta County, Virginia

### Don S. Reid
BORN: June 5, 1945, Staunton, Virginia

### Harold W. Reid
BORN: August 21, 1939, Augusta County, Virginia

The Statler Brothers are made up of the Reid brothers, Lew DeWitt, Phil Balsley, and absolutely no one named Statler. It was DeWitt, with his composition "Flowers on the Wall" that made the group famous. It became a smash hit in 1965, and the group, which formed in the early sixties (all the boys knew each other as teen-agers), signed with Columbia originally, leaving in 1969 to work for Mercury. Among their hits: "Bed of Roses," "Class of 1957," "New York City," and "You Can't Have Your Kate and Edith, Too." For a time the Statlers were part of the *Johnny Cash Show*, but recently they have been touring under their own banner, to perform for audiences who turn out in droves to see them, and to buy their best-selling albums.

The Statler Brothers: Lew is seated, and from the left, standing, are Don, Phil, and Harold.

## STEAGALL, RED [Russell Steagall]
BORN: Gainesville, Texas

Red Steagall is one of Capitol's newer artists, though he's been on the country scene awhile writing hits like "Here We Go Again" and "Alabama Woman" for Glen Campbell, Dean Martin, and Jeannie C. Riley. Torn between a career in agriculture or in music, Steagall graduated from West Texas University with a degree in agriculture. He got a job as a soil-chemistry expert for a large company but played weekends at country dances. Eventually he quit his weekday job, formed a group, and was booked in all the ski-resort clubs in the Rocky Mountain area. In 1965 he came to California, wrote for two music publishers, Tree and Combine, signed with Capitol Records, and made a beginning splash with "Party Dolls and Wine" and

"Somewhere My Love." Red Steagall's 1973 album, "If You've Got the Time, I've Got the Song," gives promise of better things to come.

Steagall claims a great love for the Southwest, and this remembrance, written by him for a magazine article, gives some insight into his character:

"One of my favorite pieces of art is entitled 'The Cowboy's Christmas Ball.' This pen-and-ink sketch by Harold Bugbee depicts a group of horses and buggies in a winter setting with folks just gathered at a ranch house on the Texas plains for an evening of barbecued beef, potato salad, fiddle music, and a whole lotta joy.

"Christmas at our house, like most of the families I knew when I was growin' up on the Texas plains, was relatively simple, but by far the richest time of the year. And on Christmas Eve we liked to sit around the piano or a guitar

265

and sing Christmas carols, or listen to some member of the family read the Christmas stories from the Bible. There wasn't much in the way of material gifts, but then we didn't expect much. And I know that you've heard a million times that we had so much more: we had love and

Red Steagall: Would you believe a soil chemist?

each other, but I think at Christmastime those are the two things that all of us are most grateful for, regardless of where we live.

"It doesn't take long for those festivities and tables of food to disappear and the worries of weather and bills to take the upper hand. But for awhile at Christmastime, the whole world seems at ease. We know of course that every day can't be as carefree as Christmastime, but isn't it great to have Christmas to look forward to, to relax and enjoy bein' one of the folks, and to take time to thank God for all the privileges and pleasures that have been ours?''

## STEWART, WYNN
BORN: June 7, 1934, Morrisville, Missouri

Wynn Stewart had the number-one hit in the U.S.A. in 1967, lasting on the country charts for twenty-two weeks: "It's Such a Pretty World Today." In fact, Wynn Stewart numbers (recorded for Capitol) have been on the country hit parades since 1959 and many people wonder why he hasn't achieved greater prominence. Stewart, along with Merle Haggard and Buck Owens, is responsible for the popularity of the "California Sound," and his influence and value have far outweighed his commercial recognition. Stewart's band, featuring guitarists like Ralph Mooney, is described by country-music historian Bill C. Malone as playing in an "uptempoed, supercharged, strident manner with their instruments tuned to an almost ear-splitting pitch." Merle Haggard got his start playing bass for Stewart.

Wynn Stewart made his first recording at fifteen (Intro Records) and was nineteen when he signed with Capitol ("Strollin' " was his first release). A number of his early recordings feature singer Jan Howard. For a spell, he ran the country-music-oriented Nashville-Nevada Club in Las Vegas. Serious students of country music should study Stewart records for the origins of a lot of today's groovy country sounds.

## STONE, CLIFFIE
BORN: March 1, 1917, Burbank, California
MARRIED: w. Dorothy Darling
CHILDREN: s. Stevie, two other brothers; d. Linda

One of my first real jobs, while I was in college,

was to write profiles of local southern California radio and TV personalities for a now-long-defunct magazine called *Televiews.* I hung around Los Angeles studios talking to such personalities as Larry Cotton (*The Singing Chef*) and Peter Potter (*Peter Potter's Platter Parade*) —but my favorite assignment (and I was always thinking up excuses to cover the show) was *Hometown Jamboree,* starring "California's gift to country music," Cliffie Stone. Stone was a singer, bandleader, composer, bass violist, comedian, and disc jockey. Everybody, in the early fifties, knew Cliffie Stone. And as I remember him (he hasn't been in the public eye for some time now), he was a jolly, moon-faced character, friendly, with a pleasant if not spectacular voice. His other show, *Town Hall Party,* introduced country music to a lot of urban dwellers. It featured Spade Cooley and Lefty Frizzell, and introduced Dallas Frazier, Molly Bee, and Jeannie Black.

Cliffie Stone was born into country music: His father, who called himself Herman the Hermit, was a well-known country comic. Unlike most country stars, Cliffie didn't start playing the guitar at thirteen. His instrument was the trom-

bone, and when he mastered that, he went on to the bass viol. For a spell he played bass with dance bands, but in 1935 he became a leading country-western disc jockey, and "falling in love" with the music, he dedicated himself to the country field. From 1943 to 1947 he was master of ceremonies for twenty-eight western radio shows a week. In 1946 he joined Capitol Records as a consultant on "folk and hillbilly artists," working with Tennessee Ernie Ford, Hank Thompson, and others. Cliffie Stone also recorded for Capitol, singing his own compositions: "No Vacancy," "Divorce Me C.O.D.," and "So Round, So Firm, So Fully Packed." One of the Stone's great contributions to the field: He hated the use of the word "hillbilly" to describe the music he sang and played, and convinced Capitol to use "country music" instead.

## STRINGBEAN [David Akeman]
BORN: June 17, 1915, Annville, Kentucky
MARRIED: w. Estelle
DIED: November 10, 1973, Goodlettsville, Kentucky

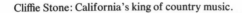

Cliffie Stone: California's king of country music.

Stringbean (left) with Grandpa Jones: Nashville tragedy.

A few weeks before I completed this encyclopedia, I was in Nashville watching the taping of a segment of the *Hee Haw* show. During a break, I spoke to Stringbean. "Well, now," he said, "I don't buy many encyclopedias, but this is one that I am a-gonna git. You can bet on it." A few days later he was dead.

Marshal Fallwell, Jr., the Nashville photographer, called to tell me about it. "I was taking pictures backstage at Grand Ole Opry and was talking to Stringbean just before he went home. He invited me to come over in a few days to take some more pictures, and then he and his wife drove off to Goodlettsville—that's where they lived—to go to bed early. Stringbean was going fishing with his fellow Grand Ole Opry performer, Grandpa Jones, the next morning. Only there never was another morning for Stringbean. They drove into their driveway, caught thieves robbing them, and the thieves shot Stringbean and his wife, both of them. Both dead. It's a real tragedy." Stringbean never wanted to harm a fly —just to entertain people, and that's what he did, and superbly, in the tradition of Uncle Dave Macon, who was his mentor. (When Macon died, he willed a banjo to Stringbean.)

Born and raised on a farm in Kentucky, David Akeman grew up to the music of his father's banjo. He bought his own banjo when he was fourteen, and four years later he began picking professionally in Lexington, Kentucky, at station WLAP, and touring with Bill Monroe, Ernest Tubb, Red Foley, and others. He became an Opry regular and performed on Red Foley's TV show as well. For a long time Stringbean's trademark was an odd costume featuring a shirt that extended to his knees and pants that began where the shirt ended. On *Hee Haw* he wore his curled-up porkpie hat and plain overalls—as well as his characteristic horn-rimmed glasses. "They make me look like a professor," he would explain, smiling and picking his banjo.

# STUCKEY, NAT

BORN: December 17, 1937, Cass County, Texas

MARRIED: w. Carolyn Ann

During the early days of country music, many of the performers considered themselves lucky if they had a high school education. As the music

changes, and more people listen to it in places like New York and San Francisco, the personnel change too—and college graduates aren't so rare. Nat Stuckey, an example of the new breed of country entertainers, hit the country charts in 1966 with "Sweet Thang" and has had popular hits ("Plastic Saddle," "Joe and Mabel's 12th Street Bar and Grill," etc.) ever since.

Writer Don Rhodes profiled Stuckey in a magazine article:

"Most entertainers find the time just before they are introduced on stage pretty nerve-racking. Some kill time by watching television in their motel rooms or on private buses. Others play cards. And still others tune their guitars, or just talk with anybody who happens to be handy: stage managers, doormen, reporters, sidemen, fans.

"It was during such a conversation a few years back that Nat Stuckey learned a valuable lesson—one he frequently likes to recall. Stuckey had been chatting with a stage manager, who remarked casually, 'Well, I finally discovered how a person becomes a success in this business.'

"Stuckey's ears perked up, and he forgot about what he was going to do when he hit that stage. 'Would you care to share that bit of valuable information with me?' he asked the seasoned veteran. With a knowledgeable air about him, as if he were about to deliver a college lecture, the stage manager said in a near-monotone, 'The secret is that you have to wait your turn.'

"Stuckey has waited nearly ten years for his turn. It is just now starting to come. All those road dates and recording sessions are finally proving fruitful, with Stuckey continuously clicking on the charts in the past year or so with such numbers as 'Is It Any Wonder,' 'Only a Woman Like You,' 'Forgive Me for Calling You Darling,' 'She Wakes Me with a Kiss Every Morning,' and 'Take Time to Love Her.' The long list of hits has helped ease the memory of knocking on studio doors in Nashville and being turned down by every major label, including RCA at that time. Other memories of trying to make it big in the business go back as far as his days of growing up in Texas.

"In 1952 Stuckey finished high school and continued his education at the University of Texas at Arlington. There he earned a degree in radio and television. His job after his college years was with radio station KALT back in Atlanta, Texas, where he worked for two years before going into the army. His army days found him working in radio and television both in New York and in Korea. After his military discharge, he worked at station KALT for two more years before moving to Shreveport, Louisiana, and joining radio station KWKH.

" 'Shreveport is the home of the *Louisiana Hayride* show, and draws people in the business like Nashville does,' Stuckey said. 'I got into radio because it was the closest I could be to what I wanted to get into. It was a lot of good preparation, because I learned not to be afraid of a microphone. Besides if you want to pick peaches, you go to a peach orchard.'

"For eight years Stuckey worked in Shreveport as a disc jockey. Gradually he began getting his foot in the country-music door as a songwriter, turning out songs which were picked up by major artists. Ricky Nelson recorded 'Be True to Me,' Ray Price had a hit with 'Don't You Believe Her,' Jim Ed Brown did well with Stuckey's 'Pop a Top,' and Buck Owens latched onto a smash with the Stuckey original 'Waitin' in Your Welfare Line.'

" 'Writing, to me, is not only a desire, it's a need,' Stuckey said. 'It's like a letter to the editor. A song is a letter to the world. It's something inside you that you feel like saying aloud.'

"Like many songwriters, Stuckey yearned for the recording end of the business; Nashville, however, apparently didn't yearn for Stuckey to record. The doors stayed shut in his face. 'I remember one person told me that I would make it as a writer, but not as a singer. I later saw him and he was out of work. He asked me what was I doing now. I told him I was making hit songs.'

"With the major studios rejecting him, Stuckey said he began looking for a 'back door' to Nashville. He found his back door with a small label called Paula Records. He cut one record on Paula that didn't quite make it, but for his second Paula release he enlisted five rock musicians called The Uniques. One member of the Uniques at that time was Joe Stampley—now making it big himself with hits like 'Soul Song' and 'Bring It On Home.'

"On that second release, Stuckey and the Uniques cut a novelty song Stuckey had com-

Nat Stuckey: Wakes up to a kiss every morning.

posed. The song was 'Sweet Thang,' and it turned out to be a chart-buster and a star-maker. Not so long afterwards, Stuckey hitched his star to RCA Records, with Jerry Bradley as his producer.

"Stuckey's early RCA releases were good-selling, up-tempo numbers like 'Plastic Saddle,' 'Cut Across Shorty,' 'Don't Pay the Ransom,' and 'I'm Gonna Act Right.' But his ballad release of 'She Wakes Me with a Kiss Every Morning' broke the mold. Most of his recent ballads have been delivered from the standpoint of a man deeply in love with a woman. Stuckey's woman is his wife, Ann, whom he met in Shreveport during his disc jockey days. 'We met at a New Year's Eve party on December 31, 1961, and were married two months and nine days later,' Ann recalls. While Stuckey is on the road, Ann generally is busy putting out one of the best fan-club mimeographed monthly news-letters and quarterly journals in the business, and circulating 'Stuck on Stuckey' badges.

I hit Stuckey with the question if he thought top entertainers deserved pay in the thousands of dollars for each concert. He shot back, "In the entertainment business, there is no retire-ment pay, no sick leave and no unemployment compensation. An entertainer, other than a few overnight hits, spends a lot of time and money getting to where he is. Entertainers are basically a hearty lot. They work many times when they are sick when the average person would stay at home and go to bed. But, most of all, the entertainment business is one business where you can't say, 'Well, I'm here and I'm going to be here.' All you can say is, 'I'm here for right now.'"

## THOMPSON, HANK
BORN: September 3, 1925, Waco, Texas
MARRIED: w. Dorothy Jean Ray

From 1953 to 1965, Hank Thompson's Brazos Valley Boys were voted by numerous country polls as America's Number One Western Band. Texas considers him (proudly) a native son—but he's lived in Oklahoma for a long time. And he went to college, too—Princeton University, surprisingly, on the GI Bill. (He also attended Southern Methodist University and the Univer-sity of Texas, as well.) He is in the top dozen of country artists with the most records on the country hit parades. He has had a number of top-ten hits: "Wild Side of Life," "Rub-a-Dub-Dub," "Wake Up Irene," "Oklahoma Hills," "Annie Over," "A Fooler and a Faker," and "Smoky the Bear." When Bob Dylan went to Nashville to cut a record, he told the local press that he had "never felt at home with the New York crowd" because one of the major influ-ences on him had been Hank Thompson.

I myself have only seen Thompson once in person, in 1954, in Palestine, Texas. I had been

sent on a minor military mission (the minor-est) from Fort Bliss, Texas, and having a night to kill, I attended a Hank Thompson dance at a local dance hall. Texas has always been kind to men in uniform, even Yankee soldiers like myself, and the woman at the box office wouldn't accept my money. "I didn't think northern boys liked this kind of music," she said, letting me in. Everybody was dancing. These days, when people go to *listen* to country music, they forget that during the 1940s and 1950s people *danced*, slowly, to country music

Hank Thompson: The Brazos Valley Boys get around.

—in the case of Thompson, western swing music. The whole town seemed to be there— toothless farmers in overalls and scuffed shoes, their overstuffed wives in print dresses and black oxfords, young cowboys, and a number of people all dressed up. Everybody danced, ex-cept me. It was never one of my strong points, but a nice woman in her forties came over with her husband. "Why aren't you dancing?" she asked.

"Well, I'm not very good at it," I said, shyly. "I'd just like to listen to the music."

She pulled me onto the dance floor. "Nonsense, soldier," she insisted, "anybody can dance to Hank Thompson." (She learned that anybody could, except me.)

Thompson grew up listening to the Grand Ole Opry, and his first instrument was a harmonica, which he played well enough to win contests. But when he saw a Gene Autry movie for the first time, he decided to get a guitar. His parents bought him a four-dollar secondhand model for Christmas. He practiced diligently while other kids played baseball, hoping to "perform before an audience." While in high school, he sang for a Waco station as "Hank the Hired Hand." When he finished high school, World War II was on, and he enlisted in the navy. Thompson and his guitar crossed the Pacific several times. "A lot of people heard Hank Thompson for the first time on ships," he recalls. "They didn't have much choice unless they wanted to jump overboard." After the service, he went to college for a few years, but returned to Waco to do a live noonday radio show. "Just me and my guitar," he says. Some of his original compositions reached the ears of the owners of Globe Records in Dallas and they asked him to record. Thompson took along his group, The Brazos Valley Boys (a steel guitar, electric standard, fiddle, and bass). He had written two songs, "Whoa, Sailor" and "Swing Wide Your Gate of Love." They were put on a record by Globe. Both sides were hits, and Thompson still sings both at all his performances. Country star Tex Ritter heard the songs, liked them, and introduced Thompson to producers at Capitol Records. He signed a contract, and stayed with Capitol for eighteen years (he now records for Dot). His first Capitol discs all were smash hits: "Humpty-Dumpty Heart" and "Today." When he left Capitol, he had sold more than 30 million records. Throughout the 1950s and 1960s Thompson appeared on major TV shows and toured with the Brazos Valley Boys from Texas to Europe, the Far East, and Latin America. He often travels in his own Cessna-112.

"Throughout the years I have seen country music become more homogenized," Thompson says, "and the lines dividing it and other types of music are not so well defined. But by broadening its base, country music now embraces an international audience and enjoys a recognition and dignity not prevalent during my early years in the business. I feel proud to have grown with an industry to which I could fully lend myself and which in return has given me so much." Currently Hank Thompson is starring in a syndicated TV show, featuring major guest stars and filmed at Circle R Ranch near Tulsa, which is owned by Thompson, *Hee Haw* star Roy Clark, and Thompson's manager, Jim Halsey.

## TILLIS, MEL

BORN: August 8, 1932, Pahokee, Florida
MARRIED: w. Doris
CHILDREN: s. Melvin, Jr.; d. Pam, Connie, Cindy

Mel Tillis has already written 450 songs that have been recorded by big stars like Webb Pierce, Ray Price, Carl Smith, and Burl Ives. Among them: "Detroit City," "Ruby, Don't Take Your Love to Town," "One More Time," "Heart Over Mind," and "Take Time."

Mel Tillis stutters badly except when he sings. Journalist Paul Hemphill reports on Tillis telling a friend about a song he'd written, "Who's Julie?" which tells about a man who talks in his sleep and is asked by his wife "over coffee this morning" who is the girl he was talking about. "My wife doesn't care for it much," said Tillis. "When it first came out, she asked me, 'Who is Julie?' and I told her, 'Oh, i-it-s just my r-racehorse up in Kentucky.' Well, I went on the r-road for a couple of w-weeks, and when I got back home my wife said, 'You had a c-call while you were gone,' and I said, 'Wh-who was it?' and she said, 'Y-y-your racehorse.' "

Tillis uses his stuttering as part of the "comic" portion of his well-choreographed shows. While on assignment to interview Hank Williams, Jr., I caught the Mel Tillis show in Hartford, Connecticut, and though I knew about Tillis and his songs, and his many appearances on TV shows, I hadn't realized how polished he was, and how smooth his band, The Statesiders, were. The audience, New Englanders, loved his southern humor, and they knew the words to all his songs.

Mel Tillis: He t-t-talks in his ss-ss-sleep.

Born in rural Florida, Tillis grew up listening to country songs, and before he was a teen-ager he'd written several songs of his own. He headed for Nashville as soon as he was of age, and started passing out his compositions. It took very little time for Tillis to be recognized as a songwriter, and Columbia signed him as a recording artist. He stayed with Columbia five years and then recorded for Kapp; he is currently with MGM.

## TRASK, DIANA
BORN: Warburton, Australia
MARRIED: h. Tom Ewen

Diana Trask wanted to be a singer when she was five years old. Her mother taught voice and piano, and Diana recalls standing in the back-

Diana Trask: Australia's gift to country music.

ground during lessons and thinking how much better *she* could sing the note her mother was teaching someone else to sing. When she was sixteen she won a major talent contest in her native Australia. A year later she was a national celebrity, singing jazz and pop songs, and opening shows for visiting American superstars like Frank Sinatra and Sammy Davis, Jr. The record-buying population in Australia couldn't support Diana's talent in the degree she envisioned for herself, however, and in 1966 she came to the United States with her American husband, Tom Ewen, seeking that old dream of fame and fortune.

After "starving in New York," according to a Dot Records publicist, Diana and Tom made their way to Nashville for the 1966 Country Music Association convention. "Country music spoke for the heart of America," Diana is quoted as saying. In any case, she soon met many Nashville music moguls and, in due time, signed to tour with Hank Williams, Jr. Thus began her long climb toward acceptance by the country-music audience.

In 1973 her career took a distinct upward turn with the release of two singles, "Say When" and "It's a Man's World," and frequent appearances on network television shows. She had recorded several albums on the Dot label prior to that time, but "It's a Man's World" boosted her reputation as a sure seller.

The Dot Records publicity department likes to refer to Diana as "Miss Country Soul." She is certainly the most "southern born" country singer in existence, but the title "Miss Country Soul" belongs to Jeannie Seely, who has a letter from the Patent Office to prove it.

## TRAVIS, MERLE

BORN: November 29, 1917, Rosewood, Kentucky

MARRIED: w. Bettie Morgan

CHILDREN: s. Dennis; d. Mildred, Pat, Cindy, Merlene

Old Merle Travis, now. There's more'n a few Nashville pickers who think he is just the best picker in the entire world, and if not the number-one picker, then he'd be in the top six of anybody's list. Chet Atkins claims he picked up

Merle Travis: Chet and Doc learned from Merle.

his guitar style from Travis, and Doc Watson named his son Merle so some of the talent might wear off, and one of Donna Fargo's pickers proudly announced that his son's name was Merle, too, named after the hero he'd never met. Alas, I've not had that pleasure, either, though I've seen him close up, backstage at Carnegie Hall some years ago, at the first Flatt and Scruggs concert there. Merle, now, he was calm as Hickory Lake in Nashville on a hot summer day, and he stood before that packed New York house chewing gum, smiling, and joking with the audience, making his guitar do tricks, say words, imitate birds and animals, and sing. "Didn't know a GIT-ar could sing, I'll betcha," he laughed. And the damn thing sang.

Born in the coal-mining regions of Kentucky, Merle Travis spent the majority of his professional career in California, and garnered his biggest successes through singing western and honky-tonk songs. But Travis' influence is definitely traditional. "His highly intricate and complex guitar style, among the most accomplished in country music," writes historian Bill C. Malone, "was nonetheless derived from folk sources in western Kentucky, particularly from the playing of such home-grown talent as Mose Rager, Ike Everly, and Arnold Schultz." (Travis techniques have been copied by thousands of latter-day guitar enthusiasts.)

"Folk Songs from the Hills" was one of the first 78-rpm albums I ever bought. It was filled with great songs written and sung by Travis: "Nine-Pound Hammer," "Dark as a Dungeon" (yes, Merle Travis wrote that—it *isn't* a folk song), "I Am a Pilgrim," and "Sixteen Tons" (another Travis composition, the one that made Tennessee Ernie Ford famous and Travis a bit of cash).

Merle left Kentucky with his Gretsch guitar during the darkest Depression days, traveled the United States singing on street corners, and finally got himself a job on station WLW in Cincinnati, where he remained until World War II. After his discharge from the marines he settled in California, working with artists like Tex Ritter and Cliffie Stone. For Capitol he recorded a number of hits: "No Vacancy," "So Round, So Firm, So Fully Packed," "Divorce Me C.O.D.," and "Old Mountain Dew." He appeared on all the West Coast country TV shows and was featured playing the guitar in the

Academy Award winning film *From Here to Eternity*. He has been living in Nashville lately, and at this writing, the great, the wonderful, the magnificent Merle Travis is not under contract to a record company. He did appear with the Nitty Gritty Dirt Band on its album "Will the Circle Be Unbroken?" and for that reason alone it is worth having (though there are many other reasons to own that album also).

## TUBB, ERNEST

BORN: February 9, 1914, Crisp, Texas
MARRIED: w. Elaine (divorced) (s. Justin Tubb); Olene Adams

What can you say about Ernest Tubb? He certainly is a king of country music. He has to be listed in anybody's top-ten list of great performers. Tubb was a conduit of Jimmie Rodgers-ism into the contemporary. He was among the first bandleaders to develop the "honky-tonk" style, a fusion of western-swing and country-vocal ways of singing and playing. And the electric guitar as a country instrument is almost (if not quite) a Tubb innovation. My own impressions of Tubb, the first time I saw him, in his celebrated record store in Nashville, were jotted down in a small notebook: "Tall, darker than I thought . . . more and bigger teeth than most people have . . . doesn't he ever take that huge white hat off? . . . looks like a modern Abe Lincoln."

Ernest Tubb was born on a farm near Crisp, Texas. As a boy he listened to the recordings of Jimmie Rodgers. Tubb legend has it that he once walked twelve miles to town to hear Rodgers on a radio show. "I was consumed by Rodgers music," Tubb says, "and I spent what was considerable money in those days, fifty dollars, to buy a guitar." Friends recall that Tubb would practice until his fingertips were bleeding. And he practiced yodeling, so he could sound like his hero. "I just wanted to sing like Jimmie and didn't really have any idea of making a living with my singing when I first started out. I just kept practicing and working at odd jobs." The odd jobs included selling mattresses, managing a drugstore, and digging ditches for the Works Progress Administration set up by President Franklin D. Roosevelt in 1935 to ease the massive unemployment created by the Depression. Tubb also played the guitar and sang (in imitation of Jimmie Rodgers) at oil-field honky-tonks at $1.25 a night. "I wanted to play on the radio, and I offered my services for free, generally only to be turned down," he recalls.

In the mid-1930s Tubb noticed a San Antonio phone book in the bus depot and, having some time to kill, opened to "Rodgers" and found a listing for "Mrs. Jimmie Rodgers." "It was just a fluke," he says now. "I figured she would have moved back to Mississippi after Jimmie's death." He called her and asked for a personal interview, and after three hours Mrs. Rodgers, impressed with Tubb's sincerity and listening to him sing, and convincing him that he didn't sound a bit like Jimmie Rodgers, offered to help him with his career. "Whatever success I've had, I owe to Mrs. Jimmie Rodgers," Tubb says repeatedly. She helped him get some recordings distributed, but nothing much happened. At Mrs. Rodgers' suggestion, he drove to Fort Worth, and got a job singing at KGKO at $20 a week. "I turned professional then, I was twenty-six years old," Tubb relates. And then Tubb was asked by Decca to record two songs he had written: "Blue-Eyed Elaine" and "I'll Get Along Somehow." Not too many records were sold, but their appearance did enable KGKO to find Tubb a sponsor, and he became known as "the gold-chain troubadour." But $75 a week wasn't enough to feed his growing family, and he considered giving up music and taking a job in a defense plant. At the time, he was fooling around with a new song about frustrated love. He called it "I'm Walking the Floor over You," Decca recorded it, and it sold more than 3 million records. Few songs are more closely identified with an artist than "I'm Walking the Floor over You" with Ernest Tubb. Other singers, including Bing Crosby, recorded it, and Hollywood became interested. Tubb was signed for two Durango Kid westerns (starring Charles Starrett): *Fighting Buckaroo* and *Ridin' West*. Hollywood, and the world, realized that Tubb would never be a John Barrymore or even a George Gabby Hayes, but Nashville heard about him at this time, and Grand Ole Opry beckoned. He drove to the Opry, so the story goes, in a 1932 Chevrolet, and wound up with four curtain calls, a steady job, and the beginning of endless royalty checks for "I'm Walking the Floor over You." He formed a band, 'The

Texas Troubadours, and he began his years of travel, two or three hundred nights on the road annually (and the road has taken him to fifty states, all of Canada, Europe, Japan, Korea, and South America). The first country performer to appear in Carnegie Hall, he opened his performance with the oft-quoted line "My, my, this place sure could hold a lot of hay." He recorded hit after hit: "Blue Christmas," "Missing in Action," "Show Her Lots of Gold," "Mr. Juke Box," "Thanks Alot," "It Don't Hurt Anymore," and dozens of others.

Tubb has sung a number of duets with Red Foley ("Tennessee Border No. 2" and "Good Night, Irene"), Loretta Lynn ("Mr. and Mrs. Used-to-Be"), the Wilburn Brothers ("Hey, Mr. Bluebird"), and, wonders of wonders, the Andrews Sisters ("Don't Rob Another Man's Castle").

Tubb, who says he is a Bing Crosby fan and likes Perry Como and some of Frank Sinatra, is still loyal to country music: "Country music over the years has been the most successful type and I neither intend to knock it or to give it up. There are those who cross over the bridge and mix their music, but I personally have no desire to do this. Country music is good. It is humble, simple, and honest and relaxed. It is a way of life. It is not confined to any segment of the country. We see young faces and we see old faces—and many in-between faces. Therefore, country music must have a general appeal to all ages, to all sections. I like it, the people like it and I'll stick to it."

Bernard Henry, the British music critic, can't understand Tubb's success. "He sings like an owl with emphysema," Henry wrote, "and occasionally misses notes and doesn't pronounce his words right." A standing joke in Nashville is that "the reason ol' Ernie Tubb is successful is because of tavern beer drinkers who like to listen to him because they figure they can sing better drunk or sober." But whatever Ernest Tubb does, it seems to work. "I don't care whether I hit the right note or not," he says. "I don't read music and I'd fight the man who tried to teach me. I'm not looking for perfection of delivery—thousands of singers have that. I'm looking for individuality. I phrase the way I want to; I sing the way I feel like singing at the moment."

Ernest Tubb was elected to the Country Music Hall of Fame in 1965.

Ernest Tubb: Owes it all to Mrs. Jimmie Rodgers.

## TUBB, JUSTIN

BORN: August 20, 1935, San Antonio, Texas
MARRIED: w. Carolyn McPherson
CHILDREN: d. Leah, Lisa

In the early 1950s Ernest Tubb's oldest son, Justin, left the University of Texas to become a disc jockey. On his program, he occasionally sang his own compositions, attracting the attention of record companies. "Oo-la-lah" and "The Story of My Life" were released by Decca, and he joined Goldie Hill to hit the top-ten lists with "Looking Back to See" and "Sure-Fire Kisses." He made the charts again in 1963 with "Take a Letter, Miss Gray" for Groove and a few more sides in the mid-sixties for RCA Victor. He has written numerous hits for other performers, but has the difficult job of being in his father's business, when his father was one of the founding fathers.

## TUCKER, TANYA

BORN: October 10, 1958, Seminole, Texas

Charlie Rich is there, because it is his party, and Freddie Weller and Barbara Mandrell and a host of other Nashville celebrities. But gathered near the refreshment table, by the huge bowl packed with pink-red shrimp, is the biggest crowd: reporters, record-company executives, and disc jockeys, all talking to a slender, ash-blonde girl in a short, simple blue dress, with an engaging smile. The trace of a slight adolescent complexion problem (after all, she only is fifteen years old) is easily hidden under a simple make-up base. She is more sophisticated than one would imagine, and she answers a New York promoter, who has asked her to appear as a number-three act on a bill with a well-known country music queen: "Well, I sell as many records as she does, so if I appear, I want co-billing." He is dumbfounded at her reply. In the background, her father, Bo Tucker, in a lively double-knit suit, pops a dumpling into his mouth, while her sister LaCosta, a bit more physically mature as well as older, laughs. Tanya Tucker, *wunderkind* of country music, looks at me (we had been introduced a few minutes earlier) and winks. "Outasight," I think. But then, that's really not strange. Half the stars in country music have begun their professional careers in their pre-

teens, but most of them don't hit it big as fast as Tanya Tucker. And there's a simple reason. Tanya Tucker *is* out of sight! Stupendous! And she certainly doesn't sing kiddie hits. Her biggest seller, and the one that popped her into the super-starlette category, was Alex Harvey's Faulknerian saga of "Delta Dawn," a song about a woman "they used to call Delta Dawn," who is "forty-one but her daddy still calls her baby." She walks around Brownsville, Texas, "with a suitcase in her hand," waiting for a long-lost lover. Tanya's rendition of this song bounded to the top of the country charts, beating out versions by Kitty Wells, Jody Miller, Waylon Jennings, and Bobby Bare. (Helen Reddy recorded it for pop fans, but her version pales into insignificance compared to Tanya's throaty, lusty, almost poetically cruel version.)

At the party, we learn that Tanya Tucker has finally quit school to sing full-time. "It was my decision," she said bluntly, "and a good one." I am an advocate of higher education for one and all, but I had to agree that her decision was wise. My prophecy quotient isn't too hot, but I'll make a prediction. Within five years, unless she loses her voice, or her heart to some male chauvinist piglet, Tanya Tucker will be the undisputed "queen of country music."

Presently, when she's not traveling and singing, Tanya Tucker lives with her family in a modest, double-width mobile home, complete with a green metal canopy for a garage and a small plot of Henderson, Nevada–style desert grass out front. J. R. Young reported on Tanya Tucker for a magazine article:

"Tanya is a most ordinary and most extraordinary young lady at the same time," Young writes. "One minute she is giggling and blushing behind her flashing blue eyes, and the next minute—by just the tilt of her head or the hint of a smile—she is calm and serious in the manner of a woman twice her age. The story of Tanya Tucker isn't so much the story of Tanya herself as it is the story of the entire Tucker family, again a most ordinary and extraordinary household that deserves the collective credit for the success of its youngest daughter. Music has always been a part of the Tucker clan; Tanya's older sister, LaCosta, started singing before Tanya did.

" 'We all thought LaCosta was great. And she is,' Bo Tucker, Tanya's father, drawled as he

Tanya Tucker: One of her first horses is named Delta Dawn.

leaned back in his easy chair in the paneled room of the trailer.

" 'I guess Tanya got tired of listening to LaCosta all the time,' Bo Tucker continued. 'She came up to me one day and said, "Daddy, you want to hear me sing a song?" I said, "Sweetheart, you couldn't sing your way out of a paper sack." ' Tanya giggled as her father smiled. 'Well, she backed up a couple of steps and sang a song. And I said, "Boy, that sounds pretty good. Sing another one." So she did, and I seen real soon that she was going to be a singer.'

"Tanya was eight at the time, but Bo claims to know a country voice when he hears one. And that's what he heard—a real good country voice, as anyone who has heard Tanya singing 'Delta Dawn,' 'Jamestown Ferry,' or 'What's Your Mama's Name?' will testify.

" 'She said to me, "Daddy, I want you to hear me sing 'Your Cheatin' Heart,' " and I said, "Now don't start that. There never has been a girl who could sing Hank Williams numbers." I've heard them try, but never any who could really do it. But Tanya proved me wrong again.' And by the time Bo asked his 'Your Cheatin' Heart' girl what she wanted to be, he figured he knew the answer. 'A country singer,' little Tanya answered, with all the gusto only an eight-year-old could muster. And with all the confidence that perhaps only a father could muster, Bo Tucker decided to help Tanya become just that.

"He became at once Tanya's singing coach, chauffeur, promoter, and whatever else he had to be to get his daughter's career going. He didn't know anything about the country-music business, but he was willing to learn.

"Jesse 'Bo' Tucker was born in Colgate, Oklahoma, 'a long time ago,' he says, and Juanita Tucker ('the Mrs.') was born in Abilene, Texas. They both grew up in Denver City, Texas, and, as Mrs. Tucker admits with a shy smile, 'I didn't like him much until he got out of the army.' Soon after she got to liking him, they got married and began moving around the Southwest. Tanya's official biography reads: '. . . Bo is a heavy-equipment operator in the construction industry. There have been good times, financially, and bad times for the Tuckers, and the elder Tucker's work forced them to move frequently.' But it was really much more complicated than that.

"Tanya, the youngest of the three Tucker children, was born in 1958 in the small, dusty west Texas town of Seminole. She did most of her growing up in Wilcox, Arizona, where her family moved shortly after she was born.

"Bo Tucker was always a great country-music fan. 'The closest I ever got to singing myself, though,' Bo recalls, 'was in the car, as me and my buddies would drive around. You know how that is. I did a pretty good imitation of Ernest Tubb, but that was about it. But I always had a good ear for music.'

"The only radio station in Wilcox at that time was a country-music station, and between her daddy's records and the one radio station, Tanya fell easily into that good ol' country sound. 'Me and my sister would sing around the house for as far back as I can remember, and it was always country music. The first song I remember is "Sad Movies" by the Lennon Sisters. Country music was all there was, and that's the only thing I've known.'

" 'I don't like rock-and-roll,' Tanya says rather bluntly and matter of factly, but catching herself sounding a little severe, she cocks her head a bit and tempers the answer. 'Oh, there are some things I like, but nothing like country. Rock may be good to dance to for the kids, but I still like the country dances.'

"When Tanya was ten, she began entering talent shows soon after the family moved to Phoenix in 1969. She never won any. But Bo Tucker still knew he heard 'something in her voice that sounded right,' and he set out to get people to hear it. On a trip to Nashville, Bo got producer Danny Davis to listen to some home-made tapes. Danny said, 'Well, I think she'll be a whiz,' but that's as far as it got. The next time Bo saw Danny Davis was when Tanya walked on stage at the Grand Ole Opry to sing 'Delta Dawn.'

"Bo took Tanya to Nashville another time to try and get someone with the right connections to listen to her, but the musical doors of Nashville seemed steadfastly closed. He finally took some of the homemade tapes to a prominent Nashville record store owner for any kind of an opinion. The owner listened a few minutes and then looked over at his secretary and said,

'If you just got $50,000 in the mail today, would you put one penny in this girl's singing career?'

" 'Nope,' the secretary announced coolly.

" 'Does that answer your question?'

" 'Yessir,' said Bo.

" 'I'd try and get people like that store owner to listen to her,' Bo recalled, 'but they'd say, "Who is she?" "Well," I'd say, "my daughter." And that ruined it.' Bo smiled with the confidence of three-plus years' distance from those trying days. ' "Yeh, I've got a daughter, too!" they'd say.'

"In the meantime, Tanya had sung a couple of songs on a local variety show in Phoenix, and as a result of that appearance she became a regular on the *Lew King Show*, a kids' talent show. In August 1970 the Tuckers again had to move, this time following the construction crew to St. George, Utah, a small town in the southwest corner of the state. The job was a good one, almost $9 an hour. St. George wasn't exactly the place for Tanya to break into show business, but it was at this time that she received her first real break.

"Country singer Judy Lynn was going to play the Arizona State Fair. Incredible as it may seem, the day before the fair opened Bo and Tanya jumped in the family car and drove almost 300 miles to Phoenix on the chance that they might be able to use Tanya on that show. There they met Tanya's brother, who just walked backstage to Miss Lynn's trailer and said his little sister was out front and wanted to be on the show.

" 'He must have been persuasive or something,' Tanya laughed, 'because they said they'd listen to me. I came backstage and sang something and then they talked it over. Finally they said yes. I heard later that Judy herself didn't think it was such a hot idea because then a lot of other kids would want to be on the show. And sure enough, the next day eight other kids came in and auditioned after I was on the show.' When the show ended, however, Bo and Tanya got right back in the car and drove back to St. George and, as Tanya puts it, 'goofed off for more than a year before really trying to get started again.'

"If that singular drive to Phoenix seems rather incredible, then the permanent move to Henderson, Nevada, south of Las Vegas, in the fall of 1971, was even more mind-boggling. 'My family didn't move to Henderson because we wanted to move here,' Tanya says with a characteristic frankness. 'We moved here because of me. My life's goal was still to be a country singer. Las Vegas was a good place to get started.'

" 'I've quit some awful good jobs to go help her,' Bo Tucker drawled. 'I automatically quit them to try and take her future on to where I knew it should be.'

"Bo had met some music agents from Las Vegas who talked a good game, and who said they could help Tanya get the break she needed if she moved to Las Vegas. That initial contact fell through, but since the mobile home was already purchased and installed up on the hill in nearby Henderson, they stayed on and began looking elsewhere in the neon city. Bo chanced upon the name of Dolores Fuller, onetime agent for pop star Johnny Rivers, a songwriter and a woman who just might have the contacts they needed.

" 'When we heard about her,' Bo said, 'we just looked her up in the phone book one day.' At that time, Tanya had six demo tapes that she had made one afternoon at United Recordings in Las Vegas with the help of musicians recruited off the street. They were rather ragged musically, and the songs rather standard ('For the Good Times,' 'Put Your Hand in the Hand,' etc.), but Dolores Fuller liked the tapes; she wanted the famed executive A & R producer for Columbia and Epic records in Nashville, Billy Sherrill, to hear them. In Nashville, Billy Sherrill listened to the tapes and liked what he heard. That in itself is compliment enough. Sherrill has one of the best track records in the business, and is the guiding hand behind Tammy Wynette's career.

"Sherrill flew to Las Vegas to talk personally with Bo and Tanya. After hearing Tanya sing in person, he signed her on the spot. A month later, Tanya found herself standing in Studio C at the Columbia studios in Nashville with the city's finest pickers playing behind her.

"Billy felt he had found exactly the right record for Tanya's first single, and presented it to her when she arrived in Nashville. The song, of course, was Alex Harvey's 'Delta Dawn.'

" 'He could tell I could sing it right away,' Tanya says delightedly. 'But when Billy heard my demo tapes, he heard my sound. Everybody says I sound older and look older than I really am, but I think being only fourteen was really an advantage. People hear my records and then see me. It's hard for them to believe.' ''

Since J. R. Young interviewed Tanya, she has toured with a number of major stars. She is growing up faster than her former schoolmates, and she lives in an adult world. When I asked her about boyfriends, she smiled. ''I'd like to get married when I'm twenty-five.'' Her songs have heavy sexual connotations: ''Jamestown Ferry'' is about being left in the lurch; ''What's Your Mamma's Name?'' deals with a down-and-outer named Beaufort Wilson who asks green-eyed little girls about their mother's name (he had a liaison with a local woman some years back and he knows he has a child with ''eyes of Wilson green''). And ''Blood Red and Goin' Down'' is narrated by a young girl who goes with her father on a search for her errant mother, only to see her father shoot her mother and her lover as father and daughter catch them in a motel. Heavy stuff for a fifteen-year-old. Tanya wouldn't discuss her songs, or even her whiskey-throated, country-jazz style of singing. She did say she had a new horse that was called Delta Dawn.

# TWITTY, CONWAY [Harold Jenkins]
BORN: September 1, 1933, Friars Point, Mississippi
MARRIED: w. Georgia
CHILDREN: s. Conway, Jr.; d. Cathy

Conway Twitty sold 16 million rock records before he returned to his country roots, and has probably sold millions more country records since the mid-sixties. From 1968 to 1971 his records consistently reached number one, two, or three on the charts (''Next in Line,'' ''Hello, Darlin','' ''How Much More Can She Stand?'' and others). His duets with Loretta Lynn have been tremendously popular. ''After the Fire Is Gone'' and ''Lead Me On'' both reached number one in 1971, and in 1973 ''Mississippi Woman, Louisiana Man'' not only reached number one on the charts, but the Country Music Association cited the Lynn-Twitty team as the Best Country Duet, and Conway Twitty's composition, the controversial ''You've Never

Been This Far Before,'' catapulted to premiere chart position, despite numerous disc jockeys refusing to air the song because of its suggestive lyrics. Twitty is among the top fifteen country artists with the most number-one records. He is one of the few major country stars who steadfastly refuses to live in Nashville. His home is in Oklahoma City.

In November 1973 Conway Twitty recalled his career in an exclusive, never-published taped interview with columnist Patrick Carr:

''Yes, I used to play baseball quite a bit. I had a contract with the Phillies when I got drafted and had to go in the army, and after I got in the army, I played for the post team and it's really what I'd planned on doing when I got out. But I had a band—I've had one since I was ten years old—my own group, but it was strictly as a hobby. I'd never thought about music as a profession. All I knew back then was country music, and that's what I grew up on. I had my heroes when I was growing up—people I really liked, like Hank Williams and Roy Acuff. The thought of competing with these people just never crossed my mind. You take people like that, that you really like, and you put them up here somewhere on a pedestal out of reach of everything else. I loved them so much that the thought of competing with those people just never crossed my mind at all. Even though I loved music, had my own band and played for all kinds of things, it was strictly a hobby, something I liked to do. Baseball I was serious about. Like I said, I got drafted, went into the army, played baseball and music in the army, and while I was in the army I met a fellow who asked me if I ever thought about music as a profession and I said No. I remembered that, but it went in one ear and out the other. When I got out of the army—I was stationed in Japan for a year—I came back to the States, and the first thing I heard when I got off the ship was an Elvis Presley song, and that type of music was just getting started. It was a song called 'Mystery Train.' I'm from the Memphis area—born in Mississippi and raised in Arkansas just outside of Memphis. Then I heard Carl Perkins' record 'Blue Suede Shoes' and that really knocked me out. I thought this was a young type of music and I thought I could do this, not taking anything away from the early rock stuff.

''So I got a little group together—the same one I got now—and we started playing in

Conway Twitty: Harold Jenkins made it big.

Conway Twitty and Loretta Lynn at a recording session.

nightclubs and on street corners and under shade trees—anywhere they'd let us play down in Arkansas and Tennessee and the Mississippi area. We finally got to where we'd play in the same clubs as Johnny Cash was playing, and Elvis, and Jerry Lee [Lewis], and all those people, without a record. But I did go to Memphis and talk to Sam Phillips, the fellow that owns Sun Records, which is the label that Elvis was on. I went into the studio and recorded day after day for about twelve hours a day. I'd write songs and record and write and record again, trying to get something that he thought was sellable, but I never could come up with anything that they liked. About three months after I got out of the army, I remember a fellow called me from New York and he said he'd talked to a man who knew me in the army. It was the same guy that had asked me if I'd ever thought about music as a profession. He asked me if I was playing this new kind of music they got down in Memphis and I said I was. He suggested I make a demonstration tape and send it to him. So I did. I went to Sun and told them what I was doing, and they said Okay. So I cut a demo tape and sent it up there and then I forgot all about it. I figured that was the end of that. I kept on trying to get started down there where I was. About a month later this fellow called me back and said he thought he could get me a contract, but he said he didn't want to do it with Sun. He said he'd get me with somebody else, but I wanted to get with Sun. But then I figured, What the heck, any label would be all right. So he did —he got me with Mercury, but he said he thought I should change my name. I thought, Why would a guy want to do that? He explained to me that the disc jockeys get from 50 to 100 new records a week and they've got their play list and they may put five new records on it a week. So you can see that it's a tremendous problem. They get all these records in, and out of seventy or so, four or five of them are going to be established artists, and you can see the problem they have—and you've got a problem too, getting air play. So he said maybe if we come up with a name that's real different, then when they're flippin' through those things, they might come across this name and say, 'Maybe I ought to play this.'

"So we started thinking about all kinds of names, and to make a long story short, what I finally wound up doing was, I got the map out and there's a place called Twitty, Texas. Then I thought if I could get something different to go with this, it might be something. I finally got the map of Arkansas and started looking through that, and there're towns in Arkansas like Baldknob, Walnut Creek, Smackover, and all kinds of crazy names like that. But right outside of Little Rock there's a town called Conway, and that's how it came about—Conway, Arkansas, and Twitty, Texas. So we all agreed that that was an unusual name, and my first record was with Mercury under the name of Conway Twitty. I didn't agree with the idea first because my main interest was I was worried about the people in my hometown that wouldn't know who Conway Twitty is, and I wanted all them to know I had a new record out. So that was what I was worried about. But I finally realized what the fellow was talking about and I decided he was right, so we went with Conway Twitty. I had maybe three releases on Mercury, but nothing seemed to come of it. I was still looking for a style and nothing happened.

"So I went to Canada. None of the southern-style rock singers had ever been up there. There was a club called The Flamingo Lounge in Hamilton, Ontario. To make a long story short, me and my band stayed at that one club eighteen straight weeks, and were sold out every night, Monday through Saturday. That's where I wrote 'It's Only Make-Believe,' and a lot of songs I had out, I wrote during that eighteen-week period right there in that club. I developed myself a style there—I developed the growl thing I do. I had done it on stage before but I'd never recorded it. So I called my manager in New York and told him I had a lot of songs and a few hit songs. He said Okay and he called MGM, and he talked to the president of MGM and a fellow who went on to become my A & R man for years, a man named Jim Vinneau. They set up a recording session in Nashville and the way MGM was gonna produce the thing. If we came up with anything, then we'd sign a contract and I'd be on the label. If we didn't, then they blew a session. So we went to Nashville and I recorded 'It's Only Make-Believe' and a couple of other songs. During the session, for one of the cuts we did on 'It's Only Make-Believe' I did that growl thing I always do on the stage. So Jim came down from the control room and he said, 'What was that thing you did?' And I said, 'I don't know,' and he said, 'Well, just do it again, because I like it.' So we cut the thing again, and I really put it in like I wanted to, and it came out good. So that was the beginning of what separated me from the rest of the singers I guess. Everybody says Elvis and I sound alike—of course we were born about forty miles apart—we even talked alike back then. I didn't purposely sound like him, it's just the way it was. In fact, I was trying not to, not because I didn't think the world of him, but I knew I'd have my own style and that little growl thing was what made the difference. I stayed in Canada until the song came out, and it took about three months before anything really happened with the song. In fact, I called New York and told my manager that if this song wasn't good enough then I don't have it.

"So I quit and went back to Arkansas out to my father-in-law's farm, and I was driving a tractor one day on his farm and somebody came out and told me I had a long-distance call from Columbus, Ohio, some disc jockey. So when I got in I returned the call, and this disc jockey on some big rock station in Columbus proceeded to tell me how 'It's Only Make-Believe' was a monster record in that town and we just had to come up there and do something because it was the biggest record they ever had in that town, and they've had some big ones. So I thought, You gotta be kiddin', and he said, 'No, I'm not kidding.' So we talked to my manager in New York and I got my group back together and we cut out to Columbus, Ohio, and it was an experience that I'll never forget. I've had a lot of experiences since then, but that was the first one, and I'll never forget it. First of all, he took us in this big radio station and we did an all-afternoon thing with them. I only had one record out, but I was up there all afternoon being interviewed and playing that record. Then we talked some more and played the record—he must have played it twenty times that afternoon. Then he had a show set up for that night—there was a disc jockey called Dr. Bock—and he did a show off the top of a drive-in restaurant. We were supposed to be there at a certain time, and we got in the car and headed in that direction. We got about a mile from the restaurant and we started running into all these people. People in

the street, on the sidewalk, cars parked that far away and it took us a solid hour to get that last mile, there were so many people. We just had to ease along through there. People would bang along the side of the car and they'd rock it and holler.

"It was a fantastic experience. But that's how I started in the rock-music business, but eventually I wanted to get back into country music. I recorded 'It's Only Make-Believe' in 1958, which was a number-one country record. It was also number one in the blues and rock fields. That's what made it such a big record—it was a hit in all fields—and it was number one in twenty-two different countries. I went to the people at MGM and said I'd like to do some country stuff too, not much but just a little bit. They said Okay, but then they wouldn't let me do it. The way I felt about it, I had to get out there and really experience life before I could really get into country music, if I ever did. But the thought was beginning to cross my mind after about a year in the business. So after I'd been with MGM for about eight years, I felt like I had lived long enough and had experienced enough of the things that a country song is all about to compete with the different country singers that I thought were great. Not taking anything away from the rock thing, but I feel like I started off with rock and worked my way up to country music, and I really feel that way. I don't mean that to put rock-and-roll music down. But I love country music so much and I think it's so much a part of everybody's everyday life that it's like Coke—it's the real thing. Feeling that way about it, I knew I had to really experience all these things before I could get out there and sing a country song. But I felt like I had reached that point, and my contract was up, so I quit.

"I was thirty-two years old and still playing the rock shows, and I was beginning to feel out of place. I wanted to get in the country thing so bad. So I got ahold of a friend of mine here in Nashville, Harlan Howard, the songwriter, and I told him I was ready to get into country music. He had been trying to get me to for a couple of years, but it's hard—you have a lot of people through the years who come to depend on a Conway Twitty or somebody like Conway Twitty. You have a manager, a booking agency, a family, a band, and disc jockeys all around the country who're used to Conway Twitty as he is, and it's like being on a merry-go-round and you can't get off. I'd really been trying for two years to quit and I couldn't. So I told my manager that at the end of the summer, that's it. I quit, and don't obligate me anywhere, because I'm gonna go into country music. He said Okay. I was playing at a place in Somers Point, New Jersey —Tony Marts's club out there on the ocean— and all the college kids came there, and we played it for a year. Tony was a good friend of mine. I was up on stage and I don't know what we were playing—I forget what it was—and in the middle of the song I thought, I can't take it anymore. That day, though, I had gotten about a hundred contracts booking me up until the next year—that day—and I began to realize that there's no way these people are ever gonna let me quit, there's no way I can get out of it where everybody will be happy, so I'm just gonna have to do what I think is right for Conway Twitty. So when the set was over I walked off the stage and went back and told Tony Marts that I was leaving. I explained it to him briefly, and he said, 'Don't worry about it, Conway, I understand, you do what you think you gotta do.' So I did. So I went up to the apartment and threw my things in the car and told the boys I'd see them back in Arkansas, and I cut out and went home.

"I got ahold of Harlan Howard and told him what I'd done, and he said, 'Come on over here to Nashville.' Harlan took a tape I had written of country songs over to Owen Bradley, who is my producer now, and he played the tape for Owen, and it was like he was pitching songs to Owen. Owen said, 'Well, the songs are pretty good, but who is that singing?' Harlan said, 'Never mind who that is singing, how do you like the song?' And Owen repeated, 'The songs are pretty good, but who's singing?' He says, 'You mean you don't know?' And Owen says, 'No, I don't know.' He said, 'Well, he's a good friend of yours; he records in your studio here,' and he said, 'Well, I don't know, who is it?' And he told him it was Conway Twitty, and he said, 'I can't believe that's Conway—he sings country music like that?' And Harlan says, 'Yes, he's not with MGM anymore and he wants to cut country music.' So Owen said, 'Okay, bring him over here and we'll cut a country song,' and I

went over and did my first country session, which was one of the happiest days of my life."

Conway Twitty's children appear to be following in his footsteps. His fourteen-year-old daughter Cathy is, according to Twitty, "knockin' 'em out on the stage," and Conway Twitty, Jr., still unsure of himself as a performer, is nonetheless building up a following of his own.

## TYLER, T. TEXAS [David Luke Myrick]

BORN: June 20, 1916, Mena, Arkansas
DIED: 1971
MARRIED: w. Claudia Louise Foster (deceased)
CHILDREN: s. David Luke, Jr., Rodger

T. Texas Tyler, may he rest in peace, was billed as "that man with a growl in his voice and a million friends." One of the first country talk-songs I ever heard was Tyler's best-selling "Deck of Cards." During World War II Tyler spent several years in the service, and the talk-song came out of his experience. It tells the story of a soldier who is admonished by his commanding officer for playing cards during a church service, and the soldier explains why the deck of cards is his almanac, diary, and Bible. Tyler ends the song with, "And Ah know that story's true, cause Ah *was* that soldier boy."

Born in Arkansas and raised in Texas, Tyler formed a band after the war and signed in Los Angeles with Four Star Records. "Deck of Cards" and "Daddy Gave My Dog Away" were big hits in the late forties. Tyler had his own radio program from Hollywood, *Range Round-up*, and he appeared in several western films, the most prominent of which was *Horsemen of the Sierras*. He recorded a number of hits for Decca, Capitol, King, and Starday: "Remember Me," "Oklahoma Hills," "Bumming Around," "Courtin' in the Rain," and several others. One of the first country stars to appear in Carnegie Hall, Tyler was typically accompanied by brash, country honky-tonk instrumentation, and every song featured his distinctive growl. In the late sixties, before he died, Tyler experienced a strong religious conversion, and only recorded hymns and spirituals.

Leroy Van Dyke: Wanted to be an auctioneer.

recording on Mercury, Kapp, and Decca, to resist any thoughts of entering the field of agriculture (he has a degree in agriculture from the University of Missouri). For a spell, before he entered the music business full-time, Van Dyke worked as a farm reporter for a Missouri paper, and thought about becoming an auctioneer. The Korean war broke out, and Van Dyke found himself in Korea, working for army intelligence and occasionally entertaining the troops. When he returned home, he entered a song he'd written, "Auctioneer," in a contest, resulting in a bid from Arthur Godfrey's *Talent Scouts* and subsequently a place on Red Foley's TV show. He is part of Grand Ole Opry, and in 1967 won the Connie B. Gay Award for his "outstanding contribution to the furthering of country music."

# V

## VAN DYKE, LEROY

BORN: October 4, 1929, Spring Fork, Missouri
MARRIED: w. Carol Sue Greathouse
CHILDREN: s. Lee, Adam; d. Carla

Leroy Van Dyke's "Walk on By" is one of those great country songs dealing with the lure of illicit love. The narrator asks the woman to walk on by; he loves her, but they are "strangers when we meet." The song, one of the top dozen records appearing on the country charts for thirty weeks or more in 1961, boosted Van Dyke to stardom, and he followed with another top-ten hit, "If a Woman Answers." In the following ten years, Van Dyke, who sings in a country-pop fashion, has continually made the charts, but never reaching as high as his first efforts. However, he has done well enough,

# W

## WAGONER, PORTER

BORN: August 12, 1927, West Plains, Missouri
MARRIED: w. Denise Mayree
CHILDREN: s. Richard; d. Denise, Debra

It's only a terrifying dream, but I have it night after night. There's Porter Wagoner in a posh barbershop, attended by sissified tonsorial artists, intent on transforming his corn-yellow pompadour into the hairstyle affected by the Hagers (which is nice for them). When he rises from the barber chair, he is wearing an Ivy League suit with a tattersall vest. "I've thrown away all my sequined and embroidered clothes," he tells me, unapologetically. "They don't like them over at the music conservatory." Fortunately, it's only a nightmare. Of all the consistently successful country stars, few have been so loyal to his rural roots as Porter Wagoner. "One day I was out there plowin'—I was daydreaming out loud," Wagoner recalls, "like I often did. I didn't know there was anyone else around, but there was—a neighbor boy, and he heard me talkin' to myself. He asked me what I was doin' and I told him I was

Porter Wagoner chats with Dolly Parton on the set of his TV show.

pretending I was at the Grand Ole Opry and introducing my special guest, Roy Acuff. And he laughed and said, 'You'll still be plowing these mules when you're eighty.' Of course, it's a big joke between us now."

Wagoner is a big star. He is one of the most heavily booked stars in the country firmament. He's recorded for RCA for more than twenty years. Since the first day he performed "Jimmy Brown the Newsboy" for his RCA audition, Porter Wagoner has never thought about being a pop star. His repertory is wide, diverse, and interesting, but it all stays within the realm of country music. He sings mountain songs, gospel, honky-tonk. The songs he likes best deal with "the cold hard facts of life." Country-music historian Bill C. Malone writes: "With the possible exception of Merle Haggard, Wagoner has done most to chronicle in song the tragic foibles and failures of humanity: the condemned prisoner of 'The Green Grass of Home,' the distraught husband who murdered his unfaithful wife and her lover in 'The Cold Hard Facts of Life,' and the pitiful creature who went insane as he watched his beautiful sweetheart 'Julie' turn progressively 'wayward and wild.' " Porter Wagoner has one of the most successful country TV shows, sponsored by the Chattanooga Medicine Company, creators of rural southern medicines, "Black Draught" and "The Wine of Cardui." (Originally, Norma Jean was the female star of the show, but when she decided to put marriage before a career, Dolly Parton took her place, and won her place as a real contender for "queen of country music.") Wagoner's band, The Wagonmasters, features some of the best Nashville musicians: Mack MaGaha, the former Don Reno and Red Smiley fiddler, and Buck Trent, the man who electrified the banjo. Wagoner is in the top twenty of stars with the most charted records, and he has had scores of big-selling hits, including "Satisfied Mind," "Skid Row Joe," "Big Wind," "Carroll County Accident," and "Misery Loves Company." His marvelous duets with Dolly Parton include the best-selling "The Last Thing on My Mind," "We'll Get Ahead Someday," "Just Someone I Used to Know," and "If Teardrops Were Pennies."

Growing up was hard for Porter Wagoner. When he was six, his father was crippled by arthritis. And Charlie Wagoner's illness forced Porter to drop out before he was half finished with grade school: "My brother and me were the only two left at home. Had to do the biggest part of the hard work of the farm, because Dad couldn't. I had to help plant the crops and help with the harvesting. Later my brother got sick with an incurable heart ailment, so that left nearly all the work for me. We lived a long way from town and it would have been impossible for me to go to high school. So most of the education I've gotten is just the knowledge the good Lord gave me—common sense, I guess you'd call it—and what I've learned from other people. When I was ten I asked my mother to order a guitar for me, an $8 guitar. I paid her back with money I got from selling rabbits I trapped. They'd sell anywhere from eight cents to twelve cents apiece. I paid for the guitar that way and my brother and I would play it. And boy, it sure sounded beautiful. I still have the guitar, incidentally."

Wagoner listened to Grand Ole Opry on a battery radio, the only one in the area. "Whenever we listened to the radio, there'd be sixteen or eighteen folks, all neighbors, at our house, because we was the only ones who had a radio. Everybody would sit around real quiet and listen to the music. We had to keep quiet cause the reception would fade in and out. I sang all the time by myself, but I still had a problem when I got in front of people. When I was by myself I'd take my guitar and go out in the woods and I'd *sing.* But if there was people around, I'd choke up. I took a job in a butcher market, and the owner, Sid Vaughan, liked my singing real well. He liked the old songs like 'Jimmy Brown' and 'The Birmingham Jail' and he'd ask me to sing these to him. I learned them from Momma mostly, she knew most of the old songs and she taught the biggest part of them to me. Well, one day I was singing some of them and Sid said, 'You know, we ought to put these songs on radio and advertise the things we got for sale at the store.' He went out to the radio station in West Plains and talked to them about buying a fifteen-minute time slot in the early morning. We broadcast from the store. They brought up a microphone and set it up, and I asked him who'd do the commercials. He said, 'You'll do them. You tell them what our specials are and sing a few songs. We managed to get through the first days okay, but the people must have felt sorry for me because it was just unbelievable the amount of mail I got. So then, once I got mail, I had something to talk about. It became easier. I didn't make much money with these shows. Just expenses, but each show gave me more confidence. One morning I went down to the store to open up to do the radio show and there was this big black Lincoln setting in front of the store. This guy sitting in the car came by and introduced himself. 'I'm Lou Black, program director of KWTO in Springfield, and I've come down to hear you sing.' "

Thus began the career of Porter Wagoner at $70 a week. Shortly after he came to the station, Red Foley formed his *Ozark Jubilee* TV show in Springfield, taking Wagoner on as a regular. By 1955, through the help of Si Siman, co-owner of KWTO, who knew Steve Sholes of RCA Victor, Wagoner signed his contract with RCA. The rest is country-music history. And my dream is just a dream. Porter Wagoner will never throw away his Nudie suits and multicolored boots. Wagoner is a man who sticks to his guns. In the mid-fifties, when country music was in trouble, Steve Sholes advised Wagoner to do some rock stuff if he wanted to make any money. "I told him I couldn't," Porter Wagoner states firmly. "It just didn't suit my personality. I couldn't sing the songs."

Jimmy Wakely: Sang duets with Margaret Whiting.

## WAKELY, JIMMY

BORN: February 16, 1914, Mencola, Arkansas
MARRIED: w. Inez Miser
CHILDREN: s. Johnny; d. Deanna, Carol, Linda

Jimmy Wakely hasn't been on the country charts for many years, but there was a period when everybody was singing his "I Wish I Had a Nickel," "Beautiful Brown Eyes," and "My Heart Cries for You." With pop star Margaret Whiting, he made all the hit parades with "Slippin' Around" and "I'll Never Slip Around Again." He appeared in seventy-two (mostly forgettable) films such as *Twilight on the Trail, Silver Bullet,* and *Song of the Range.* Often he played a character called The Melody Kid, and he had a number of comic sidekicks like George Gabby Hayes and Andy Clyde.

Wakely grew up in a log cabin in Arkansas, tried out for and won an amateur contest in Oklahoma, and in 1937, with Johnny Bond and Scott Harrel, formed the Wakely Trio, which was hired by Gene Autry for his CBS *Melody Ranch* show. Wakely left Autry to form his own band, the graduates of which form a *Who's Who* of southern California country: Merle Haggard, Wesley Tuttle, Spade Cooley, and Cliffie Stone. Though he never reached the popularity of Gene Autry or Roy Rogers, Wakely had his moments. And the duets with Maggie Whiting were warm and pleasant 1940s music. If you ever see a single of their "Beyond the Sunset" in a golden-oldie shop, snap it up at any cost!

291

## WALKER, BILLY

BORN: January 14, 1929, Ralls, Texas
MARRIED: w. Sylvia Dean Smith ("Boots")
CHILDREN: d. Judy, Deana, Lina, Julie

Billy Walker's had a lot more hits than one would imagine, with a couple of really big ones like "Charlie's Shoes" and "Cross the Brazos at Waco," as well as "A Million and One," "She Goes Walking Through My Mind," and "I'm Gonna Keep On Loving You." Born in Texas and raised in Texas and New Mexico, Walker began as a rancher, but having played and sung since childhood, he decided to form his own band to tour the Southwest. He joined the cast of the *Big D Jamboree* radio show in Dallas, where he was billed as "the traveling Texan, the masked singer of country songs." He also appeared on a Waco, Texas, radio show and on *Louisiana Hayride,* which led to a Columbia contract. Billy Walker has recorded for Monument, and since 1970 for MGM. With that terrific lineup of hits over the years, there must be a valid reason why he isn't considered a country superstar. But even if there's something some of us don't know, Billy Walker can belt out a damn good song, hoss.

## WALKER, CHARLIE

BORN: November 11, 1926, Collin County, Texas
MARRIED: w. Shirley
CHILDREN: s. Art, Ronnie; d. Carrie Lucinda

Charlie Walker, like Billy Walker, has a lot more chart action than his publicity lets us know. Charlie Walker is one of the South's leading disc jockeys and sports announcers, and considered one of the best play-by-play men in the business. For several years he was the MC at Las Vegas' Golden Nugget. He is a championship golfer, to boot—winning, among others, the Sahara Invitational Tournament in Las Vegas. Born in Texas, he originally was a member of Bill Boyd's Cowboy Ramblers. His first chart hit, for Columbia, was "Pick Me Up on Your Way Down," and during the sixties he scored with "Who'll Buy the Wine?" and "Don't Squeeze My Sharman." Charlie Walker occasionally sings "drinking" songs, like "The Lord Knows I'm Drinkin'," and he does them as smoothly as anyone in the business.

Charlie Walker: Sings, talks good, and plays mean golf.

# WATSON, DOC

BORN: March 2, 1923, Deep Gap, North Carolina

MARRIED: w. Rosalie

CHILDREN: s. Merle

Doc Watson's never had a hit on the country charts, and he's most often associated with bluegrass or the urban folk revival. I first heard of him in the early sixties at Israel Young's Folklore Center in Greenwich Village, a place where folk singers "hung out." Joan Baez walked in one evening and looked over some of the guitars hanging behind the counter, pointed at one, and took out her checkbook. "But I better try the guitar first," she said, and began singing a country song. "I love country music," she explained, "and this guitar is a Christmas present for Doc Watson." When I asked her who Doc Watson was, she looked at me quizzically and said, "Buy one of his records from Izzy." I did, and the next week I went to see him in person at Gerde's Folk City, which is also in "the Village."

Doc Watson is blind. But it hasn't been a complete handicap. While he was at a school for the blind in Raleigh, North Carolina, his father bought him a guitar, and from records of the Carter Family and Gid Tanner and His Skillet Lickers, he learned country favorites. When Doc was seventeen, he played at the fiddler's convention in Boone, North Carolina, and from then on didn't miss a local music festival. Most of the music he originally played was country-western commercial, but when a recording group came down to tape some picking at Clarence Ashley's, Doc was there, and when the Ashley group went to New York, Doc joined them. The response to the concert was tremendous, Watson was invited back, and soon he was appearing as the second act with Bill Monroe. For a while he recorded old-timey songs for Folkways and then was signed by Vanguard. His most recent appearance is with his son Merle on the Nitty Gritty Dirt Band album "Will the Circle Be Unbroken?" I've always felt Watson would not sacrifice his quality at all if he sang commercial country. He has a clear, pure voice and is a master guitarist (as his son Merle is, too). But even though his renditions of simple, old-timey country tunes like "The Train That Carried My Girl to Town" are pleasant to hear and authentic mountain songs, it would be nice to hear some unusual contemporary phrasing from Watson.

Doc Watson: A superb guitar player.

Freddy Weller: Sings sexy songs about "perfect strangers."

## WELLER, FREDDY

BORN: September 9, 1947, Atlanta, Georgia

Freddy Weller writes some pretty nifty songs, many of them dealing with that fine old titillating country song subject sex with a stranger. One big hit, "A Companion for the Evening," is about a man who meets a virgin in Atlanta, seduces her, and then has some remorse when she talks about the white dress her mother had made for her wedding. When he hears she is married, a tear forms in his eye and he recalls that night in Georgia: "I ain't saying how I know it, but some old boy's sure got himself a prize." The other big Freddy Weller hit, sung in a clear country voice that sometimes could use a bit more animation, is "The Perfect Stranger." In this song, Weller convinces a girl to come to his motel room and share his bottle of vodka and his body. There's a moral ending to this one, since the perfect stranger becomes his perfect wife. "No wonder Freddy Weller's songs are more up-front about sexual mores," critic Bernard Henry writes. "He really isn't a country singer and his background is steeped in rock music, where sex was never perfect nor a stranger." It's true. Freddy Weller was a member of Paul Revere and the Raiders. He also collaborated with pop writer/singer Tommy Roe on a number of songs, and played guitar for Joe South, who is only peripherally country. Yet Weller claims devotion to country, and he sounds like a country singer. Moreover, every one of his records on Columbia ("Games People Play," "These Are Not My People," "Indian Lake," and "Another Night of Love") made the top-ten country lists and the fans consider him country. Also, a man who can write a single song that contains religion, infidelity, a hint of murder, and lesbianism, can't be all bad.

294

## WELLS, KITTY [Muriel Deason]

BORN: August 30, 1919, Nashville, Tennessee
MARRIED: h. Johnny Wright
CHILDREN: s. Bobby; d. Ruby, Carol Sue

There is an old Carter Family tune called "I'm A-Goin' to Marry Kitty Wells." And Johnny Wright, who knew this tune, met a country singer named Muriel Deason in Mt. Juliet, Tennessee. Johnny Wright was a singing partner of Jack Anglin (they billed themselves as "Johnny and Jack"), and Johnny courted and married Muriel. At the time, Muriel was appearing on station WSIX in Nashville. Johnny convinced her to leave her show and join his act as a gospel singer, with a new name—and remembering the old tune, Johnny chose "Kitty Wells," never thinking at the time that she would be the first "queen of country music" (and in the hearts of many of her older fans, the *only* queen). For several years, while she was raising her family, Kitty sang with the act, and occasionally on radio programs, in Memphis, Nashville, and Knoxville. In 1947 Grand Ole Opry invited her to make guest appearances, and shortly afterward she joined *Louisiana Hayride.* Within two years she emerged not only as the highest-rated female country singer but as a strong rival to male singers. She remains the only woman in the top-ten country artists of all time with the most hits on the charts. She is high among the top ten artists with the most recorded sides, but Loretta Lynn has more number-one hits. That fact doesn't faze Kitty too much. "Kitty Wells," a professional Nashville gossip claims, "is the richest of the country queens because she works more." When she signed with Decca, in 1952, her first release was "It Wasn't God Who Made Honky-Tonk Angels" (she was thirty-three years old, with a family). And the record exploded, staying on the top for sixteen profitable weeks. "It Wasn't God Who Made Honky-Tonk Angels" (though Gloria Steinem doesn't know it) was probably the first woman's lib country song. It was an angry answer to Hank Thompson's "Wild Side of Life," which claimed that wicked, unfaithful women were a creation of God. Kitty disagreed, and claimed, in the song, that "it was men to blame." Obviously, the country fans sided with Kitty, because they immediately declared their fealty. "She has

Kitty Wells was the first female artist to have a number-one hit on the country charts: "It Wasn't God Who Made Honky-Tonk Angels" gave her a million-seller in 1952.

neither true pitch nor a good sense of rhythm," a Nashville musicologist once wrote, "but her nasal, straight-from-the-Appalachians twang is the most distinctive female sound in the business and has kept her such a big favorite in rural areas for so long that nobody can argue with her success." And this tribute was written when she was well over fifty and the mother of three children (one of them, Bobby, played a leading role in the *McHale's Navy* TV show). "I have always taken time to be a good mother," Kitty claims. All of her children have married, and she has seven grandchildren.

Originally, Kitty Wells was part of the *Johnny and Jack Show*, but when Jack Anglin was killed in an auto accident (country music has a high death rate among its always-on-the-go performers), the name of the show was changed to the *Johnny Wright–Kitty Wells Family Show*, and Johnny Wright seems to have happily fallen into the role of prince consort (though his own records have always done well). No queen spends more time among her subjects. She makes almost 300 personal appearances a year, mostly one-nighters in places like Hatch, New Mexico, and Runge, New Hampshire, and Pogosa Springs, Colorado. "My record sales have been pretty good," she admits. Her producers say they have been so "outstanding that no one knows the exact total, which runs into the many millions." When she is called a "queen," Kitty tells this story: Once, while she was on tour, her bus stopped in a little Minnesota town, and she went into a grocery store. As she was paying for her purchases, she looked up and saw the bus pull away without her. "I had to wait an hour before they realized I wasn't on the bus and they came back to get me. That's not the way queens are treated."

Kitty Wells recorded for MCA, and her numerous hits on that label include "You Don't Hear," "Will Your Lawyer Talk To God?", "Heartbreak, U.S.A.," "A Woman Half My Age," and "Meanwhile, Down at Joe's." She has also recorded duets with Roy Drusky, Red Foley, and Webb Pierce, and in 1968, with her husband, Johnny, she waxed a prophetic "We'll Stick Together."

In 1974 she signed with Capricorn Records. Her first release was Bob Dylan's "Forever Young," a song which seems to fit her personality.

## WEST, DOTTIE

BORN: October 11, 1932, McMinnville, Tennessee

MARRIED: h. Bill West (divorced) (s. Dale, Kerry, William M. III; d. Shelly); h. Byron Allen

Whenever there's a newspaper piece about Dottie West, the writer invariably remarks about her beauty. She's in her late thirties now, and no longer wears crinolines or bright orange plastic jackets over patterned bell-bottoms. Her hair is reddish blonde now, instead of dark brown. She generally wears crushed-velvet suits, and in front of sophisticated audiences (her favorite artists these days include Helen Reddy, a non-country singer, and Bread, a rock group) she wears tight white hot-pants under a slit skirt. Country-music queen Dottie West isn't afraid to be sexy.

She had regal confidence from the beginning. When she finished Tennessee Tech (she is one of the few country songstresses with an A.B. in music), she decided that her church-soprano voice should be heard by one and all, and announcing that fact to Starday record executives, they had no recourse but to sign her up. Success came quickly. She married a school chum, Bill West, an engineer as well as guitarist. Together they wrote "Here Comes My Baby," which made high scores on the charts. Dottie duetted with Jim Reeves for the top ten again with "Love Is No Excuse." and she was a regular on the Grand Ole Opry TV show. She had other big hits such as "Paper Mansions" and "Mommy, Can I Still Call Him Daddy?" The last one was prophetic. Dottie and Bill were subsequently divorced, but Dottie doesn't talk about the breakup openly. "Bill last played with my show two days before our twentieth wedding anniversary," she says. Her associates claim that Dottie has retained her emotional stability and regained much happiness by immersing herself deeper into her music. And she has remarried a much younger man—Byron Allen, her road manager and drummer. She and Byron appear on her latest album cover, looking happily and romantically into each other's eyes. "The look of love is no coincidence and no put-on," claims writer Don Rhodes. "She has turned to bearded Byron during many a performance and sung, 'Funny Face, I love you.'"

Dottie West: Just "full of country sunshine."

Rhodes continues: "Her success is due equally to her records and to her seemingly tireless
stage appearances. During one six-night week in
Augusta, Georgia, she did twenty-three shows.
First show at 10:00 P.M. Last show ending
around 2 A.M. She puts her all into her work—as
trite as that sounds—and gives the same show to
a room of thirty people as she does to a stadium
of twelve thousand. Last year, at the 1973
Country Music Festival in Wembley, England,
the crowd gave her four standing ovations when
she sang 'Six Weeks Every Summer.' Dottie
said, 'I couldn't get off the stage, they liked that
song so.'

"Now, strangely enough, it is the Coca-Cola
Company that has her career off and running.
Her 'I'm Your Country Girl' commercial (the
one that has a closeup of a girl gardening with
the camera fading away to show her on a tall
New York building) was placed high on the
annual Cleo Awards balloting (for the best radio
and television nationally broadcast commercials): number two in the television category and
number three in the radio category. One of her
biggest hits this year has been her 'Country
Sunshine' Coke commercial, which has Dottie
singing, 'I was raised on country sunshine, and
I'm happy with the simple things,' while 'Hen-

297

ry's Taxi' brings a young girl home down a dusty road.

" 'We record the songs for my Coke commercials in some Nashville recording studio, using musicians who are generally with me on my RCA sessions,' she says. 'The only thing different from my regular sessions is that Billy Davis does the producing rather than my regular producer, Jerry Bradley. We don't have any written arrangements—just head arrangements. You know, Coke's not a jingle. It's a song. Each of the commercials tells a story. I just cut 'Country Sunshine' as a single record for RCA. When we finished, it sounded just like the commercial.'

"Does Dottie have to get in the mood to sing the praises of a soft drink? 'It's easy to get in the mood. It's easy to put sincerity in the commercial because the product is one that all the world knows. I feel everyone knows what I'm singing about, and that the product is good.

" 'A few years ago I thought a Big Orange was everything,' Dottie admits, 'but now, of course, things are different.'

"The song that led to her Coke commercials, 'Country Girl,' has become an anthem for Dottie—her personal statement of what the whole country-girl life-style is all about. 'I got to thinking that any time a song was written about a country girl, it ended sad,' she says. 'I thought of the things I remembered about being a country girl, and it was, and is, a happy time of my life. So, I wrote about the pretty things I remembered.' "

## WHEELER, BILLY EDD

BORN: December 9, 1932, Whitesville, West
Virginia
MARRIED: w. Mary Mitchell
CHILDREN: d. Lucy

It was in Brooklyn, New York, that I met Billy Edd Wheeler. Clarence Cooper of the Tarriers took us over to meet him. "He's marvelous," Clarence said. "The real country boy. A real honest-to-goodness country boy, and you know where he's living? In Brooklyn, that's where. And do you know where that real honest-to-goodness country boy went to school? Well, man, I'll tell you. He went to the Yale Graduate School of Theater. That's where." We found

Billy Edd Wheeler: A Yale grad from the mountains of West Virginny.

Billy Edd to be quiet, reserved, and charming, and he played a little song for us. I don't remember the title, but it had something to do with "There's nothin' I like better'n girls, unless it's a horse, of course . . . ." He was part of the folk scene at that time and had written the Kingston Trio hit "The Reverend Mr. Black." His own recording of "The Little Brown Shack Out Back" did fairly well.

Born and raised in "the mountain part" of West Virginia, he picked and sang at high school fairs and local clubs. After college in Berea, Kentucky, and at Yale, he served in the navy, then came to New York to try his hand at playwriting and performing and writing songs. He also appeared in religious dramas, and some of his songs were performed in the sixties by the Lexington, Kentucky, symphony orchestra. Among his compositions is "Jackson," recorded by Johnny and June Carter Cash. He is now part of the Cash "family." Billy Edd Wheeler considers himself a "country music" person, lives in North Carolina, is interested in the folklore of the area, and is creator of the Billy Edd Wheeler Music Room in the Mountain Hall of Fame in Richwood, West Virginia. Billy Edd

has recorded for Kapp ("I Ain't the Worryin' Kind") and United Artists ("Fried Chicken and a Country Tune"), and now has signed with RCA.

## WHITMAN, SLIM [Otis Dewey]
BORN: January 20, 1924, Tampa, Florida
MARRIED: w. Jerry
CHILDREN: d. Charlene

Yodelin' Slim Whitman, self-styled protégé of that other Slim (Montana Slim—Wilf Carter), has crowded the country charts since 1952, when his "Indian Love Call" remained high on the lists for six months. Whitman has a high, clear tenor voice and a style that was quite original in the 1950s, when he was at the height of his popularity. He specialized in the sentimental and sad love song. Some of his songs, such as "I'm Casting My Lasso Toward the Sky," were western. Some were old standbys like "Danny Boy." "Indian Love Call" came from a Broadway musical (which must establish some kind of country-music first). Whitman not only yodeled himself, but his backing had anoth-

Slim Whitman: A yodelin' protégé of Wilf Carter.

er "yodeling" characteristic—a "crying" steel guitar.

Born and brought up in western Florida, Whitman planned a career in baseball, and actually pitched for the Plant City Berries of the Orange Belt League (his pitching record was 11-1, and he batted .360). At night he played local clubs. In 1949, after playing on local radio stations, he was asked to appear on *Louisiana Hayride.* Whitman traveled extensively, and many of his songs achieved hit status in Europe, Asia, and Australia as well as in the United States. He was the first country artist to appear at the London Palladium.

## THE WILBURN BROTHERS

### Doyle Wilburn
BORN: July 7, 1930, Hardy, Missouri

### Teddy Wilburn
BORN: November 30, 1931, Hardy, Missouri

Teddy and Doyle Wilburn were introduced to the public through the medium of television. They had made country recordings, but they weren't particularly successful, and occasionally bordered on pop. But their TV show proved their loyalty to their country roots. They were born in a farm family that sang gospel and played old-time melodies. The entire family were performers at one time or another, but in 1954 the brothers formed their duo and joined the Webb Pierce troupe. They recorded "Go Away with Me," which gained quick popular acceptance, followed by a succession of other hits: "Which One Is to Blame," "Roll, Muddy River" and "Hurt Her Once for Me," among others. In addition to an occasional pop tune, the Wilburns have a huge repertory. Their show is sponsored by Garrett snuff and Bull-of-the-Woods tobacco, and for a long time the show featured Loretta Lynn as a "permanent guest star," the banjo playing of Harold Morrison, and the steel-guitar playing of Don Helms, who backed Hank Williams. Every show has a honky-tonk number, a gospel song, a traditional song, and a "contemporary" song.

Along with Jim and Jesse McReynolds and the Osbornes, the Wilburns continue the long tradition of country-singing brother acts.

The Wilburn Brothers: Have a huge repertory of country songs.

# WILLIAMS, HANK

BORN: September 15, 1923, Georgiana, Alabama

DIED: January 1, 1953, West Virginia

MARRIED: w. Audrey Shepard (divorced) (s. Randall Hank; d. Lycrecia Ann); w. Billie Jean Jones

Hank Williams, an extraordinary artist, died on January 1, 1953, of "too much living, too much sorrow, too much love, too much drink and drugs." He couldn't read or write music, but his 125 compositions include many classics of popular music. He was the first country musician and writer whose songs were eagerly grabbed by pop singers. The twenty years since his death haven't diminished his stature. Millions of his albums are still sold, and millions more will be sold.

Hank Williams was born in a two-room log cabin to the poverty-stricken family of a shell-shocked veteran of World War I. When he was seven, his mother gave him a $3.50 guitar. His music lessons came from a black street singer who taught him while Hank shined shoes or sold peanuts on Montgomery street corners. When he was twelve, he won a songwriting contest with "WPA Blues." With the $15 prize he decided to form a band, The Drifting Cowboys. (He had always dreamed, he said, of becoming a cowboy.) At seventeen, he tried rodeoing in Texas and was thrown from a horse, and back trouble plagued him all his life. He joined a medicine show, selling and singing, and met Audrey Shepard. After a stormy courtship, he married "Miss Audrey." Meanwhile, his reputation was growing. Ernest Tubb heard him and tried to get Grand Ole Opry to sign him on, but Williams' reputation as a "womanizing, hard-drinking wild man" preceded him, and Opry officials felt he'd be trouble. *Louisiana Hayride* had no such reservations and Hank joined the show. He kept writing songs; met Fred Rose, Roy Acuff's music-publishing partner. Hank sang a lot of songs for Rose, including "Move It On Over," "I Saw the Light," and "Honky-Tonkin'." Rose was impressed, signed Williams to an exclusive contract, and arranged for Hank to meet Frank Walker of MGM Records. His records sold, from the beginning, like the proverbial hotcakes. Grand Ole Opry relented, and

on June 11, 1949, Hank sang "Lovesick Blues" at the Opry and stopped the show "colder than it had ever been stopped in its thirty-one years." He was forced to sing an unprecedented six encores. The money began to pour in, and Hank checked his drinking. For two or three years, the happiest in his life, he traveled, sang and recorded, and enjoyed his money. But when he broke up with Audrey, in 1952, he began to fall apart. He was divorced and immediately married Billie Jean Jones, a singer, on the stage of a theater, as part of the act. He was on his way to West Virginia for a performance when he died on the back seat of his Cadillac. That year his record "I'll Never Get Out of This World Alive" outsold all his previous discs. To list his compositions would take all the pages of this article: "Wedding Bells," "Lost Highway," "Long-Gone Lonesome Blues," "Your Cheatin' Heart," "Jambalaya," "Kawliga," and "I'm So Lonesome I Could Cry" are only a few of them.

I consider myself lucky that I once met Hank Williams. It is a meeting I will never forget:

I received a letter recently from a twenty-one-year-old Harvard student who claimed he'd "just read" an article of mine in "an old copy of *Esquire*"—an article in which I mentioned that as a teen-ager in the late 1940s, I'd listened to, met, and interviewed the late Hank Williams for my high school newspaper. My correspondent was in the midst of completing "a thesis on American folk-poets" and he considered Hank Williams on a par with "Bob Dylan, Phil Ochs, and Buffy St. Marie." Would I "open up" about my "friendship" with Hank Williams?

I wish I *could* say I was his friend.

I was an admirer and still remain an ardent fan.

I think, in his time, no other performer—country, folk, or pop—could come within a country mile of Hank Williams.

A number of musicians have asked me, "What kind of *vibes* did Hank give off?" I always reply, "Williams was special, different."

I only spent about six hours with him, saw him twice in person, once only as a member of the audience—and that was more than twenty years ago. I wrote him two letters and he answered both of them with scrawled postcards.

Hank Williams when he was singing for the Mother's Best Flour show.

One was from Beaumont, Texas, and the other from Wheeling, West Virginia. When my parents moved to a new house while I was at college, the postcards disappeared.

The memory of my afternoon, though, with Hank Williams remains as vivid as if it were yesterday.

Two old friends, Vern Young and Annie, occasionally promoted traveling "hillbilly music" shows in my hometown, and it was from one of their posters that I first heard of Hank Williams. "If you never get to see another southern singer, boy," Vern Young insisted, "get over this weekend somehow and listen to Hank Williams. He's gonna be one of the big ones." He pointed to the bottom of the poster, which listed a number of performers then touring the area. It read, in the smallest typeface, *Extra Added Attraction: Hank Williams.*

I was an editor of my high school newspaper, and one of my "innovations" was to interview visiting celebrities about their own adolescence. The results proved to be quite popular. I had interviewed Vaughn Monroe, the Boswell Sisters, and Frankie Laine.

"I have to interview Hank Williams," I told my mother.

"Who?" my mother asked, innocently.

"Hank Williams. He's appearing at Max Raney's in East Bloomfield on Saturday."

"East Bloomfield?" My mother was incredulous. "That's about fifty miles. Your father will never let you have the car all day on Saturday."

"I have enough money for gas and tickets."

"Ask your father," my mother said, but it didn't look very good.

"I *have* to interview Hank Williams for the paper at school," I insisted (lie). "Miss ———— (the paper's adviser) is really excited about the interview."

He let me have the car—a green Buick. I drove over country roads, past neat red barns and through herds of grazing Brown Swiss and Holstein dairy cows. I cross the Erie Canal at the West Henrietta locks and cut my speed through the picturesque main streets of little towns like Honeyoye Falls, following the hand-made signs: *Hillbilly Jamboree This Way.*

When the traffic grew heavier and the sound of electric guitars grew louder, I knew I'd arrived. Hundreds of cars, some bearing license plates from as far away as Pennsylvania and Canada, were already parked in an empty corn-field, plowed down to make it into a parking lot. In the distince was a miniature impromptu fairground and a huge tent, emblazoned with a badly painted sign: *This Is It!*

Many of the cars had picnic blankets spread out next to them on the still-wet field; whole families were squatting and talking and eating sandwiches from abundant picnic baskets and drinking out of huge thermos jugs. There were people of all ages, from toothless old grandfathers in faded engineer's caps to healthy kids in well-worn hand-me-downs and Momma-scissored haircuts. Judging by their complexions, they spent a lot more time outdoors than I did. (To this day, visitors are surprised to find out how rural most of New York State really is.)

I remember what I wore: a wide-shouldered, double-breasted, one-button roll, blue serge suit and a bulky red knit tie. As was the city style in those days, the cuffs of my trousers were pegged to sixteen inches. The knee was about

Hank sporting a western "zoot" suit.

303

twenty inches. Outfits with pants like this were called zoot suits, and they looked as if they had been designed by Al Capp for Evil-Eye Fleagle. Among the farmers in overalls that day, I was unusually conspicuous and I felt ill at ease.

I paid my dollar to get into the "This Is It" tent and found a single seat—an uncomfortable wooden folding chair—in the third row. A local country band was already on the stage, playing "Pistol Packing Mama" and other popular western-swing hits. They probably weren't so hot, but I thought they were nifty.

There were several performers on the bill that day, some of whom probably have gone on to fame and Nashville-style fortune, but I can't honestly remember much about them except that they were lively, professional, and entertaining. Whatever talents they had were obscured by the Hillbilly Jamboree's "added attraction." He climbed onto the stage, carrying his guitar, and gave some sheet music to the house band. He was lanky, hungry-looking, and ill at ease. He wore a huge Roy Rogers–style hat, white as snow. His suit, which made the padded shoulders on my own pale to insignificance, was also white, and embroidered with butterflies. His face was slightly misshapen, pale as if it had been taken out of the oven too soon—but his expression was clear even to the least astute observer in the audience; it spoke of pain and sorrow and loneliness.

"Here's a boy you might be hearin' a lot about," the MC announced. "He was just signed on by *Louisiana Hayride*, and you can buy his recording of 'Move It On Over' on the MGM label. He's a boy who's gonna go far in our kind of music. Folks, let's give a great big upstate New York hand to that lonesome drifter from Alabama, Hank W-i-l-l-i-ams!"

Upstate New Yorkers, Pennsylvanians, and Canadians aren't given to outbursts of emotion. Throughout the earlier part of the show the audience had been attentive and courteous, and had applauded generously. When Hank Williams was introduced, a smattering of handclapping filled the tent. Then Williams adjusted the microphone. "My own boys couldn't make it this trip and we haven't had a chance to rehearse. I come here by bus and the roads ain't so good (trickle of laughter). But I'd like to play you a number to start that I've written and am going to record. It's called 'Lovesick Blues.' "

From the very first crack of "sweet d-a-a-a-a-ady," the audience exploded. They stood on their chairs. They howled at "Howling at the Moon" and they screamed at "Why Don't You Love Me Like You Used to Do?" And I was screaming with them. THE MAN WAS GREAT. Nobody has ever successfully explained the quality that deserves the term "great." But whatever it is, Hank Williams had it. He was supposed to have twenty minutes on the program. The audience wouldn't let him go for almost an hour. Though the "star" of the Jamboree was yet to come, I left my seat as soon as Williams left the stage. I followed him to the "dressing room," a screened-off area in the far corner of the tent. At first he thought I wanted an autograph and then I explained that I was an editor of my high school paper and wanted to interview him.

"Well, well," he said, looking at me. "How old are you?"

I told him.

"Hell's bells," he said. "Writin' for a newspaper at that age. When I was your age I couldn't much write." He enjoyed his joke. He handed me his guitar while he opened his collar and took off his tie and jacket. He was wearing brown, clip-on suspenders and was sweating. His hair was already thinning.

"They sure are nice folks," he said, "that audience." He picked up a half-empty bottle of orange soda. "It's warm," he said. "Why don't you and me go get us a cold one."

We walked toward a stand selling hot dogs. "W-h-i-t-e Hots," he said deliberately, reading a sign. "What are white hots?"

"Pork hots," I said. "It's a specialty of the area." (They still are a specialty of Monroe County, New York, where white hot-dogs seem to outsell the red ones. I've never seen them anywhere else.)

"Instead of you writin' for the high school paper," he said, as we walked around the fairgrounds, Williams eating his hot dog and drinking a bottle of Queen-O Orange, "you should go into business sellin' these things in other parts of the country. Maybe I should quit the music business and become a white-hot performer instead of a red-hot one." He looked to see if I was going to laugh.

I didn't. I was too intent on taking notes.

"Why don't you put that notebook away so

we can talk.'' Williams looked around. ''Mighty pretty country. It's all mighty pretty country.'' He pointed to a big tree. ''Let's us sit under that 'un,'' he said, tossing the bottle into a waste bin. ''I like to relax between shows.''

I asked him if he thought country music would sweep America. ''I don't know what you mean by country music,'' he said. ''I just make music the way I know how. Singin' songs comes natural to me the way some folks can argue law or make cabinets. It's all I know. It's all I care about.''

I gave him the inevitable press question to a number-one singer: ''Where do you get ideas for your songs?'' He smiled (he kept smiling—not a nervous smile, but a natural one) and said, ''I don't know how to answer that. Sometimes I make 'em up. Other times they just come to me. And other times I listen to people and try to understand how they feel about things. Feelings about things. That's what songs should be about.'' I was busy taking notes. ''If I could write that fast,'' he said, ''I'd have written 500 songs by now.''

We talked about growing up. About parents and their desires for children and how parents didn't really understand kids and that he probably would be a parent someday and hoped his kids would turn out okay.

''What do you mean, 'okay'?''

''Well, if I had a son,'' he said slowly, ''I wouldn't mind if he growed up like you.'' I was embarrassed. ''I'm not sure you know me well enough,'' I said, trying to be cool. But that was disconcerting, and I stopped taking notes and we just continued talking. He told me a little about his growing up, about his listening to black singing (''that's real natural music''), about starting his own band when he was only fourteen (''A man has to know what he wants to do, and then do it and keep your mind on it, and don't let nothing else get in the way to clutter up your life''). We talked about cars, about America, and how the people were the same wherever he went, about the funny way people dress, about girls (he was willing to talk about women, but I was prudish and uncomfortable), about whiskey (''Don't you start drinkin' now, just because your friends do it''), and about religion.

''Are you a God-fearin' boy?'' he asked. It was a question I didn't expect. ''I really don't know how to answer that,'' I said. ''I don't think

much about fearing God.''

''Well, boy,'' he offered deliberately. ''Don't let it trouble you none. I ain't afraid of God, either.''

We were interrupted by a shout. ''Where the hell are you hidin', Hank?'' It was the MC. ''I thought you'd run out on us. It's almost time for the next show.''

''I been bein' interviewed,'' Williams replied.

''Interviewed?'' the MC said. ''What paper?''

''It's for a high school newspaper, his paper.'' He pointed to me.

''You mean you disappear for hours just to give some high school kid an interview?''

''He ain't just some kid,'' Williams said. ''We're buddies, aren't we, buddy?'' I nodded.

The MC tried to pull Williams away. ''Hey, you'll send me a copy of the interview when it's published, won't you?'' Williams said to me. He quickly scratched his address and went off. ''Next time *you* buy the white-hots.''

My father was angry and my mother worried sick when I got home, hours later than they expected. Undaunted, I went to my room and typed out my interview—it was long and detailed and it totally praised Hank Williams and I believed every word.

On Monday morning I turned the story into Miss ———, and the next day she called me into her office. She was rejecting the story. ''I don't know how an intelligent mind like yours can deal with such superfluous things as hillbilly singers.''

She pronounced the word ''hillbilly'' in a way to make you crawl—filled with disgust and loathing. ''Furthermore,'' she said sternly, ''none of the other students at Monroe High School will find your story has any value at all.'' She tossed it back to me.

Poor Miss ———. I wonder if she knows now, as she teaches grammar to illiterate angels in some heavenly schoolroom, that in 1973 Harvard students were writing theses about that ''hillbilly.'' Dear Miss ——— (May She Rest in Peace). What a sock she must have had when she slipped a golden nickel into one of the celestial juke boxes and the first sounds she heard were '' a fiddle and a git-tar with a honky-tonk sound . . .''

I wrote a long letter to Hank Williams explaining what an idiot Miss ——— was and that I was sorry I'd wasted his time and wasn't able to give him the publicity I'd promised. Two months later, in an almost unintelligible scrawl, Hank Williams wrote me: "Don't sweat, buddy. The world's not yet lonesome for me."

I've just read over what I've written. If all I did twenty-five years ago was sit under an elm tree near the Erie Canal with Hank Williams, talking about things I talk to everybody about every day, why do I almost totally recall the experience? The answer is simple. Hank Williams was one of those rare persons who projected: "I am special. I am different. I only do what I know how to do, and something drives me to do it better than anybody else. Why do you want me to be just like you? Lord knows, I don't want you to be like me. Why do you not accept me as God made me?"

Through the years, as the Williams legend has grown, a lot of things, probably more profound than on these pages, have been written about the meaning of Hank Williams' music and the whys of his existence. There is always the undercurrent of ugliness: drugs, insanity, liquor, wild women, drugs, brutality, drugs, overdose.

He probably wasn't perfect. But from my personal experience that afternoon more than two decades ago, you couldn't find that out from me. I remember him as a man of undisputed genius who treated an excited teen-age reporter as an equal (in a time when teen-agers didn't make the headlines very often). I tried to see him once more, backstage in Los Angeles, in 1950. He was already a superstar by this time and I was reporting for my college newspaper. Only I couldn't get by the guards. ("Just give him this note," I pleaded. "He knows me." But they wouldn't believe me, and the girl I was with didn't believe me, either.) And when I wrote Hank Williams that I had tried to get backstage, his postcard, in an even wilder script than his first one, said, "Buddy, life gets tougher all the time."

# WILLIAMS, HANK, JR. [Randall Hank Williams]

BORN: May 26, 1949, Shreveport, Louisiana
MARRIED: Gwen Yeargain
CHILDREN: s. Hank Williams III

The first thing I scrawled in my notebook when I

got a good look at Hank Williams, Jr., was: *Why isn't he a bag of bones like his father?*

He stood about fifteen feet away from me, wearing a neat pair of cream-colored bell-bottoms and an open-collared shirt. He was shaking hands with some of the backstage people, and then, removing his banjo from its case, he began to pace back and forth, plucking away all the time.

Now Hank Williams, Jr., isn't fat. That isn't it at all. It's just that he isn't skeletal like his father was. Hank, Jr., wouldn't be cast as the scarecrow in *The Wizard of Oz*. Hank, Sr., could have been a serious contender. You know that Hank, Jr., had all the milk and protein he needed when he was a kid. And that's the way it should be. But the minute I saw him, I broke an oath: *I, Melvin B. Shestack, had solemnly sworn that I would not compare Hank Williams, Jr., to Hank Williams, Sr.*

It was a noble gesture—but impossible in the light of what had happened to me during the past four months. The previous summer, I had burst into the offices of *Country Music* magazine, offering the story I'd been unable to sell for twenty years: my meeting with Hank Williams when I was a writer for my high school newspaper. I sold the story (*Country Music*, January 1973) and my life changed considerably. First, the mail came—in bushels. I heard from several people who had been at the same concert and were anxious to have a get-together. Vic Willis, of the great Willis Brothers, was kind enough to point out some obvious errors in my memory. I've received pecan cookies and cured Virginia hams from fans of Hank's and I've been asked to speak at colleges on Hank Williams' influence on American popular music. I even had one proposal of marriage (my wife didn't appreciate that one), and an Arkansas farmer offered a weekend of possum hunting, should I ever get down to Crockett's Bluff. Vern Young, the man who had insisted I go to a Hank Williams concert all those years ago, read the article and contacted me, and we've made plans for a reunion.

So Hank Williams had touched *my* life—and now I was meeting his son, little "Bocephus," as he had called him, the joy of *his* life. (Anyone who could write a song like "My Son Calls Another Man Daddy" knows the rewards and

Hank Williams, Jr. (center), discusses his father with TV host Mike Douglas (left) and George Hamilton, Jr., who portrayed Hank, Sr., on the screen.

pains of fatherhood.)

"I'd sure like to talk to you this minute," Hank, Jr., told me as I waited backstage with my wife. (I tried to think: What had his father's voice been like? Was it higher-pitched?) "But I gotta couple of things to do first. You all come up to my dressing room in ten minutes."

"Why are you so nervous?" asked my wife, who is always cool and logical.

I tend toward the dramatic, and Hartford, Connecticut, where Hank, Jr., was singing,

seemed the wrong place to interview him. I had planned to catch a later concert of his in Rochester, New York, because that was where I had met his father. But circumstances prevented it. Not that Rochester, New York, is typical country-music country. I mean, Merle Haggard wouldn't write "I'm Just an Okie from Rochester," but it would have been better than being in New England. For a complicated reason, I felt Connecticut was a damn poor place to encounter the son of "Luke the Drifter." I was suffering from a case of the "Long-Gone Lone-some Blues."

We had arrived early and silently. Bushnell Memorial Auditorium is Hartford's old opera house, a tarnished but still oddly elegant alliance of American Colonial style and Gallic rococo, and haunted by the dim ghosts of now-forgotten musical luminaries of the last seventy-five years.

I thought, Had Hank Williams, Sr., ever graced these ornate walls? I doubted it. But the doorman, whose enthusiastic remarks belied his Hibernian grimace, told us, "Sold out. Both concerts."

The hall was empty save for two solitary figures. One, a listless attendant, shuffled through the empty rows of seats, bending occasionally to scrape gum from lifted chair bottoms; the other was a sideman from one of the groups making up the afternoon's show. He was short and wiry and he carried a fiddle. In a Chaplinesque gesture, he waddled to the shadowy center stage, made a deliberate bow to the imaginary, white-tie audience, placed his instrument confidently under his chin, and guiding his bow over the strings, filled the vacant hall with strains of Tchaikowsky's "Winter Dreams," motivating the attendant to snap to bewildered attention.

The fiddler stopped in mid-chord. His face reddened as two more denim-clad musicians broke the silence, their arms clumsily wrapped around amplifiers and drum cases. Dashing by us, and seeing us for the first time, the fiddler offered an embarrassed "Just clownin', folks," and calming down, "You here to see Mel [Tillis]?"

"We're here to listen to Tillis and talk to Hank, Jr."

"Hank ain't here yet," he told us. "Their bus is a little bit late."

The stage door opened to admit a smiling young woman. She was thin and dark-haired and wore the kind of dark glasses movie stars often wear. I was struck by her thinness and felt I should offer her a candy bar or something. But even if she was hungry, she had a fine reason for smiling. The previous night in Nashville she'd won her first Grammy Award, and for the moment at least, she was the happiest girl in the whole USA.

"Who's that guy with Donna Fargo?" someone beside me asked.

The guy was an intense man whose face served as a greenhouse for a tremendous jungle of black whiskers, growing like a rain forest, and long enough to leave scratch marks on his new, soft-as-velvet brushed-suede jacket. It was Stan Silver, Donna Fargo's manager (and a brilliant one, too, I am informed by very important sources) as well as her husband. With him, carrying a guitar case and sporting what, by the time this is in print, will be a curly red beard, was the great Texas sideman Odell Martin. "I'm lookin' for pickers," he confided to a Mel Tillis bandsman, who knew him. "Gonna put together a group for Donna." Martin's boots are deserving of mention: scuffed black leather, but tipped at the points with an armor plate of tooled Mexican silver. Out of sight!

I was about to join Donna Fargo's well-wishers when the "Cheatin' Heart Special" pulled up next to the stage door. A number of young men in denim got out of the bus and entered the back stage; none were Hank, Jr. I was on the lookout for Jerry Rivers, road manager and fiddler, and one of Hank Williams, Sr's, *original* Drifting Cowboys. Promoter Abe Hansa collared a man with longish white hair. "This guy's looking for you, Jerry."

During our introduction (I learned that Hank, Jr., had come to Hartford by plane and would be arriving any minute); I spotted a familiar face. "Who's that?" I asked Jerry.

"He's our driver and jack-of-all-trades," Jerry Rivers replied, admiringly. "We couldn't do without him."

"I mean, what's his name?"

"Okie Jones," Jerry told me. "He's been with us five years."

Okie Jones, indeed. This certainly was turning out to be a banner day.

Okie Jones.

Probably no one remembers him much now—outside of Nashville—but when I was stationed at Fort Bliss, Texas, during the last days of the Korean War, Okie Jones was the post celebrity. I was editor of the Fort Bliss *News* and we often took photos of Private Okie Jones with generals and congressmen and visiting celebrities. Before being drafted, Okie Jones had recorded a number of hits, and everybody at Fort Bliss believed

Okie would become a country superstar.

"Okie," Jerry Rivers said, bringing us together, "this fellow is here to interview Hank, Jr., and he claims he was in the army with you."

"Yeah?" Okie Jones said, smiling like a chipmunk. "I'll be darned." He worked on the bus as we talked, but he was reluctant to talk about himself. "I drove for Marty Robbins a long time," Okie told me. "But when Marty had his heart attack, I didn't want to just hang around the ranch or nothin' so I joined Hank, Jr. I like drivin' the bus."

"I don't know what we'd do without ol' Okie," one of the Cheatin' Hearts (Hank, Jr.'s, group) offered. "He's just a bag of smiles an' there don't seem nothin' that ever bothers him."

One of the Cheatin' Hearts passed me, carrying a couple of costumes (bright green, embroidered with red hearts). A Tillis man said, "Now that Donna's on her way, Hank's really got to push his performance."

"Don't you worry none about ol' HWJR," the Williams advocate replied, confidently. "He's got all the breedin' he needs."

Hank's voice, rich and deep, boomed, "Why don't you and your wife come upstairs where it's quiet and we can talk." The dressing room, empty and nondescript, looked like the kind of room always used by criminals in the 1940s second-feature movies. The plaster was cracked. There were no curtains on the windows. The furniture was peeling and a shadeless 75-watt bulb dangled from a single cord.

"Oh, hell, I been in worse than this," Hank, Jr., assured us. "Mostly, I dress on the bus, anyway." (I wrote in my notebook: *Hank, Jr.'s, clothes fit so well. Hank, Sr., probably had tailor-made clothes, too, but poor boys don't have tailor-made physiques. Wears rings. Two: one a jeweled "HW," the other a jeweled "JR." For no reason at all I'm reminded of the words from "Wedding Bells": "I . . . I even bought a little band of gold./I thought some day I'd place it on your finger,/but now the future looks so dark and cold . . . "*

"Did you know that Daddy's album, the one they advertised on TV, has sold one million in three months," Hank, Jr., told us proudly. "That's pretty darn good for a man dead twenty years."

"Did he ever win a Grammy?" my wife asked. Hank, Jr., answered the question with another: "Did you watch the Grammies? Didn't you think Don McLean should've won something?" Someone poked his head in the door. "Tillis is leading off, then Donna, who's gonna use our musicians, and then you end the show, Hank." Hank, Jr., smiled at the face and nodded.

"Do you do many personal appearances a year?"

"Oh, somewhere between 220 and 230 shows a year," he remarked happily. "You don't get the bookings, you're not going to sell records." He went on: "I played my first show at eight with Grandpa Jones, my sister, and Momma. Between the ages of eight and fourteen, I did about thirty to fifty shows a year. When I was fourteen, I hit the Ed Sullivan show and the Jimmy Dean show. People in the audience always asked for Daddy's songs. 'Let's go, Hank Williams' son.' I didn't think much of my first records. 'Standing in the Shadows' was the changeover; that is, I liked it. But I've always worked—ever since I could remember, I worked, and when I didn't work I played sports and still do, but at school I played sports. And I studied. It was expected of me, and I expected it of myself.

"You know, I play six instruments. And I was taught by the best, like Earl Scruggs. He'd come over and show me a couple of things. People like that. I knew everybody in Nashville, and I still do.

"Boy, I'm country. I play a little rockabilly and rock-and-roll and I like hymns and all kinds of music, but I'm country.

"Didn't I say I knew everybody in Nashville? Well, that's not exactly true anymore. There are so many new people. I grew up knowin' the Tubbs' and Stringbean and those people. But there are so many new faces, and when I see 'em on the street, we just nod. I feel bad. I don't know who they are.

"Do you know, I grew up not knowin' any young people except the girls I took out. I was always with older people. I'd go fishin' with my father's friends and I still go fishin' with them. I fish in Kentucky Lake. I flew down to Mexico to go fishin'. I can't wait to take Hank Williams III fishing. He's over two years old now.

"People think I was born in Nashville, but I

was born in Shreveport. Daddy was with *Louisiana Hayride* there, you know. People say, 'Hank, Jr.'s, pretty good, but never as good as his daddy.' Well, *are you out of your mind*? I mean, there was only *one* Hank Williams. But I play a lot of instruments and I write songs. I have a new song I'm working on which talks about my life.''

(From my notebook: *He smiles through the monologue. His speaking voice is as rich as his singing voice. He's a man with a vocation. If anyone can be said to have been born to the business, HWJR certainly was. He's not sad inside like his father, but why the hell should he be? Why should I expect him to be a carbon copy?*)

"I can't think of anything I'd rather do than do what I do. And that's to sing and know other singers and to hunt and fish, except that the singing keeps me from doing as much fishing as I'd like.

"Did I tell you I collect guns? I've got a great collection ... '' The door burst open and in came a tall, big man with black curly hair and very white teeth. He was wearing a king-size blue crushed-velvet jacket. "Oh, I didn't know you had company,'' he said, his voice equally as deep as Hank, Jr.'s.

"This is Merle Kilgore,'' Hank, Jr., said. Kilgore smiled, "You got a nice magazine,'' he said to me.

"Merle Kilgore,'' I told my wife. "He wrote 'Wolverton Mountain.' ''

"Merle and I wrote a good song on the bus,'' Hank, Jr., said, picking up his guitar. The strap was of tooled leather and "Bocephus'' was cut into the leather. "That's the name Daddy called me. I don't know exactly how you pronounce it. It was Alexander the Great's horse. Anyway, lemme play you this song. We like it. It's called 'Country Music, Those Tear-Jerkin' Songs.' ''

Hank, Jr., played and sang a duet with Merle Kilgore, a *private* concert—one of the things that makes *my* job so special.

"Country music—those tear-jerkin' songs
About life the way it really is
He's not happy at home so he'll play those
    old songs
And dance with someone who's not his
    . . . ''

"There's a great jug sound in the cut we recorded,'' Hank said.

"You bet,'' Kilgore added. "It's Oswald playing the jug.''

Pete "Oswald'' Kirby was a regular on Grand Ole Opry in its infancy, a dobro-playing member of Roy Acuff's band who merited top billing along with Clayton McMichen, Eddy Arnold, Chuck Wiggins, and San Antonio Rose. "Oswald hasn't done much recording lately,'' Hank said, "and I invited him to join us for the tear-jerkin'-songs number.''

Kilgore interrupted. "He *makes* the song on the record. You get that record and listen. At the end of the cut, there's a weird laugh—he-he-he-haw—well, that's Oswald, doing his number. Anybody who's an Opry fan'll know that laugh.''

"He-he-he-haw,'' Hank, Jr., said.

"What I came in to tell you, Hank, was to get ready for the show,'' Kilgore said.

"C'mon down to the Cheatin' Heart Special,'' Hank said. "I need some help, anyway.''

All country-music buses are interesting, and each has its own character. We squeezed through the "parlor'' with its booths for card playing, reading, or writing songs, through the "dormitory'' with only one of the bunks made, and happily, a copy of *Country Music* sticking out from under a pillow. The back of the bus is Hank, Jr.'s, private domain, with a radio and TV set, and a parlor all its own. There were a couple of framed photos of Hank Williams, Sr., and titles of a number of songs had been carefully painted on the walls. "What I need you to help me with is to get this on me.'' He pointed to a handsome black leather shirt. "I work hard to make my hair look good. That's one thing I have in common with Daddy, having thin hair.'' He laughed, held his hands against his hair and said, "Let 'er go.'' I carefully lowered the shirt over his head, hoping not to touch his hair. "Perfect,'' he said. His eyes hit another magazine, which he picked up. "This is a newsletter from Africa,'' he told us. "I spent a month there hunting. It was wonderful. Here's my picture, right here. That's me. H. Williams of Tennessee.

"You know, I didn't sing for a long time in Africa, and I missed it. I missed singing. And one day, I found this old seventeen-dollar guitar and I picked it up and sang for them Africans, country music, and they didn't go for it at all. So I sang that song—remember it? 'The Witch Doctor'—oo-oo-ee-ee-ah-ah-ug-ug, and that sort of stuff. Well, they went crazy. Ate it up. Loved every bit. But I don't think I'll ever be able to go for a month without picking again.''

We walked toward the stage door. ''After this Northeast tour I have one on the West Coast, and there's special concerts, I occasionally play those, but I won't play clubs. I can't stand playing to an empty room. I like Fats Domino a lot, and in Las Vegas I saw him play to an empty room and it was awful. Not me. No, sir. Not HWJR.''

He loped onto the stage, sang ''Your Cheatin' Heart,'' and the audience loved it. He sang ''Eleven Roses'' and a couple of other hits, and they stamped their feet (these Connecticut hillbillies and Yale students, bless them) and shouted and screamed and sang along. Hank, Jr., played the acoustic guitar, the banjo, the steel guitar and the electric guitar, and then he headed for the piano and, Jerry Lee Lewis style—no, let's make that Hank Williams, Jr., style—started banging away. He forgot his carefully prepared hair and shook his head as his fingers pounded the keys. I turned to the man next to us in the wings. He was a security guard in his midfifties, portly and gray. ''That's the son of Hank Williams,'' I said.

''Who?'' the guard said. ''I don't care whose son he is. That boy is really very good. What did you say his name was?''

## WILLIAMS, TEX [Sol Williams]
BORN: August 23, 1917, Ramsey, Illinois
MARRIED: w. Dallas Orr

Tex Williams appeared in scores of movies with Tex Ritter, Buster Crabbe, and Charles Starrett (the Durango Kid) between the years 1935 and 1955. Raised in rural Illinois, he had his own one-man-band show when he was thirteen and eventually joined the Reno Racketeers, a Washington, D.C., country band that moved its base to California. Besides acting, Williams formed his twelve-piece band, the Western Caravan, and signed with Capitol Records. ''Smoke, Smoke, Smoke'' (the Tex Ritter–Merle Travis composition) was a huge hit for Williams and he catapulted to national fame. During the late forties the Western Caravan played to huge audiences from Chicago to Los Angeles, and non-country stars like Dinah Shore and Jo

Stafford appeared with Williams. His popularity dwindled as a bandleader, but he has kept singing, making the charts sporadically. In 1971, for Monument, he caused a little flurry with a humorous song called ''The Night Miss Nancy Ann's Hotel for Single Girls Burned Down.''

## THE WILLIS BROTHERS
### Guy Willis
BORN: July 15, 1915, Alex, Arkansas

### Skeeter Willis
BORN: December 20, 1907, Coalton, Oklahoma

### Vic Willis
BORN: May 31, 1922, Schulter, Oklahoma

During the past year I've been in postal contact with Vic Willis, who often corrects factual mistakes in articles I write for *Country Music*

The Willis Brothers: Give them forty acres . . .

magazine. I've never met Vic in person, but I've seen the Willis Brothers in operation on a few occasions, and they are among the pioneer groups in country music. (They were the first group to back Hank Williams, which is some kind of country-music milestone.) The Willis boys grew up in Oklahoma during the Depression years. Always devoted to country music, they played and sang; eventually they landed a job at KGEF in Shawnee, Oklahoma, and they began traveling through the Midwest. Many of the Willis Brothers' songs were original Guy Willis compositions: "I Miss Old Oklahoma," "Drive My Blues Away," and "My Heart Is Tired." After World War II (during which time the trio was temporarily suspended) they joined Eddy Arnold and toured with him for several years. They are members of Grand Ole Opry, and have taken their act, which features imitations of other country bands, to places as disparate as Holland, Newfoundland, and Puerto Rico. An unusual feature of the Willis outfit is that each brother is trained to sing solo lead. Willis Brothers hits for Starday Records include "Give Me Forty Acres to Turn This Rig Around," "Bob," and "Somebody Knows My Dog."

## WILLS, BOB

BORN: March 6, 1906, Limestone County, Texas

Bob Wills was elected to the Country Music Hall of Fame in 1968, and no wonder. He's one of the most important figures in country music. He's called "the king of western swing," and if he didn't inaugurate the style, he certainly was the most influential performer. His composition "San Antonio Rose" is one of the most popular songs of all time. Bob Wills wrote the song in less than thirty minutes, because a producer wanted one more song for a recording session. Countless singers, from Tex Ritter to Bing Crosby, have recorded it, and country-music stations still play the original Wills version. Astronaut Pete Conrad played the song from space. Sheet music doesn't sell like hotcakes these days, but Southern Music Company still sells thousands of copies a year (thirty-five years after the song was written). George Car-

mack of the *San Antonio Express News* wrote that during World War II, he was watching a special services movie on the island of Leyte. The movie was *Pygmalion* and "there was some applause. The crowd started to leave when the operator called out that he had a short subject. Soon the screen lighted up and on came 'Bob Wills and the Texas Playboys and "San Antonio Rose."' Soldiers started hollering, shouting, standing up, and pounding each other on the back. You would have sworn the Japanese would have heard it back in Tokyo. As the song continued, the 'Ah—ah-haaaa' went up at every appropriate moment, and what a shout as Bob came forth with his famous 'Take it away, Leon.' Most of those soldiers had never been to San Antonio, but to them 'San Antonio Rose' meant the United States." And in the United States during the years before and during World War II, Bob Wills and his Texas Playboys *were* country music to many thousands of southwesterners.

The novelist J. R. Goddard told Robert Shelton (and reported in "The Country Music Story") about his memories of Bob Wills: "Imagine a Saturday night at a dance hall in Norman or Muskogee, Oklahoma. There might be 1,200 people jammed in the hall, some of whom drove 150 miles for the dance. Some were hard-shell Baptists, oil workers, and mule farmers. Most of Bob Wills's fans were poor working class. They were just coming out of the Depression, out of the worst sort of rural isolation, just beginning to get electricity in their homes.

"Wills dressed conservatively in a starched white shirt, but maybe he wore a $100 pair of boots or a $100 cowboy hat. He had bought a big bus to take his band around, a bus with a big longhorn steer head on the front. The people had never seen anything quite like that. Wills could provide a visual style as well as a musical style. He was sort of a folk hero, but a reachable hero who gave these people something to live up to and look up to. His old theme went something like, 'Howdy, everybody from near and far/You want to know just who we are?/We're the Texas Playboys from the Lone Star' . . . Those dances had incessant music. You could hear the feet of the dancers stomping on the old wooden floor. Up near the bandstand were fifty or sixty people standing, hollering, trying to give Wills cigars.

Bob Wills and The Texas Playboys got together a couple of years ago for a reunion. Standing, left to right, are Al Strickland, Glen Rhees, Sleepy Jackson, Joe Ferguson, Smokey Dacus, Leon McAuliff, Andy Jackson (*not* a Playboy, but a disc jockey from KBUC, Texas, radio) Leon Rausch, Keith Coleman, and Johnnie Lee Wills; seated are Laura Lee McBride, the band's female singer for many years, Bob Wills (confined to a wheelchair after suffering a stroke), Joe Andrews, and Jesse Ashlock.

There was a down-home grandmother wearing a thirty-dollar set of false teeth. They had a strong need to get in contact with him. . . .''

At the same time Benny Goodman and Glenn Miller were popularizing urban swing in the east, Wills and other southwestern bandleaders were playing country-western music with a strong swing beat for dancing in rural areas. As country-music historian Bill C. Malone writes: ''His western swing stressed a heavy insistent beat, the jazz-like improvisations of the steel guitar, and the heavily bowed fiddle. It was a rhythmically infectious music designed for

dancing, but it also stressed lyrics, rendered usually by a vocalist such as Tommy Duncan.''

Bob Wills was born and brought up on a Texas ranch, where all his relatives were farmers, barbers, or musicians. He learned to play the fiddle at ten, and in country music star tradition was playing at local stations by the time he was in his teens. In the late 1920s Wills, with a friend, Herman Arnspiger, began playing in the Fort Worth area as The Wills Fiddle Band. By 1931 they had been joined by Milton Brown, and they called themselves Aladdin's Laddies. The Light Crust Flour Company hired the band to broadcast for it over KFJZ in Fort Worth (and to work for the company as truck drivers and unloaders) and changed the group's name to The Light Crust Doughboys. The flour company executive who hired them was Wilbert Lee ("Pappy") O'Daniel, who was also a song-writer and singer, and who performed with the Light Crust Doughboys. (O'Daniel eventually used his musical ability to help his political career, becoming a Texas senator and then governor of Texas.) By 1933 Wills had left the Doughboys to found his own organization. In 1934 he moved to Tulsa, Oklahoma, to broad-cast from KVOO. Talent scout Art Satherly heard Wills and signed him for Okeh records. Wills's show on KVOO became the most popu-lar radio show in Oklahoma, and the Red Star Milling Company offered him a percentage of the profits from all the flour sales promoted on his show. Wills eventually bought his own flour mill and began advertising his flour throughout Oklahoma, and in addition he bought a ballroom where each appearance drew more than 2,000 people. His repertory was wide, including old-time fiddle pieces like "White River Stomp" and numerous country-style jazz pieces like "Basin Street Blues" and "Troubles in Mind." During the height of his popularity Wills appeared in sixteen movies, mostly second-feature westerns like *Take Me Back to Oklahoma.* And during his heyday, Wills reputedly paid more income tax than any other performer in America—popular as well as country. Long after the western-swing band had declined in popularity, the Wills "beat" and style influenced country musicians. In 1969 Governor Preston Smith of Texas and both houses of the Texas legislature honored a number of Texas-born musicians: Tex Ritter, Ernest Tubb, and Bob Wills. That day, Wills suffered a stroke, and since then he has been confined to a bed in the hospital, or at home. He can no longer play, and because of failing eyesight he is unable to watch television. He spends his time listening to country music on radio.

## WISEMAN, MAC

BORN: March 23, 1925, Crimora, Virginia

From time to time, during my travels in the country-music world, I have been mistaken for

Mac Wiseman: All-around music man.

Mac Wiseman. Neither of us is particularly svelte, and both of us sport a handsome set of whiskers. The resemblance ends there: Mac Wiseman plays a great bluegrass guitar and is one of the five or six great bluegrass singers in America. He grew up in the Shenandoah Valley of Virginia, listening to country music, and after being taught to play a few guitar chords by a roving evangelist, he managed to get a Sears-Roebuck guitar. By the time he was in high school, Wiseman was a member of a country band (in the style of Ted Daffan/Bob Wills) called The Hungry Five. Local success brought him to the attention of Molly O'Day (one of the first women to lead a country band), who offered Wiseman the chance to join her as lead singer. He remained with the O'Day group until Lester Flatt and Earl Scruggs, who had just left the Bill Monroe organization, asked Wiseman to be-come a part of The Foggy Mountain Boys. He left Flatt and Scruggs to star on his own program in Atlanta and to act as front man and lead singer for Bill Monroe. Landing a personal contract with Dot Records, his first release, " 'Tis Sweet to Be Remembered," was a major hit. Wiseman followed with a succession of successful records: "Wildfire," "Four Walls Around Me," and "I'll Still Write Your Name in the Sand." All the Wiseman hits were backed up with a bluegrass band featuring twin fiddles. Dot Records asked Wiseman to head its country-music division, but rock-and-roll was cutting into country sales, and after a few years Wiseman returned to Nashville. "At that time," he recalls, "a thing took place that really was just a fortunate stroke of luck for me. It's when the folk trend started to develop in colleges. And without any effort at all, I was fortunate enough that the colleges picked up a lot of my old bluegrass catalog and adapted it in their folk collection. Places that had never really paid a whole lot of attention to this thing, as a bluegrass thing, or even before it was called bluegrass, now picked it up and I started playing some of the colleges ... even Carnegie Hall." Wiseman recorded the Carter Family hit "Jimmy Brown the Newsboy" for Dot. It was a hit, but Wiseman left Dot for Capitol, because it actively promoted country artists. In 1965 Wiseman moved to Wheeling to coproduce and star on the WWVA *Jamboree* and to have his own show, *Mac Wiseman's Record Shop*, which he still sponsors. In 1969 Wiseman signed with RCA and produced "Johnny's Cash and Charley's Pride," a straight country tune. Wiseman told producer Chet Atkins that he'd prefer to do some bluegrass numbers. "Lester Flatt and I were on the same bluegrass festival in Myrtle Beach, South Carolina," Wiseman says, "and he mentioned just in passing, 'Hey, we're both on the same label, we ought to get together and do an album.' And I said, 'Well, that'd be fine.' And when the MC had introduced him, he went onstage and did his show almost on down to the end and called me out to do the old 'We'll Meet Again, Sweetheart' which we'd done on Mercury twenty years ago, which we do often at festivals. When he introduced me to come back out and do the duet with him, he said, 'Hey, we were just thinking about doing an album together for Victor'—we got a standing ovation out of it! So we took it back to Nashville, and RCA was in favor of it, and in February of '71 we cut the first album." As it turns out, two albums have resulted ("Lester and Mac" and "On the Southbound").

These days Wiseman makes personal appearances with and without Lester Flatt. He has recorded his own album, "Concert Favorites," and keeps his *Mac Wiseman Record Shop*. He told writer Doug Green, "It's like a little bit of insurance on the side, and while it isn't anything that will scare Rockefeller to death, it'll keep me off those icy roads in the wintertime!" Wiseman also runs the annual bluegrass festival in Renfro Valley, Kentucky.

## WOOLEY, SHEB

BORN: April 10, 1921, Erick, Oklahoma
MARRIED: w. Beverly Addison
CHILDREN: d. Christie

Sheb Wooley was one of the bad guys in the great western film *High Noon*, and he played the part of Pete Nolan for several years on TV's *Rawhide* (which starred Clint Eastwood). He wrote the popular novelty song of the 1950s "The Purple People Eater," and as the comic Ben Colder, released a number of country parody records. For MGM he has come up with sporadic hits over the years: "The One-Man Band," "That's My Pa" (number one on the country charts), and "Tonight's the Night My Angel's Halo Fell."

## WORTH, MARION

BORN: Birmingham, Alabama
MARRIED: h. Happy Wilson
CHILDREN: d. Joyce Lea

For a spell during the late fifties and early sixties, Marion Worth recorded successful songs for Columbia and Decca, such as "I Think I Know" and "The French Song." As a girl in Alabama she memorized country songs and sang them for relatives, and then sang locally with her sister. She signed, originally, with Happy Wilson's Guyden label and had a hit with "That's My Kind of Love." Apparently it was (she married Happy Wilson). Marion Worth had a burst of popularity, recorded a best-selling duet with George Morgan ("Slipping Around"), and made numerous personal appearances. Now she is heard mostly around Christmas, with her country holiday perennial "Shake Me, I Rattle."

## WRIGHT, JOHNNY

BORN: May 13, 1914, Mt. Juliet, Tennessee
MARRIED: w. Kitty Wells
CHILDREN: s. Bobby; d. Ruby, Carol Sue

Johnny Wright and Jack Anglin (who billed themselves as "Johnny and Jack") were among the top duos during the fifties, with numerous hits for RCA Victor, including many they wrote themselves, such as "Ashes of Love" and "One By One." When Jack was killed in an auto crash in 1963, Johnny reorganized the act, which he produces for television as *The Johnny Wright–Kitty Wells Family Show.*


## WYNETTE, TAMMY [Wynette Pugh]

BORN: May 4, 1942, Itawamba County, Mississippi
MARRIED: h. George Jones
CHILDREN: d. Georgette

My life is really incomplete, at least as far as country music is concerned: I have *never* seen Tammy Wynette perform in person, I have never met her. I did see her hand out an award at the Country Music Awards show in 1973. And I have most of her records, some of which I love more than others, which is natural. Tammy Wynette is a very important star—she is generally accepted by a non-country audience and is, in fact, *the* country star (and she's very, very country-rooted) that most non-country fans can name. When she and her husband, George Jones, were reputedly about to break up, it was front-page news on all major city dailies, and CBS' Walter Cronkite made special note of it. Fortunately, Tammy decided to stand by her man after all, appearing publicly with him in regular concerts and special events such as the Macy's department store Thanksgiving Parade in New York City.

Because Tammy Wynette warrants the full country-queen treatment, John Gabree, noted editor, author, and lecturer who is writing a book on women in country music, has supplied this entry:

"It's just part of the Nashville legend: The Day Billy Sherrill Discovered Tammy Wynette. By now probably nobody remembers it just as it happened. It's been told so many times.

"Billy himself—head of production for Columbia and Epic records in Nashville—is modest enough about it. Something just told him to take a chance, so a chance is what he took. Not much of a chance, though, when you think about it. If it hadn't worked out, he'd have been down maybe a couple of hours of studio time. Hindsight says that's an acceptable risk.

"So Billy brought Tammy into the studio. Her first song 'Apartment Number 9,' went to number 43 on the national charts. 'Your Good Girl's Gonna Go Bad,' her second record, went to number one. Nowhere to number one. Rags to riches. An hour with Billy Sherrill and a star is born.

"It was not, of course, quite that simple. It never is.

" 'I kept getting breaks that didn't quite happen,' says Tammy Wynette. 'In early 1965 I moved in with my grandparents in Birmingham. I had an uncle who was chief engineer at Channel 6, WBRC-TV. He got me an audition and I became a regular on the *Country Boy Eddy Show.* I was getting up at 4 A.M., getting to the station by 6, then working 8 A.M. till 6 P.M. in a beauty parlor. Nothing happened. Then in October the next year I sang at the Disc Jockey Convention in Nashville. Porter Wagoner heard me and liked me enough to have me do several shows with him after Norma Jean left him and before he found Dolly Parton. Nothing happened. Early in 1967, I moved to an efficiency apartment in East Nashville. By the time I met Billy in the lobby at Columbia, I had already been to five record companies. Nobody but Billy was willing to really listen.'

"The Wynette-Sherrill team followed 'Your Good Girl's Gonna Go Bad' with fifteen straight number-one singles, a streak that was broken only when an inspirational tune, 'The Wonders You Perform,' went to number two. That shouldn't really count. In all, Tammy and Billy have been together on twenty-one number-one songs.

"Ironically, Tammy's most and least favorite songs, respectively, are 'D-I-V-O-R-C-E' and 'Stand By Your Man,' the two hits by which she is best known. 'D-I-V-O-R-C-E' probably graced the juke box in every honky-tonk from Augusta to Amarillo. And 'Stand By Your Man,' which sold more than 2 million copies, is the biggest single by a woman in the history of country music. They are both classic Wynette.

" 'D-I-V-O-R-C-E' is sung by a young woman, presumably in her late twenties, the same age as much of Tammy's audience.

Tammy Wynette: Billy is always right.

Our D-I-V-O-R-C-E
Becomes final today
And me and Little J-O-E
Will be going away
I know that this will be
pure H-E-double-L for me
I wish that we could stop this
D-I-V-O-R-C-E

"Tammy and Billy pull out all the stops on this one. The singer holds nothing back, draining emotion from herself, the song and her listeners. 'I think I've always liked it best,' she says.

" 'Stand By Your Man' is another matter. 'I didn't like the song very much when Billy and I wrote it. I had been married about two weeks (on August 22, 1968, to be exact) and I took it home and showed it to George [Jones]. When he didn't like it either, I guess I got prejudiced toward it. But Billy is always right. He's a genius. If he came in and told me to record "Yankee Doodle," I'd do it.'

"A lot of people in Nashville think Billy Sherrill is a genius. But then a lot of people think he's a lousy SOB. Watching him work in the studio, you'll probably decide that his fans are right. You'll also probably find it harder and harder to agree with his critics.

"As a producer, Billy Sherrill is without equal. As head of production for Columbia and Epic in Nashville, he oversees the album making of more than thirty artists. Besides Tammy, he personally produces records for some of the best country artists, performers like Charlie Rich, Jody Miller, Sandy Posey, Johnny Paycheck and Freddy Weller. By the industry's standards, he is the best there is: Nobody has scored number one more consistently than he has. And though he isn't extremely prolific as a writer, only fifty or so songs, nearly everything he writes turns to gold. 'He has an uncanny ear for good material,' says Tammy, 'his own and other people's.'

"In other ways, however, Billy Sherrill is his own worst enemy. He has acquired, for example, an uncommon suspicion of the press. It's true that he has been bagged a couple of times by unscrupulous reporters. But it is equally true that he says most of those awful things they say he says. Billy seems to have no idea what his jokes will sound like in print. Most of the time he *is* kidding, and besides, what he says is often no worse than what other people in the music business might say. Only Billy gets quoted.

"Studio B at Columbia's Sixteenth Street headquarters is beginning to fill with musicians. Billy Sherrill is in the control booth with engineer Lou Bradley, heavy into a discussion. From the outside it looks like they're hard at work, and they are. But what they're talking about is football. Billy is a football nut and a betting nut, and the previous weekend he had won a bundle on Miami over Washington in the Super Bowl. He is asking Lou Bradley, as he has asked everyone he's met all day, whether he'd won or lost on the game. Bradley, a lanky, soft-spoken man in his thirties, is noncommittal; mostly, he just lets Billy talk. Billy tells a visitor he'd like to bet on some hockey matches. 'What do you know about hockey?' his friend wants to know. 'What the hell do I know about basketball either?' says Billy. 'I just like to bet.'

"The thing Billy liked best about the Dolphins-Redskins game, besides winning, was that most of the 'experts' picked the other side. Billy likes beating the experts. His first hit was a smash even though the experts said it should have been impossible. Don't cut a waltz, they told him, keep it under two and a half minutes, get the punch line up front, and never feature a steel guitar. So Billy recorded David Houston singing 'Almost Persuaded,' a waltz over three minutes long with the punch line two minutes into the record and featuring a steel guitar. It sold a million. Billy really likes beating the experts.

"In the studio, Tammy Wynette is tucked away in a corner, peering around a partition at George Jones, who is working out an arrangement with the musicians. Tammy is talking about two of her favorite topics, George and Billy.

" 'Billy is doing wonderful things for George. George never recorded on more than one track before he came to Epic. He knows how much Billy has done for me and he trusts him completely. George has been a star for eighteen years, so it's not that Billy had anything to teach him about performing. It's just that Billy's way of producing is better than a lot of other people's.'

"Billy is snaking in and out among the musicians, offering a greeting here, a bit of advice or a joke there. Mostly he's talking about the barium treatment he's received the day before. He looks older than his thirty-five years, and tired and frail among the hearty, fleshy sessionmen.

"Earlier Tammy had been over-dubbing part of her newest single when Billy broke in from the control room: 'Can you just talk that line there instead of singing it?'

"'I don't know, Billy, you know I hate to talk.' But she did it, and of course the cut was much improved. 'I really hate to talk,' she is saying now, 'I just am not very good at it. The only time I ever argued with Billy was once when he wanted me to do "Cry," the old Johnny Ray song, and sort of talk my way through it. I really disagreed. I didn't think it was my type of song and I got this mental block against it. I couldn't get the melody in my mind. But we finally got it down and it was such a good sound. Billy was right. In the studio he really is always right.'

"Tammy Wynette is an extraordinarily attractive woman. When she talks to you, she fixes you with two of the saddest and most beautiful eyes in Creation. Here, in street clothes instead of the costumes she wears on stage, she looks like any moderately prosperous young woman, albeit a very lovely one, like Eva Marie Saint playing Tuesday Weld. Her manner is direct, open, and intelligent.

"To a lot of people, Tammy Wynette *is* country music. She has had a greater impact on country and its image than any other woman performer. Genius or not, Billy Sherrill had a lot to work with in Tammy. She has a strong, clear voice, maybe the best female voice in Nashville, and she knows how to wield it with great dramatic and emotional effect. When they wanted to epitomize country music, the producers of the film *Five Easy Pieces* used the record of Tammy Wynette singing 'Stand By Your Man.' Karen Black played a character who wanted to *be* Tammy Wynette, as thousands of women around the country also must. Her records are made by a great producer, but they feature a great singer.

"'The hardest thing about making records is finding the songs. George and I listen to everything that's sent to us. A while back we got a tape from California with no return address on it. We liked one of the songs and I wanted to do it. All we had was a name, J. Judy Kay, and the postmark, so we called agents and promoters on the Coast until we tracked her down. Then I recorded the song, "Bridge of Love." Billy's best at picking songs, though. And of course he's written most of our biggest ones. We had a survey that showed most of our listeners were women between twenty-two and forty-five years old. In the past couple of years we have been getting more and more college kids and that makes me really happy. But most of the people who like our records are probably married, so we try to find material they'll like.

"'"Stand By Your Man" was so big because country people aren't attracted to women's lib. They like to be able to stand by their man. And of course the men liked the idea that their women would stand by them. I try to find songs that express down-to-earth, honest feelings.

"'That's why I like Tom T. Hall so much as a songwriter. He's the storyteller of all storytellers. When we're on the road, George and I will stay in the bus or the dressing room until just before we go on. But if Tom's playing, we'll always go out and listen. Some of his songs are corny, but they always brighten your day a bit.

"'We don't travel more because it's so nerve-wracking. I love to perform for live audiences, to get to see real people. But sometimes you'll feel bad and you'll still have to go on out and smile. You'll want to scream, pull hair and run and say you don't feel like it. But you owe it to people to come see them and you want to do it. I get very nervous just before a show. You wonder if you're going to do the job. You want to and people expect you to. That's why I always open with a fast song, to cover my nervousness. If I tried to open with something slow I'd be shaking so much I couldn't sing.'

"Billy is back in the control room and ready to roll. George is at the mike. There'll be no more talking for a while.

"'Why don't you come out and see the farm in the morning?' Tammy says to me.

"That's a date.

"'The farm' is a fifteen-room mansion on 340 acres of prime land about thirty miles south of Nashville in Maury County. Tammy and George have only owned it a couple of months. They are still redecorating. The new carpets are so thick that the man answering the door can hardly get it open.

"'I'm Foy Lee,' he says, 'Tammy's father [stepfather]. This is Mrs. Lee. Come on in.'

"As she pours a couple of cups of coffee, Mildred Lee, a short, plump, energetic woman, talks about her daughter. 'Tammy was an only child and we tried to be real good to her. I was a schoolteacher and Mr. Lee worked the farm. There wasn't any town. It was all farm. There weren't but 800 people in all of Itawamba County. When Tammy turned eighteen, she got married, moved to Tupelo, and went to work for a beauty shop.'

"Mrs. Lee turns her attention to Tammy's maid's son, who has stayed home from school with a bad cold. She is trying to get him to eat something to keep up his strength. 'His Ma and Pa haven't come up from Florida yet,' she explains.

"Florida is where the Joneses and the Lees had been living for the last few years. Tammy and George bought an old plantation about forty miles from Tampa, in Lakeland. They put in a bandshell, and every couple of weeks they'd put on a big Nashville show starring themselves and whichever of their friends—Porter Wagoner and Dolly Parton, Conway Twitty, ole Waylon Jennings—could make it. But they found it meant too much traveling. Besides being on the road, they had to be in Nashville to record, rehearse, and find songs. So they've moved back home to Music City.

"Foy Lee offers to conduct a tour of the new house, beginning in the cellar. 'They kept the slaves down here,' he says, pointing to the barred windows. The masonry walls and oak beams, almost 140 years old, are in perfect shape. Pointing to rows of scratches over the fireplace, he adds, 'See, here's where they kept count of the days by marking the wall. They used to work them like horses during the day, then ring that big old bell out there in the evening and herd them in down here.' These are working-class people and they haven't forgotten how hard life can be. There is real sympathy in Foy Lee's voice, just as there will be later when Tammy says, 'That cellar gives you a creepy feeling. It's a terrible thing to lock anybody up like that.'

"It is a relief to get your feet into the thick carpet upstairs. The carpet stretches wall to wall in every room, including the kitchen. It changes color every time you go through a doorway— pink here, blue there—but nowhere do your feet touch solid ground.

"The front hall is two and a half stories high, with an enormous wooden door with the 140-year-old key still in the lock. Painters and carpenters are busy in several of the rooms. One painter is uncomfortably high up near the ceiling. A carpenter is putting extra closets into one of the guest rooms.

"'The house has a lot of history in it,' Mr. Lee is saying. 'The State even put a historical marker about it out by the highway. It was General John Hood's headquarters during the War Between the States. One story is that five generals spent the night here and then all went out and were killed at the battle of Franklin the next day. I don't know if that's true or not.'

"Back downstairs in the kitchen, George and Tammy have arrived from Nashville. With them is baby Georgette, and she gets a lot of grandmotherly attention from Mrs. Lee. George goes off to get one of the carpenters to plane the door so it won't be scraping the rug. Tammy runs up to her suite to get several framed photographs showing the house as it looked a hundred or so years ago. The big magnolias that dominate the front yard were just sprouts then.

"The suite that George and Tammy share has been decorated in Spanish modern, like a lot of the rest of the house. 'George is actually the decorator. He picks everything out. But I love Spanish. I think it is really beautiful.' Over the fireplace in the den, above the gas-powered logs, George has hung a collection of mounted prize-winning fish, all stuffed so that they look like they are leaping in the air. Over the door is a beautiful hand-decorated Spanish sword.

"Tammy goes outside for another session with the photographer. Dressed in yellow slacks and a yellow top under her blond hair, she is fabulous. George is talking management problems with one of the hands, discussing the herd of Black Angus cattle he has begun to assemble. 'We have about sixty head now,' he tells a visitor. 'I'm not sure of the exact number because we keep having calves. We lost two calves during the snow in January because we didn't have the cattle indoors. The previous owners hadn't moved theirs out yet, but every-

George Jones was her childhood hero.

thing is fine now. We'd like to get up to about 300 head. Originally we thought we'd just buy a herd, but we found out you get a lot of old cows that way. So now we're buying a few at a time when we find some good ones.'

"George is chewing on a little black cigar. 'We gave up smoking this morning,' says Tammy. 'I've tried before, but this time I'm going to do it. George didn't have any trouble giving up drinking a couple of years ago, but this seems a lot harder. We won't start again. George has a little touch of emphysema and it just makes me feel bad to smoke. So we've stopped.'

"Georgette has followed her mother out into the yard, and Tammy calls her over to have her picture taken. The Joneses have six other children, three each by previous marriages. The oldest is a legal secretary in Nashville, the rest are in school. Georgette is a beautiful, serious-looking child. She has her mother's sad eyes, and today she has decided not to smile. 'Georgette got her first s-p-a-n-k-i-n-g yesterday,' says Tammy. 'Mommy was washing her hair and Georgette wanted to do her hair the same way, so I gave her a shampoo and fixed her hair. She liked it so much that she gave herself three more shampoos in the commode. I finally lost my temper.'

"At two, Georgette has already started to sing. The only song in her repertoire so far is 'Funny Face.'

"Georgette is being followed around by a skinny mongrel who looks like he invented the hangdog look. Mrs. Lee is following him: 'This is Lucky. We found him abandoned when we moved in. He was so weak he couldn't walk, but I've been feeding him and taking care of him and he's starting to get better. I call him Lucky

321

'cause he's lucky we found him.'

" 'Imagine leaving an animal to starve like that,' adds Tammy, as Lucky lopes off after one of the fat squirrels that live in the yard.

"Tammy Wynette has been on top for almost five years. Even though it looks like George might, she knows nobody can stay on top forever. 'I'm completely happy,' she says. 'I have no other goal than to keep doing what I'm doing. I always wanted to be a singer, but I never dreamed I'd become rich and famous. I always expected to have a hard country life. George and I are really happy. We have a nice home for the kids. Now that we're back in Nashville, we're going to join the Opry again. We can perform and we can get the insurance. [The Opry is owned by an insurance company, and performers get big life policies.] We're on the road so much and we want to make sure the kids are taken care of if anything should ever happen to us. A lot of people love us, and we'll just go on making records and singing for people who want to hear us. I love music and I love performing, but if I never had another hit it would be all right.' "

# Y

## YOUNG, FARON

BORN: February 25, 1932, Shreveport, Louisiana

MARRIED: w. Hilda Margot Macon

CHILDREN: s. Damion Ray, Robin Farrell, Kevin Robert; d. Alana

Faron Young has had a lot of hits. Indeed, he is in the top ten of artists with the most records on the country hit charts, with many, many on the top-ten lists and a number of number-one hits, too: "Hello, Walls" in 1957 and "It's Four in the Morning" in 1971 (a really big one, with almost a million records sold in the continental United States and 500,000 in England). Unlike many country performers, Young was born in a fairly large city, but his father bought a farm when he was very young. As a child he got his first guitar and he spent "many hours figuring

out chords and fingering with a herd of cattle as an audience." As a student at Fair Park High School in Shreveport, he formed his own group, playing at school functions, dances, and country fairs. Although he planned to complete college (he entered Centenary College in 1950), the lure of music was too strong, and he'd become too well known in the Louisiana area and received too many good reviews to give up music. Station KWKH asked him to perform, and shortly afterward he joined *Louisiana Hayride*, where he impressed the star, Webb Pierce. Pierce not only featured Young on the program, but hired him to be one of the singers on his own traveling show. Capitol Records signed him in 1951, and his first two songs, "Tattletale Tears" and "Have I Waited Too Long?" brought him national attention. *Variety* reported, "Young Rising like a Country Meteor," but the Korean War intervened and Young was drafted, and after winning an army talent show he spent his time entertaining troops and singing on an army recruiting program. "Goin' Steady," which he wrote and recorded before he was drafted, made the country charts in 1953, and when he was mustered out, Grand Ole Opry beckoned.

Young's career boomed, and *Billboard* reports that hardly a week went by in twenty years when Young was not represented on that magazine's country hit charts. He appeared on the hit TV show *Daniel Boone* and acted in a number of films, including the odd second-feature *Country Music Holiday*, in which he shared billing with Ferlin Husky and Zsa Zsa Gabor. During the sixties Young moved from traditional country to a more contemporary style. Country-music historian Bill C. Malone writes: "At first accompanied by the standard honky-tonk instrumentation of fiddle and steel guitar, Young moved from *Louisiana Hayride* to the Grand Ole Opry. Possessed of a strong, virile voice and a style that ranged from rock-and-roll to an almost Frank Sinatra type of phrasing, Faron Young bore greater resemblance to the popular crooners than did most of the other country singers. By 1961, with his renditions of 'Hello, Walls' and 'The Yellow Bandana,' his appeal had gone far beyond the country audience." Nonetheless, Faron Young considers himself a country singer, headquarters himself in Nashville on an eight-and-a-half-acre estate. Nashville gossips consider Young a "family man," and he has had a successful marriage with "seventeen happy years."

Faron Young's manager, Billy Deaton, claims Young is, if not the king of country music, "king of the state-fair circuit." Hap Peebles, who probably books talents for more country fairs than any other man in Nashville, says Young is "the best box-office attraction of any country act playing the fairs in the continental United States." Young is the star of the BC Headache Powder commercials (five years at this writing) and has done commercials for Ford and other companies. He has appeared on all the national variety TV shows, as well as a number of the talk shows. Young is often cited for his interest in upcoming country talent. Some years ago he spoke with a bellhop in the old Andrew Jackson hotel in Nashville who asked him for a job with his Country Deputies band as a drummer. The drummer's name (and he worked with Young for two years, during which time he wrote songs for him): Roger Miller. Willie Nelson was having difficulty establishing himself as a songwriter until Young bought and recorded the great "Hello, Walls." Faron Young is president of *Music City News*, a Nashville monthly, and he is co-owner with Billy Deaton and Billy Grammer of the Faron Young Recording Studio. Faron Young plays golf and has shiny dark hair, which makes him look like one of the handsome models in the 1930s hair-tonic ads. Faron's no hippie.

Faron Young: Sits for his official portrait.

# Discography

The discography does not contain listings for albums that have been dropped from manufacturers' catalogs, nor does it list each and every album on which the artists contained in this encyclopedia performed. The discography attempts to offer the reader a list of album titles that are representative of the artist's work and are readily available for purchase.

Many of the record labels in this list have been abbreviated, as follows:

Amp.: Ampex
Arhoo.: Arhooley
At.: Atlantic
Barn.: Barnaby
Blue.: Bluebonnet
Cam.: Camden
Cambr.: Cambridge
Cap.: Capitol
Cart.: Cartwheel
Cinn.: Cinnamon
Col.: Columbia
Dec.: Decca
Elek.: Elektra
Folk.: Folkways
Har.: Harmony
Hick.: Hickory
Hill.: Hilltop
KC: Kash Country

Lib.: Liberty
Mer.: Mercury
Metro.: Metromedia
Mon.: Monument
Mus.: Musicor
Nash.: Nashville
Nug.: Nugget
Pick.: Pickwick
Pop.: Poppy
Reb.: Rebel
Rep.: Reprise
Roy. Am.: Royal American
Sma.: Smash
Star.: Starday
UA: United Artists
Van.: Vanguard
Voc.: Vocalion
Warn.: Warner Brothers

# DISCOGRAPHY

## ACUFF, ROY

| TITLE | LABEL | RECORD NO. |
|---|---|---|
| Greatest Hits | Col. | CS-1034 |
| "Great Speckled Bird" and Other Favorites | Col. | HS-11289 |
| Night Train to Memphis | Col. | HS-11403 |
| Waiting for My Call to Glory | Col. | HS-11334 |
| Roy Acuff and the Smoky Mountain Boys | Cap. | DT-1870 |
| All-Time Greatest Hits | Hick. | LPS-109 |

## ALAN, BUDDY

| | | |
|---|---|---|
| Best of Buddy Alan | Cap. | ST-11019 |

## ALLEN, REX

| | | |
|---|---|---|
| Mister Cowboy | Dec. | 78776 |
| Sings and Tells Tales | Mer. | 16324 |

## ANDERSON, BILL

| | | |
|---|---|---|
| Still | MCA | DL-7-4427 |
| I Love You Drops | MCA | DL-7-4771 |
| Greatest Hits | MCA | MCA-13 |
| Where Have All Our Heroes Gone? | MCA | DL-7-5254 |
| Always Remember | MCA | DL-7-5275 |
| Greatest Hits, Vol. 2 | MCA | DL-7-5315 |
| All the Lonely Women in the World | MCA | DL-7-5344 |
| Don't She Look Good | MCA | DL-7-5383 |
| The Bill Anderson Story | MCA | MCA-2-4001 |
| Bill | MCA | MCA-320 |
| Bill Anderson's Country Style | MCA | VL-7-3835 |
| Just Plain Bill | MCA | VL-7-3927 |
| I Can Do Nothing Alone | MCA | CB-20002 |
| For Loving You (with Jan Howard) | MCA | DL-7-4959 |
| Bill and Jan (with Jan Howard) | MCA | DL-7-5293 |
| Singing His Praise (with Jan Howard) | MCA | DL-7-5339 |
| That Casual Country Feeling (Bill Anderson's Po' Boys) | MCA | DL-7-5278 |
| The Rich Sound of Bill Anderson's Po' Boys | MCA | MCA-337 |
| Christmas | MCA | DL-75161 |

## ANDERSON, LIZ

| | | |
|---|---|---|
| If the Creek Don't Rise | RCA | 4222-H |

## ANDERSON, LYNN

| TITLE | LABEL | RECORD NO. |
| --- | --- | --- |
| The Christmas Album | Col. | C-30957 |
| Cry | Col. | KC-31316 |
| Greatest Hits | Col. | KC-31641 |
| How Can I Unlove You? | Col. | C-30925 |
| Keep Me in Mind | Col. | KC-32078 |
| Listen to a Country Song | Col. | KC-31647 |
| Rose Garden | Col. | C-30411 |
| A Woman Lives for Love | Har. | KH-30760 |
| The World of Lynn Anderson | Col. | G-30902 |
| You're My Man | Col. | C-30793 |

## ARNOLD, EDDY

| All-Time Favorites | RCA | LSP-1223 |
| --- | --- | --- |
| Anytime | RCA | LSP-1224 |
| The Chapel on the Hill | RCA | LSP-1225 |
| A Dozen Hits | RCA | LSP-1293 |
| Eddy Arnold Sings Them Again | RCA | LSP-2185 |
| Christmas with Eddy Arnold | RCA | LSP-2554 |
| Cattle Call | RCA | LSP-2578 |
| Faithfully Yours | RCA | LSP-2629 |
| Pop Hits from the Country Side | RCA | LSP-2951 |
| My World | RCA | LSP-3466 |
| The Best of Eddy Arnold | RCA | LSP-3565 |
| The Romantic World of Eddy Arnold | RCA | LSP-4009 |
| The Warmth of Eddy | RCA | LSP-4231 |
| The Best of Eddy Arnold, Vol. 2 | RCA | LSP-4320 |
| Welcome to My World | RCA | LSP-4570 |
| Loving Her Was Easier | RCA | LSP-4625 |
| Lonely People | RCA | LSP-4718 |
| Eddy Arnold Sings for Housewives and Other Lovers | RCA | LSP-4738 |
| The Best of Eddy Arnold, Vol. 3 | RCA | LSP-4844 |
| The World of Eddy Arnold | RCA | APL-1-0239 |
| This is Eddy Arnold | RCA | VPS-6032 |
| The Everlovin' World of Eddy Arnold | RCA | LSP-3931 |

## ASHLEY, CLARENCE

| Old-Time Music at Clarence Ashley's | Folk. | 2355 |
| --- | --- | --- |

## ASHWORTH, ERNIE

| Talk Back, Trembling Lips | Hick. | 118 |
| --- | --- | --- |

# DISCOGRAPHY

## ATCHER, BOB

| TITLE | LABEL | RECORD NO. |
|---|---|---|
| Bob Atcher, Dean of Cowboy Singers | Col. | CS-9032 |
| Bob Atcher's Best Early American Folk Songs | Har. | HL-7313 |

## ATKINS, CHET

| | | |
|---|---|---|
| Stringin' Along with Chet Atkins | RCA | LSP-1236 |
| Finger-Style Guitar | RCA | LSP-1383 |
| Christmas with Chet Atkins | RCA | LSP-2423 |
| Down Home | RCA | LSP-2450 |
| Chet Atkins Plays Back-Home Hymns | RCA | LSP-2601 |
| Guitar Country | RCA | LSP-2783 |
| The Best of Chet Atkins | RCA | LSP-2887 |
| Reminiscing (with Hank Snow) | RCA | LSP-2952 |
| Chet Atkins Picks on the Beatles | RCA | LSP-3531 |
| The Best of Chet Atkins, Vol. 2 | RCA | LSP-3558 |
| It's a Guitar World | RCA | LSP-3728 |
| Chet Atkins Picks the Best | RCA | LSP-3818 |
| Class Guitar | RCA | LSP-3885 |
| Solid Gold '68 | RCA | LSP-4061 |
| Lover's Guitar | RCA | LSP-4135 |
| Solid Gold '69 | RCA | LSP-4244 |
| C.B. Atkins and C.E. Snow by Special Request | RCA | LSP-4254 |
| Me and Jerry (with Jerry Reed) | RCA | LSP-4396 |
| "For the Good Times" and Other Country Moods | RCA | LSP-4464 |
| Pickin' My Way | RCA | LSP-4585 |
| Me and Chet (with Jerry Reed) | RCA | LSP-4707 |
| Chet Atkins Picks on the Hits | RCA | LSP-4754 |
| Alone | RCA | APL-1-0159 |
| This Is Chet Atkins | RCA | VPS-6030 |
| Chet Atkins—Now and Then—Special Anniversary Issue | RCA | VPSX-6079 |
| The "Pops" Goes Country (with Arthur Fiedler, Boston Pops) | RCA | LSC-2870 |
| Chet Picks on the Pops (with Arthur Fiedler, Boston Pops) | RCA | LSC-3104 |
| My Favorite Guitars | RCA | LSP-3316 |
| Hometown Guitar | RCA | LSP-4017 |

## AUTRY, GENE

| | | |
|---|---|---|
| Back in the Saddle Again | Col. | HS-11276 |
| Country Music Hall of Fame Album | Col. | CS-1035 |
| "You Are My Sunshine" and Other Great Hits | Col. | HS-11199 |

## BARE, BOBBY

| | | |
|---|---|---|
| What Am I Gonna Do | Mer. | SR-61363 |

| TITLE | LABEL | RECORD NO. |
|---|---|---|
| Tunes for Two (with Skeeter Davis) | RCA | LSP-3336 |
| The Best of Bobby Bare | RCA | LSP-3479 |
| The Real Thing | RCA | LSP-4422 |
| "I Hate Goodbyes"/"Ride Me Down Easy" | RCA | APL-1-0040 |
| This Is Bobby Bare | RCA | VPS-6090 |

## BEAVERS, CLYDE

| | | |
|---|---|---|
| The Love and Hurting Side of Clyde Beavers | KC | K-1001 |

## BEE, MOLLY

| | | |
|---|---|---|
| Swingin' Country | MGM | E/SE-4423 |

## BELEW, CARL

| | | |
|---|---|---|
| Twelve Sides of Carl Belew | RCA | LSP-3919 |
| Another Lonely Night | Pick. | (S)6013 |

## BOGGS, DOCK

| | | |
|---|---|---|
| Dock Boggs | Folk. | 2351 |
| Legendary Dock Boggs | Verve/Fore | (S)9025 |
| Interview (w. Mike Seeger) | | |
|    Vol. 1 | Folk. | 2132 |
|    Vol. 2 | Folk. | 2392 |

## BOND, JOHNNY

| | | |
|---|---|---|
| Johnny Bond | Star. | (S)147 |
| Songs That Made Him Famous | Star. | 227 |
| Best of Johnny Bond | Har. | 7308 |

## BOOTH, TONY

| | | |
|---|---|---|
| On the Right Track | MGM | 4704 |
| Key's in the Mailbox | Cap. | ST-11076 |
| Lonesome, 7-7203 | Cap. | ST-11126 |

# DISCOGRAPHY

## BOWMAN, DON

| TITLE | LABEL | RECORD NO. |
|---|---|---|
| Funny Folk Flops | RCA | LSP-3920 |

## BRITT, ELTON

| | | |
|---|---|---|
| Elton Britt Yodel Songs | RCA | LPM-1288 |
| The Best of Elton Britt, Vol. 2 | RCA | LSP-4822 |

## BROWN, JIM ED

| | | |
|---|---|---|
| Just for You | RCA | LSP-4366 |
| Morning | RCA | LSP-4461 |
| She's Leavin' | RCA | LSP-4614 |
| Evening | RCA | LSP-4713 |
| Brown Is Blue | RCA | LSP-4755 |
| Barrooms and Pop-A-Tops | RCA | APL-1-0172 |

## BUFFETT, JIMMY

| | | |
|---|---|---|
| Down to Earth | Barn. | Z-30093 |
| A White Sport Coat and a Pink Crustacean | ABC | DSV-50150 |

## BUSH, JOHNNY

| | | |
|---|---|---|
| Here Comes the World Again | RCA | ALP-0216 |
| Whiskey River/There Stands the Glass | RCA | LSP-4817 |

## BUTLER, CARL AND PEARL LEE

| | | |
|---|---|---|
| Honky-Tonkin' | Col. | 9769 |

## CAMPBELL, ARCHIE

| | | |
|---|---|---|
| Golden Years | RCA | LSP-3892 |

## CAMPBELL, GLEN

| | | |
|---|---|---|
| Wichita Lineman | Cap. | ST-103 |
| Galveston | Cap. | ST-210 |

| TITLE | LABEL | RECORD NO. |
|---|---|---|
| Glen Campbell "Live" | Cap. | STBO-268 |
| Try a Little Kindness | Cap. | SW-389 |
| Oh Happy Day | Cap. | SW-443 |
| The Glen Campbell Goodtime Album | Cap. | SW-493 |
| The Last Time I Saw Her | Cap. | SW-733 |
| Glen Campbell's Greatest Hits | Cap. | SW-752 |
| Anne Murray/Glen Campbell | Cap. | SW-869 |
| Gentle on My Mind | Cap. | ST-2809 |
| Time I Get to Phoenix | Cap. | ST-2851 |
| Glen Travis Campbell | Cap. | SW-11117 |
| I Knew Jesus (Before He Was a Superstar) | Cap. | SW-11185 |

## CARGILL, HENSON

| | | |
|---|---|---|
| Coming on Strong | Col. | SLP-18103 |
| The Uncomplicated Henson Cargill | Col. | SLP-18137 |
| Welcome to My World | Har. | KH-31397 |
| This is Henson Cargill Country | At. | SD-7279 |

## CARLISLE, BILL

| | | |
|---|---|---|
| Best of Bill Carlisle | Hick. | (S)129 |

## CARSON, MARTHA LOU

| | | |
|---|---|---|
| Martha Carson Sings | Cam. | CAS-906 |
| Satisfied | Cap. | T-1507 |
| Talk with the Lord | Cap. | T-1607 |

## THE CARTER FAMILY

| | | |
|---|---|---|
| The Best of The Carter Family | Col. | CS-9119 |
| The Famous Carter Family | Col. | HS-11332 |
| I Walk the Line | Col. | HS-11392 |
| Travelin' Minstrel Band | Col. | KC-31454 |
| Give My Love to Rose | Har. | KH-31256 |
| 'Mid the Green Fields of Virginia | RCA | LPM-2772 |
| Mother Maybelle Carter (2 records) | Col. | KG-32436 |

## CARTER, WILF (MONTANA SLIM)

| | | |
|---|---|---|
| No Letter Today | Cam. | CAS2171 |
| Thirty-two Wonderful Years | Cam. | 847 (s) |
| Living Legend | Star. | 300 |

331

# DISCOGRAPHY

## CARVER, JOHNNY

| TITLE | LABEL | RECORD NO. |
|---|---|---|
| Tie a Yellow Ribbon | ABC | X-792 |

## CASH, JOHNNY

| | | |
|---|---|---|
| America/A 200-Year Salute | Col. | KC-31645 |
| Any Old Wind that Blows | Col. | KC-32091 |
| At Folsom Prison | Col. | CS-9639 |
| At San Quentin | Col. | CS-9827 |
| Ballads of the True West | Col. | C2S-838 |
| Bitter Tears/Ballads of the American Indian | Col. | CS-9048 |
| Blood, Sweat and Tears | Col. | CS-8730 |
| Carryin' on with J. Cash and June Carter | Col. | CS-9528 |
| Christmas | Col. | KC-31754 |
| The Christmas Spirit | Col. | CS-8917 |
| Everybody Loves a Nut | Col. | CS-9292 |
| Give My Love to Rose | Har. | KH-31256 |
| The Gospel Road | Col. | KG-32253 |
| Greatest Hits, Vol. 1 | Col. | CS-9478 |
| Greatest Hits, Vol. 2 | Col. | KC-30887 |
| The Holy Land | Col. | CS-9726 |
| Hymns by Johnny Cash | Col. | CS-8125 |
| Hymns from the Heart | Col. | CS-8522 |
| I Can See Clearly Now | Epic | NE-31607 |
| I Walk the Line | Col. | CS-8990 |
| The Johnny Cash Show | Col. | KC-30100 |
| The Johnny Cash Songbook | Har. | KH-31602 |
| Man in Black | Col. | C-30550 |
| Mean as Hell/Ballads from the True West | Col. | CS-9246 |
| Orange Blossom Special | Col. | CS-9109 |
| Ride This Train | Col. | CS-8255 |
| Ring of Fire | Col. | CS-8853 |
| A Thing Called Love | Col. | KC-31332 |
| This is Johnny Cash | Col. | HS-11342 |
| Understand Your Man | Har. | KH-30916 |
| The Walls of a Prison | Har. | KH-30138 |
| The World of Johnny Cash | Col. | GP-29 |

## CASH, TOMMY

| | | |
|---|---|---|
| The American Way of Life | Epic | E-30860 |
| The Best of Tommy Cash, Vol. 1 | Epic | KE-31995 |

## CLARK, ROY

| | | |
|---|---|---|
| Urban Suburban/The Fantastic Guitar of Roy Clark | Dot | DLP-25863 |
| Yesterday When I Was Young | Dot | DLP-25953 |

| TITLE | LABEL | RECORD NO. |
|---|---|---|
| The Everlovin' Soul of Roy Clark | Dot | DLP-25972 |
| The Other Side of Roy Clark | Dot | DLP-25977 |
| I Never Picked Cotton | Dot | DLP-25980 |
| The Best of Roy Clark | Dot | DOS-25986 |
| The Incredible Roy Clark | Dot | DOS-25990 |
| Magnificent Sanctuary Band | Dot | DOS-25993 |
| Roy Clark Country | Dot | DOS-25997 |
| Roy Clark Live! | Dot | DOS-26005 |
| Superpicker | Dot | DOS-26008 |
| Roy Clark's Greatest! | Cap. | SKAO-369 |
| Lightning Fingers of Roy Clark | Cap. | ST-1780 |
| Roy Clark Guitar Spectacular | Cap. | ST-2425 |
| Come Live with Me | Dot | DOS-26010 |

## CLINE, PATSY

| | | |
|---|---|---|
| The Patsy Cline Story | MCA | DXSB-7176 |
| Patsy Cline Showcase | MCA | DL-74202 |
| Sentimentally Yours | MCA | DL-74282 |
| A Portrait of Patsy Cline | MCA | DL-74508 |
| Greatest Hits | MCA | MCA-12 |
| Here's Patsy Cline | MCA | VL-73753 |

## COCHRAN, HANK

| | | |
|---|---|---|
| Hits from the Heart | RCA | LSP-3303 |
| Going in Training | RCA | LSP-3431 |

## COOPER, WILMA LEE AND STONEY

| | | |
|---|---|---|
| Sunny Side of the Mountain | Har. | HS-1178 |

## COPAS, COWBOY

| | | |
|---|---|---|
| All-Time Hits | King | 553 |
| Country Gentleman | King | 817 |
| As You Remember | King | 824 |

## THE COUNTRY GENTLEMEN

| | | |
|---|---|---|
| The Country Gentlemen | Van. | VSD-79331 |
| The Award-Winning Country Gentlemen | Reb. | 1506 |
| Yesterday and Today | Reb. | 1521 |

# DISCOGRAPHY

## CRADDOCK, BILLY "CRASH"

| TITLE | LABEL | RECORD NO. |
|---|---|---|
| Knock Three Times | Cart. | 037-001 |
| Mr. Country Rock | ABC | X-788 |

## CRAMER, FLOYD

| | | |
|---|---|---|
| Floyd Cramer Goes Honky-Tonkin' | MGM | 4666 |
| Last Date | RCA | LSP-2350 |
| I Remember Hank Williams | RCA | LSP-2544 |
| Cramer at the Console | RCA | LSP-2883 |
| The Best of Floyd Cramer | RCA | LSP-2888 |
| Hits from the Country Hall of Fame | RCA | LSP-3318 |
| We Wish You a Merry Christmas | RCA | LSP-3828 |
| Floyd Cramer Plays Country Classics | RCA | LSP-3935 |
| The Best of Floyd Cramer, Vol. 2 | RCA | LSP-4091 |
| More Country Classics | RCA | LSP-4220 |
| The Big Ones, Vol. 2 | RCA | LSP-4312 |
| Floyd Cramer with the Music City Pops | RCA | LSP-4364 |
| Class of '70 | RCA | LSP-4437 |
| Sounds of Sunday | RCA | LSP-4500 |
| Class of '71 | RCA | LSP-4590 |
| Floyd Cramer Detours | RCA | LSP-4676 |
| Class of '72 | RCA | LSP-4773 |
| Best of the Class of | RCA | LSP-4821 |
| Super Country Hits | RCA | APD-1-0155 |
| This Is Floyd Cramer | RCA | VPS-6031 |

## CURLESS, DICK

| | | |
|---|---|---|
| Hard, Hard Traveling Man | Cap. | ST-552 |
| Doggin' It | Cap. | ST-689 |
| Comin' On Country | Cap. | ST-792 |
| Tombstone Every Mile | Cap. | ST-11011 |
| Stonin' Around | Cap. | ST-11087 |
| Live at Wheeling Jamboree | Cap. | ST-11119 |

## DAVIS, DANNY (THE NASHVILLE BRASS)

| | | |
|---|---|---|
| The Nashville Brass Play the Nashville Sound | RCA | LSP-4059 |
| The Nashville Brass Featuring Danny Davis Play More Nashville Sounds | RCA | LSP-4176 |
| Movin' On | RCA | LSP-4232 |
| Hank Locklin and Danny Davis and the Nashville Brass | RCA | LSP-4318 |

| TITLE | LABEL | RECORD NO. |
|---|---|---|
| You Ain't Heard Nothin' Yet | RCA | LSP-4334 |
| Christmas with Danny Davis and the Nashville Brass | RCA | LSP-4377 |
| Down Homers | RCA | LSP-4424 |
| Somethin' Else | RCA | LSP-4576 |
| Super Country | RCA | LSP-4571 |
| Nashville Brass Turns to Gold | RCA | LSP-4627 |
| Live—In Person! | RCA | LSP-4720 |
| Turn On Some Happy! | RCA | LSP-4803 |
| Travelin' | RCA | APD-1-0034 |
| Caribbean Cruise | RCA | APL-1-0232 |

## DAVIS, JIMMIE

| | | |
|---|---|---|
| Sweet Hour of Prayer | MCA | DL-7-4087 |
| How Great Thou Art | MCA | DL-7-4322 |
| Highway to Heaven | MCA | DL-7-4432 |
| Singing the Gospel | MCA | DL-7-4976 |
| Greatest Hits | MCA | DL-7-4978 |
| Let Me Walk with Jesus | MCA | DL-7-5085 |
| Songs of Consolation | MCA | DL-7-5199 |
| Old Baptizing Creek | MCA | DL-7-5273 |
| What a Happy Day | MCA | DL-7-5331 |
| Near the Cross | MCA | DL-7-5184 |
| You Are My Sunshine | MCA | DL-7-8896 |
| Suppertime | MCA | DL-7-8953 |
| Memories Coming Home | MCA | DL-7-5387 |
| God's Last Altar Call | MCA | MCA-323 |
| Amazing Grace | MCA | VL-7-3863 |
| No One Stands Alone | MCA | VL-7-3676 |
| In My Father's House | MCA | VL-7-3878 |
| Country Side of Jimmie Davis | MCA | CB-20004 |
| By Popular Demand | MCA | DL-74429 |

## DAVIS, MAC

| | | |
|---|---|---|
| I Believe in Music | Col. | C-30926 |
| Baby, Don't Get Hooked on Me | Col. | KC-31770 |

## DAVIS, SKEETER

| | | |
|---|---|---|
| Here's the Answer | RCA | LSP-2327 |
| Tunes for Two (with Bobby Bare) | RCA | LSP-3336 |
| The Best of Skeeter Davis | RCA | LSP-3374 |
| Hand in Hand with Jesus | RCA | LSP-3763 |
| A Place in the Country | RCA | LSP-4310 |

# DISCOGRAPHY

| TITLE | LABEL | RECORD NO. |
|---|---|---|
| It's Hard to Be a Woman | RCA | LSP-4382 |
| Skeeter | RCA | LSP-4486 |
| Love Takes a Lot of My Time | RCA | LSP-4557 |
| Bring It on Home to Me | RCA | LSP-4642 |
| Skeeter Sings Dolly | RCA | LSP-4732 |
| The Hillbilly Singer | RCA | LSP-4818 |
| The Best of Skeeter Davis, Vol. 2 | RCA | APL-1-0190 |
| The End of the World | RCA | CAS-2607 |

## DEAN, JIMMY

| | | |
|---|---|---|
| The Country's Favorite Son | Col. | HS-11270 |
| Gotta Travel On | Col. | HS-11356 |
| Greatest Hits | Col. | CS-9285 |
| Hymns by Jimmy Dean | Col. | HS-11042 |
| My Country Music | Col. | HS-11208 |
| "Most Richly Blessed" and Other Great Inspirational Songs | RCA | LSP-3824 |
| The Jimmy Dean Show Recorded Live At Harrah's Club, Reno | RCA | LSP-3890 |
| Everybody Knows | RCA | LSP-4511 |
| These Hands | RCA | LSP-4618 |

## THE DELMORE BROTHERS

| | | |
|---|---|---|
| Stars of the Grand Ole Opry (this album includes a few cuts of the Delmore Brothers) | RCA | LCM-6015 |

## DENVER, JOHN

| | | |
|---|---|---|
| Rocky Mountain High | RCA | LSP-4731 |
| Poems, Prayers and Promises | RCA | LSP-4499 |

## DEXTER, AL

| | | |
|---|---|---|
| Pistol Packin' Mama | Har. | 7293 |

## DICKENS, LITTLE JIMMY

| | | |
|---|---|---|
| Greatest Hits | Col. | LE-10106H |
| Best of Little Jimmy Dickens | Har. | 7311 |

## THE DILLARDS

| TITLE | LABEL | RECORD NO. |
|---|---|---|
| Wheatstraw Suite | Elek. | 74035 |

## DIXON, DORSEY

| | | |
|---|---|---|
| Dorsey Dixon | Test | 3301 |

## DOLLAR, JOHNNY

| | | |
|---|---|---|
| Big Rig Rollin' Man | Chart | S-1023 |

## DRIFTWOOD, JIMMY

| | | |
|---|---|---|
| Best of Jimmy Driftwood | Mon. | (1)8043 |

## DRUSKY, ROY

| | | |
|---|---|---|
| My Grass Is Green | Mer. | 61233 |
| I'll Make Amends | Mer. | 61260 |
| All My Hard Times | Mer. | 61306 |
| Yesterday's Gone | Mer. | 60919 |
| Country Special | Voc. | 73909 |
| Doin' Something Right | Mer. | 61377 |
| El Paso | Hill. | S-6091 |

## DUDLEY, DAVE

| | | |
|---|---|---|
| The Original Traveling Man | Mer. | 61365 |
| The Best of Dave Dudley | Mer. | SR-61268 |
| Greatest Hits | Mer. | SR-61046 |

## DUNCAN, JOHNNY

| | | |
|---|---|---|
| There's Something About a Lady | Col. | C-30618 |

## EDWARDS, JONATHAN

| | | |
|---|---|---|
| Honky-Tonk Stardust Country | At. | 7015 |

# DISCOGRAPHY

## EDWARDS, STONEY

| TITLE | LABEL | RECORD NO. |
| --- | --- | --- |
| Country Singer | Cap. | ST-741 |
| Down Home in the Country | Cap. | ST-834 |
| Stoney Edwards | Cap. | ST-11090 |

## EVANS, DALE
*See Roy Rogers*

## THE EVERLY BROTHERS

| | | |
| --- | --- | --- |
| End of an Era (2 records) | Barn. | 26-80260 |
| Hit Sound | Warn. | 1676 |
| Pass the Chicken and Listen | RCA | LSP-4781 |
| Roots | Warn. | WS-1752 |

## FAIRCHILD, BARBARA

| | | |
| --- | --- | --- |
| Someone Special | Col. | C-30123 |
| A Sweeter Love | Col. | KC-31720 |
| Kid Stuff | Col. | KC-32711 |

## FARGO, DONNA

| | | |
| --- | --- | --- |
| The Happiest Girl in the Whole U.S.A. | Dot | DOS-26000 |
| My Second Album | Dot | DOS-26006 |
| All About a Feeling | Dot | DOS-26019 |

## FELTS, NARVEL

| | | |
| --- | --- | --- |
| Drift Away | Cinn. | 5000 |

## FLATT, LESTER
*(see also Flatt and Scruggs)*

| | | |
| --- | --- | --- |
| Flatt on Victor | RCA | LSP-4495 |
| Lester 'n' Mac (with Mac Wiseman) | RCA | LSP-4547 |
| Kentucky Ridgerunner | RCA | LSP-4633 |

| TITLE | LABEL | RECORD NO. |
|---|---|---|
| On the South-Bound (with Mac Wiseman) | RCA | LSP-4688 |
| Foggy Mountain Breakdown | RCA | LSP-4789 |
| Country Boy, featuring "Feudin' Banjos" | RCA | APL-1-0131 |
| Over the Hills (with Mac Wiseman) | RCA | APL-1-0309 |

## FLATT AND SCRUGGS
*(see also Lester Flatt; Earl Scruggs)*

| | | |
|---|---|---|
| Flatt and Scruggs | Col. | HS-11314 |
| At Carnegie Hall | Col. | CS-8845 |
| Changin' Times | Col. | CS-9596 |
| The Fabulous Sound of Flatt and Scruggs | Col. | CS-9055 |
| Foggy Mountain Chimes | Col. | HS-11401 |
| Greatest Hits | Col. | CS-9370 |
| Hard Travelin' | Col. | CS-8751 |
| Sacred Songs/Great Original Recordings | Col. | HS-11202 |
| Songs to Cherish | Col. | HS-11265 |
| The Story of Bonnie and Clyde | Col. | CS-9649 |
| Twenty All-Time Great Recordings | Col. | GP-30 |
| Wabash Cannonball | Har. | KH-30932 |
| When the Saints Go Marching In | Col. | CS-9313 |
| The World of Flatt and Scruggs | Col. | KG-31964 |

## FOLEY, RED

| | | |
|---|---|---|
| Songs of Devotion | MCA | MCA-86 |
| Beyond the Sunset | MCA | MCA-147 |
| I Believe | MCA | CB-20059 |
| The Red Foley Story | MCA | DXSB-7177 |
| I'm Bound for the Kingdom | MCA | VL-73745 |
| Red Foley | MCA | VL-73751 |
| Kitty Wells and Red Foley's Golden Favorites | MCA | DL-74109 |

## FORD, TENNESSEE ERNIE

| | | |
|---|---|---|
| Holy, Holy, Holy | Cap. | ST-334 |
| America the Beautiful | Cap. | STAO-412 |
| Tennessee Ernie Ford | Cap. | STBB-506 |
| Everything Is Beautiful | Cap. | ST-583 |
| Abide with Me | Cap. | ST-730 |
| Tennessee Ernie Ford Hymns | Cap. | ST-756 |
| Tennessee Ernie Ford Spirituals | Cap. | ST-818 |
| C-h-r-i-s-t-m-a-s | Cap. | ST-831 |
| The Folk Album | Cap. | ST-833 |
| Near the Cross | Cap. | ST-1005 |

# DISCOGRAPHY

| TITLE | LABEL | RECORD NO. |
|---|---|---|
| A Friend We Have | Cap. | ST-1272 |
| Sixteen Tons | Cap. | DT-1380 |
| Sing a Hymn with Me | Cap. | ST-1679 |
| Book of Favorite Hymns | Cap. | ST-1794 |
| God Lives! | Cap. | ST-2618 |
| Tennessee Ernie Ford Deluxe Set | Cap. | STCL-2942 |
| Mr. Words and Music | Cap. | ST-11001 |
| It's Tennessee Ernie Ford | Cap. | ST-11092 |

## FRIEDMAN, KINKY

| | | |
|---|---|---|
| Sold American | Van. | VSD-79333 |

## FRIZZELL, LEFTY

| | | |
|---|---|---|
| The Legendary Lefty Frizzell | ABC | X-7999 |
| Greatest Hits | Col. | CS-9288 |
| Signed, Sealed, and Delivered | Col. | HS-11260 |

## GENTRY, BOBBIE

| | | |
|---|---|---|
| Patchwork | Cap. | ST-494 |
| Sittin' Pretty/Tobacco Road | Cap. | STBB-704 |

## GIBSON, DON

| | | |
|---|---|---|
| Don Gibson | MGM | 138 |
| The Two of Us Together (with Sue Thompson) | Hick. | LPS-168 |

## THE GLASER BROTHERS

| | | |
|---|---|---|
| Now Country | MGM | 4620 |
| The Award Winners | MGM | 4775 |
| Tompall and the Glaser Brothers Sing Great Hits from Two Decades | MGM | 4888 |

## GLASER, TOMPALL

| | | |
|---|---|---|
| Charlie | MGM | SE-4918 |

## GRAMMER, BILLY

| TITLE | LABEL | RECORD NO. |
|---|---|---|
| Travelin' On | Mon. | (1)8039 |

## GRAY, CLAUDE

| | | |
|---|---|---|
| Claude Gray Sings | Dec. | 74882 |
| Easy Way | Dec. | 75963 |
| Treasure of Love | Hill. | S-6051 |

## THE GREENBRIAR BOYS

| | | |
|---|---|---|
| Best of the Greenbriar Boys | Van. | 79317 |

## GREENE, JACK

| | | |
|---|---|---|
| There Goes My Everything | MCA | DL-7-4845 |
| I Am Not Alone | MCA | DL-7-5080 |
| Greatest Hits | MCA | DL-7-5208 |
| There's a Whole Lot About a Woman a Man Don't Know | MCA | DL-7-5283 |
| Greene Country | MCA | DL-7-5308 |
| The Last Letter | MCA | VL-7-3926 |
| Love Stories | MCA | CB-20009 |
| Jack Greene and Jeannie Seely | MCA | DL-7-5171 |
| Two for the Show (with Jeannie Seely) | MCA | DL-7-5392 |

## GUTHRIE, WOODY

| | | |
|---|---|---|
| Dust Bowl Ballads | RCA | LPU-502 |
| Library of Congress Recordings (3 records) | Elek. | 271-2 |

## THE HAGERS

| | | |
|---|---|---|
| Countryside | Barn. | 15002 |
| Motherhood, Apple Pie, and the Flag | Cap. | ST-783 |

# DISCOGRAPHY

## HAGGARD, MERLE

| TITLE | LABEL | RECORD NO. |
|---|---|---|
| Pride in What I Am | Cap. | SKAO-168 |
| Same Train, Different Time | Cap. | SWBB-223 |
| A Portrait of Merle Haggard | Cap. | ST-319 |
| Okie from Muskogee | Cap. | ST-384 |
| Fightin' Side of Me | Cap. | ST-451 |
| Tribute to Best Fiddle Player | Cap. | ST-638 |
| Sing a Sad Song (2 records) | Cap. | STBB-707 |
| Hag (with The Strangers) | Cap. | ST-735 |
| Many Churches (2 records) | Cap. | SWBO-803 |
| Someday We'll Look Back | Cap. | ST-835 |
| Let Me Tell You About Song | Cap. | ST-882 |
| Strangers | Cap. | ST-2373 |
| Swinging Doors (with The Strangers) | Cap. | ST-2585 |
| I'm a Lonesome Fugitive | Cap. | ST-2702 |
| Branded Man (with The Strangers) | Cap. | ST-2789 |
| Sing Me Back Home | Cap. | ST-2848 |
| The Best of Merle Haggard | Cap. | SKAO-2951 |
| Mama Tried | Cap. | ST-2972 |
| Best of the Best of Merle Haggard | Cap. | ST-11082 |
| It's Not Love | Cap. | ST-11127 |
| Totally Instrumental | Cap. | ST-11141 |

## HALL, TOM T.

| | | |
|---|---|---|
| The Ballad of Forty Dollars and His Other Great Songs | Mer. | SR-61211 |
| Homecoming | Mer. | SR-61247 |
| I Witness Life | Mer. | SR-61277 |
| Tom T. Hall Sings "One Hundred Children" | Mer. | SR-61307 |
| In Search of a Song | Mer. | SR-61350 |
| We All Got Together and . . . | Mer. | SR-61362 |
| The Storyteller | Mer. | SR-61368 |
| Greatest Hits | Mer. | SR-61369 |
| The Rhymer and Other Five-and-Dimers | Mer. | SRM-1-668 |

## HAMBLEN, STUART

| | | |
|---|---|---|
| It Is No Secret | RCA | LPM-1253 |
| Spell of the Yukon | Col. | CS-8388 |

## HAMILTON, GEORGE, IV

| | | |
|---|---|---|
| Country Music in My Soul | RCA | LSP-4700 |
| Down Home in the Country | RCA | LSP-4435 |

| TITLE | LABEL | RECORD NO. |
|---|---|---|
| Early Morning Rain | Cam. | S-2468 |
| International Ambassador | RCA | LSP-4826 |
| West Texas Highway | RCA | LSP-4609 |

## THE HARDEN TRIO

| | | |
|---|---|---|
| Tippy-toeing | Col. | CS-9306 |

## HART, FREDDIE

| | | |
|---|---|---|
| Just Us Three (with Sammi Smith, Jerry Reed) | Har. | H-31499 |
| Lonesome Love | Har. | KH-31165 |
| The World of Freddie Hart | Col. | G-31550 |
| California Grapevine | Cap. | ST-593 |
| Easy Loving | Cap. | ST-838 |
| My Hang-up Is You | Cap. | ST-11014 |
| Bless Your Heart | Cap. | ST-11073 |
| Super Kind of Woman | Cap. | ST-11156 |
| Got the All-Overs for You | Cap. | ST-11107 |
| Born a Fool | MCA | CB-20011 |
| Straight from the Heart | MCA | VL-73929 |

## HAWKINS, HAWKSHAW

| | | |
|---|---|---|
| Hawkshaw Hawkins | King | 592 |
| All New | King | 808 |
| Hawkshaw Hawkins and Cowboy Copas | King | 835 |
| Bandstand | King | 847 |
| The Legend | King | 850 |

## HELMS, BOBBY

| | | |
|---|---|---|
| Fraulein | Har. | 11209 |

## HILL, GOLDIE

| | | |
|---|---|---|
| Heartaches | Dec. | (7)4148 |

# DISCOGRAPHY

## HOLLY, DOYLE

| TITLE | LABEL | RECORD NO. |
|---|---|---|
| Just Another Cowboy Song | Barn. | BR-15001 |

## HOMER AND JETHRO

| | | |
|---|---|---|
| The Best of Homer and Jethro | RCA | LSP-3474 |

## HORTON, JOHNNY

| | | |
|---|---|---|
| The Battle of New Orleans | Har. | KH-30394 |
| Greatest Hits | Col. | CS-8396 |
| Honky-Tonk Man | Col. | CS-8779 |
| Johnny Horton Makes History | Col. | CS-8269 |
| The Legendary Johnny Horton | Col. | HS-11384 |
| On Stage | Col. | CS-9366 |
| The Spectacular Johnny Horton | Col. | CS-8167 |
| The Unforgettable Johnny Horton | Col. | HS-11291 |
| The World of Johnny Horton | Col. | G-30884 |

## HOUSTON, DAVID

| | | |
|---|---|---|
| David Houston | Col. | HS-11412 |
| David Houston | Col. | EG-30437 |
| The Day That Love Walked In | Epic | KE-31385 |
| Gentle on My Mind | Har. | H-31027 |
| Good Things | Epic | KE-32189 |
| Greatest Hits | Col. | BN-26342 |
| The Many Sides of David Houston | Har. | KH-31778 |
| Old-Time Religion | Har. | KH-32287 |
| A Perfect Match (with Barbara Mandrell) | Epic | KE-31705 |

## HOWARD, JAN

| | | |
|---|---|---|
| Love Is Like a Spinning Wheel | MCA | DL-7-5333 |
| Bad Seed | MCA | CB-20007 |
| For Loving You (with Bill Anderson) | MCA | DL-7-4959 |
| Bill and Jan (with Bill Anderson) | MCA | DL-7-5293 |
| Singing His Praise (with Bill Anderson) | MCA | DL-7-5339 |

## HUSKY, FERLIN

| TITLE | LABEL | RECORD NO. |
|---|---|---|
| The Best of Ferlin Husky | Cap. | SKAO-143 |
| Just Plain Lonely | Cap. | ST-11069 |
| True True Lovin' | ABC | X-776 |
| One More Time | Cap. | ST-768 |
| Green, Green Grass of Home | Hill. | S-6086 |

## IAN AND SYLVIA

| | | |
|---|---|---|
| Great Speckled Bird | Amp. | 10103 |
| Greatest Hits, Vol. 1 (2 records) | Van. | VSD-5/6 |
| Greatest Hits, Vol. 2 (2 records) | Van. | VSD-23/4 |
| Ian and Sylvia | MGM | GAS-115 |

## IVES, BURL

| | | |
|---|---|---|
| Payin' My Dues Again | MCA | MCA-318 |
| Greatest Hits | MCA | MCA-114 |
| Song Book | MCA | CB-20029 |
| The Best of Burl Ives | MCA | DXSB-7167 |
| Sons of the West | MCA | DL-74179 |
| The Best of Burl's for Boys and Girls | MCA | DL-74390 |
| Burl Ives Sings Pearly Shells | MCA | DL-74578 |
| Have a Holly Jolly Christmas | MCA | DL-74689 |
| Greatest Hits | MCA | MCA-114 |

## JACKSON, STONEWALL

| | | |
|---|---|---|
| The Exciting Stonewall Jackson | Col. | HS-11187 |
| Greatest Hits | Col. | CS-9177 |
| Greatest Hits, Vol. 2 | Col. | CS-9770 |
| I Pawned My Past Today | Col. | HS-11324 |
| Me and You and a Dog Named Boo | Col. | C-30924 |
| Recorded Live at the Grand Ole Opry | Col. | C-30469 |
| Thoughts of a Lonely Man | Col. | HS-11256 |
| Waterloo | Har. | H-30936 |
| The World of Stonewall Jackson | Col. | KG-31411 |

## JACKSON, WANDA

| | | |
|---|---|---|
| I Wouldn't Want You Any Other Way | Cap. | ST-11096 |
| Leave My Baby Alone | Hill. | S-6074 |

# DISCOGRAPHY

| TITLE | LABEL | RECORD NO. |
|---|---|---|
| Praise the Lord | Cap. | ST-11023 |
| We'll Sing in the Sunshine | Hill. | 6116 |

**JAMES, SONNY**

| | | |
|---|---|---|
| The Greatest Country Hits of 1972 | Col. | KC-32028 |
| When the Snow is on the Roses | Col. | KC-31646 |
| Astrodome Presents Sonny James | Cap. | ST-320 |
| Sonny James | Cap. | STBB-535 |
| Sonny James Sings No. 1 Country Hits | Cap. | ST-629 |
| The Biggest Hits of Sonny James | Cap. | ST-11013 |
| Traces | Cap. | ST-11108 |
| Empty Arms | Cap. | ST-734 |
| Young Love | Cap. | ST-11196 |
| The Gentleman from the South | Cap. | ST-11144 |

**JEAN, NORMA**

| | | |
|---|---|---|
| Jackson Ain't a Very Big Town | RCA | LSP-3836 |
| The Only Way to Hold Your Man | RCA | APL-1-0170 |
| The Best of Norma Jean | RCA | LSP-4227 |
| It's Time for Norma Jean | RCA | LSP-4446 |
| Norma Jean | RCA | LSP-4510 |
| Norma Jean Sings | RCA | LSP-4587 |
| Thank You for Loving Me | RCA | LSP-4691 |
| I Guess That Comes from Being Poor | RCA | LSP-4745 |

**JENNINGS, WAYLON**

| | | |
|---|---|---|
| Waylon | RCA | LSP-4260 |
| The Best of Waylon Jennings | RCA | LSP-4341 |
| Singer of Sad Songs | RCA | LSP-4418 |
| The Taker/Tulsa | RCA | LSP-4487 |
| Cedartown, Georgia | RCA | LSP-4567 |
| Good-Hearted Woman | RCA | LSP-4647 |
| Ladies Love Outlaws | RCA | LSP-4751 |
| Lonesome, On'ry and Mean | RCA | LSP-4854 |
| Honky-Tonk Heroes | RCA | APL-1-0240 |

**JIM AND JESSE (McREYNOLDS)**

| | | |
|---|---|---|
| Diesel on My Tail | Col. | BN-26314 |
| Wildwood Flower | Col. | HS-11399 |

346

## JONES, GEORGE

| TITLE | LABEL | RECORD NO. |
| --- | --- | --- |
| Let's Build a World Together (with Tammy Wynette) | Epic | KE-32113 |
| Me and the First Lady (with Tammy Wynette) | Epic | KE-31554 |
| A Picture of Me (Without You) | Epic | KE-31718 |
| We Go Together (with Tammy Wynette) | Epic | KE-30802 |
| We Love to Sing About Jesus (with Tammy Wynette) | Epic | KE-31719 |
| First in the Hearts of Country Music Lovers | RCA | LSP-4672 |
| The Best of George Jones, Vol. 1 | RCA | LSP-4716 |
| Poor Man's Riches | RCA | LSP-4725 |
| I Made Leaving (Easy for You) | RCA | LSP-4726 |
| Country Singer | RCA | LSP-4727 |
| George Jones "And Friends" | RCA | LSP-4733 |
| Four-O-Thirty-Three | RCA | LSP-4785 |
| Tender Years | RCA | LSP-4786 |
| Take Me | RCA | LSP-4787 |
| Wrapped Around Her Finger | RCA | LSP-4801 |
| I Can Still See Him in Your Eyes | RCA | LSP-4847 |
| Nothing Ever Hurt Me (Half as Bad as Losing You) | Epic | KE-32412 |

## JONES, GRANDPA

| | | |
| --- | --- | --- |
| Everybody's Grandpa | Col. | SLP-18083 |
| Hits from *Hee Haw* | Col. | SLP-18131 |
| Live | Har. | H-31396 |
| Pickin' Time | MCA | VL-73900 |

## THE JORDANAIRES

| | | |
| --- | --- | --- |
| Monster Makers | Stop | 10010 |

## KAZEE, BUELL

| | | |
| --- | --- | --- |
| Songs and Music of Buell Kazee | Folk. | 3810 |

## KERSHAW, DOUG

| | | |
| --- | --- | --- |
| Devil's Elbow | Warn. | 2649 |
| Doug Kershaw | Warn. | S-1906 |
| Spanish Moss | Warn. | S-1861 |
| Swamp Grass | Warn. | BS-2581 |

# DISCOGRAPHY

### KILGORE, MERLE

| TITLE | LABEL | RECORD NO. |
|---|---|---|
| Ring of Fire | Hill. | S-6084 |
| Merle Kilgore | Mer. | 13661 |

### KINCAID, BRADLEY

| Mountain Ballads and Old-Time Songs | | |
|---|---|---|
| Vol. 1 | Blue. | 105 |
| Vol. 2 | Blue. | 107 |
| Vol. 3 | Blue. | 109 |
| Vol. 4 | Blue. | 112 |

### KING, CLAUDE

| | | |
|---|---|---|
| Tiger Woman | Col. | CS-9215 |
| Meet Claude King | Col. | CL-1810 |
| Chip 'n' Dale's Place | Col. | C-30804 |

### KING, PEE WEE

| | | |
|---|---|---|
| "Tennessee Waltz" and "Slowpoke" | Nash. | 2042 |
| Country Barn Dance | Camb. | CAS-876 |
| Pee Wee King and Redd Stewart | Star. | 284 |

### KRISTOFFERSON, KRIS

| | | |
|---|---|---|
| Border Lord | Mon. | KZ-31302 |
| Jesus was a Capricorn | Mon. | KZ-31909 |
| Me and Bobby McGee | Mon. | Z-30817 |
| Silver-tongued Devil and I | Mon. | Z-30679 |

### LANE, RED

| | | |
|---|---|---|
| The World Needs a Melody | RCA | LSP-4576 |

### LEE, BRENDA

| | | |
|---|---|---|
| Memphis Portrait | Dec. | 75232 |
| Ten Golden Years | MCA | DL-7-4757 |

| TITLE | LABEL | RECORD NO. |
|---|---|---|
| Brenda | MCA | MCA-305 |
| Here's Brenda Lee | MCA | VL-7-3795 |
| Let It Be Me | MCA | VL-7-3890 |
| The Brenda Lee Story/Her Greatest Hits | MCA | MCA-2-4012 |
| Merry Christmas from Brenda Lee | MCA | DL-74583 |

## LEE, DICKEY

| | | |
|---|---|---|
| Never-Ending Song of Love | RCA | LSP-4637 |
| Ashes of Love | RCA | LSP-4715 |
| Baby, Bye-Bye | RCA | LSP-4791 |
| Crying over You | RCA | LSP-4857 |

## LEWIS, JERRY LEE

| | | |
|---|---|---|
| Live at The International, Las Vegas | Mer. | SR-61278 |
| Touching Home | Mer. | SR-61343 |
| Would You Take Another Chance on Me? | Mer. | SR-61346 |
| Who's Gonna Play This Old Piano . . . (Think About It, Darlin') | Mer. | SR-61366 |
| The "Killer" Rocks On | Mer. | SRM-1-637 |
| The Golden Rock Hits of Jerry Lee Lewis | Sma. | SRS-67040 |
| The Greatest Live Show on Earth | Sma. | SRS-67056 |
| All Country | Sma. | SRS-67071 |
| By Request: More of the Greatest Live Show on Earth | Sma. | SRS-67086 |
| Another Place, Another Time | Sma. | SRS-67104 |
| She Still Comes Around (to Love What's Left of Me) | Sma. | SRS-67112 |
| Jerry Lee Lewis Sings The Country Music Hall of Fame Hits, Vol. 1 | Sma. | SRS-67117 |
| Jerry Lee Lewis Sings The Country Music Hall of Fame Hits, Vol. 2 | Sma. | SRS-67118 |
| Together (with Linda Gail Lewis) | Sma. | SRS-67126 |
| She Even Woke Me Up to Say Good-bye | Sma. | SRS-67128 |
| The Best of Jerry Lee Lewis | Sma. | SRS-67131 |
| The Session | Mer. | SRM-2-803 |

## LINDSAY, LA WANDA

| | | |
|---|---|---|
| Pickin' Wild Mountain Berries | Chart | S-1030 |
| Swingin' and Singin' My Song | Chart | S-1015 |
| We'll Sing in the Sunshine | Chart | S-1035 |

## LOCKLIN, HANK

| | | |
|---|---|---|
| The Best of Hank Locklin | RCA | LSP-3559 |
| Hank Locklin and Danny Davis and the Nashville Brass | RCA | LSP-4318 |

# DISCOGRAPHY

| TITLE | LABEL | RECORD NO. |
|---|---|---|
| Bless Her Heart . . . I Love Her | RCA | LSP-4392 |
| The First Fifteen Years | RCA | LSP-4604 |
| The Mayor of McLellan, Florida | RCA | LSP-4800 |
| Send Me the Pillow You Dream On | RCA | CAS-2562 |

## LONZO AND OSCAR

| | | |
|---|---|---|
| Lonzo and Oscar | Star. | 244 |
| Country Comedy Time | Dec. | 4363 |

## LORD, BOBBY

| | | |
|---|---|---|
| You and Me Against the World | Dec. | 75246 |

## LOUDERMILK, JOHN D.

| | | |
|---|---|---|
| Elloree, Vol. 1 | Warn. | WS-1922 |
| Sings a Bizarre Collection | RCA | LSP-3497 |
| Suburban Attitudes in Country Verse | RCA | LSP-3807 |

## THE LOUVIN BROTHERS (see also Charlie Louvin)

| | | |
|---|---|---|
| The Great Gospel Singing of the Louvin Brothers | Cap. | ST-11193 |
| Tragic Songs of Life | Cap. | T-769 |

## LOUVIN, CHARLIE (see also The Louvin Brothers)

| | | |
|---|---|---|
| The Best of Charlie Louvin | Cap. | ST-11112 |
| Lonesome Is Me | Cap. | ST-2482 |

## LULUBELLE AND SCOTTY

| | | |
|---|---|---|
| Lulubelle and Scotty | Star. | 351 |

## LUMAN, BOB

| | | |
|---|---|---|
| Bob Luman | Har. | KH-32006 |
| A Chain Don't Take to Me | Col. | E-30923 |

| TITLE | LABEL | RECORD NO. |
|---|---|---|
| Lonely Women Make Good Lovers | Epic | KE-31746 |
| Neither One of Us | Epic | KE-32192 |
| When You Say Love | Epic | KE-31375 |

## LYNN, JUDY

| | | |
|---|---|---|
| Caesar's Palace | Col. | 9879-H |
| Parts of Love | AMA | 5011 |

## LYNN, LORETTA

| | | |
|---|---|---|
| Blue Kentucky Girl | MCA | DL-7-4665 |
| Hymns | MCA | DL-7-4695 |
| You Ain't Woman Enough | MCA | DL-7-4783 |
| Don't Come Home A-Drinkin' | MCA | DL-7-4842 |
| Who Says God Is Dead | MCA | DL-7-4928 |
| Fist City | MCA | DL-7-4997 |
| Greatest Hits | MCA | MCA-1 |
| Your Squaw Is on the Warpath | MCA | DL-7-5084 |
| Woman of the World—To Make a Man | MCA | DL-7-5113 |
| Wings Upon Your Horns | MCA | DL-7-5163 |
| Loretta Writes 'Em and Sings 'Em | MCA | DL-7-5198 |
| Coal Miner's Daughter | MCA | DL-7-5253 |
| I Wanna Be Free | MCA | DL-7-5282 |
| You're Lookin' at Country | MCA | DL-7-5310 |
| One's on the Way | MCA | DL-7-5334 |
| God Bless America Again | MCA | DL-7-5351 |
| Here I Am Again | MCA | DL-7-5381 |
| Entertainer of the Year | MCA | MCA-300 |
| Here's Loretta Lynn | MCA | VL-7-3853 |
| Alone with You | MCA | CB-20064 |
| The Ernest Tubb-Loretta Lynn Story | MCA | MCA-2-4000 |
| Only Make Believe (with Conway Twitty) | MCA | DL-7-5251 |
| Lead Me On (with Conway Twitty) | MCA | DL-7-5326 |
| Louisiana Woman—Mississippi Man | MCA | MC-335 |
| Love Is the Foundation | MCA | MCA-355 |
| Here's Loretta Lynn | MCA | CB-20056 |
| Country Christmas | MCA | DL-74817 |
| Alone With You | MCA | CB-20064 |

## McAULIFF, LEON

| | | |
|---|---|---|
| Golden Hits | Dot | 3689 |
| Western Swing | Star. | 171 |

# DISCOGRAPHY

## McCLINTOCK, HARRY K. (HAYWIRE MAC)

| TITLE | LABEL | RECORD NO. |
|---|---|---|
| Haywire Mac | Folk. | FD-5272 |

## McCLINTON, O. B.

| | | |
|---|---|---|
| Obie from Senatobie | Ent. | ENS-1029 |

## MACON, UNCLE DAVE

| | | |
|---|---|---|
| Uncle Dave Macon | Dec. | 4760 |
| Uncle Dave Macon | Folk. | RF-51 |

## McCOY, CHARLIE

| | | |
|---|---|---|
| The Fastest Harp in the South | Col. | KZ-32749 |
| Good-Time Charlie | Col. | KZ-32215 |
| The Real McCoy | Col. | Z-31329 |

## MADDOX, ROSE

| | | |
|---|---|---|
| Rose Maddox's Best | Har. | HL-7312 |
| Rosie | Star. | S-463 |

## MAINER, J.E.

| | | |
|---|---|---|
| J. E. Mainer and His Mountaineers | Arhoo. | 500 |

## MANDRELL, BARBARA

| | | |
|---|---|---|
| Treat Him Right | Col. | C-30967 |
| Midnight Oil | Col. | KC-32743 |

## MAPHIS, JOE AND ROSE LEE

| | | |
|---|---|---|
| Hi-fi Holiday for Banjo | Col. | HS-11032 |
| Joe and Rose Lee Maphis | Star. | 286 |

## MILLER, JODY

| TITLE | LABEL | RECORD NO. |
|---|---|---|
| The Best of Jody Miller | Cap. | ST-11169 |
| Good News! | Epic | KE-32386 |

## MILLER, ROGER

| | | |
|---|---|---|
| Golden Hits | Sma. | SRS-67073 |
| Best of Roger Miller | Mer. | 61361 |
| Walkin' in Sunshine | Sma. | 67092 |
| The Return of Roger Miller | Sma. | SRS-67061 |
| Dear Folks | Col. | KC-32449 |

## MILSAP, RONNIE

| | | |
|---|---|---|
| Where My Heart Is | RCA | APL-1-0338 |

## MONROE, BILL

| | | |
|---|---|---|
| Mr. Bluegrass | MCA | MCA-82 |
| Bluegrass Ramble | MCA | DL-7-4266 |
| Bluegrass Special | MCA | DL-7-4382 |
| I'll Meet You in Church Sunday Morning | MCA | DL-7-4537 |
| Bluegrass Instrumentals | MCA | DL-7-4601 |
| The High Lonesome Sound | MCA | DL-7-4780 |
| Bluegrass Time | MCA | MCA-116 |
| Greatest Hits | MCA | MCA-17 |
| Bill and Charlie Monroe | MCA | DL-7-5066 |
| A Voice from On High | MCA | DL-7-5135 |
| Kentucky Bluegrass | MCA | MCA-136 |
| Country Music Hall of Fame | MCA | DL-7-5281 |
| Uncle Pen | MCA | DL-7-5348 |
| I Saw the Light | MCA | DL-7-8769 |
| Sings Country Songs | MCA | VL-7-3702 |
| Bluegrass Style | MCA | VL-7-3870 |
| Father and Son (with James Monroe) | MCA | MCA-310 |
| Bill Monroe and his Bluegrass Boys | Col. | HS-11335 |
| Sixteen All-Time Greatest Hits (with the Bluegrass Boys) | Col. | CS-1065 |

## MONTANA, PATSY

| | | |
|---|---|---|
| Sweetheart | Star. | 376 |

# DISCOGRAPHY

### MONTGOMERY, MELBA

| TITLE | LABEL | RECORD NO. |
|---|---|---|
| Melba Montgomery | Elek. | EKS-75069 |
| Hallelujah Road | Mus. | 3097 |

### MULLICAN, MOON

| | | |
|---|---|---|
| Unforgettable Great Hits | Star. | 398 |

### MURRAY, ANNE

| | | |
|---|---|---|
| Snowbird | Cap. | ST-579 |
| Anne Murray | Cap. | ST-667 |
| Danny's Song | Cap. | ST-11172 |

### THE NASHVILLE BRASS, *see Davis, Danny*

### NELSON, RICK

| | | |
|---|---|---|
| Rick Nelson Country (2 records) | MCA | 4004 |
| In Concert | MCA | MCA-3 |
| Garden Party | MCA | DL-7-5391 |

### NELSON, WILLIE

| | | |
|---|---|---|
| Willie Nelson and Family | RCA | LSP-4489 |
| Yesterday's Wine | RCA | LSP-4568 |
| The Words Don't Fit the Picture | RCA | LSP-4653 |
| The Willie Way | RCA | LSP-4760 |
| Shotgun Willie | At. | SD-7262 |

### NEWBURY, MICKEY

| | | |
|---|---|---|
| Heaven Help the Child | Elek. | EKS-75055 |
| Sings His Own | RCA | LSP-4675 |

### NEWMAN, JIMMY "C."

| | | |
|---|---|---|
| Born to Love You | Dec. | 75065 |
| World of Music | Dec. | 74885 |

## THE NITTY GRITTY DIRT BAND

| TITLE | LABEL | RECORD NO. |
|---|---|---|
| Will the Circle be Unbroken | UA | UAS-9801 |

## ORBISON, ROY

| | | |
|---|---|---|
| Roy Orbison's Many Moods | MGM | 4636 |
| The Great Songs of Roy Orbison | MGM | 4659 |
| Hank Williams the Roy Orbison Way | MGM | 4683 |
| Roy Orbison Sings | MGM | 4835 |
| Memphis | MGM | 4867 |
| All-Time Greatest Hits | Col. | KZG-31484 |
| Greatest Hits | Col. | SLP-18000 |
| More Greatest Hits | Col. | SLP-18024 |
| The Very Best of Roy Orbison | Col. | SLP-18045 |

## THE OSBORNE BROTHERS

| | | |
|---|---|---|
| Voices in Bluegrass | MCA | DL-7-4602 |
| Up This Hill and Down | MCA | DL-7-4767 |
| Modern Sounds of Bluegrass | MCA | DL-7-4903 |
| Yesterday, Today and The Osborne Brothers | MCA | DL-7-4993 |
| Favorite Hymns | MCA | MCA-125 |
| Up to Date and Down to Earth | MCA | DL-7-5128 |
| Ru-Beeee | MCA | MCA-135 |
| The Osborne Brothers | MCA | DL-7-5271 |
| Country Roads | MCA | DL-7-5321 |
| Bobby and Sonny | MCA | DL-7-5356 |
| Midnight Flyer | MCA | MCA-311 |
| Bluegrass Express | MCA | CB-20003 |
| Cuttin' Grass Osborne Brothers Style | MGM | 4149 |
| The Osborne Brothers | MGM | 140 |

## OWENS, BONNIE

| | | |
|---|---|---|
| Bonnie Owens | Cap. | ST-2403 |

## OWENS, BUCK

| | | |
|---|---|---|
| Best of Buck Owens, Vol. 3 | Cap. | SKAO-145 |
| Tall Dark Stranger | Cap. | ST-212 |
| We're Gonna Get Together | Cap. | ST-448 |
| Country Christmas (2 records) | Cap. | STBB-486 |

# DISCOGRAPHY

| TITLE | LABEL | RECORD NO. |
|---|---|---|
| Buck Owens | Cap. | STBB-532 |
| Great White Horse (with Susan Raye) | Cap. | ST-558 |
| Buck Owens and the Buckaroos (3 records) | Cap. | STCL-574 |
| Buck Owens' Ruby | Cap. | ST-795 |
| Merry Christmas from Owens and Raye | Cap. | ST-837 |
| The Best of Buck Owens and Susan Raye | Cap. | ST-11084 |

## OVERSTREET, TOMMY

| | | |
|---|---|---|
| Tommy Overstreet | Dot | DOS-25992 |
| This Is Tommy Overstreet | Dot | DOS-25994 |
| Heaven Is My Woman's Love | Dot | DOS-26003 |

## PARSONS, GRAM

| | | |
|---|---|---|
| GP | Warn./Rep. | 2123 |
| Grievous Angel | Rep. | MS-2171 |

## PARTON, DOLLY

| | | |
|---|---|---|
| Just Between You and Me (with Porter Wagoner) | RCA | LSP-3926 |
| Just Because I'm a Woman | RCA | LSP-3949 |
| Just the Two of Us (with Porter Wagoner) | RCA | LSP-4039 |
| Always, Always (with Porter Wagoner) | RCA | LSP-4186 |
| My Blue Ridge Mountain Boy | RCA | LSP-4188 |
| Porter Wayne and Dolly Rebecca (with Porter Wagoner) | RCA | LSP-4305 |
| A Real Live Dolly | RCA | LSP-4387 |
| Once More (with Porter Wagoner) | RCA | LSP-4388 |
| Golden Streets of Glory | RCA | LSP-4398 |
| The Best of Dolly Parton | RCA | LSP-4449 |
| Two of a Kind (with Porter Wagoner) | RCA | LSP-4490 |
| Joshua | RCA | LSP-4507 |
| The Best of Porter Wagoner and Dolly Parton | RCA | LSP-4556 |
| Coat of Many Colors | RCA | LSP-4603 |
| The Right Combination/Burning the Midnight Oil (with Porter Wagoner) | RCA | LSP-4628 |
| Touch Your Woman | RCA | LSP-4686 |
| Dolly Parton Sings "My Favorite Songwriter, Porter Wagoner" | RCA | LSP-4752 |
| Together Always (with Porter Wagoner) | RCA | LSP-4761 |
| We Found It (with Porter Wagoner) | RCA | LSP-4841 |
| My Tennessee Mountain Home | RCA | APL-1-0033 |
| Love and Music (with Porter Wagoner) | RCA | APL-1-0248 |

## PAYCHECK, JOHNNY

| TITLE | LABEL | RECORD NO. |
|---|---|---|
| She's All I Got | Col. | E-31141 |
| Somebody Loves Me | Epic | KE-31707 |
| Someone to Give My Love To | Epic | KE-31449 |
| Mr. Lovemaker | Epic | KE-32387 |

## PAYNE, LEON

| | | |
|---|---|---|
| Leon Payne (2 records) | Star. | 231/236 |

## PEARL, MINNIE

| | | |
|---|---|---|
| Cousin Minnie Pearl | Star. | 224 |

## PERKINS, CARL

| | | |
|---|---|---|
| Brown-Eyed Handsome Man | Har. | KH-31179 |
| Carl Perkins | Col. | HS-11385 |
| Greatest Hits | Har. | KH-31792 |

## PHILLIPS, BILL

| | | |
|---|---|---|
| Action | Dec. | 75022 |
| Style | Dec. | 74897 |

## PIERCE, WEBB

| | | |
|---|---|---|
| Greatest Hits | MCA | DL-7-4999 |
| Webb Pierce Road Show | MCA | DL-7-5280 |
| I'm Gonna Be a Swinger | MCA | DL-7-5393 |
| Webb Pierce | MCA | VL-7-3766 |
| Country Songs | MCA | VL-7-3830 |
| Country Favorites | MCA | VL-7-3911 |
| Without You | MCA | CB-20025 |

## PILLOW, RAY

| | | |
|---|---|---|
| Slippin' Around | Mega | M-31-1017 |

# DISCOGRAPHY

## PRESLEY, ELVIS

| TITLE | LABEL | RECORD NO. |
|---|---|---|
| Elvis Presley | RCA | LSP-1254 |
| Elvis | RCA | LSP-1382 |
| Loving You | RCA | LSP-1515 |
| Elvis' Golden Records | RCA | LSP-1707 |
| King Creole | RCA | LSP-1884 |
| For LP Fans Only | RCA | LSP-1990 |
| A Date with Elvis | RCA | LSP-2011 |
| 50,000,000 Elvis Fans Can't Be Wrong—Elvis' Gold Records, Vol. 2 | RCA | LSP-2075 |
| Elvis is Back! | RCA | LSP-2231 |
| G. I. Blues | RCA | LSP-2256 |
| His Hand in Mine | RCA | LSP-2328 |
| Something for Everybody | RCA | LSP-2370 |
| Blue Hawaii | RCA | LSP-2426 |
| Pot Luck | RCA | LSP-2523 |
| Girls! Girls! Girls! | RCA | LSP-2621 |
| "Fun in Acapulco" | RCA | LSP-2756 |
| Elvis' Golden Records, Vol. 3 | RCA | LSP-2765 |
| "Kissin' Cousins" | RCA | LSP-2894 |
| Roustabout | RCA | LSP-2999 |
| Girl Happy | RCA | LSP-3338 |
| Elvis For Everyone! | RCA | LSP-3450 |
| Paradise Hawaiian Style | RCA | LSP-3643 |
| How Great Thou Art | RCA | LSP-3758 |
| Elvis' Gold Records, Vol. 4 | RCA | LSP-3921 |
| Speedway | RCA | LSP-3989 |
| Elvis—TV Special | RCA | LPM-4088 |
| From Elvis in Memphis | RCA | LSP-4155 |
| On Stage (February 1970) | RCA | LSP-4362 |
| Elvis in Person at the International Hotel, Las Vegas, Nevada | RCA | LSP-4428 |
| Elvis Back in Memphis | RCA | LSP-4429 |
| Elvis—That's the Way It Is | RCA | LSP-4445 |
| Elvis Country | RCA | LSP-4460 |
| Love Letters from Elvis | RCA | LSP-4530 |
| Elvis Sings the Wonderful World of Christmas | RCA | LSP-4579 |
| Elvis Now | RCA | LSP-4671 |
| He Touched Me | RCA | LSP-4690 |
| Elvis as Recorded Live at Madison Square Garden | RCA | LSP-4776 |
| Elvis | RCA | APL-1-0283 |
| From Memphis to Vegas/From Vegas to Memphis | RCA | LSP-6020 |
| Elvis' Worldwide Fifty Gold Award Hits, Vol. 1 | RCA | LPM-6401 |
| Elvis—Aloha from Hawaii Via Satellite | RCA | VPSX-6089 |
| Separate Ways | RCA | 2611 |

## PRICE, KENNY

| | LABEL | RECORD NO. |
|---|---|---|
| The Red Foley Songbook | RCA | LSP-4469 |
| Northeast Arkansas Mississippi County Bootlegger | RCA | LSP-4373 |
| Walking on New Grass | RCA | LSP-4425 |

## PRICE, RAY

| TITLE | LABEL | RECORD NO. |
|---|---|---|
| All-Time Greatest Hits | Col. | KG-31364 |
| Born to Lose | Col. | HS-11240 |
| Burning Memories | Col. | CS-9089 |
| Christmas Album | Col. | CS-9861 |
| Collector's Choice | Col. | HS-11172 |
| Danny Boy | Col. | CS-9477 |
| For the Good Times | Col. | C-30106 |
| Greatest Hits | Col. | CS-8866 |
| Greatest Hits, Vol. 2 | Col. | CS-9470 |
| I Fall to Pieces | Col. | HS-11373 |
| I Won't Mention It Again | Col. | C-30510 |
| She's Got to Be a Saint | Col. | KC-32033 |
| Take Me as I Am | Col. | CS-9606 |
| Touch My Heart | Col. | CS-9406 |
| Welcome to My World | Col. | G-30878 |
| The World of Ray Price | Col. | GP-28 |
| You Wouldn't Know Love | Col. | CS-9918 |

## PRIDE, CHARLEY

| | | |
|---|---|---|
| (Country) Charlie Pride | RCA | LSP-3645 |
| Pride of Country Music | RCA | LSP-3775 |
| The Country Way | RCA | LSP-3895 |
| Make Mine Country | RCA | LSP-3952 |
| Songs of Pride . . . Charley, That Is | RCA | LSP-4041 |
| Charley Pride—in Person | RCA | LSP-4094 |
| The Sensational Charley Pride | RCA | LSP-4153 |
| The Best of Charley Pride | RCA | LSP-4223 |
| Just Plain Charley | RCA | LSP-4290 |
| Charley Pride's Tenth Album | RCA | LSP-4367 |
| Christmas in My Home Town | RCA | LSP-4406 |
| From Me to You | RCA | LSP-4468 |
| Did You Think to Pray? | RCA | LSP-4513 |
| I'm Just Me | RCA | LSP-4560 |
| Charley Pride Sings Heart Songs | RCA | LSP-4617 |
| The Best of Charley Pride, Vol. 2 | RCA | LSP-4682 |
| A Sunshiny Day with Charley Pride | RCA | LSP-4742 |
| Songs of Love by Charley Pride | RCA | LSP-4837 |
| Sweet Country | RCA | APL-1-0217 |

## PRUETT, JEANNE

| | | |
|---|---|---|
| Love Me | MCA | DL-7-5360 |
| Satin Sheets | MCA | MCA-338 |

# DISCOGRAPHY

## RAINWATER, MARVIN

| TITLE | LABEL | RECORD NO. |
|---|---|---|
| Marvin Rainwater | MGM | 4046 |

## RANDOLPH, BOOTS

| | | |
|---|---|---|
| Yakety Sax | Col. | SLP-18002 |
| Boots With Strings | Col. | SLP-18066 |
| More Yakety Sax | Col. | SLP-18037 |

## RAYE, SUSAN

| | | |
|---|---|---|
| One-Night Stand | Cap. | ST-543 |
| Great White Horse (with Buck Owens) | Cap. | ST-558 |
| Pitty, Pitty, Patter | Cap. | ST-807 |
| Merry Christmas from Owens and Raye | Cap. | ST-837 |
| (I've Got a) Happy Heart | Cap. | ST-875 |
| The Best of Buck Owens and Susan Raye | Cap. | ST-11084 |
| Wheel of Fortune | Cap. | ST-11106 |
| Love Sure Feels Good | Cap. | ST-11135 |
| Cheating Game | Cap. | ST-11179 |

## REED, JERRY

| | | |
|---|---|---|
| The Unbelievable Guitar and Voice of Jerry Reed | RCA | LSP-3756 |
| Nashville Underground | RCA | LSP-3978 |
| Alabama Wild Man | RCA | LSP-4069 |
| Better Things in Life | RCA | LSP-4147 |
| Jerry Reed Explores Guitar Country | RCA | LSP-4204 |
| Cookin' | RCA | LSP-4293 |
| Georgia Sunshine | RCA | LSP-4391 |
| Me and Jerry (with Chet Atkins) | RCA | LSP-4396 |
| When You're Hot, You're Hot | RCA | LSP-4506 |
| Ko-Ko Joe | RCA | LSP-4596 |
| Smell the Flowers | RCA | LSP-4660 |
| Me and Chet (with Chet Atkins) | RCA | LSP-4707 |
| The Best of Jerry Reed | RCA | LSP-4729 |
| Jerry Reed | RCA | LSP-4750 |
| Hot A' Mighty! | RCA | LSP-4838 |
| Lord, Mr. Ford | RCA | APL-1-0238 |

## REEVES, DEL

| | | |
|---|---|---|
| Before Good-bye | UA | 6830 |
| The Best of Del Reeves, Vol. 2 | UA | 6758 |
| Friends and Neighbors | UA | 6789 |
| Out in the Country | Sun | 5321 |

## REEVES, JIM

| TITLE | LABEL | RECORD NO. |
|---|---|---|
| Jim Reeves | RCA | LPM-1576 |
| God Be with You | RCA | LSP-1950 |
| Songs to Warm the Heart | RCA | LSP-2001 |
| The Intimate Jim Reeves | RCA | LSP-2216 |
| He'll Have to Go | RCA | LSP-2223 |
| Tall Tales and Short Tempers | RCA | LSP-2284 |
| Talkin' to Your Heart | RCA | LSP-2339 |
| A Touch of Velvet | RCA | LSP-2487 |
| We Thank Thee | RCA | LSP-2552 |
| Gentleman Jim | RCA | LSP-2605 |
| The International Jim Reeves | RCA | LSP-2704 |
| Twelve Songs of Christmas | RCA | LSP-2758 |
| Moonlight and Roses | RCA | LSP-2854 |
| The Best of Jim Reeves | RCA | LSP-2890 |
| The Jim Reeves Way | RCA | LSP-2968 |
| Jim Reeves Up Through the Years | RCA | LSP-3427 |
| The Best of Jim Reeves, Vol. 2 | RCA | LSP-3482 |
| Distant Drums | RCA | LSP-3542 |
| Blue Side of Lonesome | RCA | LSP-3793 |
| My Cathedral | RCA | LSP-3903 |
| A Touch of Sadness | RCA | LSP-3987 |
| The Best of Jim Reeves, Vol. 3 | RCA | LSP-4187 |
| Jim Reeves Writes You a Record | RCA | LSP-4475 |
| Something Special | RCA | LSP-4528 |
| My Friend | RCA | LSP-4626 |
| Missing You | RCA | LSP-4749 |
| Am I That Easy to Forget | RCA | APL-1-0039 |

## RICE, BOBBY G.

| | | |
|---|---|---|
| Hit After Hit | Roy. Am. | 1003 |
| You Lay So Easy on My Mind | Metro. | EML-1-0186 |

## RICH, CHARLIE

| | | |
|---|---|---|
| Behind Closed Doors | Epic | KE-32247 |
| The Best of Charlie Rich | Epic | KE-31933 |
| I Do My Swingin' at Home | Har. | KH-32166 |
| Tomorrow Night | RCA | APL-1-0258 |

## RILEY, JEANNIE C.

| | | |
|---|---|---|
| Give Myself a Party | MGM | 4805 |
| Down to Earth | MGM | 4849 |
| When Love Has Gone Away | MGM | SE-4891 |

# DISCOGRAPHY

## RITTER, TEX

| TITLE | LABEL | RECORD NO. |
|---|---|---|
| Hillbilly Heaven | Cap. | ST-1623 |
| The Best of Tex Ritter | Cap. | DT-2595 |
| Supercountrylegendary | Cap. | ST-11037 |

## ROBBINS, MARTY

| | | |
|---|---|---|
| This Much a Man | MCA | DL-7-5389 |
| All-Time Greatest Hits | Col. | KG-31361 |
| Bound for Old Mexico | Col. | KC-31341 |
| Devil Woman | Col. | CS-8718 |
| The Drifter | Col. | CS-9327 |
| El Paso | Har. | KH-30316 |
| Favorites | Har. | KH-31257 |
| From the Heart | Har. | KH-30756 |
| Greatest Hits | Col. | CS-8639 |
| Greatest Hits, Vol. 3 | Col. | C-30571 |
| Gunfighter Ballads and Trail Songs | Col. | CS-8158 |
| I've Got a Woman's Love | Col. | KC-31628 |
| I Walk Alone | Col. | CS-9725 |
| Marty's Country | Col. | GP-15 |
| More Greatest Hits | Col. | CS-8435 |
| More Gunfighter Ballads and Trail Songs | Col. | CS-8272 |
| My Woman, My Woman, My Wife | Col. | CS-9978 |
| Return of the Gunfighter | Col. | CS-8872 |
| Singing the Blues | Col. | HS-11338 |
| The Song of Robbins | Col. | CS-9421 |
| Song of the Islands | Har. | H-31258 |
| The Story of My Life | Col. | HS-11409 |
| "Streets of Laredo" and Other Ballads | Har. | KH-32286 |
| Tonight Carmen | Col. | CS-9525 |
| What God Has Done | Col. | CS-9248 |
| The World of Marty Robbins | Col. | G-30881 |
| Marty Robbins | MCA | MCA-342 |

## RODGERS, JIMMIE

| | | |
|---|---|---|
| Never No Mo' Blues | RCA | LPM-1232 |
| Train Whistle Blues | RCA | LPM-1640 |
| My Rough and Rowdy Ways | RCA | LPM-2112 |
| Jimmie the Kid | RCA | LPM-2213 |
| Country Music Hall of Fame | RCA | LPM-2531 |
| The Short but Brilliant Life of Jimmie Rodgers | RCA | LPM-2634 |
| My Time Ain't Long | RCA | LPM-2865 |
| The Best of the Legendary Jimmie Rodgers | RCA | LSP-3315 |
| This Is Jimmie Rodgers | RCA | VPS-6091 |

## RODRIGUEZ, JOHNNY

| TITLE | LABEL | RECORD NO. |
|---|---|---|
| Introducing, Johnny Rodriguez | Mer. | SR-61378 |
| All I Ever Meant to Do Was Sing | Mer. | SRM-1686 |

## ROGERS, DAVID

| | | |
|---|---|---|
| Farewell to the Ryman | At. | SD-7283 |
| Need You | Col. | KC-31506 |
| She Don't Make Me Cry | Col. | C-30972 |

## ROGERS, ROY

| | | |
|---|---|---|
| The Country Side of Roy Rogers | Cap. | ST-594 |
| A Man from Duck Run | Cap. | ST-785 |
| The Bible Tells Me So (with Dale Evans) | Cap. | ST-1745 |
| Take a Little Love | Cap. | ST-11020 |

## RUSSELL, JOHNNY

| | | |
|---|---|---|
| Mr. and Mrs. Untrue | RCA | LSP-4588 |
| Catfish John/Chained | RCA | LSP-4851 |
| Rednecks, White Socks, and Blue-Ribbon Beer | RCA | APL-1-0345 |

## SCRUGGS, EARL (see also Flatt and Scruggs)

| | | |
|---|---|---|
| Dueling Banjos | Col. | C-32268 |
| His Family and Friends (with Joan Baez, Bob Dylan, the Byrds, et al.) | Col. | C-30584 |
| I Saw the Light (with Linda Ronstadt, et al.) | Col. | KC-31354 |
| Earl Scruggs Live at Kansas State | Col. | KC-31758 |
| Nashville's Rock | Col. | CS-1007 |

## SEALS, TROY

| | | |
|---|---|---|
| Now Presenting | At. | SD-7281 |

## SEELY, JEANNIE

| | | |
|---|---|---|
| Jack Greene and Jeannie Seely | MCA | DL-7-5171 |
| Two for The Show (with Jack Greene) | MCA | DL-7-5392 |

# DISCOGRAPHY

| TITLE | LABEL | RECORD NO. |
|---|---|---|
| Greatest Hits | Col. | KZ-31911 |
| Little Things | Col. | SLP-18104 |
| Make the World Go Away | Har. | H-31029 |

## SHAVER, BILLY JOE

| | | |
|---|---|---|
| Old Five-and-Dimers | Mon. | KZ-32293 |

## SHEPARD, JEAN

| | | |
|---|---|---|
| Slippin' Away | UA | LA-144-F |
| Here and Now | Cap. | ST-738 |
| Just Like Walkin' in the Sunshine | Cap. | ST-11049 |

## SIMPSON, RED

| | | |
|---|---|---|
| I'm a Truck | Cap. | ST-881 |
| The Very Real Red Simpson | Cap. | ST-11093 |
| Trucker's Christmas | Cap. | ST-11231 |

## SMITH, CAL

| | | |
|---|---|---|
| The Best of Cal Smith | MCA | KS-3642 |
| I've Found Someone of My Own | MCA | MCA-56 |
| Swinging Doors | MCA | CB-20008 |
| Cal Smith | MCA | MCA-344 |

## SMITH, CARL

| | | |
|---|---|---|
| Faded Love and Winter Roses | Col. | 10112-H |
| Tribute to Roy Acuff | Col. | 9870 |
| I Love You Because | Col. | 9898 |
| Carl Smith and the Tunesmiths | Col. | 30215 |
| The Tall, Tall Gentleman | Col. | LE-10025-H |
| Country Gentleman Sings His Favorites | Col. | LE-10111-H |
| Kisses Don't Lie | Col. | LE-10031-H |
| Don't Say You're Mine | Col. | C-31277 |
| If This Is Good-bye | Col. | KC-31606 |

## SMITH, CONNIE

| TITLE | LABEL | RECORD NO. |
|---|---|---|
| Connie Smith Sings Great Sacred Songs | RCA | LSP-3589 |
| The Best of Connie Smith | RCA | LSP-3848 |
| Sunday Morning with Nat Stuckey and Connie Smith | RCA | LSP-4300 |
| The Best of Connie Smith, Vol. 2 | RCA | LSP-4324 |
| I Never Once Stopped Loving You | RCA | LSP-4394 |
| Where is My Castle? | RCA | LSP-4474 |
| Just One Time | RCA | LSP-4534 |
| Come Along and Walk With Me | RCA | LSP-4598 |
| Ain't We Havin' Us a Good Time | RCA | LSP-4694 |
| "If It Ain't Love" and Other Great Dallas Frazier Songs | RCA | LSP-4748 |
| Love Is the Look You're Looking For | RCA | LSP-4840 |
| Dream Painter | RCA | APL-1-0188 |
| A Lady Named Smith | Col. | KC-32185 |

## SMITH, SAMMI

| The Toast of '45 | Mega | M-31-1021 |
|---|---|---|
| Help Me | Mega | M-31-1000 |
| Best of Sammi Smith | Mega | M-31-1019 |

## SNOW, HANK

| Hank Snow Souvenirs | RCA | LSP-2285 |
|---|---|---|
| Together Again (with Anita Carter) | RCA | LSP-2580 |
| I've Been Everywhere | RCA | LSP-2675 |
| Songs of Tragedy | RCA | LSP-2901 |
| Reminiscing (with Chet Atkins) | RCA | LSP-2952 |
| Hank Snow Sings Your Favorite Country Hits | RCA | LSP-3317 |
| The Best of Hank Snow | RCA | LSP-3478 |
| C.B. Atkins and C.E. Snow by Special Request | RCA | LSP-4254 |
| Hank Snow Sings in Memory of Jimmie Rodgers (America's Blue Yodeler) | RCA | LSP-4306 |
| Tracks and Trains | RCA | LSP-4501 |
| Award Winners | RCA | LSP-4601 |
| The Jimmie Rodgers Story, featuring Albert Fullam | RCA | LSP-4708 |
| The Best of Hank Snow, Vol. 2 | RCA | LSP-4798 |
| This Is My Story | RCA | LSP-6014 |
| Hank Snow Sings Grand Ole Opry Favorites | RCA | APL-1-0162 |

## SONS OF THE PIONEERS

| Favorite Cowboy Songs | RCA | LPM-1130 |
|---|---|---|
| Cool Water | RCA | LSP-2118 |

# DISCOGRAPHY

| TITLE | LABEL | RECORD NO. |
|---|---|---|
| Lure of the West | RCA | LSP-2356 |
| The Sons of the Pioneers Sing Legends of the West | RCA | LSP-3351 |
| The Best of the Sons of the Pioneers | RCA | LSP-3476 |
| The Sons of the Pioneers Sing Campfire Favorites | RCA | LSP-3714 |
| Tumbling Tumbleweeds | RCA | LSP-4119 |
| Tumbleweed Trails | MCA | VL-73715 |

## SOUTH, JOE

| | | |
|---|---|---|
| Introspect | Cap. | ST-108 |
| Games People Play | Cap. | ST-235 |
| Don't It Make You Want to Go Home? | Cap. | ST-392 |
| Joe South's Greatest Hits | Cap. | ST-450 |
| So the Seeds Are Growing | Cap. | ST-637 |

## SOVINE, RED

| | | |
|---|---|---|
| That's Truck Drivin' | Star. | S-357 |
| Country Way | Voc. | 73829 |
| Giddyup Go | Star. | S-363 |

## STAMPLEY, JOE

| | | |
|---|---|---|
| If You Touch Me (You've Got to Love Me) | Dot | DOS-26002 |
| Soul Song | Dot | DOS-26007 |

## THE STATLER BROTHERS

| | | |
|---|---|---|
| Big Country Hits | Har. | H-30610 |
| The Big Hits | Col. | CS-9519 |
| Flowers on the Wall | Col. | CS-9249 |
| How Great Thou Art | Har. | KH-31560 |
| The World of the Statler Brothers | Col. | KG-31557 |
| Bed of Rose's | Mer. | SR-61317 |
| Pictures of Moments to Remember | Mer. | SR-61349 |
| Innerview | Mer. | SR-61358 |
| Country Music Then and Now | Mer. | SR-61367 |
| The Statler Brothers Sing Country Symphonies in E Major | Mer. | SR-61374 |

## STEAGALL, RED

| TITLE | LABEL | RECORD NO. |
|---|---|---|
| Somewhere My Love | Cap. | ST-11162 |
| If You've Got the Time | Cap. | ST-11228 |

## STEWART, WYNN

| | | |
|---|---|---|
| Baby, It's Yours | Cap. | ST-687 |
| It's a Beautiful Day | Cap. | ST-561 |
| Something Pretty | Cap. | 2921 |
| In Love | Cap. | 113 |
| O Beautiful Day | Cap. | 561 |
| Love's Gonna Happen | Cap. | 2849 |

## STONE, CLIFFIE

| | | |
|---|---|---|
| The Party's on Me | Cap. | T-1080 |

## STRINGBEAN (DAVID AKEMAN)

| | | |
|---|---|---|
| Me and My Ole Cow | Nug. | 102 |

## STUCKEY, NAT

| | | |
|---|---|---|
| Sunday Morning With Nat Stuckey and Connie Smith | RCA | LSP-4300 |
| Country Fever | RCA | LSP-4389 |
| She Wakes Me with a Kiss Every Morning | RCA | LSP-4477 |
| Only a Woman Like You | RCA | LSP-4559 |
| Forgive Me for Calling You Darling | RCA | LSP-4635 |
| Is It Any Wonder That I Love You | RCA | LSP-4743 |
| Take Time to Love Her/I Used It All on You | RCA | APD-1-0080 |

## THOMPSON, HANK

| | | |
|---|---|---|
| Hank Thompson Sings the Gold Standards | Dot | DLP-25864 |
| On Tap, in the Can, or in the Bottle | Dot | DLP-25894 |
| Hank Thompson Salutes | Dot | DLP-25971 |
| The Countrypolitan Sound of Hank Thompson | Dot | DLP-25978 |
| Next Time I Fall In Love | Dot | DOS-25991 |
| Greatest Hits | Dot | DOS-26004 |

# DISCOGRAPHY

| TITLE | LABÈL | RECORD NO. |
|---|---|---|
| The Hank Thompson Twenty-Fifth Anniversary Album | Dot | DOS-2-2000 |
| Cab Driver—A Salute to The Mills Brothers | Dot | DOS-25996 |
| The Best of Hank Thompson | Cap. | DT-1878 |

## TILLIS, MEL

| | | |
|---|---|---|
| Mel Tillis and The Statesiders on Stage— at the Birmingham Municipal Auditorium | MGM | 4889 |
| I Ain't Never/Neon Rose | MGM | 4870 |
| Would You Want the World to End? | MGM | 4841 |
| Living and Learning/Take My Hand (with Sherry Bryce) | MGM | 4800 |
| Live at the Sam Houston Coliseum | MGM | 4788 |
| One More Time | MGM | 4681 |
| Greatest Hits | MCA | KS-3589 |
| Mel Tillis and Bob Wills "in Person" | MCA | KS-3639 |
| Greatest Hits, Vol. 2 | MCA | KS-3653 |
| Big 'n' Country | MCA | VL-73914 |
| Walking on New Grass | MCA | VL-73928 |

## TRASK, DIANA

| | | |
|---|---|---|
| It's a Man's World | Dot | DOS-26016 |

## TRAVIS, MERLE

| | | |
|---|---|---|
| The Best of Merle Travis | Cap. | DT-2662 |
| Great Songs of the Delmore Brothers | Cap. | ST-249 |
| Strictly Guitar | Cap. | ST-2938 |

## TUBB, ERNEST

| | | |
|---|---|---|
| Golden Favorites | MCA | DL-7-4118 |
| Just Call Me Lonesome | MCA | DL-7-4385 |
| The Family Bible | MCA | DL-7-4397 |
| Blue Christmas | MCA | DL-7-4518 |
| Greatest Hits | MCA | MCA-16 |
| Greatest Hits, Vol. 2 | MCA | DL-7-5252 |
| One Sweet Hello | MCA | DL-7-5301 |
| Say Something Sweet to Sarah | MCA | DL-7-5345 |
| Baby, It's So Hard to Be Good | MCA | DL-7-5388 |
| The Ernest Tubb Story | MCA | DXSB-7159 |
| Ernest Tubb and His Texas Troubadours | MCA | VL-7-3684 |
| Stand By Me | MCA | VL-7-3765 |

| TITLE | LABEL | RECORD NO. |
|---|---|---|
| Great Country | MCA | VL-7-3877 |
| The Ernest Tubb-Loretta Lynn Story | MCA | MCA-2-4000 |
| I've Got All the Heartaches I Can Handle | MCA | MCA-341 |

## TUBB, JUSTIN

| | | |
|---|---|---|
| That Country Style | Voc. | 73802 |
| Things I Remember Well | Dot | 25922 |

## TUCKER, TANYA

| | | |
|---|---|---|
| Delta Dawn | Col. | KC-31742 |
| What's Your Mama's Name? | Col. | KC-32272 |

## TWITTY, CONWAY

| | | |
|---|---|---|
| Lead Me On (with Loretta Lynn) | MCA | DL-7-5326 |
| Louisiana Woman—Mississippi Man (with Loretta Lynn) | MCA | MC-335 |
| Greatest Hits | MGM | 3849 |
| You Can't Take the Country Out of Conway | MGM | 4650 |
| Conway Twitty Hits | MGM | 4799 |
| Conway Twitty Sings the Blues | MGM | 4837 |
| Twenty Great Hits by Conway Twitty (2 records) | MGM | SES-4884 |
| Conway Twitty | MGM | 110 |
| Look into My Teardrops | MCA | DL-7-4828 |
| Conway Twitty Sings | MCA | DL-7-4724 |
| Conway Twitty Country | MCA | DL-7-4913 |
| Here's Conway Twitty and His Lonely Blue Boys | MCA | DL-7-4990 |
| Next in Line | MCA | DL-7-5062 |
| Darling, You Know I Wouldn't Lie | MCA | CL-7-5105 |
| I Love You More Today | MCA | DL-7-5131 |
| To See My Angel Cry/That's When She— | MCA | DL-7-5172 |
| Hello, Darling | MCA | DL-7-5209 |
| Fifteen Years Ago | MCA | DL-7-5248 |
| How Much More Can She Stand? | MCA | DL-7-5276 |
| I Wonder What She'll Think About Me Leaving | MCA | DL-7-5292 |
| I Can't See Me Without You | MCA | DL-7-5335 |
| Greatest Hits, Vol. 1 | MCA | DL-7-5352 |
| I Can't Stop Loving You/Her Love on Our First Date | MCA | DL-7-5361 |
| She Needs Someone to Hold Her | MCA | MCA-303 |
| I'm So Used to Loving You | MCA | CB-20000 |
| Only Make Believe (with Loretta Lynn) | MCA | DL-7-5251 |
| You've Never Been This Far Before | MCA | 359 |

# DISCOGRAPHY

## TYLER, T. TEXAS

| TITLE | LABEL | RECORD NO. |
|---|---|---|
| Great Hits | Hill. | S-6042 |

## VAN DYKE, LEROY

| | | |
|---|---|---|
| Country Hits | Warn. | S-1652 |
| I've Never Been Loved | Har. | 11308 |

## WAGONER, PORTER

| | | |
|---|---|---|
| The Grand Old Gospel (and The Blackwood Brothers Quartet) | RCA | LSP-3488 |
| The Best of Porter Wagoner | RCA | LSP-3560 |
| Confessions of a Broken Man | RCA | LSP-3593 |
| "Soul of a Convict" and Other Great Prison Songs | RCA | LSP-3683 |
| More Grand Old Gospel (and The Blackwood Brothers Quartet) | RCA | LSP-3855 |
| Just Between You and Me (with Dolly Parton) | RCA | LSP-3926 |
| Porter Wagoner and The Blackwood Brothers Quartet in Gospel Country | RCA | LSP-4034 |
| Just the Two of Us (with Dolly Parton) | RCA | LSP-4039 |
| The Carroll County Accident | RCA | LSP-4116 |
| Always, Always (with Dolly Parton) | RCA | LSP-4186 |
| Porter Wayne and Dolly Rebecca (with Dolly Parton) | RCA | LSP-4305 |
| The Best of Porter Wagoner, Vol. 2 | RCA | LSP-4321 |
| Skid Row Joe—Down in the Alley | RCA | LSP-4386 |
| Once More (with Dolly Parton) | RCA | LSP-4388 |
| Two of a Kind (with Dolly Parton) | RCA | LSP-4490 |
| Simple as I Am | RCA | LSP-4508 |
| The Best of Porter Wagoner and Dolly Parton | RCA | LSP-4556 |
| Porter Wagoner Sings His Own | RCA | LSP-4586 |
| The Right Combination/Burning the Midnight Oil (with Dolly Parton) | RCA | LSP-4628 |
| What Ain't to Be, Just Might Happen | RCA | LSP-4661 |
| Ballads of Love | RCA | LSP-4734 |
| Together Always (with Dolly Parton) | RCA | LSP-4761 |
| Experience | RCA | LSP-4810 |
| We Found It (with Dolly Parton) | RCA | LSP-4841 |
| I'll Keep On Lovin' You | RCA | APL-1-0142 |
| Love and Music (with Dolly Parton) | RCA | APL-1-0248 |

## WAKELY, JIMMY

| | | |
|---|---|---|
| Heartaches | Dec. | 75077 |
| Here's Jimmy Wakely | Voc. | 73857 |
| I'll Never Slip Around Again | Hill. | S-6063 |
| Show Me the Way | Voc. | 73855 |

## WALKER, BILLY

| TITLE | LABEL | RECORD NO. |
|---|---|---|
| Billy Walker's All-Time Greatest Hits | MGM | 4887 |
| Billy Walker—Live! | MGM | 4789 |
| The Billy Walker Show (with The Mike Curb Congregation) | MGM | 4863 |
| I'm Gonna Keep On Lovin' You/She Goes Walking Through My Mind | MGM | 4756 |
| When a Man Loves a Woman | MGM | 4682 |

## WALKER, CHARLIE

| I Don't Mind Goin' Under (If It'll Get Me Over You) | RCA | LSP-4737 |
|---|---|---|
| Break Out the Bottle—Bring on the Music | RCA | APL-1-0181 |

## WATSON, DOC

| Then and Now | Pop. | PP-LA022-F |
|---|---|---|
| Elementary | Pop. | 5703 |
| On Stage (2 records) | Van. | VSD-9/10 |

## WELLER, FREDDY

| Games People Play | Col. | 9904 |
|---|---|---|
| Too Much Monkey Business | Col. | KC-32218 |
| Roadmaster | Col. | KC-31769 |

## WELLS, KITTY

| Greatest Hits | MCA | DL-7-5001 |
|---|---|---|
| Your Love Is the Way | MCA | DL-7-5245 |
| They're Stepping All Over My Heart | MCA | DL-7-5277 |
| Pledging My Love | MCA | DL-7-5313 |
| Heart-Warming Gospel Songs (with Johnny Wright) | MCA | DL-7-5325 |
| Sincerely | MCA | DL-7-5350 |
| Dust on the Bible | MCA | DL-7-8858 |
| Kitty Wells Story | MCA | DXSB-7174 |
| I've Got Yesterday | MCA | DL-7-5382 |
| Yours Truly | MCA | MCA-330 |
| Kitty Wells | MCA | VL-7-3786 |
| Country Heart | MCA | VL-7-3875 |
| Kitty Wells and Red Foley's Golden Favorites | MCA | DL-74109 |

# DISCOGRAPHY

## WEST, DOTTIE

| TITLE | LABEL | RECORD NO. |
|---|---|---|
| Careless Hands | RCA | LSP-4482 |
| Have You Heard . . . Dottie West? | RCA | LSP-4606 |
| I'm Only a Woman | RCA | LSP-4704 |
| The Best of Dottie West | RCA | LSP-4811 |
| If It's All Right with You/Just What I've Been Looking For | RCA | APD-1-0151 |
| Country Sunshine | RCA | APL-1-0344 |

## WHEELER, BILLY EDD

| | | |
|---|---|---|
| Love | RCA | LSP-4491 |
| I Ain't the Worryin' Kind | Kapp | 3567 |
| Nashville Zodiac | UA | 6711 |

## WHITMAN, SLIM

| | | |
|---|---|---|
| The Best of Slim | UA | 6832 |
| Guess Who | UA | 6783 |
| It's a Sin to Tell a Lie | UA | 6819 |
| Ramblin' Rose | Sun | 5320 |
| Yodeling | Lib. | LP-9235 |

## THE WILBURN BROTHERS

| | | |
|---|---|---|
| It's Another World | Dec. | 74954 |
| Need More Happiness | Dec. | 75087 |
| Looks Like the Sun's Gonna Shine | Dec. | 75123 |
| Little Johnny Down the Street | Dec. | 75173 |
| Take Up Thy Cross | MCA | DL-7-4464 |
| That She's-Leaving Feeling | MCA | DL-7-5291 |
| A Portrait | MCA | MCA-2-4011 |
| Carefree Moments | MCA | VL-7-3691 |
| That Country Feeling | MCA | VL-7-3876 |
| I Walk the Line | MCA | VL-7-3889 |

## WILLIAMS, HANK, JR.

| | | |
|---|---|---|
| Hank Williams, Jr., Sings Songs of Hank Williams | MGM | 4213 |
| Hank Williams' Life Story—<br>   Music from the Motion Picture *Your Cheatin' Heart* | MGM | 4260 |
| Hank Williams, Sr., and Hank Williams, Jr. | MGM | 4276 |

| TITLE | LABEL | RECORD NO. |
|---|---|---|
| Ballads of the Hills and Plains | MGM | 4316 |
| Again | MGM | 4378 |
| The Best of Hank Williams, Jr. | MGM | 4513 |
| My Songs | MGM | 4527 |
| A Time to Sing | MGM | 4540-ST |
| Luke the Drifter, Jr. | MGM | 4559 |
| Songs My Father Left Me | MGM | 4621 |
| Hank Williams, Jr., Live at Cobo Hall, Detroit | MGM | 4644 |
| Greatest Hits | MGM | 4656 |
| Sunday Morning | MGM | 4657 |
| Luke the Drifter, Jr. | MGM | 4673 |
| Singing My Songs, (signed) Johnny Cash | MGM | 4675 |
| Removing the Shadow (with Lois Johnson) | MGM | 4721 |
| All for the Love of Sunshine (with The Mike Curb Congregation) | MGM | 4750 |
| I've Got a Right to Cry/They All Used to Belong to Me | MGM | 4774 |
| Sweet Dreams (with The Mike Curb Congregation) | MGM | 4798 |
| Greatest Hits, Vol. 2 | MGM | 4822 |
| Eleven Roses | MGM | 4843 |
| Send Me Some Lovin'/Whole Lotta Lovin' (with Lois Johnson) | MGM | 4857 |
| Hank Williams/Hank Williams, Jr.—The Legend of Hank Williams in Song and Story (2 records) | MGM | SES-4865 |
| Hank Williams, Jr. | MGM | 119 |

## WILLIAMS, HANK, SR.

| | | |
|---|---|---|
| I Saw the Light | MGM | 3331 |
| The Unforgettable Hank Williams | MGM | 3733 |
| Wait for the Light to Shine | MGM | 3850 |
| Greatest Hits | MGM | 3918 |
| Le Me Sing a Blue Song | MGM | 3924 |
| Wanderin' Around | MGM | 3925 |
| I'm Blue Inside | MGM | 3926 |
| First, Last, and Always | MGM | 3928 |
| The Spirit of Hank Williams | MGM | 3955 |
| On Stage | MGM | 3999 |
| Greatest Hits, Vol. 2 | MGM | 4040 |
| On Stage, Vol. 2 | MGM | 4109 |
| Greatest Hits, Vol. 3 | MGM | 4140 |
| The Very Best of Hank Williams | MGM | 4168 |
| The Very Best of Hank Williams, Vol. 2 | MGM | 4227 |
| "Lost Highway" and Other Folk Ballads | MGM | 4254 |
| Hank Williams, Sr., and Hank Williams, Jr. | MGM | 4276 |
| Hank Williams Sings "Kaw-Liga" and Other Humorous Songs | MGM | 4300 |
| The Legend Lives Anew | MGM | 4377 |
| Again | MGM | 4378 |
| Luke the Drifter | MGM | 4380 |
| I Won't Be Home No More | MGM | 4481 |
| Hank Williams and Strings, Vol. 3 | MGM | 4529 |
| In the Beginning | MGM | 4576 |

# DISCOGRAPHY

| TITLE | LABEL | RECORD NO. |
|---|---|---|
| The Essential Hank Williams | MGM | 4651 |
| Life to Legend | MGM | 4680 |
| Twenty-four of Hank Williams' Greatest Hits | MGM | 4755-2 |
| Hank Williams/Hank Williams, Jr.—The Legend of Hank Williams in Song and Story (2 records) | MGM | SES-4865 |

## WILLIAMS, TEX

| | | |
|---|---|---|
| A Man Called Tex | Mon. | 5044 |
| Tex Williams | Sun | 5144 |

## THE WILLIS BROTHERS

| | | |
|---|---|---|
| The Best of the Willis Brothers | Star. | S-466 |
| Bummin' Around | Star. | S-442 |
| For the Good Times | Star. | S-473 |

## WILLS, BOB

| | | |
|---|---|---|
| The History of Bob Wills and The Texas Playboys | MGM | 4866 |
| A Tribute to Bob Wills | MGM | 141 |
| Greatest String Band Hits | MCA | MCA-152 |
| The Best of Bob Wills | MCA | MCA-153 |
| Bob Wills and His Texas Playboys | MCA | DL-78727 |
| King of Western Swing | MCA | KS-3523 |
| Time Changes Everything | MCA | KS-3569 |
| The Living Legend | MCA | KS-3587 |
| Mel Tillis and Bob Wills "in Person" | MCA | KS-3639 |
| The Best of Bob Wills | MCA | MCA-153 |
| Western Swing | MCA | VL-73735 |

## WISEMAN, MAC

| | | |
|---|---|---|
| Golden Hits | Dot | DLP-25896 |
| Concert Favorites | RCA | LSP-4845 |
| Over the Hills (with Lester Flatt) | RCA | APL-1-0309 |
| Lester 'n' Mac (with Lester Flatt) | RCA | LSP-4547 |
| On the South-Bound (with Lester Flatt) | RCA | LSP-4688 |

## WOOLEY, SHEB

| | | |
|---|---|---|
| The Very Best of Sheb Wooley | MGM | 4275 |

## WORTH, MARION

| TITLE | LABEL | RECORD NO. |
|---|---|---|
| Woman Needs Love | Dec. | 74936 |

## WRIGHT, JOHNNY

| | | |
|---|---|---|
| Heart-Warming Gospel Songs (with Kitty Wells) | MCA | DL-7-5325 |
| Favorites | Dec. | 75019 |
| Wright Way | Dec. | 74846 |

## WYNETTE, TAMMY

| | | |
|---|---|---|
| Bedtime Story | Epic | KE-31285 |
| Christmas with Tammy | Col. | E-30343 |
| D-I-V-O-R-C-E | Col. | BN-26392 |
| The First Songs of the First Lady | Col. | KEG-30358 |
| Greatest Hits | Col. | BN-26486 |
| Greatest Hits, Vol. 2 | Col. | E-30733 |
| Inspiration | Col. | BN-26423 |
| It's Just a Matter of Time | Har. | KH-30914 |
| Kids Say the Darndest Things | Epic | KE-31937 |
| Let's Build a World Together (with George Jones) | Epic | KE-32113 |
| Me and the First Lady (with George Jones) | Epic | KE-31554 |
| My Man | Epic | KE-31717 |
| Stand By Your Man | Col. | BN-26451 |
| Take Me to Your World | Col. | BN-26353 |
| Tammy Wynette | Har. | KH-30096 |
| Tammy's Touch | Col. | BN-26549 |
| The Ways to Love a Man | Col. | BN-26519 |
| We Go Together (with George Jones) | Epic | KE-30802 |
| We Love to Sing About Jesus (with George Jones) | Epic | KE-31719 |
| We Sure Can Love Each Other | Col. | E-30658 |
| The World of Tammy Wynette | Col. | EGP-503 |
| Your Good Girl's Gonna Go Bad | Col. | BN-26305 |

## YOUNG, FARON

| | | |
|---|---|---|
| The Best of Faron Young | Mer. | SR-61267 |
| Step Aside | Mer. | SR-61337 |
| Faron Young Sings "Leavin' and Sayin' Good-bye" | Mer. | SR-61354 |
| It's Four in the Morning with Faron Young | Mer. | SR-61359 |
| Faron Young Sings "This Little Girl of Mine" | Mer. | SR-61364 |
| This Time the Hurtin's on Me | Mer. | SR-61376 |

# COUNTRY RADIO STATIONS
# UNITED STATES, PUERTO RICO, AND CANADA

According to the Country Music Association, the following radio stations program country music at least eight hours a day.

## UNITED STATES

| Call Letters | Spot on Dial | Call Letters | Spot on Dial |
|---|---|---|---|
| **ALABAMA** | | | |
| *Country Exclusively* | | WBAM | 740 |
| WARI | 1480 | WHHY-FM | 102 |
| WARI-FM | 94.3 | WHIY | 1500 |
| WAAO | 1530 | WAOA | 1520 |
| WANA | 1490 | WAYD | 1190 |
| WRAB | 1380 | WOAB-FM | 104.9 |
| WJMW | 730 | WVSM | 1500 |
| WBCA | 1110 | WWWR | 920 |
| WYAM | 1450 | WELR | 1360 |
| WYDE | 850 | WELR-FM | 95.3 |
| WBTS | 1480 | WCNA-FM | 98.3 |
| WYBE | 1370 | WSHF | 1290 |
| WCOX | 1540 | WTUN | 100.1 |
| WAGC | 1560 | WEYY | 1580 |
| WEIS | 990 | WTLS | 1300 |
| WBIB | 1110 | WACT | 1420 |
| WKLF | 980 | WACT-FM | 105.5 |
| WDRM-FM | 102.1 | WRCK | 1410 |
| WHOS | 800 | WRCK-FM | 106.3 |
| WAGF | 1320 | WETU | 1250 |
| WTVY-FM | 955 | WRMG | 1430 |
| WIRB | 600 | WEZQ | 1300 |
| WBLO | 1470 | | |
| WXOR | 1340 | *13 Hours Daily* | |
| WZOB | 1250 | WAMA | 1340 |
| WGEA | 1150 | | |
| WGEA-FM | 93.5 | *12 Hours Daily* | |
| WERH | 970 | WAAX | 570 |
| WERH-FM | 92.1 | | |
| WBHP | 1230 | *9 Hours Daily* | |
| WHOD | 1290 | WKLF | 980 |
| WHOD-FM | 104.9 | WROS | 1330 |
| WARF | 1240 | | |
| WLVN | 1080 | *8 Hours Daily* | |
| WZAM | 1270 | WPRN | 1240 |
| WLIQ | 1360 | WEIS | 990 |
| WUNI | 1410 | WTBF | 970 |
| | | WVNA | 1590 |

| Call Letters | Spot on Dial | Call Letters | Spot on Dial |
|---|---|---|---|
| **ALASKA** | | *16 Hours Daily* | |
| | | KLCN-FM | 96.1 |
| *Country Exclusively* | | *12 Hours Daily* | |
| KYAK | 650 | KDEW | 1470 |
| KIAK | 970 | KDEW-FM | 96.7 |
| KINY | 800 | *9 Hours Daily* | |
| KJNP | 1170 | KFFA | 1360 |
| *8 Hours Daily* | | *8 Hours Daily* | |
| KBYR | 700 | KGMR-FM | 100.3 |
| KNOM | 780 | KPCA | 1580 |
| **ARIZONA** | | **CALIFORNIA** | |
| *Country Exclusively* | | *Country Exclusively* | |
| KCUZ | 1490 | KFYV | 1280 |
| KCKY | 1150 | KUZZ | 800 |
| KAPR | 930 | KZIN-FM | 107.9 |
| KAFF | 930 | KIOT | 1310 |
| KJJJ | 910 | KROP | 1300 |
| KNIX-FM | 102.5 | KEAP | 980 |
| KRDS | 1190 | KMAK | 1340 |
| KTUF | 1580 | KIEV | 870 |
| KCUB | 1290 | KNGS | 620 |
| KHOS | 940 | KBVM | 1380 |
| KHIL | 1250 | KFOX | 1280 |
| | | KFOX-FM | 100.3 |
| *12 Hours Daily* | | KLAC | 570 |
| KCYN | 1240 | KMPC | 710 |
| | | KWIP | 1580 |
| *10 Hours Daily* | | KLOC | 920 |
| KDJI | 1270 | KDOL | 1340 |
| | | KDOL-FM | 97.7 |
| *8 Hours Daily* | | KGUY | 1270 |
| KNOT | 1450 | KKAR | 1220 |
| KVSL | 1450 | KWOW | 1600 |
| | | KCLM | 1330 |
| **ARKANSAS** | | KACE | 1570 |
| *Country Exclusively* | | KACE-FM | 92.7 |
| KMCW | 1190 | KPSC-FM | 96.9 |
| KBBA | 690 | KRAK | 1140 |
| KAMD | 910 | KTOM | 1380 |
| KVEE | 1330 | KRSA | 1570 |
| KVEE-FM | 105.1 | KCKC | 1350 |
| KCAB | 980 | KOZN-FM | 103.7 |
| KCAB-FM | 102.3 | KSON | 1240 |
| KFAY | 1250 | KSAY | 1010 |
| KTCS | 1410 | KEEN | 1370 |
| KTCS-FM | 99.9 | KGUD | 990 |
| KBHS | 590 | KGUD-FM | 99.9 |
| KXOW | 1420 | KZON | 1600 |
| KLRA | 1010 | KVRE | 1460 |
| KZOT | 1460 | KGEN | 1370 |
| KBIB | 1560 | KCEY | 1390 |
| KBHC | 1260 | KCIN | 1590 |
| KCCL | 1460 | | |
| KADL | 1270 | *9 Hours Daily* | |
| KADL-FM | 94.9 | KCNO | 570 |
| KCLA | 1400 | KBPK-FM | 90.1 |
| KUOA | 1290 | | |
| KSUD | 730 | | |

| Call Letters | Spot on Dial | Call Letters | Spot on Dial |
|---|---|---|---|
| **COLORADO** | | WCEA-FM | 95.9 |
| | | WQIK | 1090 |
| *Country Exclusively* | | WQIK-FM | 99.1 |
| KPIK-FM | 94.3 | WVOJ | 1320 |
| KPIK | 1580 | WDSR | 1340 |
| KSSS | 740 | WGRO | 960 |
| KLAK | 1600 | WLIZ | 1380 |
| KLAK-FM | 107.5 | WWAB | 1330 |
| KQIL | 1340 | WZST | 1410 |
| KSTR | 620 | WTAI | 1560 |
| KREX-FM | 92.3 | WTAI-FM | 107.1 |
| KYOU | 1450 | WYRL-FM | 102.3 |
| KPUB | 1480 | WWOK | 1260 |
| KWYD-FM | 105.5 | WXBM-FM | 102.3 |
| KUAD | 1170 | WWSD | 1090 |
| | | WGUL-FM | 105.5 |
| *19 Hours Daily* | | WMOP | 900 |
| KGEK | 1230 | WOKC | 1570 |
| | | WLMC-FM | 103.1 |
| *12 Hours Daily* | | WFIV | 1080 |
| KIUP | 930 | WHOO | 990 |
| | | WHOO-FM | 96.8 |
| *8 Hours Daily* | | WPAP-FM | 590 |
| KBRN | 800 | WSCM | 1290 |
| | | WNVY | 1230 |
| | | WPFA | 790 |
| **CONNECTICUT** | | WGKR | 1310 |
| | | WPLA | 910 |
| *Country Exclusively* | | WJOE | 1080 |
| WCDQ | 1220 | WAOC | 1420 |
| WFIF | 1500 | WELE | 1590 |
| WIOF-FM | 104.1 | WSAF-FM | 102.5 |
| WEXT | 1550 | WMEN | 1330 |
| | | WOMA-FM | 94.9 |
| | | WQYK | 1110 |
| **DELAWARE** | | WQYK-FM | 99.5 |
| | | WHBO | 1050 |
| *Country Exclusively* | | WYOU | 1550 |
| WAFL-FM | 97.7 | WMEN | 1313 |
| | | WFSH | 1340 |
| | | WEAT | 850 |
| **FLORIDA** | | | |
| | | *17 Hours Daily* | |
| *Country Exclusively* | | WPXE | 1490 |
| WTWB | 1570 | | |
| WAPR | 1390 | *14 Hours Daily* | |
| WBAR | 1460 | WPAS | 1400 |
| WPUL | 1130 | | |
| WSWN | 900 | *12 Hours Daily* | |
| WSBP | 1580 | WBGC | 1240 |
| WWBC | 1510 | WTYS | 1340 |
| WAAZ-FM | 104.9 | | |
| WCNU | 1010 | *11 Hours Daily* | |
| WDCF | 1350 | WSUZ | 800 |
| WELE | 1590 | | |
| WDLF-FM | 105.9 | *8 Hours Daily* | |
| WKKX | 1310 | WKMK | 1000 |
| WEXY | 1520 | WJSB | 1050 |
| WDVH | 980 | WMAF | 1230 |
| WHAN | 930 | | |
| WGMA | 1320 | | |
| WCOF | 1490 | | |

379

| Call Letters | Spot on Dial | Call Letters | Spot on Dial |
|---|---|---|---|
| **GEORGIA** | | *10 Hours Daily* | |
| | | WPCH-FM | 94.9 |
| *Country Exclusively* | | WHIE | 1320 |
| WJAZ | 960 | | |
| WMES | 1570 | *9 Hours Daily* | |
| WDOL | 1470 | WBBK | 1260 |
| WNGC-FM | 95.5 | WKRW | 1270 |
| WPLO | 590 | WOKA | 1310 |
| WFNL | 1600 | WFDR | 1370 |
| WGUS | 1380 | WMTM | 1300 |
| WACX | 1600 | WBRO | 1310 |
| WAZA | 1360 | | |
| WMGR | 930 | *8 Hours Daily* | |
| WEBS | 1110 | WRWH | 1350 |
| WVMG | 1440 | WDWD | 990 |
| WVMG-FM | 96.7 | WSEM | 1500 |
| WCLS | 1580 | WSYL | 1490 |
| WHYD | 1270 | WTIF | 1340 |
| WHYD-FM | 107.3 | | |
| WPNX | 1460 | **HAWAII** | |
| WFAV-FM | 98.3 | | |
| WRCD | 1430 | *Country Exclusively* | |
| WDGL | 1520 | KAHU | 940 |
| WSSA | 1570 | | |
| WNRJ | 1130 | **IDAHO** | |
| WNMT | 1520 | | |
| WKOG | 1560 | *Country Exclusively* | |
| WGRI | 1410 | KBRJ | 950 |
| WCEH | 610 | KGEM | 1140 |
| WLOP | 1370 | KGVM-FM | 99.1 |
| WLAG-FM | 104.1 | KUPI | 980 |
| WDEN-FM | 105.3 | KART | 1400 |
| WDEN | 1500 | KMCL | 1240 |
| WBIE-FM | 101.5 | KPST | 1340 |
| WBIE | 1080 | KSPT | 1400 |
| WNGA | 1600 | KBRV | 790 |
| WPGA | 980 | | |
| WLAQ | 1410 | *13 Hours Daily* | |
| WBYG | 1450 | KYET | 1450 |
| WEAS | 900 | | |
| WYNX | 1550 | *10 Hours Daily* | |
| WMCD-FM | 100.1 | KTEE | 1260 |
| WTGA | 1590 | | |
| WLOR | 730 | *8 Hours Daily* | |
| WLET | 1420 | KAYT | 970 |
| WGOV-FM | 92.9 | | |
| WJEM | 1150 | **ILLINOIS** | |
| WBMK | 1310 | | |
| | | *Country Exclusively* | |
| *19 Hours Daily* | | WFVR | 1580 |
| WXLI | 1230 | WKZI | 800 |
| WXLI-FM | 92.7 | WCCR | 1580 |
| | | WJJD | 1160 |
| *13 Hours Daily* | | WJJD-FM | 104.3 |
| WBHF | 1450 | WHOW | 1520 |
| WMTM-FM | 93.9 | WIAI-FM | 99.1 |
| | | WNOI-FM | 103.9 |
| *12 Hours Daily* | | WGIL-FM | 94.9 |
| WLOV | 1370 | WGNU | 920 |
| WLOV-FM | 100.1 | WJIL | 1550 |
| | | WKAK-FM | 99.9 |

| Call Letters | Spot on Dial |
|---|---|
| WDDD-FM | 107.1 |
| WMCL | 1060 |
| WAKC | 1440 |
| WXCL | 1350 |
| WROK | 1440 |
| WFMB-FM | 104.5 |
| WIZZ | 1250 |
| WIZZ-FM | 97.7 |
| WPMB | 1500 |

*12 Hours Daily*

| | |
|---|---|
| WSOY-FM | 102.9 |

*10 Hours Daily*

| | |
|---|---|
| WCRA-FM | 95.7 |
| WGNU-FM | 106.5 |
| WAKO910 | |
| WVJC | 89.1 |
| WRTL | 1460 |
| WSDR | 1240 |

*8 Hours Daily*

| | |
|---|---|
| WESN-FM | 88.1 |
| WJBD | 1350 |
| WJBD-FM | 100.1 |

## INDIANA

*Country Exclusively*

| | |
|---|---|
| WIFF | 1570 |
| WSCH-FM | 99.3 |
| WWCM | 1130 |
| WCSI | 1010 |
| WROZ | 1400 |
| WFWR | 1090 |
| WIRE | 1430 |
| WNIR | 1590 |
| WWKI-FM | 100.5 |
| WVAK | 1560 |
| WVAK-FM | 95.3 |
| WARU | 1600 |
| WARU-FM | 98.3 |
| WGLM-FM | 96.1 |
| WSLM-FM | 98.9 |
| WMPI | 100.9 |
| WSVL-FM | 97.1 |
| WRBR-FM | 103.9 |
| WPFR | 102.7 |

*12 Hours Daily*

| | |
|---|---|
| WLCL-FM | 107.1 |
| WOCH | 1460 |
| WOCH-FM | 106.1 |

*10 Hours Daily*

| | |
|---|---|
| WSLM | 1220 |

*8 Hours Daily*

| | |
|---|---|
| WILO | 1570 |

| Call Letters | Spot on Dial |
|---|---|
| WILO-FM | 99.7 |
| WSMJ | 99.5 |
| WJOB | 1230 |
| WORX | 1270 |
| WORX-FM | 96.7 |
| WIBW | 580 |

## IOWA

*Country Exclusively*

| | |
|---|---|
| KKUZ | 1150 |
| KHAK | 1360 |
| KHAK-FM | 98.1 |
| KWKY | 1150 |
| WDBQ-FM | 105.3 |
| KWMT | 540 |
| KOUR | 1220 |
| KOUR-FM | 95.3 |
| KSMN | 1010 |
| KXEL | 1540 |
| KOEL-FM | 92.3 |
| KLEE | 1480 |
| KFNF | 920 |

*14 Hours Daily*

| | |
|---|---|
| KTOF-FM | 104.5 |

*13 Hours Daily*

| | |
|---|---|
| KNEI | 1140 |

*12 Hours Daily*

| | |
|---|---|
| KVDB | 1090 |

*11 Hours Daily*

| | |
|---|---|
| WHO | 1040 |

*8 Hours Daily*

| | |
|---|---|
| KHBT-FM | 97.7 |

## KANSAS

*Country Exclusively*

| | |
|---|---|
| KKOY-FM | 105.5 |
| KWBW-FM | 103 |
| KCKN | 1340 |
| KCKN-FM | 94.1 |
| KCLO | 1410 |
| KLIB | 1470 |
| KFDI | 1070 |
| KFDI-FM | 101.3 |
| KJCT-FM | 95.1 |
| KWBB | 1410 |

*9 Hours Daily*

| | |
|---|---|
| KALN | 1370 |
| KFLA | 1310 |

*8 Hours Daily*

| | |
|---|---|
| KUPK | 1050 |
| KUPK-FM | 97.3 |
| KJCK | 1420 |

| Call Letters | Spot on Dial | Call Letters | Spot on Dial |
|---|---|---|---|
| **KENTUCKY** | | *9 Hours Daily* | |
| | | WGOH | 1370 |
| *Country Exclusively* | | WMIK | 560 |
| WTCR | 1420 | | |
| WYWY | 950 | *8 Hours Daily* | |
| WLJC-FM | 102.3 | WKCB | 1540 |
| WIBJ | 1410 | WVKY | 1270 |
| WIBJ-FM | 96.7 | WDOC | 1310 |
| WKDZ | 1110 | WDOC-FM | 95.5 |
| WKDZ-FM | 106.3 | WPRT | 960 |
| WTCO | 1450 | WPRT-FM | 105.5 |
| WCAK | 92.7 | WCND | 940 |
| WSTL | 1600 | | |
| WKYW-FM | 104.9 | | |
| WGGC-FM | 95.1 | | |
| WLLS | 1600 | | |
| WLLS-FM | 106.3 | **LOUISIANA** | |
| WKCM | 1140 | | |
| WKIC | 1390 | *Country Exclusively* | |
| WSON | 860 | WABL | 1570 |
| WEKG | 810 | KVOB | 1340 |
| WJRS-FM | 103.1 | WYNK | 1380 |
| WIXI | 1280 | WYNK-FM | 101.5 |
| WAXU | 1580 | KCTO | 1540 |
| WINN | 1240 | WSLG | 1090 |
| WTMT | 620 | WLBI | 1220 |
| WFMW | 730 | KFNV-FM | 93.5 |
| WFTM-FM | 95.9 | WFCG | 1110 |
| WFLW | 1360 | KCIL-FM | 107.1 |
| WNKY | 1480 | KJEF | 1290 |
| WBKR-FM | 92.5 | KXKW | 1520 |
| WNVL | 1250 | KIKS | 1310 |
| WKYX-FM | 93.3 | KLCL | 1470 |
| WBGR | 1440 | KREB-FM | 106.1 |
| WBGR-FM | 96.7 | WSHO | 800 |
| WDHR | 106.3 | KREH | 900 |
| WTJM | 106.3 | KDBH | 97.7 |
| WCBR | 1110 | WNOE-FM | 101.1 |
| WCBR-FM | 101.7 | KJOE | 1480 |
| WRSL | 1520 | KRMD | 1340 |
| WKKS | 1570 | KRMD-FM | 101.1 |
| WTCW | 920 | KAGY | 1510 |
| WTCW-FM | 103.9 | KUZN | 1310 |
| WEZJ | 1440 | KVCL | 1270 |
| | | *12 Hours Daily* | |
| *16 Hours Daily* | | KWCL | 1280 |
| WVCM | 100.1 | KWCL-FM | 96.7 |
| | | | |
| *12 Hours Daily* | | *11 Hours Daily* | |
| WLCK | 1250 | WFPR | 1400 |
| WLCK-FM | 99.3 | | |
| WSEK-FM | 96.7 | *10 Hours Daily* | |
| | | KWKH | 1130 |
| *11 Hours Daily* | | | |
| WRVK | 1460 | *9 Hours Daily* | |
| | | KALB | 580 |
| *10 Hours Daily* | | | |
| WANY | 1390 | *8 Hours Daily* | |
| WANY-FM | 106.3 | KTRY | 730 |
| WTKY | 1370 | WWL | 870 |
| WTKY-FM | 92.1 | KSLO | 1230 |

| Call Letters | Spot on Dial |
|---|---|
| **MAINE** | |
| *Country Exclusively* | |
| WFAU | 1340 |
| WFAU-FM | 101.3 |
| WBGW | 97.1 |
| WPOR | 1490 |
| WPOR-FM | 101.9 |
| WJAB | 1440 |
| **MARYLAND** | |
| *Country Exclusively* | |
| WBMD | 750 |
| WTRI | 1520 |
| WCEM-FM | 1240 |
| WFRB | 560 |
| WFRB-FM | 105.3 |
| WISZ | 1590 |
| WISZ-FM | 95.9 |
| WICO | 1320 |
| WICO-FM | 94.3 |
| WYII-FM | 95.9 |
| WDON | 1540 |
| **MASSACHUSETTS** | |
| *Country Exclusively* | |
| WCOP | 1150 |
| WFMP-FM | 104.5 |
| WMAS | 1450 |
| *10 Hours Daily* | |
| WBET | 1460 |
| *8 Hours Daily* | |
| WREB | 930 |
| WOCB-FM | 94.9 |
| **MICHIGAN** | |
| *Country Exclusively* | |
| WNRS | 1290 |
| WNRZ-FM | 102.9 |
| WXOX | 1250 |
| WBRN | 1460 |
| WBRN-FM | 100.9 |
| WANG-FM | 98.5 |
| WDEE | 1500 |
| WEXL | 1340 |
| WCZN | 1570 |
| WKMF | 1470 |
| WJEF | 1230 |
| WJCO | 1510 |
| WBUK | 1560 |
| WITL | 1010 |
| WITL-FM | 100.7 |
| WSMA | 1590 |
| WKBZ | 850 |
| WAOP | 980 |
| WSJM-FM | 107.1 |

| Call Letters | Spot on Dial |
|---|---|
| WMIC | 1560 |
| WMIC-FM | 97.7 |
| WSMM | 92.7 |
| WSDS | 1480 |
| WZND | 99.3 |
| *14 Hours Daily* | |
| WILS-FM | 101.7 |
| *12 Hours Daily* | |
| WJML | 1110 |
| *10 Hours Daily* | |
| WVOC | 1500 |
| *8 Hours Daily* | |
| WNMR-FM | 90.1 |
| WSOO | 1230 |
| **MINNESOTA** | |
| *Country Exclusively* | |
| WXOX | 1250 |
| KLIZ | 1380 |
| KRWC | 1360 |
| KDAN | 1370 |
| WDSM | 710 |
| KAOH | 1390 |
| KRAD | 1590 |
| WMFG | 1240 |
| KEYL | 1400 |
| KTCR | 690 |
| KTCR-FM | 97.1 |
| KTMF | 1350 |
| KFIL | 1060 |
| KLOH | 1050 |
| KOLM | 1520 |
| WVAL | 800 |
| *13 Hours Daily* | |
| KDHL | 920 |
| KDHL-FM | 95.9 |
| *12 Hours Daily* | |
| WHLB | 1400 |
| *11 Hours Daily* | |
| KQDE-FM | 92.1 |
| *8 Hours Daily* | |
| KAGE-FM | 95.3 |
| **MISSISSIPPI** | |
| *Country Exclusively* | |
| WMPF-FM | 105.5 |
| WAMY | 1580 |
| WVMI | 570 |
| WRKN | 970 |
| WMBC | 1400 |

383

| Call Letters | Spot on Dial | Call Letters | Spot on Dial |
|---|---|---|---|
| WCHJ | 1470 | **MISSOURI** | |
| WJRL | 1530 | | |
| WDSK | 1410 | *Country Exclusively* | |
| WCMA | 1230 | KWAT | 1370 |
| WWTX-FM | 95.3 | KPCR | 1530 |
| WDMS-FM | 100.7 | KZYM | 1220 |
| WGVM | 1260 | KDKD | 1280 |
| WRIL-FM | 100.1 | KHAD | 1190 |
| WBKH | 950 | KDFN | 1500 |
| WJQS | 1400 | KFMO | 1240 |
| WLAV | 1430 | KFTW | 1450 |
| WRBE | 1440 | KFAL | 900 |
| WCOC | 910 | KBTC | 1250 |
| WOKK | 1450 | KJFF-FM | 106.9 |
| WJXN | 1450 | WMBH | 1450 |
| WNAU-FM | 103.2 | KBIL | 1140 |
| WCIS | 1460 | KBOA | 830 |
| WKPO | 1510 | KTMO-FM | 98.9 |
| WJLJ | 1060 | KEMM | 1510 |
| WTUP | 1490 | KRES-FM | 1230 |
| WKYV-FM | 106.7 | KPWB | 1140 |
| WVLY | 1320 | KWOC | 903 |
| WIGG | 1420 | KYRO | 1280 |
| WJNS-FM | 92.1 | KZNN-FM | 105.3 |
| | | KUSN | 1270 |
| *13 Hours Daily* | | WGNU | 920 |
| WABG | 960 | WIL | 1430 |
| WNAT | 1450 | KSMO-FM | 95.9 |
| WROB | 1450 | KDRO | 1490 |
| | | KMPL-FM | 97.1 |
| *12 Hours Daily* | | KTTS | 1400 |
| WVMI-FM | 93.7 | KTTS-FM | 94.7 |
| WCJU | 1450 | KWTO | 560 |
| WSEL | 1440 | KALM | 1290 |
| WSEL-FM | 96.7 | KFBD | 1270 |
| | | KFBD-FM | 97.7 |
| *11 Hours Daily* | | | |
| WOOR-FM | 1420 | | |
| | | *18 Hours Daily* | |
| *10 Hours Daily* | | WGNU-FM | 920 |
| WHII | 1570 | | |
| WSJC-FM | 107.5 | | |
| WMLC | 1270 | *14 Hours Daily* | |
| WBKN | 1410 | KGMO | 810 |
| | | | |
| *9 Hours Daily* | | *10 Hours Daily* | |
| WXTN | 1000 | KLRS | 1360 |
| WMLC | 1270 | KFBD-FM | 97.7 |
| WABO | 990 | KWPM | 1450 |
| WABO-FM | 105.5 | | |
| | | *9 Hours Daily* | |
| *8 Hours Daily* | | KMRN | 1360 |
| WBIP | 1400 | KTUI | 1560 |
| WFTO | 1330 | | |
| WMDC | 1220 | | |
| WMDC-FM | 100.9 | *8 Hours Daily* | |
| WVOM | 1270 | KNIM-FM | 95.3 |
| WLSM | 1270 | KNIM | 1580 |
| WQMA | 1520 | KRMS | 1150 |
| WBFN | 1500 | KWRE | 730 |
| WNJC | 90.1 | | |

| Call Letters | Spot on Dial | Call Letters | Spot on Dial |
|---|---|---|---|
| **MONTANA** | | WOTW-FM | 106.3 |
| | | WCNL-FM | 104.9 |
| *Country Exclusively* | | | |
| KANA | 580 | *10 Hours Daily* | |
| KFLN | 960 | WLTN | 1400 |
| KBMY | 1240 | | |
| KOYN | 910 | *8 Hours Daily* | |
| KMON | 560 | WBBX | 1380 |
| KLYQ | 980 | | |
| KHDN | 1230 | **NEW JERSEY** | |
| KGMY | 1450 | | |
| KYSS | 930 | *Country Exclusively* | |
| KVCK | 1450 | WSUS-FM | 102.3 |
| | | WDLV | 1270 |
| *16 Hours Daily* | | | |
| KGEZ | 600 | *12 Hours Daily* | |
| | | WDVL-FM | 92.1 |
| *13 Hours Daily* | | | |
| KXXL | 1450 | **NEW MEXICO** | |
| | | | |
| *11 Hours Daily* | | *Country Exclusively* | |
| KWYS | 920 | KCCC | 930 |
| | | KRZE | 1280 |
| *8 Hours Daily* | | KCIA | 1110 |
| KBMN | 1230 | KGRD-FM | 103.9 |
| KGCX | 1480 | KENM | 1450 |
| | | KRSY | 1230 |
| | | KAFE | 810 |
| **NEBRASKA** | | KNFT | 950 |
| | | KCHS | 1400 |
| *Country Exclusively* | | KTNM | 1400 |
| KAMI | 1580 | | |
| KGMT | 1310 | *13 Hours Daily* | |
| KRVN | 880 | KBIM-FM | 94.9 |
| KECK | 1530 | | |
| KHAT-FM | 106.3 | *8 Hours Daily* | |
| KEYR | 690 | KWEW | 1480 |
| | | KAFE-FM | 97.3 |
| *16 Hours Daily* | | | |
| WJAG-FM | 106.7 | **NEW YORK** | |
| | | | |
| *9 Hours Daily* | | *Country Exclusively* | |
| WJAG | 780 | WOKO | 1460 |
| | | WSEN | 1050 |
| *8 Hours Daily* | | WSEN-FM | 92.1 |
| KBBB | 1400 | WGHT | 1380 |
| KGFW | 1340 | WKOP | 1360 |
| | | WWOL | 1120 |
| | | WWOL-FM | 104.1 |
| **NEVADA** | | WBZA-FM | 107.1 |
| | | WQIX-FM | 100.9 |
| *Country Exclusively* | | WIZR-FM | 104.9 |
| KPTL | 1300 | WXRL | 1300 |
| KPTL-FM | 97.3 | WHN | 1050 |
| KVLV | 980 | WEAV | 960 |
| KRAM | 1340 | WPDH-FM | 101.5 |
| KONE | 1450 | WADR | 1480 |
| | | WNYR | 680 |
| | | WGNA-FM | 107.7 |
| **NEW HAMPSHIRE** | | WHAZ | 1330 |
| | | WGMF | 1500 |
| *Country Exclusively* | | | |
| WDNH-FM | 97.5 | | |

| Call Letters | Spot on Dial | Call Letters | Spot on Dial |
|---|---|---|---|
| *12 Hours Daily* | | WTRQ | 1560 |
| WXXY-FM | 104.9 | WEEW | 1320 |
| | | WETC | 540 |
| *8 Hours Daily* | | WKLM | 980 |
| WTHE | 1520 | WHSL | 1490 |
| | | WWIL-FM | 97.3 |
| | | WLLY | 1350 |
| | | WBTE | 990 |
| **NORTH CAROLINA** | | WKBX | 1500 |
| | | WYDK | 1480 |
| *Country Exclusively* | | | |
| WCSE-FM | 92.3 | *13 Hours Daily* | |
| WSKY | 1230 | WIZS | 1450 |
| WWNC | 570 | WRDX-FM | 106.5 |
| WBYP | 1130 | | |
| WPTL | 920 | *12 Hours Daily* | |
| WAME | 1480 | WBMA | 1400 |
| WKTC | 1310 | WMBL-FM | 95.9 |
| WSOC | 103.7 | | |
| WPEG-FM | 97.9 | *11 Hours Daily* | |
| WQTI-FM | 103.1 | WFMA | 100.7 |
| WTIK | 1310 | WADE | 1210 |
| WEAF-FM | 94.5 | | |
| WLOE | 1490 | *10 Hours Daily* | |
| WWKO | 1480 | WELS | 1010 |
| WFAG | 1250 | WSAT | 1280 |
| WFAI | 1230 | | |
| WQSM-FM | 98.1 | *9 Hours Daily* | |
| WFSC | 1050 | WDJS | 1430 |
| WAKS | 1460 | | |
| WLTC | 1370 | *8 Hours Daily* | |
| WFMC | 730 | WGNC | 1450 |
| WKJK | 900 | WGNC-FM | 101.9 |
| WGBG | 1400 | WBBO-FM | 93.3 |
| WPXY | 1550 | WNNC | 1230 |
| WKDX | 1250 | WMPM | 1270 |
| WXNC | 92.5 | | |
| WXRC-FM | 95.7 | | |
| WNOS | 1590 | **NORTH DAKOTA** | |
| WNOS-FM | 100.3 | | |
| WLAS | 910 | *Country Exclusively* | |
| WRCM-FM | 92.1 | KBMR | 1130 |
| WRKB | 1460 | KFGO | 790 |
| WRKB-FM | 99.7 | KSJB | 600 |
| WKTE | 1090 | KMAV | 1520 |
| WKMT | 1220 | KTYN | 1430 |
| WRNS-FM | 95.1 | KGCA | 1450 |
| WKGX | 1080 | KTGO | 1090 |
| WIXE | 1190 | | |
| WHIP | 1350 | *9 Hours Daily* | |
| WHIT | 1450 | KNDK | 1080 |
| WKBC | 810 | | |
| WYNA | 1550 | *8 Hours Daily* | |
| WREV | 1220 | WDAY | 970 |
| WRXO-FM | 96.7 | | |
| WWGP | 1050 | **OHIO** | |
| WWGP-FM | 105.5 | | |
| WBZB | 1090 | *Country Exclusively* | |
| WDBM | 550 | WSLR | 1350 |
| WSTH | 860 | WNCO-FM | 101.3 |
| | | WBWC-FM | 88.3 |

| Call Letters | Spot on Dial | Call Letters | Spot on Dial |
|---|---|---|---|
| WMGS | 730 | **11 Hours Daily** | |
| WCLU | 1320 | KNED | 1150 |
| WUBE | 1230 | KCES-FM | 102.3 |
| WUBE-FM | 105.1 | KMUS | 1380 |
| WELW-FM | 107.9 | | |
| WCOL-FM | 92.3 | **10 Hours Daily** | |
| WMNI | 920 | KEOR | 1110 |
| WWOW | 1360 | | |
| WONE | 980 | **9 Hours Daily** | |
| WCNW | 1560 | KCRC-FM | 96.9 |
| WFOL-FM | 94.9 | KRBB-FM | 95.9 |
| WITO-FM | 107.1 | | |
| WLMJ | 1280 | **8 Hours Daily** | |
| WHOK | 95.5 | KTJS | 1420 |
| WLNO-FM | 106.3 | | |
| WBRJ | 910 | **OREGON** | |
| WMPO-FM | 92.1 | | |
| WOBL | 1570 | **Country Exclusively** | |
| WTOD | 1560 | KRKT | 990 |
| WMWM | 1090 | KCMX | 580 |
| | | KVAS | 1230 |
| **10 Hours Daily** | | KNND | 1400 |
| WBCO | 1540 | KATR | 1320 |
| WKBN | 570 | KRDR | 1230 |
| | | KLAD | 960 |
| **9 Hours Daily** | | KMCM | 1260 |
| WOUB | 1340 | KSHA | 860 |
| WOUB-FM | 91.3 | KWJJ | 1080 |
| WSRW | 1590 | KPRB | 1240 |
| WSRW-FM | 106.7 | KRNR | 1490 |
| | | KGAY | 1430 |
| **OKLAHOMA** | | KORE-FM | 93.1 |
| | | KORE | 1050 |
| **Country Exclusively** | | KFIR | 1370 |
| KRPT | 850 | KTDO | 1230 |
| KLTR | 1580 | | |
| KXXX-FM | 105.5 | **12 Hours Daily** | |
| KWPR | 1270 | KOHU | 1360 |
| KADS | 1240 | | |
| KCRC | 1390 | **8 Hours Daily** | |
| KOKC | 1490 | KWRC | 940 |
| KCCO-FM | 98.1 | | |
| KMAD | 1550 | **PENNSYLVANIA** | |
| WNAD | 640 | | |
| KEBC-FM | 94.7 | **Country Exclusively** | |
| KJAK-FM | 100.5 | WHOL | 1600 |
| KLPR | 1140 | WVAM-FM | 100.1 |
| KINB-FM | 107.3 | WASP | 1130 |
| KRBB | 1560 | WIOV-FM | 105.1 |
| KTOW | 1340 | WSKE | 1050 |
| KVOO | 1170 | WHYP | 1530 |
| KWLG | 1530 | WHYP-FM | 100.9 |
| | | WRCP | 1540 |
| **18 Hours Daily** | | WWML | 1470 |
| KGLC | 910 | WKBI-FM | 94.3 |
| | | WGBI | 910 |
| **12 Hours Daily** | | WVSC | 990 |
| KGWA | 960 | WGMR-FM | 101.1 |
| KGYN | 1213 | WNOW | 1250 |
| KTOK | 1000 | | |
| KRBB | 1560 | **16 Hours Daily** | |
| | | WILQ-FM | 105.1 |

387

| Call Letters | Spot on Dial | Call Letters | Spot on Dial |
|---|---|---|---|
| *11 Hours Daily* | | *10 Hours Daily* | |
| WHJB | 620 | WPUB | 1130 |
| | | WCRE | 1420 |
| *10 Hours Daily* | | WAGI-FM | 105.3 |
| WCBG | 1590 | | |
| WPHB | 1260 | *8 Hours Daily* | |
| | | WDSC | 800 |
| *8 Hours Daily* | | WDSC-FM | 92.9 |
| WCVI | 1340 | | |
| WWGO | 1450 | | |
| WHON | 1150 | **SOUTH DAKOTA** | |
| WHON-FM | 106.3 | | |
| | | *Country Exclusively* | |
| | | KOBH | 580 |
| | | KBJM | 1400 |
| **RHODE ISLAND** | | KGFX | 1060 |
| | | KXRB | 1000 |
| *Country Exclusively* | | KBHB | 810 |
| WHIM | 1110 | WNAX | 570 |
| WHIM-FM | 94.1 | | |
| | | *12 Hours Daily* | |
| | | KWAT-FM | 96.1 |
| | | | |
| | | **TENNESSEE** | |
| **SOUTH CAROLINA** | | *Country Exclusively* | |
| | | WSLV | 1110 |
| *Country Exclusively* | | WYXI | 1390 |
| WHPB | 1390 | WBOL | 1560 |
| WCAY | 620 | WFWL | 1220 |
| WEZL-FM | 103.5 | WDOD | 1310 |
| WQSN | 1450 | WMOC | 1450 |
| WCMJ-FM | 99.3 | WDXN | 540 |
| WCOS-FM | 97.9 | WCLE | 1570 |
| WDAR | 1350 | WYSH | 1380 |
| WDAR-FM | 105.5 | WAEW | 1330 |
| WSHG-FM | 106.3 | WAEW-FM | 99.3 |
| WESC | 660 | WCSV | 1520 |
| WCKI | 1300 | WDNT | 1280 |
| WEAB | 800 | WDSG | 1450 |
| WLCM-FM | 107.1 | WIXC | 1140 |
| WVAP | 1510 | WAGG | 950 |
| WTWE-FM | 92.1 | WIZO | 1380 |
| WBER | 950 | WAMG | 1130 |
| WKMG | 1520 | WOFM-FM | 94.9 |
| WKTM-FM | 102.5 | WSMG | 1450 |
| WKKR | 1540 | WHAM | 1580 |
| WASC | 1530 | WIRJ-FM | 102.3 |
| | | WTJS | 1390 |
| *18 Hours Daily* | | WTJS-FM | 104.1 |
| WKDY | 1400 | WJCW | 910 |
| | | WGOC | 1090 |
| *16 Hours Daily* | | WIVK | 850 |
| WCJM-FM | 99.3 | WIVK-FM | 107.7 |
| | | WKCS | 91.1 |
| *14 Hours Daily* | | WLIV | 920 |
| WDKD | 1310 | WBMC | 960 |
| | | WKYZ | 1250 |
| *13 Hours Daily* | | WGAP | 1400 |
| WFGN | 1570 | KWAM-FM | 101.1 |
| | | | |
| *12 Hours Daily* | | | |
| WESC-FM | 92.5 | | |

388

| Call Letters | Spot on Dial | Call Letters | Spot on Dial |
|---|---|---|---|
| WMC | 790 | WDXL | 1490 |
| WMQM | 1480 | WLIJ | 1580 |
| WKBJ | 1600 | WJLE | 1480 |
| WKBJ-FM | 92.3 | WSMT | 1050 |
| WAKI | 1230 | WSMT-FM | 105.5 |
| WMTN | 1300 | | |
| WMTS | 810 | **TEXAS** | |
| WENO | 1430 | | |
| WKDA | 1240 | *Country Exclusively* | |
| WSIX-FM | 97.9 | KWKC | 1340 |
| WLIK | 1270 | KOPY | 1070 |
| WTPR-FM | 105.5 | KDJW | 1010 |
| WTBP | 1550 | KZIP | 1310 |
| WTRB | 1570 | KOKE | 1370 |
| WRCS | 1370 | KVET | 1300 |
| WQTM | 1130 | KIOX | 1270 |
| WNTT | 1250 | KLVE | 560 |
| WECO | 940 | KTRM | 990 |
| WPHC | 1060 | KTRM-FM | 95.1 |
| WAAN | 1480 | KTON | 940 |
| | | KTON-FM | 106.3 |
| *15 Hours Daily* | | KHEM | 1270 |
| WBNT | 1310 | KFYN | 1420 |
| | | KQTY | 1490 |
| *14 Hours Daily* | | KBAN | 1410 |
| WJJM-FM | 94.3 | KSTB | 1430 |
| WJJM | 1490 | KEAN | 1240 |
| | | WTAW | 1150 |
| *13 Hours Daily* | | KHLB | 1340 |
| WEDG | 1240 | KMIL | 1330 |
| | | KCAN | 1550 |
| *12 Hours Daily* | | KDET | 930 |
| WDEB | 1500 | KCTX | 1510 |
| WDEB-FM | 100.1 | KCAR | 1350 |
| WHDM | 1440 | KSTA | 1000 |
| WSM | 650 | KCOM | 1550 |
| WCDT | 1340 | KMCO | 900 |
| | | KIKN | 1590 |
| *10 Hours Daily* | | KBSN | 970 |
| WLAF | 1450 | KIVY | 1290 |
| WBLC | 1360 | KCFH | 1600 |
| WTBP | 1550 | KBOX | 1480 |
| WTNE | 1500 | KWMC | 1490 |
| | | KSPL | 1260 |
| *9 Hours Daily* | | KDHN | 1470 |
| WPTN | 1550 | KHEY | 690 |
| WPTN-FM | 88.5 | KZOL | 1570 |
| WHMT | 1190 | KFLP | 900 |
| WKTA-FM | 106.9 | KBUY | 1540 |
| | | KSCS-FM | 96.3 |
| *8 Hours Daily* | | WBAP | 820 |
| WKBL | 1250 | KBRZ | 1460 |
| WKBL-FM | 93.5 | KGAF | 1580 |
| WIDD | 1520 | KGAF-FM | 94.5 |
| WCPH | 1220 | KSWA | 1330 |
| WCLC | 1260 | KCLW | 900 |
| WJFC | 1480 | KRME | 1460 |
| WDXE-FM | 95.9 | KENR | 1070 |
| | | KIKK-FM | 95.7 |

| Call Letters | Spot on Dial | Call Letters | Spot on Dial |
|---|---|---|---|
| KIKK | 650 | *13 Hours Daily* | |
| KNUZ | 1230 | KCIR-FM | 107.9 |
| KPET | 690 | KSNY | 1450 |
| KETX | 1440 | | |
| KETX-FM | 92.1 | *12 Hours Daily* | |
| KEES | 1430 | KWBA | 1360 |
| KDAV | 580 | KZZN | 1490 |
| KLLL | 1460 | KOYL-FM | 97.9 |
| KLLL-FM | 96.3 | KGRO | 1230 |
| KDOX | 1410 | KBMF-FM | 98.3 |
| KNEL | 1490 | | |
| KBGH | 1130 | *11 Hours Daily* | |
| KWFA | 1500 | KIBL | 1490 |
| KJBC | 1150 | KBUS | 1590 |
| KMOO | 1510 | | |
| KORC | 1140 | *10 Hours Daily* | |
| KRAN | 1280 | KEAN | 1240 |
| KSFA | 860 | KTXJ | 1350 |
| KNBO | 1530 | KOLJ | 1150 |
| KOYL | 1310 | KFRD | 980 |
| KPRE | 1250 | KFRD-FM | 104.9 |
| KCAW | 1510 | KVOU | 1400 |
| KCAW-FM | 93.3 | | |
| KPOS | 1370 | *9 Hours Daily* | |
| KOLJ | 1150 | KSAM | 1490 |
| KSOX | 1240 | KOOI-FM | 106.5 |
| KYAL | 1600 | KULG-FM | 104.9 |
| KPEP | 1420 | | |
| KTEO | 1340 | *8 Hours Daily* | |
| KBER | 1150 | KPSO | 1260 |
| KBER-FM | 100.3 | KHRB | 1060 |
| KBUC | 1310 | KLBK | 1340 |
| KBUC-FM | 107.5 | KRBA | 1340 |
| KKYX | 680 | KMHT | 1450 |
| KIKZ | 1250 | KSEY | 1230 |
| KSHN-FM | 96.7 | KTAE | 1260 |
| KTXO | 1500 | | |
| KCAS | 1050 | **UTAH** | |
| KDWT | 1400 | | |
| KSTV | 1510 | *Country Exclusively* | |
| KCMC | 740 | KBRE | 940 |
| KTLW | 920 | KMOR | 1230 |
| KTUE | 1260 | KSVN | 730 |
| KZAK | 1330 | KIXX | 1400 |
| KZAK-FM | 93.1 | KRGO | 1550 |
| KNAL | 1410 | KSOP | 1370 |
| KWBY | 1130 | KSOP-FM | 104.3 |
| WACO-FM | 1460 | KONI | 1480 |
| KAWA | 1010 | KONI-FM | 106.3 |
| KBGO | 1580 | KDYL | 990 |
| KBEC | 1390 | | |
| KRGV | 1290 | *12 Hours Daily* | |
| KLUR-FM | 99.9 | KFMC-FM | 96.1 |
| | | *8 Hours Daily* | |
| *16 Hours Daily* | | KURA | 1450 |
| KOKE-FM | 95.5 | | |
| | | **VERMONT** | |
| *14 Hours Daily* | | *10 Hours Daily* | |
| KOGT | 1600 | WJSC-FM | 90.1 |

| Call Letters | Spot on Dial | Call Letters | Spot on Dial |
|---|---|---|---|
| **VIRGINIA** | | **WASHINGTON** | |
| *Country Exclusively* | | *Country Exclusively* | |
| WPIK | 730 | KBKW | 1450 |
| WXRA-FM | 105.9 | KBFW | 930 |
| WKDE | 1000 | KELA-FM | 102.9 |
| WODY | 900 | KCVK | 1430 |
| WBLT | 1350 | KSMK | 1340 |
| WKEX | 1430 | KBAM | 1270 |
| WKJC | 106.3 | KAPS | 1470 |
| WZAP | 690 | KWIQ | 1260 |
| WODL | 1230 | KWIQ-FM | 100.3 |
| WKBY | 1080 | KARY | 1310 |
| WSVS-FM | 104.7 | KPOR | 1370 |
| WPED | 810 | KAYO | 1150 |
| WDVA | 1250 | KQIN | 800 |
| WKCY | 1300 | KGA | 1510 |
| WSVA-FM | 100.7 | KSPO | 1230 |
| WOHN | 1440 | KTNT-FM | 97.3 |
| WBRG | 1050 | KMO | 1360 |
| WWOD | 1390 | KUEN | 900 |
| WOLD | 1330 | KAAR-FM | 104.1 |
| WSIG | 790 | KUTI | 980 |
| WCMS | 1050 | | |
| WCMS-FM | 100 | *10 Hours Daily* | |
| WTID | 1270 | KAOS | 89.3 |
| WPVA | 1290 | | |
| WWOC | 1400 | **WEST VIRGINIA** | |
| WBLB | 1510 | | |
| WEET | 1320 | *Country Exclusively* | |
| WTVR | 1380 | WJLS | 560 |
| WXGI | 950 | WCAW | 680 |
| WSLC | 610 | WPDX | 750 |
| WAFC | 900 | WELD | 690 |
| WSGM-FM | 93.5 | WNST | 1600 |
| WKCW | 1420 | WKYG | 1230 |
| | | WKYG-FM | 103.1 |
| | | WAEY | 1490 |
| *12 Hours Daily* | | WMOV | 1360 |
| WBBI | 1230 | WWVA | 1170 |
| | | | |
| | | *10 Hours Daily* | |
| *10 Hours Daily* | | WMTD | 1380 |
| WRAA | 1330 | WRDS | 1410 |
| WNVA | 1350 | WXEE | 1430 |
| WNVA-FM | 106.3 | | |
| WQVA | 1530 | *9 Hours Daily* | |
| | | WBTH | 1400 |
| | | | |
| *9 Hours Daily* | | *8 Hours Daily* | |
| WRIC | 540 | WSCB | 1490 |
| WHEO | 1270 | | |
| | | **WISCONSIN** | |
| *8 Hours Daily* | | *Country Exclusively* | |
| WHHV | 1400 | WAPL | 1570 |
| WSWV | 1570 | WAXX | 1150 |
| WKBA | 1550 | WDMP | 810 |
| WTZE | 1470 | WEAU-FM | 104.5 |
| WTZE-FM | 100.1 | WBAY | 1360 |
| WNNT-FM | 100.9 | WMIR | 1550 |

| Call Letters | Spot on Dial | Call Letters | Spot on Dial |
|---|---|---|---|
| WMAD | 1550 | **CANADA** | |
| WMAD-FM | 106.3 | | |
| WXMT-FM | 93.5 | **ALBERTA** | |
| WBCS-FM | 102.9 | | |
| WOSH-FM | 103.9 | *Country Exclusively* | |
| WPLY | 1420 | CFAC | 960 |
| WGLB | 1560 | CFCW | 790 |
| WGLB-FM | 100.1 | | |
| WEVR | 1550 | *12 Hours Daily* | |
| WEVR-FM | 106.3 | CKSA | 1080 |
| WDUX | 800 | CKRD | 850 |
| WLKE | 1170 | | |
| WXCO | 1230 | *8 Hours Daily* | |
| | | CKYL | 610 |
| *10 Hours Daily* | | | |
| WAPL-FM | 105.7 | **BRITISH COLUMBIA** | |
| WLDY | 1340 | | |
| WTCH | 960 | *Country Exclusively* | |
| | | CJJC | 800 |
| *9 Hours Daily* | | CHQB | 1280 |
| WISS | 1090 | CJVI | 900 |
| WISS-FM | 102.3 | | |
| WYLO | 540 | *13 Hours Daily* | |
| | | CKSP | 1450 |
| *8 Hours Daily* | | | |
| WCCN | 1370 | *10 Hours Daily* | |
| WCCN-FM | 107.5 | CKNL | 560 |
| WOCO | 1260 | CJCI | 620 |
| WOCO-FM | 107.1 | | |
| | | *8 Hours Daily* | |
| | | CKAY | 1500 |
| **WYOMING** | | | |
| | | **MANITOBA** | |
| *Country Exclusively* | | | |
| KVOC | 1230 | *Country Exclusively* | |
| KCGO | 1530 | CJOB-FM | 97.5 |
| KVWO | 1370 | | |
| KSGT | 970 | *12 Hours Daily* | |
| KOVE | 1330 | CFRY | 920 |
| KTHE | 1240 | | |
| | | **NEW BRUNSWICK** | |
| *14 Hours Daily* | | | |
| KRAL | 1240 | *12 Hours Daily* | |
| | | CHSJ | 1150 |
| *9 Hours Daily* | | | |
| KOJO | 1490 | *10 Hours Daily* | |
| | | CJCJ | 920 |
| *8 Hours Daily* | | | |
| KODI | 1400 | *8 Hours Daily* | |
| KEVA | 1240 | CFNB | 550 |
| KVOW | 1450 | | |
| KWOR | 1340 | **NEWFOUNDLAND** | |
| | | | |
| | | *13 Hours Daily* | |
| **PUERTO RICO** | | CFCB | 570 |
| | | CFGN | 1230 |
| *Country Exclusively* | | CFSX | 910 |
| WCID | 1460 | CFLW | 1340 |

| Call Letters | Spot on Dial | Call Letters | Spot on Dial |
|---|---|---|---|
| *12 Hours Daily* | | *12 Hours Daily* | |
| CKGA | 730 | CHIC | 790 |
| CKCM | 620 | CHYM-FM | 1490 |
| *10 Hours Daily* | | *9 Hours Daily* | |
| CJCN | 680 | CHEX | 980 |
| *8 Hours Daily* | | | |
| CJOX | 710 | **QUEBEC** | |
| | | *Country Exclusively* | |
| **NORTHWEST TERRITORIES** | | CFOX | 1470 |
| *8 Hours Daily* | | *12 Hours Daily* | |
| CFCT | 600 | CKRB | 1460 |
| **NOVA SCOTIA** | | | |
| *Country Exclusively* | | **SASKATCHEWAN** | |
| CHFX-FM | 96.1 | *Country Exclusively* | |
| *10 Hours Daily* | | CKRM | 980 |
| CJCB | 1270 | CKKR | 1330 |
| | | *14 Hours Daily* | |
| **ONTARIO** | | CJNB | 1050 |
| *Country Exclusively* | | *8 Hours Daily* | |
| CHOO | 1390 | CHAB | 800 |
| CHYM-FM | 96.7 | CJGX | 940 |
| CHID | 1450 | | |
| CFGM | 1310 | | |
| CKEY | 590 | **YUKON TERRITORY** | |
| CHOW | 1470 | | |
| *18 Hours Daily* | | *9 Hours Daily* | |
| CKSL | 1410 | CKRW | 610 |
| CKBY | 105.3 | | |

# A Sampling of Country Songs

The origins of country music, as detailed elsewhere in this book, are relatively easy to trace. The songs of the Carter Family, for instance, bear strong resemblance to the Anglo-Saxon ballads brought here by the earliest settlers. But the Carters' distinctively southern harmonies and instrumentation put these gentle ballads and pastoral airs into a different mode, foreshadowing the mixture we now call *country music*. Ever since the Carters and their contemporaries brought these tunes into America's musical mainstream in the 1920s, country music has been slowly responding to the different styles, the different *folk*, it encounters along the way. The mingling of a field hand's shout and a southern gentleman's fiddle playing, sooner or later, inspired someone to write a song incorporating both styles. As the music evolved, it formed a circle, threading its way through the South and across the Texas plains to California, and finally, with some help from Hollywood, beginning to move back across the heartland, riding the media with its singing cowboys. The circle is now closing. Country music is a worldwide phenomenon.

The songs in this section reflect the changes country music has gone through as the circle forms. Notice the unmistakable Dixieland influence on Jimmie Rodgers' "In the Jailhouse Now." See how Kitty Wells's version of "It Wasn't God Who Made Honky-Tonk Angels" blends elements of white gospel singing, traditional ballads, and cowboy songs into a classic country tune. (This particular song also marked a departure from the male-oriented romantic double-standard, and was, in fact, written in response to a song that reflected such an attitude.) Willie Nelson's songs, "Night Life" and "Funny How Time Slips Away," display his personal style. At first glance, their structure bears scant resemblance to traditional country music, but Willie's ultra-relaxed, laconic delivery—and his philosophical stance are grounded in country. He's a bit bluer than most, but that's part of the honky-tonk tradition that Willie often represents.

Loretta Lynn's song, "Coal Miner's Daughter," is self-explanatory. Finally, we come to The Statler Brothers' "The Class of '57," closing this particular circle and coming back to the roots. Here we find the gentle harmonies of the Carter Family's balladsinging mixed with the rolling rhythms of pop, as interpreted by a quartet from the Shenandoah Valley. The subject matter is highly contemporary; the approach is wistfully traditional. "The more things change . . ."

As you sing these songs, or pick out their melody on a guitar, think about where they came from. Think of the people who sang them first, and who are probably still singing them. There's a wealth of information, hope, and understanding here. Let the music play.

# KEEP ON THE SUNNYSIDE

Words and Music by
A.P. CARTER &
GARY GARETT

**Verse**

1. There's a dark and trou-bled side of life, One that's filled with care and strife,
2. When life's storm-y let faith a-bide, And you'll al-ways turn the tide,
3. Just re-mem-ber to sing out strong, When you find the road is long,

Then the side that plays a hap-py part;_____ Till your
Light your hopes and you'll come smil-in' through;_____ In each
And your bur-den won't be hard to bear;_____ If you

span of life is done, Find your place be-neath the sun, And the
life there must be rain, But you'll ban-ish ev-'ry pain, If you
learn to wear a smile, You will short-en ev-'ry trial, For the

sun-shine will bright-en up your heart._____
pic-ture that rain-bow in the blue._____
laugh-ter will drive a-way your care._____

**Chorus**

KEEP ON THE SUN-NY SIDE, Al-ways on the sun-ny side,

KEEP ON THE SUN-NY SIDE of life;_____ It will help you ev-'ry

day, It will bright-en all the way, If you KEEP ON THE

*1 & 2.*
SUN-NY SIDE of life._____ 2. When life's
*To Verse* *Fine*
life._____
3. Just re-

# Will The Circle Be Unbroken?

Words and Music by
A.P. Carter

Moderately (In 2)

Instrum. Intro.

1. I was stand-in'_____ by my win-dow_____ on one cold and cloud-y day,_____ When I saw this_____ hearse come roll-in'_____ for to car-ry my moth-er a-way._____ Will the Cir-cle_____ Be Un-bro-ken_____ Bye and bye, Lord, bye and bye;_____ There's a bet-ter_____ home a-wait-ing,_____ In the

sky, Lord, in the sky.

Instrumental (ad lib) (15 bars) Verse 2.

2. Lord, I told the un-der-

tak-er, "Un-der-tak-er, please drive slow;

For this bod-y you are haul-in' Lord, I

hate to see her go. (Repeat chos) Will the

Verse 3

3. I will fol-low close be-hind her, Try to

hold off and be brave; But I could not

hide my sor-row When they laid her in her

Chorus Verse 4

grave. Will the I went back home, Lord,

my home was lone-some, Miss my moth-er, she was gone; All my

broth-ers, sis-ters cry-in', What a home so sad and lorn. Will the

399

# IN THE JAILHOUSE NOW

Moderately, with a "beat"

Words and Music by
JIMMIE RODGERS

1. Well I had a friend called Ram-bl-in' Bob,— Who used to steal gam-ble and rob;— He thought he was the smart-est guy in town;— But I found out last Mon-day,— That Bob got locked up Sun-day;— They got him in the jail-house way down town.

2. Well I went out last Tues-day,— Met a girl named Su-sie,— I told her I was the swell-est man a-round;— We start-ed to spend my mon-ey,— She start-ed in to call me "Hon-ey";— We took in ev-'ry Honk-y Tonk in town.

**Chorus**

{He's / We're} IN THE JAIL-HOUSE NOW,_____ {He's / We're} IN THE JAIL-HOUSE NOW;— {I / They told} {him / us} once— or twice,— to quit play-in' cards— and shoot-in' dice; _____ {He's / We're} IN THE JAIL-HOUSE NOW.—

(to Verse)

shoot-in' dice, We're IN THE JAIL HOUSE NOW. _____

400

# IT WASN'T GOD WHO MADE HONKY TONK ANGELS

Tune Ukulele A D F# B

Words and Music by
J.D. MILLER

1. As I sit here to-night, the juke-box play-ing, The tune a-bout the wild side of life; As I lis-ten to the words you are say-ing, It brings mem'-ries when I was a trust-ing wife.

2. It's a shame that all the' blame is on us wo-men, It's not true that on-ly you men feel the same; From the start most ev-'ry heart that's ev-er bro-ken, Was be-cause there al-ways was a men to blame.

**CHORUS**

IT WAS-N'T GOD WHO MADE HONK-Y TONK AN-GELS As you said in the words of your song; Too man-y times mar-ried men think they're still sin-gle; That has caused man-y a good girl to go wrong. 2.It's a wrong.

# COAL MINER'S DAUGHTER

LORETTA LYNN

1. Well, I was born a coal__ min - er's daugh - ter,__
2. (My) dad - dy worked all night__ in the fam - 'ly coal - mine,__

In a cab - in on a hill in Butch - er Hol - ler.
All day long in a field hoe - in' corn.__

We were poor but we had love, That's the
Mom - mie rocked the ba - by at night, Read the

one thing that dad - dy made sure of. He shov - eled coal to
Bi - ble by a coal - oil light, ___ And ev - 'ry - thing would start all

**1.-5.**

**6.**

make a poor man's dol - lar. ___  2. My
o - ver come break of morn. ___

3. Daddy loved and raised eight kids on a coal miner's pay,
Mommie scrubbed our clothes on a wash board.
I've seen her fingers bleed; To complain there was no need,
She'd smile in Mommie's understanding way.

4. In the summer time we didn't have shoes to wear,
But in the winter time we'd all get a brand new pair.
From a mail order catalog, money made by selling a hog,
Daddy always managed to get the money somewhere.

5. I'm proud to be a coal miner's daughter,
I remember well the well where I drew water.
The work we done was hard; At night we'd sleep 'cause we were tired;
I never thought I'd ever leave Butcher Holler.

6. But a lot of things has changed since 'way back then,
And it's so good to be back home again.
Not much left but the floor; Nothin' lives here anymore;
Just a memory of a coal miner's daughter.

403

# NIGHT LIFE

By WILLIE NELSON, PAUL BUSKIRK,
and WALT BREELAND

When the eve-ning sun goes down, you will find me hang-in' round; The NIGHT LIFE ain't a good life, but it's my life.

Man-y peo-ple just like me dream-in' of old used to be's; The NIGHT LIFE ain't a good life, but it's my life.

Lis-ten to the blues they're play-in', lis-ten to what the blues are say-in'. My, it's just an-oth-er scene from the world of brok-en dreams; The NIGHT LIFE ain't a good life, but it's my life.

# FUNNY HOW TIME SLIPS AWAY

By WILLIE NELSON

Lyrics:

1. Well, hel - lo there, my it's been a long, long time.
(B) How's your new love, I hope that he's do - in' fine.
2. Got - ta go now, guess I'll see you a - round,

"How'm I do - in'?" Oh, I guess that I'm do - in'
Heard you told him that you'd love him till the end of
Don't know when tho', nev - er know when I'll be back in

fine. It's been so long now and it seems that it was
time. Now, that's the same thing that you told me, seems like
town. But re - mem - ber what I tell you, that in

on ly yes - ter - day. Gee, ain't it FUN - NY HOW
just the oth - er day. Gee, ain't it FUN - NY HOW
time you're gon - na pay, And it's sur - pris - ing how

TIME SLIPS A - WAY. (To (B))
TIME SLIPS A - WAY. (To Vs. 2)
time slips a- way.

 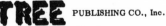

# THE CLASS OF '57

Words and music by
Harold Reid and Don Reid
"of The Statler Brothers"

1. Tom-my's sell - in' used cars, Nan - cy's fix - in' hair;
2. Hel - en is a hos - tess, Frank works at the mill;

Har - vey runs a gro - cery store___ and Mar - garet does - n't care;___
Jan - et teach - es grade school___ and prob - 'ly al - ways will;___

Jer - ry drives a truck for Sears,___ and Char - lotte's on the make;___ And
Bob works for the cit - y,___ and Jack's in lab re - search;___ And

Paul sells life in - sur - ance and part - time real es - tate.
Peg - gy plays or - gan at the Pres - by - ter - ian church.

And the class of fif - ty sev - en had it's dreams _____
And the class of fif - ty sev - en had it's dreams _____

_____ but we all thought we'd change the world _____ with our great works and
_____ but liv - in' life day to day _____ is nev - er like it

deeds; _____ Or may - be we just thought the world _____ would change _____
seems _____ Things get com - pli - ca - ted _____ when you _____

3. Betty runs a trailer park, Jan sells Tupperware;
   Randy's on an insane ward, and Mary's on welfare;
   Charlie took a job with Ford, and Joe took Freddie's wife;
   Charlotte took a millionaire, and Freddie took his life.

4. John is big in cattle, Ray is deep in debt;
   Where Mavis finally wound up is anybody's bet;
   Linda married Sonny, and Brenda married me;
   And the class of all of us is just part of history.
   *(to 2nd Chorus)*

# Photo Credits

The publisher wishes to thank the following for permission to use photographs: Roy Acuff, courtesy *Country Music* magazine; Buddy Alan, Emerson-Loew; Bill Anderson, Marshall Fallwell, Jr.; Lynn Anderson, Tuberculosis League of Pittsburgh; Eddy Arnold, Marshall Fallwell, Jr.; Chet Atkins, Marshall Fallwell, Jr.; Gene Autry, CBS Radio; Bobby Bare, Marshall Fallwell, Jr.; Tony Booth, Capitol Records; Jim Ed Brown, Yvonne Hannemann; Jimmy Buffett, Don Light Talent, Inc.; Pearl Lee and Carl Butler, *Country Music* magazine; Archie Campbell, WSM / Nashville; Glenn Campbell, Marshall Fallwell, Jr.; Henson Cargill, Marshall Fallwell, Jr.; The Carter Family, *Country Music* magazine; Johnny Cash, Alan David Whitman; Tommy Cash, Alan David Whitman; Roy Clark, *Hee Haw*; Patsy Cline, Decca Records; The Country Gentlemen, Vanguard Records; Billy Craddock, ABC Records; Floyd Cramer, RCA Records; Dick Curless (with Red Sovine), Andy Lloyd; Danny Davis, RCA Records; Jimmie Davis, Don Light Talent, Inc.; Mac Davis, Mike O'Mahony; Skeeter Davis, Marshall Fallwell, Jr.; Jimmy Dean, RCA Records; John Denver, RCA Records; Roy Drusky, Mercury Records; Dave Dudley, Andy Lloyd; Stoney Edwards, Owen Cartwright / *Nashville Banner*; The Everly Brothers, Slick Lawson; Barbara Fairchild, Marshall Fallwell, Jr.; Donna Fargo, Emerson-Loew; Flatt and Scruggs at Newport Folk Festival, David Gahr; Tennessee Ernie Ford, Capitol Records; Kinky Friedman, Vanguard Records; Lefty Frizzell, ABC-Dunhill Records; Tompall Glaser, Marshall Fallwell, Jr.; The Glaser Brothers, *Country Music* magazine; Grand Ole Opry (Ryman Auditorium), Marshall Fallwell, Jr.; the new Grand Ole Opry, courtesy Opryland; Claude Gray, Decca Records; Jack Greene, Top Billing, Inc.; The Hagers, *Hee Haw*; Merle Haggard, Paul Levine / Tree; Tom T. Hall (with Jeanne Pruett and Archie Campbell), Marvin Cartwright / WSM; George Hamilton IV, RCA Records; Freddie Hart, *Country Music* magazine; Hawkshaw Hawkins, Starday / King Records; *Hee Haw* cast, courtesy *Hee Haw*; Doyle Holly, John Duggleby; Homer and Jethro, RCA Records; David Houston, Epic Records; Jan Howard, Marshall Fallwell, Jr.; Ferlin Husky, Richard Luongo; Burl Ives, *Country Music* magazine; Stonewall Jackson, Moeller Talent, Inc.; Sonny James, courtesy Sonny James; Norma Jean, RCA Records; Waylon Jennings, Raeanne Rubinstein.

Also: Jim and Jessie, *Country Music* magazine; George Jones, Paul Levine; Doug Kershaw, Anthony Korody / Fourth Estate Press; Merle Kilgore, Bill Preston / *Nashville Tennessean*; Kris Kristofferson, Steve Ditlea; Brenda Lee, IFA; Dicky Lee, Marshall Fallwell, Jr.; Jerry Lee Lewis, Emerson-Loew; Hank Locklin, RCA Records; Lonzo and Oscar, General

Recording Corporation; The Louvin Brothers, Country Music Foundation; Bob Luman, Marshall Fallwell, Jr.; Judy Lynn, Country Music Foundation; Loretta Lynn, *Country Music* magazine; O. B. McClinton, Enterprise Records; Charlie McCoy, Marshall Fallwell, Jr.; Uncle Dave Macon, Country Music Foundation; Barbara Mandrell, Marshall Fallwell, Jr.; Jody Miller, RCA Records; Roger Miller, Columbia Records; Ronnie Milsap, Marshall Fallwell, Jr.; Bill Monroe, Howard Wight Marshall; Patsy Montana, Country Music Foundation; Melba Montgomery, *Country Music* magazine; Anne Murray, Marshall Fallwell, Jr.; Rick Nelson, MCA Records; Willie Nelson, Marshall Fallwell, Jr.; The Nitty Gritty Dirt Band, United Artists Records; The Osborne Brothers, MCA Records; Tommy Overstreet, Alan David Whitman; Bonnie Owens, Country Music Foundation; Gram Parsons, Warner Brothers Records; Dolly Parton, Bill Preston / *Nashville Tennessean*; Johnny Paycheck, Epic Records; Carl Perkins, Marshall Fallwell, Jr.; Webb Pierce, Country Music Foundation; Elvis Presley, MGM; Kenny Price, RCA Records; Charley Pride playing baseball, courtesy Charley Pride; Charley Pride with guitar, Quesada / Burke & Burke; Jeanne Pruett, MCA Records; Boots Randolph, Monument Records; Jerry Reed, Alan David Whitman; Del Reeves, Alan David Whitman; Jim Reeves, RCA Records; Charlie Rich, Alan David Whitman; Jeannie C. Riley, Marshall Fallwell, Jr.; Tex Ritter in *Ridin' the Cherokee Trail* and in *Trouble in Texas*, Tex Ritter Official Fan Club, Carrollton, Texas; Marty Robbins, Geoff Winningham; Jimmie Rodgers, *Country Music* magazine; Johnny Rodriguez (with Happy Shahan and Joaquin Jackson), Richard Harbert; David Rogers, Atlantic Records; Roy Rogers (with Dale Evans), Republic Pictures; Earl Scruggs and sons, Scruggs Talent Agency; Troy Seals, Atlantic Records; Jeannie Seely, Marshall Fallwell, Jr.; Billy Joe Shaver, Marshall Fallwell, Jr.; Jean Shepard, United Artists Records; Red Simpson, Capitol Records; Cal Smith, MCA Records; Connie Smith (with her new husband), Joe Rudis / *Nashville Tennessean*; Sammi Smith, Chuck Gist; Hank Snow, Marshall Fallwell, Jr.; Sons of the Pioneers, RCA Records; Joe Stampley, Dot Records; The Statler Brothers, Mercury Records; Red Steagall, Capitol Records; Cliffie Stone, Country Music Foundation; Stringbean (with Grandpa Jones), *Hee Haw*; Nat Stuckey, RCA Records; Hank Thompson, Dot Records; Mel Tillis, Paul Levin / *Tree*; Diana Trask, Dot Records; Merle Travis, Country Music Foundation; Ernest Tubb, MCA Records; Tanya Tucker, *Country Music* magazine; Conway Twitty, MCA Records; Conway Twitty (with Loretta Lynn), Bill Goodman / *Nashville Banner*; LeRoy Van Dyke, Decca Records; Porter Wagoner (with Dolly Parton), Bill Preston / *Nashville Tennessean*; Jimmy Wakely, Country Music Foundation; Charlie Walker, Al Stephenson / *Atlanta Journal-Constitution*; Doc Watson, Jamie Parslow / *Country Music* magazine; Freddy Weller, Columbia Records; Ketty Wells, MCA Records; Dottie West, Alan David Whitman; Billy Edd Wheeler, Country Music Foundation; Slim Whitman, Country Music Foundation; The Wilburn Brothers, MCA Records; Hank Williams, MGM Records; Hank Williams, Jr. (with Mike Douglas and George Hamilton, Jr.), The Mike Douglas Show; The Willis Brothers, Country Music Foundation; Bob Wills and The Texas Playboys, Wolf-Robeson; Mac Wiseman, Marshall Fallwell, Jr.; Tammy Wynette, Marshall Fallwell, Jr.; Tammy Wynette (with George Jones), Alan David Whitman; Faron Young, Mercury Records; Buck Owens, Emerson-Loew.